Federal Courts

Federal Courts

Larry W. Yackle

Professor of Law
Boston University

CAROLINA ACADEMIC PRESS
Durham, North Carolina

ISBN 0-89089-999-1
LCCN 98-89641

CAROLINA ACADEMIC PRESS
700 Kent Street
Durham, North Carolina 27701
Telephone (919) 489-7486
Fax (919) 493-5668
E-mail: cap@cap-press.com
www.cap-press.com

Printed in the United States of America

For Jeanette

Contents

Acknowledgments   xi
Foreword   xiii

Chapter I   Methodology   3
   A.   Constitutional Interpretation   3
      1.   Separation of Powers   3
      2.   Federalism   6
      3.   The "Greater Power" Syllogism   8
   B.   Statutory Construction   8
      1.   Textualism   9
      2.   The Doctrine of Clear Statement   12
   C.   Conceptual Perspectives   13
      1.   The Hart and Wechsler Paradigm   13
      2.   The Private Rights Model   15
      3.   The Process Model   18
      4.   The Public Rights Model   19
      5.   The Parity Debate   23

Chapter II   Historical Background   27
   A.   The Colonial Period   27
   B.   The Articles of Confederation   28
   C.   The Constitutional Convention   29
   D.   Ratification and the Federalist Papers   32
   E.   The Judiciary Acts of 1789–1793   36
   F.   Reconstruction   40
   G.   The Modern Structure   41
   H.   The Caseload Crisis   43

Chapter III   Judicial Independence   47
   A.   Selection of Supreme Court Justices   48
   B.   Selection of Inferior Court Judges   51
   C.   Removal by Impeachment   53
   D.   Alternative Means of Discipline   55

Chapter IV   Article III Courts   57
   A.   Inferior Article III Courts   58
   B.   Inferior Court Jurisdiction   60

	1. Jurisdiction Within Article III Limits	60
	2. Apportionment of Article III Jurisdiction	62
	3. Jurisdiction Outside Article III Limits	64
C.	Supreme Court Jurisdiction	66
D.	Outcome-Determinative Jurisdictional Limits	71
E.	Preclusion of Jurisdiction	73
F.	Academic Theories	75
Chapter V	**Legislative Courts**	**79**
A.	Theoretical Models	80
B.	Adjuncts to Article III Courts	87
C.	Legislative Courts	92
	1. Familiar Illustrations	92
	2. Public Rights Cases	94
	3. The Balancing Approach	97
D.	Trial by Jury	104
Chapter VI	**Federal Questions in State Court**	**105**
A.	State Court Authority	105
B.	State Court Obligation	114
C.	State Courts and Federal Officials	125
D.	Protections for State Court Jurisdiction	128
	1. Limited Removal	128
	2. Limited Appellate Review	135
	3. Preclusion	136
Chapter VII	**The Supreme Court**	**143**
A.	Original Jurisdiction	143
B.	Appellate Review of State Judgments	148
C.	Federal Questions	151
	1. The Preservation Requirement	151
	2. The Final Judgment Requirement	152
D.	State Questions	157
E.	Independent State Grounds	161
	1. Parallel State and Federal Issues	161
	2. State and Federal Issues in Tandem	164
	3. Hybrid Cases	166
	4. Ambiguous State Court Decisions	168
F.	Adequate State Grounds	170
G.	Standards of Review	175
H.	Appellate Review of Federal Judgments	176
I.	Discretionary Review	177
Chapter VIII	**Federal Questions in Federal District Court**	**183**
A.	Cases Arising Under Federal Law	183
B.	Federal Common Law	189
C.	Federal Rights of Action	196
	1. Rights of Action Implied in Federal Statutes	202
	2. Rights of Action Implied in the Constitution	207

D.	Statutory Jurisdiction	212
E.	Rights of Action Revisited	224
F.	Declaratory Judgment Actions	228
	1. Potential Defenses	232
	2. Claims by Defendants	234
G.	Preemption	240
H.	Supplemental Jurisdiction	242

Chapter IX Justiciability — 247

A.	Basic Doctrines	248
	1. Advisory Opinions	248
	2. Finality	252
	3. Political Questions	254
B.	Standing: Background	258
C.	Standing: Constitutional Prerequisites	268
	1. Injury in Fact	268
	2. Causation	276
	3. Redressability	280
D.	Standing: Non-Constitutional Prerequisites	283
	1. Third Party Claims	284
	2. The Zone Test	288
E.	Standing: Congressional Power	293
F.	Standing and the Merits	300
G.	Ripeness	303
	1. Relevant Considerations	303
	2. Ripeness and Remedies	306
H.	Mootness	308

Chapter X Suits Against the Government — 311

A.	Suits Against the Federal Government	312
	1. Officer Suits	312
	2. Waivers of Immunity	315
B.	Suits Against a State	317
	1. The Eleventh Amendment	317
	2. Alternative Interpretations	320
	3. Abrogation by Congress	323
	4. Categorical Exceptions	327
	5. Waivers of Immunity	329
C.	Officer Suits	331
	1. Suits for Injunctive Relief	331
	2. Suits for Compensatory Relief	337
	3. Suits to Enforce State Law	340
D.	The Ku Klux Klan Act	342
	1. Suits Against Cities and Counties	346
	2. Constitutional Torts	348
E.	Official Immunity	355
	1. Absolute Immunity	356
	2. Qualified Immunity	358

Chapter XI   Abstention   363
   A.   Statutory Limitations   364
       1.   The Anti-Injunction Act   364
       2.   Other Statutes   368
   B.   Exhaustion of Non-Judicial Remedies   369
   C.   State-Question Abstention   373
       1.   Prerequisites   376
       2.   Procedure   379
   D.   Special State Interests   380
       1.   State Administrative Interests   380
       2.   State Sovereign Interests   384
       3.   Parallel Litigation in State Court   386
   E.   Federal-Question Abstention   388
       1.   The Process Model   395
       2.   Anticipatory Actions   399
       3.   Civil Proceedings in State Court   406
       4.   State Administrative Proceedings   412
       5.   State Executive Activities   414

Chapter XII   Habeas Corpus   417
   A.   Function and History of the Writ   417
       1.   The Suspension Clause   419
       2.   Challenges to Executive Detention   422
       3.   Challenges to Criminal Convictions   423
   B.   Prerequisites   429
       1.   The Custody Doctrine   429
       2.   The Exhaustion Doctrine   430
   C.   Procedural Default in State Court   437
   D.   Evidentiary Hearings   445
       1.   State Court Findings of Fact   445
       2.   Procedural Default Revisited   447
   E.   Cognizable Claims   448
       1.   Constitutional Claims   449
       2.   Non-Constitutional Claims   450
       3.   Harmless Error   451
   F.   New Rules of Law   452
   G.   Previous Adjudication in State Court   460
       1.   State Court Mistakes of Law   463
       2.   State Court Mistakes of Fact   469
   H.   Multiple Petitions   471
   I.   The Ku Klux Klan Act Revisited   473

Table of Cases   477
Index   489

Acknowledgments

I received advice and criticism from Susan A. Bandes, Jack M. Beermann, Robert G. Bone, Clark Byse, Ronald A. Cass, Michael G. Collins, Donald L. Doernberg, Frederick M. Lawrence, Evan Tsen Lee, James S. Liebman, Daniel G. MacLeod, Daniel J. Meltzer, William E. Ryckman, Jr., Lawrence G. Sager, David J. Seipp, Aviam Soifer, Michael Wells, and Jeanette F. Yackle. I had excellent research assistance from Richard Bowman, Stuart S. Koonce, Melissa Mandroc, Joshua Perlman, and Alfred Saikali. I had equally fine administrative help from Sebastian Bach, Mark Barasso, Sara Cunningham-Cooper, Charlotte Gliksman, Linda Skinner, Edith Solomon, and Elizabeth Texiera. And I enjoyed extremely valuable library support from Marlene Alderman, Terri Geiger, Dan J. Freehling, Joshua Kantor, and Russell Sweet.

Foreword

I mean in this book to offer a concise introductory account of the constitutional, statutory, and judge-made law governing federal courts—the tribunals that exercise the judicial power of the United States. I will chiefly be concerned with the federal courts' authority to adjudicate questions of federal law, especially questions touching individual constitutional rights. I will guide readers along the path a litigant must follow, and over the hurdles a litigant must clear, to obtain a federal court decision on the merits of a federal claim. In that sense, I will investigate and explicate matters of genuine operational meaning in the world. Still, my goal is not to brief students and lawyers on the procedures that govern federal legal practice. I want to examine the federal courts as *institutions*, functioning alongside other centers of governmental power within an overarching constitutional framework.

I lean heavily and shamelessly on the prodigious research and insightful analysis that others have displayed in course materials prepared for law school classes. Inasmuch as those materials form the basis of university education regarding the federal courts, they have *become*, in effect, the corpus of this field. I mean this book to be a supplemental text that helps students work their way through the course books they are asked to master. Accordingly, I often track the subject headings, principal decisions, and commentaries that the authors of law school course books employ.[1]

I do not promise to answer all the questions that may arise. Neither my own discussion nor my references to the work of others can hope to be exhaustive or anything like it. I do believe, however, that what I have to say about the federal courts will be of help to readers who wish to consult a text that organizes and elucidates basic ideas. In aid of brevity and coherence, I will deliberately sacrifice some scope. I will give only piecemeal attention to the federal courts' jurisdiction

---

1. The first great course book, The Federal Courts and the Federal System, is now in its fourth edition. Previous editors (Henry M. Hart, Jr., Herbert Wechsler, Paul J. Mishkin, and Paul M. Bator) set a standard of excellence that the current editors (Richard H. Fallon, Jr., Daniel J. Meltzer, and David L. Shapiro) have somehow managed to maintain. Other excellent course books also organize and analyze masses of materials: Federal Courts: Theory and Practice (Robert N. Clinton, Richard A. Matasar & Michael G. Collins eds.); Federal Jurisdiction: Policy and Practice (Howard P. Fink & Mark V. Tushnet eds.); Federal Courts: Cases, Comments, and Questions (Martin H. Redish & Susanna Sherry eds.); Federal Courts and the Law of Federal-State Relations (Peter W. Low & John C. Jeffries, Jr. eds.); Federal Courts, Federalism and Separation of Powers: Cases and Materials (Donald L. Doernberg & C. Keith Wingate eds.); Federal Courts: Cases and Comments on Judicial Federalism and Judicial Power (Louise Weinberg ed.); and Cases and Materials on Federal Courts (Charles T. McCormick, James H. Chadbourn & Charles A. Wright eds.).

in "diversity" cases to enforce state law claims in disputes between citizens of different states and very little attention to the rules under which cases are processed. I will tailor my account to the typical academic course on the subject, which shares little in common with civil procedure and often spills over into constitutional law and theory.

Federal courts are the product of history, politics, and shifting and developing theoretical understandings of law and legal institutions in the modern world. Small wonder they defy easy description and may at first appear curious, even incomprehensible. To understand them, it is essential to appreciate both their relationship to the legislative and executive branches of the national government and their intercourse with the states and state courts. Accordingly, I will devote substantial space to the authority that Congress enjoys to establish federal courts in the first instance and to prescribe their purview, to the authority that state courts retain to adjudicate federal questions, and to the structural arrangements the resulting allocation of power both reflects and fortifies. I will dedicate even more space to the role federal courts play in protecting individual federal rights against excesses of state power. The operative constitutional themes are everywhere apparent: the separation of powers, federalism, individual liberty, and the unique form of democracy that has developed in this country.

My approach is descriptive, not prescriptive.[2] That will be apparent from the manner in which I try to weave materials together in pursuit of a coherent whole. I scarcely expect many readers to devour this book from start to finish. Some will take it a chapter at a time, perhaps with some backing and filling. Others will dip into it for guidance on particular points. Yet over the years, I have become convinced that these ideas can best be digested in the order I adopt here. I mean, then, to offer a linear treatment, which builds on itself as the manuscript progresses. The law in this field is not a seamless web. I will do my best to present an organized treatment without imposing discipline where the materials themselves resist.

Having stated my expository objectives, I hasten to say that the really important and interesting aspects of this subject invariably lurk beneath the surface. Decision-makers commonly wrestle with delicate questions of substance indirectly, by contesting what appears to be only the procedural question whether an issue is subject to judicial resolution and, if so, whether a federal court or some alternative tribunal (typically a state court) should bear the adjudicatory responsibility.

To put the point bluntly, the doctrines I will examine in this book are not always the value-neutral administrative devices they seem to be. They often reflect ideological perspectives on what the American governmental structure should be and how it should function. And in some instances at least, they are instruments for advancing or discouraging the claims in issue. When, for example, a citizen asks a federal court for help in checking the excesses of government, the judge charged to say whether the court's doors are open cannot be (and in the real world is not) indifferent to the possibility that the answer may determine whether the government's actions are constrained at all.

The law touching federal courts bears profound significance for the very nature and character of the American order of things. Certainly, this body of law

---

2. I collected my personal views on selected issues in Reclaiming the Federal Courts (1994).

adjusts the distribution of power within the national government and between the national government and the states. Behind those structural arrangements lies another delicate balance—between governmental power of any stripe, on the one hand, and individual rights and interests, on the other. I will not attempt to resolve the ideological controversies these materials evoke. Yet I will certainly identify and explore them. To do otherwise would be to miss half the picture (and nearly all the fun).

Federal Courts

Chapter I

Methodology

The law governing federal courts is largely concerned with allocating power among the three branches of the national government and between the national government and the states. To understand the way in which those allocations are made, it is essential to master the methodology the Supreme Court employs in resolving actual cases as they arise. Specifically, it is vital to develop a facility for using the sources the Court regards as authoritative and the policy arguments the Court finds persuasive.

A. Constitutional Interpretation

The Court invariably begins with the relevant constitutional provisions. Of course, the Constitution rarely commands any particular answer to a close question. The judicial article, Article III, is notoriously opaque. Justices who hope to read that Article according to its "original understanding" find the relevant historical materials obscure and scarcely dispositive.[1] So the Court's constitutional decisions with respect to the purview of the federal courts depend in the main on the Court's best judgment in the circumstances and thus are neither more nor less manageable and predictable than its constitutional decisions in other contexts. The Court relies primarily on inferences it draws from the constitutional structure as a whole and from interpretive techniques the Court finds especially helpful. Two structural ideas predominate: the separation of powers and federalism. One interpretive technique is extremely common: the syllogism that the "greater" power ineluctably includes any "lesser" power subsumed within it.

1. Separation of Powers

The Constitution does not distribute authority and responsibility among the legislative, executive, and judicial branches of the national government in so many words.[2] Yet the theme of separation is everywhere apparent. The organiz-

---

1. See Chapter II, notes 10-52 and accompanying text.

2. In response to Anti-Federalist demands that the Constitution should state the separation idea expressly, James Madison prepared an amendment that would have articulated the principle as tautology: "The powers delegated by the Constitution to the government of the United States shall be exercised as therein appropriated, so that the Legislative shall never exercise the powers vested in the Executive or Judicial; nor the Executive the powers vested

ing articles differentiate both the three powers and the institutions in which those powers "shall be vested."[3] There is, then, a federal judicial power (of some character) that is distinguishable (in some fashion) from the legislative and executive powers. Courts organized under Article III (not Congress or the President) are supposed to exercise that judicial power. And those courts are not supposed to be doing the jobs assigned to the other two branches. These premises in place, the interpretive difficulties are only beginning.

The existence of a power identified as judicial begs for some definition. That definition demands, in turn, some conceptual understanding of the way the three species of power fit together. History provides no answer. The rough idea of separation was popular in the founding period, but historians have discovered no genuine consensus on what it really meant to the public men who promoted it. They probably drew no clear distinction between distributing legislative, executive, and judicial power within the new national government and allocating any kind of authority among other groups—social and economic classes, for example.[4]

It is unrealistic to think that each of the three national powers occupies its own distinctive turf and that any incursion is an offense to the separation principle. If the judicial power had such absolute boundary lines with the legislative and executive powers, it would be necessary to spell out what those lines are in the abstract, so that decision-makers (namely, courts) might know a trespass when they see one. Any attempt to do that would be futile. Conventionally, the judicial function embraces three tasks: (1) ascertaining the facts; (2) identifying the applicable legal standard; and (3) applying that standard to the facts. Yet executive officers perform each of those duties on a daily basis. When, for example, a federal inspector visits a factory to enforce federal safety standards, the officer ascertains the factual circumstances on the shop floor, identifies the controlling regulation, and applies that regulation to the facts. Thus the conventional, three-step understanding of the judicial function collapses into routine executive activity. In reality, our notions about what counts as adjudication (as opposed to legislation and execution) rest on experience and pragmatic judgment. They are not logically preordained.[5]

Even if an abstract definition of judicial power could be formulated, it would defy practical implementation. If we had a system in which the legislative, executive, and judicial powers were relentlessly isolated and we permitted none of the

---

in the Legislative or Judicial; nor the Judicial the powers vested in the Legislative or Executive." IV Documentary History of the First Federal Congress of the United States of America, 1789-1791, 45-48 (Bickford & Veit eds. 1986). That amendment was not adopted. See Chapter II, text accompanying note 34.

3. U.S. Const. art. I, § 1 (stating that "[a]ll legislative Powers herein granted shall be vested in a Congress"); U.S. Const. art. II, § 1 (stating that "[t]he executive Power shall be vested in a President"); U.S. Const. art. III, § 1 (stating that "[t]he judicial Power of the United States, shall be vested in one supreme Court, and in such inferior Courts as the Congress may from time to time ordain and establish").

4. See generally Gerhard Casper, Separating Power: Essays on the Founding Period 7-22 (1997).

5. Paul M. Bator, *The Constitution as Architecture: Legislative and Administrative Courts Under Article III*, 65 Ind. L.J. 233, 264 (1990). See text accompanying notes 50-53 (explaining that this same three-step conception of adjudication also involves policy-making—a function typically regarded as legislative in character).

three to rub shoulders with the others, then we would have a recipe for "*impasse* reminiscent of the Nebraska statute which decreed that when two trains met at a crossing, neither could start until the other had moved on."[6] In fact, the three branches must cooperate. The separation principle is tempered by "checks and balance," by which each department routinely exercises significant authority with respect to affairs primarily assigned to the others.[7] Moreover, wholly apart from the formal way in which the Constitution requires cooperation, the three branches have to work together in order to get anything accomplished.

There are modern decisions in which the Supreme Court has attempted to define and enforce formal conceptual spheres for Congress and the President.[8] And some of the justices would plainly prefer an even more rule-oriented approach.[9] On the whole, though, the Court is more flexible. The idea of separated powers is not so much a hard "rule of decision"[10] as it is an extremely influential consideration in cases in which the Court must determine the proper allocation of power within the national government.

This certainly is true with respect to the Court's treatment of judicial power. The Court recognizes a significant role for Congress with respect to the judicial function. The cases permitting Congress to restrict the federal courts' jurisdiction illustrate the point,[11] as do less celebrated decisions allowing Congress to assign adjudicative functions to agencies other than Article III courts.[12] In other instances, the Court allows federal courts to fashion common law, which provides substantive rules of decision when Congress has enacted no controlling rules by statute. In those cases, the courts plainly perform a legislative function.[13] The decisions on litigant "standing" to appear in federal court explicitly rest on the separation theme. By restricting Article III courts to the adjudication of disputes that demand and justify judicial settlement, standing doctrine keeps those courts from establishing legal rules and principles in the abstract, thus interfering with the

---

6. Edward S. Corwin, *Tenure of Office and the Removal Power Under the Constitution*, 27 Colum. L. Rev. 353, 385 (1927) (dismissing "the notion—or superstition—that the Constitution effects such a nice apportionment of the total field of governmental activity among the three departments").

7. See Alan L. Feld, *Separation of Political Powers: Boundaries or Balance?*, 21 Ga. L. Rev. 171 (1986).

8. E.g., *INS v. Chadha*, 462 U.S. 919 (1983) (invalidating a congressional encroachment on the executive branch); *Bowsher v. Synar*, 478 U.S. 714 (1986) (invalidating an executive encroachment on the legislative branch). Many of these decisions have been criticized for being overly formalistic and for claiming support in historical materials that is not there to be found. E.g., Jack M. Beermann, *"Bad" Judicial Activism and Liberal Federal-Courts Doctrine: A Comment on Professor Doernberg and Professor Redish*, 40 Case W. Res. L. Rev. 1053 (1990); Erwin Chemerinsky, *A Paradox Without A Principle: A Comment on the Burger Court's Jurisprudence in Separation of Powers Cases*, 60 So. Calif. L. Rev. 1083 (1987).

9. Justice Scalia in particular has rather firm views regarding the powers that each branch enjoys. E.g., *Morrison v. Olson*, 487 U.S. 654, 697 (1988) (dissenting opinion).

10. Philip B. Kurland, *The Rise and Fall of the "Doctrine" of Separation of Powers*, 85 Mich. L. Rev. 592, 603 (1986).

11. See Chapter IV, notes 19-40, 48-72 and accompanying text.

12. See Chapter V; Harold J. Krent, *Separating the Strands in Separation of Powers Controversies*, 74 Va. L. Rev. 1253 (1988); Peter L. Strauss, *Formal and Functional Approaches to Separation-of-Powers Questions—A Foolish Inconsistency?*, 72 Cornell L. Rev. 488 (1987).

13. See Chapter VIII, notes 32-78 and accompanying text.

legislative function assigned to Congress. At the same time, Congress retains some authority to confer standing on litigants, thus permitting private citizens to invoke judicial power to test the validity of governmental action.[14]

It is not enough simply to mouth the separation principle and insist that it *means* that an action by one of the branches has unconstitutionally trespassed on another's preserve. It is essential to dig beneath the rhetoric of separation and to ask precisely *how* the other branch is affected. That is the level at which an argument either has genuine substance or, instead, merely offers an apparently neutral excuse for siding with one party or claim over another. There is, of course, the danger that the effect of individual actions in isolation may seem negligible, but that, over time, one branch may achieve hegemony over another incrementally. But the possibility that any of the branches is suffering death by a thousand pin pricks is itself a factor to be considered.[15]

2. Federalism

The Constitution nowhere mentions federalism, but nonetheless clearly contemplates an important role for the states. The system thus demands some distribution of authority and responsibility between the central government and autonomous states. As a matter of fact, the lion's share of the law associated with federal courts is concerned with reconciling two parallel sets of courts, one federal and the other state, coexisting in a single political framework.[16]

Here, too, definitional problems abound, and abstract reasoning from formal conceptual premises produces irreconcilable conflict. The Supreme Court's allocations of authority between the federal and state courts may perhaps be explained by the general perspective on federal-state relations that the Court brings to bear. In some periods, and in some individual cases, the Court adopts a decidedly "nationalist" perspective and regards federal courts as the tribunals of choice. In other periods and cases, the Court is comparatively "federalist" in its approach and tends to prefer the state courts. It is hardly surprising, then, that the precedents appear to be inconsistent and federal courts doctrine unstable.[17]

---

14. See Chapter IX, notes 204-50 and accompanying text.

15. See Chapter V, notes 95-106 and accompanying text (noting the way the Court attempts to handle this problem when Congress confers judicial authority on "legislative" courts).

16. But see Edward L. Rubin & Malcolm Feeley, *Federalism: Some Notes on a National Neurosis*, 41 UCLA L. Rev. 903 (1994) (offering an engaging *refutation* of federalism as an important American theme).

17. This is Professor Fallon's assessment. He elaborates and defends it in Richard H. Fallon, Jr., *The Ideologies of Federal Courts Law*, 74 Va. L. Rev. 1141 (1988). Fallon's nomenclature can be confusing. The perspective he calls "federalist" does not necessarily correspond to the attitudes typically ascribed to Federalists in the early years of the Republic and may, in fact, more closely approach the views associated with the Anti-Federalists in that era. See Chapter II, note 29 and accompanying text. Fallon makes it clear that his "nationalist" and "federalist" models are "ideal types" that may be helpful in analyzing the Court's decisions, but do not purport actually to track the precedents. As a matter of fact, neither comes even close to that mark—which tends to prove, in Fallon's view, that the Court has lurched back and forth between extremes that resist reconciliation. Professor Redish thinks Fallon's two categories are insufficient and that as many as seven considerations together are needed to explain the Court's decisions: "cross-pollenization, systemic represen-

nationalist perspective

Decisions that reflect a more nationalist perspective take the view that state prerogatives are, or should be, subordinate to the vindication of federal rights, especially individual constitutional rights against state power established by the fourteenth amendment. The working idea is that the national government bears primary responsibility for enforcing federal rights and that litigants' desire to be in federal court should be respected. By contrast, decisions that reflect a federalist perspective regard the states as the sovereign units of government at the system's core and the state courts as the presumptive tribunals for adjudication, *ceteris paribus*. Federalist decisions thus deny that federal courts have a special purchase on the vindication of federal rights and insist that there must be some particularized justification for allowing litigants to escape or bypass state courts. In close cases, the Supreme Court needs and employs a default position, which prevails in the absence of a good reason to choose an alternative state of affairs. The Court's currently ascendant (nationalist or federalist) perspective may account for the default position the Court selects.

Federalist perspective

The task, here again, is to cut through the rhetoric down to underlying values. To argue for federalism is not invariably to insist on a generalized devolution of power to the states. In any particular instance, judicial business should be placed in one system or the other according to a careful appraisal of the interests conventionally associated with federalism in this context — namely, the extent to which state court adjudication promotes diversity, self-determination, efficiency, and civil liberties.[18] The last of these four classic values is currently in fashion. Academics and the Court alike promote federalism as a device for maintaining the lines of accountability in a democracy. Congress can obscure those lines by commandeering the states to act as its agents and making it appear to the public that the states are responsible for policies that Congress, in fact, has established.[19] The Court wrestles with federalism in a host of circumstances, but particularly in cases involving the federal courts' authority (and obligation) to abstain from exercising jurisdiction in deference to state court litigation.[20]

---

tativeness, litigant choice, litigation efficiency, fundamental fairness, institutionalism, and logical consistency." Martin H. Redish, *Reassessing the Allocation of Judicial Business Between State and Federal Courts: Federal Jurisdiction and "The Martian Chronicles,"* 78 Va. L. Rev. 1769, 1770-71 (1992). Professor Wells argues that the Court's results, if not its stated explanations, probably turn on the justices' desire to channel litigation to the courts likely to reach the judgment the justices themselves think is correct. In Wells' view, the Warren Court typically routed cases to federal courts in hopes those courts would favor civil rights and civil liberties claims, while the current Court more often sends cases to state courts in the expectation that those courts will side with the government in individual liberty cases. See, e.g., Michael Wells, *Naked Politics, Federal Courts Law, and the Canon of Acceptable Arguments*, 47 Emory L.J. 89 (1998); Michael Wells, *Rhetoric and Reality in the Law of Federal Courts: Professor Fallon's Faulty Premise*, 6 Const. Comm. 367 (1989).

18. See generally Ann Althouse, *Variations on a Theory of Normative Federalism: A Supreme Court Dialogue*, 42 Duke L.J. 979 (1993); Deborah Jones Merritt, *The Guarantee Clause and State Autonomy: Federalism for a Third Century*, 88 Colum. L. Rev. 1, 3-10 (1988); Michael W. McConnell, *Federalism: Evaluating the Founders' Design*, 54 U. Chi. L. Rev. 1484, 1491-1511 (1987). See generally David L. Shapiro, Federalism: A Dialogue (1995); Barry Friedman, *Valuing Federalism*, 82 Minn. L. Rev. 317 (1997).

19. See generally Vicki C. Jackson, *Federalism and the Uses and Limits of Law: Printz and Principle?*, 111 Harv. L. Rev. 2181 (1998) (collecting a host of authorities).

20. See Chapter XI. Professor Wells proposes that in the interests of candor and clear thinking, the Court should entertain express arguments that sending a case to federal or state court is likely to affect the result that will be reached. Wells, *Naked Politics*, note 17, at 92.

3. The "Greater Power" Syllogism

In coming to terms with constitutional questions touching federal courts, the Court routinely employs a range of familiar interpretive techniques.[21] Yet one device in particular is ubiquitous: the proposition that if a unit of government (typically Congress) enjoys a "greater" (encompassing) power to take or forbear some significant action, it follows as a logical imperative that it also enjoys a "lesser" (subset) power to take or forbear some less sweeping action. The "greater power" syllogism is appealing inasmuch as it promises an irrefutable, deductive answer to a legal problem and thus makes it unnecessary to offer additional persuasive reasoning. Despite its allure, however, the syllogism almost always constitutes a mistake in legal analysis.

In some contexts, the "greater power" proposition is perfectly logical. If the Mighty Casey has the physical strength to smack a baseball over the left field wall at Fenway Park, it follows that he also has the physical strength to slap a ball onto the grass in front of the wall. Legal power is not physical strength. In federal courts cases, "greater power" arguments often rest on an invalid premise. Typically, the power said to be the "greater" does exist, but the power said to be the "lesser" is not (as a logical matter) a subset power at all. Instead, it is a different (though related) power. It may well exist, but it *does* require additional justification. The Supreme Court often relies on the "greater power" syllogism to reach perfectly sound results despite its flawed reasoning. The classic illustrations are the Court's decisions on the power of Congress to prescribe the jurisdiction of inferior federal courts.[22]

B. Statutory Construction

Statutes are typically more definitive than the Constitution. Yet the enactments in this field are often vague and ambiguous. They, too, require creative exegesis. In some important instances, the Supreme Court self-consciously takes it

---

21. For example, the Court commonly invokes the prudential considerations that Justice Brandeis identified in the *Ashwander* case: Upon the whole, the Court hesitates to address a constitutional question unless and until it appears necessary to do so. To that end, the Court will prefer a non-constitutional ground of decision when it is available, it will construe statutes in a way that avoids constitutional questions, and, when it does decide a constitutional issue, it will not formulate a rule of decision that is broader than needed to dispose of the matter immediately at hand. *Ashwander v. TVA*, 297 U.S. 288, 346 (1936) (concurring opinion). See Lisa A. Kloppenberg, *Avoiding Constitutional Questions*, 35 B.C. L. Rev. 1003 (1994). These are not rules, of course, but persuasive considerations that are given significant weight, if sometimes in the breach.

22. See Chapter IV, notes 21-31 and accompanying text. There are many other illustrations. See, e.g., Chapter V, text accompanying note 6 (describing this kind of argument with respect to Congress' power to create "legislative" courts); Chapter VI, text accompanying notes 128-29 (describing a similar argument on behalf of Congress' power to confer "protective" jurisdiction on federal courts). For a discussion of the "greater power" proposition in constitutional law generally, see Michael Herz, *Justice Byron White and the Argument That the Greater Includes the Lesser*, 1994 B.Y.U. L. Rev. 227

upon itself to elaborate statutes according to its own sense of proper policy. The best illustrations are the Court's decisions regarding 28 U.S.C. § 1331 (the basic statute conferring jurisdiction on federal district courts to entertain federal question cases) and the decisions regarding 42 U.S.C. § 1983 (the general statute authorizing private litigants to sue state officials for violations of their federal rights).[23] In other instances, the Court invokes the usual canons of statutory construction, coupled with two techniques: (1) special attention to the text of enacted statutes; and (2) the doctrine of "clear statement."

1. Textualism

Traditional statutory construction draws on numerous sources. In recent years, however, and particularly in cases in this field, the Supreme Court has focused primarily (though not exclusively) on the text of the statutes that Congress actually places in the United States Code.[24] Occasionally, the Court expresses its focus on a statute's text in the familiar language of the "plain meaning" rule, which has it that "where language is plain and admits of no more than one meaning, the duty of interpretation does not arise."[25] That is misleading. Individual statutory terms and provisions *have* no meaning in isolation.[26] The Court's textualism is much more sophisticated. It begins with particular terms and their accepted dictionary definitions, but also takes account of the context in which terms appear in a statute, as well as the statute's fit with other related statutes.[27]

The practical significance of textualism is that the Court attaches little or no value to "legislative history"—background materials like committee reports and floor speeches. Even when the Court insists it is interested in Congress' "inten-

---

23. See Chapter VIII, text accompanying note 170 (§ 1331); Chapter X, text accompanying note 204 (§ 1983). See also Chapter XII (describing the Court's free-wheeling interpretations of the habeas corpus statutes).

24. For discussions of the relationship between literary theory and the interpretive function in law, see Richard A. Posner, Law and Literature: A Misunderstood Relation (1988); Robert M. Cover, *Foreword: Nomos and Narrative*, 97 Harv. L. Rev. 4 (1983); *Symposium, Interpretation*, 58 So. Calif. L. Rev. 1 (1985).

25. *Caminetti v. United States*, 242 U.S. 470, 485 (1917).

26. Cass R. Sunstein, The Partial Constitution 8 (1993) (explaining that there is no such thing as "preinterpretive meaning"); Frank H. Easterbrook, *Statutes' Domains*, 50 U. Chi. L. Rev. 533, 536 (1983) (crediting Wittgenstein with the insight that isolated words do not have "intrinsic meanings"). Professor Schauer does not disagree, but contends that people who share a common language can communicate with one another in an ordinary vocabulary, which can be the starting point for further interpretive work. Frederick Schauer, *Statutory Construction and the Coordinating Function of Plain Meaning*, 1990 Sup. Ct. Rev. 231.

27. E.g., *Textron Lycoming Reciprocating Engine Div. v. UAW*, 118 S. Ct. 1626, 1629 (1998) (moving quickly from dictionary definitions to context); *King v. St. Vincent's Hosp.*, 502 U.S. 215, 221 (1991) (explaining that the meaning of statutory language "plain or not" depends on the context in which the language is used); *United States Savings Ass'n v. Timbers of Inwood Forest Ass'n*, 484 U.S. 365, 371 (1988) (explaining that a statutory provision "that may seem ambiguous in isolation is often clarified by the remainder of the statutory scheme"); *West Va. Univ. Hosp. v. Casey*, 499 U.S. 83, 100-01 (1991) (explaining that the Court will construe ambiguous statutory terms "to contain that permissible meaning which fits most logically and comfortably into the body of both previously and subsequently enacted law...[in order to] make sense rather than nonsense out of the *corpus juris*"). See generally George H. Taylor, *Structural Textualism*, 75 B.U. L. Rev. 321 (1995).

tions" in enacting a statute, the Court regards the language actually placed on the books as the best evidence of those intentions.[28] Better said, the Court looks not for the intentions of the people who drafted or voted for a bill, but for the intentions of the enacted statute itself. What matters is the point of its text, derived exclusively from the text.[29] Legislators who propose or oppose public polices typically come to naught if they merely record their views in reports and speeches, but lack the political muscle it takes to put hard language in the text of an enacted statute.[30]

There is a way in which the Court's textualism reflects democratic values. Congress is empowered to make public policy jointly with the President. Proponents of a bill must marshal majority votes in both the House and the Senate, present their product to the President, and achieve at least his acquiescence.[31] In

---

28. See generally William N. Eskridge, Jr., *The New Textualism*, 37 UCLA L. Rev. 621 (1990). Justice Scalia, the chief exponent of textualism, would discard all talk of legislative "intent" and focus, instead, on legislative "meaning." Antonin Scalia, *Common-Law Courts in a Civil- Law System: The Role of United States Federal Courts in Interpreting the Constitution and Laws* 22-23, in A Matter of Interpretation (Gutmann ed. 1997). Justice Scalia quotes Holmes approvingly: "We do not inquire what the legislature *meant*; we ask only what the statute *means*." Oliver Wendell Holmes, Collected Legal Papers 207 (1920) (emphasis added). According to Justice Scalia, if a court attempts to discover what the legislature "*meant*" (rather than what it said), the court is likely to end up with what a "wise and intelligent" person "*should* have meant," which will turn out to be what the court itself thinks is a good idea. Scalia, at 18. Other justices continue to refer to legislative "intent," even as they increasingly rely primarily on statutory text. E.g., *Thompson v. Thompson*, 484 U.S. 174, 179 (1988) (professing to be investigating legislative "intent" but explicitly declining to ask what members of Congress "actually had in mind").

29. See Taylor, note 27, at 338. The extent to which this kind of textualism departs significantly from classic accounts of statutory interpretation can be debated. When Justices Jackson and Frankfurter called on courts to identify a statute's "purpose," they contemplated that the text of the statute under review would provide the guide (as opposed to background materials). E.g., *D'Oench, Duhme & Co. v. FDIC*, 315 U.S. 447, 465 (1942) (Jackson, J., concurring); Felix Frankfurter, *Some Reflections on the Reading of Statutes*, 47 Colum. L. Rev. 527, 538 (1947). The Legal Process school, too, eschewed any search for the subjective desires of a statute's authors and also regarded courts' function as identifying a more objective "purpose" for a statute. Henry M. Hart, Jr. & Albert M. Sacks, The Legal Process: Basic Problems in the Making and Application of Law 1378 (Eskridge & Frickey eds. 1994).

30. See *Morse v. Republican Party*, 517 U.S. 186, 276 n.18 (1996) (Thomas, J., dissenting) (explaining that there are "myriad reasons" why a majority of the members of Congress might have "wanted" to enact a bill that never became law but that the Court "must look to the extant text of the statute and see what Congress has in fact...enacted"). Justice Breyer insists that courts should not abandon legislative history entirely. Stephen Breyer, *On the Uses of Legislative History in Interpreting Statutes*, 65 So. Calif. L. Rev. 845 (1992). By one account, both justices who take account of legislative history and those who ignore it actually share a single interpretive methodology, which regards courts as "agents" of the legislature, obliged to be guided *by* the legislature in some way or other. The Federal Courts and the Federal System 758 (Fallon, Meltzer & Shapiro eds. 1996). This "agency theory" of statutory interpretation probably does not help to analyze the differences between the justices over the value of legislative history. Yet it may help to distinguish the text-based interpretive methodology most of the justices employ from other approaches suggested in the academic literature—approaches that deny that courts are agents of the enacting legislature and argue for a more "dynamic" and "creative" role for the judiciary in the elaboration of policy. Id. at 760-61. See note 35.

31. *Landgraf v. USI Film Products*, 511 U.S. 244, 263 (1994).

a formal sense, only a statute enacted in that way qualifies as law. Background materials have no such status. They have not survived the crucible of the actual law-making process, but may, instead, be manipulated by individual members of Congress and their staffs,[32] as well as courts searching for excuses to set aside the text actually enacted.[33] The Court's strict textualism can thus be defended for respecting only the formal law that Congress and the President forge in the constitutionally prescribed manner.[34] At the same time, however, by declining to consider background materials, the Court necessarily shoulders responsibility for elaborating an ambiguous statute's meaning in the exercise of its own judgment.[35]

Textualism as a statutory construction methodology does not, in itself, entail any particular allocation of power among the three departments of the national government or between the central government and the states. The results the Court reaches depend on the values and policies that textualism allows the Court to introduce when statutes are susceptible to more than one interpretation. The Court does not always specify what those extra-text considerations may be, but buries them beneath intricate arguments about what the text alone truly means. This is the pattern,

---

32. Professor Manning contends that the Court's textualism is best understood as a refusal to permit Congress essentially to delegate legislative power to the professional staff who prepare background materials. John F. Manning, *Textualism as a Non-delegation Doctrine*, 97 Colum. L. Rev. 673 (1997).

33. Committee reports and floor speeches can be voluminous and internally inconsistent, tempting courts to select what they like and leave the rest. Judge Harold Leventhal once described the use of legislative history as "the equivalent of entering a crowded cocktail party and looking over the heads of the guests for one's friends." See *Conroy v. Aniskoff*, 507 U.S. 511, 519 (1993) (Scalia, J., concurring).

34. Scalia, note 28, at 22 (explaining that "[t]he text is the law... and it is the text that must be observed"). See *Musick, Peeler & Garrett v. Employ. Ins.*, 508 U.S. 286, 305-06 (1993) (Thomas, J., dissenting) (insisting that "[c]ourts should not treat legislative... silence as a tacit license to accomplish what Congress... [is] unable or unwilling to do"). In some instances, the Supreme Court acknowledges that statutory construction must take account of the complex way in which public policy is fashioned by and through administrative agencies. In *Chevron v. Natural Resources Defense Council*, 467 U.S. 837 (1984), the Court held that courts should ordinarily accept "reasonable" agency interpretations of the statutes the agencies are charged to implement—on the theory that Congress has delegated legislative authority to the agencies concerned. See Chapter V, note 39. Professor Pierce argues that the Court often undermines *Chevron* by concluding that a statute's meaning is clear and, accordingly, that an administrative agency's interpretation is entitled to no special consideration. See Richard J. Pierce, Jr., *The Supreme Court's New Hypertextualism: An Invitation to Cacophony and Incoherence in the Administrative State*, 95 Colum. L. Rev. 749 (1995).

35. Commentators offer a variety of answers to this dilemma. Professor Eskridge proposes that courts should decide close cases by reading statutes to comport with courts' best understanding of the public good. William N. Eskridge, Jr., Dynamic Statutory Interpretation (1994); William N. Eskridge, Jr., *Public Values in Statutory Interpretation*, 137 U. Pa. L. Rev. 1007 (1989). Professor Sunstein argues that courts should construe statutes in a way that reflects the needs and requirements of the modern administrative state. Cass R. Sunstein, *Interpreting Statutes in the Regulatory State*, 103 Harv. L. Rev. 405 (1989). Public choice adherents debate the way in which courts should contend with statutes that, in their view, merely reflect the bargained-for results of legislative deals. Compare Posner, note 24, at 245 (arguing that courts should explore the intentions of "those who wrote the provision that is being interpreted"), with Easterbrook, note 26, at 539 (insisting that only the text of a statute should ordinarily be consulted). See William N. Eskridge, Jr. & Philip P. Frickey, *Legislative Intent and Public Choice*, 74 Va. L. Rev. 423 (1988).

for example, in cases in which the justices argue among themselves over whether statutes authorize citizens to file private enforcement lawsuits in federal court.[36]

2. The Doctrine of Clear Statement

In many cases touching federal courts, the Supreme Court resolves statutory construction problems by insisting that a statute must spell out a policy in an exacting way, else the Court will assign it a different meaning.[37] The idea of demanding a clear statement from Congress regarding an allocation of judicial power is attractive. Precise language demonstrates awareness, confidence, and resolve. So when the Court demands clarity from a statute and finds it, the Court has every justification for accepting the policy that Congress has so plainly demonstrated it wants to advance. In the run of cases, however, the Court itself effectively assumes the responsibility for making policy choices.

In this context, too, the Court selects a default position—here, the construction the Court will place on a statute in the absence of clarity. If, for example, the Court announces that federal courts can entertain a class of cases if Congress is clear (but only if Congress is clear), it follows that if Congress is not clear (enough), state courts will handle those cases. The choice of a default position is not self-evident, and it is not value-neutral. When the Court makes such a choice, it selects the allocation of judicial power it thinks best. If, then, the Court demands a clear statement from Congress before permitting federal courts to handle lawsuits, it is because the Court has decided, as an anterior matter, that those suits should not be heard in federal court. Otherwise, the Court would have chosen the opposite baseline and allowed the federal courts to proceed in the absence of a clear statute stating that they cannot.[38]

In practice, the default position the Court chooses is likely to prevail, because Congress is so rarely clear. The legislative process runs on compromise. When a power-allocation question excites controversy, Congress typically submerges disagreement in statutory language that is deliberately inexact. If, then, the Court wants to achieve a particular distribution of power, the Court can invoke a clear statement rule, which establishes the state of affairs the Court prefers as the default position and challenges anyone who disagrees to get Congress clearly to insist on a different policy—the very thing Congress is unlikely to do.[39]

---

36. See Chapter VIII, notes 104-34 and accompanying text.

37. The doctrine of clear statement is not reserved for legislation affecting federal courts. Yet it is deployed routinely in this field, typically to divert judicial business *away* from federal courts. William N. Eskridge, Jr. & Philip P. Frickey, *Quasi-Constitutional Law: Clear Statement Rules as Constitutional Lawmaking*, 45 Vand. L. Rev. 593 (1992).

38. Justice Scalia acknowledges that the clear statement rule "load[s] the dice" and thus requires independent justification. Scalia, note 28, at 28-29.

39. Professor Shapiro regards this effect as typically conservative inasmuch as it makes "radical change less likely by raising interpretive barriers to such a change." David L. Shapiro, *Continuity and Change in Statutory Interpretation*, 67 N.Y.U. L. Rev. 921, 941 (1992). Professor Bandes argues that the Court's insistence on clear legislative language "ratifies the choices of the powerful, and relegates the powerless to explicit legislative remedies they are unlikely to secure." Susan Bandes, *Reinventing Bivens: The Self-Executing Constitution,* 68 So. Calif. L. Rev. 289, 314 (1995).

The Court employs the doctrine of clear statement in a variety of contexts. The Court insists, for example, that if Congress wishes to give federal courts exclusive jurisdiction over a class of cases, carving state courts out of the picture entirely, only a clear statement will do.[40] The default position in that context, accordingly, is that state courts enjoy concurrent jurisdiction. That is the state of affairs the Court thinks is preferable (for a host of good reasons). Similarly, the Court demands that Congress use exacting statutory language if it means to subject the states themselves to suit in federal court.[41] Otherwise, the default position is that the states enjoy immunity. There, too, the Court's own predilections are plainly on display.

C. Conceptual Perspectives

Usually, the Supreme Court finds itself unable to anchor decisions in preexisting authority alone and therefore must exercise even more judgment. The literature in point suggests several models that help to explain both the way in which the Court proceeds and its results.

1. The Hart and Wechsler Paradigm

A particular set of underlying assumptions supplies the paradigm within which thinking about federal courts occurs and, in many instances, Supreme Court analysis proceeds.[42] Those assumptions are ascribable to Professor Henry Hart and Professor Herbert Wechsler, who built them into the original edition of their great course book.[43] In a real sense, Hart and Wechsler *defined* the federal courts field by focusing their work (and the work of everyone else to follow) on allocations of power within the federal system and, concomitantly, by contending that power distributions are defensible only if they conform to presuppositions that Hart and Wechsler themselves viewed as proper.[44]

Commentators describe the Hart and Wechsler assumptions in a variety of ways. In the main, however, the idea boils down to this. Power should *not* be allocated according to a self-conscious purpose to ensure that federal claims receive a generous interpretation. Instead, power should be distributed (both among the branches of the national government and between the national government and the states) according to policies that are neutral with respect to the issues to be decided and the results to be reached. The law should assign a matter to the branch of government, or the court system, that is institutionally most competent to address it.[45]

---

40. See Chapter VI, notes 34-36 and accompanying text.

41. See Chapter X, notes 102-04 and accompanying text.

42. Professor Fallon initially offered this characterization. Richard H. Fallon, Jr., *Reflections on the Hart and Wechsler Paradigm*, 47 Vand. L. Rev. 953 (1994).

43. The Federal Courts and the Federal System (Hart & Wechsler eds. 1953).

44. Fallon, note 42, at 961-63.

45. Hart and Wechsler's commitment to neutrality was not complete, but it was certainly characteristic of their work. Their particular aim to achieve a body of consistent, neutral policies to control adjudication was a product of the Legal Process movement in the

In the Hart and Wechsler view, legislatures are chiefly competent to make substantive value choices, while courts are competent to resolve disputes. Accordingly, the law should leave it to Congress to define national public policies and should prevent the federal courts from adjusting those policies by means of creative interpretation. Equally, the law should ensure that federal courts can adjudicate disputes independently and should prevent Congress from interfering with the courts' adjudicative function. The law should also assign judicial business to federal or state courts in light of neutral administrative policies: the extent to which one set of courts or the other can offer special expertise regarding the questions presented, protect individual and societal interests in finality and repose, resolve matters with a minimum of friction, ensure the uniformity of federal law, and dispose of a legal matter more efficiently. Typically, according to the paradigm, state courts offer an adequate opportunity for "full and fair" adjudication, even in cases implicating questions of federal law.[46]

According to the Hart and Wechsler paradigm, the law of federal courts is and should be indifferent to the result that a court reaches in a case. Once the proper court has been given authority to adjudicate a matter, that court's judgment on the merits is entitled to be accepted. This is so not because that outcome *is* right in an absolute sense, but rather because a result that has been generated by a court with properly assigned authority to make a decision should be *taken* as right—for the necessary and sufficient reason that we have no better measure of the way things *should* turn out.[47] Importantly, according to the paradigm, there is no reason to think that the judgment a federal court reaches on an issue, even an issue of federal law, is any better than the judgment a state court produces. Both are subject to appellate review, but until an appellate court finds a decision to be erroneous, it is entitled to be accepted.

According to the paradigm, the Constitution itself recognizes the primacy of state law. The states preexisted the Constitution and the new central government it created. They were previously entitled to fashion public policy on the basis of their police power, and they retain that general law-making power today. State law, in turn, forms the general background web of standards to which society looks, as an initial matter, to test the legal effects of human behavior. Federal law, on the other hand, is by nature "interstitial," consisting of fragments sprinkled over the corpus of state law in places where national standards are needed.[48] By this account, the complex modern judicial system is nonetheless basically the decentralized common law regime that has always prevailed. The task at hand is to adjust that common law framework to accommodate a body of legislative and

---

1940s and 1950s, to which both Hart and Wechsler contributed. For an account of the jurisprudential background, see William N. Eskridge, Jr. & Gary Peller, *The New Public Law Movement: Moderation as a Postmodern Cultural Form*, 89 Mich. L. Rev. 707 (1991). Professor Fallon argues that Hart and Wechsler did not celebrate neutrality to a fault, but offered an approach whose very strength lay in its sensitivity to the interactions between substantive and procedural values. Richard H. Fallon, Jr., *Comparing Federal Courts "Paradigms,"* 12 Const. Comm. 3, 6 (1995).

46. See also notes 62-63 and accompanying text (discussing this proposition as the key feature of the process model).

47. Professor Fallon explains that the paradigm's "single, controlling insight" is that "authority to decide must...include authority to decide wrongly." Fallon, note 42, at 962.

48. The Federal Courts and the Federal System, note 43, at 435.

administrative activity, particularly at the federal level, which brings new centripetal pressure to bear on the traditional order.

Positing the primacy of state law (and the contingent, supplemental nature of federal law), it follows naturally enough, according to the paradigm, that state courts (exercising judicial authority given them by state law) constitute our first-line adjudicative mechanisms when disputes arise. Federal courts (exercising a much more limited jurisdiction) are summoned to service only in exceptional circumstances.[49]

2. The Private Rights Model

Power allocations in this field also reflect the "private rights" or "dispute resolution" model of adjudication, which posits that the role of courts, as opposed to legislatures and executive officers, is to resolve actual disputes between contending parties. By this account, the parties come to a court for help not when they want to change the law, but when they have a quarrel over existing law. When asked to decide who has the better legal position, a court undertakes the familiar duties of adjudication.[50] Initially, the court determines the material facts. The court examines any evidence the parties offer, decides who is telling the truth, and ascertains the state of affairs on which the law must be brought to bear. Next, the court identifies the controlling legal standard: the substantive law governing the parties' rights in circumstances of the relevant kind. Finally, the court applies that legal standard to the facts of the particular dispute at hand.[51]

Conventionally, when a court decides what has transpired to give rise to the parties' dispute, the court is said to be determining basic, primary, historical facts—this is to say, descriptions of historical events.[52] When the court articu-

---

49. Professor Hart reached the same conclusion by another route in a famous law review article in which he produced a lively dialogue between fictional antagonists, one (a student or colleague) pressing the other (Hart's alter ego) on whether a citizen with a federal claim is entitled to proceed in a federal court rather than a state court. That question quickly reduced to whether Congress can constitutionally deny such a litigant a federal forum. Given the explicit text of Article III, Hart found it inescapable that no litigant can claim a federal forum if Congress does not provide one. See Chapter IV, text accompanying notes 19-20; Chapter VI, notes 67, 77 and accompanying text. Hart was equally sure, however, that no litigant can be denied access to *all* courts to press a federal claim. Consequently, if Congress withholds a federal forum, the state courts must be open. "In the scheme of the Constitution," Hart's alter ego declared, state courts are "the primary guarantors of constitutional rights, and in many cases they may be the ultimate ones." Henry M. Hart, Jr., *The Power of Congress to Limit the Jurisdiction of the Federal Courts: An Exercise in Dialectic*, 66 Harv. L. Rev. 1362, 1401 (1953).

50. See text accompanying note 5.

51. Obviously, a court cannot isolate these steps from each other and take them one at a time in this order. When, for example, the court sets about to find the basic facts, it must already have in mind the legal standard that is applicable. Otherwise, the court can have no idea what facts are legally relevant and thus need finding. Moreover, all three steps run together at the fringes. In particular, one must understand that the difference between a legal standard and its application in particular instances is elusive. A legal rule, articulated in the abstract, is only a generalized account of the way a series of cases should be resolved.

52. Professor Monaghan describes this fact-finding step as a "case-specific inquiry into *what happened here.*" Henry P. Monaghan, *Constitutional Fact Review*, 85 Colum. L. Rev. 229, 235 (1985) (emphasis in original).

lates the controlling legal standard, it is said to be deciding an abstract or pure question of law. And when the court applies that legal standard to the facts of the particular case at hand, the court is said to be deciding a "mixed" question of law and fact—that is, the legal significance of the basic, primary, historical facts.[53] These duties entail judicial law-making. When courts ascertain applicable legal standards, they necessarily elucidate preexisting authorities of various kinds, assigning meaning to those sources of abstract law. And when courts apply abstract legal standards to the facts of particular cases, they necessarily elaborate and enrich the law, even as they add to its corpus an additional precedent on which future courts will rely. According to the private rights model, this much judicial law-making is appropriate and legitimate inasmuch as it is essential to the resolution of disputes for which courts exist and to which their authority is limited.

The most famous illustration of the private rights model is *Marbury v. Madison*.[54] In that case, John Marshall held that the Supreme Court had authority to invalidate a federal statute the Court found to conflict with the Constitution. He gave as his chief reason that it was essential for the Court to elaborate the Constitution's meaning in order to resolve an actual dispute between two litigants. On one side, William Marbury claimed he had been named a justice of the peace in the District of Columbia and had a right to his commission. On the other, James Madison (the Secretary of State) had refused to give Marbury the commission and thus, by Marbury's account, had violated Marbury's legal right to it. According to Marbury, § 13 of the Judiciary Act of 1789 established the Supreme Court's jurisdiction to adjudicate his dispute with Madison as an "original" matter (not on appeal from some inferior court), because he was pursuing a writ of mandamus instructing Madison to deliver the commission.[55]

Chief Justice Marshall held, first, that Marbury had a legal right to the commission, and, second, that a writ of mandamus was an appropriate judicial remedy for a violation of that right. A federal court of proper jurisdiction, accordingly, might have issued the writ and thus ordered a governmental official like Madison to do his duty by delivering the commission to Marbury.[56] Marshall concluded, however, that § 13 failed to supply the needed jurisdiction, because that provision of the 1789 Act was unconstitutional: It purported to grant the

---

53. The classic explanation of the categories is Justice Frankfurter's opinion in *Brown v. Allen*, 344 U.S. 443, 506 (1953) (concurring opinion). The classic statement of the private rights model is Lon Fuller, *The Forms and Limits of Adjudication*, 92 Harv. L. Rev. 353 (1978). Professor Bone contends that Fuller's theory was more fluid than others have suggested. See Robert G. Bone, *Lon Fuller's Theory of Adjudication and the False Dichotomy Between Dispute Resolution and Public Law Models of Litigation*, 75 B.U. L. Rev. 1273 (1995).

54. 5 U.S. (1 Cranch) 137 (1803).

55. See Chapter IV, text accompanying note 5 (identifying the elements of the Court's original jurisdiction); Chapter VII, notes 1-39 and accompanying text (offering a more complete account).

56. See Chapter X, note 19 and accompanying text. On the other hand, the statutes in place at the time did not clearly confer jurisdiction on any inferior federal court, either. See Akhil R. Amar, *Marbury, Section 13, and the Original Jurisdiction of the Supreme Court*, 56 U. Chi. L. Rev. 443, 461 & n.90 (1989).

Court original jurisdiction of a case that was not among those that Article III would permit the Court to consider as an original matter.[57] In the end, accordingly, Marshall interpreted the Constitution in *Marbury* only because it was necessary to do so to resolve the dispute at hand. Unfortunately for Marbury himself, when Marshall turned to the Constitution for that reason, he decided that the Court had no jurisdiction to give Marbury what he wanted after all and thus was obliged to dismiss his complaint.[58]

The private rights model corresponds to the separation of national powers. It contemplates a role for federal courts that is analytically distinct from the functions left to the other two branches of the national government. Modern cases on "standing" provide the best illustrations.[59] In those cases, the Supreme Court insists that federal judges are not elected and thus should not develop substantive law to promote their own notions of good public policy in an affirmative, freewheeling way. They can elaborate the law only when they adjudicate actual "cases" and "controversies" involving adverse parties whose personal interests in the results establish their standing to appear in an Article III court. Then (and only then) is the federal courts' authority to create law both justified and limited by the necessity of resolving disputes. By this account, judicial law-making is contingent and incidental; it is a by-product of courts' primary adjudicative responsibility.

The private rights model also corresponds with the role the Hart and Wechsler paradigm contemplates for federal courts. According to the paradigm, courts are not suited to making public policy for the future, but are competent to settle disputes that have already arisen regarding the law as it is. Courts are not good at assessing the popular will and identifying the public interest. Courts are good at marshaling evidence, making credibility choices, analyzing precedents, and elaborating legal rules and principles in particular circumstances. It follows that courts should leave legislating to Congress, that they should confine themselves to resolving actual disputes, and that when they make law they should do it only as a necessary incident of dispute resolution.

Inasmuch as the private rights model regards dispute resolution as the only judicial function to be performed, this model, like the Hart and Wechsler paradigm to which it is so closely linked, contemplates that state courts can and will shoulder responsibility for most judicial business, irrespective of subject matter. State courts of general jurisdiction are typically open to adjudicate any disputes that come through the door. Federal courts, by contrast, are reserved for special circumstances in which they, rather than the state courts, are suited to provide the adjudication required.[60]

---

57. See Chapter VII, notes 12-13 and accompanying text (elaborating this point).

58. But see notes 72-76 and accompanying text (discussing an alternative perspective on *Marbury*).

59. See Chapter IX.

60. Academics debate the extent to which the Hart and Wechsler paradigm tends to prefer state courts over federal courts. Professor Wells contends that the paradigm is systematically biased in favor of state court adjudication. Wells, *Rhetoric and Reality*, note 17. Professor Fallon contends that the paradigm is neutral in this respect, but that the great capacity of state courts understandably attracts considerable business. Fallon, note 42.

3. The Process Model

Both the private rights model of adjudication and the Hart and Wechsler paradigm contemplate occasions on which federal courts are needed. Certain subjects plainly invite national tribunals: cases involving foreign affairs, for example. And in some instances, the policy considerations the paradigm invokes will select federal courts. This will be true, in the main, when the premise on which the Hart and Wechsler paradigm ordinarily proceeds does not obtain—namely, when state courts fail to provide the kind of process that is needed to reach an acceptable result.

Recall that the working idea in the paradigm is that jurisdictional power should be allocated on the basis of outcome-neutral criteria in the expectation that the results on the merits will be unaffected. Then, when any court (but often a state court) produces a result, that decision is entitled to respect *because* it is the product of an appropriate decision-making process. If, however, state court process is flawed, so that the matter is denied "full and fair" adjudication, the situation is altered.[61] A state court judgment cannot be *taken* to be right on the ground that it was generated in a procedurally proper way, if it is clear in the circumstances of a case that the state court has not delivered the caliber of process on which its claim to adjudicate depends.

Herein the "process model" in the law of federal courts, which supplies what the private rights model and the Hart and Wechsler paradigm plainly require: a subordinate model for deciding when the ordinary expectation of state court adjudication should give way to adjudication in federal court. The process model answers that federal courts may properly be called to duty when the procedural machinery in state court breaks down. Like the private rights model and the Hart and Wechsler paradigm, the process model attends exclusively to *process*. It summons the federal courts not because those courts are thought to be superior to state courts, nor because they are more likely to reach objectively correct decisions, nor, certainly, because they are more likely to render judgments more favorable to federal claims. The process model engages federal courts not when state court *results* are unpalatable, but rather when the *processes of adjudication* in state court are inadequate. Outcomes the state courts reach by procedurally irregular means are not, by hypothesis, entitled to the respect that outcomes reached via procedurally sound adjudication routinely receive.[62]

The Supreme Court employs the process model in a variety of contexts. In "abstention" cases, for example, the Court allows federal courts to enjoin state

---

61. See Paul M. Bator, *Finality in Criminal Law and Federal Habeas Corpus for State Prisoners*, 76 Harv. L. Rev. 441, 462 (1963).

62. Professor Bator explained that the idea is to set aside any debate over the substantive accuracy of outcomes and to focus, instead, on "arrangements and procedures which provide a reasoned and acceptable probability that justice will be done." Id. at 448. The process model's insistence on "full and fair" adjudication does not address the general question whether state courts are fungible with federal courts, but only tests whether, in some case or class of cases, state courts do not or cannot offer the process required. Paul M. Bator, *The State Courts and Federal Constitutional Litigation*, 22 Wm. & Mary L. Rev. 605, 626-27 (1981).

proceedings if it appears that state courts have denied a litigant an opportunity for "full and fair" adjudication of a federal claim.[63] The process model also figures in the Court's decisions on whether federal courts can consider federal claims that were, or might have been, considered previously in state court,[64] as well as in the cases on whether the Supreme Court can review state court judgments that purport to rest on adequate state grounds of decision.[65]

4. The Public Rights Model

Together, the Hart and Wechsler paradigm, the private rights model, and the process model undoubtedly help to explain a large measure of federal courts law. Yet they do not capture everything federal courts do. Moreover, they have come under attack for failing to appreciate fundamental changes that have occurred in the American legal culture since Hart and Wechsler fashioned their understanding of legal institutions a half century ago.[66] By some accounts, a competing "public rights" model offers both a better explanation of the federal courts' work in some instances and a better normative vision of what the federal courts *should* be about.

The idea of "public rights" is elusive. In a line of decisions stretching back to the Nineteenth Century, the Supreme Court has used the public rights label to refer to routine fact-based claims arising from federal regulatory schemes. Matters of that nature have negligible significance for the federal legal system as a whole. According to some authorities, Congress might dispose of them without involving the courts at all.[67] In the modern era, however, courts and commentators use the same public rights designation to identify extremely important cases that can have profound implications for the body of federal law and the framework for its enforcement. Some of the new public rights cases are the very disputes with the federal government that previously were thought to be *de minimis*, but are now understood in a different light. Some have an entirely different shape and scope. In all instances, however, cases that reflect the public rights model invite federal courts to enforce federal law not merely as the by-product of isolated dispute-resolution, but for its own sake, or better said, for the sake of the public at large.

When the Court first applied the public rights label to trivial individual claims that citizens had against federal bureaucrats, it did not seem important that the courts should be involved. Then, the private rights model captured the work that federal courts performed. Superintending the conduct of government agents was no essential part of that work. Today, by contrast, the public rights model depicts the legal system in a quite different way. Federal courts are not limited to settling quarrels between individual litigants, and they do not merely

---

63. See Chapter XI, notes 164-89 and accompanying text.
64. See Chapter VI, notes 159-60, 175-79 and accompanying text.
65. See Chapter VII, notes 143-44 and accompanying text.
66. Professor Amar contends that the assumptions associated with Hart and Wechsler were out of date even in 1953, when their case book was published. Akhil R. Amar, *Law Story*, 102 Harv. L. Rev. 688, 710 (1989).
67. See Chapter V, notes 64-75 and accompanying text.

fill gaps that state courts leave open. Rather, federal courts have a special office within the American political structure. They are in place to enforce federal statutes and the Constitution and thus to hold governmental power in check in a wide range of circumstances.

The Hart and Wechsler paradigm and the private rights model focus on the separation of powers, federalism, and efficient judicial methodology. They contemplate that power should be allocated with those structural and functional values in mind. By contrast, the public rights model celebrates access to federal courts for the vindication of federal claims.[68] Two related developments suggest that the public rights model helps to explain the role federal courts now play.

First, the rise of the administrative state since the 1930s has transformed the very nature and character of American law. In many contexts, the law is no longer largely comprised of rights and duties that common law courts enforced on behalf of individuals. Instead, much of the substantive law in place today is federal constitutional law (which has exploded in the wake of *Brown v. Board of Education*) and federal regulatory law (often administered in the first instance by federal administrative agencies). Different forms of law and legal institutions place novel demands on federal courts to perform in ways that would have been alien to the common law.[69]

Second, many of the disputes with which federal courts contend are not between private litigants at all, but between private citizens, groups, and corporations, on the one hand, and governmental officers, on the other. In many instances, private litigants continue to advance particularized individual claims that fit the private rights model. Often, however, litigants insist more generally that governmental officers should simply respect the law. Modern class actions challenge governmental activities on a wide scale and demand broad-gauged equitable relief that can affect millions of lives. The claims in those cases are less personal than the private rights recognized at common law. They may better be understood as public rights inasmuch as they are in service of the public interest in seeing that the law is enforced.[70]

---

68. Professor Bandes contends that by adopting a public rights model of this kind, the Court could rationalize the very idea of a constitutional "case" for resolution in federal court. See Susan Bandes, *The Idea of a Case*, 42 Stan. L. Rev. 227 (1990).

69. For an account of these developments, see Eskridge & Peller, note 45. For an argument that federal courts have necessarily come to forge public policy straightforwardly, see Malcolm M. Feeley & Edward L. Rubin, Judicial Policymaking and the Modern State: How the Courts Reformed America's Prisons (1998). Professor Resnik adds that the domain of federal courts law today must take greater account of the judicial work performed by magistrate judges, bankruptcy judges, administrative law judges, and tribal courts. Judith Resnik, *Rereading "The Federal Courts": Revising the Domain of Federal Courts Jurisprudence at the End of the Twentieth Century*, 47 Vand. L. Rev. 1021 (1994).

70. Here, too, conventional jargon can be confusing. Previously, the Supreme Court denominated matters as "public rights" cases because they involved disputes with federal bureaucrats as opposed to other private citizens. See text accompanying note 67. The new public rights cases are "public" not only because they turn on federal law and involve government officials as defendants, but also because they are pursued in the general public interest. American jurisprudence distinguishes between an *interest* and a *right*, the one being a human concern or desire of any kind, the other capturing only an entitlement, guaranteed by law, to demand a particular form of treatment by another. Mutt has an *interest* in attending a Red Sox game with Jeff, an interest that will be injured if Jeff decides (inexplicably) to go to the ballet, instead. But, *ceteris paribus*, Mutt has no *right* to demand that Jeff keep their date at Fenway Park. Nevertheless, when courts and commentators use the phrase "public rights," they typically do not mean the public equivalent of private individual *rights*,

According to the public rights model, federal law is no longer typically the exception, but is now very often the rule. Superintending the conduct of government officials is no longer a minor matter, but has become the central function that federal courts perform. Federal injunctive relief no longer demands special justification, but is typically necessary to force government officials to conform their behavior to law. The task at hand now is not to teach a basically common law system to accommodate new developments. It is to understand and nourish the new federal public law system in light of its stubborn common law past.[71]

There is a way in which the public rights model arguably has figured in a variety of traditional cases, even *Marbury v. Madison*.[72] After all, John Marshall was scarcely dragged kicking and screaming through his analysis in that case. He might have made quick work of Marbury's claim, simply by holding that Marbury had no right to the commission until it was delivered or that mandamus was not an appropriate remedy. Certainly, Marshall might have construed § 13 of the Judiciary Act to authorize the Court to issue the writ of mandamus only in appellate cases, thus reaching the same result (that the Court had no original jurisdiction to entertain Marbury's application) on a statutory ground.[73] Instead, Marshall wrote a lengthy opinion in which he not only *exercised* judicial power to give the Constitution its authoritative meaning, but also *asserted* judicial power (in a case of proper jurisdiction) to issue orders to a member of the President's cabinet.[74] In those early years, that was judicial muscle-flexing of an extra-

---

but rather the public *interest*. Likewise, when courts and commentators refer to litigation in the "public interest," they typically have in mind litigation conforming at least roughly to the model of public *rights*. But see Chapter IX, note 96 and accompanying text (discussing the way in which law may affect what society considers to *be* a *de facto* interest).

71. The idea of "public law" litigation is also elusive. In the main, plaintiffs in public rights lawsuits attempt to force government officials to comply with federal law (the Constitution or a federal statute) and do not attempt to force other private actors to behave. That is an important sense in which both the litigation and the law to be enforced are *public*. Nevertheless, courts and commentators may well place some suits against private actors in the public law category (e.g., suits to force corporations to comply with federal civil rights and environmental legislation). The more fundamental point of the label "public rights" is to distinguish these policy-oriented suits, which typically are in the class action form and invariably seek injunctive or declaratory relief, from the comparatively simple suits envisioned by the model of private rights, which are discrete disputes between self-interested litigants that can be resolved without implicating the public at large in any self-conscious way and in which compensatory damages ordinarily supply a sufficient remedy. Judge Oakes has explained it this way: "[W]e no longer think in simple terms of adjudication based on retrospective, self-contained, party-initiated and controlled bipolar lawsuits seeking to constrain power. We now recognize a form of public law litigation which enforces affirmative values running to groups and which needs prospective judicial enforcement." James L. Oakes, *The Proper Role of the Federal Courts in Enforcing the Bill of Rights*, 54 N.Y.U. L. Rev. 911, 918 (1979). For good sources, see Bruce A. Ackerman, Reconstructing American Law (1984); Owen M. Fiss, The Civil Rights Injunction (1978); Abram Chayes, *The Role of the Judge in Public Law Litigation*, 89 Harv. L. Rev. 1281 (1976).

72. See notes 54-58 and accompanying text.

73. Marshall thus reached out to decide constitutional questions that might easily have been avoided. Cf. note 21 (discussing the Court's usual caution). See generally William W. Van Alstyne, *A Critical Guide to Marbury v. Madison*, 1969 Duke L.J. 1, 16. Professor Amar argues that § 13 was not a jurisdictional provision at all, but only authorized the Court to issue the writ of mandamus as a remedy. Amar, note 56, at 456.

74. According to Professor McCloskey, Marshall's opinion was a "masterwork of indirection, a brilliant example of Marshall's capacity to sidestep danger while seeming to court

ordinary order.[75] Accordingly, even as Marshall insisted that his task was only to settle the dispute at bar, he seized the opportunity to project judicial power a good deal further: "It is emphatically the province and duty of the judicial department to say what the law is."[76]

The modern Supreme Court's decisions allocating judicial power often defy explanation as the product of outcome-neutral policies of the kind that the Hart and Wechsler paradigm and the private rights model make central. By all accounts, the Warren Court of the 1950s and 1960s encouraged citizens to go to federal court seeking injunctive orders that would desegregate the public schools, restructure the administration of prisons and mental hospitals, and enforce federal civil rights and environmental legislation. If the liberal justices then sitting did not always endorse the ends that the plaintiffs in those cases hoped to achieve, they plainly thought it was appropriate that the federal courts should be open to public rights litigation with public objectives in view. By most accounts, the Court became uncomfortable with suits of that nature in the 1970s. If the more conservative justices then sitting did not always disapprove of the goals the plaintiffs in public rights suits were seeking, they thought it was inappropriate that the plaintiffs should advance their contentions in federal court, instead of pressing them on Congress or state legislatures.[77]

Today, by most accounts, the Court is divided over the legitimacy and advisability of public rights litigation. Individual justices undoubtedly attach different significance and weight to the outcome-neutral concerns they debate with such vigor. Yet there is no escaping the suspicion that they are moved by deeper attitudes regarding both the substantive goals and values at stake in litigation and the role of federal courts in the system. In many minds, then, the law of federal courts is more result-oriented than the Hart and Wechsler paradigm and the private rights model can readily explain. The genuine explanation for the justices' performance may lie in their attempts, individually and collectively, to wrestle with the

---

it, to advance in one direction while his opponents [were] looking in another." Robert G. McCloskey, The American Supreme Court 40 (1960).

75. At the time *Marbury* was decided, Jefferson had just become President and Republicans were taking over in Congress. The outgoing Federalists were attempting to retain (and expand) their power in the judicial branch. When the Court first took up the case, it issued a "show cause" order to Madison, instructing him to appear and explain why a writ of mandamus should not issue. Madison ignored that order and gave every appearance that he would also ignore an actual writ if the Court should send him one. The really contentious issue in the case, then, may not have been the Court's power to interpret the Constitution, but its power to demand that the executive branch carry out judicial orders. Given that Madison (and Jefferson) were poised to rebuff any order the Court might issue, Marshall may have thought it prudent (and politically expedient) merely to *say* that the Court might have issued a writ of mandamus in a proper jurisdictional posture, but to find an excuse for withholding an order that Madison would disregard. The *Marbury* decision thus may have been an attempt to strengthen and protect the federal judiciary at one and the same time. See James O'Fallon, *Marbury*, 44 Stan. L. Rev. 219 (1992). These points granted, Professor Alfange argues that *Marbury* is still best understood as the classic precedent on the power of judicial review. See Dean Alfange, Jr., *Marbury v. Madison and Original Understandings of Judicial Review: In Defense of Traditional Wisdom*, 1993 Sup. Ct. Rev. 329.

76. 5 U.S. at 177.

77. For an account of the Warren Court's ideological orientation, see Morton J. Horwitz, The Warren Court and the Pursuit of Justice (1998). For a discussion of the Burger Court, see The Burger Court: The Counter-Revolution That Wasn't (Blasi ed. 1983).

implications of the public rights model and its distinctive vision for the Article III judiciary. The very decisions that illustrate the current Court's commitment to the private rights model reflect these divisions inasmuch as the justices in the majority typically take pains to explain why they reject the competing public rights model.[78]

5. The Parity Debate

When arguments about power allocations between the federal and state courts become more ideological, they commonly take the form of a candid debate over whether courts in the two systems are likely to reach the same judgments in federal question cases. If they are, then, by hypothesis, channeling jurisdictional power in one direction or the other will have no effect on outcomes. The Supreme Court can sensibly allocate power exclusively on the basis of the considerations captured in the Hart and Wechsler paradigm. To put the point the other way, the paradigm rests on the premise that the federal and state courts are interchangeable. That is *why* the paradigm conceives that jurisdiction can be distributed on outcome-neutral grounds without concern that federal rights will suffer in the process.[79]

If, however, there is no parity between federal and state courts, then the premise of the Hart and Wechsler paradigm is unsound, and allocations of power without consideration of the effect on results make little sense. Obviously, a great deal turns on the question of parity. Many observers are convinced that federal and state courts are not fungible at all and that, with few exceptions, federal courts are better adjudicators—in general and especially in cases involving individual federal rights. The question does not lend itself to empirical testing.[80] Arguments for and against parity rest on formal arrangements, experience, and intuition. The Hart and Wechsler paradigm takes parity as a given.[81] Yet there are reasoned arguments on both sides.

The case *against* parity goes this way. Initially, it is said that the Constitution deliberately makes federal courts more independent than state courts.[82] Article III judges are appointed (not elected). They serve (in effect) for life and thus need not answer for their decisions either in Congress or at the polls. Their salaries cannot be diminished while they are in office. These structural devices insulate

---

78. See text accompanying note 59 (citing the Court's decisions on "standing" as illustrations). Professor Wells insists that the jurisdictional policies that the Hart and Wechsler paradigm embraces do not account for the Court's results and that a more pragmatic perspective is required to get at the "real differences between jurisdictional law and the law of primary rights and obligations." Michael Wells, *Busting the Hart & Wechsler Paradigm*, 11 Const. Comm. 557, 586 (1995).

79. See text accompanying notes 46-47.

80. Efforts have been made to test the parity thesis empirically, but the methodological difficulties render the results unreliable. Compare Michael E. Solimine & James L. Walker, *Constitutional Litigation in Federal and State Courts: An Empirical Analysis of Judicial Parity*, 10 Hastings Const. L.Q. 213 (1983) (reporting no pattern of state court hostility to federal rights), with Erwin Chemerinsky, *Parity Reconsidered: Defining a Role for the Federal Judiciary*, 36 UCLA L. Rev. 233 (1988) (identifying methodological flaws in the Solimine/Walker study).

81. See text accompanying note 46.

82. Geoffrey C. Hazard, Jr., *Reflections on the Substance of Finality*, 70 Cornell L. Rev. 642, 646-47 (1985); see Chapter III, text accompanying note 3.

the federal courts from political accountability and thus enable them to vindicate unpopular civil rights and civil liberties claims without concern for political repercussions. State court judges are typically elected. They rarely enjoy the same safeguards once they are on the bench. And they thus labor under the threat of reprisals if their judgments displease politicians or the public at large.[83]

In addition, and on a different level, it is said that in a host of other ways federal courts are superior institutions. The federal judiciary is small, making it comparatively easy to achieve a high level of quality among individual members; the ranks of state judges are legion, making quality control comparatively difficult. Federal judges are underpaid, but still receive significant salaries; state judges are typically less handsomely compensated. Federal court appointments are enormously prestigious; state court positions, at least at the trial level, enjoy less public repute. Federal judges are appointed under a scheme that, for all its faults, takes some account of professional qualifications; state judges often are selected under systems heavily influenced by political patronage. Federal judges are assisted by excellent young law clerks; state judges typically are served by career staff with less rigorous training. Federal judges face a large but tolerable case load; state judges are swamped with work. Federal judges are generally able to prepare reasoned opinions to guide the public and to explain results to higher courts; state judges are, on the whole, less proficient. In all these ways, federal judges are said to be more capable of interpreting federal rights generously, provided they choose to do so.[84]

Many observers are convinced that federal judges *do* choose to be more hospitable to individuals in federal question cases. They succeed to a unique perspective on the federal system, which generates an expansive understanding of federal claims. Federal judges operate within a grand tradition as an elite core of jurists with the duty and responsibility to implement federal law; state judges lack the same tradition and sense of responsibility. By this account, the federal courts' tradition in service of individual liberty supersedes even the personal ideological inclinations that judges exhibited before they were appointed to the federal bench—arousing men and women who, as lawyers, represented the haves of society to champion, as judges, the interests of society's have-nots. Acting on these presuppositions, lawyers advancing civil rights and civil liberties claims often prefer to be in federal court, simply to gain a "litigating edge."[85]

---

83. See Stephen B. Bright, *Can Judicial Independence Be Attained in the South? Overcoming History, Elections, and Misperceptions About the Role of the Judiciary*, 14 Ga. St. L. Rev. 817 (1998); Chapter III, text accompanying notes 1-2 (describing the benefits of federal judicial independence).

84. See generally Burt Neuborne, *The Myth of Parity*, 90 Harv. L. Rev. 1105 (1977). The appointment of federal judges and the (typical) election of state judges arguably transcends the structural and other conditions that (arguably) produce a superior federal bench. Judges who run for office must raise the capital essential to an effective campaign in the first instance, and, once in office, they must continue to invest time and effort in preparation for the next election. The practical requirement of campaigning obviously does not discourage all good candidates from seeking state judicial office. But it may discourage some.

85. Michael Wells, *Behind the Parity Debate: The Decline of the Legal Process Tradition in the Law of Federal Courts*, 71 B.U. L. Rev. 609, 611 (1991). For differing accounts

Defenders of parity insist, by contrast, that there are valid reasons for accepting the fungibility of federal and state courts—if not as extant reality, then at least as a worthy objective.[86] It is said that a gross comparison of *all* state judges with *all* federal judges ignores variations in quality from state to state and within individual state systems. Moreover, even if state trial judges do not compare well with federal district judges, the same cannot be said (so easily) about the judges who sit on state appellate courts. It is said that the quality of state judges has improved over time. So the case against parity, whatever its strength, is now presumably weaker than at any time in the past. If, indeed, state courts are getting better, there is all the more reason to set aside previous doubts about them and to establish incentives for continued improvement.

Defenders of parity contend that if civil rights and civil liberties plaintiffs prefer to be in federal court, it is because they are understandably concerned only with vindicating their own claims *against* state power. They thus neglect other constitutional values that state courts, operating from a different perspective, are peculiarly positioned to appreciate: values like federalism and the autonomy of the states. It is said, accordingly, that the case against parity suffers from a normative bias *in favor* of individual constitutional claims to be free of state power and *against* countervailing (but equally constitutional) values served by (or at least reflected in) the exercise of state authority.[87]

The parity debate provides the backdrop for many of the Supreme Court's decisions allocating judicial authority. Until recently, the Court declined to discuss the parity question openly in its opinions. Yet it is frankly hard to account for many of the Warren Court's decisions, except as a reflection of that Court's sense that federal claims would be more warmly received in federal court.[88] Today, the Court often declares its conviction that state courts are perfectly willing to vindicate federal rights.[89] Accordingly, the current Court typically explains its judgments on the basis of the outcome-neutral policies associated with the Hart and Wechsler paradigm—which, again, rests on the premise that parity

---

of the implications of allowing litigants to choose where they will press their claims, compare Martin H. Redish, *Judicial Parity, Litigant Choice, and Democratic Theory: A Comment on Federal Jurisdiction and Constitutional Rights*, 36 UCLA L. Rev. 329 (1988), with Erwin Chemerinsky, *Federal Courts, State Courts, and the Constitution: A Rejoinder to Professor Redish*, 36 UCLA L. Rev. 369 (1988).

86. Bator, note 62, at 623-35.

87. Id. at 631-35.

88. See *Dombrowski v. Pfister*, 380 U.S. 479, 498 (Harlan, J., dissenting) (expressing this assessment at the time); accord Owen M. Fiss, *Dombrowski*, 86 Yale L.J. 1103 (1977).

89. See, e.g., *Stone v. Powell*, 428 U.S. 465, 494 n.35 (1976) (insisting that there is no reason to think that a federal court is a more competent or conscientious adjudicator in federal question cases than a state court).

does, indeed, exist. In all candor, however, many observers question whether those considerations genuinely explain the Court's decisions in politically sensitive cases.[90] The best critiques and defenses of the Court's work question what normative, ideological influences lie muted just beneath the surface.[91]

---

90. Professor Nichol laments "how little honest, straightforward, old-fashioned, explanation-giving is ever attempted." Gene R. Nichol, *Is There a Law of Federal Courts?*, 96 W. Va. L. Rev. 147, 166 (1993). Professor McManamon argues that "[w]hen one looks beyond the so-called neutral Federal Courts principles...one sees that the Supreme Court's choices are value-laden." Mary Brigid McManamon, *Challenging the Hart and Wechsler Paradigm*, 27 Conn. L. Rev. 833, 839 (1995).

91. Professor Wells and Professor Matasar call for more explicit attention to the likelihood that the Court distributes jurisdictional power on the basis of unstated predictions that state and federal courts will *not* reach the same outcomes. Michael Wells, *Who's Afraid of Henry Hart?*, 14 Const. Comm. 175 (1997); Wells, *Naked Politics*, note 17; Richard A. Matasar, *Treatise Writing and Federal Jurisdiction: Does Doctrine Matter When Law is Politics?*, 89 Mich. L. Rev. 1449 (1991). Professor Althouse promotes doctrinal devices that draw out the best in state courts, but laments the harsh consequences that often befall litigants who are denied access to a federal tribunal. Ann Althouse, *Late Night Confessions in the Hart and Wechsler Hotel*, 47 Vand. L. Rev. 993, 1003-04 (1994).

Chapter II

Historical Background

The extent to which history affects (or should affect) modern thinking about federal courts is debatable. Originalists insist on beginning with historical materials as the anchor for analysis. Yet few observers believe the founding generation had any definite vision for federal courts. Fewer still believe that, if such a vision existed then, it is retrievable now. Historians do agree, however, on some important features of the historical backdrop. And it is *de rigueur* to take stock of what little we know, or think we know, of the relevant history.

A. The Colonial Period

The early colonists probably had no developed conception of the judicial function. They only dimly perceived the difference between the King's executive power and any separate legislative power that the emerging Parliament presumed to exercise. To the extent they grasped the idea of judicial power at all, they probably regarded adjudication as a species of administration.[1] The judges the colonists knew were the socially connected landowners whom the Crown commissioned to serve in the American provinces. Those royal judges superintended public affairs in an informal way. They imposed taxes, supervised public works projects, and generally presided over their communities.[2]

The royal judges did settle disputes, and the colonists recognized that they might abuse that authority. The colonists thus insisted that judges were empowered only to apply irrefutable legal rules to undisputed facts. If any serious question arose, regarding either the law or the facts, a jury made the necessary judgment. It may be, then, that the colonists either considered juries actually to *be* the courts on which they might rely or saw themselves as participating in judicial decisions by means of jury service. In any case, they regarded judges not as professionals who would protect them and their rights, but rather as instruments of the ruling class — against which ordinary citizens needed protection.[3]

---

1. Jack N. Rakove, Original Meanings: Politics and Ideas in the Making of the Constitution 297-300 (1996).

2. Gordon S. Wood, The Radicalism of the American Revolution 71-72, 82 (1992).

3. Rakove, note 1, at 300-02, 305-06; William E. Nelson, Americanization of the Common Law: The Impact of Legal Change on Massachusetts Society, 1760-1830, 18-35 (1994). The procedural arrangements under which early courts operated were quite different from anything we would recognize today. Professor Bilder illustrates the general point in her his-

Early on, the King surrendered absolute power to name and remove judges in England. Pursuant to the Act of Settlement in 1701, English judges held office during "good behaviour."[4] In the colonies, however, the King insisted on appointing judges to serve at his pleasure (or that of his royal governors) and gave the colonial assemblies no say in the matter.[5] It is hardly surprising, then, that the Declaration of Independence condemned George III for naming judges "dependent on his will alone, for the tenure of their offices, and the amount & paiment of their salaries." Some early state constitutions adopted the "good behavior" standard for judges. Most gave state legislatures authority both to select and to remove judges, typically by means of impeachment.[6]

B. The Articles of Confederation

After the Revolution, the states established the semblance of unified government under the Articles of Confederation. The Articles made no provision for national courts. They routed border disputes between states to a complicated arbitration scheme and relied on state courts for any adjudicative functions required in other situations. In maritime cases, state court judgments were subject to review by a special Court of Appeals for Cases of Capture (staffed by judges but answerable to Congress). State courts entertained any legal actions the central government brought to enforce its laws and claims.[7] The experience under the Articles was not good, and part of the reason may have been the absence of national courts. Chiefly, however, the Articles failed because the member states refused to cooperate with the weak national legislature.[8] Virginia ultimately lost patience and invited the other states to a convention that would explore ways to reform the Articles. That meeting in Annapolis in 1786 produced a call for the Constitutional Convention, which convened the following year in Philadelphia.

The chief task was to devise some means to discipline the states, whose divisive activities frustrated common interests. At the time, even the most insightful of future "framers," James Madison, had no expectation that national courts would be of much help in that effort. Madison, for his part, hoped to fashion a viable union by means of a strong central political structure that could bypass the states and address the people directly. He doubted that courts could curb

---

tory of the idea of "appeal" in early American jurisprudence. Mary S. Bilder, *The Origins of Appeal in America*, 48 Hastings L. Rev. 913 (1997).

4. Joseph H. Smith, *An Independent Judiciary: The Colonial Background*, 124 U. Pa. L. Rev. 1104-12 (1976).

5. Martha Andes Ziskind, *Judicial Tenure in the American Constitution: English and American Precedents*, 1969 Sup. Ct. Rev. 135.

6. Gerhard Casper, *The Judiciary Act of 1789 and Judicial Independence*, in Origins of the Federal Judiciary: Essays on the Judiciary Act of 1789, at 281, 284 (Marcus ed. 1992).

7. Hampton L. Carson, The Supreme Court of the United States 44-64 (1891).

8. The Continental Congress lacked sufficient power to enforce the Treaty of Paris, to raise the revenues needed for westward expansion, and to regulate commerce with other nations and among the states. The Articles required a vote of nine states to take significant action and unanimity for amendments. See Rakove, note 1, at 25-28.

state abuses and envisioned, instead, a congressional veto over ill-advised state legislation. Madison anticipated using Supreme Court justices only as members of a council of revision, which would review statutes the new national legislature enacted before they became effective.[9]

C. The Constitutional Convention

The delegates to the Convention in Philadelphia focused on the powers that would be given to the new Congress and on the creation of a national executive. Yet both Randolph's Virginia plan and Patterson's New Jersey plan proposed to establish a federal judiciary as well. The delegates accepted the idea of at least a single Supreme Court. They debated whether other federal tribunals, inferior to the Supreme Court, should also be established.

Nationally inclined delegates, whom we now (oddly) call "Federalists,"[10] argued that the Constitution should mandate a full complement of inferior federal courts. Delegates more concerned with preserving state prerogatives insisted that the state courts already in existence would suffice. In the debate that ensued, Madison and other Federalists contended that state courts could not be relied upon to protect federal interests when those interests conflicted with the concerns of individual states.[11] According to conventional wisdom, the *impasse* was broken by the "Madisonian Compromise," under which the delegates agreed that the Constitution would permit, but would not require, the new Congress to cre-

---

9. Id. at 51-54.

10. It is conventional to refer to the more nationally oriented delegates in Philadelphia as Federalists but unconventional to label their adversaries Anti-Federalists. Only three delegates present at the final meaning refused to sign the new Constitution. The "Anti-Federalist" designation is typically reserved for delegates to the state ratifying conventions, who openly opposed the Constitution. See note 29 and accompanying text.

11. Max Farrand, The Framing of the Constitution 80 (1913). By some accounts, Madison meant that state courts could not be trusted to enforce federal *law*, including the new Constitution, and that the Supreme Court alone would be unable to bring them to heel. E.g., Casper, note 6, at 286. Accordingly, he anticipated that inferior federal courts would be important to the development of the national framework the Federalists envisioned. By other accounts, Madison had no expectation that a significant body of federal law, as distinguished from the common law or state law, would be developed—by any court. Instead, he was concerned that state courts would not protect federal *interests*. They might fail to appreciate the unity of the nation under the new Constitution and thus might favor their own citizens in disputes with citizens of other states. That was the kind of provincialism that had made the Articles of Confederation unworkable, and Madison hoped to avert it by the introduction of new federal courts that would be free of local bias. See Carl McGowan, The Organization of Judicial Power in the United States 26-28 (1967) (making this point with respect to Madison's similarly ambiguous argument during the debate on the Judiciary Act of 1789). If Madison was worried about substantive law at all, he anticipated that state legislatures would enact statutes in violation of vaguely defined natural rights that Americans had always claimed (entitlements reflected in the rights of Englishmen that colonists insisted were theirs) and that state courts would be unable to stand in their way. Even as to those rights, Madison put his trust primarily in structural limitations on power rather than on federal courts simply enforcing rights in the teeth of political opposition. Rakove, note 1, at 290, 314-16.

ate inferior federal courts.[12] The implication is that, even today, the very existence of lower federal courts may not be constitutionally guaranteed, but may be contingent on Congress' policy predilections.[13]

Inasmuch as the Supreme Court itself was sure to be created, the Convention took responsibility for specifying its purview, at least in broad outline. The delegates agreed that the Court should function in the main as an appellate body, correcting the mistakes made by lower courts. In some narrow circumstances, however, they concluded that the Court should have original jurisdiction to determine matters not previously examined below. Those instances were unremarkable: disputes involving states as parties or implicating representatives of foreign governments.[14] The delegates left the shape of the Supreme Court largely undefined. Nothing in Article III specified the size of the Court, for example, or so much as mentioned its presiding officer.[15]

The delegates argued at some length about the means by which Supreme Court justices would be chosen. There was no suggestion that the justices might be *elected*; the question was how they would be *appointed*—and by whom.[16] The original Virginia Plan contemplated that the full Congress would make selections. Madison preferred the Senate, perhaps because the smaller body might be less inclined to name justices on the basis of personal friendship or talents for legislative, as opposed to judicial, service. His view prevailed on the whole. Yet in the end, after the Convention decided that Senate membership would be apportioned by states rather than by population, Madison and others evidently concluded that a nationally elected officer, namely the President, should share the responsibility. That is the implication typically drawn from the scheme established by the Appointments Clause.[17]

---

12. Rakove, note 1, at 172. Accord Farrand, note 11, at 155. Some delegates may have hoped that new federal courts would not be created, but that state courts would be commissioned to act as federal tribunals. Federalists almost certainly would have opposed a scheme of that kind and may have thwarted the idea by dropping early language indicating that federal courts would be "appointed" and substituting the language ultimately adopted—by which Congress was given authority to "ordain and establish" inferior federal tribunals. That language arguably connotes new federally chartered institutions, not new authority for existing state judges. See Michael G. Collins, *Article III Cases, State Court Duties, and the Madisonian Compromise*, 1995 Wis. L. Rev. 39, 112-26. Nevertheless, Madison evidently suggested to the Virginia ratifying convention that at least some state courts might be recruited for federal duty. Of course, Madison might have been willing to stretch the truth a bit in aid of getting Virginia into line behind the new Constitution. See McGowan, note 11, at 21-22.

13. See Chapter IV, notes 8-9 and accompanying text (elaborating this point).

14. U.S. Const. art. III, § 2, cl.2. Professor Collins speculates that the Convention may have circumscribed the Supreme Court's original jurisdiction in order to reinforce the Madisonian Compromise. If original jurisdiction had been more expansive, the Court might itself have functioned in the manner of a full body of federal tribunals—by dividing itself into numerous panels for conducting trials. Collins, note 12, at 107-10.

15. Article I designates the chief justice to preside at any Senate impeachment trial of the President. U.S. Const. art. I, § 3, cl.6. See John Niven, Salmon P. Chase: A Biography 415-32 (1995) (describing the one instance in which such a trial was conducted: the trial of Andrew Johnson).

16. The election of judges in this country was a Nineteenth Century idea, the product of Jacksonian populism. See Mary Volcansek & Jacqueline Lafon, Judicial Selection: The Cross-Evolution of French and American Practices 75-98 (1988).

17. U.S. Const. art. II, § 2, cl.2. See Chapter III, notes 4-18 and accompanying text (describing the appointment of Supreme Court justices today).

The means by which justices would be held accountable also excited attention. On that point, the colonies' history with King George was paramount. The delegates agreed that Supreme Court justices (as well as any inferior court judges who were ultimately appointed) would not be subject to removal at will (by either the President or Congress). Instead, adopting language directly from the English Act of Settlement, the delegates proposed that judges would serve "during good Behaviour" and would receive salaries that could not be reduced during their tenure.[18] Both justices and judges would be removable, but only for misconduct and then only by impeachment.

Some points of vital conceptual importance apparently aroused no substantial controversy. The delegates readily agreed, for example, that the Supreme Court would have authority to review state court decisions. Perhaps in light of that authority, they rejected Madison's idea for a congressional veto over errant state statutes. Instead, the delegates adopted the Supremacy Clause, which contemplated that the Supreme Court would review state court judgments to ensure that state judges respected federal law, anything to the contrary in state law notwithstanding.[19] By some accounts, it was the delegates who most feared the expansion of federal power in general who least resisted that innovation in particular. To them, it was easier to accept that the state courts would be subject to the Supreme Court's appellate supervision than it was to tolerate the obvious alternative: a constitutionally mandated body of inferior federal courts. The thinking leading to the Supremacy Clause was thus linked with the Madisonian Compromise.[20]

The delegates also agreed that the Supreme Court would have authority to determine the Constitution's meaning. It was for that reason, perhaps, that they rejected Madison's idea for a council of revision (whose membership would have included sitting members of the Court) to pass on federal legislation. The justices scarcely needed to examine legislation as soon as it was enacted if they would have ample opportunity to pass on its validity later.[21] Moreover, the delegates may have thought that involving federal judges in the legislative process was inconsistent with the developing (though as yet still primitive) sense that governmental power in the new framework should not be concentrated in any one place.[22] The Convention's answer to ill-considered federal legislation was, instead, the President's veto power.[23]

The delegates expressed no clear view regarding the conditions under which the Supreme Court, or any inferior courts Congress created, would exercise judi-

---

18. U.S. Const. art. III, § 1. See Chapter III, notes 26-40 and accompanying text (describing impeachment and alternative means of discipline now in place).

19. U.S. Const. art. VI, cl.2.

20. Rakove, note 1, at 171-77.

21. This is not to say that the delegates regarded the Supreme Court's power of judicial review as particularly important or that they anticipated that the Court's unifying force would hold the country together. It is more likely that the delegates put their faith in various structural devices built into the constitutional scheme, which constantly divided and subdivided power in an apparent attempt to achieve a shifting yet viable balance. See Robert A. Burt, The Constitution in Conflict 46, 56-72 (1992); Gordon S. Wood, The Creation of the American Republic, 1776-1787, 549-50 (1969). See Chapter I, note 4 and accompanying text (noting the early appreciation for the separation principle).

22. Casper, note 6, at 286. See James T. Barry, *The Council of Revision and the Limits of Judicial Power*, 56 U. Chi. L. Rev. 235, 253-54 (1989).

23. U.S. Const. art. I, § 7.

cial power. At one point, Madison said that the federal judiciary should be limited to cases of a "Judiciary Nature."[24] Yet it is unclear what he meant by that characterization. Certainly, it is unclear what anyone else understood him to mean. Recall in this vein that the preexisting royal courts had routinely performed duties that today would be regarded as legislative or executive in nature.[25]

The Committee on Detail produced a draft, under which federal judicial power might be exercised in nine overlapping categories of "cases" and "controversies." By most accounts, the draft (and ultimately Article III) used the terms "case" and "controversy" interchangeably.[26] In some instances, Article III defined "cases" or "controversies" according to their subject matter. That was true, for example, with respect to "cases arising under this Constitution, the Laws of the United States, and Treaties made, or which shall be made, under their Authority."[27] In other instances, Article III defined "cases" or "controversies" according to the identity or alignment of the parties. That was true with respect to what we now call "diversity" jurisdiction over "Controversies...between Citizens of different States."

Once the delegates approved a final document, they asked the Continental Congress to transmit it to specially formed state ratifying conventions. Importantly, they insisted that the Constitution must be presented as an indivisible whole, not subject to amendment. That take-it-or-leave-it strategy evoked significant opposition. But it worked. Ultimately, all the states accepted the full document without insisting on changes as a condition of ratification.[28]

D. Ratification and the Federalist Papers

At some of the state ratifying conventions, the Constitution encountered opposition from detractors, grouped under the label "Anti-Federalists." Roughly speaking, the Anti-Federalists were the conservatives of their day. They were sus-

---

24. Max Farrand, II The Records of the Federal Constitution of 1787, at 430 (1937).

25. See text accompanying note 2.

26. Alternatively, it has been suggested that a "case" could be a criminal proceeding, but a "controversy" was necessarily civil. See William A. Fletcher, *Exchange on the Eleventh Amendment*, 57 U. Chi. L. Rev. 131, 133 (1990); Daniel J. Meltzer, *The History and Structure of Article III*, 138 U. Pa. L. Rev. 1569, 1575-76 & nn. 18 & 22 (1990). Professor Pushaw argues that the founding generation regarded a "case" as an occasion for resolving important public questions, but regarded a "controversy" as an occasion for resolving a private dispute between self-interested advocates. Robert J. Pushaw, Jr., *Article III's Case/Controversy Distinction and the Dual Functions of Federal Courts*, 69 Notre Dame L. Rev. 447 (1994); see Chapter IX, note 8 (discussing the implications of Pushaw's research for the modern justiciability doctrines). Professor Pfander argues that the distinction between "cases" and "controversies" fortifies his (revisionist) account of the Supreme Court's original jurisdiction. See Chapter VII, note 9.

27. See Chapter IV, note 3 and accompanying text; Chapter VIII (elaborating the federal courts' jurisdiction to decide federal question cases).

28. Rakove, note 1, at 100-16.

picious of change, ever mindful of stability, and fearful that the new Constitution would subvert state autonomy.[29]

Where the delegates in Philadelphia had focused no great attention on the judicial branch, Anti-Federalist delegates to the state ratifying conventions made the prospect of a powerful federal judiciary a major focus of their attack. They charged that the Supreme Court and any inferior courts that might be established would be insulated from political constraints. Courts with that kind of independence would know no other authority but themselves.[30] Recall that the colonial courts had exercised broad governmental power and that one of the chief objections to that regime had always been that those courts were free from any legislative check.[31] Moreover, the new Constitution did not clearly preserve the right to jury trial and thus threatened to discard the only safeguard against judicial power with which the colonists were familiar.[32]

The Anti-Federalists did not defeat ratification of the Constitution. But they did persuade many ratifying conventions to urge the new Congress to give early consideration to several amendments regarding the federal judiciary. There were proposals, for example, to specify the separation-of-powers principle more explicitly, to delimit the federal courts' purview, to eliminate the Supreme Court's authority to review determinations of *fact* as well as *law*, and to confirm the right to trial by jury expressly. Several conventions also offered amendments that would have immunized the states from suit in federal court.[33]

Madison collected the proposals advanced by the ratifying conventions, sifted them into categories, and developed a list of amendments for submission to Congress. Ten were adopted in 1791. The first eight formed the Bill of Rights. In some instances, those early amendments addressed the ratifying conventions' concerns about the federal judicial branch. The provisions for trial by jury in the sixth and seventh amendments fit that description. In other instances, state concerns were overlooked or deliberately neglected. Madison himself almost certainly thought that no explicit acknowledgment of the separation principle was needed or desirable. He nonetheless drafted an innocuous amendment to satisfy others' concerns. The House accepted it, but the Senate did not.[34] Madison declined to prepare an amendment regarding state sovereign immunity—an issue that was revisited when the eleventh amendment was promulgated.[35]

---

29. The "Anti-Federalist" label has always been confusing. Professor Storing explains that delegates to whom it was applied "usually denied, in fact, that the name was either apt or just, and seldom used it." According to Storing, the Anti-Federalists "often claimed" they were "the true federalists." Yet the "pro-Constitution party" saw "the advantage of a label that would suggest that those who opposed the Constitution also opposed such a manifestly good thing as federalism.... But what has not been sufficiently understood is that the term 'federal' had acquired a specific ambiguity that enabled [pro-Constitution delegates] not merely to take but to keep the name." Herbert J. Storing, What the Anti-Federalists Were For: The Political Thought of the Opponents of the Constitution 7-9 (1981).

30. See Casper, note 6, at 288-89 (collecting relevant primary materials).

31. See notes 4-6 and accompanying text.

32. See note 3 and accompanying text.

33. See Rakove, note 1, at 318-21.

34. See Chapter I, note 2 and accompanying text.

35. See text accompanying note 68; see Chapter X, notes 46-63 and accompanying text (discussing the later adoption of the eleventh amendment).

The ratification debates produced more than formal adoption of the Constitution. They also generated the Federalist Papers: thoughtful and illuminating essays about the Constitution by Madison, Alexander Hamilton, and John Jay. The Federalist Papers were neither disinterested appraisals of the new Constitution's meaning nor neutral recollections of the actual deliberations in Philadelphia. They were works of advocacy—political tracts meant to dispel Anti-Federalist objections. Nevertheless, they are typically cited in modern arguments about constitutional interpretation. For as Madison, Hamilton, and Jay responded to the concerns raised by their Anti-Federalist adversaries, they developed what many now regard as the United States' unique contribution to political theory.[36]

Most of the Federalist Papers explored structural themes in the Constitution: the separation of powers, as well as federalism and the idea of republicanism.[37] Some addressed questions raised at the state conventions about the new federal judiciary. Hamilton in particular made a series of related points about the judicial branch.

The status of the federal courts. By Hamilton's account, it would be "essential to the idea of law" in the new constitutional system "that it be attended by a sanction, or, in other words, a penalty or punishment for disobedience."[38] Adjudication in the courts would provide the only available vehicle for ensuring that law was respected. Hamilton recognized that courts would have no physical power to force the states and the other two branches of the national government to cooperate, but would have to depend on Congress (which would control the public purse) and the President (who would control the sword). Thus the judiciary must always be, in Hamilton's memorable description, the "least dangerous" feature of the new framework.[39]

The independence of federal courts. By Hamilton's account, an independent federal judiciary would not be a vice, but a virtue. He insisted that the country could not depend entirely on state courts, but would need national tribunals that would be insulated from parochial interests. In the same vein, he argued that federal courts must be free from manipulation by the elected branches of the national government. It was to ensure judicial independence that the new Constitution guaranteed that federal judges would serve for life (given good behavior) and would receive irreducible salaries. Hamilton insisted that "a power over a man's subsistence amounts to a power over his will."[40] Without personal protections for individual judges, federal courts would be forced to "consult popularity" as well as "the constitution and the laws" in reaching judicial decisions.[41] They would be at the mercy of the President and Congress and would be unable to enforce checks on governmental power.[42]

---

36. See generally Bernard Bailyn, The Ideological Origins of the American Revolution (1977).
37. E.g., Federalist 10, 51 (Madison).
38. Federalist 15.
39. Federalist 78.
40. Federalist 79.
41. Federalist 78.
42. Federalist 78, 79. Hamilton added that federal judges would need an extended tenure in order to gain and retain command of the precedents that would develop as the nation grew. Good candidates might be discouraged from accepting federal appointments and

The removal of federal judges. Hamilton acknowledged that federal judges could be forced from office. But he contended that the only means available would be formal impeachment (as prescribed in Article I of the Constitution) and that the only permissible basis would be "mal-conduct"[43]—by which he probably meant "Treason, Bribery, or other high Crimes and Misdemeanors" (as prescribed in Article II).[44] Hamilton justified severe limits on removal as a further safeguard for judicial independence. So intent was he on protecting the judiciary from the other branches that he resisted even the possibility that Article III judges should be unseated for "inability." A standard of that kind might tempt the President or Congress to declare unpopular judges incompetent and thus to deprive them of their offices by indirection. For Hamilton, only "insanity" could be "safely pronounced a virtual disqualification."[45]

The supremacy of federal law. In Hamilton's view, the federal courts would certainly have jurisdiction to adjudicate cases implicating the new Constitution. That power would be especially important to ensure that the federal judiciary could force state legislatures and state courts to conform to the Constitution as the supreme law of the land. Otherwise, the states might continue to obstruct national unity as they had under the Articles of Confederation.[46]

The uniformity of federal law. By Hamilton's account, federal judicial power must be co-extensive with federal legislative power. This is to say, the federal courts must be able to handle the judicial business generated when Congress enacted federal statutes. Otherwise, state courts would have to do service, and it would be difficult to obtain consistent interpretations of federal law in all the states.[47]

Cases in which the United States is a party. Under the Articles of Confederation, attorneys representing the national government had been forced to sue in state court. That, in Hamilton's view, not only jeopardized the supremacy and uniformity of federal law, but also offended proper "decorum."[48] Under the new Constitution, it would be vital that the federal courts have jurisdiction in cases in which the United States itself was a party.

Diversity jurisdiction. According to Hamilton, the federal courts must have authority to adjudicate disputes that cut across state boundary lines, especially disputes between two states as parties, as well as cases involving foreign nations and their citizens. There, too, Hamilton thought state courts would be incapable of providing the necessary independence, national perspective, and respect for

---

achieving expertise in federal materials, if they risked losing their positions after an ordinary term of office. Federalist 78.

43. Federalist 79; U.S. Const. art I, § 3.

44. U.S. Const. art. II, § 4. See Chapter III, notes 29-33 and accompanying text (discussing the grounds for impeachment today).

45. Federalist 79.

46. Federalist 80.

47. In this, Hamilton embraced the understanding, common in the period, that a government's legislative and judicial powers must be coterminous. That may have suggested to Anti-Federalists that the more expansive the power Hamilton contemplated for the judicial branch, the more expansive, in turn, the power he must contemplate for Congress. See G. Edward White, *Recovering Coterminous Power Theory: The Lost Dimension of Marshall Court Sovereignty Cases*, in Origins, note 6, at 66, 93-94.

48. Federalist 80.

the status and dignity of other states and nations. Hamilton referred to suits against *unconsenting* states, but only elliptically. He may have meant to paper over the controversial question of sovereign immunity.[49]

The state courts. Hamilton recognized that state courts had jurisdiction, grounded in state law, to handle a wide range of cases having nothing to do with the new national framework. Article III authorized Congress to establish new federal tribunals to adjudicate some of those same cases — for example, disputes between citizens of different states. But Article III did not purport to make federal jurisdiction of those cases exclusive and thus to divest the state courts of the power they had previously had under state law. Hamilton acknowledged that the Constitution might be read to preclude state court jurisdiction implicitly inasmuch as Article III declared that the federal judicial power "shall" be vested in Article III courts. Yet he insisted that Article III should not be construed to alienate the state courts' prior jurisdiction by implication. In this, Hamilton stated the general proposition that, *ceteris paribus*, the state courts and any new federal courts would function side-by-side, typically with concurrent jurisdiction over the same subject matter and parties.[50]

Exclusive federal jurisdiction. By Hamilton's account, Congress would have authority to make the federal courts' jurisdiction exclusive (and thus to foreclose the state courts from acting) in cases or controversies arising entirely from the new federal framework. But he insisted that state courts would have concurrent jurisdiction, unless and until Congress "expressly" barred them from entertaining specified business. He thus carved out a significant measure of congressional power, but at the same time also conditioned that power on Congress' willingness (and ability) to satisfy a clear statement rule.[51]

Supreme Court jurisdiction to review state judgments. Again to ensure the supremacy and uniformity of federal law, Hamilton explained that the Supreme Court would have appellate jurisdiction to review state court judgments regarding cases and controversies subject to federal judicial power. He insisted that Article III's express reference to the Court's appellate jurisdiction plainly contemplated that appeals from state courts might be heard. Moreover, it was implicit in the underlying plan that state courts, as well as any inferior federal courts that might be created, were elements of a single judicial system and thus were naturally subject to the final discipline that a single Supreme Court would provide.[52]

E. The Judiciary Acts of 1789–1793

After the new government was assembled, Congress made the creation of the judicial branch a priority. The Judiciary Act of 1789 established both the

---

49. Id. See also Federalist 81.

50. Federalist 82.

51. Id. See Chapter I, notes 37-41 and accompanying text (discussing the clear statement doctrine and its function).

52. Federalist 82. Elaborating this point, Hamilton conceded that Article III left it to Congress to decide whether to create inferior federal courts with appellate jurisdiction to review state court judgments.

Supreme Court and a body of inferior federal courts: district courts (with only original jurisdiction) and circuit courts (with both original and appellate jurisdiction). The circuit courts were assigned no judges of their own and had to be staffed by district judges and Supreme Court justices, who, in turn, traveled very significant distances to sit periodically on the circuit bench.[53] The particulars of the jurisdictional grants to the early district and circuit courts are unimportant today.[54] But some general points are of crucial conceptual significance.

The Judiciary Act of 1789 conferred substantial jurisdictional power on the federal judicial branch, covering most of the categories that Hamilton had identified as crucial.[55] Most of the jurisdictional assignments depended on the status or alignment of the parties. For example, the Act gave the Supreme Court original jurisdiction over civil controversies in which a state was a party. And it gave district and circuit courts authority (concurrent with state courts) to entertain cases involving parties of diverse citizenship and, as well, cases in which the United States was the plaintiff. The Act also extended federal judicial power to cases identified by subject matter. For example, the Act granted the district and circuit courts federal jurisdiction over admiralty cases and federal criminal prosecutions. And it gave both those inferior courts and the Supreme Court authority to entertain petitions for the writ of habeas corpus from prisoners who claimed that federal officials were detaining them in violation of federal law.[56] Those grants of jurisdiction ensured that the federal judiciary would have a significant role to play, especially in cases implicating individual liberty.[57]

---

53. Itinerant judges had been common in England, and Congress may have chosen the same pattern without considering the burdens on justices in a much larger country. Historians report that some candidates for the Court declined to be considered rather than face "riding circuit." Those who served complained bitterly. The notorious "Midnight Judges Act" of 1801 assigned the old circuit courts their own judges and eliminated circuit-riding for a brief period. But that action by the outgoing Federalists was immediately reversed by the incoming Jeffersonians, who jettisoned the 1801 Act (and circuit judgeships with it) in 1802—as part of the episode that produced *Marbury v. Madison*. See Chapter I, notes 54-58 and accompanying text. Circuit-riding survived (at least formally) until 1891. Professor Amar suggests that the circuit-riding idea may have had conceptual significance as an indication that Supreme Court justices were not on a different hierarchical plane from district court judges. That, he thinks, is why justices could be expected to staff lower court positions routinely. Akhil R. Amar, *Jurisdiction Stripping and the Judiciary Act of 1789*, in Origins, note 6, at 40, 58-60.

54. For a more detailed summary, see Wilfred J. Ritz, Rewriting the History of the Judiciary Act of 1789, 63-70 (Holt & LaRue eds. 1990).

55. See text accompanying notes 46-52. Typically, the Act restricted jurisdiction to cases involving specified monetary amounts in controversy. For example, the circuit courts could review district court judgments only if the amount in controversy exceeded $50.

56. The Constitution bars the suspension of the "privilege" of the writ of habeas corpus, "unless when in Cases of Rebellion or Invasion the public Safety may require it." U.S. Const. art. I, § 9, cl.2. The Supreme Court suggested in *Ex parte Bollman*, 8 U.S. (4 Cranch) 75 (1807), that the statutory provision in the Judiciary Act was necessary to confer jurisdiction on the federal courts to issue the writ. That understanding of the Suspension Clause has been questioned. For a discussion of the Suspension Clause generally, see Chapter XII, notes 15-33. See also Chapter IV, note 70.

57. The 1789 Act also introduced the idea of removal jurisdiction—by which lawsuits initiated in state court can sometimes be transferred (removed) to federal court. See Chapter VI, notes 116-48 and accompanying text (discussing modern removal statutes and describing the relationship between removal and original jurisdiction in federal question cases).

The Act nevertheless stopped short of conferring on the federal courts the full measure of judicial power specified in Article III. Academians have identified numerous instances in which the Act might have extended the federal courts' authority further than it did. Congress evidently understood that it had discretion to create courts, but at the same time to withhold from the courts it created at least some parts of (indeed, large chunks of) the business that Article III potentially made available as a constitutional matter.[58]

The gaps between the jurisdiction that Article III would have allowed Congress to assign and the jurisdiction that Congress actually conferred were extremely significant. The chief example is the Judiciary Act's failure to give the district and circuit courts a general jurisdiction to entertain cases "arising under" federal law. That is the one basis of jurisdiction one might have expected the Act to recognize—for the reasons that Hamilton and others had articulated. In 1789, there was no substantial body of federal law (as distinct from state law or English common law) to enforce in any court. Moreover, the district and circuit courts were positioned to address issues of federal law that appeared in cases within their party-based jurisdiction.[59] Nevertheless, the Act's omission of a general jurisdiction in federal question cases appears to be important.[60]

The 1789 Act gave the Supreme Court jurisdiction (via the writ of error) to review civil judgments rendered either in the lower federal courts or in the highest state courts.[61] There, too, however, the Act withheld the full appellate power

---

58. See Chapter IV, notes 19-31 and accompanying text (elaborating this point).

59. See Akhil R. Amar, *A Neo-Federalist View of Article III: Separating the Two Tiers of Federal Jurisdiction*, 65 B.U. L. Rev. 205 (1985).

60. See Meltzer, note 26, at 1585; Chapter IV, notes 90-105 and accompanying text (discussing the implications of congressional power to withhold jurisdiction in civil liberties cases). Professor Holt argues that some members of Congress hesitated to give inferior federal courts a general jurisdiction in federal question cases, in fear that those courts would serve as collection agencies for Revolutionary War debts based on treaties. Wythe Holt, *To Establish Justice: Politics, the Judiciary Act of 1789, and the Invention of the Federal Courts*, 1989 Duke L.J. 1421. See Chapter X, notes 75-76 and accompanying text (discussing the relationship between the war debt cases and the eleventh amendment). Because the Judiciary Act of 1789 came so early, and because so many members of Congress at the time had also been delegates to the Constitutional Convention, the state ratifying conventions, or both, the Act is often cited as evidence of what the founding generation thought the Constitution itself contemplated. E.g., *Wisconsin v. Pelican Ins. Co.*, 127 U.S. 265, 297 (1888). Maeva Marcus and Natalie Wexler have discovered evidence that many members neglected the text of Article III and, instead, made pragmatic judgments about the jurisdiction the federal courts needed to safeguard federal interests. Maeva Marcus & Natalie Wexler, *The Judiciary Act of 1789: Political Compromise or Constitutional Interpretation?*, in Origins, note 6, at 24. It appears, then, that the Act may not have simply embodied what Congress took to be the meaning of the cases and controversies to which Article III referred. It does seem clear that Congress read the Constitution to leave the particulars of the federal courts' purview to legislation—within the outer limits established by Article III. Perhaps relatedly, the Act *did* contain what we now call the Rules of Decision Act, which specifies that "the laws of the several states" typically provide the "rules of decision" in "civil actions in the courts of the United States." See Chapter VIII, notes 34-35, 55 and accompanying text (discussing the Rules of Decision Act in connection with the federal courts' authority to create federal common law).

61. The Act conferred no appellate jurisdiction on the Court in federal criminal cases. *United States v. More*, 7 U.S. (3 Cranch) 159 (1805); see Marc M. Arkin, *Rethinking the Constitutional Right to a Criminal Appeal*, 39 UCLA L. Rev. 503, 521-22 (1992). Professor Liebman has shown that the Court was able to exercise review by means of its jurisdiction

that Article III would have permitted. The Act pointedly restricted the Court's purview to judgments in which a party had advanced a federal claim below and *lost*. If, instead, the lower court had sustained a federal claim (over, for example, an opponent's state law defense), the Act made no provision for Supreme Court review. The implication was that the Court had appellate jurisdiction to ensure that federal law was held *supreme*, but not to ensure that federal law was interpreted *uniformly*.

In addition to creating new federal tribunals and prescribing their jurisdiction, the Judiciary Act of 1789 attended to various other organizational and logistical matters. Inasmuch as the Constitution prescribed no set number of justices for the Supreme Court, Congress necessarily exercised its own judgment regarding that practical problem. The 1789 Act fixed the number at six. In 1801, Congress (then controlled by Federalists) reduced the Court to five seats, apparently to prevent the newly elected Jefferson from naming a replacement for Justice Cushing, who was ill at the time. Thereafter, Congress increased the number of justices—to seven, to nine, and to a high of ten during Lincoln's tenure. After the Civil War, Congress reduced the Court back to seven seats, apparently to keep Andrew Johnson from advancing any nominations at all. The number returned to nine with Grant's election and has remained there ever since.[62]

The 1789 Act left other important matters to be resolved by custom and practice. Like the Constitution itself, the Act largely neglected the Supreme Court's presiding officer, acknowledging only that one of its members would be chief justice.[63] From there, things might have developed in any number of directions.[64] In the event, President Washington specifically identified his choice for chief justice (John Jay). Since then, the custom has been that candidates are nominated, confirmed, and appointed to that particular office—and then hold it for life (barring impeachment).[65]

After affirmatively establishing the federal court system and prescribing its many authorities in 1789, Congress turned to housekeeping amendments and a series of restrictive measures. The Judiciary Acts of 1790 and 1793 contained both a version of what is now the Anti-Injunction Statute, 28 U.S.C.

---

to issue writs of habeas corpus. James S. Liebman, *Apocalypse Next Time? The Anachronistic Attack on Habeas Corpus/Direct Review Parity*, 92 Colum. L. Rev. 1997, 2058-59 (1992).

62. Franklin Roosevelt asked Congress to increase the number of justices, ostensibly to ensure that elderly members were not overworked but, by all accounts, actually to achieve a majority to sustain the New Deal. That effort failed and is now widely regarded as an attempt to undermine the Court's independence. See Chapter III, note 2.

63. See note 15 and accompanying text.

64. To name only a few, the President might have named six justices and left them to choose their own presiding officer, perhaps according to seniority or by election. The chief judges of the modern district courts and circuit courts of appeals are determined by seniority. 28 U.S.C. §§ 45(a)(1), 136(a)(1). Alternatively, the President might have named one of the six as chief justice, but with the understanding that the justice selected would preside for a fixed term or, perhaps, during the President's own term of office. The Lord Chancellor of England is obliged to surrender his office with a change in the British government. Henry Cecil, The English Judge 19-20 (1970).

65. The current statute only identifies the chief justice as a distinct member of the Court. 28 U.S.C. § 1. See Chapter III, notes 4-18 and accompanying text (discussing the appointment process).

§ 2283,[66] and the Full Faith and Credit Statute, 28 U.S.C. § 1738.[67] Concomitantly in 1793, Congress took the initial steps toward the eleventh amendment, which was formally proposed in 1794 and ultimately ratified in 1798.[68]

While the Capitol was under construction in Washington, the new national government established itself in New York City, where the Continental Congress had been located. The Supreme Court met for the first time in 1790 in a room in the Royal Exchange Building on Broad Street. There were no cases, and the Court summarily adjourned. There were still no cases the following year, when the government moved to Philadelphia. Over the next ten years, the justices routinely surrendered their quarters to city and state courts, which had comparatively heavy caseloads to manage. It was well into the Nineteenth Century before either the Supreme Court or the lower federal courts handled a significant body of judicial business beyond maritime and real property disputes.[69]

When the Capitol was completed in 1800, Congress had a home, but the Supreme Court still did not. The justices took a spare room on the first floor of the Capitol building, but often found that space intolerably dry and preferred to conduct what little business they had across the street at Long's Tavern, where the Library of Congress now stands. Later, the Court used another room just beneath the Senate chamber. Legend has it that when British troops burned the Capitol in 1814, they used some of the Court's official documents as tinder. There is no commonly accepted account of whether the papers were missed. The Court moved to the building it now occupies in 1935.

The federal judiciary's structure and jurisdiction changed comparatively little for three quarters of a century. On a number of occasions, Congress extended the federal courts' authority to issue the writ of habeas corpus. During Reconstruction, however, the federal courts' place in the system was altered in ways that can only be regarded as revolutionary.

F. Reconstruction

The Reconstruction period is aptly named. That brief span of years, 1865-1876, produced a fundamental transformation of the relations between the central government and the states. The post-Civil War constitutional amendments, particularly the fourteenth, together with a host of civil rights statutes, established crucial new federal restraints on state power. Simultaneously, numerous new statutes extended the jurisdiction and the remedial authority of the federal

---

66. See Chapter XI, notes 8-30 and accompanying text.
67. See Chapter VI, notes 156-87 and accompanying text.
68. See Chapter X, notes 46-63 and accompanying text.
69. John P. Frank, *Historical Bases of the Federal Judicial System*, 13 Law & Contemp. Prob. 3, 15-18 (1948). Early on, the Supreme Court's station was such that John Rutledge, named as one of the first associate justices, promptly resigned to become chief justice of the Supreme Court of South Carolina. Henry J. Abraham, *Justices and Presidents: A Political History of Appointments to the Supreme Court* 65, 71 (3d ed. 1992).

courts, in order that they might provide the adjudicative machinery needed to enforce the new federal rights.

The Reconstruction Congress enacted the Habeas Corpus Act of 1867, 28 U.S.C. § 2241, *et seq.* (which authorized the federal courts to entertain petitions from prisoners held in *state*, as well as federal, custody in violation of federal law);[70] the Civil Rights Removal Statute, 28 U.S.C. § 1443 (which allowed defendants sued in state court to remove the actions against them to federal court on a showing that they would be denied their federally protected civil rights in state court);[71] and the Judiciary Act of 1875, containing 28 U.S.C. § 1331 (which finally assigned the federal courts a general jurisdiction in civil actions "arising under" federal law).[72] In 1871, Congress enacted the Ku Klux Klan Act, 42 U.S.C. § 1983, which (fortified by an accompanying jurisdictional statute)[73] authorized federal courts to entertain civil actions on behalf of anyone claiming to be deprived of federal rights by a person acting under color of state law.[74] By means of that Act and others, the Reconstruction Congress charged the federal courts to shoulder new and enormously important authority and responsibility for securing individuals' civil rights against state power.[75]

G. The Modern Structure

In the wake of Reconstruction, the federal courts' role in American public life became ever more significant. At the end of the Nineteenth Century, Congress finally discarded much of the framework erected in 1789 in favor of a more rational and coherent structure. Statutes enacted between 1887 and 1925, particularly the Evarts Act in 1891 and the Judges Bill in 1925, established the basic elements of the modern scheme. During the same period, Congress extended the federal courts' purview in extremely important ways. In 1934, Congress enacted

---

70. See Chapter IV, notes 54-72 and accompanying text (discussing the classic habeas corpus cases that soon followed); Chapter XII (discussing modern habeas corpus).

71. See Chapter VI, notes 133-48 and accompanying text.

72. See Chapter VIII, notes 166-287 and accompanying text.

73. E.g., 28 U.S.C. § 1343. See Chapter VIII, note 94 (discussing the interplay between § 1343 and § 1331 in § 1983 cases).

74. See Chapter VI, notes 49-53 and accompanying text (discussing the argument that state courts are obligated to entertain § 1983 actions); Chapter VIII, notes 90, 93-94, 125-34 and accompanying text (discussing § 1983 as an authorization to enforce federal rights in court); Chapter X, notes 188-244 and accompanying text (discussing § 1983 as a vehicle for suing state officers); Chapter XI, notes 17-20 and accompanying text (discussing § 1983's exemption from the Anti-Injunction Act); Chapter XII, notes 240-53 and accompanying text (discussing the relationship between § 1983 and habeas corpus).

75. Robert J. Kaczorowski, The Politics of Judicial Interpretation: The Federal Courts, Department of Justice and Civil Rights, 1866-1876 (1985). Professor Gressman contends that Congress actually enacted only a "pitiful handful" of measures that, in turn, were narrowly construed by the unsympathetic justices who sat on the Supreme Court in the post-War period. Eugene Gressman, *The Unhappy History of Civil Rights Legislation*, 50 Mich. L. Rev. 1323, 1357 (1952).

the Declaratory Judgment Act, 28 U.S.C. § 2201,[76] and in 1946 the judicial review provision of the Administrative Procedure Act, 5 U.S.C. § 702.[77]

Today, five kinds of federal courts are organized under the authority of Article III to exercise the federal judicial power: (1) district courts (which handle most trial-level work in the federal system); (2) courts of appeals for each of the twelve regional circuits (which have appellate jurisdiction to review district court judgments and some orders issued by federal administrative agencies); (3) the Court of Appeals for the Federal Circuit (which has responsibility for appeals in cases involving claims against the United States, customs matters, and patent and trademark disputes); (4) the Court of International Trade (which handles matters touching customs duties, import quotas, and international trade agreements); and (5) the Supreme Court itself (which now has a largely discretionary appellate jurisdiction to review most federal question judgments from most courts, irrespective of whether the party claiming under federal law won or lost below).[78]

The district courts enjoy the services of adjunct officers who perform judicial functions under the auspices of, and subject to control by, the Article III judges they attend. Magistrate judges fit that description.[79] In addition, Congress has created other tribunals that exercise judicial authority but are not Article III courts inasmuch as their decision-making officers are appointed for limited terms and receive salaries that are subject to diminution. Those so-called "legislative" courts include territorial courts, military courts, local courts in the District of Columbia, the Court of Federal Claims, and the Tax Court.[80]

Where once the federal courts functioned as autonomous entities, today they are linked in an integrated system. This structural reformation is in major part due to the creation of several administrative institutions that have unified the federal judicial branch more, perhaps, than anyone might have envisioned. In 1922, Congress established the Conference of Senior Circuit Judges to serve as a governing body for the federal judiciary as a whole. Since renamed the Judicial Conference of the United States, that body not only establishes policy within the judicial branch, but also speaks for the judiciary in Congress. In 1939, Congress established the Administrative Office of United States Courts to provide the judiciary with administrative support, and in 1967 the Federal Judicial Center to

---

76. See Chapter VIII, notes 92, 98-103, 231-73 (discussing § 2201's effect on jurisdiction pursuant to 28 U.S.C. § 1331); Chapter IX, notes 11-16, 286-90 and accompanying text (discussing the relationship between declaratory judgment actions and the advisory opinion and ripeness doctrines).

77. See Chapter VIII, notes 91, 95-97 and accompanying text (discussing § 702 as an authorization to sue); Chapter IX, notes 82-93 and accompanying text (discussing § 702 as a congressional grant of standing).

78. See Chapter VII, notes 57-58 and accompanying text (discussing the Court's authority to review state court judgments), 178-81 and accompanying text (discussing the Court's authority to review inferior federal court judgments).

79. See Chapter V, notes 29-35 and accompanying text. Bankruptcy judges, too, are units of the district courts. The current arrangement is a product of the Supreme Court's decision invalidating the previous scheme on Article III grounds. See Chapter V, note 51.

80. See Chapter V, notes 23-26 and accompanying text (discussing the constitutional difficulties with "legislative" courts).

conduct research and educational programs. Those institutions bring federal judges together on a regular basis to discuss common problems and formulate recommendations for reform.[81]

H. The Caseload Crisis

In recent years, the common problem the federal courts have emphasized is the volume of business they are asked to do. Well over ninety percent of the litigation in the United States occurs in state, not federal, court.[82] Nevertheless, by some accounts, federal dockets have expanded to crisis proportions.[83] The reasons are clear enough: population growth, the rise of the federal administrative state, and the "federalization" of American law.[84] The national government now routinely assumes responsibility for matters that historically were left to the states (and the state courts). In particular, federal criminal jurisdiction is much more extensive than it was in the past.[85] Concerns about caseload may be inflated.[86] Yet they must be taken seriously.

Remedies for the caseload problem fall into four broad categories: (1) more judges to do the work assigned to the federal judiciary; (2) better case management to improve the productivity of the judges already in place; (3) structural reforms to distribute business more efficiently within the federal judicial branch; and (4) reductions in the federal courts' jurisdiction.

Additional judges. Congress has steadily increased the number of Article III judgeships. The Judiciary Act of 1789 provided for only 19, with 6 of those set aside for the Supreme Court. By 1970, there were 500, and today the number of authorized positions is about 1,000. The number will almost certainly go higher. There is strong sentiment, however, for keeping the size of the federal judiciary small—both to maintain the quality of the federal bench and to avoid creating even more work simply by introducing more opportunities for disagreement.[87]

---

81. For a description of the Judicial Conference, the Administrative Office, and the Judicial Center and their (sometimes fractious) relations with Congress, see Charles G. Geyh, *Paradise Lost, Paradigm Found: Redefining the Judiciary's Imperiled Role in Congress,* 71 N.Y.U. L. Rev. 1165 (1996).

82. Professor Baker explains that "[w]hile state courts of general jurisdiction have 15 times as many judges as the U.S. district courts, state trial judges handle 83 times as many criminal cases and 41 times as many civil cases as their federal colleagues." Thomas E. Baker, *A View to the Future of Judicial Federalism: "Neither Out Far Nor In Deep,"* 45 Case Western Res. L. Rev. 705, 716 (1995).

83. E.g., Report of the Federal Courts Study Committee 109 (1990).

84. See William W. Schwarzer & Russell R. Wheeler, On the Federalization of the Administration of Civil and Criminal Justice (1994).

85. Baker, note 82, at 752.

86. Jack M. Beermann, *Crisis? What Crisis?,* 80 Nw. U. L. Rev. 1383 (1986). Judge Posner subtitled the original edition of his book "Crisis and Reform." He now believes that by various means the "crisis" has been averted, justifying a change in title: Richard A. Posner, The Federal Courts: Challenge and Reform xiii (1996). By contrast, Professor Baker predicts an increase in federal litigation of various kinds. Baker, note 82.

87. Study Committee, note 83, at 7.

Not everyone shares these concerns in equal measure.[88] Nevertheless, respected observers warn that simply increasing the number of judges will not answer.[89]

Improved productivity. By all accounts, district courts have become "managerial" in an attempt to streamline litigation and encourage settlement.[90] They now make extensive use of magistrate judges and staff lawyers, alternative dispute-resolution devices, mediation conferences, and various other mechanisms for conserving the judicial effort required to dispose of cases.[91] Pursuant to the Civil Justice Reform Act of 1990, the district courts rely on local advisory groups to formulate case management programs. If anything, the courts of appeals are even more creative. All the circuits have local rules and plans for resolving appeals via truncated process. Most appeals are now considered without benefit of oral argument and, more importantly, are decided without published opinion.[92] The Supreme Court has relied upon its discretion to diminish the sheer number of cases to which it gives full dress review.[93] Many of these developments are controversial.[94]

Structural reform. Specialized Article III courts might bring experience and expertise to certain technical fields. Yet many observers insist that the federal courts' tradition as generalists is extremely valuable and should not be compromised.[95] Chief Justice Burger's idea for a unique Article III court of appeals for

---

88. The risk that digging deeper into the talent pool would compromise quality is debatable. Professor Wells argues that the country would not have to settle for lesser lights if federal judgeships lost their "snob appeal." Michael Wells, *Against an Elite Judiciary: Comments on the Federal Courts Study Committee*, 1991 B.Y.U. L. Rev. 923, 937.

89. See, e.g., Jon O. Newman, *Restructuring Federal Jurisdiction: Proposals to Preserve the Federal Judicial System*, 56 U. Chi. L. Rev. 761 (1989); Jon O. Newman, *1,000 Judges — The Limit for an Effective Federal Judiciary*, 76 Judicature 187 (1993).

90. See Judith Resnik, *Managerial Judges*, 96 Harv. L. Rev. 374 (1982). Compare Robert F. Peckham, *The Federal Judge as a Case Manager: The New Role in Guiding a Case from Filing to Disposition*, 69 Calif. L. Rev. 770 (1981) (offering a favorable appraisal), with Owen M. Fiss, *Against Settlement*, 93 Yale L.J. 1073 (1984) (responding in the negative).

91. See Owen M. Fiss, *The Bureaucratization of the Federal Judiciary*, 92 Yale L.J. 1442 (1983).

92. Thomas E. Baker, Rationing Justice on Appeal: The Problems of the U.S. Courts of Appeals 105-139 (1994) (offering an examination of these and other management tools).

93. In recent years, the Court has received more and more petitions for review, but has actually accepted fewer and fewer. By limiting the number of cases it decides, the Supreme Court may concomitantly limit its capacity to referee the justice system. Professor Hellman reports that during the year ending in June of 1996, the Court considered only half the number of cases it reviewed in a single year during the 1970s and 1980s. Arthur D. Hellman, *The Shrunken Docket of the Rehnquist Court*, 1996 Sup. Ct. Rev. 403. See Chapter VII, notes 182-201 (discussing the discretionary nature of the Court's appellate jurisdiction).

94. For example, the Civil Justice Reform Act decentralizes federal rule-making and thus compromises the uniformity of federal law. See Linda S. Mullenix, *The Counter-Reformation in Procedural Justice*, 77 Minn. L. Rev. 375, 379 (1992); Lauren Robel, *Fractured Procedure: The Civil Justice Reform Act of 1990*, 46 Stan. L. Rev. 1447 (1994). The practice of deciding cases without signed published opinions has deeper significance. The public depends on the courts' published explanations for their actions as a check on federal judicial power, and lawyers and courts depend on reported cases as the material for *stare decisis* arguments. See Baker, note 92, at 130; William L. Reynolds & William M. Richman, *An Evaluation of Limited Publication in the United States Courts of Appeals: The Price of Reform*, 48 U. Chi. L. Rev. 573 (1981).

95. See, e.g., Judicial Conference of the United States, Long Range Plan for the Federal Courts 43 (1995) (recommending the preservation of "generalist" courts of appeals — apart from the Court of Appeals for the Federal Circuit already in place). On specialized Article III

the resolution of intercircuit conflicts has won only limited academic support.[96] The Freund Committee's proposal for a "National Court of Appeals" to screen cases for the Supreme Court has evoked arguments that it may be unconstitutional.[97] Current initiatives concentrate on modest adjustments in the way the district and circuit courts address classes of cases that may be especially suited for streamlined adjudication.[98]

Reductions in jurisdiction. Forthright reductions in jurisdiction may be the most controversial remedies for the workload problem. All the plans in this vein share a common theme: The federal courts should be reserved for those matters in which there is sufficient federal interest to justify the deployment of Article III resources. Other business should be channeled either to alternative federal tribunals and agencies or to the state courts.[99] The Judicial Conference has adopted that theme as its primary policy recommendation.[100] The implications are both conceptual and practical. Decisions must be made regarding what matters *are* of such national interest to warrant federal jurisdiction. And alternative tribunals, typically state courts, must accept responsibility for the overflow.

Many observers have attempted to identify the ideal allocation of jurisdiction between the federal and state courts.[101] Yet no plan is value-neutral. At some point, everyone makes a normative judgment about what the federal courts *ought* to do and what, in consequence, *ought* to be left to other institutions.[102] Agreement on matters of that kind does not come easily.[103] The Judicial Confer-

---

courts, see Posner, note 86, at 244-70; Paul M. Bator, *The Judicial Universe of Judge Posner*, 52 U. Chi. L. Rev. 1146 (1985); Judith Resnik, *History, Jurisdiction, and the Federal Courts: Changing Contexts, Selective Memories, and Limited Imagination*, 98 W. Va. L. Rev. 171 (1995); Richard L. Revesz, *Specialized Courts and the Administrative Lawmaking System*, 138 U. Pa. L. Rev. 1111 (1990).

96. Warren Burger, *Annual Report on the State of the Judiciary*, 69 A.B.A. J. 442 (1983); see Thomas E. Baker & Douglas D. McFarland, *The Need for a New National Court*, 100 Harv. L. Rev. 1400 (1987).

97. Report of the Study Group on the Caseload of the Supreme Court (1972). See Charles L. Black, Jr., *The National Court of Appeals: An Unwise Proposal*, 83 Yale L.J. 883, 885-87 (1974) (insisting that such a court would violate the Article III mandate that there shall be "one" Supreme Court). Numerous other ideas have been advanced. See Note, *Of High Designs: A Compendium of Proposals to Reduce the Workload of the Supreme Court*, 97 Harv. L. Rev. 307 (1983).

98. The Federal Courts Study Committee recommends changes in the way certain Social Security, taxation, and employment cases are handled. Study Committee, note 83.

99. E.g., American Law Institute, Study of the Division of Jurisdiction Between State and Federal Court 1-6 (1969).

100. Long Range Plan, note 95, at 23 (encouraging Congress to "conserve the federal courts as a distinctive federal forum of limited jurisdiction" and to assign civil and criminal jurisdiction to the federal courts "only to further clearly defined and justified national interests").

101. E.g., Henry J. Friendly, Federal Jurisdiction: A General View (1973).

102. See Erwin Chemerinsky & Larry Kramer, *Defining the Role of the Federal Courts*, 1990 B.Y.U. L. Rev. 67, 76-77; Martin H. Redish, *Reassessing the Allocation of Judicial Business Between State and Federal Courts: Federal Jurisdiction and "The Martian Chronicles,"* 78 Va. L. Rev. 1769 (1992).

103. Diverting judicial business to other federal bodies raises a host of vexing constitutional problems. See Chapter V, notes 23-26 and accompanying text. State courts of general jurisdiction are formally open to receive any business that is channeled their way. See Chapter VI, notes 3-36 and accompanying text. By some accounts, however, state courts face an even more serious workload crisis than the federal courts.

ence has targeted two categories of cases to be shifted in whole or in part to state court: criminal prosecutions having no peculiar national character and civil cases in which federal jurisdiction is based on the parties' diverse citizenship.[104] Congress, for its part, has steadily *expanded* the federal courts' criminal docket and has been willing to adjust the workload in diversity cases only by raising the required amount that must be in controversy to invoke a district court's jurisdiction.[105]

The federal courts are acutely aware that the decisions they make with respect to their jurisdiction inevitably have implications for their crowded dockets. There is a way, then, in which questions regarding resources can influence the substantive and procedural law the federal courts are constantly developing and applying in the cases that come before them.[106]

---

104. Long Range Plan, note 95, at 24-33. Accord Study Committee, note 83, at 14-17, 35-42.

105. See 110 Stat. 3850 (1996) (raising the amount to $75,000).

106. See Chapter V, note 22 and accompanying text (discussing the possibility that concerns about docket congestion have led the Court to approve legislative courts more readily); Chapter IX, note 2 (noting the possibility that similar concerns may have led the Court to establish stringent justiciability doctrines). For a general appraisal of current thinking within the federal judiciary, see Judith Resnik, *The Federal Courts and Congress: Additional Sources, Alternative Texts, and Altered Aspirations*, 86 Gtn. L.J. 2589 (1998).

Chapter III

Judicial Independence

The Anti-Federalists may have been troubled by the idea that federal judges should be free of political influence.[1] Yet today that idea is received wisdom. Judicial independence: (1) ensures that federal courts can check the excesses of the President and Congress (as well as the states); (2) insulates the courts from public pressure to reach popular judgments (particularly in civil rights and civil liberties cases involving *un*popular claims and individuals); (3) promotes confidence in federal courts and enhances their prestige (which, in turn, makes judicial service attractive to qualified candidates for federal judgeships); and (4) protects individual judges from their colleagues on the bench (and thus promotes honesty and creativity).[2]

The Constitution itself establishes structural safeguards for judicial independence. Article III judges are neither elected in the first instance nor answerable at the polls thereafter. They are appointed pursuant to a scheme that captures and channels political and ideological considerations. Once seated, they have no fixed terms but serve, effectively, for life. Federal judges can be disciplined within the judicial branch, but they are not subject to penalties imposed unilaterally by the President or Congress. They are subject to removal only by means of impeachment.[3]

---

1. See Chapter II, note 30 and accompanying text.

2. This fourth virtue has implications for modern disciplinary procedures. See note 44 and accompanying text; see generally Irving R. Kaufman, *The Essence of Judicial Independence*, 80 Colum. L. Rev. 671 (1980). Professor Redish explains that federal judges have "institutional" independence in order that they can have "decisional" independence. Martin H. Redish, *Federal Judicial Independence: Constitutional and Political Perspectives*, 46 Mercer L. Rev. 697, 698-99 (1995). See *Symposium, Judicial Review and Judicial Independence*, Ga. St. L. Rev. v (1998). The classic illustration of the nation's commitment to judicial independence is Franklin Roosevelt's failure to win support for his plan to "pack" the Supreme Court. The President presented his proposal (to add as many as seven justices to the Court) as a means of helping elderly justices keep up with their workload. Yet the practical effect would have been to give FDR a large number of places to fill with nominees likely to validate his New Deal programs. See William E. Leuchtenberg, The Supreme Court Reborn: The Constitutional Revolution in the Age of Roosevelt 82-162 (1995); Frank Freidel, Franklin D. Roosevelt: A Rendezvous with Destiny 226-39 (1990).

3. In what may be a telling recent incident, members of Congress urged President Clinton to ask Judge Harold Baer for his resignation after Baer rendered an unpopular decision in a search and seizure case. Initially, the White House press secretary suggested that the President might well do so. The President's counsel soon explained, however, that while Clinton thought Baer's decision was erroneous, he supported "the independence of the federal judiciary" and would simply instruct the prosecutors to appeal if Baer declined to change his position. Meanwhile, Senator Dole, then campaigning against Clinton for the presidency, declared that if Baer did not resign, he should be impeached. When other federal judges asked Clinton and Dole to reconsider their "rhetoric," both responded with assurances that they thought it inappropriate for elected officials to coerce a judge into changing a ruling. Judge Baer ultimately withdrew his order, ostensibly on the basis of new evidence.

A. Selection of Supreme Court Justices

The Supreme Court is the only federal tribunal that Article III makes mandatory.[4] Apparently for that reason, the Appointments Clause speaks expressly only to the selection of justices who serve the Supreme Court itself. The President "shall *nominate*, and by and *with the advice and consent of the Senate*, shall *appoint* Ambassadors, other public Ministers and Consuls, *Judges of the supreme Court*, and all other Officers of the United States, whose Appointments are not herein otherwise provided for, and which shall be established by Law."[5] That language distributes authority for selecting justices in a complex way that reflects important structural themes.

On one level, the Appointments Clause incorporates the separation principle, tempered by checks and balances. Both the President and the Senate have their own roles in the selection of justices, but they ultimately share responsibility for the candidates who actually obtain seats on the Court—the one branch balancing (and checking) the other. The result is that the players must cooperate. Neither can unilaterally appropriate the Court to its own agenda.[6] On another level, the Appointments Clause acknowledges the balance between popular democracy and federation. The President's role reflects the former, the Senate's the latter. Since the Senate's membership is apportioned by state, rather than by population, the Senate's authority in this instance (to the exclusion of the House of Representatives) ensures that the states as corporate entities can influence the selection of Supreme Court justices.[7]

The Appointments Clause specifies no eligibility standards for Court membership. There is no age limit, nor any requirement that justices have professional credentials of any kind. In the absence of constitutional guidance, the "qualifications" that the President and the Senate can or should seek in candidates are endlessly debated. Most authorities converge on the same list of desirable attributes: integrity, intelligence, education, experience, temperament, technical competence, and physical stamina.[8] Yet the really crucial question is intensely controversial: whether, or the extent to which, a candidate's ideological views may properly be considered.

Some observers argue that ideological considerations should be ruled out of order.[9] That view has appeal for at least two related reasons. First, it seems to promote the impartiality expected of judges. It would not do to appoint zealots

---

The episode received widespread publicity. The correspondence is reproduced in Jon O. Newman, *The Judge Baer Controversy*, 80 Judicature 156 (1997).

4. See Chapter II, notes 10-13 and accompanying text (explaining that the debate was over the creation of inferior courts).

5. U.S. Const. art. II, § 2, cl.2 (emphasis added).

6. See Chapter I, notes 2-15 and accompanying text (discussing the separation principle).

7. David Strauss & Cass R. Sunstein, *The Senate, the Constitution and the Confirmation Process*, 101 Yale L.J. 1491 (1992).

8. See Larry W. Yackle, *Choosing Judges the Democratic Way*, 69 B.U. L. Rev. 273, 307-10 (1989).

9. E.g., Bruce Fein, *A Circumscribed Senate Confirmation Role*, 102 Harv. L. Rev. 672 (1989).

who are predisposed to favor some litigants or claims over others and thus to undermine the judiciary's neutrality and integrity. Second, the view that ideology should not be considered seems consistent with a commonly held conception of the judicial function. Adjudication, by that account, is an exercise of disinterested judgment in light of preexisting legal standards — as distinguished from the exertion of political will. Accordingly, candidates for the Court should not be chosen because their philosophical views are in harmony with those of the President or the Senate, but rather because they have talents that will enable them to perform distinctly judicial duties. The President and the Senate corrupt the judicial branch if they treat judicial candidates as potential policy-makers in robes.[10]

Other observers dismiss that kind of thinking as either hopelessly naive or dangerously duplicitous. Some critics argue that judicial impartiality is a myth, that the justices make policy with no more constraint than the President or Congress, and that any argument for banishing ideological considerations from judicial selection is mere pretense. Thus the system should frankly recognize that candidates' values matter, the better to identify those values before justices are seated (for life).[11]

Most observers settle into a comfortable middle ground, nodding respectfully in each direction. No one really thinks that human beings can set aside their personal predilections entirely. Everyone, including a Supreme Court justice, brings a certain amount of ideological baggage to every task. Yet American society routinely depends on professional jurists to discipline themselves against bias and prejudice, to restrict attention to the evidence presented, and to respect authoritative legal materials. Accordingly, the President and the Senate can select justices on the basis of ideology without undermining the Court's integrity in the adjudication of individual cases.

It may be that some ideologies are so alien to the adjudicatory function as to be disabling. But a candidate's political allegiances are not typically of that caliber, or anything like it. Similarly, a candidate's generalized views about an issue do not necessarily command a foreseeable result in some identifiable case in which that issue may arise. It is one thing, then, to consider a candidate's general respect for individual liberty as a selection criterion and quite another to condition confirmation on the candidate's promise to sustain an individual's claim in some hypothetical case.[12]

---

10. Professor Carter acknowledges that this conception of the judicial function may be aspirational. But he insists that the Senate should not "surrender the myth." Stephen Carter, *The Confirmation Mess*, 101 Harv. L. Rev. 1185, 1201 (1988). Carter argues that the Senate should eschew an exploration of candidates' ideological views and concentrate, instead, on their capacity for "moral reflection." Id. at 1199.

11. Professor Nagel argues that the Senate should use the confirmation process to exert "overt pressure" on the Court to chart a course the Senate finds politically satisfying. Robert F. Nagel, *Advice, Consent, and Influence*, 84 Nw. U. L. Rev. 858, 874 (1990).

12. By convention, the Senate Judiciary Committee leaves it to its members to decide what questions they will ask, and to nominees to decide which, if any, questions they will answer. Still, it is bad form for a senator to ask flatly how a nominee would vote on some controversial matter, and when any question comes at all close to that description, candidates routinely respond that they will not prejudge issues that are likely to come before the Court. In a celebrated incident in 1985, Senator Denton sent a candidate for a circuit judgeship, Andrew Frey, a lengthy questionnaire meant to pin Frey down on the abortion issue. That action was widely regarded as an inappropriate effort to manipulate the judicial branch through the confirmation process. See 131 Cong. Rec. S21662-63 (July 31, 1985).

Adjudication *is* different from legislation in a variety of ways. But in no sense is it a logical or mechanical function, devoid of any need to bring values into play. At the Supreme Court level in particular, justices face extraordinarily difficult issues that demand sound human judgment to resolve. By taking account of candidates' views in the selection process, the President and the Senate may improve the chances of selecting men and women with a sufficient grip on moral and social reality to make those decisions responsibly.[13]

Positing that justices of the Supreme Court will inevitably fashion public policy from the bench, it still is incorrect to regard them as of a piece with ordinary public officials who (properly) must stand for election. The justices' policy-making authority only warrants the President and the Senate to subject candidates to some form of political screening to ensure, at least, that the justices who are selected begin on the same page with the executive and one house of Congress. That measure of electoral control, albeit at several steps removed, may even mitigate the counter-majoritarian difficulty that attends the very existence of unelected, life-tenured justices.[14]

Finally, the Constitution's silence with respect to qualifications may actually speak volumes. Since the Appointments Clause prescribes no value-neutral criteria for selecting justices, and since it assigns the nomination and approval of candidates to demonstrably political entities, it invites the inference that justices are supposed to be selected with politics and ideology in view. At the same time, however, the Appointments Clause forces the President and the Senate to share in the ultimate decision and thus disciplines their ability to bring political influence to bear. Candidates can win seats on the Court only if they demonstrate the attributes and talents that everyone agrees are needed to perform the judicial function.[15]

As a practical matter, candidates' views have always figured in the selection of Supreme Court justices.[16] Presidents have routinely exercised ideological judg-

---

Professor Lubet contends that it may be unethical for candidates to "evince a settled intention to decide certain cases in a certain manner." Steven Lubet, *Advice and Consent: Questions and Answers*, 84 Nw. U. L. Rev. 879, 882 (1990).

13. But see Carter, note 10 (contending that the Senate should concern itself only with candidates' moral fitness for judicial judgment).

14. Henry P. Monaghan, *The Confirmation Process: Law or Politics?*, 101 Harv. L. Rev. 1202, 1203 (1988). Chief Justice Rehnquist takes the view that "a president who sets out to pack the Court does nothing more than...appoint people...who are sympathetic to his...principles"—which allows "public opinion" to have "some say in who shall become judges of the Supreme Court." William H. Rehnquist, The Supreme Court 235-36 (1987).

15. Professor Monaghan thinks that the founding generation may have regarded the President's power to nominate candidates to be tantamount to an authority actually to make appointments. Yet he explains that in modern times the absence of constitutional criteria for the Senate's confirmation decision leads ineluctably (and properly) to a much more active (and political) role for the Senate. Monaghan, note 14, at 1204-08.

16. When John Jay resigned, President Washington recalled John Rutledge to succeed him as chief justice. Rutledge had been intimately involved in the formulation of the judicial branch and, indeed, had chaired the Committee on Detail in Philadelphia. Moreover, he had been confirmed as one of the original associate justices (albeit he had not actually served in that capacity). See Chapter II, note 69. Nevertheless, the Senate refused to confirm him as chief justice, primarily because he had opposed the Jay Treaty. Henry J. Abraham, Justices and Presidents: A Political History of Appointments to the Supreme Court 73 (3d ed. 1992). Two recent nominees, Robert Bork and Clarence Thomas, faced fierce opposition on ideological grounds. Bork and Thomas were regarded as conservative and were opposed by more liberal critics. See *Symposium, Confirmation Controversy: The Selection of a Supreme Court Justice*, 84 Nw. U. L. Rev. 832 (1990); *Symposium, Gender, Race and the Politics of*

ment in naming nominees in the first instance, and the Senate has often countered the President's strategy with its own. This is not to suggest, of course, that the selection of Supreme Court justices is merely a matter of patronage. Men and women whose views make them appealing also may offer other talents that excellent jurists need. Moreover, the mortality of justices and the general vagaries of life make it virtually impossible to manipulate the Court's decisions over time simply by choosing new members with particular points of view.[17]

Proceeding from the skeletal baseline fixed by the Appointments Clause, the President and the Senate have developed the modern selection process by custom. When an opening appears on the Court, the President chooses a nominee to fill the position, typically relying on the advice he receives from legal advisors like the Attorney General. The President submits the nominee to the Senate Judiciary Committee, which screens the candidate on behalf of the Senate as a whole. The committee conducts an investigation which, in modern times, invariably includes public hearings at which the nominee is asked to respond to questions.[18]

B. Selection of Inferior Court Judges

The Appointments Clause does not establish that judges assigned to inferior Article III courts must be selected by the mechanism prescribed for Supreme Court justices. By some accounts, an affirmative answer has been assumed.[19] Yet a presidential nomination coupled with senatorial advice and consent is explicitly mandated only for "principal" officers: Supreme Court justices, ambassadors, and "other public Ministers and Consuls."[20] Federal judges serving lower federal courts fit none of those categories.[21] The presidential nomination/senatorial con-

---

Supreme Court Appointments: The Impact of the Anita Hill/Clarence Thomas Hearings, 65 So. Calif. L. Rev. 1279 (1992). In previous episodes, liberal or progressive nominees provoked a similar reaction, albeit from conservative quarters. Louis Brandeis and Felix Frankfurter are the classic illustrations. See Abraham, at 180-84; 220-25; see generally Charles L. Black, Jr., A Note On Senatorial Consideration of Supreme Court Nominees, 79 Yale L.J. 657 (1970); Paul A. Freund, Appointments to the Supreme Court: Some Historical Perspectives, 101 Harv. L. Rev. 1146 (1988).

17. See Bruce A. Ackerman, Transformative Appointments, 101 Harv. L. Rev. 1164, 1183 (1988); Richard D. Friedman, Tribal Myths: Ideology and the Confirmation of Supreme Court Nominations, 95 Yale L.J. 1283, 1291 (1986).

18. Nominees did not appear at confirmation hearings in person until Frankfurter broke from tradition in 1939. The absence of candidates did not keep hearings calm, however. The hearings on Brandeis' nomination resembled a trial in absentia. Brandeis himself was not there, but he was formally represented by counsel—as was the organized opposition. See Leonard S. Baker, Brandeis and Frankfurter: A Dual Biography 103-11 (1984).

19. E.g., Richard A. Posner, The Federal Courts: Challenge and Reform 16 n.17 (1996) (citing no authority).

20. Buckley v. Valeo, 424 U.S. 1, 132 (1976). See John M. Burkoff, Appointment and Removal Under the Federal Constitution: The Impact of Buckley v. Valeo, 22 Wayne L. Rev. 1335 (1976).

21. The possibility that judges in the lower courts are "other public Ministers" is foreclosed by the very next subdivision of Article II, which specifies that the President is to "receive Ambassadors and other public Ministers." U.S. Const. art. II, § 3. That provision plainly refers to "public Ministers" as representatives of foreign nations. It seems to follow

sent scheme *may* also be employed in the selection of "all other Officers of the United States, whose Appointments are not herein otherwise provided for." But according to a further proviso in the Appointments Clause, Congress may "by Law vest the Appointment of such inferior Officers, as they think proper, in the President alone, in the Courts of Law, or in the Heads of Departments." The "Appointments" of inferior court judges are "not herein otherwise provided for."[22] Lower court judges may be "inferior Officers" who can be chosen by some alternative means.[23]

Whatever alternatives the Constitution may permit, Congress has in fact specified that judges serving the district courts and the courts of appeals are to be selected in the same way that Supreme Court justices are chosen.[24] The selection process at this different level is more bureaucratic. The President typically depends on political relationships in individual states to generate nominees. Senators of the President's party have historically exercised significant influence. The American Bar Association Standing Committee on the Federal Judiciary also appraises nominees' qualifications and offers recommendations both to the President and to the Senate.[25]

---

that when the Appointments Clause uses the same label, it contemplates similar officers of the United States—i.e., officers with authority for foreign affairs.

22. The officers whose appointments *are* "herein otherwise provided for" include the President himself and the Vice President, as well as the members of the House and Senate and the constitutionally prescribed officers in each—all of whom are selected by means specified elsewhere in the Constitution. The Constitution also prescribes the way in which officers of the state militia and the members of the electoral college are to be chosen. But since those authorities are selected by the states concerned, they are not officers "of" the United States at all. *Fitzgerald v. Green*, 134 U.S. 377 (1890) (holding as much with respect to electoral college members).

23. Congress might turn the duty over to the President alone or allow the judicial branch to fill openings in its own ranks. See Burke Shartel, *Federal Judges—Appointment, Supervision, and Removal—Some Possibilities Under the Constitution*, 28 Mich. L. Rev. 485, 488-92 (1930). Or Congress might recruit the "Head" of some "Department" to duty. The Attorney General presides over the Department of Justice and thus might be available. Or Congress might establish a new department to assume this responsibility. Whether Congress might mix and match selection schemes is problematic. Consider, for example, the possibility that Congress might give the Supreme Court authority to fill vacancies in the lower courts, but only subject to the Senate's "advice and consent." See Yackle, note 8, at 322-26 (offering wild speculation).

24. 28 U.S.C. § 133(a) (district judges); 28 U.S.C. § 44(a) (circuit judges).

25. The formal procedural mechanisms for identifying and screening candidates for inferior court judgeships are anything but constant. Most modern Presidents have established special offices in the Justice Department for the purpose. President Carter supplemented that model with nominating commissions, charged to seek out qualified women and members of minority groups as potential nominees. During the Carter years, the number of women and African Americans on the federal bench increased dramatically. President Reagan rescinded Carter's executive orders in favor of an advisory group located in the Justice Department's Office of Legal Policy. President Bush used a similar Justice Department division, but also relied on a deputy attorney general and the Office of White House Counsel. President Clinton has employed the Office of Policy Development at the Justice Department, working jointly with the Office of White House Counsel. For an account of the judicial selection process and its results in the modern era, see Sheldon Goldman, Picking Federal Judges (1997). For a discussion of the federal appointments process generally, see Michael J. Gerhardt, *Toward a Comprehensive Understanding of the Federal Appointments Process*, 21 Harv. J. Law & Pub. Policy 467 (1998).

C. Removal by Impeachment

Since the Constitution empowers the President to appoint confirmed candidates, it might have been expected that it would equally empower the President to remove them—the one authority implying the other.[26] Instead, Article III states that all judges appointed under its authority hold office "during good Behaviour" and, in addition, are entitled to an irreducible salary while they are on the bench. Plainly, then, the Constitution separates the appointment and removal powers where Article III judges are concerned.[27] In this way, too, federal judges enjoy independence from the political branches.

The Constitution does not squarely address judicial removal or discipline in so many words. But the last section in Article II provides for impeaching "the President, Vice President, and *all civil Officers of the United States.*" Article III judges have always been understood to be "civil Officers" within the meaning of that provision.[28] Three further questions remain controversial: (1) the grounds that warrant impeachment; (2) the process that impeachment cases must follow; and (3) the extent to which removal can be based on prior criminal proceedings.

Grounds for impeachment. Article II specifies that "civil Officers" can be removed if the House of Representatives impeaches them for, and the Senate convicts them of, "Treason, Bribery, or other high Crimes and Misdemeanors." By negative inference, it appears that judges cannot be forced from office on some other basis.[29] Yet the phrase "high Crimes and Misdemeanors" is ambiguous. The definition of "impeachable" offenses has been debated in cases involving executive officers, and the answer in that context may ultimately be that anything will do if it wins sufficient votes in the House of Representatives. Equally in the context of judicial officers, it has been said that an "impeachable" offense is "whatever a majority of the House...considers [it] to be at a given moment in history."[30]

That assessment may reflect political reality, but not history. The first federal judge to be impeached, John Pickering, was by all accounts mentally disturbed and thus unable to perform judicial duties. Pickering was ultimately convicted, but only after a lengthy (and inconclusive) debate over whether incompetence

---

26. See *Myers v. United States*, 272 U.S. 52, 122 (1926) (stating in connection with the removal of an executive officer that "[t]he power of removal is incident to the power of appointment"—even if the appointive power is conditioned on the Senate's "advice and consent").

27. See Edward S. Corwin, *Tenure of Office and the Removal Power Under the Constitution*, 27 Colum. L. Rev. 353, 379 n.69 (1927).

28. U.S. Const. art. II, § 4. See Chapter II, notes 43-45 and accompanying text (discussing Hamilton's views in Federalist 79).

29. Peter M. Shane, *Who May Discipline or Remove Federal Judges? A Constitutional Analysis*, 142 U. Pa. L. Rev. 209, 218-19 (1993).

30. This was Gerald Ford's famous statement during the debates on whether Justice William O. Douglas should be impeached because of his personal lifestyle. 116 Cong. Rec. H11913 (April 15, 1970). See Robert Kramer & Jerome A. Barron, *The Constitutionality of Removal and Mandatory Retirement Procedures for the Federal Judiciary: The Meaning of "During Good Behaviour,"* 35 Geo. Wash. L. Rev. 455 (1967); Paul S. Fenton, *The Scope of the Impeachment Power*, 65 Nw. U. L. Rev. 719 (1970).

alone was sufficient.[31] The only Supreme Court justice ever to be impeached, Samuel Chase, was charged both with criminal conduct and with mishandling James Callender's celebrated sedition trial. In truth, Chase had made himself a target by attacking Republican policies from the bench. He was acquitted in the Senate, and his case is now regarded as having settled, in American culture if not formally in American law, that federal judges are not subject to removal on the basis of their decisions.[32] All the lower court judges impeached in recent years were charged with personal misbehavior (usually criminal offenses) said to undermine their integrity and impartiality.[33]

The impeachment process. The Constitution prescribes the general process for impeachment cases in bare outline. The House of Representatives has "the sole Power of impeachment" and thus lays formal charges.[34] The Senate has "the sole Power to try all Impeachments" and thus determines whether a judge should actually be removed from office.[35] The Supreme Court held in *Nixon v. United States*[36] that the Senate can determine for itself whether to delegate responsibility for holding hearings to a committee.[37]

Reliance on criminal prosecutions. The Constitution neither insulates federal judges from criminal charges nor specifies that they must be impeached before, rather than after, prosecution.[38] If a judge has already been found guilty of serious crime, but nonetheless declines to resign, the House and Senate are likely to impeach and convict in short order. It is debatable whether the prior judicial determination of guilt can be given preclusive effect in impeachment proceedings, such that the House and Senate have nothing independently to decide.[39] Yet by extension, the Court's decision in *Nixon* may leave the resolution of that issue to the Senate.[40]

---

31. Richard Ellis reports that Pickering's opponents doubted that he could be impeached for insanity and thus were forced into the awkward posture of insisting that he was lucid and thus able to commit "high Crimes and Misdemeanors." See Richard E. Ellis, The Jeffersonian Crisis: Courts and Politics in the Young Republic 69-75 (1971).

32. Report of the National Commission on Judicial Discipline and Removal 11 (1993). See William H. Rehnquist, Grand Inquests: The Historic Impeachments of Justice Samuel Chase and President Andrew Johnson (1992); Suzanna Sherry, *Judicial Independence: Playing Politics With the Constitution*, 14 Ga. St. L. Rev. 795 (1998).

33. National Commission, note 32, at 44-45.

34. U.S. Const. art. I, § 2, cl.5.

35. U.S. Const. art. I, § 3, cl.6.

36. 506 U.S. 224 (1993); see Chapter IX, notes 49-56 and accompanying text.

37. See National Commission, note 32, at 27-82 (reviewing existing House and Senate rules and offering modest recommendations for reform).

38. *United States v. Claiborne*, 727 F.2d 842, 846 (9th Cir.), *cert. denied*, 469 U.S. 829 (1984); *United States v. Hastings*, 681 F.2d 706, 709 (11th Cir. 1982). See Shane, note 29, at 223-32.

39. See National Commission, note 32, at 45-47 (recommending that some form of preclusion be accepted). An obstreperous judge can remain in office while impeachment proceedings are under way. That is possible even if the judge is first convicted and sent to prison. Yet experience shows that judges under fire almost always resign. Emily Field Van Tassel, *Resignations and Removals: A History of Federal Judicial Service — and Disservice — 1789-1992*, 142 U. Pa. L. Rev. 333, 337-38 (1993). Any practical difficulties in this vein can probably be resolved by reassigning cases to others. See National Commission, note 32, at 15-16; notes 42-46 and accompanying text.

40. It has been suggested that Congress might short circuit the impeachment process entirely by making forfeiture of a judge's office part of the penalty for a serious crime. That

D. Alternative Means of Discipline

The Judicial Councils Reform Act charges judicial councils in all circuits to investigate both complaints that judges are unable to discharge their duties because of mental or physical disability and allegations that judges have engaged in conduct "prejudicial" to the administration of justice.[41] Those judicial councils cannot *remove* judges in the constitutional sense of depriving them of their offices and salaries. But they can reprimand judges found to have misbehaved and, perhaps more importantly, they can temporarily reassign a judge's official duties to others while investigations are under way.[42] This system of legislatively prescribed, but judicially administered, discipline is far less cumbersome than the impeachment process, but still minimizes the concerns about legislative overreaching.

Objections can be raised. Depriving judges of case assignments may amount to removal—in fact, if not in form. If Congress truly is restricted to impeachment as a means of discharging miscreant judges, a statute authorizing judicial councils to achieve the same end in a different way may be invalid.[43] Leaving it to other judges to decide whether to reassign a judge's cases responds to most of the values associated with judicial independence. Yet it arguably neglects one important item on that list: the idea that individual judges have tenure and salary

---

would involve Congress in the removal of a judge without benefit of impeachment, but it would be neutral with respect to the judge's exercise of judicial power and thus would not present the risks of legislative overreaching that the (deliberately difficult) impeachment process presumably hopes to forestall. Moreover, the courts superintend criminal prosecutions. If Congress achieves removal by means of judicial action, the concerns that unilateral congressional steps evoke are, once again, defused. There is already a statute that disqualifies a judge who is convicted of bribery from holding office. See 18 U.S.C. § 201. But see Raoul Berger, Impeachment: The Constitutional Problems 141-53 (1973) (explaining that § 201 has never been utilized). All this said, the fact remains that the Constitution clearly separates impeachment from criminal prosecutions. That suggests that the one cannot do service for the other. And by most accounts, impeachment is the only valid means by which the legislative branch can drive a federal judge from office. See National Commission, note 32, at 23; Philip B. Kurland, *The Constitution and the Tenure of Federal Judges: Some Notes from History*, 36 U. Chi. L. Rev. 665 (1969).

41. 28 U.S.C. § 372(b)-(c). Judge Edwards has criticized the Act as a misuse of judicial resources. He would prefer informal means of persuading judges to behave properly. Harry T. Edwards, *Regulating Judicial Misconduct and Divining 'Good Behavior' for Federal Judges*, 87 Mich. L. Rev. 765 (1989).

42. 28 U.S.C. § 372(c)(6)(B). In *Chandler v. Judicial Council*, 398 U.S. 74 (1970), the Supreme Court bypassed an opportunity to decide whether reassigning a judge's cases constitutes removal in substance and whether, accordingly, removal at the hands of other judges (rather than via impeachment) is valid. Dissenting in that case, Justices Douglas and Black reached the merits of those questions and insisted that depriving judges of their caseloads in the absence of impeachment is unconstitutional. Id. at 136-37. In a concurring opinion, Justice Harlan concluded that a judicial council's reassignment of a case constitutes part of the adjudicative process in that case, so that such an order is reviewable as judicial action by an Article III court. Id. at 110. See Chapter IV, notes 41-47 and accompanying text (discussing the constitutional questions raised when Article III courts undertake administrative functions apart from their judicial duties).

43. See Lynn A. Baker, *Unnecessary and Improper: The Judicial Councils Reform and Judicial Conduct and Disability Act of 1980*, 94 Yale L.J. 1117 (1985).

protections to protect them from overbearing colleagues, as well as from the executive and legislative branches.[44] Despite these theoretical difficulties, the Act is probably valid—provided, of course, that judicial councils do not abuse their authority in an effort to affect the outcomes that Article III judges can reach.[45] There is no definitive Supreme Court authority on the constitutionality of the judicial disciplinary scheme the Act establishes.[46]

44. See text accompanying note 2; Michael J. Gerhardt, The Federal Impeachment Process: A Constitutional and Historical Analysis 101 (1996). See Shane, note 29, at 235 n.104 (collecting authorities contending that judicial branch discipline jeopardizes individual judges' independence). But see National Commission, note 32, at 15-16 (acknowledging but rejecting those arguments).

45. Appellate court judges have a more appropriate remedy for what they regard as an erroneous judicial decision. They can reverse.

46. But see note 42 (noting the positions that Justices Black and Douglas took in the *Chandler* case).

Chapter IV

Article III Courts

The Constitution establishes only the bare outlines of the federal judiciary's structure and purview. Article III states that "the judicial Power" of the United States "*shall* be vested" in "one supreme Court" and in "such inferior Courts as the Congress *may* from time to time ordain and establish."[1] The federal judicial power "*shall* extend" to "*all* Cases"[2] in three categories (most of them defined by subject matter): (1) "all Cases, in Law and Equity, arising under this Constitution, the Laws of the United States, and Treaties made, or which shall be made, under their Authority;" (2) "all Cases affecting Ambassadors, other public Ministers and Consuls;" and (3) "all Cases of admiralty and maritime Jurisdiction."[3]

In addition, the judicial power extends to "controversies" in six other categories (all of them defined by the identity or alignment of the parties): (1) "Controversies to which the United States shall be a Party;" (2) "Controversies between two or more States;" (3) "[Controversies] between a State and Citizens of another State;" (4) "[Controversies] between Citizens of different States;" (5) "[Controversies] between Citizens of the same State claiming Lands under the Grants of different States;" and (6) "[Controversies] between a State, or the Citizens thereof, and foreign States, Citizens or Subjects."[4]

The Supreme Court has original jurisdiction over only a very few matters: "all Cases affecting Ambassadors, other public Ministers and Consuls, and those in which a State shall be a Party."[5] With respect to "the other Cases before mentioned," the Court's jurisdiction is appellate, "with such *Exceptions*, and under such *Regulations*, as the Congress shall make."[6] Operating within this general framework, Congress fills in the details by statute. Questions regarding congressional power fall under two headings: (1) Congress' discretion to create (or to eschew) federal courts inferior to the Supreme Court; and (2) Congress' authority to prescribe the jurisdiction that any inferior federal courts, as well as the Supreme Court, will enjoy.

---

1. U.S. Const. art. III, § 1 (emphasis added).
2. U.S. Const. art. III, § 2 (emphasis added).
3. See Chapter VIII, notes 5-31 and accompanying text (discussing cases "arising under" federal law).
4. See notes 20-22 and accompanying text (discussing diversity jurisdiction).
5. See Chapter VII, notes 1-39 and accompanying text.
6. U.S. Const. art. III, § 2, cl.2 (emphasis added).

A. Inferior Article III Courts

Congress' authority to establish federal courts in the first instance is unremarkable. Legislation is obviously needed to erect governmental institutions of any stripe. The Constitution nowhere expressly authorizes Congress to establish the Supreme Court. Yet by all accounts Congress was not only entitled, but dutybound, to do that. Article III contemplates that Congress may "ordain and establish" other federal courts, and Article I explicitly grants Congress authority "[t]o constitute Tribunals inferior to the supreme Court."[7] Congress' authority to decide *in favor* of creating inferior federal courts is therefore perfectly clear.

Congress' authority to decide *against* creating inferior courts is more problematic. If the federal judiciary were limited to the Supreme Court alone, the significance of the judicial branch would be seriously diminished. Congress established inferior federal courts in 1789 and has maintained them ever since. So any question about whether Congress might have left them out of the mix arouses only academic interest today.[8] Still, by most accounts, Congress was initially obliged only to create the Supreme Court itself and might have chosen to forego lower federal courts entirely—at least so long as state courts were able to take up the slack. That, after all, was the point of the Madisonian Compromise.[9]

History aside, the proposition that Congress can choose whether or not to create inferior federal courts is neither surprising nor (necessarily) troubling. In a democracy, controversial issues are usually left to politically accountable institutions. Congress' power with respect to the courts may be regarded as no more than another legislative check on the judicial branch—the kind of device that does not undercut, but only further defines, the separation principle.[10] Federal courts are not subservient to Congress after they are in place, but are structurally insulated from politics in order that they can exercise independent judgment in the cases that come before them.[11] It may be sensible, then, that Congress should exercise a political check at a prior stage, when the question is whether the country should have inferior federal courts to conduct its judicial business (independently).[12] Moreover, Congress is unlikely to use its discretion regarding inferior courts to undermine the judicial branch. Congress often needs those courts to implement its legislative policies.[13]

---

7. U.S. Const. art. I, § 8, cl.9.

8. See Chapter II, text accompanying notes 53-65 (discussing the Judiciary Act of 1789).

9. See Chapter II, text accompanying note 12 (discussing the Compromise).

10. See Chapter I, text accompanying note 7 (discussing the "checks and balances" idea).

11. See Chapter III, notes 1-2 and accompanying text (describing the values associated with judicial independence).

12. Professor Black argued that Congress' authority with respect to the courts mitigates the "counter-majoritarian difficulty" attending judicial decisions that override legislation. If the courts are in a position to invalidate statutes only because Congress has created them and given them the necessary jurisdiction, there is a way in which Congress bears indirect responsibility for what the courts do with the power they are assigned. Charles L. Black, Jr., Decision According to Law 18 (1981).

13. In many instances, however, Congress may rely on non-Article III tribunals to dispose of disputes arising from the implementation of legislative programs. When Congress chooses

There is an argument that Congress was required to create inferior courts, the Madisonian Compromise notwithstanding. Justice Story made the case for mandatory inferior courts in his opinion for the Court in *Martin v. Hunter's Lessee*.[14] The judgment in that case touched only the Supreme Court's jurisdiction to review state court judgments. Story's discussion of the lower federal courts was dicta. Nevertheless, the points he made retain significance for modern analysis.

Story began with the first line of Article III, which states that the judicial power of the United States "shall be vested" in the Supreme Court and any inferior courts that Congress creates.[15] He took "shall" in that line to establish a constitutional mandate that the entire judicial power must be "vested" in some federal court or courts—either in the Supreme Court alone or in the Supreme Court supplemented by inferior federal courts. Turning to the content of the judicial power to be vested, Story focused on the adjective "all," which appears before the items identified in Article III as "cases," but not before the entries identified as "controversies."[16] Taking that modifier to heart, Story interpreted the judicial power of the United States to extend to "all" the *cases* on the list, but not to "all" the *controversies*. Returning to his initial premise, he said that Congress could satisfy the command that the entire judicial power "shall be vested" by conferring jurisdiction on the Supreme Court (and any inferior courts) to determine "all" the cases, but not (necessarily) "all" the controversies described in Article III.

Next, Story considered whether responsibility for "all" those cases could be given to the Supreme Court alone, so that Congress need not create any lower federal courts to share the load. He recognized that the Court could entertain some cases as an original matter. But most would have to reach the Court on appeal from some other court. Story conceded that the state courts could do service in most instances. In his view, however, some of the cases on the Article III menu could not be adjudicated originally in state court and therefore could not reach the Supreme Court on appeal from those courts. Those cases would be left out entirely, unless Congress established some inferior federal court to consider them in the first instance. The cases Justice Story had in mind were federal criminal prosecutions. He argued that state courts could not enforce another system's penal laws and that inferior federal courts were constitutionally mandated at least to deal with those cases. On that point, Story was wrong. There is no *constitutional* reason why state courts cannot handle federal criminal prosecutions.[17] Neat and tidy as Story's deductive logic may have seemed to him, it collapsed in the end and is now generally rejected.[18]

---

that course, the integrity and independence of Article III courts may be threatened. See Chapter V.

14. 14 U.S. (1 Wheat.) 304 (1816).

15. See text accompanying note 1.

16. See text accompanying note 2.

17. Recall that under the Articles of Confederation the central government was forced to take its lawsuits to state court. See Chapter II, text accompanying note 7. Early statutes under the new Constitution contemplated that certain federal criminal offenses would be prosecuted in state court. Even today, it is occasionally proposed to revive that idea in the interest of solving the caseload crisis in the federal system. See Chapter II, note 104 and accompanying text; Chapter VI, note 13 and accompanying text.

18. Professor Goebel argued that the forceful "ordain and establish" language in Article III connotes obligation rather than discretion. Julius Goebel, History of the Supreme Court of the United States: Antecedents and Beginnings to 1801, at 247 (1971). Professor Collins

B. Inferior Court Jurisdiction

Congress' authority to prescribe the jurisdiction of inferior courts poses different questions: (1) whether Congress can give those courts it creates only part of the jurisdiction that Article III permits; (2) whether Congress can apportion jurisdiction for Article III business between different inferior courts; and (3) whether Congress can assign inferior courts jurisdiction over matters that are not mentioned in Article III.

1. Jurisdiction Within Article III Limits

Congress can create inferior Article III courts and give them jurisdiction in only some of the cases and controversies listed in Article III. Recall that the Judiciary Act of 1789 left a number of matters out in the very beginning.[19] That has always been the pattern. Moreover, the opposite proposition (that the federal courts must have authority to determine all the various cases and controversies on the Article III menu) would have implausible implications.[20]

The leading case is *Sheldon v. Sill*.[21] A bank in Michigan assigned a bond to a New York citizen, who filed suit to recover the amount of the bond in a federal court in Michigan, naming a Michigan citizen as the defendant and invoking the court's diversity jurisdiction (now prescribed by 28 U.S.C. § 1332). The defendant objected to the federal court's jurisdiction on the ground that a related statute barred a litigant like the bank from assigning an instrument for the sole purpose of manufacturing diversity.[22] In response, the New York plaintiff insisted that Article III allowed for diversity jurisdiction in such a case and that Congress had no power to define the court's power more narrowly. The Supreme Court rejected that argument.

---

contends that, at the time Story wrote, many people took the view that state courts were unable to adjudicate all the cases identified in Article III—thus making inferior federal courts essential. Michael G. Collins, *Article III Cases, State Court Duties, and the Madisonian Compromise*, 1995 Wis. L. Rev. 39, 58-78. Professor Eisenberg argues that if inferior federal courts were not constitutionally obligatory in 1789, they nonetheless are today inasmuch as the country has grown so large and diverse that the Supreme Court cannot manage the judicial branch alone. Theodore Eisenberg, *Congressional Authority to Restrict Lower Federal Court Jurisdiction*, 83 Yale L.J. 498 (1974).

19. See Chapter II, text accompanying notes 58-61.

20. Notice, for example, that Article III places a controversy between citizens of different states within the federal judicial power. See text accompanying note 4. If the federal courts were constitutionally entitled (and obligated) to entertain all diversity matters that fit that description, they would have jurisdiction in any lawsuits in which only two of what may be dozens of parties reside in different states. It would make little sense to saddle the federal courts with "minimal diversity" jurisdiction as a matter of policy, far less as an interpretation of Article III. See *Strawbridge v. Curtis*, 7 U.S. (3 Cranch) 267 (1806) (reading *statutory* diversity jurisdiction to require "complete" diversity).

21. 49 U.S. (8 How.) 441 (1850).

22. For the current provision, see 28 U.S.C. § 1359 (barring district court jurisdiction if a party is joined by assignment for the purpose of "improperly or collusively" invoking § 1332 jurisdiction).

Unfortunately, the Court in *Sill* explained its result, at least in part, on the basis of the "greater power" syllogism.[23] Positing that Congress had the "greater" power to decide in the first instance whether to create lower federal courts at all, the Court said it followed "as a necessary consequence" that Congress had power to establish such courts, but to give them only part of the authority the Constitution would allow. Of course, that was not a "necessary consequence" at all. The authority to decide whether to establish courts is certainly a significant (settled) power. But the power to prescribe jurisdiction is not a subset power at all. It is a different power.

It would have been perfectly *logical* in *Sill* to interpret Congress' power in another way. Article III might give Congress a choice—either to create federal courts with jurisdiction over all the cases and controversies the Constitution allows, or to establish no inferior federal courts at all and to rely entirely on state courts. That interpretation would actually flow more easily from the text of Article I, which refers expressly only to Congress' power to "constitute" inferior courts and says nothing about power to prescribe their jurisdiction.[24] Moreover, this alternative interpretation would be consistent with the "checks and balances" motif. It would give Congress a check on the courts at one level (the power to decide whether to create inferior federal courts at all). But it would balance that check at another level (by insisting that the courts Congress creates have more jurisdiction than Congress might choose to assign them—thus preventing Congress from having its cake and eating it, too).

This is not to say that *Sill* was wrongly decided. Nobody seriously takes that position.[25] It makes sense that Congress should have authority to adjust the federal courts' jurisdiction to ensure that their resources are not squandered on matters that are within the outer reaches of the federal judicial power described in Article III, but can be left to state courts without jeopardizing federal interests. The problem with *Sill* is that the Court reached the right outcome for the wrong reason and thus failed to grapple with the serious interpretive question presented.[26]

Poorly reasoned cases like *Sill* beg the question whether there are constitutional limits on Congress' power to prescribe inferior court jurisdiction. The problem is serious not only because a really sweeping power might tempt Congress to overreach the judicial branch, but also because an ability to bar access to inferior federal courts may affect the substantive claims that litigants wish to advance. When Congress closes federal courts, state courts typically remain open.

---

23. See Chapter I, text accompanying notes 21-22.

24. See text accompanying note 7.

25. Professor Bator insisted that it would make "nonsense" of the Madisonian Compromise to read Article III to give Congress an "all-or-nothing" power to decide whether "*none* or *all*" the cases and controversies listed warrant a federal forum. Paul M. Bator, *Congressional Power Over the Jurisdiction of the Federal Courts*, 27 Vill. L. Rev. 1030, 1031 (1982) (emphasis in original).

26. The Court so committed itself to the "greater power" syllogism that it declared at one point that a jurisdictional statute written by Congress could be unconstitutional only if it purported to assign the federal courts jurisdiction beyond the boundaries fixed by Article III. 49 U.S. at 449. That neglected the possibility that a jurisdictional statute might run afoul of an external restraint on congressional power—for example, due process. See text accompanying note 93.

If, however, there is no parity between federal courts and state courts, the substantive rights federal courts would otherwise enforce may suffer for being channeled into a less inviting forum.[27] Over the years, Congress has considered (but never enacted) measures that would withdraw the federal courts' jurisdiction to address controversial questions (like organized prayer in public schools, the apportionment of state legislatures, desegregation, and abortion).[28] The idea was to attack federal court judgments on those questions indirectly—by depriving federal courts of jurisdiction and routing cases to state courts, where proponents hoped different results would be forthcoming.

By some accounts, there is little risk that Congress might use its authority over the federal courts' jurisdiction to frustrate those courts and the rights they vindicate. A statute depriving federal courts of jurisdiction in a category of cases is a poor instrument for changing unpopular results. Once jurisdiction is withdrawn, the very judgments Congress finds objectionable are frozen in place. Even if the courts are inclined to reconsider, they have no ability to do so.[29] Congress' refusal to enact restrictive bills in the past may be evidence that Congress sees this point.[30] Nevertheless, many observers regard Congress' power as a looming threat to manipulate and compromise the judicial branch. The possibility that Congress might yet strip federal courts of jurisdiction in civil rights and civil liberties cases fuels both the debate over parity and the search for judicially enforceable limits on congressional authority regarding the federal judiciary.[31]

2. Apportionment of Article III Jurisdiction

Congress can allocate Article III cases and controversies among different inferior federal courts. In *Lockerty v. Phillips*[32] and *Yakus v. United States*,[33] the Supreme Court upheld the Emergency Price Control Act of 1942, which established a system for controlling inflation during World War II. That Act authorized a federal administrative agency to issue regulations fixing the maximum prices that manufacturers could charge for their goods. It was a criminal offense to violate a price regulation, and anyone who did so could be prosecuted in a district court. Nevertheless, the Act explicitly denied the district courts any author-

---

27. See Chapter I, text accompanying notes 79-91 (discussing the parity debate). Proposals to withdraw federal court jurisdiction in controversial cases usually make no attempt to affect state court jurisdiction to decide those same cases. Proponents may hesitate to restrict state court jurisdiction, either in deference to state prerogatives or in (unstated) recognition that depriving *all* courts of jurisdiction raises independent constitutional questions. See notes 83-89 and accompanying text.

28. See Ronald D. Rotunda, *Congressional Power to Restrict the Jurisdiction of the Lower Federal Courts and the Problem of School Busing*, 64 Gtn. L.J. 839 (1976); Robert B. McKay, *Courts, Congress, and Reapportionment*, 63 Mich. L. Rev. 255 (1964).

29. This point is all the more powerful with respect to congressional attempts to undermine decisions of the Supreme Court by making "exceptions" to the Court's appellate jurisdiction and thus leaving state courts free to reach different conclusions. See note 52.

30. Professor Gunther argues that Congress is in the driver's seat, but that the dangers are not grave. Gerald Gunther, *Congressional Power to Curtail Federal Court Jurisdiction: An Opinionated Guide to the Ongoing Debate*, 36 Stan. L. Rev. 895 (1984).

31. See notes 90-105 and accompanying text.

32. 319 U.S. 182 (1943).

33. 321 U.S. 414 (1944).

ity to determine the validity of price regulations. Instead, the Act granted a special Article III court (the Emergency Court of Appeals) exclusive jurisdiction to decide whether regulations were lawful—subject to appellate review in the Supreme Court.

In *Lockerty*, meat packers filed a civil action in a district court, seeking an injunction against a United States attorney who threatened to prosecute them for violating price regulations they contended were unconstitutional. The Court held that the district court lacked jurisdiction, because Congress had chosen, in its discretion, to channel attacks on price regulations to the Emergency Court.[34] In *Yakus*, a manufacturer charged with violating a price regulation built its defense on an argument that the regulation was invalid. The Court held that, under the Act, the district court handling the criminal prosecution had no jurisdiction to inquire into the lawfulness of the regulation—so long as the defendant had received an "adequate" opportunity to raise that question in a prior civil action in the Emergency Court. Between them, *Lockerty* and *Yakus* held that Congress could apportion jurisdiction between the two tribunals—giving the Emergency Court exclusive authority to determine the *validity* of regulations and giving the district courts authority to determine whether particular manufacturers had *violated* regulations.[35]

---

34. The meat packers argued that a suit in the Emergency Court would not protect their constitutional rights, because that court had no authority to insulate them from prosecution while it considered their claims. The Supreme Court responded that the Act's prohibition on interlocutory relief did not condemn the basic allocation of jurisdiction between the Emergency Court and the district courts. Even if that feature of the scheme was problematic, it was separable from the rest. The Court hinted that the meat packers might be able to contest the Act's prohibition on interlocutory relief in some other court. Professor Hart suggested that an action of that kind might have been filed in state court, notwithstanding that the Act equally purported to deprive the state courts of any jurisdiction to entertain lawsuits attacking price regulations. In his view, it would have been unconstitutional for Congress to foreclose all judicial avenues for advancing a constitutional claim. Henry M. Hart, Jr., *The Power of Congress to Limit the Jurisdiction of Federal Courts: An Exercise in Dialectic*, 66 Harv. L. Rev. 1362, 1401 (1953). See notes 83-86 and accompanying text. It is hard to think that Congress meant to route interlocutory relief questions to the state courts rather than to some federal tribunal—if not the Emergency Court, then a federal district court. Nevertheless, *Lockerty* suggests that neither the Emergency Court nor a district court had jurisdiction to consider the meat packers' argument that they were entitled to protection while their lawsuit was pending.

35. Of these two cases, *Yakus* was the more significant inasmuch as the Court held in that case that Congress could subject a defendant to criminal liability in a federal district court, while withholding from that court any ability to determine the validity of the regulation the defendant was charged with violating. More recently, the Court has said that *Yakus* presupposed a "meaningful" previous opportunity to test the validity of a regulation in some other court. *United States v. Mendoza-Lopez*, 481 U.S. 828, 837-38 (1987). In *Mendoza-Lopez*, the Court concluded that an alien who claimed that a deportation order was invalid had not had such an opportunity and therefore could attack the regulation as a defense to the criminal charge of re-entering the country after deportation. In two conscription cases during and after World War II, *Falbo v. United States*, 320 U.S. 549 (1944), and *Estep v. United States*, 327 U.S. 114 (1944), the Court wrestled with a similar attempt by Congress to keep the district courts from considering the validity of orders that defendants were charged with violating. In *Estep*, the Court said that Congress could insist that defendants exhaust administrative remedies before attacking induction notices as defendants in criminal prosecutions, but that anyone who did that could argue that a draft board had acted beyond its jurisdiction in ordering a defendant to report for military duty. It is hard to say what light those war time cases throw on the current Court's thinking.

In at least one instance, *Lauf v. Shinner*,[36] the Supreme Court arguably approved a federal scheme depriving *all* inferior federal courts of jurisdiction over certain constitutional claims and leaving those claims exclusively to state courts, subject to appellate review in the Supreme Court. Previously, the Court had held that state statutes prohibiting state courts from enjoining unlawful labor union activities violated the fourteenth amendment.[37] In *Lauf*, however, the Court held that the Norris-LaGuardia Act validly barred the federal courts from issuing injunctions in the very same circumstances.

The implications of *Lauf* are debatable. By some accounts, that case is authority for the proposition that Congress can absolutely deny the federal courts jurisdiction in a class of constitutional cases, provided state courts remain open for that business.[38] By other accounts, *Lauf* merely recognized that Congress can adjust the *remedies* that federal courts provide to plaintiffs in constitutional cases.[39] By still other accounts, *Lauf* is best understood as an illustration of the Court's developing acceptance of regulatory legislation in the 1930s. The previous cases holding that state courts could not refuse to enjoin unlawful strikes were part of the Court's economic due process excesses in the 1920s, while *Lauf*, decided in 1938, formed part of the Court's post-New Deal jurisprudence. By this last account, *Lauf* is more significant for what it implied about Congress' power to regulate national economic affairs than for what it said about Congress' power to prescribe the federal courts' jurisdiction.[40]

3. Jurisdiction Outside Article III Limits

Congress (probably) cannot give inferior Article III courts (or the Supreme Court) jurisdiction to entertain matters that are not on the Article III menu. Chief Justice Marshall virtually said as much in *Hodgson v. Bowerbank*,[41] when he disapproved a provision in the Judiciary Act of 1789 purporting to give lower federal courts jurisdiction over state law disputes between two aliens.[42] Moreover, the modern Court insists that Congress can confer "standing" on litigants to press their claims in an Article III court only if the actions affected are "cases" or "controversies" within the meaning of Article III.[43] Those decisions proceed

36. 303 U.S. 323 (1938).

37. *Truax v. Corrigan*, 257 U.S. 312 (1921).

38. Hart, note 34, at 1363; see Chapter VI, notes 78-88 and accompanying text (providing a more complete account of the argument that Congress can impose jurisdiction on state courts).

39. See Chapter VI, note 60 (discussing various meanings for the term "remedy"); Chapter VIII, note 80 (noting further complications).

40. See Gordon G. Young, *A Critical Reassessment of the Case Law Bearing on Congress's Power to Restrict the Jurisdiction of the Lower Federal Courts*, 54 Md. L. Rev. 132, 176-78 (1995).

41. 9 U.S. (5 Cranch) 303 (1809).

42. Professor Mahoney contends that Marshall actually construed the Judiciary Act not to extend the courts' jurisdiction that far. Dennis J. Mahoney, *A Historical Note on Hodgson v. Bowerbank*, 49 U. Chi. L. Rev. 725 (1982).

43. See Chapter IX, notes 219-21 and accompanying text.

from the premise that it would be unconstitutional for Congress to assign Article III courts jurisdiction to perform duties that Article III does not mention.[44]

The leading case in point, *Nat'l Mutual Ins. Co. v. Tidewater Transfer Co.*,[45] honored this proposition, albeit in the breach. In a prior decision, the Court had held that the District of Columbia was not a "State" within the meaning of the provision in Article III providing for federal jurisdiction between citizens of different "States." In 1940, Congress nonetheless enacted a jurisdictional statute authorizing federal district courts to entertain suits between citizens of the District and citizens of ordinary states. In *Tidewater*, a citizen of the District relied on that statute to sue a Maryland citizen in a district court in Maryland. The Supreme Court sustained the district court's jurisdiction, but without a majority opinion.

Justice Jackson announced the Court's judgment in an opinion joined by two other justices. He acknowledged that the suit was not a diversity action within the contemplation of Article III. Nevertheless, he said that Congress could confer extra-Article III jurisdiction on Article III courts as an exercise of other congressional powers collected in Article I. In *Tidewater*, then, three justices said that Article III does *not* fix the outer boundaries of the work that Congress can assign to Article III courts. Four other members of the Court dissented—both from the Court's judgment and from Justice Jackson's view that Article III courts can be given non-Article III business. The decisive votes rested with the two remaining justices. They concurred in Jackson's result, but dissented from his analysis.[46] In the end, accordingly, six members of the Court explicitly disclaimed the proposition that Congress can assign Article III courts jurisdiction of matters not on the Article III menu.

The dangers that would be presented if Congress could routinely channel non-Article III business to Article III courts are obvious enough. Just as Congress might upset the balance between the legislative and judicial branches by depriving the courts of jurisdiction in important cases, Congress might equally upset the balance by swamping the courts with unimportant duties. As a matter of experience, however, Congress has never attempted to do any such thing, and the system has operated since *Tidewater* without serious difficulty—despite the Court's failure to revisit the issue in that case and spell out the controlling principle.[47]

---

44. The obscure decision in *Hayburn's Case*, 2 U.S. (2 Dall.) 408 (1792), also stands for this proposition—to the extent the judges in that case said that Article III courts could be assigned only "judicial" duties. See Chapter IX, notes 25-29 and accompanying text.

45. 337 U.S. 582 (1949).

46. Rutledge and Murphy argued that the precedents were wrong, that the District of Columbia *is* a "State" within the meaning of Article III, and that the new statute giving the district courts jurisdiction of disputes between citizens of the District and citizens of other "States" did not attempt to give the district courts jurisdiction of matters outside Article III's limits.

47. A few precedents indicate that Congress *can* give Article III courts assignments beyond Article III, but they are confined to narrow circumstances. In *O'Donoghue v. United States*, 289 U.S. 516 (1933), for example, the Court held that Congress could give the local courts in the District of Columbia (then understood to be Article III courts) certain administrative tasks falling outside Article III. Congress' special relationship to the District may cabin that precedent. Today, the local courts in the District are legislative tribunals that can be given non-Article III duties without raising the same questions. See Chapter V, text accompanying notes 57-58. By some accounts, federal courts breach Article III boundaries

C. Supreme Court Jurisdiction

The Constitution is more explicit regarding the Supreme Court's jurisdiction and Congress' authority to affect it. Article III fixes the Court's original jurisdiction and gives Congress no power either to add to that jurisdiction or to detract from it.[48] That much was decided in *Marbury v. Madison*.[49] The Court's appellate jurisdiction is subject to the "Exceptions Clause," which authorizes Congress to make "Exceptions" and "Regulations" that limit the Court's ability to reach all the cases and controversies on the Article III menu.[50]

In the main, the Supreme Court has indulged Congress. In *Durousseau v. United States*,[51] the Court explained that Article III itself establishes the Court's appellate jurisdiction and that the power left to Congress is only to make "Exceptions" from that constitutionally derived judicial power. The Court acknowledged, however, that Congress typically enacts legislation that appears to grant jurisdiction to the Court affirmatively—as though Congress had authority to determine the Court's appellate jurisdiction in the first instance in the same way that it prescribes the jurisdiction of the inferior federal courts. Deferring to Congress' preferred style, the Court said that it would not insist that jurisdictional statutes be stated as negative "Exceptions" to Article III power, but would read affirmative statutory grants of jurisdiction to make "Exceptions" for any jurisdiction omitted.[52]

The Court has adopted a different attitude when jurisdictional statutes threaten to deprive the Court of appellate jurisdiction in sensitive constitutional

---

when they engage in rule-making or other ostensibly legislative activities. The Court has not found arguments of that kind persuasive. In *Mistretta v. United States*, 488 U.S. 361 (1989), the Court held that individual federal judges can be appointed to the United States Sentencing Commission. As commissioners, those individuals perform non-judicial functions. But they do so as presidential appointees, not as Article III judges. See Chapter III, note 42 (noting Justice Harlan's discussion of these problems in the *Chandler* case).

48. See Chapter VII, notes 1-39 and accompanying text (discussing modern decisions on original jurisdiction).

49. See Chapter I, text accompanying note 54-58.

50. See text accompanying note 6.

51. 10 U.S. (6 Cranch) 307 (1810).

52. As a practical matter, Congress cannot easily thwart unpopular Supreme Court decisions by making exceptions to the Court's jurisdiction. Professor Wechsler insists that if the Court's jurisdiction were withdrawn, state courts would be duty-bound to follow the very Supreme Court precedents to which Congress objects. Herbert Wechsler, *The Courts and the Constitution*, 65 Colum. L. Rev. 1001, 1006-07 (1965). Professor Caminker argues, however, that state courts would be free to depart from existing Supreme Court precedents to the extent state courts are convinced that the Court itself would—if it had jurisdiction to revisit earlier decisions. Evan H. Caminker, *Why Must Inferior Courts Obey Superior Court Precedents?*, 46 Stan. L. Rev. 817, 837-38, 868-69 (1994). Professor Sager acknowledges that if Congress withholds Supreme Court jurisdiction, state courts might be tempted to ignore existing precedents with which they disagree—knowing that the Court is no longer in a position to reverse them. Congress may anticipate that response and thus withdraw jurisdiction from the Court with a "lewd wink" at the state courts waiting in the wings. Lawrence G. Sager, *Foreword: Constitutional Limitations on Congress' Authority to Regulate the Jurisdiction of the Federal Courts*, 95 Harv. L. Rev. 17, 41 (1981).

cases. The Court has never held that Congress cannot make outcome-neutral "Exceptions" that bar the Court from deciding constitutional issues. But the Court has made it clear that Congress operates close to the frontiers of its authority when it attempts to exercise its power in that way. The means the Court employs to check congressional overreaching is familiar: a doctrine of clear statement. Unless a statute explicitly negates the Court's appellate jurisdiction in a constitutional case, the Court reads it to preserve jurisdiction. In adopting a clear statement rule of this kind, the Court reminds Congress of the serious constitutional question looming in the background, but avoids formally passing on that question.[53]

The classic illustrative cases were decided in the Reconstruction Era and are difficult to extract from the politically charged atmosphere in which they arose. Combined with more recent precedents, however, they paint a fairly clear picture. Beginning with *Ex parte McCardle*,[54] the Court has allowed Congress to withdraw one basis of appellate jurisdiction in federal question cases, but has declined in the absence of clear statement to surrender jurisdiction entirely.

Recall that the Judiciary Act of 1789 gave both the lower federal courts and the Supreme Court jurisdiction to entertain habeas corpus petitions filed by prisoners claiming to be held in the custody of federal officers in violation of federal law.[55] After the Civil War, the Reconstruction Congress enacted the Habeas Corpus Act of 1867, which extended the federal courts' jurisdiction in habeas corpus cases by removing the requirement that petitioners be in the custody of federal officers. Under the 1867 Act, federal courts could entertain petitions from prisoners held by either federal or state officers, so long as the prisoners alleged that they were deprived of their freedom in violation of federal law. The Act explicitly provided that prisoners who failed to win their freedom in the lower courts could appeal to the Supreme Court.[56] The point of the 1867 Act was to make federal courts, including the Supreme Court, accessible to African Americans in the South, who were often deprived of their liberty despite formal emancipation. Simultaneously, Congress enacted the Military Reconstruction Act, which installed martial law in the states of the former Confederacy.

While those and similar measures were popular in the Republican Congress, they evoked passionate resentment in the South. President Andrew Johnson sympathized with southerners and resisted significant aspects of the Reconstruction program. Ultimately, he was impeached in the House and made to stand trial in the Senate. Meanwhile, the Supreme Court, too, expressed doubts about Congress' actions and let it be known that the Military Reconstruction Act might be held unconstitutional.[57]

---

53. See Chapter I, text accompanying notes 37-41 (discussing the way the doctrine of clear statement functions).

54. 74 U.S. (7 Wall.) 506 (1869).

55. See Chapter II, text accompanying note 56.

56. See Chapter II, text accompanying note 70. Specifically, the 1867 Act gave the federal courts, including the Supreme Court, jurisdiction "in addition to the authority already conferred by law," to grant writs of habeas corpus in "all cases where any person may be restrained of his or her liberty in violation of the Constitution, or of any treaty or law of the United States." 15 Stat. 44.

57. *Ex parte Milligan*, 71 U.S. (4 Wall.) 2 (1867).

McCardle was a newspaper editor who wrote editorials condemning martial law in Mississippi.[58] Federal military authorities arrested him and charged him with disturbing the peace, libel, and a variety of other offenses, including incitement to insurrection. Today, McCardle's case would present a straightforward first amendment issue; then, it supplied a vehicle for challenging the Military Reconstruction Act. Awaiting trial in a military brig, McCardle filed a habeas corpus petition in federal court, complaining that the military authorities who held him in custody lacked authority to do so and relying on the newly enacted 1867 Habeas Corpus Act to invoke the federal court's jurisdiction. The district court denied his petition, and McCardle appealed to the Supreme Court—now relying on the specific provision of the 1867 Act granting the Court appellate jurisdiction in habeas corpus cases.

When the case was initially argued, Lyman Trumball contended on the government's behalf that McCardle's petition was not covered by the 1867 Act. Trumball, a sitting senator who had himself largely written that Act, explained that it was meant not for white southerners contesting the actions of *federal* officials, but rather for recently freed slaves seeking the federal courts' protection from *state* authorities. The Court rejected that argument: By its terms, the Act authorized the federal courts to entertain petitions from prisoners challenging any kind of custody (state or federal), provided the basis of the challenge was an alleged violation of federal law.[59] At that point, it appeared that the Court would reach the merits of McCardle's claims against the Military Reconstruction Act and, in all probability, would hold that martial law in the South was unconstitutional.

Trumball promptly went back to Congress and ushered through yet another statute in 1868, this one expressly repealing that part of the 1867 Habeas Corpus Act giving the Supreme Court appellate jurisdiction in cases arising under that Act. Then, when the Court reconvened, Trumball argued that Congress had exercised its power under the Exceptions Clause to withdraw the Court's jurisdiction over the McCardle case itself. The circumstances were extraordinary. On at least one occasion, Chief Justice Chase had to excuse himself in order to preside in Johnson's impeachment trial, then under way in the Senate. No one could have failed to comprehend Congress' determination to have its way.[60] In the end, Chase wrote a brief opinion for a unanimous Court, deferring to Congress' power under the Exceptions Clause and dismissing McCardle's appeal for want of jurisdiction to consider it further.

The McCardle decision is widely cited for the proposition that the Exceptions Clause grants Congress extensive power to limit the Supreme Court's appellate jurisdiction. After all, in that case the Court approved an "Exception" in a case implicating free speech, after the case had been argued and it appeared the Court would reach a decision that Congress disapproved. The repealer was outcome-neutral on its face, but there is no question that it was enacted to achieve (or avoid) a particular result on the merits. If Congress was successful in McCar-

---

58. See generally William W. Van Alstyne, *A Critical Guide to Ex parte McCardle*, 15 Ariz. L. Rev. 229 (1973).

59. *Ex parte McCardle*, 73 U.S. (6 Wall.) 318 (1868).

60. One of the counts in the President's indictment was his unsuccessful veto of the 1868 repealer.

dle, it appears that Congress should be equally successful in most other instances *a fortiori*.[61] Nevertheless, there are two reasons to doubt that *McCardle* actually stands for such a broad proposition. One, of course, is that the special circumstances in which the case was decided make it an unreliable precedent for ordinary cases in which the Court is under less pressure to pacify Congress.[62]

The other reason for pause is the Court's own warning that the *McCardle* decision was less sweeping than it appeared to be. Near the end of his opinion, Chase said that the parties apparently assumed that the provision in the 1867 Act giving the Supreme Court appellate jurisdiction over cases filed under that Act was the only jurisdictional basis available, so that if the repealer was valid there was no other jurisdictional hook on which the Court could rely. That, he said, was untrue. The repealer in 1868 had no effect on "the jurisdiction which was previously exercised."[63] By that, Chase meant the jurisdiction the Court had always had pursuant to the Judiciary Act of 1789. In *McCardle*, where the petitioner claimed to be held in unlawful *federal* custody, he might have proceeded under that earlier statute—without relying on the 1867 Act and thus without running into the 1868 repealer of the Supreme Court's appellate jurisdiction under that Act.[64]

The Court thus hinted in *McCardle* itself that, in another case, it might read the 1868 repealer to leave the Court's jurisdiction under the 1789 Act in place— so that, by switching jurisdictional horses, the Court might yet exercise appellate jurisdiction in the same kind of situation. In *Ex parte Yerger*,[65] decided shortly thereafter, the Court did precisely that.[66] It appears, then, that the Court in *McCardle* did not actually face the constitutional question whether Congress has power to withdraw every basis of appellate jurisdiction in a controversial constitutional case. Instead, the Court may only have addressed a far less significant issue: whether Congress can change the jurisdictional basis on which the Court can proceed—by eliminating the jurisdictional statute that initially authorized the Court to hear a case and leaving the Court to act on the basis of another, unaffected jurisdictional statute. A statute that simply shifts pending cases from one jurisdictional anchorage to another presents no obvious constitutional difficulty.

The Court followed *Yerger* in a recent habeas corpus case, *Felker v. Turpin*,[67] involving yet another statute eliminating one appellate avenue to the Court without expressly withdrawing another. Under the Antiterrorism and Effective Death Penalty Act of 1996, prisoners who wish to file more than one habeas corpus pe-

---

61. But see note 77 and accompanying text (discussing the *Klein* case).

62. Justice Douglas once suggested that *McCardle's* conclusion would not be accepted today. *Glidden Co. v. Zdanok*, 370 U.S. 530, 606 (1962) (dissenting opinion).

63. *McCardle*, 74 U.S. at 515.

64. The 1867 Act arguably supported this thesis inasmuch as it conferred new jurisdiction on the federal courts "in addition to the authority already conferred by law." See note 56. And Chase was surely right that the repealer in 1868 expressly eliminated only "so much [of the 1867 Act] as authorized an appeal from the judgment of the Circuit Court to the Supreme Court of the United States." 74 U.S. at 508.

65. 75 U.S. (8 Wall.) 85 (1869).

66. The Court still did not determine the constitutionality of the Military Reconstruction Act in *Yerger*, because the authorities released the prisoner before the Court could reach a decision.

67. 518 U.S. 651 (1996).

tition must obtain permission to do so from a panel of three circuit judges.[68] The AEDPA explicitly states that if the panel refuses, the disappointed prisoner cannot seek review of the panel's decision in the Supreme Court in the customary way—by filing a petition for *certiorari*.[69] In *Felker*, however, the Court explained that the Act does not mention the Court's independent jurisdiction to entertain habeas corpus petitions "as an original matter." That independent basis of jurisdiction survives.[70]

The *Yerger* and *Felker* decisions indicate that the Supreme Court is reluctant actually to make the judgment for which *McCardle* is typically cited—namely, that Congress has power to eliminate entirely the Court's appellate jurisdiction in sensitive constitutional cases. The Court strains to read jurisdictional statutes not to preclude appellate jurisdiction and thus not to present that troubling question for decision. Unless a statute expressly states that another basis of jurisdiction, too, is withdrawn, the Court reads the statute to leave that alternative jurisdiction in place.[71] The practical result is that Congress is kept at bay without a formal constitutional decision holding any particular limitation on appellate jurisdiction invalid.[72]

---

68. 28 U.S.C. § 2244(b)(3).

69. 28 U.S.C. § 2244(b)(3)(E). See Chapter VII, text accompanying notes 178-81 (discussing the Supreme Court's jurisdiction to review lower federal court decisions under 28 U.S.C. § 1254); Chapter XII, notes 230-39 and accompanying text (discussing other issues touching multiple habeas corpus petitions from a single prisoner).

70. The prisoner in *Felker* was held in state custody. Accordingly, the Court could not reach back to the 1789 Act for its authority to entertain his petition, but had to rely on the 1867 Act. See Chapter II, text accompanying note 56 (explaining that the 1789 Act conferred jurisdiction only to grant habeas corpus relief to prisoners in federal custody). That presented no difficulty, however, since the AEDPA was silent with respect to the Court's "original" jurisdiction under the 1867 statute. For a discussion of *Felker*, see Mark V. Tushnet, *The King of France With Forty Thousand Men: Felker v. Turpin and the Supreme Court's Deliberative Processes*, 1996 Sup. Ct. Rev. 163. The Court's jurisdiction to entertain a habeas corpus petition "as an original matter" (i.e., without taking the case on appellate review from a lower court) is problematic. Recall that the Court held in *Marbury* that Congress cannot confer original jurisdiction outside the narrow limits prescribed in Article III. A petition for a writ of habeas corpus is no more one of the cases that Article III assigns to the Court's original jurisdiction than is a petition for a writ of mandamus. See Chapter I, text accompanying note 57. John Marshall defused the tension with *Marbury* in *Ex parte Bollman*, 8 U.S. (4 Cranch) 75 (1807), where he said that when a prisoner files a petition for a writ of habeas corpus in the Supreme Court without first applying to a lower court, the Court's jurisdiction is nonetheless appellate in nature—because somewhere along the line some lower court, state or federal, has typically had a hand in the prisoner's detention and the Supreme Court is now being asked to review that court's action, at least indirectly. Professor Paschal speculates that Marshall overlooked the Court's "original" habeas corpus jurisdiction when he wrote the *Marbury* opinion and then, in *Bollman*, contrived a way to accommodate habeas corpus to his analysis in *Marbury*. Francis Paschal, *The Constitution and Habeas Corpus*, 1970 Duke L.J. 605, 651.

71. *Felker*, 518 U.S. at 660-61.

72. Professor Friedman understands this pattern to reflect a "dialogic" approach to congressional and judicial power, under which both Congress and the Court contribute to the development of the law and neither ultimately asserts dominance over the other. Barry Friedman, *A Different Dialogue: The Supreme Court, Congress and Federal Jurisdiction*, 85 Nw. U. L. Rev. 1 (1990). For criticism, see Michael Wells, *Congress's Paramount Role in Setting the Scope of Federal Jurisdiction*, 85 Nw. U. L. Rev. 465 (1990).

D. Outcome-Determinative Jurisdictional Limits

In another line of cases beginning with *United States v. Klein*,[73] the Court has explicitly invalidated, or threatened to invalidate, attempts by Congress simply to tell an Article III court what result to reach in a case. As Union troops advanced into the Confederacy during the last years of the Civil War, they confiscated valuable property. The Abandoned Property and Collection Act of 1863 authorized federal agents to sell that property and deposit the proceeds in the United States Treasury. The Act allowed for compensation claims to be filed in the Court of Claims, but conditioned all claims on loyalty to the Union. Claimants were out of luck if they had given aid or comfort to the Confederacy.

John Klein filed a claim on behalf of Victor Wilson, whose cotton had been seized and sold pursuant to the Act. The government resisted payment on the ground that Wilson had signed a surety bond for two Confederate officers—demonstrating that he was disloyal to the Union. Klein produced a presidential pardon, issued to Wilson after the date on which he had signed the bonds. According to the Supreme Court's then-recent decision in *United States v. Padleford*,[74] that pardon rendered Wilson loyal in law, if not in fact, inasmuch as it forgave any allegiance he had shown the rebel cause. The Court of Claims accepted the pardon as a legal basis for Klein's loyalty claim and ordered compensation to be paid. The government sought appellate review in the Supreme Court.

While the *Klein* case was working its way to the Court, Senator Trumball sponsored new legislation plainly meant to thwart the claim in that case. Having just succeeded in withdrawing the Court's jurisdiction in *McCardle*, Trumball tried the same strategy with respect to *Klein*. This time, however, Congress went much further. The new law, enacted in 1870, was not merely a facially outcome-neutral repealer of the statute on which the Court's jurisdiction depended. It declared that an individual could not rely on a pardon to demonstrate loyalty under the 1863 Act, that the existence of a pardon actually proved disloyalty, and that in any case in which an individual had won compensation in the Court of Claims on the basis of a pardon, the Supreme Court had no jurisdiction of the matter on appeal and must dismiss "same" for want of power to act.[75]

When the Supreme Court turned to the *Klein* case some time later, Chief Justice Chase held the 1870 Act unconstitutional and affirmed the lower court's judgment in Klein's favor. The opinion Chase wrote for the Court is impenetrable and appears to stand for a variety of questionable propositions. Chase said, for example, that jurisdictional legislation cannot be "a means to and end."[76] That suggests that even outcome-neutral limits on jurisdiction are

---

73. 80 U.S. (13 Wall.) 128 (1871).
74. 76 U.S. (9 Wall.) 531 (1869).
75. See Gordon G. Young, *Congressional Regulation of Federal Courts' Jurisdiction and Processes: United States v. Klein Revisited*, 1981 Wis. L. Rev. 1189.
76. 80 U.S. at 145-46.

invalid if they are motivated by a desire to affect judicial results. Given the difficulties of any search for congressional motives, it is hard to think that a proposition like that can be sustained.[77] In addition, Chase faulted the 1870 Act for attempting to "prescribe rules of decision" for the courts to follow.[78] That idea is also hard to take seriously. Congress certainly can establish substantive legal rules to govern cases, even cases already under way.[79] That, after all, is the principal (and legitimate) function performed by the legislative branch.

Looking back at *Klein* more recently, the Court has read that case to stand for different, though extremely important, propositions—pertinent both to Congress' power to make "Exceptions" from the Supreme Court's appellate jurisdiction and to Congress' power to prescribe the jurisdiction of inferior Article III courts:

Congress cannot employ its authority over jurisdiction to undermine the effect of a presidential pardon. The Court had decided in *Padleford* that a pardon rendered a claimant eligible for compensation under the 1863 Act, and the 1870 repealer proposed to defeat that interpretation of the President's power. This understanding seems artificial inasmuch as it turns on the peculiar subject matter in *Klein*. Yet it illustrates a more general idea: Jurisdictional statutes, like all other enactments, are subject to restraints located elsewhere in the Constitution.[80]

Congress cannot manipulate jurisdiction to ensure that the government wins. This proposition is more significant inasmuch as it bars Congress from en-

---

77. If a purpose to affect the Court's results were sufficient to invalidate otherwise neutral jurisdictional legislation, then presumably *McCardle* was wrongly decided. See text accompanying note 61. But see Eugene Gressman & Eric K. Gressman, *Necessary and Proper Roots of Exceptions to Federal Jurisdiction*, 51 Geo. Wash. L. Rev. 495, 520-23 (1983) (arguing that *McCardle* did not address an exception meant to weaken the Court and that *Klein* did establish that congressional motivation is "relevant to the inquiry" whether an exception is valid).

78. 80 U.S. at 146.

79. Federal courts routinely apply the law in place at the time of decision, even if it is changed while a case is pending. See *Landgraf v. USI Film Products*, 511 U.S. 244 (1994).

80. See note 93 and accompanying text. Professor Sager sees deeper meaning in the Court's objection in *Klein* to being made a party to Congress' scheme to defeat the proper effect of a pardon. Since the Court had previously held that a pardon rendered a claimant loyal as a matter of federal constitutional law, the 1870 Act instructed the Court to participate in a scheme that denied that very interpretation of the Constitution. For it called on the Court to receive evidence that a pardon existed and then, because of its existence, to wash its hands of a case and thus to deny the very relief that the pardon, were it given its rightful effect, would command. According to Sager, the principal import of *Klein* is that the Court refused to participate in a process in which it would be called upon to speak and act in conflict with its own understanding of the Constitution. Lawrence G. Sager, *Klein's First Principle: A Proposed Solution*, 86 Gtn. L.J. 2525 (1998). See also Christopher L. Eisgruber & Lawrence G. Sager, *Why the Religious Freedom Restoration Act is Unconstitutional*, 69 N.Y.U. L. Rev. 437 (1994) (offering a similar reading of *Klein*). Professor Meltzer agrees that Congress cannot force the Court to "speak a constitutional untruth." But he thinks that Sager's interpretation of *Klein* is unsound (and dangerous) in that it draws into question congressional enactments that achieve results, by statute, that could not be reached in reliance on the Constitution alone. Meltzer cites, for example, the Voting Rights Act of 1992, which outlaws voting rules having a discriminatory *effect* on minority voters, while the fifteenth amendment itself condemns only voting rules having a discriminatory *purpose*. Daniel J. Meltzer, *Congress, Courts, and Constitutional Remedies*, 86 Gtn. L.J. 2537, 2538-49 (1998).

acting self-serving jurisdictional limits that skew judicial results in the government's favor.[81]

Congress cannot use its authority regarding jurisdiction to tell an Article III court what decision to reach in a case. This is by far the most powerful lesson to be drawn from *Klein*. Congress may have authority to limit a federal court's jurisdiction at the outset in an outcome-neutral way—provided that the statute enacted is sufficiently clear. Congress may change the substantive law governing a case and, in that way, affect the judgment a court will reach. But Congress cannot allow an Article III court to exercise jurisdiction, leave the controlling law unchanged, and simply tell the court what judgment to render.[82]

E. Preclusion of Jurisdiction

The question whether Congress can absolutely foreclose all judicial consideration of federal questions remains open. In some instances, the Court has appar-

---

81. E.g., *United States v. Sioux Nation of Indians*, 448 U.S. 371, 405 (1980). Recall that in *Klein* the individual had won in the lower court, and it was the government that appealed. Ordinarily, a statute depriving the Supreme Court of jurisdiction would preserve the lower court judgment. That is what happened in *McCardle*. In *Klein*, however, the 1870 repealer did not merely withdraw the Court's jurisdiction of the government's appeal, but reached back to the judgment below in Klein's favor and instructed the Court to dismiss "same." In that way, then, Congress attempted to manipulate things in its own favor. See Young, note 75, at 158-59.

82. See *Plaut v. Spendthrift Farm*, 514 U.S. 211, 226-27 (1995) (explaining that Congress cannot wait until Article III courts have reached final judgments and *then* attempt to alter their results by retroactively changing the applicable law). This is the way the court of appeals read *Klein* in *Robertson v. Seattle Audubon Society*, 503 U.S. 429 (1992), and that interpretation is surely correct. The Supreme Court ultimately concluded that the statute in *Robertson* altered the substantive law governing the case and thus legitimately affected the result. Ordinarily, Congress enacts general legal standards to govern a field of play and leaves it to the courts to decide how those standards work in particular instances. That pattern comports with conventional understandings of the differences between legislative power to prescribe substantive law and judicial power to adjudicate disputes over how that law applies in individual cases. See Martin H. Redish, *Federal Judicial Independence: Constitutional and Political Perspectives*, 46 Mercer L. Rev. 697, 718-21 (1995). Congress may choose, however, to enact much more detailed statutes that are so finely tuned to a particular set of circumstances that they effectively prescribe their own effect, leaving little for a court to decide. When that happens, the courts must determine whether Congress has been uncharacteristically (but legitimately) particular in specifying the controlling law or has (illegitimately) pushed beyond its legislative function and presumed to adjudicate disputes as well. In *Robertson*, the Court understood Congress to have done the former and thus avoided any question under *Klein*. Of course, the insight that the legislative and judicial functions run together in the end is nothing new, but always lurks in the background of any argument over the separation of powers. See Chapter I, text accompanying note 5. It is in part because Congress can alter the substantive law applicable to a case that Professor Sager contends that *Klein*'s principal point is not that Congress must couch legislation in that form, but rather that the Court will not be placed in a position in which it cannot keep faith with its own interpretation of the Constitution. Sager, note 80, at 2527-28. Professor Meltzer finds more significance in the formal difference between statutes that purport merely to make public policy legislatively, on the one hand, and statutes that purport to interpret the Constitution, on the other. Meltzer, note 80, at 2549.

ently held that due process requires the states (and presumably the federal government) to offer litigants some access to courts to vindicate certain federal constitutional claims.[83] And in a host of other cases, the Court has gone to great lengths to read statutes to contemplate some form of judicial review for other constitutional questions. In this context, too, the Court applies a clear statement rule that preserves access in the absence of exacting language to the contrary.[84] If Congress were to *be* sufficiently clear in a particular instance, some justices plainly would permit Congress to insulate constitutional issues from judicial examination entirely.[85] Others are doubtful.[86]

In one famous lower court case, *Battaglia v. General Motors*,[87] the Second Circuit grappled with the problem, but ultimately rested its decision on a distinction that is difficult to credit. In previous decisions, the Supreme Court had held that the Fair Labor Standards Act entitled workers to be paid while they traveled through underground mines to the place where they would actually set to work.[88] Those decisions made both private employers and the federal government liable for billions of dollars in back wages. To avert that liability, Congress enacted the Portal-to-Portal Act of 1947. That Act purported not only to abrogate any claims that workers had, but also to withdraw the jurisdiction of *any* court to entertain suits by workers seeking any kind of relief.

The court in *Battaglia* nonetheless entertained a suit by workers claiming back wages. Without mentioning Article III, the court reasoned that a withdrawal of jurisdiction having the effect of depriving workers of their property without due process of law would itself violate due process. Turning to the merits, the court held that the abrogation of the workers' claims did *not* violate due process. Then, in an ironic twist, the court said that it was unnecessary to decide whether the Act's attempt to withdraw jurisdiction from the courts would have been successful if the workers' underlying due process claims had been meritorious.

The principal holding in *Battaglia* is compelling. Jurisdictional statutes, like any other form of legislation, must conform to the Constitution. And the courts must be institutionally capable of ensuring that they do. Accordingly, courts must have threshold jurisdiction to decide whether any particular jurisdictional

---

83. See Chapter VI, notes 54-77 and accompanying text.

84. E.g., *Webster v. Doe*, 486 U.S. 592 (1988) (reading a statute not to preclude judicial review of a constitutional challenge to the decision of the Director of the CIA to dismiss an employee); *Franklin v. Massachusetts*, 505 U.S. 788 (1992) (allowing Massachusetts to press constitutional claims regarding the way in which federal officers conduct the census); *Dalton v. Specter*, 511 U.S. 462 (1994) (construing the Defense Base Closure Act to preclude judicial review only of statutory claims against actions taken by the Secretary of Defense).

85. See, e.g., *Webster*, 486 U.S. at 612 (Scalia, J., dissenting) (contending that Congress can put some constitutional questions "beyond judicial review"). Cf. *Bartlett v. Bowen*, 816 F.2d 695, 719-20 (D.C. Cir. 1987) (Bork, J., dissenting) (arguing that Congress can foreclose judicial review in reliance on sovereign immunity).

86. E.g., *Webster*, 486 U.S. at 603 (Rehnquist, C.J.) (stating that an attempt by Congress to bar all judicial review of a constitutional question would itself "raise a serious constitutional question").

87. 169 F.2d 254 (2d Cir. 1948).

88. E.g., *Tennessee Coal, Iron & R. Co. v. Muscoda Local No. 123*, 321 U.S. 590 (1944).

statute confers on them all the jurisdiction the Constitution requires.[89] The court's discussion, however, is problematic in two respects. First, inasmuch as the court relied exclusively on the fifth amendment, it implied that Article III poses no bar to federal statutes that bar all courts from adjudicating constitutional claims. Second, inasmuch as the court suggested that it might have lacked jurisdiction if the workers' claims had been good, it implied that the question whether Congress can withhold jurisdiction may be contingent on the validity of the governmental action that a withdrawal of jurisdiction attempts to shield. It is hard to think that Congress can carve all courts, federal and state, out of the picture — but only when those courts would disapprove the activity under attack if they had jurisdiction to consider it. That would be circular.

F. Academic Theories

The Supreme Court's failure to elaborate clear limits on Congress' power invites academicians to fill the vacuum with theoretical accounts of their own. The resulting literature is rich in detail, typically combining intricate analysis of historical materials with explicit normative arguments about the way the legislative and judicial branches can best function together.[90] Academics tend to agree that Congress' authority to adjust and allocate jurisdiction threatens the system's balance and therefore must have limits. If Congress had plenary power to reduce the Supreme Court's purview dramatically and simply to eliminate wholesale the lower federal courts' jurisdiction (or, indeed, the lower courts themselves), the system's basic structure might be radically changed at any time. Moreover, Congress' manipulation of jurisdiction may have implications for the vindication of individual rights that Article III courts ordinarily enforce.[91]

Academics also tend to agree that the policy Congress adopts in one context typically has implications for the policies it simultaneously adopts in another. It is one thing, for example, for Congress to deny lower federal courts jurisdiction in some category of Article III business (even cases involving federal constitutional rights) — so long as Congress permits the Supreme Court to consider cases of that kind on appeal from state courts.[92] It is another thing for Congress to withhold ju-

---

89. See Richard H. Fallon, Jr., *Some Confusions About Due Process, Judicial Review, and Constitutional Remedies*, 93 Colum. L. Rev. 309, 368 (1993) (crediting Professor Hart with this insight).

90. Professor Wells and Professor Larson have criticized the "originalist premises" of much of this literature and argued that commentators would do better to fashion principles that take greater account of modern circumstances. Michael Wells & Edward J. Larson, *Original Intent and Article III*, 70 Tulane L. Rev. 75 (1995).

91. See text accompanying notes 27-31.

92. In fact, Congress does this all the time. For example, the basic statute on which district courts rely for jurisdiction in federal question cases, 28 U.S.C. § 1331, typically demands that a federal issue appear on the face of the plaintiff's properly pleaded complaint. Yet Article III allows Congress to give district courts a more extensive jurisdiction. See Chapter VIII, notes 5-31 and accompanying text. Ordinarily, when a case is not within the district courts' jurisdiction pursuant to § 1331 and thus is heard in state court, the Supreme Court has appellate jurisdiction to review any decisive state court judgment on a federal question. See Chapter VII, notes 57-79 and accompanying text.

risdiction from both lower federal courts and the Supreme Court, thus leaving federal constitutional cases entirely to state courts. It is still another thing for Congress to strip all courts, federal and state, of jurisdiction to adjudicate constitutional claims. Those are the problems the Supreme Court has largely skirted.

Academics identify two kinds of limits the Constitution places on congressional power: "external" limits and "internal" limits. External limits typically rest on rights-bearing provisions of the Constitution that Congress must respect when it enacts any kind of legislation. The fifth amendment's Due Process Clause and the first amendment's Free Exercise Clause are common examples. Obviously, a statute depriving district courts of jurisdiction in cases in which the plaintiff is African-American would violate due process. Equally, a statute making an "Exception" to the Supreme Court's appellate jurisdiction for cases involving Jews would violate free exercise. The jurisdictional character of a statute does not shield it from external restraints of that kind.[93]

Internal limits flow from the scope of the legislative authority Congress purports to exercise; they are tied up in the very definition of that power and limit Congress even when no external restraint is implicated. Congress has explicit power to create tribunals inferior to the Supreme Court and implicit power to prescribe the jurisdiction those courts will enjoy within the boundaries established by Article III. Congress also has explicit power to make "Exceptions" from the Supreme Court's appellate jurisdiction. Those powers have not only an affirmative side (what they allow Congress to do), but also a negative side (what they do not authorize Congress to do). Any interpretation of them must therefore contemplate that some congressional actions will reach beyond the scope of the power Congress purports to be exercising and thus exceed the limits "internal" to that power.

Of the two kinds of constitutional limits, internal limits are the more difficult to elaborate. The most influential academic accounts of internal restraints fall under three headings: (1) essential function theories; (2) zero-sum theories; and (3) judicial independence theories.

Essential Function Theories. Many academicians are content with a large measure of congressional control over lower federal courts, but insist that Congress' ability to make "Exceptions" from the Supreme Court's appellate jurisdiction is subject to significant restraints. As a matter of grammar alone, an *exception* presupposes a body of jurisdiction from which Congress removes some piece. Accordingly, Congress cannot make "Exceptions" for the entirety of the appellate jurisdiction that Article III prescribes, leaving nothing behind.[94] Congress cannot meet this grammatical objection simply by allowing the Court some trifle of jurisdiction while making "Exceptions" for everything else. Congress' power under the Exceptions Clause must be reconciled

---

93. See Richard H. Fallon, Jr., *The Ideologies of Federal Courts Law*, 74 Va. L. Rev. 1141, 1221 (1988). Professor Tribe contends that foreclosing federal jurisdiction of cases involving a specified individual right and thus shifting adjudication of that right to state court imposes a "burden" that violates the right itself. Laurence H. Tribe, *Jurisdictional Gerrymandering: Zoning Disfavored Rights Out of the Federal Courts*, 16 Harv. C.R.—C.L. L. Rev. 129 (1981). That argument is attractive, particularly if it is true (as it invariably is) that proponents of the limitation on federal jurisdiction hope the state courts will be less generous to the federal right in issue. If, however, federal and state courts are fungible in constitutional cases, Professor Tribe's argument is less compelling.

94. This was Professor Hart's approach to the problem. Hart, note 34, at 1365.

with the constitutional framework within which it is located and therefore must respect the Supreme Court's role in the tripartite system. Congress' power must therefore be limited to adjustments that are not disabling, but rather preserve the Court's ability to perform its "essential functions."[95] What counts as an essential function can be controversial. It seems clear, however, that the Court's crucial role concerns matters of federal law, particularly constitutional law. The Court must serve as the judicial system's ultimate referee, ensuring that federal law is accurately elaborated, that it is held supreme over state law, and that it is uniformly understood and enforced throughout the country.[96]

The essential function thesis has the virtue of being consistent with the Supreme Court's precedents. Then again, Congress has not (yet) enacted jurisdictional legislation that genuinely threatens the Court's capacity to referee the system in federal question cases. Most observers endorse this theory as a minimalist account of the constitutional limits on congressional power. Yet many doubt its sufficiency without more. As a practical matter, the essential functions limit may be unenforceable. It would be hard to say that any particular, isolated restriction on the Supreme Court's jurisdiction is in itself disabling. The essential functions limiting principle may thus be evaded if Congress enacts a series of modest restrictions that are devastating only in cumulative effect.

Zero-Sum Theories. Other academics advance alternative theories, which attempt to delineate both Congress' authority to make "Exceptions" from the Supreme Court's appellate jurisdiction and Congress' authority to prescribe the jurisdiction of inferior federal courts. Zero-sum theories proceed from Justice Story's premise that the term "shall" in the first section of Article III establishes a constitutional mandate that the judicial power of the United States *must* be vested in Article III courts.[97]

By one account, Congress must give Article III courts jurisdiction in all the (non-trivial) cases and controversies listed in Article III. If Congress creates only the Supreme Court, that single tribunal must be able to reach everything, either by exercising original jurisdiction or by taking appeals from state courts. In that instance, Congress' power to make "Exceptions" from the Court's appellate jurisdiction is limited to allocating business between the Court's original and appellate dockets. It is a zero-sum game. Everything must be in one place or the other, with nothing (or almost nothing) entirely omitted. If, on the other hand, Congress creates inferior federal courts, then by this account Congress can deny the Supreme Court either original or appellate jurisdiction of some case or controversy and channel that business to those inferior courts. The constitutional mandate is satisfied so long as everything can reach *some* Article III court in *some* way.[98]

---

95. Id.

96. See Leonard Ratner, *Congressional Power Over the Appellate Jurisdiction of the Supreme Court*, 109 U. Pa. L. Rev. 157, 161 (1960).

97. See text accompanying note 15.

98. This is the understanding that Professor Clinton ascribes to the founding generation. Of course, he explains and defends it in much finer detail. Robert N. Clinton, *A Mandatory View of Federal Court Jurisdiction: A Guided Quest for the Original Understanding of Article III*, 132 U. Pa. L. Rev. 741 (1984). See also Robert N. Clinton, *A Mandatory View of Federal Court Jurisdiction: Early Implementation of and Departures from the Constitutional Plan*, 86 Colum. L. Rev. 1515 (1986).

A second zero-sum account builds on Story's observation that only the "cases" on the Article III menu are preceded by the modifier "all."[99] By this second account, Congress is obliged only to allow the Supreme Court (together with inferior federal courts if they are created) jurisdiction in those *cases*—and not the *controversies* on the Article III list. Article III thus establishes two "tiers" of matters over which Article III courts *can* exercise jurisdiction. The cases in the one tier (preceded by "all") are especially important and thus must be vested. The controversies listed further down are of another order and need not have access to an Article III forum.[100]

These theories have appeal, but they are also open to criticism. By contrast to the essential functions thesis, they plainly depart from established precedent. The Supreme Court has often permitted Congress to make net withdrawals of Article III jurisdiction from federal courts and thus has implicitly rejected the zero-sum baseline. The first zero-sum account has it that the federal courts must constitutionally be given much more jurisdiction than they have ever had. If Congress were to place the entirety of that business in the Supreme Court itself, the burden would be enormous—and extremely difficult to justify.[101] The second zero-sum account would be easier to implement. But that approach, too, insists that Article III courts must shoulder much more responsibility than may be either wise or practical.[102]

Judicial Independence Theories. Still other academics insist that Congress' power to prescribe the jurisdiction of federal courts must be reconciled with constitutional safeguards for the independence of those courts: Congress cannot have such plenary authority to withhold jurisdiction that it can defeat Article III's tenure and salary protections by indirection, simply by channeling judicial business to state judges who stand for popular election.[103] According to this last the-

---

99. See text accompanying note 16.

100. This is a nutshell of Professor Amar's thesis. He, too, elaborates his argument in much greater depth. See Akhil R. Amar, *A Neo-Federalist View of Article III: Separating the Two Tiers of Federal Jurisdiction*, 65 B.U. L. Rev. 205 (1985). Amar fortifies his theory of Article III with a related argument that it conforms (in most respects) to the Judiciary Act of 1789. Akhil R. Amar, *The Two-Tiered Structure of the Judiciary Act of 1789*, 138 U. Pa. L. Rev. 1499 (1990). See Chapter II, notes 53-65 and accompanying text. For criticism, see John Harrison, *The Power of Congress to Limit the Jurisdiction of Federal Courts and the Text of Article III*, 64 U. Chi. L. Rev. 203 (1997); Martin H. Redish, *Text, Structure, and Common Sense in the Interpretation of Article III*, 138 U. Pa. L. Rev. 1633 (1990); Daniel J. Meltzer, *The History and Structure of Article III*, 138 U. Pa. L. Rev. 1569 (1990). For Professor Amar's response, see Akhil R. Amar, *Reports of My Death Are Greatly Exaggerated: A Reply*, 138 U. Pa. L. Rev. 1651 (1990).

101. If Congress creates no inferior federal courts and, under Clinton's theory, must confer "minimal" diversity on the Supreme Court, then the Court would have jurisdiction to accept appeals from the state courts in a wide range of cases controlled by state law. See note 20; Chapter VII, notes 92-94 (discussing the understanding that state courts are authoritative with respect to state law). Professor Harrison contends that Clinton's theory would "fill the federal courts with diversity cases." Harrison, note 100, at 207.

102. Professor Amar has it that federal question cases are among those that must be vested in some Article III court. That seems attractive. Yet under the precedents a case "arises under" federal law not only when it actually implicates a federal issue, but also when a federal question may potentially appear. That, suffice it to say, is a lot of cases. See note 92. Professor Harrison contends that Amar reads too much into the term "all." See Harrison, note 100, at 233.

103. Professor Sager is the principal proponent of this position. Sager, note 52. He, too, explains his approach in much more detail. For criticism, see Martin H. Redish, *Constitu-*

ory, Congress can deny federal courts significant portions of the power that Article III would allow. But Congress cannot deprive the federal judiciary of the capacity to handle critical constitutional cases. This theory also conflicts with established precedent. Observers who are comfortable with the Hart and Wechsler paradigm and the private rights model will find it unattractive, as will observers who accept the parity of the state and federal courts.[104] Observers who embrace the public rights model may find it appealing.[105]

---

tional Limitations on Congressional Power to Control Federal Jurisdiction: A Reaction to Professor Sager, 77 Nw. U. L. Rev. 143 (1982).

104. See Chapter I, text accompanying notes 42-60,79-91.

105. See Chapter I, text accompanying notes 66-78.

Chapter V

Legislative Courts

The Supreme Court and the inferior federal tribunals organized under Article III are the "constitutional" or "Article III" courts in which "[t]he judicial Power of the United States...shall be vested." Congress often creates other federal officers, agencies, and tribunals and gives them authority to perform adjudicative functions. Those entities differ from Article III courts in one crucial respect: Their decision-makers do not enjoy the life tenure and salary protections that the Constitution guarantees to Article III judges. Instead, they serve for a term of years, and their compensation can be reduced.

Some of the bodies in question are officers or units operating within Article III courts. Others form the legions of federal administrative agencies located within the executive branch, but performing legislative and judicial functions as well. Agencies forge federal policy to govern their respective fields—both when they promulgate formal rules (in proceedings that look and feel legislative) and when they apply statutes and rules in particular instances (in proceedings that look and feel adjudicative). Plainly, whenever agencies determine facts and apply the law to those facts, they engage in adjudication.[1]

Early in this century, federal agencies were thought to be constitutionally troubling both because they combine executive, legislative, and judicial functions under one roof and because, with respect to adjudication, they trespass into territory occupied by the Article III judiciary. The Supreme Court defused those concerns in the 1930s, and for many years thereafter agency adjudication was rarely questioned. The great mass of modern administrative law developed to assimilate agencies into the constitutional framework.[2] Recently, however, the Supreme Court has revisited the tension between the judicial work that agencies do and the Constitution's contemplation that judicial power lies with Article III courts.

The occasion for this reassessment is Congress' increasing reliance on non-Article III adjudicators called "legislative" or "Article I" courts.[3] Legislative

---

1. See Chapter I, text accompanying note 5.
2. See notes 36-44 and accompanying text (discussing *Crowell v. Benson*). For a discussion of the development and significance of administrative agencies, see Chapter VIII, notes 82, 91, 95-97 and accompanying text; Chapter IX, notes 60-95 and accompanying text.
3. Labels can be confusing. Non-Article III adjudicators are not called "legislative" courts because they themselves exercise legislative functions (any more than do Article III courts), but because Congress creates them in service of its legislative programs. Nor are legislative courts called "Article I" courts because they are created pursuant to U.S. Const. art. I, § 8, cl. 9, which gives Congress power to "constitute Tribunals inferior to the supreme Court." That clause authorizes Congress to create Article III courts. *Glidden Co. v. Zdanok*, 370 U.S. 530, 543 (1962). Legislative courts are called "Article I" courts because, here again, Congress claims power to create them as an exercise of various other legislative pow-

courts are not units of Article III courts and thus cannot easily be justified as auxiliary staff. They occupy their own precincts and resolve legal disputes independently, without any expectation that Article III courts need be involved prior to an appellate stage. In most respects, legislative courts are conceptually indistinguishable from administrative agencies performing adjudicative functions. Yet the Supreme Court has worried at length over whether they can be squared with Article III. The Court's concerns about legislative courts, in turn, rekindle similar concerns about agencies.

One might have expected the Court to be especially suspicious of Congress' use of non-Article III tribunals in cases in which the federal government is a party and may wish to appear before judges more susceptible to influence.[4] As a matter of fact, the Court indulges Congress' use of legislative courts in cases of that kind with equanimity and reserves its concern for cases in which Congress employs legislative courts to resolve disputes between private litigants. It is in those cases, perhaps, that legislative courts seem most clearly to be doing the work historically regarded as judicial—thus poaching on Article III courts' preserve.[5]

A. Theoretical Models

Analysis of non-Article III tribunals is both energized and handicapped by two competing models: (1) the simple Article I model; and (2) the simple Article III model. No one offers either model as a comprehensive basis for deciding whether any particular assignment of jurisdiction is valid. Yet both plainly animate the arguments that are advanced in the cases and in the accompanying academic literature.

The simple Article I model. According to the simple Article I model, legislative courts present no great constitutional difficulty. Since Article I gives Congress power to make substantive law in a variety of fields, Congress must also have the implied power to choose the means by which its regulatory mandates will be carried out. Under the simple Article I model, Congress need not rely on Article III courts to elaborate the meaning of federal legislation and to settle any disputes.

---

ers, typically (though not always) enumerated in Article I—for example, the commerce power. Legislative courts are nonetheless "Courts of Law" within the meaning of the Appointments Clause, U.S. Const. art. II, § 2, cl.2, and therefore can be assigned the authority to appoint inferior legislative court judges. *Freytag v. Commissioner*, 501 U.S. 868 (1991).

4. See Chapter III, text accompanying note 2 (identifying the values associated with the independence of Article III courts); Chapter IV, notes 27-31 and accompanying text (describing the implications of congressional power to withhold jurisdiction from federal courts in sensitive cases).

5. Professor Resnik has noted the "irony" of reading the Constitution to give litigation between private citizens the strongest claim to an Article III tribunal. Judith Resnik, *The Mythic Meaning of Article III Courts*, 56 U. Colo. L. Rev. 581, 600 (1985). Professor Redish finds it "bizarre" that the Court overlooks cases in which the threat of congressional overreaching is greatest and focuses, instead, on cases that are "barely within any of the . . . categories" of cases and controversies that Article III includes in the federal judicial power. Martin H. Redish, *Legislative Courts, Administrative Agencies, and the Northern Pipeline Decision*, 1983 Duke L.J. 197, 208-09.

Instead, Congress can choose to implement statutes by other means—namely, by channeling disputes to non-Article III adjudicative bodies created for the purpose.

The simple Article I model is a classic illustration of a "greater power" mistake.[6] It posits that Congress' power to establish a regulatory scheme under Article I constitutes a "greater" power, which necessarily includes as a "lesser" power the authority to create and use a legislative court. That rationale is unsound. It may be perfectly sensible to interpret a legislative power to include the power to create a legislative court. But it is not logically imperative that Article I powers must be interpreted that way. The Constitution might also be read to authorize Congress to fashion substantive policies to govern a field, but to specify that if Congress wants federal tribunals to resolve any disputes that arise in connection with its regulation, Congress must rely on independent Article III courts. A requirement that Congress use Article III courts exclusively might be a check that balances Congress' power to make and implement policy in the first instance. In any case, the simple Article I model fixes no apparent limits and thus ignores the separation principle altogether. There must be some check on non-Article III adjudicators. Otherwise, Congress would be able to carve Article III courts out of the picture entirely.

The simple Article III model. According to the simple Article III model, legislative courts conflict with fundamental constitutional principles. The Constitution unmistakably places the federal judicial power in the hands of Article III courts alone, and Congress must make do with those courts or none at all. To allow Congress to create other tribunals and to route federal judicial business to them is to invite Congress to bypass independent Article III courts at will, to ignore the federal judicial branch that Article III envisions, and thus to dismantle the fundamental tripartite framework of the national government.[7]

The simple Article III model is an example of separation-of-powers formalism. It proceeds from a contestable interpretation of Article III's text and an equally contestable inference from the constitutional structure. Recall that what qualifies as judicial business is not logically determinable, but turns on conventional practices and pragmatic judgment.[8] If there is no principled line between adjudication and everything else, it is useless to insist that only Article III judges can perform judicial functions. Moreover, the simple Article III model is infeasible. Federal agencies with adjudicative authority are vital to the modern administrative state—a complex political and economic order unknown to the common law and unmanageable by common law courts.[9] The country might get along without so many agencies doing judicial work. And Congress might meet the constitutional difficulties with some agencies simply by making their decision-making officers Article III judges. Yet the charge the simple Article III model lays

---

6. See Chapter I, notes 21-22 and accompanying text.

7. Professor Fallon calls this point of view "Article III literalism." Richard H. Fallon, Jr., *Of Legislative Courts, Administrative Agencies, and Article III*, 101 Harv. L. Rev. 915, 918 (1988). Professor Bator called it the "Simple Model." Paul M. Bator, *The Constitution as Architecture: Legislative and Administrative Courts Under Article III*, 65 Ind. L.J. 233, 235 (1990).

8. See Chapter I, note 5 and accompanying text.

9. Agencies might still perform legislative functions by formal rule-making. But they would lose the ability to resolve problems arising at the implementation stage.

against agencies runs deep. It condemns all adjudicative action by non-Article III bodies and thus could presumably be answered only if all federal officers performing judicial functions were given Article III judgeships.[10]

Struck by the obvious deficiencies in the simple models, many academics urge the Court to hold that non-Article III adjudicators are valid, so long as Article III courts can reexamine their decisions in some kind of appellate capacity.[11] Congress typically makes judgments by legislative courts final (if unchallenged), but subject to review in an Article III court. Parties who are displeased by what legislative courts decide thus bear the burden of pressing on to the Article III judiciary. Congress usually specifies that administrative agency judgments are *not* immediately effective. Agencies must ordinarily file independent lawsuits in the Article III courts, seeking judicial orders enforcing their decisions. Article III courts must therefore participate if agencies are to bring coercive power to bear on individuals. The form that Article III court review takes may have practical significance for the litigants involved. Yet by most accounts, the *constitutional* point is that Article III courts perform a serious supervisory function—whoever has the burden of bringing them into play.[12] The real question, then, is the *scope* of Article III court review. Asking Article III courts essentially to rubberstamp the work of non-Article III bodies would make the courts superfluous. Asking them to review all issues *de novo* would defeat the point of introducing non-Article III adjudicators in the first place.[13]

The Supreme Court plainly finds Article III court involvement critical. If the courts serve in an appellate capacity, the Court is ambivalent about whether it is

---

10. The point is not that federal officers other than Article III judges must be employed at will. Most already enjoy a large measure of job security under the civil service system. The point is not even (entirely) that the application of the various trappings attending federal judgeships to ordinary officers in the executive branch would rework well-established schemes for the appointment, retention, compensation, and dismissal of federal employees—from desk clerks to FBI agents. The real point is that making ordinary federal executive officers Article III judges would fundamentally transmute the nature of their offices. They would no longer serve within a hierarchical system, taking orders in the ordinary course from their superiors, but would occupy their own independent preserves and would be answerable in the much different manner of inferior Article III judges, whose judicial actions are subject to reversal only for *error* on appeal to a higher court. Any attempt by superiors within an executive branch or agency to reexamine the *wisdom* of their decisions would presumably constitute executive revision in violation of Article III. See Chapter IX, notes 23-29 and accompanying text. Professor Stern insists that Article III can be read literally without such dire consequences—merely by defining the exercise of federal judicial power according to the identity of the officer concerned (rather than the function the officer performs). By his account, executive officers may routinely perform adjudicative functions without implicating Article III, because they (not being Article III judges) do not exercise federal judicial authority. Craig A. Stern, *What's a Constitution Among Friends?—Unbalancing Article III*, 146 U. Pa. L. Rev. 1043 (1998). Stern claims that Justice Scalia essentially adopted that position in his concurring opinion in *Freytag.* 501 U.S. at 911.

11. Professor Fallon, for example, contends that Article III court review is not only a necessary, but a sufficient, response to Article III difficulties generally. Fallon, note 7. Professor Stern disparages the appellate review approach, but nonetheless appears to be content that Article III is satisfied so long as the "ultimate" decision-maker is an Article III judge. Stern, note 10, at 1047, 1073-74.

12. See Redish, note 5, at 216-17. Professor Meltzer also doubts that the constitutionality of non-Article III adjudication should turn on "which party has the burden of seeking judicial review." Daniel J. Meltzer, *Legislative Courts, Legislative Power, and the Constitution,* 65 Ind. L.J. 291, 303 n.61 (1990).

13. See note 106 (elaborating this point of view).

preferable that individuals or non-Article III bodies have the burden of seeking judicial review. The Court is not convinced, however, that *any* form of after-the-fact review is sufficient in itself. By contrast, the Court insists that the Constitution imposes limits of some kind on *original* adjudication by non-Article III entities.[14] Accordingly, the Court has set about the task of finding its own middle passage between the simple Article I and Article III models. The first order of business is to look behind the models themselves and to identify and evaluate the reasons for employing legislative courts, on the one hand, and the genuine problems and hazards they present, on the other.

In many instances, legislative courts have obvious advantages and pose very few risks. Some of them are nothing new at all, but are quite old and familiar.[15] They operate in fields in which Congress has special constitutional authority and responsibility, handling business for which Article III courts are not suited.[16] Legislative courts can serve a temporary purpose that demands no Article III courts to achieve. It makes sense, then, to allow Congress to employ decision-makers for fixed terms and thus to avoid building up a battery of life-tenured Article III judges whose services may not always be needed.[17] Some legislative courts have jurisdiction over a limited geographic area and thus have little capacity to extend their influence beyond fixed borders. While they may handle cases implicating legal standards of wider applicability, they rarely affect the national adjudicative system as a whole.[18] Most legislative courts have jurisdiction over a limited subject matter;[19] many offer special expertise with respect to the jurisdiction they exercise.[20] Legislative courts sometimes dispose of comparatively routine, fact-sensitive matters expeditiously, without the expenditures and delays that often accompany ordinary litigation.[21] Finally, legislative courts can mitigate the caseload crisis simply by assuming adjudicative responsibility that Article III courts would otherwise have to shoulder.[22]

---

14. See text accompanying note 104.

15. Territorial courts may be the best example under this heading, but military courts, too, are typically explained in this way. See notes 53-56, 59-62 and accompanying text.

16. Once again, territorial and military courts are illustrations. See notes 56, 59-60 and accompanying text.

17. Early territorial courts met this description, though the territorial courts we now have may not. See note 55 and accompanying text. Temporary tribunals established *ad hoc* to handle cases in other nations may be the best illustrations. But see Maryellen Fullerton, *Hijacking Trials Overseas: The Need for an Article III Court*, 28 Wm. & Mary L. Rev. 1 (1986).

18. Territorial courts and the courts of the District of Columbia share this feature. See notes 53-58 and accompanying text.

19. Military courts martial are restricted to armed forces personnel, for example, and the Tax Court of the United States is limited to taxation cases. See note 60 and accompanying text.

20. Numerous modern tribunals fit under this heading. By contrast, there is strong sentiment that Article III judges should be generalists. See Chapter II, note 95 and accompanying text.

21. Classic examples include federal pension cases, customs disputes, and some immigration cases—in which truncated procedures are thought to be expedient. See Bator, note 7, at 261-62; but see note 68 (regarding immigration cases). The Court of Federal Claims and the Benefits Review Board illustrate the kind of specialized tribunals that may be established to hear claims against the federal government.

22. See Chapter II, notes 82-106 and accompanying text. This justification for legislative courts is open to debate. Professor Meltzer argues that if Congress is unprepared to in-

Legislative courts nonetheless entail problems and potential perils. Since their decision-makers lack the salary and tenure protections enjoyed by Article III judges, their independence from political pressure is less secure. That, in turn, threatens both structural arrangements on which society as a whole depends and the personal rights of individuals to appear before life-tenured federal judges—if they appear before federal adjudicators at all. The Constitution does not systematically guarantee anyone a right to litigate in an Article III court.[23] Nevertheless, if Congress chooses to provide a federal forum, the independence of the judge who sits is Article III-sensitive.[24] Legislative courts' vulnerability to political pressure may rob their proceedings of fairness and thus violate due process.[25] Finally, legislative courts typically rely exclusively on professional decision-makers and therefore may compromise litigants' independent seventh amendment right to trial by jury.[26]

To accommodate these competing interests and concerns, the Supreme Court has relied on two distinct theories of its own creation: (1) the "adjunct" theory, which justifies non-Article III adjudicators as arms of the Article III judiciary; and (2) a much more complex theory, which justifies legislative courts as independent tribunals, though typically subject to appellate supervision by an Article III court.[27]

---

crease the number of Article III judgeships, judicial independence might better be served by diverting the overflow into state court. Meltzer, note 12, at 293-94.

23. In many instances, individuals must proceed in state court. Few state judges have tenure and salary safeguards, and it would be extravagant to argue that, for that reason, their adjudicative functions violate Article III. See Chapter IV, text accompanying notes 19-20 (explaining that Congress routinely gives federal courts less jurisdiction than Article III would allow); Chapter VI, notes 3-36 and accompanying text (discussing the presumptive authority of state courts to entertain federal question cases).

24. State judges may have no structural safeguards to ensure their independence, but they do not depend on Congress for their maintenance, either. Larry Kramer, *The Constitution as Architecture: A Charette*, 65 Ind. L.J. 283, 286 (1990).

25. This point draws on the same theme as the previous point. Yet the argument from fairness is more conventional inasmuch as it rests on a principle of individual liberty (due process) rather than on a structural theme (the separation of powers reflected in Article III). Justice Brandeis contended that if an individual litigant has any constitutional complaint about the status of the judge assigned to determine a case, that complaint must be anchored in due process rather than in Article III. *Crowell v. Benson*, 285 U.S. 22, 87-88 (1932) (dissenting opinion). Yet the modern Court has acknowledged that an individual has a (waivable) Article III right to appear before a judge who is protected from the influences of other branches. See note 94.

26. See note 34 (discussing the authority of magistrate judges to conduct jury trials); notes 110-31 and accompanying text (discussing the tension between the constitutional right to trial by jury and non-Article III adjudication in which juries are not available). This point, too, can be debated. Recall that trial by jury was understood historically as a democratic safeguard against powerful judges, answerable to the Crown or, after 1787, only to themselves. See Chapter II, notes 30-33 and accompanying text. There is an argument, then, that the seventh amendment right to jury trial is chiefly at risk when cases are adjudicated by life-tenured Article III judges.

27. Professor Strauss explains that "the whole point" is that "*no judicial involvement at all*" is required before a legislative court can coerce a litigant to conform to its orders. Peter L. Strauss, *The Place of Agencies in Government: Separation of Powers and the Fourth Branch*, 84 Colum. L. Rev. 573, 632 (1984) (emphasis in original).

B. Adjuncts to Article III Courts

Under the adjunct theory, the Supreme Court finds that non-Article III adjudication is essentially consistent with the simple Article III model. The officers and entities concerned are conceptualized as auxiliary elements of Article III courts. If adjunct officers or bodies perform adjudicative duties *for* Article III courts, there is no serious conflict with Article III, and the separation of powers is preserved.[28]

Magistrate judges. The best illustrations of adjunct officers are magistrate judges. They have been in place since the Judiciary Act of 1789, albeit traveling under different names.[29] Magistrate judges handle misdemeanor criminal trials, preliminary proceedings in serious criminal cases, habeas corpus hearings, a wide range of civil matters, and any "additional duties as are not inconsistent with the Constitution and laws of the United States."[30] In *United States v. Raddatz*,[31] the Supreme Court held that a district judge could rule on a criminal defendant's motion to suppress incriminating evidence on the basis of a magistrate's report, without independently seeing the witnesses. Neither the Due Process Clause nor Article III required the district judge to hold another hearing, even though the defendant's constitutional rights were at stake. It was enough that the district judge was empowered to "accept or reject" the magistrate's recommendations and might have *chosen* to "hear the evidence *de novo*." Since the magistrate judge acted under the district court's "total control," all constitutional requirements were satisfied.[32]

The Court has never specified the nature and scope of the review that district courts must give, or be empowered to give, to the original judgments that magistrate judges reach.[33] And the Court has yet to explain fully the effect the parties'

---

28. Professor Bator acknowledged (but derided) the adjunct theory as a device for finding non-Article III bodies to be "in harmony with the fundamentals of the Simple Model." Bator, note 7, at 253.

29. See Linda J. Silberman, *Masters and Magistrates, Part II: The American Analogue*, 50 N.Y.U. L. Rev. 1297 (1975). Under current law, magistrate judges are appointed for eight-year terms by the Article III district court judges whose courts they serve. Those same district judges may remove them for "incompetency, misconduct, neglect of duty, or physical or mental disability." 28 U.S.C. § 631 (e), (i).

30. 28 U.S.C. § 636(b)(3). The Court held in *Wingo v. Wedding*, 418 U.S. 461 (1974), that previous law did not permit magistrates to conduct evidentiary hearings in habeas corpus cases. Thereafter, Congress expanded their authority to handle a host of proceedings—subject to reconsideration by district judges if it is "shown" that a magistrate's order is "clearly erroneous or contrary to law." 28 U.S.C. § 636(b)(1)(A). Magistrate judges prepare reports setting forth proposed findings of fact and recommendations for disposition. If parties object, district judges make *de novo* determinations. When the parties consent (and the court directs), magistrate judges can fully dispose of any civil case. In that instance, any appeal lies not to a judge of the district court, but directly to the appropriate circuit court of appeals. 28 U.S.C. § 636(b)-(c). The lower courts have upheld these provisions against constitutional attack, albeit frequently citing the parties' consent. E.g., *Pacemaker Diagnostic Clinic of Amer. v. Instromedix*, 725 F.2d 537 (9th Cir. 1984), *cert. denied*, 469 U.S. 824 (1985).

31. 447 U.S. 667 (1980).

32. Id. at 681.

33. Since district judges now have authority to reexamine magistrate judge actions top to bottom, the Court has had no occasion to decide whether some lesser measure of district

consent to magistrate judge activities may have on the validity of those actions under Article III.[34] In light of the caseload crisis, it is likely that the tasks assigned to magistrate judges will continue to grow and that the Supreme Court will approve so long as Article III judges retain theoretical control and responsibility.[35]

Administrative agencies. In some instances, administrative agencies are also understood to perform adjudicative functions as adjuncts of Article III courts. In *Crowell v. Benson*,[36] the Supreme Court held that when agencies determine facts related to "private rights," they, like magistrate judges, may do so as instruments of Article III courts — performing judicial duties, but leaving "the essential attributes of judicial power" to the courts.[37] Knudsen claimed he had been injured in a maritime accident while employed by Benson. He filed a complaint with the Employees Compensation Commission, seeking compensation from Benson. Crowell, a deputy commissioner, heard the evidence and concluded that Knudsen was entitled to recover. Benson then sued Crowell in federal district court, seeking an injunction against enforcement of the judgment in Knudsen's favor.[38] Benson contended, first, that Crowell had acted beyond his jurisdiction (because Knudsen had not been in Benson's employ at the time of the accident) and, second, that Crowell's actions on behalf of the Commission violated both due process and Article III. The district court held a *de novo* hearing, concluded that Knudsen had not been employed by Benson at the time of the accident, and on that basis enjoined enforcement of the Commission's order.

-----

court supervision would satisfy the Constitution. The Court has equally failed to specify minimal standards of judicial review in other contexts, in which Article III courts have less sweeping supervisory authority and in which, accordingly, the need for greater clarity is more urgent. See notes 104-06 and accompanying text. For an argument that magistrate judges receive too little Article III oversight, see Note, *The Boundaries of Article III: Delegation of Final Decisionmaking Authority to Magistrates*, 52 U. Chi. L. Rev. 1032 (1985).

34. In *Peretz v. United States*, 501 U.S. 923 (1991), the Court held that district courts can allow magistrate judges to conduct jury selection hearings in criminal cases in which defendants consent. By giving consent, defendants waive any personal Article III or due process claim they have to an Article III judge. The Court had no occasion in *Peretz* to decide whether Article III allows magistrate judges to select juries in criminal cases when defendants refuse to consent. Nor has the Court decided whether, under current statutes, magistrate judges can conduct jury trials (in either criminal or civil cases) without the relevant party's consent. The Court expressly bypassed that question in *McCarthy v. Bronson*, 500 U.S. 136 (1991), where the parties had waived jury trial. The Federal Courts Improvement Act of 1996 authorizes magistrate judges to conduct trials in petty criminal cases without the defendant's consent. 28 U.S.C. § 636(a)(3). The Court has elaborated the role that consent plays in Article III cases in other contexts. See note 94.

35. The Administrative Office of United States Courts reports that the magistrate system is operating well. Report, *A Constitutional Analysis of Magistrate Judge Authority*, 150 F.R.D. 247 (1993). By some accounts, however, the district courts' increasing reliance on magistrate judges threatens to relegate vulnerable litigants (e.g., prison inmates) to non-Article III judges. Reinier H. Kraakman, *Article III Constraints and the Expanding Civil Jurisdiction of Federal Magistrates: A Dissenting View*, 88 Yale L.J. 1023 (1979).

36. 285 U.S. 22 (1932).

37. Id. at 51.

38. The deputy's award was not immediately effective, but had to be enforced in a separate lawsuit in the appropriate district court. See text accompanying notes 11-12 (discussing the form that Article III court involvement typically takes in cases in which agencies make original determinations). Either the Commission itself or the beneficiary of an award could sue to enforce it. Anyone found liable could sue to enjoin it. That is what Benson did in *Crowell*.

The Supreme Court sustained the district court in a famous opinion by Chief Justice Hughes. Initially, Hughes distinguished between questions of law, on the one hand, and questions of fact, on the other. Regarding questions of law, he said that the district court was entitled and obligated to exercise its own independent judgment. The statute in *Crowell* was clear (enough) on that point, and Hughes hinted that the Constitution would have called for independent judicial judgment on legal questions in any event.[39] The decisive issue in *Crowell*, then, was whether Congress could give the Commission authority to determine the underlying facts.

Chief Justice Hughes took it to be significant that the case was "one of private right, that is, of the liability of one individual to another."[40] In private rights cases, he said, the Constitution places limits on Congress' power to assign adjudicative power to a non-Article III adjudicator. Otherwise, Congress might "oust the courts of all determinations of fact by vesting the authority to make them with finality in its own instrumentalities or in the executive department." Those limits, however, leave agencies with a good deal of work to do. Chief Justice Hughes recognized that the very point of the scheme in *Crowell* was to provide workers like Knudsen with a streamlined administrative procedure for determining their claims and, concomitantly, to relieve Article III courts of the responsibility to handle such routine matters. To make that plan work, it was essential that the courts should treat Commission findings of fact as final, provided they were supported by substantial evidence. Hughes therefore allowed Congress to give the Commission authority for ordinary fact-finding, subject to judicial review in an Article III court.[41]

Chief Justice Hughes used the *Crowell* case to fashion a pragmatic compromise of enormous power and influence. To protect the independent role of the federal judiciary, he insisted that agency declarations of *law* must be open to *de novo* judicial examination. Yet to reap the advantages of administrative adjudication, he characterized agencies as adjuncts of the courts—able to find the *facts* in particular cases, subject to judicial review and ultimate responsibility.[42] It is

---

39. This feature of *Crowell* may survive today, but in an altered form. In *Chevron v. Natural Resources Defense Council*, 467 U.S. 837 (1984), the Court held that when the statute an agency is charged to enforce is unclear, a reviewing Article III court may not simply substitute its judgment for that of the agency, but must sustain the agency's interpretation if it is based on a permissible construction of the statute. Properly understood, *Chevron* does not command an Article III court to defer to an agency's interpretation of a federal statute. Rather, *Chevron* recognizes that Congress has implicitly delegated to the agency a measure of legislative authority to interpret its organic act. When a court accepts the product of the agency's permissible exercise of that authority, the court merely effectuates the prior delegation. Henry P. Monaghan, *Marbury and the Administrative State*, 83 Colum. L. Rev. 1, 27-28 (1983).

40. 285 U.S. at 45, 57.

41. Id. at 51, 64.

42. The compromise in *Crowell* was actually more complex. The Court said that an Article III court must exercise independent judgment on "jurisdictional" facts (the facts on which the Commission's jurisdiction depended) and on "constitutional" facts (the facts related to constitutional claims). Since the question whether Knudsen had been in Benson's employ at the time of the accident went to the Commission's authority to entertain Knudsen's claim, it was one of "jurisdictional" fact. Accordingly, the Court approved the district court's *de novo* assessment of that question. 285 U.S. at 65. In dissent, Justice Brandeis dismissed the distinction between ordinary facts and "constitutional" facts as inconsequential and insisted that if the "jurisdictional" fact category was important in some cases, it was not so in *Crowell* itself—because Knudsen's employment status went only to the applicability of

debatable whether administrative agencies operating in their own regulatory environment can persuasively be analogized to auxiliary officers acting under the watchful eye of a district court.[43] Nevertheless, the adjunct theory on which Chief Justice Hughes relied in *Crowell* has shown genuine staying power.[44]

Bankruptcy courts. The Supreme Court declined to find the adjunct theory sufficient to sustain an important feature of the Bankruptcy Act of 1978. That Act established bankruptcy courts in each federal district and gave those courts jurisdiction not only over bankruptcy proceedings, but also over other civil proceedings "arising in or related to" bankruptcies.[45] Bankruptcy court judgments were final when issued and required no further enforcement actions in an Article III court. A disappointed party could appeal a bankruptcy court order to a panel of three other bankruptcy judges—and then, if necessary, to a court of appeals. That court, however, could review bankruptcy court judgments only to decide whether they were "clearly erroneous."

In *Northern Pipeline Constr. Co. v. Marathon Pipe Line Co.*,[46] Northern initially filed a petition for reorganization in one of the new bankruptcy courts and then, three months later, added to that proceeding a lawsuit against Marathon, seeking damages for breach of a previous contract between the two companies. That contract action was governed by state law and might have been brought in state court.[47] Yet Northern contended that the bankruptcy court could entertain

---

federal substantive law, not to the Commission's jurisdiction to entertain his claim. More recently, the Court has largely abandoned any requirement that the courts always make independent judgments regarding "jurisdictional" or "constitutional" facts. See Henry P. Monaghan, *Constitutional Fact Review*, 85 Colum. L. Rev. 229 (1985); Chapter VII, text accompanying note 169. Administrative agencies now routinely determine all the facts necessary to resolve civil disputes—the very result that Brandeis and other progressives hoped to achieve.

43. Professor Bator thought it was "ludicrously inapt" and "patronizing" to conceive of administrative agencies as "adjuncts" of "some article III court," simply because that court might later review their judgments. Bator, note 7, at 252.

44. It is clear why Chief Justice Hughes thought it was essential to sustain the agency action in *Crowell*. That decision endorsed Congress' ability to depart from the common law tradition of relying exclusively on courts to perform adjudicative functions and, instead, to create administrative agencies to superintend the public law system just beginning to take shape in 1932. Even so, Justice Brandeis contended that the Court did not open its arms to the agencies widely enough. Professor Young has traced the emerging appreciation for administrative process during the period when *Crowell* was decided. Despite Brandeis' disappointment at the time, *Crowell* ultimately promoted the development of the modern administrative state. Gordon G. Young, *Public Rights and the Federal Judicial Power: From Murray's Lessee Through Crowell to Schor*, 35 Buffalo L. Rev. 765 (1986).

45. The judges who staffed the bankruptcy courts under the 1978 Act were appointed by the President after confirmation by the Senate, but they held office for fourteen-year terms and were removable by the relevant circuit judicial council for "incompetency, misconduct, neglect of duty or physical or mental disability." Previously, district courts were themselves courts of bankruptcy, albeit they employed referees to handle most of the work. The district courts had "summary" jurisdiction to dispose of property actually or constructively in their possession, but they needed the parties' consent to exercise "plenary" jurisdiction to deal with property in the hands of a third party. See Maryellen Fullerton, *No Light at the End of the Pipeline: Confusion Surrounds Legislative Courts*, 49 Brooklyn L. Rev. 207, 216-19 (1983).

46. 458 U.S. 50 (1982).

47. Actually, Northern had previously advanced the same state law claim in an independent lawsuit in a federal district court with diversity jurisdiction over the claim.

it as an action "related to" the pending petition for reorganization. Marathon responded that if the 1978 Act extended the bankruptcy court's jurisdiction that far, it violated Article III. The Supreme Court sustained Marathon's position in a plurality opinion by Justice Brennan.

Justice Brennan explained that the bankruptcy court's jurisdiction of the contract claim could not be sustained under the adjunct theory. That claim turned on state (not federal) law and, in any event, the bankruptcy court had too much authority and did not leave "the essential attributes" of judicial power with the district court.[48] Brennan distinguished both *Crowell* and *Raddatz*. In *Crowell*, the Court had allowed Congress to employ an agency as a fact-finding adjunct to an Article III court, but only with respect to a *federal* statutory claim.[49] In *Raddatz*, the Court had permitted Congress to employ a magistrate judge to determine a constitutional issue, but only where the supervising district judge made the ultimate decision. In *Northern Pipeline*, by contrast, Congress purported to give a bankruptcy court authority to determine a state law contract action and to render a judgment that would almost certainly be decisive.[50] Justice Brennan contrasted the many powers the 1978 Act assigned to bankruptcy judges with the more limited authorities exercised by the agency and the magistrate judge in *Crowell* and *Raddatz*.[51] In particular, he noted that, by contrast to *Crowell*, the

---

48. 458 U.S. at 87. Justice Brennan relied on both those grounds and thus suggested that they must be considered together and not as alternatives. Professor Redish has pointed out that if Congress is entitled to rely on non-Article III adjudicators as a means of carrying out its policies, it is unclear why an Article III court must be involved at all, let alone that such a court must retain the "essential attributes" of judicial power. And if an Article III court does make the ultimate decision, it is unclear why it makes any difference whether a case involves the implementation of a congressional regulatory scheme. Redish, note 5, at 215-16.

49. In this, Brennan appeared to rely on the "greater power" syllogism. See Chapter I, notes 21-22 and accompanying text. In dissent, Justice White said that Brennan conceded "that Congress may provide for initial adjudications by Art. I courts or administrative judges of all rights and duties arising under otherwise valid laws." 458 U.S. at 94. Justice Brennan denied any such concession, explained that he meant only to confirm *Crowell's* holding that Congress can assign "some" adjudicatory functions to non-Article III bodies, and said it was unnecessary to "specify further any limitations that may exist with respect to Congress' power to create adjuncts to assist in the adjudication of federal statutory rights." Id. at 81 n.32 (plurality opinion).

50. Justice Brennan acknowledged that many of the issues to be determined by bankruptcy courts under the 1978 Act were matters of federal law. But he distinguished Northern's state law contract action, over which the bankruptcy court had jurisdiction only because it was "related to" the pending reorganization. Id. at 84 n.36. He explained that a contract action on a "state-created right" could not become "a matter between the Government and the petitioner" [Northern] merely because Congress gave the bankruptcy court jurisdiction to hear it. In dissent, Justice White argued that most of the claims considered in a bankruptcy proceeding under the Act had previously "accrued under state law" and that it was misleading to distinguish so cleanly between federal and state issues. Id. at 96.

51. 458 U.S. at 84-86. See also Thomas G. Krattenmaker, *Article III and Judicial Independence: Why the New Bankruptcy Courts are Unconstitutional*, 70 Gtn. L.J. 297 (1981). After the decision in *Northern Pipeline*, Congress reconfigured the functions performed by bankruptcy courts in an apparent effort to conform bankruptcy judges to the adjunct model, both in name and in substance. Today, bankruptcy judges are "units" or "officers" of the district courts in which they serve. 28 U.S.C. § 151. Jurisdiction in bankruptcy cases rests with the district courts, which are authorized to refer various matters to bankruptcy judges for disposition. District courts must decline to exercise jurisdiction over state law claims that

bankruptcy court's order was final when issued. There was no need to file an enforcement action in an Article III court. Brennan acknowledged that the bankruptcy court's decision was subject to appellate review at the instance of the losing party. But he found that review too limited to satisfy Article III in itself.[52]

C. Legislative Courts

Many non-Article III adjudicative bodies resist conceptualization as adjuncts of Article III courts. They are sustained on the different theory that Congress can forthrightly assign judicial duties to legislative courts. Precisely what a given body must be or do to win approval under this second theory can be maddeningly obscure. Having set the simple Article III model to one side, the Court finds itself floating toward the simple Article I model, but laboring heroically to articulate limiting principles and considerations that keep Congress within bounds.

1. Familiar Illustrations

Some legislative courts are solidly in place. Their existence (and the justifications that fortify them) provide the analytic backdrop for more recent (and more controversial) cases.

Territorial courts. The Constitution gives Congress plenary power to provide for the territories, and it has always been thought that in the exercise of that power Congress may act for the territories in the way that state legislatures act for the states. In that capacity, Congress has authority to establish non-Article III tribunals to manage local judicial business that state courts would ordinarily do. John Marshall coined the term "legislative court" in the classic case on territorial

---

would not otherwise be within the jurisdiction of a federal court, provided an action is commenced and can be "timely adjudicated" in state court. 28 U.S.C. § 1334(b)-(c). See generally Lawrence K. Snider, et al., *The Bankruptcy Amendments and Federal Judgeship Act of 1984*, 83 Mich. L. Rev. 775 (1984). Even under the 1984 Act, some questions remain. It is not entirely clear, for example, that even a district court can adjudicate a purely state law claim in the absence of diversity merely because one of the parties is involved in bankruptcy. Justice Brennan suggested in *Northern Pipeline* that a district court may validly be given supplemental jurisdiction over such a claim. 458 U.S. at 72 n.26. Accord John T. Cross, *Congressional Power to Extend Federal Jurisdiction to Disputes Outside Article III: A Critical Analysis From the Perspective of Bankruptcy*, 87 Nw. U. L. Rev. 1188 (1993). Yet it is anything but clear what independent basis of jurisdiction there is to be supplemented. That may be why both Brennan and White agreed in *Northern Pipeline* that at least some issues in bankruptcy are matters of federal law and thus may trigger baseline federal question jurisdiction. See Chapter VIII, notes 166-210 and accompanying text (discussing the ordinary prerequisites of federal jurisdiction in federal question cases).

52. In a concurring opinion, then-Justice Rehnquist (joined by Justice O'Connor) agreed that the bankruptcy courts could not be justified as adjuncts when they took such extensive responsibility for deciding "[a]ll matters of fact and law" with respect to a state law contract action, "with only traditional appellate review by Article III courts apparently contemplated." 458 U.S. at 91.

courts, *Amer. Ins. Co. v. Canter.*[53] The validity of those courts has been settled ever since.[54] They are familiar features of the landscape, they serve important functions in a field for which Congress has special responsibility, they have historically existed only temporarily,[55] they operate within geographic limits, and they handle many matters that are not among the cases and controversies listed in Article III.[56]

The Courts of the District of Columbia. The Constitution also gives Congress general responsibility for the District of Columbia. There, too, Congress acts in the place of a state legislature. Since 1970, Congress has chosen to employ legislative courts in the District, staffed by judges serving fifteen-year terms. It cannot be said that the District's courts have always been non-Article III tribunals or that they are needed only temporarily pending the District's statehood. Yet the geographic limits are self-evident, the analogy to state courts palpable. In

---

53. 26 U.S. (1 Pet.) 511 (1828).

54. The validity of state courts staffed by judges who lack tenure and salary protections does not, in itself, equally establish the validity of territorial courts, staffed by similarly unprotected federal judges. State courts rely on their own state law status for independence from Congress.

55. The temporary nature of territorial courts was once a more significant factor in this mix than it is now. Early on, many territories were predictably on a course to statehood, and it would have been "doctrinaire in the extreme" to insist that their territorial courts must be Article III tribunals when state courts would soon be installed in their place. *Glidden Co. v. Zdanok,* 370 U.S. 530, 544-46 (1962). The territories that exist today (e.g., American Samoa, the Virgin Islands, and Guam) are not plainly on the same path.

56. It was open in *Canter* to hold that Congress can create legislative courts to determine local matters for the territories, but must rely on Article III courts to adjudicate cases and controversies listed in Article III. Marshall chose instead to analogize territorial courts to state courts and thus to allow them to do both kinds of judicial business. That approach has survived. Still, Marshall's analysis in *Canter* has drawn considerable fire. The question in that case was whether a territorial court could entertain an admiralty case—that is, a case admittedly within the federal judicial power established by Article III. Marshall responded that the territorial court could adjudicate such a case, but he insisted that, in so doing, it would not exercise "the judicial power conferred by the Constitution." That power is reserved for Article III courts, according to Marshall, and legislative courts are "incapable of receiving it." 26 U.S. at 546. Some critics read Marshall to have meant that Article III comes into play only when Congress uses Article III courts forthrightly to exercise "the judicial power conferred by the Constitution," but not when Congress chooses, instead, to create non-Article III tribunals to do the same judicial business. E.g., Stern, note 10, at 1069. That is circular. To be sure, a legislative court is not an Article III court. Yet it hardly follows that Article III has nothing to say about Congress giving such a court authority to adjudicate cases and controversies that Article III courts, too, might decide. Legislative courts obviously exercise federal judicial power given them by Congress. And when they decide cases and controversies listed in Article III, their judgments may be reviewed by Article III courts, provided Congress establishes such an appellate jurisdiction. So either Marshall was wrong, or he meant only to make the (admittedly formal) point that legislative courts, like state courts, handle cases and controversies listed in Article III on the basis of judicial power they derive from independent sources. See *Glidden,* 370 U.S. at 544-45. Professor Bator dismissed even that point as "theological." Bator, note 7, at 240-43. Today, the court systems in the territories are structured in a variety of ways. Puerto Rico has an Article III district court. Other territories have non-Article III courts, whose judgments regarding Article III matters are typically subject to appellate review in a designated circuit court of appeals. E.g., 48 U.S.C. § 1424 (Guam); 48 U.S.C. §§ 1611-13 (Virgin Islands). See 28 U.S.C. § 1291. Judgments rendered by the territorial court in American Samoa are not appealable in the ordinary fashion. For a description of the peculiar scheme for Samoa, see *Church of Latter Day Saints v. Hodel,* 830 F.2d 374 (D.C. Cir. 1987), *cert. denied,* 486 U.S. 1015 (1988).

the leading modern case, *Palmore v. United States*,[57] Justice White wrote a sweeping opinion for the Court, holding that the legislative courts in the District can handle cases and controversies listed on the Article III menu, including felony criminal prosecutions in which constitutional issues are implicated. By analogy to decisions by state courts, judgments rendered by the highest court in the District system are reviewable in the Supreme Court itself.[58]

Military courts. The Constitution also confers power on Congress to provide for the military services. Historically, the special sensitivities that attach to military discipline have been thought to warrant Congress' use of tribunals staffed by judges who lack tenure and salary safeguards.[59] Of course, military courts are not temporary, and their jurisdictional reach is geographically restricted only in the practical sense that most service-related matters arise on military reservations. Article III judges might be employed in many cases that implicate military personnel and interests.[60] At least at the highest levels, that might be in order today.[61] At present, however, the Court of Appeals for the Armed Services remains a legislative court, whose judgments are usually (but not always) reviewable in the Supreme Court.[62]

2. Public Rights Cases

Other legislative courts depend in some measure on the doctrine of "public rights." Recall that in *Crowell* the Court relied on the adjunct theory to approve agency adjudication of facts in a "private rights" setting.[63] In passing, Chief Justice Hughes said that public rights cases are different. He offered no definitive account of what public rights might be, but quoted a passage from *Murray's Lessee v. Hoboken Land & Improv. Co.*,[64] which today has come to play an important, if controversial, role in the analysis of legislative courts.

In that famous passage, Justice Curtis distinguished three kinds of questions that Congress might think to assign to courts of some ilk: (1) a "matter which,

---

57. 411 U.S. 389 (1973).

58. 28 U.S.C. § 1257(b).

59. See *Weiss v. United States*, 510 U.S. 163 (1994) (holding that military judges may be employed at the will of the commanding general). Professor Stern contends that military courts do not exercise federal judicial power at all, but serve only as "in-house—almost advisory—committees" that determine the way in which military commanders "take care of their own." Stern, note 10, at 1058. Recall that Professor Stern rejects the conventional (functional) definition of judicial power and reads Article III to exclude from its purview any adjudicative functions performed by federal officers other than Article III judges themselves.

60. Military courts can try only military personnel. *Toth v. Quarles*, 350 U.S. 11 (1955). In *O'Callahan v. Parker*, 395 U.S. 258 (1969), the Court held that a serviceman could not be tried by court martial for an offense that was not "service-connected." The Court soon thought better of that position, however, and overruled *O'Callahan* in *Solorio v. United States*, 483 U.S. 435 (1987).

61. Professor Fallon proposes that military courts martial should be retained in their conventional non-Article III form, but that their judgments in serious cases should be subject to appellate review in an Article III court. Fallon, note 7, at 973-74.

62. 10 U.S.C. § 942 (prescribing fifteen-year terms for the three judges on the court); 28 U.S.C. § 1259 (prescribing the kinds of cases in which *certiorari* review is available in the Supreme Court).

63. See text accompanying note 40.

64. 59 U.S. (18 How.) 272 (1856).

from its nature, is the subject of a suit at common law, or in equity, or admiralty;" (2) a matter "which, from its nature, is not a subject for judicial determination;" and (3) "matters, involving public rights, which may be presented in such form that the judicial power is capable of acting on them, and which are susceptible of judicial determination, but which congress may or may not bring within the cognizance of the courts of the United States, as it deems proper."[65] Congress is obliged to allow traditional courts to adjudicate cases in the first category. Congress is forbidden to ask those courts to determine cases in the second category. As to the third (public rights) category, Congress is free to choose whether to employ traditional courts or to adopt some other means of resolution.

The *Murray's Lessee* case itself involved not agency adjudication, but unilateral executive action. The Treasury Department discovered that the tax collector for the Port of New York, one Swarthout, had absconded with more than a million dollars. Pursuant to statute, Treasury issued a warrant authorizing a federal marshal to confiscate any personal property that Swarthout had left behind to offset the loss. The principal question in the Supreme Court was whether Swarthout had been denied due process, because he had been deprived of his property by executive action rather than through a judicial proceeding. After rejecting that due process claim, Justice Curtis turned to a different question implicating Article III and the separation of powers.[66] Under the statute, Swarthout was entitled to attack Treasury's action in an Article III court after the fact. Positing that Congress could involve the courts (at any stage) only if the case was "judicial" in character, the plaintiff insisted, on this related but distinct ground, that Treasury had violated Article III when it seized Swarthout's property without proceeding in an Article III court in the first instance.[67]

Justice Curtis responded that this second argument proceeded from an erroneous premise. While some matters (the subjects of suits at common law, or in equity, or admiralty) were intrinsically judicial and must be tried in court, other matters were not of that order. Some subjects were not susceptible to judicial determination at all (and thus could not be assigned to a court), while others (like the seizure of Swarthout's property) could be handled at Congress' option either by executive or judicial means. It made no difference, then, that Congress had decided as a matter of grace that a citizen in Swarthout's position could seek judicial review of a seizure at some later time. That did not mean that the seizure was an inherently "judicial controversy," such that an Article III court had to be involved when Treasury initially took action. The seizure was not by its *nature* judicial, because it was not the sort of thing that had traditionally been the basis of suits at common law, in equity, or in admiralty. It was something that Congress might have asked the courts to address. Yet it fell in that category of judicially cognizable subjects that Congress could give to Article III courts (or not) as a matter of discretion—namely, the category of public rights.

---

65. Id. at 284.

66. See Chapter VI, notes 54-77 and accompanying text (discussing the argument that due process requires a judicial forum in some circumstances).

67. The plaintiff in *Murray's Lessee* had acquired land previously owned by Swarthout. When the marshal seized that land and sold it to the defendant, the plaintiff filed an ejectment action to try the title—contending in that suit (between private parties) that the defendant's claim was invalid inasmuch as it rested on Treasury's violation of Swarthout's rights.

Classic illustrations of public rights matters are easy enough to name: claims against the federal government for money or land, for example, as well as border disputes over customs duties and some immigration matters.[68] Theoretical explanations are more difficult to supply. Academicians identify three intellectual foundations on which the public rights doctrine may rest, each with its troubling features: (1) history; (2) legislative authority; and (3) sovereign immunity.

History. Congress may be free to bypass Article III courts in any circumstances in which English law would have permitted non-judicial resolution in 1789.[69] This answer is problematic. It makes the content of public rights turn on historical understandings and practices that are difficult to retrieve today. It also makes the public rights category extremely expansive. At the dawn of the Republic, independent courts were a novel phenomenon.[70] Where they existed, they presumably *were* concerned with classic common law, equity, and maritime disputes. Yet that would have left a great deal of adjudicative business for executive officers to discharge.

Legislative authority. Congress may be able to employ non-Article III bodies to settle disputes over the largesse that Congress chooses to dispense.[71] If this is the answer, the public rights doctrine is another version of the "greater power" syllogism.[72] Positing that Congress has the "greater" power to withhold a benefit entirely, it is said that Congress must have the "lesser" power to extend the benefit on condition that any disputes that arise will be resolved outside Article III courts. That does not follow logically. The power to employ a legislative court is not (necessarily) a subset power within the power to withhold a benefit in the first instance.[73]

---

68. See generally *Ex parte Bakelite Corp.*, 279 U.S. 438, 452-58 (1929). The notion that immigration cases can be resolved administratively without involving courts is problematic. Since individual liberty is at stake in those cases, they implicate more than the usual measure of Article III sensitivity. Moreover, the Suspension Clause may place limits on congressional power to deny courts (federal or state) the authority to entertain habeas corpus petitions from would-be immigrants. See Chapter II, note 56; Chapter IV, note 70. For a discussion of the Suspension Clause and habeas corpus jurisdiction in immigration cases, see Chapter XII, notes 15-40 and accompanying text.

69. This was Professor Jaffe's understanding. Louis Jaffe, Judicial Control of Administrative Action 87-90 (1965).

70. See Chapter II, notes 1-3 and accompanying text.

71. This was Professor Hart's view. Henry M. Hart, Jr., *The Power of Congress to Limit the Jurisdiction of Federal Courts: An Exercise in Dialectic*, 66 Harv. L. Rev. 1362, 1365 (1953).

72. See Chapter I, notes 21-22 and accompanying text.

73. See Kramer, note 24, at 284. This account of the public rights doctrine reflects the discredited right/privilege distinction, which had it that government had no duty to respect procedural norms so long as it dealt with benefits it had no obligation to provide in the first place. Today, of course, the Supreme Court recognizes that the right to due process attaches to entitlements that government creates as a matter of policy. E.g., *Cleveland Bd. of Ed. v. Loudermill*, 470 U.S. 532 (1985). See William W. Van Alstyne, *The Demise of the Right-Privilege Distinction in Constitutional Law*, 81 Harv. L. Rev. 1439 (1968). Professor Woolhandler contends that it is a mistake to regard *Murray's Lessee* itself as a right/privilege doctrine case. The assets the government seized in that case can be considered largesse only because the embezzler was a government employee. Ann Woolhandler, *Judicial Deference to Administrative Action—A Revisionist History*, 43 Admin. L. Rev. 197, 231 (1991). A congressional decision to place a dispute in a non-Article III court is not, in itself, an attempt to deprive an individual of the process that is due. Agencies and legislative courts can provide due process even though their decision-making officers lack tenure and salary protections. State courts, whose judges are typically elected, can do so as well. But see Chapter IV, notes 103-05 and accompanying text (discussing the argument that Congress undermines the inde-

Sovereign immunity. The federal government need not submit to the jurisdiction of Article III courts.[74] Accordingly, Congress may be able to settle any claims that individuals advance against the government without involving those courts.[75] This last answer rests on yet another "greater power" mistake. Positing Congress' power to withhold consent to suit, it does not follow logically that Congress can agree to be sued only in the non-Article III tribunal of its choice. Here again, the two powers may go hand-in-hand, but there is no logical imperative that they do so.

The public rights doctrine has resurfaced more recently in cases concerning legislative courts. The initial occasion was *Northern Pipeline*, where the bankrupt company, Northern, argued that if the bankruptcy court could not adjudicate Northern's contract action as an adjunct of the district court, it could do so as an independent legislative court. Justice Brennan addressed that alternative theory, but rejected it in partial reliance on the public rights idea.

Justice Brennan denied that the Court's precedents supported a "broad departure from the constitutional command that the judicial power of the United States must be vested in Art. III courts." Instead, he said, the precedents in place reduced to "three narrow" exceptions to that command: territorial courts, military courts, and courts and agencies adjudicating public rights cases. Brennan explained the first two exceptions in the familiar way.[76] Turning to the public rights exception, he acknowledged the ambiguities of *Murray's Lessee*, but insisted that one thing is clear: "At a minimum," public rights cases arise "between the government and others" and do not implicate "the liability of one individual to another under the law as defined."[77] On that ground alone, Northern's contract action against Marathon could not fit the public rights category.[78]

---

pendence provisions in Article III if it shifts significant *constitutional* business to state judges who must stand for election).

74. See Chapter X, notes 7-11 and accompanying text (discussing the federal government's immunity from suit). The Court said in *Bakelite* that Congress can route public rights cases to non-Article III bodies as a "condition" attached to its "consent" to be sued at all. 279 U.S. at 452.

75. This is Justice Scalia's view. *Granfinanciera, S.A. v. Nordberg*, 492 U.S. 33, 65-66 (1989) (Scalia, J., concurring); see text accompanying note 128. Redish and LaFave have pointed out that the sovereign immunity explanation works only in cases in which the government is a defendant, not when the government is a plaintiff. Yet Justice Scalia understands that it captures all cases in which the government is a party. Martin H. Redish & Daniel J. LaFave, *Seventh Amendment Right to Jury Trial in Non-Article III Proceedings: A Study in Dysfunctional Constitutional Theory*, 4 Wm. & Mary Bill of Rts. J. 407, 438-39 (1995). Professor Stern cites Justice Scalia's opinion in *Granfinanciera* with apparent approval. Yet Stern argues that a public rights matter (within Scalia's terms) must be determined by an Article III court when (and if) it leaves the executive branch. Stern, note 10, at 1063-64.

76. See notes 53-56, 59-62 and accompanying text. Justice Brennan placed the courts in the District of Columbia in the category with territorial courts.

77. Id. at 69, quoting *Bakelite*, 279 U.S. at 451, and *Crowell*, 285 U.S. at 50. But see text accompanying note 89 (explaining that the Supreme Court has since disavowed this definition of public rights cases).

78. Despite his insistence that public rights cases must involve the government as a party, Justice Brennan conceded that the restructuring of a private bankrupt's debts and its ultimate discharge may constitute a public right. 458 U.S. at 71-72. Of course, the federal

Justice Brennan explained that the Constitution gives Congress special authority for the territories and the military services and insisted that, if bankruptcy were added to the list, there would be no stopping place.[79] He accepted the validity of the non-Article III tribunals the Court had approved in the past, but in an apparent concern that Congress might continue on the same path, he called a halt—even in a context in which it was unlikely that Congress was using legislative courts in order to exercise influence it could not bring to bear on the Article III judiciary.[80] Brennan took what he needed from the public rights doctrine, but failed to elaborate that doctrine more fully.[81] He identified the government's party status as a necessary, but not a sufficient, basis for concluding that a case fits the public rights category.[82] He explained that a criminal prosecution is not a public rights matter.[83] And he only suggested, but did not decide, that subsequent review in an Article III court is always constitutionally required.[84]

Then-Justice Rehnquist and Justice O'Connor concurred only in the judgment in *Northern Pipeline*. They declined to discuss all the powers the 1978 Act conferred on bankruptcy courts and, instead, said only that giving a bankruptcy court jurisdiction to determine Northern's traditional contract action against Marathon (without Marathon's consent) violated Article III. The claim in that lawsuit was the "stuff of the traditional actions at common law tried by the courts at Westminster in 1789" and was governed by state, not federal, law. Accordingly, that claim must be heard either in a state court or in an Article III court. It could not be heard in a bankruptcy court merely because Northern happened to be involved in a reorganization.[85]

In dissent, Justice White insisted that it was "too late" to take Article III so literally. Unless the Court meant to overrule a host of decisions approving legislative courts and agencies, White said it was "inevitable" to conclude that there is "no difference in principle" between the work that Congress can assign to legislative courts and the business the Constitution itself assigns to Article III courts. White urged the Court to discard Brennan's framework entirely and deal with legislative court cases *ad hoc*, balancing the "values Congress hopes to serve" by employing legislative courts against the consequent "burdens" on Article III "val-

---

government is not typically a party of record when a bankruptcy court enters a discharge order.

79. Professor Redish points out that the Constitution also gives Congress explicit power with respect to bankruptcy. U.S. Const. art. I, § 8, cl.3. Redish contends that Brennan might have approved bankruptcy courts on that basis without opening the floodgates to other legislative courts. Redish, note 5, at 218.

80. Professor Resnik has suggested that Brennan's opinion was a lengthy elaboration of a simple point: "hold that line." Resnik, note 5, at 598-99.

81. With respect to the public rights doctrine's conceptual origins, Brennan said only that the doctrine "may be explained in part by reference to the traditional principle of sovereign immunity," but that it also "draws upon the principle of separation of powers" and a "historical understanding that certain prerogatives were reserved" to the political branches. 458 U.S. at 67.

82. Id. at 70 n.23.

83. Id. at 70 n.24. Compare *Toth*, note 60, with *Palmore*, text accompanying note 57.

84. 458 U.S. at 70 n.23.

85. Id. at 91 (concurring opinion). Rehnquist and O'Connor thought it was unnecessary to decide whether the Court's precedents supported a general rule against legislative courts "with three tidy exceptions," or whether the public rights doctrine might justify the various other powers that Congress had bestowed on the bankruptcy courts.

ues." According to Justice White, the Court should *require* only that Congress make "ample provision" for subsequent review of a legislative court's work in an Article III court.[86]

3. The Balancing Approach

In subsequent cases, the Court largely abandoned Justice Brennan's account of legislative courts in *Northern Pipeline* in favor of the balancing approach that Justice White advocated in dissent in that case.

In *Thomas v. Union Carbide*,[87] the Court approved non-Article III adjudication of claims under recent amendments to the Federal Insecticide, Fungicide, and Rodenticide Act. Pursuant to those amendments, pesticide manufacturers needed the Environmental Protection Agency's approval before they could market their products. Companies typically invested large sums in the research necessary to convince the EPA that their chemicals were safe. Research results with respect to one product could often be useful in determining the reliability of another. When one company filed results that could bear on another company's product, the Act authorized the second company to use the first company's data rather than wasting money on redundant studies. The Act specified that the second company must compensate the first company for free-riding on its research. If the two companies could not agree on an appropriate sum, the Act required them to submit the issue to an arbiter. The arbiter's decision was final when rendered, subject to review in a federal district court for "fraud, misrepresentation, or other misconduct."

The plaintiffs in *Union Carbide* were chemical companies complaining that if their claims to compensation were handled in that way, the arbiter would undertake judicial functions that only an Article III court could perform. In light of *Northern Pipeline*, that argument had force. The arbiter plainly had adjudicative duties and was to discharge those duties independently (not as an adjunct of any Article III court). The arbiter was not a territorial or military court. And the dispute in question involved only private companies (not the federal government).

---

86. Id. at 115 (dissenting opinion). In particular, Justice White objected to the suggestion that the precedents approving the courts in the District of Columbia rested on the geographic limits on those courts' jurisdiction. Id. at 104-05. He himself had authored the Court's opinion in *Palmore*, which, in his view, stood for a much more sweeping explanation of congressional power. See text accompanying note 57. The concurring justices, Rehnquist and O'Connor, characterized White's view of the precedents as "landmarks on a judicial 'darkling plain' where ignorant armies have clashed by night." Id. at 91. Chief Justice Burger dissented separately to say that the Article III difficulties in the case, if they existed at all, could be remedied by channeling "related" state law actions like Northern's to the district court, while leaving other issues to the bankruptcy court. Id. at 92 (dissenting opinion). Burger had long opposed giving Article III judgeships to bankruptcy judges and may have worried that Congress would see that as the only course open after the *Northern Pipeline* decision. See Vern Countryman, *Scrambling to Define Bankruptcy Jurisdiction: The Chief Justice, the Judicial Conference, and the Legislative Process*, 22 Harv. J. Legis. 1 (1985). In fact, the Court stayed its order to give Congress time to enact new legislation, and Congress ultimately produced a revised scheme that preserves the non-Article III status of bankruptcy judges, but hopes to ensure that their duties regarding state law claims can be justified under the adjunct theory. See note 51.

87. 473 U.S. 568 (1985).

Nevertheless, the Supreme Court sustained the arbitration scheme in an opinion by Justice O'Connor.

Justice O'Connor limited the holding in *Northern Pipeline* to what she and Justice Rehnquist had agreed to in their concurring opinion in that case: "Congress may not vest in a non-Article III court the power to adjudicate, render final judgment, and issue binding orders in a traditional contract action arising under state law, without consent of the litigants, and subject only to ordinary appellate review."[88] Importantly, she rejected Justice Brennan's account of the public rights doctrine. Brennan had said that public rights cases form a category of judicial business (all of it involving the federal government as a party) that Congress can channel to non-Article III adjudicators. In *Union Carbide*, by contrast, Justice O'Connor reconceptualized the public rights doctrine as "a pragmatic understanding that when Congress selects a quasi-judicial method of resolving matters that 'could be conclusively determined by the Executive and Legislative Branches,' the danger of encroaching on the judicial powers is reduced."[89]

In the wake of *Union Carbide*, the public rights doctrine no longer distinguishes categorically between cases in which the government is a party and those in which it is not—permitting Congress to use non-Article III adjudicators in the former, but not in the latter. Instead, a case can implicate public rights even if the government is not a party, provided the case involves a federal regulatory scheme enacted for a *"public purpose."*[90] Justice O'Connor insisted that Brennan's analysis in *Northern Pipeline* misunderstood the "enduring lesson" of *Crowell*: Article III cases call for "practical attention to substance rather than doctrinaire reliance on formal categories."[91] Accordingly, the Court must attend to the reasons why tenure and salary protections are accorded to Article III judges. To decide concrete cases, the Court must marshal the values and interests at stake and strike a balance.[92]

Justice O'Connor solidified the balancing approach in *Commodity Futures Trading Comm'n v. Schor.*[93] Schor, an investor, filed a complaint against his brokerage house, Conti-Commodity Services, with the Commodity Futures Trading Commission in Washington, D.C. He alleged that Conti had violated the federal Commodity Exchange Act with respect to his account and that, as a result, he had lost money and was entitled to reparations under that Act. Meanwhile, Conti sued Schor in a federal district court in Illinois, invoking that court's diversity jurisdiction to determine a state law claim: Schor's account was in arrears and he had failed to make up the loss. Schor filed a counterclaim in that district

---

88. Id. at 584.

89. Id. at 589, quoting *Northern Pipeline*, 458 U.S. at 68 (plurality opinion).

90. Id. (emphasis added). Justice O'Connor noted in this connection a number of precedents in which the Court had treated disputes between private parties as public rights cases—and on that basis allowed Congress to commit them to non-Article III bodies. In *Switchmen v. Nat'l Med. Bd.*, 320 U.S. 297 (1943), for example, the Court upheld a scheme by which workers' disputes over the choice of their bargaining representatives were determined by the Mediation Board.

91. 473 U.S. at 587.

92. Justice O'Connor did not explicitly endorse the approach that Justice White had suggested in his *Northern Pipeline* dissent, but she did cite that dissent approvingly in several places. White joined O'Connor's opinion.

93. 478 U.S. 833 (1986).

court lawsuit, alleging that his losses were due to Conti's practices in violation of the federal Act. At that point, the parties' state and federal claims were properly before an Article III court for decision.

Next, however, Schor moved the district court to stay or dismiss Conti's diversity action in order that the CFTC could determine any and all claims the two parties had against each other. The district court refused either to stay or to dismiss the pending diversity action. Nevertheless, Conti withdrew its action from the district court and filed its state law claim against Schor with the CFTC as a counterclaim to Schor's federal claim for reparations. An administrative law judge at the CFTC determined both claims in Conti's favor. Schor then filed an objection to the CFTC's jurisdiction to determine Conti's state claim. In the Supreme Court, Justice O'Connor balanced a range of considerations and ultimately affirmed the CFTC's jurisdiction to determine Conti's state claim against Schor in connection with its determination of Schor's federal claim against Conti.[94]

Between them, *Union Carbide* and *Schor* identify four factors bearing on Congress' ability to assign adjudicative authority to a legislative court: (1) the source of the claim to be determined; (2) the federal government's involvement or interest; (3) the reasons for employing a non-Article III adjudicator; and (4) the form and scope of subsequent Article III court involvement. Justice O'Connor explained that "none" of the factors is "determinative."[95] Each is entitled to weight, and in the end the Court makes a reasoned judgment about whether, in cumulative effect, the circumstances of a particular assignment satisfy constitutional standards.

The source of the claim. In *Northern Pipeline*, the claim in issue was a matter of state contract law.[96] That certainly cut against the validity of legislative court adjudication. By contrast, the issue in *Union Carbide* was a matter of federal statute law. Apart from the entitlement to compensation established by the Act, the plaintiff companies would have had no right to reimbursement from other companies using their data.[97] That cut in favor of the validity of legislative court action. Justice O'Connor acknowledged that in this respect *Schor* was

---

94. Justice O'Connor recognized that parties can waive their "primarily personal" Article III right to "have" their claims "decided before judges who are free from potential domination by other branches of government." But she explained that individuals "cannot be expected to protect" the "institutional interests" that judicial independence serves and thus "cannot by consent cure" any "difficulty" with those interests. Inasmuch as Schor had known that the district court in Illinois was poised to determine Conti's state claim when he insisted that the CFTC was a better forum for resolving all the parties' differences, he waived his own Article III rights. That, however, did not resolve the structural Article III issue in *Schor*, which then turned on balancing relevant factors. See *Schor*, 478 U.S. at 848-51.

95. Id. at 851.

96. Recall that in *Northern Pipeline*, Justice Brennan cited the state law nature of Northern's contract claim as a basis for distinguishing *Crowell*, which, by Brennan's account, involved a question of federal statutory law. See text accompanying note 49. In *Union Carbide*, however, Justice O'Connor added that the federal right in *Crowell* was not entirely new with Congress, but replaced the action that Knudsen might have had against his employer under the common law of contracts for hire. In that sense, the source of the right whose related facts Congress allowed the agency to determine in *Crowell* was not so exclusively "federal" as was the right to compensation the plaintiff companies advanced in *Union Carbide*. 473 U.S. at 584.

97. Justice O'Connor explained that under state law a company that disclosed its research findings to the EPA would have placed them in the public domain and thus would have had no action against another company's use of the data for its own purposes. It was

more like *Northern Pipeline* than *Union Carbide*. Yet that was not enough to render the CFTC's jurisdiction invalid. In *Northern Pipeline*, the bankruptcy court had authority to determine a state contract claim that was "related to" the bankruptcy proceeding only because one of the parties happened to be involved in a reorganization proceeding. In *Schor*, however, Conti's state claim was, in effect, a counterclaim to Schor's federal claim for reparations.[98]

The federal government's involvement or interest. The federal government was not party to any of the three cases, *Northern Pipeline*, *Union Carbide*, or *Schor*. That cut against the validity of legislative court adjudication, but only mildly. The rights the private parties cases advanced in *Union Carbide* and *Schor* were not "purely private," but bore "many of the characteristics of a public right."[99] In both instances, the federal government's interest was substantial. In *Union Carbide*, the government had an interest in encouraging companies to share their research results as an "integral part of a program safeguarding the public health."[100] In *Schor*, the government had an interest in seeing that federal reparations claims were considered in context, along with state law counterclaims "incidental to, and completely dependent upon, adjudication of reparations claims created by federal law."[101]

The reasons for employing a non-Article III tribunal. In all three cases, Congress had neutral reasons for employing legislative courts. Congress was not attempting to manipulate the adjudicatory process by banishing independent judges and substituting tribunals on which Congress could exercise pressure. That cut in favor of approving legislative court adjudication. In *Union Carbide* and *Schor*, the reasons for introducing non-Article III adjudicators were especially obvious and powerful. The arbitration scheme in *Union Carbide* exploited the arbiter's expertise for making technical determinations of the appropriate size of compensation awards. That promoted Congress' overarching purpose to ensure that only safe products reached the market.[102] The supplemental jurisdiction

---

only the federal statute that gave a company submitting data a right to compensation from a follow-on user.

98. Essentially, then, Congress had given the CFTC supplemental jurisdiction of the state law claim. Since the federal nature of Schor's reparations claim was clear, there was no question that the district court in Illinois might have entertained both that claim and Conti's state law claim, even in the absence of diversity. See Chapter VIII, notes 288-301 and accompanying text (discussing supplemental jurisdiction under 28 U.S.C. § 1367). In *Schor*, then, the Court did not have to face the question noted in *Northern Pipeline* regarding even an Article III court's ability to adjudicate an exclusively state law dispute between non-diverse parties. See note 51.

99. *Union Carbide*, 473 U.S. at 589.

100. Id. Justice O'Connor recalled that Justice Brennan himself had conceded in *Northern Pipeline* that a bankrupt's discharge might implicate a public right even though the bankruptcy proceeding plainly would not involve the federal government as a party of record. 473 U.S. at 586; see note 78. In that small way, Brennan himself arguably signaled that some cases fit the public rights category not because the government is a party, but because the government has an interest — namely, a public purpose to advance.

101. *Schor*, 478 U.S. at 856.

102. Justice O'Connor said that Congress might have fashioned a different means of allocating the costs of pesticide research and avoided "implicating Article III." For example, Congress might have authorized the EPA simply to charge follow-on companies for permission to use research results generated by others and used the money to subsidize the companies that furnished the data. By establishing the arbitration framework, Congress merely collapsed those two steps into one and saved the EPA the time and trouble of determining the amount of compensation into the bargain. O'Connor thus invoked another "greater power"

of state law claims in *Schor* allowed litigants to resolve all their related claims in a single place. That promoted Congress' objective to create incentives for settling federal reparations claims in a prompt and inexpensive manner.[103]

The form and scope of Article III court involvement. Justice O'Connor said in *Union Carbide* that "judicial review" does not in itself meet "minimal" constitutional requirements and that it is always necessary to take other considerations into account. She thus rejected the arguments in academic circles that the Constitution permits non-Article III bodies to make original judgments, as long as there is a serious brand of after-the-fact review in an Article III court.[104] O'Connor nonetheless focused on the way in which Article III courts figured in each of the three cases. In all three, litigants disappointed with the decision rendered by a non-Article III adjudicator could complain to an Article III court. According to Justice O'Connor, the *existence* of Article III court involvement after-the-fact cut in favor of upholding legislative court adjudication, the *modest character* of that involvement against it.

In *Northern Pipeline*, the bankruptcy court's judgment was final, and appellate review in an Article III court was closely circumscribed. In *Union Carbide*, the arbiter's award was equally final, subject to equally truncated Article III court review. Nevertheless, Justice O'Connor applauded the scheme in *Union Carbide*, because it did not contemplate that the EPA would seek an enforcement order from an Article III court in the conventional manner associated with administrative agencies. O'Connor thus made a virtue of what she might have regarded as a vice. Alternatively, she might have said that Congress would have preserved judicial independence better if it had required the EPA to obtain judicial approval for its actions in the ordinary manner rather than placing the burden of seeking judicial review on the company.

Justice O'Connor was also persuaded that the scheme in *Schor* left the "essential attributes of judicial power" with Article III courts. The CFTC's adjudicative duties tracked those of the agency in *Crowell* and thus nearly met the "agency" (i.e., adjunct) model approved in that case. Like the agency in *Crowell*, but unlike the bankruptcy courts in *Northern Pipeline*, the CFTC was limited to a "particu-

---

argument—namely, that Congress' power to fix fees and subsidies was a "greater" power that subsumed a "lesser" power to force unwilling companies into an adjudicative proceeding before a non-Article III officer. In addition, O'Connor suggested that Congress might have avoided Article III by conditioning a company's ability to apply for a permit on "compliance with agency procedures." *Union Carbide*, 473 U.S. at 589. That suggested that any Article III difficulties in *Union Carbide* might have been defused by gaining party consent to the arbitration scheme. See note 94.

103. *Schor*, 478 U.S. at 855. Justice O'Connor recognized that the parties might have taken their claims to an Article III court and they had chosen to use the CFTC, instead. She explained that Congress was entitled to encourage them to resolve their dispute in a non-Article III process, just as it would have been entitled to encourage them to settle their differences by agreement without invoking any formal dispute-resolution mechanism at all. That point overlapped with O'Connor's reliance on consent to defeat any personal claim Schor had to appear before a disinterested tribunal. Yet she offered it as evidence that Congress had not attempted to banish Article III courts altogether. If Conti's counterclaim had been compulsory rather than permissive, it would have been more closely linked to Schor's federal reparations claim, thus fortifying the conclusion that Congress had given the CFTC jurisdiction of the former in service of its scheme to ensure efficient and speedy resolution of typical cases. In that event, however, Justice O'Connor would have been unable to make the different point that Congress had allowed parties the option of remaining in an Article III court.

104. *Union Carbide*, 473 U.S. at 587. See text accompanying notes 11-13.

larized area of law."[105] Justice O'Connor acknowledged that the CFTC in *Schor*, unlike the EPA in *Union Carbide*, was empowered (and required) to seek an enforcement order in an Article III court. Shifting ground, she found that feature of the scheme in *Schor* not at all troubling, but actually satisfying. In the end, then, she said in *Union Carbide* that Congress was on safer ground for *not* sending the EPA to an Article III court for an enforcement order, but, in *Schor*, she found it reassuring that Congress had specified that the CFTC would do precisely that.[106]

Justice Brennan concurred in *Union Carbide* and, in so doing, abandoned any contention that a public rights case must involve the government as a party. He said that the arbitration in that case could qualify as a public rights matter, because it arose "in the context of a federal regulatory scheme that virtually occupie[d] the field" and involved "not only the congressional prescription of a federal rule of decision to govern [the] private dispute but also the active participation of a federal regulatory agency."[107] Since the Act allowed for review in an Article III court, Brennan found it unnecessary to consider whether Congress is "always free to cut off all judicial review of decisions respecting such exercises of Art. I authority."[108] Brennan dissented in *Schor*, insisting that the Court's *ad hoc* balancing approach had started down a slippery slope and threatened to "dilute" the independence of the Article III judiciary, if not immediately then incrementally.[109]

D. Trial by Jury

After *Union Carbide* and *Schor*, it appeared that the Court was committed to *ad hoc* balancing in this field and that in future it would treat the categorical features of the doctrine it had employed in *Northern Pipeline* simply as factors for consideration. Certainly, that seemed to be true of the public rights doctrine, which had been stripped of its analytical and historical underpinnings in *Union Carbide* and then had been neglected altogether in *Schor*. Yet when Justice Brennan again wrote for the Court in *Granfinanciera, S.A. v. Nordberg*,[110] he explained that the public rights doctrine retains decision-making bite, at least in some cases. That doctrine bears both on Congress' power to confer jurisdiction on non-Article III adjudicators and on litigants' ability to invoke their right to trial by jury in "Suits at common law," guaranteed by the seventh amendment.[111]

---

105. Justice O'Connor mentioned that the CFTC could not conduct jury trials. *Schor*, 478 U.S. at 853.

106. The Court's ambivalence regarding the form of Article III court involvement suggests that the real issue is the scope of Article III court review. In that vein, Professor Fallon argues that *Northern Pipeline* was wrongly decided (because the bankruptcy court's judgment in that case was subject to sufficient review at the circuit level), that *Union Carbide*, too, was wrongly decided (because the arbiter's judgment was reviewable only for fraud and misconduct), and that *Schor* was correctly decided (because the CFTC's determinations of legal questions were subject to *de novo* review in an Article III court). Fallon, note 7, at 991.

107. *Union Carbide*, 473 U.S. at 600.

108. Id. at 601.

109. Brennan said that Schor's consent was superfluous, inasmuch as he could not surrender the institutional interests served by judicial independence. *Schor*, 478 U.S. at 866-67.

110. 492 U.S. 33 (1989).

111. See Chapter II, notes 32-35 and accompanying text.

Nordberg was a bankruptcy trustee appointed to superintend the reorganization of the Chase & Sanborn company. He sued Granfinanciera, a Columbian company, in a federal district court in Florida. He alleged that Granfinanciera had received in excess of a million dollars from Chase & Sanborn within one year prior to bankruptcy, that the deal had been actually or constructively fraudulent, and that Granfinanciera, accordingly, should repay the money so that it could be placed in the pool of assets to be divided among all the creditors. The district court referred the matter to a bankruptcy judge.[112] Granfinanciera did not object (initially), but did assert its right to trial by jury. The bankruptcy judge found the seventh amendment inapplicable, tried the issues without a jury, and entered judgment for Nordberg. In the Supreme Court, Justice Brennan said that Granfinanciera was entitled to trial by jury—if not before the bankruptcy judge, then in the district court.[113]

Initially, Justice Brennan explained that the seventh amendment guarantees trial by jury only in cases that, by their nature, would have been triable in the law courts prior to the merger of law and equity.[114] He concluded that Nordberg's fraud claim against Granfinanciera would have been one of law, not equity. That claim rested on federal bankruptcy law, but it was not formally a part of the (equitable) bankruptcy proceeding, because it had to do with computing the size of the asset pool in the first instance rather than the proper distribution of asserts once computed.[115]

Next, Justice Brennan acknowledged that Congress can deny trial by jury even in a case in which the seventh amendment would otherwise guarantee one—by channeling the claim to a non-Article III adjudicator "with which jury trial would be incompatible."[116] He explained, however, that Congress' ability to

---

112. See note 51 (discussing the Bankruptcy Act of 1984).

113. Granfinanciera conceded that it had no statutory right to jury trial under the Bankruptcy Act of 1984, but only because Nordberg had filed his action prior to the effective date of that Act. Justice Brennan accepted that concession and moved to the seventh amendment question without (expressly) deciding whether, apart from the seventh amendment, the 1984 Act either authorized the bankruptcy court to conduct a jury trial or entitled Granfinanciera to such a jury trial on a fraudulent conveyance claim. 492 U.S. at 39 n.2.

114. Litigants have a seventh amendment right to trial by jury only if their claims would have been tried in the law courts (as opposed to the courts of equity) that existed in England in 1791 (the year the seventh amendment was adopted). Claims were usually legal if the plaintiff sought money damages. If a modern plaintiff advances a statutory claim that did not exist in 1791, the Court determines whether it *would* have been tried at law if it *had* existed at that time. *Feltner v. Columbia Pictures*, 118 S.Ct. 1279 (1998); *Parsons v. Bedford*, 28 U.S. (3 Pet.) 433 (1830). The precedents do not always line up neatly. In *NLRB v. Jones & Laughlin Steel Corp.*, 301 U.S. 1 (1937), for example, the Court allowed Congress to deny trial by jury to a claim for damages, because it was "incident" to a claim for equitable relief pending before an agency that could not offer jury trial. The Court has never held that the seventh amendment right to trial by jury in common law cases is "incorporated" into the fourteenth amendment so as to be applicable in state court.

115. Justice Brennan found *Schoenthal v. Irving Trust Co.*, 287 U.S. 92 (1932), to control the historical characterization of Nordberg's fraudulent transfer claim. He acknowledged that the 1984 Act placed fraudulent conveyance actions within the "core proceedings" in which a bankruptcy judge could render final judgment (subject to review in the district and circuit courts). He also recognized Justice White's concomitant argument that the Court should defer to Congress' apparent judgment that such an action was part of the equitable bankruptcy proceeding itself. Yet Brennan insisted that Congress had no power to "re-classif[y]" a common law action and, on that basis, to evade the seventh amendment. 492 U.S. at 60.

116. 492 U.S. at 61, quoting *Atlas Roofing Co. v. Occup. Safety and Health Review Comm'n*, 430 U.S. 442, 455 (1977).

dispense with jury trial has "limits."[117] Otherwise, the seventh amendment would cease to check congressional power at all when Congress chooses to employ non-Article III bodies. Those limits are captured by the public rights doctrine: Congress can subject cases in which the seventh amendment would ordinarily mandate a jury to trial by another means, but only when Congress can validly route the case to a non-Article III adjudicator. That, in turn, is only when the case is one of public rights.[118] Since Nordberg's fraudulent transfer claim did not fall in the public rights category, Congress could not deprive Granfinanciera of the right to jury trial by assigning that claim to a non-Article III court.[119]

Justice Brennan declined to decide whether the Bankruptcy Act authorizes a bankruptcy court to conduct a jury trial or, if it does, whether a jury trial before a non-Article III judge would satisfy the seventh amendment.[120] He recognized that a bankruptcy court's judgment is reviewable by the district court, but explained that Article III oversight after trial cannot substitute for the actual conduct of a jury trial in the first instance.[121] Since *Granfinanciera*, Congress has enacted another amendment to the Bankruptcy Act, which authorizes bankruptcy judges to conduct jury trials with the express consent of the parties.[122] Given that the seventh amendment establishes a waivable personal right, the consent condition in the new statute arguably robs it of any substantive significance.[123]

---

117. Id. at 50.

118. Id. at 51. In putting the point in such an uncompromising way, Justice Brennan overlooked territorial and military courts. The Court has never decided whether Congress can deny trial by jury in those courts despite the seventh amendment. In *Pernell v. Southall Realty*, 416 U.S. 363 (1974), the Court held that the seventh amendment establishes a litigant's right to jury trial in a court in the District of Columbia.

119. In a previous case, *Katchen v. Landy*, 382 U.S. 323 (1966), the Court had rejected a creditor's seventh amendment claim to a jury trial on a similar fraudulent transfer claim. In that case, however, the creditor voluntarily entered the bankruptcy proceeding by filing a claim against the asset pool and thus placed the value of the previous transfer within the bankruptcy court's constructive possession. On that basis, *Katchen* was distinguishable. Accord *Langenkamp v. Culp*, 498 U.S. 42 (1990). Cf. *McCarthy v. Bronson*, 500 U.S. 136, 138 (1991) (confirming that individuals are free to waive seventh amendment rights). It may be that most creditors in Granfinanciera's position make claims against the bankrupt's estate. If so, the practical significance of the *Granfinanciera* decision is substantially diminished.

120. See note 113. It is questionable whether Brennan could leave the question of the bankruptcy court's power untouched. He explained that a litigant's seventh amendment right to jury trial and Congress' ability to use a non-Article III tribunal go hand-in-hand, both governed by the public rights doctrine. If that is true, then the holding that Nordberg's claim fell on the private rights side of the line would seem to preclude jurisdiction in the bankruptcy court in the first place, wholly apart from the method of trial available in that forum.

121. *Granfinanciera*, 492 U.S. at 64. If Article III courts second-guess jury verdicts in trials conducted by bankruptcy judges, they may themselves violate the seventh amendment—which states that "no fact tried by jury, shall be otherwise re-examined in any Court of the United States." That provision, in turn, responds to Anti-Federalist concerns that Article III courts would not respect the only device citizens then had to hold judges in check: juries drawn from the citizenry. See Chapter II, notes 32-33 and accompanying text. Justice Brennan had no occasion in *Granfinanciera* to decide whether Congress can mix and match—sending public rights cases to Article III courts, but barring trial by jury there. Given the historical backdrop of the jury trial provision, it is unlikely that the Court would approve a scheme of that kind.

122. 28 U.S.C. § 157.

123. See note 94.

The *Granfinanciera* decision reinvigorates a more categorical conception of public rights. Justice Brennan accommodated the balancing approach reflected in *Union Carbide* and *Schor* only insofar as he had in his concurring opinion in *Union Carbide*: A case can involve public rights even though the federal government is not a party, provided that Congress, "acting for a valid legislative purpose," creates "a seemingly 'private' right that is so closely integrated into a public regulatory scheme as to be a matter appropriate for agency resolution with limited involvement by the Article III judiciary."[124] Brennan mentioned *Schor* only in passing as a case in which the Court relied on the parties' consent.[125]

It seems plain that Justice Brennan (and the five justices who joined his opinion) hesitated to surrender the seventh amendment to the *ad hoc* balancing approach that *Union Carbide* and *Schor* apply to Article III cases in which the seventh amendment does not figure. That impulse where a provision of the Bill of Rights is at stake may be entirely understandable.[126] Yet by connecting public rights not only to the seventh amendment, but also to Article III, *Granfinanciera* reintroduced an obscure (and intellectually dissatisfying) doctrine to the body of case law on legislative courts. In dissent, Justice White warned that Brennan's analysis would prevent Congress from establishing effective non-Article III machinery in a variety of contexts.[127] Justice Scalia agreed, but drew a different conclusion. Concurring in *Granfinanciera*, he insisted that public rights cases necessarily involve the government as a party and, therefore, that both *Union Carbide* and *Schor* were wrongly decided.[128]

It is difficult to measure the predictive value of yet another complicated decision, generated by a divided vote of justices some of whom are no longer on the Court, which not only fails to continue on a linear path of doctrinal development, but actually doubles back to ideas previously discarded.[129] Certainly, it is hard to conclude that the Court has abandoned the balancing approach, albeit that approach is obviously distasteful to Justice Scalia (and perhaps to other justices now sitting) for the very reason that it is less manageable and predictable than categorical doctrinal rules.[130] It may be important that *Granfinanciera* left

---

124. 492 U.S. at 54, quoting *Union Carbide*, 473 U.S. at 586 (concurring opinion); see text accompanying note 107. Given this definition of public rights cases, it seems clear that litigants advancing constitutional claims against government remain entitled to jury trial in cases in which the seventh amendment operates. See Eric Grant, *A Revolutionary View of the Seventh Amendment and the Just Compensation Clause*, 91 Nw. U. L. Rev. 144, 207-08 (1996) (referring particularly to "takings" claims for just compensation).

125. 492 U.S. at 59 n.14. Recall that Justice Brennan dissented in *Schor*, insisting that the consent theory could not justify the Court's judgment in that case. See note 109 and accompanying text.

126. See Redish & LaFave, note 75, at 408-11.

127. Justice White argued that both Article III and seventh amendment issues should be addressed via *ad hoc* balancing. 492 U.S. at 78. Justice O'Connor joined Justice Blackmun's separate dissent, which expressed agreement with White "generally" but plainly found the particular case at bar a closer call. Id. at 91.

128. 492 U.S. at 65; see note 75 and accompanying text.

129. See text accompanying notes 90-92.

130. See *Granfinanciera*, 492 U.S. at 70 (Scalia, J., concurring). In a like manner, it may be too early to conclude that by expanding the public rights category to include cases touching federal regulatory schemes, the Court means to abandon its precedents holding that, for seventh amendment purposes, a public rights case necessarily involves the government as a party. E.g., *Atlas Roofing*, 430 U.S. at 450.

room for flexibility. Justice Brennan said that the seventh amendment would give way in a case in which jury trial would be totally "incompatible" with Congress' purpose in using a non-Article III adjudicator.[131]

---

131. *Granfinanciera*, 492 U.S. at 61 (majority opinion). In a subsequent case, Justice Brennan said that the right to trial by jury is unavailable where "Congress has permissibly delegated the particular dispute to a non-Article III decisionmaker and jury trials would frustrate Congress' purposes in enacting a particular statutory scheme." *Chauffeurs, Teamsters & Helpers Local No. 391 v. Terry*, 494 U.S. 558, 574 (1990) (Brennan, J., concurring).

Chapter VI

Federal Questions in State Court

State courts routinely entertain the kinds of cases and controversies that Article III permits federal courts to adjudicate. In most instances (and perhaps in all), state courts of general jurisdiction are constitutionally obligated to provide a forum for federal claims. State courts may lack the remedial authority that federal courts can bring to bear on officers of the federal government. But for the most part, state courts constitute an alternative judicial forum for federal question lawsuits. The omnipresence of state courts informs the statutes and doctrines that govern access to federal courts. If state courts were not routinely available, much less practical significance would attach to the Supreme Court's acceptance of the parity premise and its consequent inclination to foster federal question litigation in state tribunals.[1] As it is, the Court is free to reinforce state court authority and responsibility for conducting federal question business as coequals with the lower federal courts.

Subject to important exceptions,[2] civil litigants who find themselves in state court with a federal claim or defense will almost certainly have to be satisfied with the determination the state courts provide. They will rarely be able to escape state court and reach a federal court for an adjudication in the first instance. And after the state courts have arrived at a decision, they will rarely be able to challenge that judgment in a federal forum. The state court judgment will almost certainly be final, even though it determines the federal rights and duties of the parties. This fact of life establishes the stakes for battles over access to the federal courts as an original matter. Litigants who wish to advance a federal claim in federal court must get to a federal district court with that claim *first*, in advance of any proceedings in state court that, once begun, will almost certainly produce a decision that will conclude the matter.

A. State Court Authority

The basic proposition that state courts can handle Article III business is scarcely controversial. State courts of general jurisdiction are empowered by state

---

1. See Chapter I, notes 79-91 and accompanying text.
2. See notes 116-48 and accompanying text (discussing the possibility of removal to a federal district court); notes 156-87 and accompanying text (discussing the possibility of attacking a state court judgment collaterally in federal court); Chapter VII (discussing the possibility of appellate review in the Supreme Court of the United States).

law to adjudicate any dispute that litigants bring to them, subject only to federal constitutional limitations.[3] Nothing in the Constitution expressly bars those courts from proceeding in the ordinary course simply because a case might also have been taken to a federal tribunal. Following Hamilton, the Supreme Court has declined to interpret Article III to divest state courts of any authority they previously enjoyed to decide the kinds of cases and controversies that Article III brings within the federal judicial power.[4] Moreover, again following Hamilton, the Court has held that even with respect to cases and controversies that are peculiar to the federal constitutional system (for example, federal question cases), Article III allows state courts to act, subject to any limits that Congress may establish by statute.[5]

This construction of Article III is fortified by the Constitution's history, text, and structure. State courts' ability to do Article III business formed the premise of the Madisonian Compromise.[6] Recall the conventional understanding that federal courts inferior to the Supreme Court need never have been created. If there were no such lower federal courts, state courts would have to adjudicate Article III cases and controversies in the first instance in order to establish judgments on which the Supreme Court could exercise appellate jurisdiction.[7] The Supremacy Clause, which flowed naturally from the Compromise, states explicitly that state judges are bound by the Constitution and other "Laws of the United States" and thus plainly contemplates that state courts will adjudicate cases in which federal questions must be considered.[8] Inasmuch as the states are united in a single national structure, federal law is as much a part of their law as is local state law.[9] It only makes sense, accordingly, that the courts the states commission share responsibility for federal question litigation with the courts established by Congress under Article III.[10] Finally, it seems more practical to ad-

---

3. Formally speaking, state courts do not exercise "the judicial Power" of the United States prescribed for the federal courts by Article III. See Chapter IV, text accompanying notes 1-4. State courts need no federal footing for their existence and jurisdiction, but depend for both on independent state law. See Chapter V, note 56 (discussing a similar point regarding federal legislative courts).

4. See Chapter II, text accompanying note 50.

5. See Chapter II, text accompanying note 51.

6. See Chapter II, note 12 and accompanying text.

7. By the same token, if the cases and controversies that state courts adjudicate were not matters to which Article III extends, the Supreme Court would be unable to review the judgments the state courts reach. See Chapter V, note 56.

8. U.S. Const. art VI, cl.2. See Chapter II, text accompanying notes 19-20. Professor Collins contends that some members of the founding generation agreed with Justice Story that state courts would be unable to handle all the business included in Article III and that inferior federal courts *would* be necessary. Michael G. Collins, *Article III Cases, State Court Duties, and the Madisonian Compromise*, 1995 Wis. L. Rev. 39; see Chapter IV, notes 14-18 and accompanying text. Collins acknowledges, however, that it is "difficult if not impossible to argue today that there are areas of Article III jurisdiction within the Supreme Court's appellate jurisdiction that could not be heard in the first instance by the state courts if they were so inclined and if Congress were agreeable." Id. at 46.

9. *Claflin v. Houseman*, 93 U.S. 130, 136 (1876).

10. Not all the constitutional values typically associated with federalism are served by state court jurisdiction in federal question cases. There is no argument, for example, that state courts should participate in the resolution of federal questions in order to foster experimentation and diversity or to accommodate local sentiments not shared in other regions. By contrast, state courts, if they decide federal questions at all, must decide them in conformity

just the distribution of jurisdiction between federal and state courts by statutes (which can themselves be adjusted from time to time) than through judicial elaboration of the Constitution itself.[11]

The federal statutes in point, as well as tradition and practice, also support the understanding that state court jurisdiction is presumptively concurrent with that of federal courts. Recall that the Judiciary Act of 1789 left considerable Article III business to state courts by default and that Congress did not grant inferior federal courts a general jurisdiction in federal question cases until Reconstruction.[12] Experience shows, accordingly, that the system has often depended on state court adjudication of a significant body of federal question cases—including some federal criminal prosecutions.[13] The states typically choose local courts when they enforce local policies in litigation with individual citizens. Federal issues often arise in that context, and, when they do, state courts are positioned to address them. Any other scheme would be difficult to orchestrate. Either state officials would have to proceed in federal court in the first place, or litigation initiated in state court would have to be shifted to a federal tribunal later. At the least, significant institutional costs would accompany both possibilities.[14]

Congress has power to preempt state courts. In *The Moses Taylor*,[15] the Court said that Congress can give federal courts exclusive jurisdiction to determine "all cases to which the judicial power of the United States extends."[16] That may be an overstatement. Taken literally, it would mean that if the Constitution does not itself divest state courts of jurisdiction they had before 1787, Congress can do so by statute.[17] It would also revive the vexing constitutional questions implicated when Congress curbs the jurisdiction of the federal courts.[18] At the very least, Congress would find it infeasible to undertake such a revision of the judicial system. Consider, for example, the disruptions that would follow if Congress were to assign federal courts exclusive jurisdiction over all cases involving citizens of different states—cases in which federal courts would apply *state* law.[19]

As a practical matter, Congress rarely makes federal jurisdiction exclusive.[20] Some statutes explicitly indicate that state courts, too, have jurisdiction to pro-

---

to a uniform body of federal law. Paul M. Bator, *The State Courts and Federal Constitutional Litigation*, 22 Wm. & Mary L. Rev. 605, 608 (1981).

11. See Chapter VIII, text accompanying notes 30-31.

12. See Chapter II, notes 58-60, 72 and accompanying text.

13. See *Testa v. Katt*, 330 U.S. 386, 390 (1947); Chapter IV, note 17 and accompanying text. Today, a federal *statute* places federal criminal prosecutions exclusively within the federal courts' jurisdiction. 18 U.S.C. § 3231. But a move is afoot to amend that statute and channel some classes of federal prosecutions into state court for trial in order to conserve federal judicial resources. See Chapter II, note 104 and accompanying text.

14. Bator, note 10, at 608-09, 621.

15. 71 U.S. (4 Wall.) 411 (1867).

16. Id. at 429.

17. See text accompanying note 4.

18. See Chapter IV, notes 27-31, 90-105 and accompanying text. Consider the implications, for example, if Congress were to deny state courts jurisdiction to determine any of the cases and controversies listed in Article III and, at the same time, were to dismantle the lower federal courts—thus leaving the Supreme Court to manage what Article III business it can as an original matter.

19. See Chapter VIII, text accompanying note 34.

20. By some accounts, Congress should decline to make federal jurisdiction exclusive in any case, but should, instead, always provide for concurrent jurisdiction in both federal and

ceed. Others refer only to the federal courts, and still others ambiguously refer to courts of "competent jurisdiction." In most contexts, it does not matter. State courts are understood to have any jurisdiction that is not explicitly disclaimed — either by an express statement that federal jurisdiction is exclusive or by a statement that state court jurisdiction is foreclosed. Litigants therefore have the dominant role in deciding where a case will be resolved. When the two sides agree on the appropriate forum, there is typically no difficulty getting the case into that tribunal. When the parties disagree, various statutes and doctrines determine whose preference prevails.

The leading case is *Claflin v. Houseman*,[21] in which the Supreme Court held that state courts could entertain contract and real property suits initiated by an assignee in bankruptcy. Justice Bradley rejected the argument that state courts were deprived of jurisdiction merely because the assignee derived his procedural right to sue from the federal bankruptcy statute. That statute said nothing about state court jurisdiction. Accordingly, the occasion called for judgment regarding the proper inference to be drawn from legislative silence. Justice Bradley adopted a presumption in favor of concurrent state court jurisdiction: A federal statute should be read to allow for state court jurisdiction, unless the statute precludes that jurisdiction either "by express provision" or by "incompatibility in its exercise arising from the nature of the particular case."[22] The claims in *Claflin* were traditional common law claims over which state courts enjoyed jurisdiction prior to the Constitution. Accordingly, *Claflin* may itself be authority only for a presumption in favor of state court jurisdiction in cases of that kind. Again following Hamilton,[23] however, more recent decisions have clarified the point: State courts presumptively have concurrent jurisdiction in all cases, irrespective of subject matter.[24]

In *Gulf Offshore Co. v. Mobil Oil Corp.*,[25] the Supreme Court restated the *Claflin* doctrine as a default position, subject to three exceptions. State court con-

---

state court. The parties presumably make rational choices about the best forum in which to litigate, and it may be that a loose "market" for selecting courts will produce good results in most instances, without any attempt to control forum selection by law. In some contexts, however, special expertise or uniformity may be needed, and Congress may sensibly respond by foreclosing state court jurisdiction and forcing litigants into the federal forum. Examples include: 28 U.S.C. § 1334 (bankruptcy proceedings); 28 U.S.C. § 1355 (actions to recover fines under federal statutes); and 28 U.S.C. § 1364 (actions against insurers of foreign governments). The federal courts' exclusive jurisdiction in patent and copyright cases, 28 U.S.C. § 1338, may be more controversial inasmuch as the Supreme Court's precedents often allow for state court treatment of the same issues. See *T.B. Harms v. Eliscu*, 339 F.2d 823 (2d Cir. 1964), *cert. denied*, 381 U.S. 915 (1965) (providing a good discussion); see also Donald S. Chisum, *The Allocation of Jurisdiction Between State and Federal Courts in Patent Litigation*, 46 Wash. L. Rev. 633 (1971).

21. 93 U.S. 130 (1876).
22. Id. at 136.
23. See Chapter II, text accompanying notes 50-51.
24. E.g., *Charles Dowd Box Co. v. Courtney*, 368 U.S. 502 (1962) (holding that state courts have concurrent jurisdiction to entertain federal labor relations cases in which federal common law controls); *Garrett v. Moore-McCormack Co.*, 317 U.S. 239 (1942) (holding that state courts can handle claims under federal maritime statutes).
25. 453 U.S. 473 (1981).

current jurisdiction will be found, unless it is foreclosed by: (1) "explicit statutory" language; (2) "unmistakable implication" from legislative history; or (3) "clear incompatibility" with "federal interests."[26] The leading case on the *Gulf Offshore* formulation is *Tafflin v. Levitt.*[27] The Court held in *Tafflin* that state courts have concurrent jurisdiction to entertain civil actions under the federal Racketeering Influenced and Corrupt Organizations Act (RICO).[28] Justice O'-Connor initially found no express language in RICO purporting to deny state court jurisdiction.[29] Turning to the legislative history behind RICO, she said that "the question is not whether any intent at all may be divined from legislative *silence* on the issue, but whether Congress in its deliberations may be said to have *affirmatively* or *unmistakably* intended jurisdiction to be exclusively federal."[30] Coming to the "incompatibility" exception, O'Connor acknowledged that state jurisdiction of RICO cases would lead to state court interpretations of federal criminal offenses (which often form part of civil RICO violations). Yet she found no sufficient conflict with federal interests.[31]

Inasmuch as *Tafflin* considered all three *Gulf Offshore* exceptions, it is hard to say that any of the three can be dismissed. Nevertheless, Justice O'Connor's treatment of the latter two suggests that the first (an express statement in the text of a statute that state courts have no jurisdiction) is now predominant. Certainly, the second exception appears anomalous. Concurring in *Tafflin*, Justice Scalia urged the Court to abandon that exception entirely. In his view, Congress can deprive state courts of jurisdiction only by means of an enacted statute, not committee reports and similar background materials.[32] Justice Scalia conceded that

---

26. Id. at 478.

27. 493 U.S. 455 (1990).

28. The suit in *Tafflin* was originally initiated in a federal district court, but that court abstained in favor of pending litigation in state court. See Chapter XI (discussing the abstention doctrines). The validity of that action turned on the existence of state court jurisdiction over the plaintiff's RICO claims.

29. The relevant provision in RICO states that a plaintiff "may" sue "in any appropriate United States district court," but does not explicitly state either that federal jurisdiction is exclusive or that a plaintiff may *not* sue in state court. 493 U.S. at 460.

30. Id. at 462 (emphasis added). Justice O'Connor found no hard evidence in the legislative history to suggest that Congress so much as considered whether state courts would handle RICO cases. She might have taken the absence of any mention of state courts to imply that only federal district courts would do so. Moreover, Congress borrowed statutory language from the Clayton Act for use in RICO. Since Clayton Act cases had previously been held to be exclusively within the federal courts' jurisdiction, Justice O'Connor might have drawn the conclusion, again by implication, that Congress contemplated that the same would be true of RICO lawsuits. In the event, she declined to draw any inferences from silence in the legislative record.

31. Justice O'Connor explained that state courts handling *civil* RICO cases do not enforce federal *criminal* law directly. They are guided by the precedents set by federal courts, and, in any event, they have sufficient expertise in criminal law matters to manage RICO litigation—particularly in situations in which violations of state (as well as federal) criminal law figure in a defendant's civil liability.

32. 493 U.S. at 472. Justice Scalia recognized that the Court had previously found state court jurisdiction to be foreclosed by implication in Clayton and Sherman Act cases. Yet he criticized the reasoning in those cases and insisted that if "exclusion by implication is possible" at all, it should be possible only on the basis of what can be found implicit in the text of the statute itself, not in legislative history. Id. at 471.

the third exception may be acceptable, provided that "incompatibility" is found only when a statute "expressly mentions only the federal courts" and state court jurisdiction would "plainly disrupt" the federal statutory scheme.[33]

Justice Scalia's position reflects the kind of statutory construction analysis that now pervades Supreme Court decisions in this field: strict attention to the text of enacted statutes, disregard for legislative history, and a tendency to choose a baseline default position from which Congress can depart only by making a clear statement.[34] If the full Court did not adopt that approach in *Tafflin*, it did so in the very next case, *Yellow Freight System v. Donnelly*.[35] In *Yellow Freight*, the Court unanimously held that state courts have concurrent jurisdiction to entertain private civil actions under Title VII of the 1964 Civil Rights Act. Justice Stevens discussed the possibility that state court jurisdiction might be implicitly disclaimed by legislative history or incompatible with federal interests—but only briefly. In the main, he said that the absence of an explicit disclaimer of state court jurisdiction in the Act itself was "strong *and arguably sufficient*" evidence that state courts can entertain Title VII suits.[36]

B. State Court Obligation

The question whether state courts *must* entertain federal question lawsuits is problematic. As a practical matter, state courts of general jurisdiction are not free to turn away federal business. This is true for a host of reasons elaborated in the precedents. Still, no precedent squarely holds either that the Constitution of its own force commands state courts to handle federal question cases or that Congress can force them to do so by legislation.[37] Those ultimate questions implicate a variety of ideas: (1) the principle of national unity; (2) the principle of non-discrimination; (3) the demands of due process; (4) the scope of congressional power; (5) valid excuses for declining federal business; and (6) the place of local procedural rules.

National unity. In expansive moments, the Supreme Court is wont to conflate the state courts' constitutional *authority* to adjudicate federal question cases with a constitutional *obligation* to undertake the task. The classic illustration is

---

33. Id. at 472. But see Chapter VIII, notes 65-66, 76-78 and accompanying text (discussing Justice Scalia's controversial opinion for the Court in the *Boyle* case).

34. See Michael E. Solimine, *Rethinking Federal Jurisdiction*, 52 U. Pitt. L. Rev. 383, 385 (1991); Chapter I, notes 37-41 and accompanying text. Cf. *Village of Bolingbrook v. Citizens Utilities Co.*, 864 F.2d 481, 485 (7th Cir. 1988) (opinion of Easterbrook, J.) (proposing that the precedents holding that the anti-trust laws implicitly foreclose state court jurisdiction are now open to question). Redish and Muench argue that the Court should take greater responsibility for determining whether state court jurisdiction will satisfactorily protect federal interests. Martin H. Redish & John E. Muench, *Adjudication of Federal Causes of Action in State Courts*, 75 Mich. L. Rev. 311 (1976).

35. 494 U.S. 820 (1990).

36. Id. at 823 (emphasis added).

37. In *Nat'l Private Truck Council v. Oklahoma Tax Comm'n*, 515 U.S. 582 (1995), the Court explicitly stated that it is an open question whether state courts "generally must hear" federal question cases pursuant to the Ku Klux Klan Act, 42 U.S.C. § 1983. Id. at 587 n.4. See notes 48-53 and accompanying text (discussing the *Howlett* case).

Justice Harlan's statement in *Robb v. Connolly*: "Upon the State courts, equally with the courts of the Union, rests the *obligation* to guard, enforce, and protect every right granted or secured by the Constitution of the United States."[38] And in the leading case, *Testa v. Katt*,[39] the Court said that the precedents on state court power, particularly *Claflin*,[40] equally answer "most" of the questions regarding state courts' "duty" to enforce federal law.[41] The vision of national unity has considerable force. If the states are units of an indivisible whole, if they do not and cannot function as independent nations, and if federal law is part of their law (and, indeed, a superior form of it), it is hard to think that state courts can refuse to adjudicate claims that depend on that law.

In *Testa*, a consumer alleged that an automobile dealer had exacted a selling price that exceeded the war-time ceiling established by the federal Emergency Price Control Act. Under the provisions of that Act, the consumer was entitled to sue in "any court of competent jurisdiction" and, if successful, to obtain treble damages. The consumer chose to sue in the state courts of Rhode Island. The Rhode Island Supreme Court held that the treble damages provision was penal in character and, accordingly, that the courts of Rhode Island had no obligation to enforce it. The court relied by analogy on the settled understanding that an individual state need not give "full faith and credit" to the "penal" actions and judgments of another state or nation—if to do so would conflict with the forum state's public policy.[42]

In the Supreme Court, Justice Black assumed that the treble damages provision was penal in nature and that the Rhode Island courts might have declined to enforce it, if it had been enacted by another state or a foreign nation. But he rejected the state court's premise that it could equally refuse to enforce a federal statute. Black relied on two theories, though he failed to distinguish them one from the other. First, he implied that the Constitution of its own force obligated the Rhode Island courts to entertain the plaintiff's federal claim. Congress, he said, acted for "all the people and all the states" when it established the treble damages provision as policy for the country as a whole.[43] A state court was not free to treat a federal statute as though it were a law "emanating from a foreign sovereign," but must, instead, accept it as the supreme law of the single American nation. Second, Justice Black suggested that the Emergency Price Control Act required the state courts to entertain the

---

38. 111 U.S. 624, 637 (1884) (emphasis added).

39. 330 U.S. 386 (1947).

40. See notes 21-24 and accompanying text.

41. 330 U.S. at 391.

42. The Full Faith and Credit Clause, U.S. Const. art. IV, § 1, generally instructs the states to give "Full Faith and Credit" to the "public Acts, Records, and judicial Proceedings of every other State." See note 156. Yet states may decline to credit "penalties." E.g., *Wisconsin v. Pelican Ins. Co.*, 127 U.S. 265, 291 (1888).

43. 330 U.S. at 392, citing *Mondou v. New York R.R.*, 223 U.S. 1, 57 (1912), for the proposition that the policy reflected in a federal statute is "as much the policy of [an individual state] as if the act had emanated from its own legislature." Accord *Claflin*, 93 U.S. at 137 (explaining that state and federal law "form one system of jurisprudence"). This point is not inconsistent with the rule that a state can object to policies adopted by other states. That idea reflects a kind of horizontal federalism. It recognizes a baseline responsibility in the states to cooperate with each other, but still accommodates occasional differences in the interests of autonomy and diversity.

plaintiff's action, even if the Constitution, standing alone, did not. On this second point, Black said that the 1789 Judiciary Act and a variety of later statutes "conferred jurisdiction upon state courts to enforce" federal law and that this new statute did the same. By his account, challenges to Congress' power to "require" the state courts to entertain federal claims were essentially rejected in *Claflin*.[44]

Justice Black overlooked one alternative understanding of the Supremacy Clause and slighted (but ultimately relied on) yet another. Initially, he failed to consider whether the Supremacy Clause might demand only that state courts enforce federal law in cases the state courts voluntarily accept for consideration. If a state court chooses not to entertain a suit at all, it avoids putting itself in a position to decide whether a proposition of federal law preempts some feature of state law. Once a state court accepts a case, however, it is necessarily in such a position. At that point, it is inescapable that the court must give proper effect to federal law. Both *Testa* and subsequent precedents read the Supremacy Clause to address both a state court's decision to entertain a case in the first instance and its adjudication of a case after it has been accepted. Yet the supremacy of federal law is clearly less at risk in the former instance than it is in the latter.[45]

The Supremacy Clause might also be read to permit a state court to refuse a federal question lawsuit in the first instance, provided the court equally refuses similar cases arising under state law. Justice Black stated the question presented in *Testa* in a sweeping manner: "whether state courts may decline to enforce federal laws" on the grounds cited by the Rhode Island Supreme Court.[46] And his elaboration of the national unity principle suggested that he meant to decide the ultimate question whether the state courts must generally be open for federal question business. In the end, however, he appeared to rest the decision in *Testa* on a narrow basis—namely, that a state court cannot discriminate against federal claims.

Non-discrimination. It was conceded in *Testa* that the state courts would enforce a treble damages statute if it were enacted by the Rhode Island legislature. By refusing to enforce such a statute when it was enacted by Congress, the Rhode Island Supreme Court engaged in discrimination between state and federal law—disfavoring the latter. That is what Justice Black condemned. Accordingly, *Testa* may stand only for a non-discrimination principle: State courts cannot refuse to entertain a *federal* claim on the ground that it offends local policy, unless they also reject *state* law claims implicating a similar policy.[47]

The Court confirmed the non-discrimination principle in *Howlett v. Rose*.[48] A public school student sued school officials in a Florida state court, alleging that they had searched his car in violation of state tort law and the fourth amendment. With respect to the latter claim, the student relied on the federal Ku Klux

---

44. 330 U.S. at 389, 391.
45. But see text accompanying note 50 (noting the non-discrimination principle's basis in the Supremacy Clause).
46. 330 U.S. at 388.
47. Id. at 394. Professor Collins contends that this reading of *Testa* conforms to historical understandings of the state courts' role in the federal system. Collins, note 8, at 166-77.
48. 496 U.S. 356 (1990).

Klan Act, 42 U.S.C. § 1983, which authorizes a plaintiff to sue any "person" for violating the plaintiff's federal rights while acting "under color of state law."[49] The school officials set up state sovereign immunity as a defense. The state courts held that a state statute waived immunity with respect to state tort claims, but not with respect to federal constitutional claims. Accordingly, the state courts considered the student's state claim on the merits, but dismissed his federal claim. In the Supreme Court, Justice Stevens reversed on the grounds that discrimination *against* federal law violates the Supremacy Clause.[50]

Justice Stevens (like Justice Black before him) suggested both that the Constitution always requires state courts to entertain federal claims and that Congress can by statute command state courts to accept federal question cases. On the first point, he said that the existence of jurisdiction "creates an implication of duty to exercise it."[51] On the second, he said that § 1983 authorizes litigants to press constitutional claims in *either* federal or state court and, into the bargain, abolishes any sovereign immunity that state officials might otherwise enjoy.[52] Nevertheless, Justice Stevens set those lines of argument to one side when he explained his result in *Howlett*. He cited *Testa* and other precedents as illustrations of the non-discrimination principle.[53] And he squarely held only that the Florida courts were obligated to entertain the student's federal claim, if, at the same time, those courts were willing to consider his parallel state tort claim. Consequently, *Howlett*, too, rests on the (comparatively narrow) principle of non-discrimination.

---

49. See Chapter II, notes 73-74 and accompanying text (noting the history behind § 1983 and the many places in modern practice in which § 1983 plays a role).

50. 496 U.S. at 383.

51. Id. at 370, quoting *Mondou*, 223 U.S. at 58. Justice Stevens explained that state courts in Florida concededly had subject matter jurisdiction of the plaintiff's federal claim and that the only "jurisdictional" problem in the case resided with the sovereign immunity defense. Accordingly, he had no occasion to decide whether a state must in the first instance "establish courts competent to entertain § 1983 claims"—namely, federal claims advanced via the procedural vehicle that § 1983 provides. 496 U.S. at 378 n.20. See Chapter VIII, note 94 and accompanying text (explaining that § 1983 establishes no substantive rights and thus cannot itself be violated).

52. Justice Stevens cited *Martinez v. California*, 444 U.S. 277 (1980), for this point. There is solid supporting language in that case: "Conduct by persons acting under color of state law which is wrongful under 42 U.S.C. § 1983 ... cannot be immunized by state law." Id. at 284 n.8. Yet in *Martinez* the state courts willingly entertained a § 1983 suit, and it was in that posture that Justice Stevens (who also wrote for the Court in *Martinez*) said that state sovereign immunity did not control. Stevens intimated that the state courts in *Martinez* might have (correctly) understood that they were under an obligation to hear the § 1983 suit in order to avoid discrimination against the plaintiffs' federal claim. Id. at 283 n.7 (citing the language from *Testa* regarding discrimination). He also noted that the Court had never considered the question whether state courts *must* generally entertain § 1983 actions, discrimination to one side. That question remains open today. See note 37. For a discussion of § 1983 litigation in state court, see Steven H. Steinglass, *The Emerging State Court § 1983 Action: A Procedural Review*, 38 U. Miami L. Rev. 381 (1984).

53. In *McKnett v. St. Louis Ry.*, 292 U.S. 230 (1934), the Court found it discriminatory for a state court to reject a Federal Employers Liability Act claim filed by a non-resident when it would have accepted a similar claim if it had rested on another state's law. In *Felder v. Casey*, 487 U.S. 131 (1988), the Court found it discriminatory for a state to invoke a 120-day filing deadline to cut off a federal claim pressed in a § 1983 action, even though the same deadline applied to state law claims. The deadline frustrated federal civil rights policy.

Due Process. In some circumstances, fourteenth amendment due process requires the states to provide a means of redressing violations of federal law.[54] For
example, the fourteenth amendment incorporates the fifth amendment principle
that government cannot take private property without giving just compensation
in return. In "takings" cases, accordingly, the states are obliged to reimburse citizens and cannot set up sovereign immunity as a bar. In that instance, the Constitution itself furnishes the basis for entertaining suits against state officers and obtaining monetary relief.[55] In addition, the fourteenth amendment independently
requires the states to offer citizens a "clear and certain" remedy for taxes collected in violation of federal law.[56] The Supreme Court confirmed that point in
McKesson Corp. v. Div. of Alcoholic Beverages & Tobacco[57] and *Reich v.
Collins.*[58] By recognizing a mandatory *remedy* for unlawful taxes, *McKesson* and
Reich did not hold squarely that state *courts* must have *jurisdiction* to entertain
tax refund claims resting on federal law.[59] Remedies, judicial and non-judicial
alike, are conceptually distinct from subject matter jurisdiction.[60] Yet once it is

---

54. The states must engage some kind of process if they deprive an individual of life,
liberty, or property. States typically do so by providing a mix of administrative and judicial
proceedings. In at least some instances (e.g., criminal prosecutions) the process that is "due"
surely includes *judicial* process. In others, it is not entirely clear whether court proceedings
of some kind are constitutionally required. See Chapter IV, text accompanying notes 83-86;
cf. Chapter V, text accompanying note 65 (describing the Court's treatment of the issue in
connection with agency adjudication of public rights cases). In an ordinary due process case,
the triggering event is a deprivation of a liberty or property interest, not a violation of a federal right independent of due process. Accordingly, the familiar precedents regarding procedural due process do not establish that state courts have a threshold constitutional responsibility to adjudicate federal claims. Of course, if a state court once accepts a federal question
case, it is bound to adjudicate that case consistent with due process.

55. *First English Church v. County of Los Angeles*, 482 U.S. 304, 316 n.9 (1987). What
counts as a "taking" can be controversial—and certainly was in *First English* (an inverse
condemnation case). Professor Beermann argues that states are constitutionally required to
compensate the victims of the torts that state officers commit. He contemplates, however,
that claims of that kind should be vindicated in § 1983 actions in federal court. Jack M.
Beermann, *Government Official Torts and the Takings Clause: Federalism and State Sovereign Immunity*, 68 B.U. L. Rev. 277 (1988).

56. *Atchison, T. & S.F.R. Co. v. O'Connor*, 223 U.S. 280, 285 (1912). If a state collects
taxes that violate federal law "by coercive means," the fourteenth amendment establishes a
duty to reimburse the taxpayers concerned. *Ward v. Bd. of County Comm. of Love County*,
253 U.S. 17, 24 (1920). See Chapter VII, notes 108-09 and accompanying text (discussing
the Supreme Court's jurisdiction to review the state court's decision in *Ward* notwithstanding the argument that it rested on an adequate state ground).

57. 496 U.S. 18 (1990).

58. 513 U.S. 106 (1994).

59. In both cases, the states employed state courts for the determination of tax reimbursement claims. The possibility that exclusively administrative schemes might suffice was
not presented.

60. Loose labels can confuse this simple point. Sometimes courts use the term "remedy"
to mean a right of action—a procedural right to *pursue* a judicial *remedy* from a court.
That is the sense in which § 1983 is sometimes said to provide a "remedy" for federal rights.
E.g., *Monroe v. Pape*, 365 U.S. 167, 172 (1961). But see Chapter VIII, notes 89-90 and accompanying text (explaining that § 1983 actually establishes a right of action). Conventionally, however, a remedy is a form of relief granted to a party whose claim is judged to be
meritorious. Illustrations include compensatory damages, injunctions, declaratory judgments, and various writs. Subject matter jurisdiction, by contrast, goes to a particular court's
power to entertain a suit in which a litigant seeks some remedy. See Chapter VIII, note 80
and accompanying text.

posited that the Constitution demands a remedy, it would seem to follow that state courts must have jurisdiction either to dispense that remedy to deserving litigants in the first instance or to review the remedial actions of state administrative officers.[61] If state courts must be open for federal claims touching taxes, it may be a short step to the proposition that they must be open for other federal claims as well.

Nevertheless, there are reasons for caution. The Court did not focus on jurisdictional issues in *McKesson* and *Reich*, and those decisions cannot be cited for anything beyond their hard conclusions. The taxpayers' immediate claim was not that they had been denied an opportunity to show the state courts that they had been overcharged. It was that the states simply declined to reimburse them, irrespective of the merits of their claims. Neither the state of Florida in *McKesson* nor the state of Georgia in *Reich* attempted to shield itself from a monetary award by setting up sovereign immunity.[62] That is the form that state resistance to federal question claims typically takes. The discrimination case, *Howlett*, is an illustration.[63]

Justice O'Connor stated flatly in *Reich* that a state's failure to return money exacted by unlawful taxation violates due process, "the sovereign immunity States traditionally enjoy in their own courts notwithstanding."[64] That, however, was dictum.[65] Moreover, Justice O'Connor said in the next breath that the eleventh amendment typically bars federal courts from entertaining tax refund

---

61. See Richard H. Fallon, Jr., *The Ideologies of Federal Courts Law*, 74 Va. L. Rev. 1141, 1209 (1988); Henry P. Monaghan, *Third Party Standing*, 84 Colum. L. Rev. 277, 294 (1984). The converse is not true. Courts may have jurisdiction to adjudicate claims, but still lack authority to award prevailing litigants the remedies they seek. See Chapter XI, text accompanying notes 54-55 (discussing the prerequisites for equitable relief); see also Richard H. Fallon, Jr., *Some Confusions About Due Process, Judicial Review, and Constitutional Remedies*, 93 Colum. L. Rev. 309, 339, 370-71 (1993).

62. In *McKesson* and *Reich*, the states offered other legal and equitable justifications for refusing to reimburse taxpayers. See Vicki C. Jackson, *Seminole Tribe, the Eleventh Amendment and the Potential Evisceration of Ex parte Young*, 72 N.Y.U. L. Rev. 495, 504-05 n.40 (1997).

63. See notes 48-53 and accompanying text.

64. 513 U.S. at 110.

65. Daniel J. Meltzer, *The Seminole Decision and State Sovereign Immunity*, 1996 Sup. Ct. Rev. 1, 58. Professor Woolhandler concedes that *Reich* is "arguably" a case in which a state's consent to suit was beside the point. Yet she argues that there is also a way to read *Reich* to *depend* on state consent. The Georgia legislature established a statutory scheme by which taxpayers could sue the state itself for tax refunds. That scheme substituted for an older system in which taxpayers sued state officers on common law theories. Woolhandler contends that Georgia was constitutionally obligated to allow taxpayers to sue state officers in the traditional form. Accordingly, when the state established an alternative system, it must have implicitly agreed to forego sovereign immunity in the reimbursement actions the new scheme contemplated. Otherwise, the shift to suits against the state itself would have unilaterally eliminated a constitutional guarantee. Ann Woolhandler, *The Common Law Origins of Constitutionally Compelled Remedies*, 107 Yale L.J. 77, 150-51 (1997). In the main, Professor Woolhandler thinks that in the late Nineteenth Century state courts had a constitutional obligation to entertain tort actions against state officers. The best citation for that proposition may be *Poindexter v. Greenhow*, 114 U.S. 270 (1884), one of the Virginia cases. Professor Wolcher agrees, though he concentrates on a wide range of modern decisions (prior to *McKesson* and *Reich*). See Louis E. Wolcher, *Sovereign Immunity and the Supremacy Clause: Damages Against States in Their Own Courts for Constitutional Violations*, 69 Calif. L. Rev. 189 (1981).

claims against a state.[66] That suggested (but did not hold) that a state's constitutional obligation to entertain federal claims depends on whether the litigants concerned have access to the federal courts. It may be that if due process requires state courts to entertain federal question cases at all, it does so only when the federal courts are unavailable.[67]

The leading case on this point is *General Oil Co. v. Crain*.[68] A taxpayer sued a state officer in state court, seeking to enjoin a state tax on the theory that it violated the Commerce Clause. The state officer in *Crain*, like the defendants in *Howlett*, set up state sovereign immunity as a defense. The state courts dismissed the claim on that basis. In the Supreme Court, Justice McKenna explained that if the plaintiff's claim could be barred from state court on the basis of sovereign immunity, and if it could equally be barred from federal court on the basis of the eleventh amendment, it would go without any judicial forum at all. McKenna refused to accept the state court's determination of state sovereign immunity law as dispositive. He reached the taxpayer's federal constitutional claim and, finding it wanting, affirmed the state court's judgment on the merits.

Justice McKenna's emphasis on the risk that a federal claim might be barred from *both* state and federal court suggests that any obligation state courts have to hear federal claims is triggered only if the federal courts' doors are closed. Yet on the day the Court decided *Crain*, it also held (in *Ex parte Young*[69]) that the eleventh amendment does not bar a suit in federal court for an injunction against the enforcement of an unconstitutional state statute. Since the taxpayer in *Crain* sought only injunctive relief, the contemporaneous decision in *Young* would have allowed that action to proceed in federal court.[70] Accordingly, *Crain* itself was not driven by the need to find some tribunal for the plaintiff's claim apart from a federal trial-level court. In an important dissent in *Idaho v. Coeur d'Alene*

---

66. 513 U.S. at 110; see Chapter X, notes 166-74 and accompanying text (discussing the relevant eleventh amendment doctrine).

67. See Chapter IV, note 34 (recalling Professor Hart's argument on this point). Professor Monaghan suggests that *Reich* implicitly recognized that the eleventh amendment is a "forum selection clause," which bars federal courts from entertaining some claims, but contemplates that litigants will be entitled to advance those claims in state court. Henry P. Monaghan, *The Sovereign Immunity "Exception"*, 110 Harv. L. Rev. 102, 125 (1996). See Chapter X, notes 81-85 and accompanying text (discussing the forum-allocation theory of the eleventh amendment). In a *per curiam* in *Newsweek v. Florida Dep't of Revenue*, 118 S.Ct. 904 (1998), however, the court summarily held that Florida was obliged to give a taxpayer a post-payment opportunity to recover taxes imposed in violation of federal law — where the taxpayer had paid the contested taxes with the reasonable understanding that it would be entitled to file a later recoupment suit if its constitutional objection was sustained. The Court purported to follow *Reich*, but did not repeat the observation that the federal courts were closed. Nor did the Court address the possibility that Florida might have set up sovereign immunity to defeat the taxpayer's suit in state court.

68. 209 U.S. 211 (1908).

69. 209 U.S. 123 (1908); see Chapter X, notes 134-39 and accompanying text (discussing *Ex parte Young*).

70. At that time, moreover, Congress had not yet enacted the Tax Injunction Act, 28 U.S.C. §1341, which now bars federal district courts from restraining the assessment of state taxes if state courts are available to consider taxpayer claims. See Chapter XI, note 36 and accompanying text.

Tribe,[71] Justice Souter cited *Crain* for the general proposition that state sovereign immunity cannot "constitutionally excuse a state court of general jurisdiction from an obligation to hear a suit brought to enjoin a state official's action" on federal constitutional grounds.[72] In any case, the plaintiffs in *McKesson* and *Reich* could seek relief only in state court. They sought monetary relief that the eleventh amendment would have barred in federal court, *Ex parte Young* notwithstanding.[73]

There is an argument that Justice McKenna meant to say in *Crain* only that state sovereign immunity could not establish an adequate state ground of decision foreclosing direct review in the Supreme Court.[74] McKenna did not squarely reverse on the ground that it was constitutional error for the state court below to invoke sovereign immunity. He said that since the state court had given effect to a state tax that the plaintiff contended was unconstitutional, the state court's judgment was "reviewable." Writing for the Court in *McKesson*, Justice Brennan mentioned that the Court's appellate jurisdiction is subject to the adequate state ground doctrine, but did not link that doctrine to *Crain*.[75]

Ordinarily, it is not the Constitution that bars federal courts from entertaining federal claims, but statutes enacted by Congress.[76] Arguably, state courts should not be constitutionally obliged to conduct federal business simply because Congress withholds jurisdiction from federal courts. If the federal government wishes federal law to be enforced, it can supply federal tribunals for the purpose. At the same time, state courts hardly play a serious role in the larger national system if they can ignore federal claims that otherwise will go without judicial attention. At the least, state courts may have a blanket duty to adjudicate *constitu-*

---

71. 117 S.Ct. 2028 (1997); see Chapter X, notes 154-60 and accompanying text (discussing the *Coeur d'Alene* case).

72. 117 S.Ct. at 2057 (dissenting opinion, joined by Stevens, Ginsburg & Breyer, J.J.). In *Georgia R.R. & Banking Co. v. Musgrove*, 335 U.S. 900 (1949), the Court dismissed an appeal from a state court judgment that appeared to rest on state sovereign immunity to defeat liability for a constitutional violation. In that case, the losing party below was entitled to invoke the Court's appellate jurisdiction (under a statute since repealed). Accordingly, *Musgrove* was not a denial of *certiorari*. See Chapter VII, text accompanying notes 182-85 (explaining that the Court now can decline appellate review at its discretion). In *Coeur d'Alene*, Justice Souter said that *Musgrove* probably found a different state law ground to preclude review. See Fallon, *Ideologies*, note 61, at 1211 n.317.

73. The state argued in *McKesson* that the eleventh amendment equally should bar the Supreme Court from considering a suit for monetary relief on appeal from state court. The Court rejected that idea out of hand in light of settled precedent. *McKesson*, 496 U.S. at 26; see Chapter VII, notes 51-54 and accompanying text (discussing *Cohens v. Virginia*); Chapter X, notes 64-65 and accompanying text (also discussing *Cohens*). It is hard to think that *Crain* was itself an eleventh amendment decision, holding only that the eleventh amendment did not bar the Supreme Court from accepting appellate jurisdiction in that case. The Court must have presupposed that (previously settled) proposition and rested judgment elsewhere.

74. See Chapter VII, notes 97-177 and accompanying text (discussing the adequate state ground doctrine).

75. 496 U.S. at 29 n.12.

76. See Chapter IV (discussing Congress' authority to prescribe the federal courts' jurisdiction legislatively).

tional claims, if not federal *statutory* claims created by Congress as a matter of federal legislative policy.[77]

Congressional responsibility. If the Constitution itself imposes an obligation on state courts *ceteris paribus*, the only role for Congress is to decide whether to foreclose state court actions by making federal court jurisdiction exclusive.[78] If, by contrast, the Constitution only permits Congress to create an obligation by statute, Congress must exercise some enumerated power—subject to the internal and external restraints that attend that power.[79] Article III presumably establishes no congressional power to confer jurisdiction on *state* courts. Statutes like the Emergency Price Control Act in *Testa* rest on one or more of the legislative powers listed in Article I—for example, the power to regulate interstate commerce. It is typically easy enough to show that enactments of that kind are within the internal restraints fixed by the power Congress invokes. But statutes that prescribe jurisdictional work for state courts may touch external limitations on Congress' ability to regulate state institutions—namely, state immunity from federal regulation implied in the overarching constitutional structure (and reflected in the tenth amendment).[80]

The Court has held that Congress cannot "commandeer" state legislative and executive authorities as instruments for the enactment and administration of federal programs.[81] In those cases, the Court has distinguished *Testa* by name on the ground that the Supremacy Clause imposes obligations on state judicial authorities that no comparable constitutional provision imposes on local legislative and executive officers.[82] That distinction can be questioned.[83] Justice Frankfurter once declared that state court authority to handle federal question cases rests on state, not federal, law and that only state law can "create" state courts and "confer jurisdiction upon them."[84]

---

77. Recall that the influential Hart and Wechsler paradigm contemplates that federal statute law is interstitial by nature. See Chapter I, note 49 and accompanying text.

78. See notes 16-19 and accompanying text.

79. See Chapter IV, text accompanying note 93 (explaining internal and external restraints on congressional power).

80. U.S. Const. amend. X: "The powers not delegated to the United States by the Constitution, nor prohibited by it to the States, are reserved to the States respectively, or to the people."

81. *New York v. United States*, 505 U.S. 144 (1992); *Printz v. United States*, 117 S.Ct. 2365 (1997). See Chapter I, text accompanying note 19 (describing the prohibition on commandeering the states). See generally Evan H. Caminker, *State Sovereignty and Subordinacy: May Congress Commandeer State Officers to Implement Federal Law?*, 95 Colum. L. Rev. 1001 (1995).

82. *New York*, 505 U.S. at 178; *Printz*, 117 S.Ct. at 2381.

83. Professor Collins argues that the Court's attempt to distinguish *Testa* is unsuccessful and that the rationale in cases like *New York* provides a solid constitutional argument that Congress cannot force the states to provide state courts with the jurisdiction necessary to enforce congressional programs. Collins, note 8, at 192. It may be that the Court finds it politically appealing to vindicate some values associated with federalism by checking federal legislative power where state legislative and executive authorities are concerned, but conceives that if the same analysis were extended to state courts different values associated with federalism would be compromised. In a variety of other cases, the Court itself attempts to channel federal business into the state courts in the name of federalism. It might appear inconsistent, then, to hold that Congress offends federalism by doing essentially the same thing by statute.

84. *Brown v. Gerdes*, 321 U.S. 178, 188 (1944) (concurring opinion). In *Employees v. Dep't of Pub. Health*, 411 U.S. 279 (1973), Justice Marshall insisted that Congress has

If Congress has power to impose jurisdiction on state courts, it follows that the construction the Court places on any particular statute touches delicate federalism concerns. The occasion is ripe for the application of a doctrine of clear statement, which demands clarity regarding Congress' wishes from the text of the enacted statute.[85] As usual, the crucial policy question is the direction in which the clear statement rule should cut. Here again, the Court may be pulled in both directions. Recall that the Court already insists that Congress must specify that state court jurisdiction is *foreclosed* in favor of exclusive federal jurisdiction.[86] That understanding preserves state courts as active participants in the enforcement of federal law. By demanding a clear statement from Congress to impose an *obligation* on state courts, the Court would forego state court participation in the resolution of cases that state courts, for their own reasons, decline to entertain.[87] At the very least, a doctrine of clear statement working against mandatory state jurisdiction would produce a body of judicial business regarding

---

power both to establish substantive claims and rights of action to enforce those claims against the states and to "lift" state sovereign immunity for purposes of suits in state court. Id. at 297-98 (concurring opinion). Yet Marshall stopped short of saying that Congress can actually establish jurisdiction in state courts. Instead, he pointed out that the state in *Employees* concededly had "courts of general jurisdiction competent to hear suits of [the same] character" and insisted that those courts were obliged to enforce federal law. In that, Marshall invoked the principle of nondiscrimination. If the mere existence of the Supremacy Clause is insufficient to distinguish *Testa* from *New York* and *Printz*, there is another, more conceptual argument that may answer. Federal law does not affect the activities of state judicial authorities in the way it affects the activities of legislative and executive officers. State courts are not told that they cannot violate federal law and that they will be held to account if they do. They are told, instead, that they must embrace federal law as a rule of decision in cases that come before them. They must enforce that federal law as part of the common system of jurisprudence for which all courts, federal and state, are responsible. This is in keeping with the national unity principle, which has it that state courts are co-equal partners with federal courts. State court judgments on federal questions are subject to appellate (and sometimes collateral) review and may be overturned if found to be erroneous. But disappointed state court litigants cannot simply file federal lawsuits attacking state court decisions in the way they file suits challenging state statutes or the actions of state executive officers. If litigants could do that, state courts would cease to be co-equal judicial tribunals at all, but would instead be additional governmental units whose activities are subject to attack in *real* courts—namely, federal courts. See *Howlett*, 496 U.S. at 369 n.16 (sketching this understanding).

85. See Chapter I, notes 37-41 and accompanying text (discussing the clear statement doctrine). Some *amici* in the *Howlett* case asked the Court to hold that in order to impose an obligation on state courts to entertain litigation, Congress must use exacting language (not found in § 1983). See notes 48-53 and accompanying text (discussing *Howlett*). Justice Stevens dismissed that invitation on the ground that the state courts in *Howlett* drew their subject matter jurisdiction from state law. 496 U.S. at 370 n.17. Since § 1983 is not by nature a jurisdictional statute, it could have imposed no jurisdictional duty on the state courts in any event. See Chapter VIII, notes 93-94 and accompanying text. Still, Justice Stevens apparently found it important that § 1983 authorized the plaintiff in *Howlett* to invoke the state courts' subject matter jurisdiction (grounded in state law) to advance his fourth amendment claim.

86. See notes 35-36 and accompanying text.

87. Cf. *Gregory v. Ashcroft*, 501 U.S. 452 (1991) (acknowledging that Congress has power to establish a mandatory retirement age for state employees and to apply it to state judges—but declining to read the AEDA that way in the absence of "unmistakably clear" text). Professor Sandalow contends that the allocation of jurisdiction between federal and state courts is a legislative function and, accordingly, that the Supreme Court should not hold state courts to an obligation to entertain federal business unless Congress clearly estab-

which state court jurisdiction exists in a purely voluntary form, neither clearly precluded nor clearly demanded by the relevant federal statute.[88]

Valid excuses. Any duty that state courts may have to entertain federal business is subject to exceptions. The Court captures that idea in the valid excuse doctrine, which figures in all the decisions in this context. Arguments against a state court obligation to adjudicate invariably are couched as arguments that state courts have a valid excuse for declining. To qualify as valid, an excuse must be neutral with respect to the content and character of federal law. When the Court held in *Testa* that Rhode Island courts could not refuse to enforce a federal claim because it reflected an objectionable policy, and equally when the Court held in *Howlett* that Florida courts could not turn a claim away simply because it was federal in nature, the Court stated its conclusion as a determination that the excuses the state courts offered for their actions were invalid.[89] In other instances, the Court has found genuinely neutral excuses to be sufficient.[90]

---

lishes such a duty by statute. Terrance Sandalow, *Henry v. Mississippi and the Adequate State Ground: Proposals for a Revised Doctrine*, 1965 Sup. Ct. Rev. 187, 207.

88. Here, too, the Court must take account of the availability (or not) of jurisdiction in federal court. In most instances, Congress can and does ensure some forum by opening the federal courts. But see *Internat'l Science & Tech. Inst. v. Inacom*, 106 F.3d 1146 (4th Cir. 1997) (reading the Telephone Consumer Protection Act to establish exclusive jurisdiction of some actions in state court). Yet when the eleventh amendment bars access to federal courts (despite Congress' desires), only state courts can offer an alternative. In *Hilton v. South Carolina Pub. Ry. Comm'n*, 502 U.S. 197 (1991), the Court declined to invoke a doctrine of clear statement regarding the question whether the Federal Employers Liability Act authorizes private suits for damages against the states in state court. Justice Kennedy noted that since suits of that kind are barred from the federal courts by the eleventh amendment, a construction of the FELA that effectively foreclosed suits in state court as well would leave claimants nowhere to turn. The question in *Hilton* was not (formally) whether Congress had enacted legislation *requiring* state courts to entertain FELA claims. The state did not set up sovereign immunity to defeat the claim in that case; the state courts dismissed the plaintiff's action on the (mistaken) theory that the FELA gave the plaintiff no right of action to sue (in any court). Moreover, Justice Kennedy explained the result primarily on the ground of *stare decisis*. The Court had previously held that the FELA *does* establish a private right of action. *Parden v. Terminal Ry.*, 377 U.S. 184 (1964). Finally, Kennedy expressly stated that, apart from the special circumstances in *Hilton*, a doctrine of clear statement would make sense—bringing symmetry and predictability to the law. Nevertheless, the risk that claims might have no judicial home at all plainly affected Kennedy's conclusion that the FELA authorizes private plaintiffs to sue in state court.

89. *Testa*, 330 U.S. at 392; *Howlett*, 496 U.S. at 371. The valid excuse doctrine in this context resembles the adequate state ground doctrine in the context of Supreme Court appellate jurisdiction. See text accompanying notes 74-75; Chapter VII, notes 97-177 and accompanying text. Yet there is an important difference. If a state court's excuse for declining to entertain a federal claim is invalid, the state court has committed error and can be reversed. If, by contrast, a state court's state ground of decision is inadequate, the court has not (necessarily) committed reversible error. It is just that the inadequacy of the state ground permits the Supreme Court to exercise appellate jurisdiction regarding any otherwise dispositive federal issues.

90. In *Herb v. Pitcairn*, 324 U.S. 117 (1945), the Court held that a municipal court of limited jurisdiction had a valid excuse for declining to consider a federal FELA claim. Any obligation state courts may have to entertain federal question cases attaches to state courts of general jurisdiction and does not require the states to abandon jurisdictional limitations designed to allocate business among state courts in aid of efficiency. In *Missouri ex rel. Southern Ry. Co. v. Mayfield*, 340 U.S. 1 (1950), the Court held that a state court of general jurisdiction had a valid excuse for declining FELA claims on the theory of *forum non conveniens*, so long as the state court administered that doctrine without disfavoring federal ques-

State procedures. When state courts entertain federal question cases, they must apply the federal law that those cases necessarily entail.[91] Ordinarily, state courts are entitled to employ local procedural rules that differ from the rules that would be followed in the federal courts or in the courts in other states.[92] In keeping with the principle of non-discrimination, however, there are two conditions: (1) any rules the state courts employ must be the same rules they would apply in cases involving similar state law claims;[93] and (2) the procedural rules state courts use must not undermine the purposes furthered by the substantive federal law the state courts are enforcing.[94] Both those conditions are anchored in constitutional obligation.[95]

In most circumstances, "federal law takes the state courts as it finds them."[96] The Court might have held, on that basis, that state courts can employ any ordinary rules in federal question cases, and that if disuniformity ensues Congress is free to shift all such cases to the federal courts. The Supreme Court takes a different view, because the Court plainly *wants* to channel federal question litigation into state court—particularly litigation under the Federal Employers Liability Act (which generates much of the case law in this context). The Court thus finds it essential to keep the state courts from employing procedural rules that discourage litigants from filing suit in the state forum.[97]

C. State Courts and Federal Officials

State courts typically have jurisdiction (granted to them by state law) to adjudicate lawsuits in which federal officers are named as defendants. If the state

---

tion cases. In *Inacom*, the circuit court read the Telephone Consumer Protection Act to allow state courts to decline jurisdiction. 106 F.3d at 1157-58. According to the court, that defused any constitutional difficulty that might otherwise have attended the Act's assignment of exclusive jurisdiction to those courts. See note 88.

91. *Dice v. Akron, Canton & Youngstown R.R.*, 342 U.S. 359 (1952) (holding that federal law controlled a state court's determination whether a worker had released an employer from liability under the FELA).

92. E.g., *Minneapolis & St. Louis R.R. v. Bombolis*, 241 U.S. 211 (1916) (allowing a state court handling a FELA case to follow its usual practice of concluding civil cases on the verdict of a non-unanimous jury even though a unanimous jury would have been necessary if the case had been tried in federal court); see *Central Vermont Ry. Co. v. White*, 238 U.S. 507 (1915) (explaining that state courts can typically apply local rules governing pleading and the admissibility of evidence to FELA cases).

93. E.g., *Felder v. Casey*, 487 U.S. 131 (1988) (perceiving discrimination to the detriment of federal claims where a state court invoked a local notice rule to cut off a § 1983 suit).

94. E.g., *Brown v. Western Ry. of Alabama*, 338 U.S. 294 (1949) (holding that strict state pleading requirements imposed "unnecessary burdens" on workers' right to recovery on a FELA claim).

95. The Court appeared to rest its decision in *Felder* on the Supremacy Clause. *Felder*, 487 U.S. at 150-51.

96. Henry M. Hart, Jr., *The Relations Between State and Federal Law*, 54 Colum. L. Rev. 489, 508 (1954).

97. Professor Herman's account is exhaustive. Susan N. Herman, *Beyond Parity: Section 1983 and the State Courts*, 54 Brooklyn L. Rev. 1057 (1989).

courts determine that a litigant's claim is meritorious, they equally have power (from the same source) to award appropriate compensatory relief.[98] Nevertheless, in a line of cases stretching back to the Nineteenth Century, the Supreme Court has held that state courts have limited authority to issue coercive orders requiring federal officers to take prescribed action.[99] In two famous instances, the Court reversed state court decisions granting habeas corpus relief to prisoners in the custody of federal officers. The prisoner in *Ableman v. Booth*[100] was an antislavery activist who had been convicted in federal court for a violation of the Fugitive Slave Act. In that case, accordingly, the state court interfered with federal judicial authority. The prisoner in *Tarble's Case*[101] was a soldier who been recruited when he was too young to serve. In that case, the state court interfered with federal executive authority.[102]

Justice Field's opinion for the Court in *Tarble's Case* is a classic. Field understood the question to be of fundamental importance: whether "any judicial officer of a State" had "jurisdiction to issue a writ of habeas corpus" or "to continue proceedings under the writ when issued" where the prisoner was held under a claim of federal authority by an officer of the United States.[103] Field answered that question in the negative and gave both constitutional and statutory rationales for his judgment. Initially, he relied on the Constitution of its own force. He said that the state's ability to confer jurisdiction on its courts was "re-

98. E.g., *Teal v. Felton*, 53 U.S. (12 How.) 284 (1852); *Buck v. Colbath*, 70 U.S. (3 Wall.) 334 (1866). Federal officials may, however, avoid liability on the basis of official immunity. See Chapter X, notes 245-92 and accompanying text.

99. See Richard S. Arnold, *The Power of State Courts to Enjoin Federal Officers*, 73 Yale L.J. 1385 (1964).

100. 62 U.S. (21 How.) 506 (1859).

101. 80 U.S. (13 Wall.) 397 (1872).

102. Ordinarily, prisoners use habeas corpus to challenge unlawful detention in connection with criminal prosecutions. See Chapter XII.

103. 80 U.S. at 402. Justice Field used the term "jurisdiction" in a special way. He did not mean to suggest that the Constitution absolutely bars the states from giving their courts subject matter jurisdiction to adjudicate cases in which federal officers are named as defendants. If that were true, the federal statute giving federal officers the *option* of removing state court suits against them to federal court would be unintelligible. See text accompanying note 125. Field had in mind the special circumstances of a habeas corpus action, in which a court's authority to act (in the subject matter jurisdiction sense) is inextricably linked to its authority to issue a special kind of remedy. Under common law procedure, a court issued the writ of habeas corpus immediately upon receiving a petition. The writ's function was to require the custodian to justify a prisoner's detention. It thus immediately purported to coerce the custodian into action. If the court concluded that the custodian's explanation was inadequate, the court issued a further order actually requiring the custodian to release the prisoner. This is why Justice Field's statement of the question in *Tarble's Case* covered both the state court's issuance of the writ in the first instance and subsequent proceedings "under the writ"—including, of course, the state court's ultimate order that the soldier must be discharged. It is common to refer to a court's "jurisdiction" to issue both common law writs like habeas corpus and equitable remedies like injunctions. In the case of injunctions, use of the "jurisdiction" label traces back to the time in this country and in England when only courts of equity had power to issue equitable relief. See *Steel Co. v. Citizens for a Better Environment*, 118 S.Ct. 1003, 1010 (1998) (noting that it is "commonplace" even today to use the term "jurisdiction" to mean the authority to issue a particular form of relief).

stricted by the Constitution," which established a "sphere of action" for the federal government that was "far beyond the reach of the judicial process issued by a State judge." Wisconsin was "sovereign" within its own borders "to a certain extent," but could not authorize its courts to interfere with the affairs of another "sovereign"—namely, the nation as a whole.[104] In addition, Field insisted that Congress "certainly" had not conferred jurisdiction on state courts to entertain habeas corpus petitions from prisoners challenging the actions of federal officers. Instead, Congress had given that jurisdiction to federal courts (and thus implicitly withheld it from state courts).[105]

The result in *Tarble's Case* can readily be explained. Justice Field was plainly concerned that state courts might disrupt the federal military services by calling federal commanders to account for their recruits.[106] Yet both his rationales have been questioned. By insisting that state courts are constitutionally disabled from checking excesses of federal power, Field neglected the conventional understanding that Congress might never have created the lower federal courts and might have relied, instead, on state courts to police the system, subject to appellate review by the Supreme Court.[107] By depicting separate sovereign spheres for the states and the federal government, Field dismissed the vision of national unity that typically animates the modern Court's discussions of state court jurisdiction.[108] And by drawing a negative inference from congressional silence, he overlooked the more conventional default position: state court jurisdiction is concurrent, unless Congress specifies that federal jurisdiction is exclusive.[109] Then again, Justice Field presumably meant to hold that state court authority in *Tarble's Case* was incompatible with the federal interests at stake.[110]

It is unclear whether *Ableman* and *Tarble's Case* reach far beyond their particular context.[111] The Court held in *Donovan v. City of*

---

104. 80 U.S. at 405-06.

105. Id. See Chapter II, note 56 and accompanying text (discussing the Judiciary Act of 1789's provision for federal court jurisdiction to receive habeas corpus petitions from federal prisoners).

106. The case was decided immediately following the Civil War, and the Court explicitly recognized that "in times of great popular excitement" opponents might use state courts to "embarrass the operations of the government." 80 U.S. at 408.

107. See Chapter II, notes 12-13 and accompanying text; Chapter IV, notes 8-9 and accompanying text; Chapter XII, note 18 and accompanying text (discussing the Suspension Clause).

108. See text accompanying notes 6-14, 38-46.

109. See notes 35-36 and accompanying text. Then, too, if Field meant to acknowledge that Congress might have conferred jurisdiction on the courts of Wisconsin, it is hard to understand how he could also propose that the Constitution of its own force barred that very jurisdiction.

110. See text accompanying notes 26, 33.

111. Professor Collins cites *Tarble's Case* as evidence that state courts were not always thought to have capacity to adjudicate all the cases to which Article III extends. Collins, note 8, at 103. Redish and Woods once argued that the tension between *Tarble's Case* and the Madisonian Compromise demonstrates that Congress has a constitutional duty to establish inferior federal courts, after all—to shoulder responsibility in cases in which state courts cannot act. Martin H. Redish & Curtis E. Woods, *Congressional Power to Control the Jurisdiction of Lower-Federal Courts: A Critical Review and a New Synthesis*, 124 U. Pa. L. Rev. 45 (1975). More recently, Professor Redish has advanced the view that Congress

Dallas[112] that a state court cannot enjoin a private litigant from filing a lawsuit in federal court. In that case, Justice Black (like Justice Field before him) relied both on an apparent constitutional ground and on congressional silence. He explained that Congress had "in no way relaxed the old and well-established judicially declared rule that state courts are completely without power to restrain federal-court proceedings."[113] The Court has refused to allow a state court to direct a writ of mandamus to a federal officer, but has permitted state courts to entertain other kinds of actions in which federal officers may be given orders with which they must comply.[114] The uncertainties that attend the decisions from *Ableman* and *Tarble's Case* through *Donovan* may explain why the Court has never squarely decided whether state courts can issue injunctions directing federal officers to take specified action.[115]

D. Protections for State Court Jurisdiction

In most instances, then, state courts have both the authority and the obligation to adjudicate federal questions, and when they conclude that a federal claim is meritorious, they typically can award the winning party an appropriate remedy. The exceptions to these generalizations are important, but they are nonetheless exceptions. In keeping with this pattern, state jurisdiction, once invoked, is largely insulated from interference by the federal courts. Litigants who choose to sue in state court in the first instance can typically expect that their cases will proceed to judgment there and that the decisions the state courts render will be effectively final: (1) the removal of lawsuits to federal court for trial is tightly guarded; (2) appellate review in federal court is limited to the Supreme Court; and (3) state judgments are usually entitled to preclusive effect in later federal court actions.

---

can divest state courts of jurisdiction, if the federal courts are open. Martin H. Redish, *Constitutional Limitations on Congressional Power to Control Federal Jurisdiction: A Reply to Professor Sager*, 77 Nw. U. L. Rev. 143, 159 (1982). Professor Amar insists that *Tarble's Case* cannot be understood to deny state court jurisdiction as a constitutional matter, but can only be read to mean that Congress can make jurisdiction in that kind of case exclusive in the federal courts. Amar laments, however, any sentiment that only federal courts are suitable to police the actions of federal officers. He proposes, instead, that state courts should routinely do so on the basis of their own independent jurisdiction under state law. Akhil R. Amar, *Of Sovereignty and Federalism*, 96 Yale L.J. 1425, 1428 & 1510 (1987). Professor Fallon and Professor Meltzer understand this line of cases to represent the Court's effort to develop a federal common law of remedies that orchestrates delicate relations between the federal government and the states. See Richard H. Fallon, Jr. & Daniel J. Meltzer, *New Law, Non-Retroactivity, and Constitutional Remedies*, 104 Harv. L. Rev. 1731 (1991); Daniel J. Meltzer, *State Court Forfeitures of Federal Rights*, 99 Harv. L. Rev. 1128 (1986).

112. 377 U.S. 408 (1964).

113. Id. at 413; see Chapter XI, notes 8-30, 130-273 and accompanying text (discussing *federal* court injunctions that interfere with *state* court proceedings).

114. E.g., *Slocum v. Mayberry*, 15 U.S. (2 Wheat.) 1 (1817) (holding that a state court could issue a writ of replevin requiring federal customs officials to return property they had seized). See Arnold, note 99, at 1397 (expressing confidence that state courts can award specific relief in cases involving the possession of property).

115. Cf. *Brooks v. Dewar*, 313 U.S. 354, 360 (1941) (declining to decide the question).

1. Limited Removal

A few federal statutes authorize suits that begin in state court to be "removed" to federal court. Historically, some statutes authorized either the plaintiff or the defendant to seek removal, even after judgment in state court.[116] The statutes in place today permit only the defendant to seek removal, and then only before trial.[117] Removal is available in diversity cases, but typically bears more theoretical significance in federal question cases—where its limited scope underscores the general understanding that state court adjudication of federal claims will usually proceed undisturbed.[118]

Federal removal jurisdiction is a cousin of federal exclusive jurisdiction. The difference is that when federal jurisdiction is exclusive, Congress forecloses litigation in state court altogether and gives litigants no say in the matter. In the case of removal, state courts have jurisdiction in the first instance, but the defendant can force them to surrender that jurisdiction to federal courts. The rationale for removal jurisdiction is sometimes quite clear, sometimes obscure. Removal is ostensibly permitted when state proceedings threaten federal interests enough to warrant an exception to the usual pattern, but not enough to warrant a blanket prohibition on state court adjudication.

Removal in ordinary civil cases. The principal modern removal statute, 28 U.S.C. § 1441, is derived from the Judiciary Act of 1875 and important amendments adopted in 1887.[119] It authorizes a defendant in a civil lawsuit initiated in state court to transfer the case to a federal district court, but only if the federal court would have had jurisdiction to entertain the case if the plaintiff had chosen to go there originally.[120] This means that in federal question cases the plaintiff's claim, initially advanced in state court, must "arise under" federal law within the meaning of 28 U.S.C. § 1331, which governs the federal district courts' original jurisdiction in federal question cases.[121]

One might have expected § 1441 to allow removal at the defendant's behest if the *defendant* offers a federal theory in response to the plaintiff's allegations. A

---

116. See Michael G. Collins, *The Unhappy History of Federal Question Removal*, 71 Iowa L. Rev. 717, 720 (1986).

117. The Court held in *Shamrock Oil & Gas Corp. v. Sheets*, 313 U.S. 100 (1941), that a plaintiff cannot remove on the basis of a defendant's counterclaim.

118. Under 28 U.S.C. § 1441(c), if a "separate and independent" federal claim over which a federal court would have jurisdiction is joined in state court with a claim that would not be removable, the "entire case" can be removed. For a discussion of that provision and its controversial history, see Edward A. Hartnett, *A New Trick from an Old and Abused Dog: Section 1441(c) Lives and Now Permits the Remand of Federal Question Cases*, 63 Fordham L. Rev. 1099 (1995). The procedures for removal are prescribed by 28 U.S.C. §§ 1446-48.

119. See Chapter II, note 57 and text accompanying note 71. Professor Collins has explored the 1887 legislation. Collins, note 116, at 735.

120. Federal jurisdiction pursuant to § 1441 is constitutionally valid. The presence of the plaintiff's federal claim renders a removable lawsuit a case "arising under" federal law within the meaning of Article III. See Chapter VIII, notes 5-31 and accompanying text.

121. See Chapter VIII, notes 166-210 and accompanying text (discussing the prerequisites for original § 1331 jurisdiction); Chapter XI, text accompanying note 153 (discussing the relationship between this feature of removal under § 1441 and the federal-question abstention doctrine).

rule of that kind would ensure that litigants with affirmative federal claims can gain access to federal court. It would initially allow a plaintiff who has a federal claim the option of suing either in state or federal court, but would allow a defendant who has a federal defense or counterclaim to override the plaintiff's choice of the state forum. Instead, § 1441 makes a defendant's ability to trump the plaintiff's decision to sue in state court contingent on the nature of the *plaintiff's* claim.[122] It thus vindicates a defendant's desire to be in federal court in hopes of *defeating* a federal theory advanced by the plaintiff, but forces a defendant who has a federal theory to raise as a defense to submit that theory to the state courts.[123] The practical implication of pegging removal to the plaintiff's claim is clear. Litigants typically must advance any federal theories they wish to present in federal court as original actions filed in a district court pursuant to § 1331. If they wait to advance federal theories as defendants in state court, § 1441 will be unavailing.[124]

Removal by federal officers. Another statute, 28 U.S.C. § 1442, allows removal of either civil or criminal actions initiated in state court against the federal government itself or one of its agencies or officers. That removal provision dates from 1815.[125] It plainly reflects concern that federal interests might be compromised if federal officials were forced to defend themselves against claims and charges in state court. In *Tennessee v. Davis*,[126] a federal revenue officer was in-

---

122. The link between removal jurisdiction under § 1441 and original jurisdiction under § 1331 leads to a familiar curiosity in the law of federal courts: Questions regarding the original jurisdiction of federal district courts pursuant to § 1331 are often raised not in cases in which plaintiffs genuinely seek access to federal court, but in which they, instead, choose to proceed in state court, and *defendants* wish to transfer the litigation to the federal forum. See Chapter VIII, text accompanying notes 172-73 (explaining that the removal posture in which cases are presented can complicate the elaboration of § 1331). Moreover, in some instances, plaintiffs characterize their claims as matters of state law, and defendants attempt to recharacterize those claims as federal in nature in order to obtain removal under § 1441. On the whole, litigants are masters of the theories they wish to advance. See Chapter VIII, note 181 and accompanying text (noting the Court's classic precedents in point). Yet there are limits. Some complaints *necessarily* press federal claims, because federal law preempts any state law that would otherwise control. Where that is true, defendants may remove, even if plaintiffs themselves regard their claims as matters of state law. See Chapter VIII, notes 274-87 and accompanying text.

123. Professor Wechsler explained that § 1441 permits a litigant to invoke federal jurisdiction as a "sword," but not as a "shield." Herbert Wechsler, *Federal Jurisdiction and the Revision of the Judicial Code*, 13 Law & Contemp. Prob. 216, 234 (1948).

124. The idea may be to prevent defendants from injecting minor federal issues into cases in order to obtain removal, thus transferring lawsuits to federal court even when state issues predominate. Nevertheless, this feature of § 1441 has often been criticized. E.g., Herman L. Trautman, *Federal Right Jurisdiction and the Declaratory Remedy*, 7 Vand. L. Rev. 445, 471 (1954); Wechsler, note 123, at 224. The American Law Institute has recommended that removal be made available in most instances on the basis of a *dispositive* federal defense or counterclaim. ALI, Study of the Division of Jurisdiction Between State and Federal Courts 25 (1969). Meanwhile, the precedents relentlessly deny removal in the most compelling circumstances. In *Lear v. Adkins*, 395 U.S. 653 (1969), the Court held that a federal issue that ordinarily would be within the exclusive jurisdiction of the federal courts had to be determined in state court because it first appeared as a defense to a state court action.

125. Today, tort claims in state court against federal officers operating in the course of their official duties are handled under 28 U.S.C. § 2679, which substitutes the United States as the formal defendant and *requires* removal to federal court.

126. 100 U.S. (10 Otto) 257 (1879).

dicted for murder after a shoot-out with moonshiners in the hills of Tennessee. The Supreme Court sustained the officer's ability to remove the case to federal court.[127]

The constitutional basis of removal under § 1442 has excited theoretical interest. If the officer concerned raises an explicit federal defense, there is no difficulty. That defense supplies a federal issue on which the federal court can exercise Article III power, once the prosecution (itself anchored in state law) is removed to the federal forum. If the officer advances only a state law defense, the case is altered. In that event, the federal court's constitutional authority to adjudicate only state law issues is open to question. By some accounts, the district court can exercise "protective jurisdiction." The idea is that Congress might have enacted a body of federal substantive law to govern all aspects of a federal officer's field of operations, displacing state law and transforming all issues into federal questions. That would be extreme, however, and unwarranted as a matter of policy. Accordingly, Congress should be entitled to take the modest step of protecting federal interests by placing any disputes that arise in federal court, even though the only issues to be decided are matters of state law.[128]

The protective jurisdiction idea has considerable appeal. In *Davis*, for example, federal interests were at risk if local authorities pursued a federal revenue officer with questionable criminal charges, irrespective of the precise defense the officer raised. Local hostility to federal policies of all kinds might play itself out in a pattern of harassing state court lawsuits instituted to frustrate federal officers' enforcement efforts. Nevertheless, protective jurisdiction theory has been questioned. It reflects the "greater power" syllogism, and to that extent it is analytically troubling.[129] Moreover, it invites expansive application and ultimately threatens the body of case law regarding the prerequisites for federal question jurisdiction in the federal courts.[130] In *Mesa v. California*,[131] the Supreme Court disposed of the protective jurisdiction idea in this context by reading § 1442 to authorize removal only when a federal officer actually asserts a "colorable" federal defense.[132]

---

127. The Court rejected the contention that removal invaded state sovereignty. In this context, of course, there is no argument that Congress has "commandeered" the state courts. See notes 81-84 and accompanying text. Instead, Congress has made federal jurisdiction available for enforcing state law, albeit in circumstances in which state authorities follow the usual pattern of proceeding initially in state court.

128. See Wechsler, note 123, at 224-25; Carole Goldberg-Ambrose, *The Protective Jurisdiction of the Federal Courts*, 30 UCLA L. Rev. 542 (1983). Professor Mishkin advances the more cautious argument that protective jurisdiction can safely be acknowledged, but only if Congress gives the federal courts jurisdiction to consider state law claims in a field in which Congress has previously deployed a "developed" and "active" federal regulatory policy. Paul J. Mishkin, *The Federal "Question" in the District Courts*, 53 Colum. L. Rev. 157, 195 (1953). Professor Cross defends federal bankruptcy jurisdiction over state law claims as a species of protective jurisdiction. John T. Cross, *Congressional Power to Extend Federal Jurisdiction to Disputes Outside Article III: A Critical Analysis From the Perspective of Bankruptcy*, 87 Nw. U. L. Rev. 1188 (1993); see Chapter V, note 51. For another discussion of protective jurisdiction, see Chapter VIII, notes 20-24 and accompanying text.

129. See Chapter I, notes 21-22 and accompanying text.

130. See Chapter VIII, notes 166-210 and accompanying text (describing the relevant precedents).

131. 489 U.S. 121 (1989).

132. Id. at 139. On examination, Justice O'Connor said that the defense in *Davis* (self-defense) was essentially federal in nature inasmuch as the officer contended that he had a

Civil rights removal. One final statute, 28 U.S.C. § 1443(1), permits private litigants to remove if they are "denied or cannot enforce" a "right under any law providing for the equal civil rights of citizens of the United States."[133] That provision was originally enacted during Reconstruction, but saw little use or attention until the civil rights movement in this century.[134] In the 1960s, civil rights workers routinely invoked § 1443(1) to extricate themselves from state prosecutions arising from their participation in protest demonstrations. They insisted (with some justice) that they were being harassed for activities that were protected by the Constitution and federal civil rights laws and that state courts would not respect their federal defenses. Accordingly, they were entitled to remove the actions against them to federal court in order that the federal courts could enforce their federal rights.[135] Ultimately, the Supreme Court construed § 1443(1) so narrowly that removal under that statute became virtually impossible.

In *Georgia v. Rachel*,[136] Justice Stewart explained that it is not enough for a defendant in state court to show, on the basis of evidence in a particular case, that federal rights will not be respected in state court. Removal is available under § 1443(1) only if some state "law of general application" demonstrates that "specific" federal rights "stated in terms of racial equality" will be denied if the state prosecution is allowed to proceed.[137] In the typical case, a defendant must show that a particular federal anti-discrimination rule will not be respected in state court, because the state courts will follow a state statute or demonstrable state policy that frustrates that rule. Stewart found it insufficient that the civil rights workers in *Rachel* alleged that the state courts would not enforce their federal rights to free speech and due process. Those rights were implicated in *Rachel*, but they were not "stated in terms of racial equality" within the meaning of § 1443(1).[138] Nor did it appear that a state statute or policy would prevent the state courts from giving those rights their proper scope.

---

federal duty to respond to hostile gunfire while he was investigating an unlawful distillery. O'Connor invoked the prudential rule that statutes should be construed to avoid constitutional questions whenever possible, see Chapter I, note 21, and said that the protective jurisdiction theory *would* raise a "grave constitutional problem." Id. at 137.

133. Subsection (2) of § 1443 allows removal if defendants are prosecuted for "any act under color of authority derived from any law providing for equal rights, or for refusing to do any act on the ground that it would be inconsistent with such law." That provision is available only to federal or state officers, or private citizens acting in concert with them. *City of Greenwood v. Peacock*, 384 U.S. 808 (1966). Accordingly, it overlaps significantly with § 1442. See notes 125-32 and accompanying text.

134. See Robert D. Goldstein, *Blyew: Variations on a Jurisdictional Theme*, 41 Stan. L. Rev. 469 (1989).

135. Professor Amsterdam devised the strategy of using § 1443 in the cause of the civil rights movement. See Anthony G. Amsterdam, *Criminal Prosecutions Affecting Federally Guaranteed Rights: Federal Removal and Habeas Corpus Jurisdiction to Abort State Court Trial*, 113 U. Pa. L. Rev. 793 (1965).

136. 384 U.S. 780 (1966).

137. Id. at 800.

138. Justice Stewart did not say, nor has the Court since decided, whether the Equal Protection Clause provides a sufficiently "specific" federal anti-discrimination rule for purposes of § 1443(1). The Court has held that 18 U.S.C. § 245 does not support removal under § 1443(1). *Johnson v. Mississippi*, 421 U.S. 213 (1975). That statute bars interference with federal rights, but only "by force or threat of violence." Thus it does not immunize defendants from prosecution in state court.

Justice Stewart insisted that his interpretation of § 1443(1) would not deprive it of all meaning and that some defendants would be able to meet the admittedly stringent standards that *Rachel* put in place. To illustrate, he cited *Strauder v. West Virginia*,[139] where the Court had allowed removal to protect a criminal defendant's right to a jury chosen without discrimination on the basis of race, guaranteed by the Civil Rights Act of 1866. In that case, a West Virginia statute flatly barred African Americans from serving on juries. In *Virginia v. Rives*,[140] by contrast, the Court had denied removal where, in the absence of a similar statute, defendants could allege only that the authorities in Virginia would, in fact, select a jury in a discriminatory way. According to Justice Stewart, the difference between *Strauder* and *Rives* is crucial to removal under § 1443(1). In the one case, a state statute required the state courts to conduct a trial in violation of a federal right "stated in terms of racial equality." In the other, state law did not mandate disrespect for federal rights of that kind.

There was a plausible argument that *Rachel* itself was attracted by *Strauder* rather than *Rives*. The defendants in *Rachel* contended that the Civil Rights Act of 1964 established their right to use places of public accommodation and thus qualified as a federal anti-discrimination rule. Moreover, they were charged under a state statute making it a criminal offense to refuse to leave a restaurant on request. By their account, that statute authorized criminal prosecution for the mere exercise of rights protected by the 1964 Act. Accordingly, they were entitled to removal even under Stewart's grudging construction of § 1443(1). Stewart acknowledged that argument and remanded the case for a hearing on whether the defendants had been asked to leave "solely for racial reasons" and therefore could argue that the very initiation of state criminal proceedings violated the 1964 Act.

In a companion case, however, Justice Stewart made it clear that § 1443(1) will not allow removal in more routine cases. The civil rights workers in *City of Greenwood v. Peacock*[141] were charged with a range of state offenses, including obstructing public streets and driving without a valid operator's permit. Neither the 1964 Act nor the Equal Protection Clause insulated them from prosecution for those offenses. They were able to contend only that they were being harassed by local authorities because of their political activities and that they were likely to be convicted after a racially charged trial. Given *Rachel*, that was insufficient.

The distinction Justice Stewart drew between *Strauder* and *Rives* and, in turn, between *Rachel* and *Peacock* is problematic. The rationale is that state courts cannot be expected to defy a state statute of general application, but *can* be expected to prevent state officials from violating federal rights *ad hoc*. Yet if a state statute conflicts with federal law, the state courts may be *more* likely (not less) to recognize and enforce defendants' federal rights. Accordingly, there may be *less* (not more) reason to allow removal. If, then, the idea is to avoid disparaging state courts' ability and inclination to respect federal rights, the Court's construction of § 1443(1) is counterproductive. An alternative rationale may be more convincing. The facial validity of a statute is a legal matter that can be determined without exploring case-specific factual allegations. Accordingly, removal in that instance can

139. 100 U.S. 303 (1879).
140. 100 U.S. 313 (1879).
141. 384 U.S. 808 (1966).

be accomplished quickly and efficiently. If that is the idea, however, the Court's remand in *Rachel* is puzzling. The state statute in that case was not unconstitutional on its face, but was susceptible to unconstitutional application if invoked against customers asked to leave the premises only because of race.

The Court might have brought the process model to bear in *Rachel* and *Peacock*.[142] The Court might have read § 1443(1) to deny removal in routine cases in which defendants insist that they will be treated unfairly in state court, but to allow removal in extraordinary cases in which defendants demonstrate that state court proceedings will not provide an opportunity for "full and fair" adjudication of a federal defense.[143] It is hardly surprising that the Court declined to adopt that approach. The civil rights workers in *Rachel* and *Peacock* presented a sympathetic case for removal. Yet their arguments for wider removal authority could not easily be limited to the civil rights context and threatened to reach ordinary criminal prosecutions in which defendants assert that state courts will not properly adjudicate federal defenses.[144] The states have a powerful interest in vindicating local criminal law policy in their own courts. It would be disruptive to require state authorities to respond to allegations that state processes are flawed. Certainly, it would be revolutionary to allow defendants actually to remove ordinary prosecutions to federal court for trial.[145]

Justice Stewart explained in *Peacock* that state criminal defendants may have recourse to federal district courts by other means. In some circumstances, defendants may file suit in a federal district court pursuant to the Ku Klux Klan Act (28 U.S.C. § 1983), seeking an injunction against a state prosecution.[146] And, under some conditions, defendants who are in some form of custody may be entitled to petition a federal court for a writ of habeas corpus.[147] Those alternatives threaten the states' ability to enforce local policy in state court in much the same manner as would removal. Yet they, too, are restricted in ways that mitigate the effect on state court jurisdiction. In some respects, the process model *does* help

---

142. See Chapter I, notes 61-65 and accompanying text.

143. Martin H. Redish, *Revitalizing Civil Rights Removal Jurisdiction*, 64 Minn. L. Rev. 523 (1980).

144. Recall in this vein that defendants may often have fourteenth amendment defenses to advance, at least with respect to state court procedures. Justice Stewart was acutely aware of the risk that a more generous interpretation of § 1443(1) might open the floodgates. He noted in a footnote that the rate of removal petitions under that statute had risen dramatically in recent years — particularly in the South (where Professor Amsterdam's strategy was pursued routinely on behalf of civil rights workers). 384 U.S. at 788 n.8.

145. The Court's attention to federalism, not to mention the federal caseload crisis, counsels against such a significant departure. See Chapter I, notes 16-20 and accompanying text (discussing federalism); Chapter II, notes 82-106 and accompanying text (discussing docket congestion in the federal courts). See also Chapter XI, text accompanying note 154 (discussing the intellectual relationship between removal in criminal cases and the federal-question abstention doctrine). Alternatively, the Court might have read § 1443(1) to authorize removal for want of exacting language to the contrary. See Chapter I, notes 37-41 and accompanying text. Yet when the doctrine of clear statement appears in this context, it typically cuts in favor of state court jurisdiction. E.g., notes 35-36 and accompanying text.

146. See text accompanying note 49; Chapter II, notes 73-74 and accompanying text (noting the history behind § 1983 and the many places in modern practice in which § 1983 plays a role).

147. See Chapter XII, notes 64-71, 78-80 and accompanying text.

to explain the doctrines that attend § 1983 actions and habeas corpus petitions.[148]

In the end, the Court's general acceptance of state court authority and responsibility for federal question litigation explains why removal is not routinely available. Once it is posited (as it conventionally is) that state courts are routinely open for federal question cases, and it is assumed (as it usually is) that those courts are the equal of federal courts for these purposes, then it is unremarkable that defendants in state court should typically be unable to remove litigation to federal court. Removal jurisdiction by its nature connotes some concern that state court proceedings will put federal interests at risk. If the Court perceives no such risks, it will find no justification for reading an ambiguous statute to upset conventional arrangements.

2. Limited Appellate Review

Since removal is usually unavailable, federal question cases begun in state court typically proceed to judgment there. Litigants who are denied relief on federal claims may be able to seek appellate review in the Supreme Court.[149] But no inferior federal court has appellate jurisdiction to review state court decisions for error. In the cases confirming this understanding, *Rooker v. Fidelity Trust Co.*[150] and *District of Columbia Court of Appeals v. Feldman*,[151] two mutually enforcing theories are at work. First, the absence of inferior federal court appellate jurisdiction is in keeping with the co-equal status of state courts and lower federal courts within the constitutional framework. Neither set of courts is responsible to the other for its decisions. Both are answerable only to the Supreme Court, which sits astride the judicial system as the final unifying referee regarding questions of federal law. Second, if the Constitution would tolerate another arrangement, Congress has foreclosed it by conferring appellate jurisdiction only on the Supreme Court and denying any such jurisdiction to inferior federal courts by implication.[152] Either way, the *Rooker/Feldman* doctrine reinforces the understanding that state courts routinely adjudicate federal question cases without interference from their federal counterparts.

To implement *Rooker/Feldman*, courts must determine whether a previous proceeding in state court was sufficiently judicial in nature to warrant the conclusion that a subsequent suit in federal court is an attempt to invoke an appellate jurisdiction that the federal courts do not possess. On this count, the *Rooker* case was simple. The plaintiff there initially sought appellate review of a state court

---

148. See Chapter XI, notes 164-89 and accompanying text (discussing the role the process model plays in conditioning federal injunctions against pending state court proceedings); Chapter XII, notes 9, 72-95, 150-55 and accompanying text (discussing the process model and the exhaustion doctrine in connection with the availability of federal habeas corpus)

149. See Chapter VII.

150. 263 U.S. 413 (1923).

151. 460 U.S. 462 (1983).

152. The difference between the two theories is that the latter would admit congressional power to give the inferior federal courts appellate jurisdiction to review state court decisions. Hamilton thought Congress might do that, but he discouraged the prospect. See Chapter II, note 52.

judgment in the Supreme Court. When the Court found no basis for exercising its appellate power, the plaintiff filed suit in a federal district court, seeking a declaration that the state judgment was null and void. That action had every appearance of a request that the federal district court exercise appellate jurisdiction. It is scarcely surprising that when the case returned to the Supreme Court, Justice Van Devanter seized the occasion to make it clear that the jurisdiction of the district courts is "strictly original."[153]

The *Feldman* case was more complicated. The plaintiffs in that case asked the District of Columbia Court of Appeals (the local court for the District) to waive its rule that only graduates of accredited law schools could become members of the District bar. When that court refused, they filed suit in a federal district court, attacking the bar admission rule and its application to them on constitutional grounds. In the Supreme Court, Justice Brennan held (by analogy to *Rooker*) that the district court had no jurisdiction to review the local court's refusal to waive the rule in the plaintiffs' cases. He ruled, however, that the district court *did* have jurisdiction to entertain an original action challenging the validity of the rule on its face. The local court's handling of the plaintiffs' individual cases was a judicial act, any errors in which could be corrected on appeal only in the Supreme Court. But the bar admission rule itself was a legislative enactment, subject to attack in the ordinary course.

As *Feldman* itself demonstrates, not every action taken by courts is judicial in character for *Rooker/Feldman* purposes. State courts sometimes perform legislative and executive duties, and when they act in those different capacities disappointed parties can file original lawsuits attacking the product of their actions in federal court. In *Prentis v. Atlantic Coast Line Co.*,[154] for example, the Virginia Supreme Court exercised final legislative authority over railroad freight rates. Accordingly, Justice Holmes explained that if a railroad challenged the rates that court established in a lawsuit filed in a federal district court, the railroad would not be asking the district court to exercise an appellate jurisdiction it did not possess.[155]

3. Preclusion

Just as disappointed litigants cannot appeal state court judgments directly to the inferior federal courts, they usually cannot attack state judgments indirectly by filing additional original lawsuits in federal court that attempt, in effect, to revisit issues the state courts treated (or might have treated) previously. In subsequent lawsuits of that kind, the Full Faith and Credit Statute, 28 U.S.C. § 1738, instructs the federal courts to give previous state court judgments the preclusive effect that state law would accord them.[156]

---

153. 263 U.S. at 416.

154. 211 U.S. 210 (1908).

155. See Chapter XI, notes 40-44 (discussing other aspects of *Prentis*).

156. The Full Faith and Credit Clause, U.S. Const. art. IV, § 1, provides: "Full Faith and Credit shall be given in each State to the public Acts, Records, and judicial Proceedings of every other State." It also empowers Congress to "prescribe" the manner in which such judgments are proved "and the Effect thereof." Pursuant to that authority, Congress enacted § 1738 in 1790 as one of its first statutes touching the federal courts. Modern amendments

In effect, § 1738 incorporates state preclusion law for application in federal court. That local law can vary in its details from state to state, but typically respects central propositions. In the main, a final judgment cannot be reopened in subsequent litigation between the same parties or their privies. Along one branch of conventional doctrine, denominated "collateral estoppel" or "issue preclusion," issues of fact (or the application of law to fact) that were actually determined in an initial action may not be relitigated. Along a second branch, denominated "res judicata" or "claim preclusion," issues of fact (or the application of law to fact) that might have been (but were not) raised and determined in initial proceedings cannot be revived in a later action.[157] Of the two kinds of preclusion, claim preclusion is plainly the more powerful. Where it operates, a question may receive no judicial attention at all.[158]

Within a single jurisdiction, preclusion makes a great deal of sense. It protects the parties' reliance interests and conserves judicial resources. Any attendant unfairness can be handled by recognizing appropriate exceptions. Typically, an initial judgment is entitled to preclusive effect only if the party affected is accorded an opportunity for "full and fair" adjudication.[159] In this, state preclusion law reflects the process model, albeit in a different context and for a different purpose.[160] Across jurisdictional lines, however, the unexamined application of a particular state's preclusion doctrine can be questioned. The Full Faith and Credit Statute employs state preclusion law to adjust the relations between state and federal courts. In issue preclusion cases, it fortifies state court decisions regarding federal questions by foreclosing relitigation in federal court. In claim preclusion cases, it allows state courts to foreclose the adjudication of federal questions in any forum.

The Supreme Court has not always made it clear that § 1738 (and thus state preclusion law) controls cases in which federal courts are asked to reopen previous state court judgments. In *Allen v. McCurry*,[161] Justice Stewart suggested that a general body of preclusion law might be in play. More recently, however, the Court has insisted that state preclusion law is the first, and typically the last, authority to be consulted. In *Marrese v. Amer. Academy of Orth. Surgeons*,[162] for

---

to § 1738 specify the full faith and credit that a state owes to child support orders entered in a sister state (a good deal) and to marriages between "persons of the same sex" (none). The Full Faith and Credit Statute does not address the preclusive effects of *federal* court judgments. If a judgment by a federal court is challenged subsequently either in another federal court or in a state court, the follow-on court will give the previous judgment preclusive effect, relying on federal common law both for the initial proposition that the previous judgment is entitled to preclusive effect and for the content of the preclusion rules to be applied. E.g., *Federated Dep't Stores v. Moitie*, 452 U.S. 394 (1981); *Blonder-Tongue Laboratories v. University of Illinois Foundation*, 402 U.S. 313 (1971). For a discussion, see Stephen B. Burbank, *Interjurisdictional Preclusion, Full Faith and Credit and Federal Common Law: A General Approach*, 71 Cornell L. Rev. 733 (1986).

157. Issues of law in the pure sense are typically exempted from preclusion. Yet there is often little difference between the determination of a legal standard in the abstract and the application of that standard in a particular case. As a practical matter, then, legal determinations are not easily reopened in later litigation.

158. By hypothesis, the first court to consider the parties' dispute did not address the question, and the second court deliberately declines to consider it.

159. See *Richards v. Jefferson County*, 517 U.S. 793, 801 (1996).

160. See Chapter I, notes 61-65 and accompanying text.

161. 449 U.S. 90 (1980).

162. 470 U.S. 373 (1985).

example, a physician initially sued in state court, contending that the Academy's refusal to admit him to membership violated state law. When that lawsuit failed, he filed a new action in federal court, contending that the Academy had violated federal anti-trust laws. The state courts would have had no authority to consider the anti-trust claim if it had been advanced in the first suit. Accordingly, it was unlikely that state preclusion law would have anything to say about the effects of failing to press such a claim. Nevertheless, Justice O'Connor explained that § 1738 required the federal court to "look first to state preclusion law" in hopes that its treatment of analogous issues should throw some light on the problem.[163]

Other federal statutes can trump § 1738 and thus allow federal courts to entertain new federal actions, despite previous state court judgments. The statute conferring jurisdiction on federal courts to hear habeas corpus petitions, 28 U.S.C. § 2241, has that effect.[164] But neither the Ku Klux Klan Act (§ 1983), nor Title VII of the Civil Rights Act of 1964, exempts lawsuits filed under their authority from § 1738 and state preclusion rules.[165] In *McCurry*, a prisoner was charged with a criminal offense in state court. He moved to suppress evidence allegedly obtained by an unconstitutional search. The state courts denied the motion, and the prisoner was convicted. Ordinarily, a prisoner in custody pursuant to a state criminal conviction would have been able to petition a federal district court for a writ of habeas corpus and to revisit his federal claim in that posture.

---

163. If state preclusion law turns out to be silent on the matter, a federal court presumably must look elsewhere. Justice O'Connor suggested in *Marrese* that if the policies furthered by the federal courts' exclusive jurisdiction of a class of claims warrants it, courts may read the statutes conferring that exclusive jurisdiction to constitute an "implied repeal" of § 1738. 470 U.S. at 381. Suspending preclusion might be sensible in many contexts, but not necessarily in all. Typically, a litigant who possesses a claim over which the federal courts have exclusive jurisdiction is in a position to file a federal court suit advancing that claim in the first instance, invoking the federal court's supplemental jurisdiction of related state law claims. See Chapter VIII, notes 288-301 and accompanying text. If, then, a litigant goes first to state court, it is not always unjust to preclude resort to federal court later (and thus to foreclose the federal claim altogether). In *Matsushita Elec. Indus. Co. v. Epstein*, 516 U.S. 367 (1996), a state court approved a settlement in a class action case, which appeared to preclude members of the class from pressing federal claims against the defendant in independent litigation—including federal claims that were within the exclusive jurisdiction of the federal courts. The Supreme Court held that the preclusive effects of the state court's ruling must be determined according to the preclusion rules the state would apply to the settlement. For commentary, see Marcel Kahan & Linda Silberman, *Matsushita and Beyond: The Role of State Courts in Class Actions Involving Exclusive Federal Claims*, 1996 Sup. Ct. Rev. 219.

164. *Kremer v. Chem. Constr. Corp.*, 456 U.S. 461, 485 n.27 (1982); see Chapter XII, note 4 and accompanying text.

165. *McCurry*, 449 U.S. at 104-05 (§ 1983); *Kremer v. Chem. Constr. Co.*, 456 U.S. 461 (1982) (Title VII). In *Kremer*, a worker filed an employment discrimination claim with the appropriate state agency and, when his claim was rejected, a lawsuit in state court. When the state courts, too, denied relief, he filed a Title VII action in federal court, arguing that Title VII entitled him to *de novo* federal court consideration of his claim, despite the previous state court judgment. Justice White refused to read Title VII to "repeal" § 1738 by implication and thus instructed the district court below to consult state preclusion law. The worker would have been entitled to federal court adjudication if he had gone to federal court rather than state court to attack the state agency's unfavorable decision. When he chose the state forum at that juncture, however, he committed his claim to the state courts and could reopen the state court judgment against him in federal court only if state preclusion law would permit him to do so.

In *McCurry*, however, habeas corpus was not available.[166] Accordingly, the prisoner attempted to take his fourth amendment claim to federal court by means of a § 1983 action against the offending police officers, contending that § 1983 actions were exempt from § 1738. Justice Stewart rejected that argument on the basis of a clear statement rule: "Repeals by implication are disfavored."[167] In the absence of greater clarity in the text of § 1983 itself or its history, Stewart would not conclude that Congress "intended" § 1983 "to overrule § 1738 or the common-law rules of collateral estoppel and res judicata."[168]

The Court held in *Migra v. Warren City School Dist.*[169] that § 1738 also makes at least one kind of state claim preclusion available in § 1983 actions. A public school principal initially sued school officials in an Ohio state court, contending that she had been discharged in violation of state law. After obtaining a favorable judgment and compensatory damages from the state courts, she filed a § 1983 suit in federal court, contending that her dismissal also violated the first and fourteenth amendments and that, on that basis, she was entitled to punitive damages. She maintained that the prior state judgment did not preclude her from litigating federal claims that might have been raised and considered in state court, but in fact had been omitted from the earlier suit.[170] Justice Blackmun responded, however, that *Migra* was controlled by *McCurry*. He saw no reason to distinguish claim preclusion from issue preclusion and thus held that, pursuant to § 1738, the plaintiff's § 1983 action was subject to both kinds of state preclusion rules.[171]

The plaintiff in *Migra* was in a weak position. She herself had chosen to go to state court in the first instance, and she herself was responsible for failing to press her federal claims at that time and, instead, waiting to do so in a subsequent lawsuit in federal court. Justice Blackmun declined to say whether the Court's result would have been different if the party seeking to avoid claim preclusion in federal court had been an unwilling defendant in state court — pressed to appear in state court and unable to escape before final judgment.[172] Still, it is hard to think that Blackmun would have reached a different result in that kind of case. Recall that the reason defendants are unable to escape state court is that removal is typically unavailable on the basis of a federal defense or counterclaim. The point of § 1441 must be that defendants are expected to submit any federal theories they have to the state courts. That arrangement would

---

166. The Court had previously held that federal district courts ordinarily should not enforce the fourth amendment exclusionary rule in federal habeas corpus proceedings. *Stone v. Powell*, 428 U.S. 465 (1976); see Chapter XII, notes 150-55 and accompanying text.

167. See Chapter I, notes 37-41 (discussing the doctrine of clear statement).

168. 449 U.S. at 99. Justice Stewart distinguished *Mitchum v. Foster*, 407 U.S. 225 (1972) (holding that § 1983 *is* an express statutory exception to the Anti-Injunction Act). See Chapter XI, notes 17-20 (discussing *Mitchum*).

169. 465 U.S. 75 (1984).

170. The plaintiff in *Migra* did not argue that the Ohio courts would have declined to consider her federal claims if she had included them with her state claims in the previous lawsuit in state court. Nor did she deny that she might have sued originally in federal court rather than state court.

171. 465 U.S. at 82. There *is* a reason to distinguish claim preclusion from issue preclusion as a matter of policy, the one idea being so much more powerful than the other. Yet Justice Blackmun found nothing in § 1983 that draws that distinction.

172. Id. at 83. Blackmun had dissented in *McCurry* in part on the ground that the prisoner in that case had been an unwilling defendant in the previous state action. Id. at 85 n.7

be defeated if defendants were able to withhold federal defenses from state proceedings and reserve them for subsequent litigation in federal court.[173]

The decisions in *McCurry* and *Migra* establish only that § 1738 requires federal district courts to invoke state preclusion law. In any particular case, however, questions can arise about "how" that law applies and whether "any exceptions or qualifications" nonetheless defeat a preclusion argument.[174] Justice
Stewart explained in *McCurry*, moreover, that one exception *must* be recognized:
Preclusion rules "cannot apply when the party against whom the earlier decision
is asserted did not have a 'full and fair opportunity' to litigate that issue in the
earlier case."[175] That idea reflects the process model in a more familiar role—
namely, as a means of respecting state court adjudication in the main, but making federal courts available when the processes of adjudication in state court
break down and the outcomes reached in state court are, for that reason, unreliable.[176] Nevertheless, the Court's basis for introducing the process model here is
unclear.

There are three apparent possibilities. First, the requirement that a litigant
must have a fair opportunity to litigate a claim in state court may be a feature of
state preclusion law. If that is the answer, then by noting that requirement explicitly, Justice Stewart did not invoke a federal limitation on preclusion in § 1738
cases, but only predicted what state law is likely to entail. Second, the requirement of full and fair process in state court may mean only that state courts must
accord litigants the process that is "due" in the constitutional sense. In *Kremer v.
Chem. Constr. Corp.*,[177] Justice White said that, where the Court is "bound by
the statutory directive of § 1738, state proceedings need do no more than satisfy
the minimum procedural requirements of the Fourteenth Amendment's Due
Process Clause in order to qualify for the full faith and credit guaranteed by federal law."[178] Third, if *Kremer* does not conclude the matter, the requirement of

---

173. Professor Atwood generally defends preclusion in these circumstances. But she argues that federal courts should not be precluded from considering issues and claims in circumstances in which subsequent federal litigation does not attempt to nullify previous state
court action. In cases of that kind, according to Atwood, a litigant should be able to withhold a claim from state court proceedings and assert it later as an affirmative claim in federal court. Barbara A. Atwood, *State Court Judgments in Federal Litigation: Mapping the
Contours of Full Faith and Credit*, 58 Ind. L.J. 59, 62-63, 88-90, 98-100 (1982). The Court
embraced something of that view in *Haring v. Prosise*, 462 U.S. 306 (1983), when it held
that a litigant's previous plea of guilty to a state criminal charge did not prevent him from
suing the police in federal court for conducting an unlawful search to obtain evidence
against him. Professor Shapiro has endorsed *Haring*. See David L. Shapiro, *Should a Guilty
Plea Have Preclusive Effect?*, 70 Iowa L. Rev. 27 (1984). But see *Tower v. Glover*, 467 U.S.
914, 923 (1984) (suggesting that a prisoner who expressly raised the same claims in previous state proceedings may be precluded from pressing them again in a federal § 1983 action).

174. *McCurry*, 449 U.S. at 105 n.25, 95 n.7.

175. Id. at 95, quoting *Montana v. United States*, 440 U.S. 147, 153 (1979). Inasmuch
as *McCurry* itself concerned issue preclusion, Justice Stewart referred only to that. There is
no reason to doubt that the "full and fair opportunity" exception is equally available in
claim preclusion cases. If anything, claim preclusion presents a more compelling occasion for
making an exception in the interest of fairness.

176. See Chapter I, notes 61-65 and accompanying text.

177. 456 U.S. 461 (1982).

178. Id. at 481. Justice White explained that a federal *constitutional* definition of "full
and fair" adjudication is consistent with the premise that § 1738 makes state law control-

full and fair process in state court may rest independently on federal judge-made law. This is the most interesting of the three possibilities inasmuch as it leaves room in § 1738 cases for the operation of a generally useful device for adjusting the relations between state and federal courts.[179]

By its terms, § 1738 instructs federal courts to apply state preclusion law only with respect to judgments rendered in prior proceedings in state court. Nevertheless, the Court has held that federal courts should also consult state preclusion rules with respect to the adjudicative actions of state administrative bodies. In *University of Tennessee v. Elliott*,[180] an employee filed a race discrimination claim before the appropriate state agency, but was denied full relief after a hearing. He then filed a § 1983 action in federal court, arguing that his federal constitutional rights had been violated. In the Supreme Court, Justice White said that the findings of fact in the state administrative proceeding were entitled to the preclusive effect they would receive in a state court. White explained that in the absence of a controlling statute, the Court typically develops federal common law for preclusion issues. In *Elliott*, however, he thought it best to borrow state law as the content of that federal common law.[181] The previous state administrative proceedings in *Elliott* were sufficiently judicial in character to warrant preclusive effect. And the effect prescribed by state law was appropriate.[182]

It seems clear that the Court hopes to reduce the traffic into the district courts by insulating state adjudicative activities from federal court oversight.[183] Yet giving preclusive effect to state administrative findings may have just the opposite effect. It discourages litigants from taking their claims to state agencies established for the very purpose of handling complaints without resort to the courts and encourages them to regard immediate § 1983 actions in federal court as the primary means of vindicating their rights. There is no requirement that litigants exhaust state administrative procedures before filing § 1983 actions. So litigants in cases like *Elliott* are free to leapfrog over state administrative authori-

---

ling. The fourteenth amendment is equally a part of state law. See note 9 and accompanying text. Accordingly, the state preclusion law that § 1738 brings into play cannot contemplate giving a state court judgment any preclusive effect that the fourteenth amendment does not permit. Id. at 482.

179. But see notes 186-87 and accompanying text (noting the potential conflict with the *Rooker/Feldman* doctrine).

180. 478 U.S. 788 (1986).

181. See Chapter VIII, notes 67-75 and accompanying text (discussing the practice of borrowing state law).

182. The employee in *Elliott* had made no attempt to press his claims in state court and thus had done nothing to implicate § 1738 in the manner of the worker in the *Kremer* case. See note 165. To the extent that the employee in *Elliott* relied on Title VII in federal court, preclusion was unavailable in light of Title VII's explicit guarantee that federal court adjudication would be *de novo*. Arbitration judgments are not entitled to preclusion, because they depend on the "law of the shop" pertaining to labor contracts and therefore do not represent a reliable determination of factual issues touching a worker's Title VII race discrimination claim. *McDonald v. City of West Branch*, 466 U.S. 284 (1984).

183. Justice White once suggested that federal courts should give state court judgments *more* preclusive effect than they would enjoy under state law. *Migra*, 465 U.S. at 88 (concurring opinion). Yet White conceded that § 1738 appears to foreclose that possibility. Professor Shreve argues that § 1738 allows federal courts to give state judgments greater effect, but only if state interests are not compromised. Gene R. Shreve, *Preclusion and Federal Choice of Law*, 64 Tex. L. Rev. 1209 (1986).

ties into federal court.[184] Then again, the consequences of *Elliott* in the run of actual cases can only be determined empirically.[185]

The preclusion doctrine that § 1738 invokes must be reconciled with the *Rooker/Feldman* doctrine. On first blush, the requirement that federal courts apply state preclusion law in favor of previous state court judgments appears to be perfectly consistent with the absence of appellate jurisdiction to review state judgments directly. Yet § 1738 presupposes that federal courts have *jurisdiction* and only orchestrates the way they must exercise their power, while *Rooker/Feldman* denies the district courts any jurisdiction at all to entertain lawsuits that seek appellate review. Moreover, § 1738 establishes a *defense* that defendants may advance at their option, while *Rooker/Feldman* recognizes a jurisdictional prohibition that operates irrespective of the parties' desires and presumably must be addressed *sua sponte*.[186] In cases in which state preclusion law largely aborts federal lawsuits, these formal differences may be insignificant. But in cases in which state preclusion law leaves something for federal courts to decide, *Rooker/Feldman* threatens to bar federal adjudication nonetheless, thus undermining the framework that § 1738 envisions.[187]

---

184. *Patsy v. Bd. of Regents*, 457 U.S. 496 (1982); see Chapter XI, notes 48-52 and accompanying text.

185. In many instances, state administrative processes may be attractive on various other counts, such that litigants may choose to employ them despite the risk that they will produce unfavorable findings entitled to preclusive effect in federal court. Professor Ryckman explains, for example, that only "idealism or despair" would drive real estate developers to bypass local zoning boards and planning commissions in favor of litigation in federal court. William E. Ryckman, Jr., *Land Use Litigation, Federal Jurisdiction, and the Abstention Doctrines*, 69 Calif. L. Rev. 377 (1981).

186. See David P. Currie, *Res Judicata: The Neglected Defense*, 45 U. Chi. L. Rev. 317, 324 (1978).

187. The Supreme Court has acknowledged that § 1738 and *Rooker/Feldman* may figure in a single case, often providing alternative grounds for barring federal court action. But the Court has not grappled with the difficulties that may arise when the two ideas produce different results. In *Feldman*, the local court had already passed on the validity of the bar admission rule, and the federal district court might have been obliged to give that previous judgment preclusive effect. 460 U.S. at 487.

Chapter VII

The Supreme Court

The Supreme Court of the United States resolves very few cases on the merits. Yet the opinions the Court generates establish the baseline from which much of the law governing American public institutions proceeds. The Supreme Court thus demands attention for the systemic functions it performs, even if there is very little chance that any particular case will reach the justices for decision. The Court does the lion's share of its work as the ultimate appellate tribunal for the resolution of federal questions. In some respects, the Court's jurisdiction is governed by statutes and doctrines that bear serious study. In the main, however, the Court has discretion to set its own agenda. When the Court accepts cases for review, they become vehicles for articulating an accurate, uniform, and supreme body of federal law.

A. Original Jurisdiction

Article III establishes the menu of "cases" and "controversies" that comprise the judicial business that federal courts can handle. Article III also distributes that business between the Supreme Court's original jurisdiction, on the one hand, and its appellate jurisdiction, on the other.[1] Insofar as the *Constitution* is concerned, the Court *can* exercise jurisdiction in every "case" or "controversy" on the list, either by entertaining a suit that originates in the Court itself or, when a suit is initially filed in an inferior federal court or a state court, by reviewing the judgment reached at that level.[2] Article III specifies that the Court *can* entertain some cases as an original matter: "all Cases affecting Ambassadors, other public Ministers and Consuls, and those in which a State shall be a Party." Yet Article III does not make that original jurisdiction exclusive.[3] Nor does it bar the Court from handling those same cases, as well as the other matters on the general menu, in an appellate posture.[4]

---

1. See Chapter IV, text accompanying notes 5-6.
2. But see Chapter X, notes 46-71 (treating the way the eleventh amendment affects the scope of Article III judicial power).
3. *Bors v. Preston*, 111 U.S. 252 (1884) (holding that inferior federal courts may be given concurrent jurisdiction over cases involving foreign ambassadors and consuls); *Ames v. Kansas*, 111 U.S. 449 (1884) (holding that inferior federal courts and state courts may handle cases in which the Supreme Court also has original jurisdiction).
4. Thus when a case that might have begun in the Supreme Court as an original matter actually begins in an inferior federal court or a state court, Article III permits the Supreme Court to consider the lower court's judgment on appeal. *Cohens v. Virginia*, 19 U.S. (6 Wheat.) 264, 392-403 (1821).

Taken literally, Article III appears to say that the Supreme Court can exercise original jurisdiction of any suit on the menu, provided that a foreign emissary is involved or one of the states is a party.[5] That understanding would have provocative implications. The state is a party in an ordinary state criminal prosecution of one of its citizens. It would be extraordinary if, for that reason, local criminal cases could routinely be tried in the Supreme Court of the United States. Accordingly, the Court has given Article III a different interpretation: Original jurisdiction extends not to every case on the Article III menu in which a foreign officer happens to be involved or a state happens to be a party, but only to cases that are on the menu *because* a foreign representative is concerned or a state is a party.[6] Accordingly, original jurisdiction is limited to suits that are on the list because they are "Cases affecting Ambassadors, other public Ministers and Consuls" or "Controversies between two or more States," between "a State and Citizens of another State," or between "a State...and foreign states, Citizens, or Subjects."[7]

Original jurisdiction in the Supreme Court is a unique form of diversity jurisdiction, depending not on the nature of the issues at stake, but rather on the identity and alignment of litigants who command the Court's attention either because they represent foreign sovereigns or because they are sovereign American states themselves. The scope of original jurisdiction is negligible, its purpose largely symbolic. The explanations for its existence bear this out. Historically, original jurisdiction promised superior procedures, geographic convenience, and greater assurances of neutrality.[8] Today, it offers only the formal dignity of litigation in our most prestigious tribunal.[9]

---

5. The Court held in *Ex parte Gruber*, 269 U.S. 302 (1925), that "Ambassadors, or other public Ministers and Consuls" are representatives of foreign governments, not representatives of this country serving abroad.

6. *California v. Southern Pac. Co.*, 157 U.S. 229, 257-58 (1895). Article III establishes jurisdiction only when it identifies the nine overlapping matters that form the federal judicial power, not when it later allocates that power between the two modes of Supreme Court jurisdiction. Accordingly, the statement that the Supreme Court "shall have original Jurisdiction" in cases "in which a State shall be a Party" does not create jurisdictional power independently of the cases and controversies listed in the previous paragraph. *Pennsylvania v. Quicksilver Co.*, 77 U.S. (10 Wall.) 553, 556 (1870).

7. When, for example, Oregon challenged the validity of the eighteen-year-old vote statute on constitutional grounds, the state invoked the Supreme Court's original jurisdiction on the theory that the defendant, Attorney General Mitchell, was a citizen of Virginia — *not* on the theory that the suit arose under federal law. *Oregon v. Mitchell*, 400 U.S. 112 (1970).

8. Prior to the development of long-arm statutes, the states were unable to sue citizens of other states in their own courts, because they had no means of obtaining *in personam* jurisdiction. States and representatives of foreign nations may have found it most convenient to proceed in Washington, where their lawyers typically resided. Foreign representatives may also have preferred to appear in the Supreme Court rather than trust their fortunes to the provincialism of a state court. See Akhil R. Amar, *Marbury, Section 13, and the Original Jurisdiction of the Supreme Court*, 56 U. Chi. L. Rev. 443, 469-78 (1989) (attributing original jurisdiction largely to geography). All these explanations have weaknesses, but they probably account for the way Article III was written.

9. *California v. Arizona*, 440 U.S. 59, 65-66 (1979). Recall that Alexander Hamilton took the view that only federal courts could accord other nations the respect they were due. See Chapter II, text accompanying note 49. Professor Pfander disputes the "dignified tribunal" thesis, as well as other explanations for the conventional understanding of original jurisdiction. James E. Pfander, *Rethinking the Supreme Court's Original Jurisdiction in State-Party Cases*, 82 Calif. L. Rev. 555, 562-72 (1994). Pfander offers, instead, a revisionist

With respect to original jurisdiction, Article III is self-executing. The Court is free to exercise the power that Article III makes available, whether or not Congress enacts a statute purporting to confer original jurisdiction on the Court as a matter of legislative policy.[10] Nevertheless, Congress has enacted legislation touching the Court's original jurisdiction and thus has purported to have something to say about it.[11] There are three possibilities. Congress might wish: (1) to confer original jurisdiction that Article III does not contemplate; (2) to withhold some or all the original jurisdiction that Article III prescribes; or (3) to make some or all the Court's original jurisdiction concurrent with the jurisdiction of other courts. The first and second of these tactics are apparently foreclosed by precedent; the third is available and routinely employed.

The Court held in *Marbury v. Madison*[12] that Congress cannot *add* to the original jurisdiction fixed by Article III. That decision has often been questioned.[13] Yet it has a plausible rationale. If Congress could expand the Court's original jurisdiction, it might compromise the Court's effectiveness by swamping the justices with work.[14] It is "extremely doubtful" that Congress can *deny* the Court original jurisdiction established by Article III.[15] To avoid that "grave" constitutional question, the Court reads ambiguous statutes to make no attempt to withhold any part of original Article III jurisdiction.[16] The rationale for resisting reductions in original jurisdiction is not immediately apparent. Since the scope of original jurisdiction is so narrow in the first instance, it is hard to think that the Court's ability to perform its core functions would be impaired if some of it were lost. The Court cannot rely on original jurisdiction as a vehicle for deciding federal questions.[17] Moreover, the justices plainly do not relish original jurisdiction and exercise it only sparingly.[18] It may be, then, that the inviolate character of original jurisdiction rests largely on symbolic grounds.[19]

---

account of the history behind Article III's provision for original jurisdiction and an argument that *any* case in which a state is a party is within the Supreme Court's original jurisdiction, if the case appears on the Article III menu for *any* reason. He draws support from the text of Article III, which refers to "cases" when it prescribes the Supreme Court's original jurisdiction, but to "controversies" when it describes the diversity suits to which the conventional interpretation limits that jurisdiction. Pfander counters that when Article III refers to "cases," it means to capture matters that appear on the Article III list for different reasons — in particular, "cases" arising under federal law in which a state is a party. Id. at 600. See Chapter II, note 26 (discussing other accounts of "cases" and "controversies").

10. *Arizona v. California*, 373 U.S. 546, 564 (1963).

11. The Court insists that its appellate jurisdiction, too, is formally conferred by Article III rather than by statute. Yet the Court typically accepts the jurisdictional legislation that Congress writes in that context as authoritative. See Chapter IV, notes 51-52 and accompanying text.

12. 5 U.S. (1 Cranch) 137 (1803); see Chapter I, notes 54-58 and accompanying text.

13. E.g., William W. Van Alstyne, *A Critical Guide to Marbury v. Madison*, 1969 Duke L.J. 1.

14. But see notes 33-39 and accompanying text (explaining that litigants must have the Court's leave before filing an original action).

15. *California v. Arizona*, 440 U.S. at 66.

16. *South Carolina v. Regan*, 465 U.S. 367, 395 (1984) (O'Connor, J., concurring); see Chapter I, note 21 (discussing the practice of avoiding constitutional questions when possible).

17. See notes 5-7 and accompanying text.

18. See notes 34-37 and accompanying text

19. Professor Amar argues that (subject to other constitutional restraints) Congress *can* withhold original jurisdiction from the Court in cases in which that jurisdiction must rest on

The Court can allow inferior federal courts and state courts to entertain the kinds of cases that Article III prescribes for the Supreme Court's original jurisdiction.[20] The current statute in point, 28 U.S.C. § 1251, contemplates that the Court will have "exclusive" jurisdiction only with respect to "controversies between two or more states" and that the rest of its original jurisdiction will "not" be exclusive, but rather may be concurrent with that of other courts.[21] When Congress wishes to confer jurisdiction on inferior federal courts to entertain matters in the latter category, it is free to do so.[22] And when state courts exercise their own jurisdictional power arising from state law to adjudicate those cases, they, too, are on solid ground.[23] Since inferior federal courts and state courts often enjoy the concurrent jurisdiction required, most cases that might have been filed originally in the Supreme Court are now filed elsewhere and reach the Court, if at all, only on appellate review.[24]

The Court occasionally makes adjustments to these basic arrangements. In *United States v. Texas*,[25] the Court upheld original jurisdiction to entertain a suit by the federal government against a state. Suits in which the United States is a party are on the Article III menu, but *not* because a state is invariably a party. Accordingly, the Court was forced to carve out an exception to the usual understanding of original jurisdiction. That was not difficult to do. In the *Texas* case, the government sued to determine the boundary between Texas and the territory of Oklahoma.[26] No inferior court had jurisdiction to entertain that action, and if the Supreme Court itself was constitutionally foreclosed, the only alternative was a Texas state court. The Court found it implausible that the Constitution should force the government to submit a suit against a state to the courts of that very state. It was more sensible to infer that the national sovereign could sue in its

---

the party status of a state. He relies on the precise text of Article III, which refers to "all" cases affecting foreign envoys, but does not equally refer to "all" cases in which a state is a party. Amar, note 8, at 480-81. See also Chapter IV, notes 99-100 and accompanying text.

20. *Ames v. Kansas*, 111 U.S. 449 (1884).

21. The remaining matters to which § 1251 refers do not reach all the cases that Article III places within the Supreme Court's original jurisdiction. For example, while Article III extends original jurisdiction to all cases "affecting" foreign envoys, § 1251 acknowledges jurisdiction only in actions in which foreign representatives are "parties." If cases can *affect* foreign officers even though they are not parties, then § 1251 presents the "grave" question whether Congress can deprive the Supreme Court of original jurisdiction by statute or, better said, by negative implication from statute. See notes 15-16 and accompanying text.

22. Since § 1251 merely establishes that the Supreme Court's jurisdiction is not exclusive in most instances, that statute does not itself confer concurrent jurisdiction on any other court. Independent jurisdictional statutes are required to do that additional work. They exist in abundance. E.g., 28 U.S.C. § 1351 (conferring jurisdiction on district courts to adjudicate suits against representatives of foreign governments). District courts have jurisdiction in federal question cases in which a state is a party, albeit state immunity from suit may be asserted. 28 U.S.C. § 1331; see Chapter X, notes 46-71 and accompanying text.

23. See Chapter VI, note 3 and accompanying text.

24. See notes 40-201 and accompanying text.

25. 143 U.S. 621 (1892).

26. The law governing the boundary was federal common law. Accordingly, the suit in *United States v. Texas* was within the federal judicial power both because the United States was a party and because the suit arose under federal law. See Chapter VIII, notes 32-36 and accompanying text (explaining that a case can "arise under" federal common law).

own courts (namely, the Supreme Court itself) to settle its differences with a member state—the usual limitation of original jurisdiction to three kinds of diversity actions notwithstanding.[27]

Cases in which two states oppose each other are governed by federal common law.[28] Yet in fashioning federal law for particular occasions the Court often draws on the law of the states concerned. When local law predominates, disputes have no national consequence and thus have little purchase on original disposition.[29] They typically involve state interests in land or water,[30] or some species of contract obligation.[31] On the whole, original jurisdiction cases are notoriously dull or, if not dull, then trivial.[32] A party seeking to invoke original jurisdiction must first obtain leave to file the action.[33] The Court denies most motions without opinion. The Court has decided no cases involving foreign envoys in years and only two in its entire history.[34] In *Ohio v. Wyandotte Chemicals Co.*,[35] Justice Harlan explained that the Court can best meet its responsibilities as the system's ultimate referee by reviewing cases in an appellate posture. Moreover, as the nation has matured the historical justifications for original jurisdiction have

---

27. See text accompanying note 7. Recall that Hamilton took a similar view. See Chapter II, note 48 and accompanying text. The Court has made other adjustments that appear to conflict with one another, but probably rest on expediency. In *United States v. Wyoming*, 331 U.S. 440 (1947), the Court permitted the federal government to join private defendants to a suit against a state, even though the government plainly would not have been able to invoke the Court's original jurisdiction if it had sued those defendants alone. In *Louisiana v. Cummins*, 314 U.S. 577 (1941), however, the Court refused to allow a state to join its own citizens as defendants (thus insisting on complete diversity in original jurisdiction cases of that kind). The difference is probably that in the *Wyoming* case the Court fortified the government's ability to keep its disputes with a state in the federal forum, while in *Cummins* the Court followed its typical policy of discouraging original jurisdiction. Expediency plainly explains a third famous case, *Wisconsin v. Pelican Ins. Co.*, 127 U.S. 265 (1888), in which the Court insisted that original jurisdiction lies only for civil cases and disclaimed jurisdiction of a state's suit against a citizen of another state, seeking to impose a "penalty" for the violation of a state statute. That action may have looked too much like a local criminal prosecution, filed in the Supreme Court merely because the defendant resided in another state. Certainly, it was not the kind of matter the Court finds suitable for original jurisdiction. See text accompanying notes 5-7.

28. See *Connecticut v. Massachusetts*, 282 U.S. 660, 670 (1931).

29. *Kentucky v. Indiana*, 281 U.S. 163 (1930) (involving local contract law); *Texas v. New Jersey*, 379 U.S. 674 (1965) (involving the local law of escheat).

30. See, e.g., *Rhode Island v. Massachusetts*, 37 U.S. (12 Pet.) 657 (1838) (an early boundary dispute case); *Kansas v. Colorado*, 185 U.S. 125 (1902) (a classic western water rights case).

31. See, e.g., *Texas v. New Mexico*, 462 U.S. 554 (1983) (a suit to enforce an interstate compact).

32. In *California v. West Virginia*, 454 U.S. 1027 (1981), California asked the Court to decide whether West Virginia had breached a contract providing for football games between San Jose State and the University of West Virginia.

33. Sup. Ct. Rule 17. The Court's discretion may be justified by the equitable character of most original jurisdiction cases, or simply on an analogy to the discretion that Congress has formally allowed the Court with respect to its appellate jurisdiction. See notes 182-85 and accompanying text.

34. Vincent L. McKusick, *Discretionary Gatekeeping: The Supreme Court's Management of Its Original Jurisdiction Docket Since 1961*, 45 Me. L. Rev. 185, 187 (1993).

35. 401 U.S. 493, 497-98 (1971).

collapsed. In most instances today, an inferior federal court or a state court offers states a perfectly good forum in which to litigate.[36] Even in cases involving two disputing states (in which original jurisdiction is exclusive), the Court may force the states concerned to find another way to settle their differences.[37] In the rare cases in which the Court grants leave to file an original action, the Court invariably appoints a special master to marshal the facts and offer a recommended disposition.[38] The Court eschews any *de novo* consideration of reports by masters and typically gives them an "appellate" examination.[39]

B. Appellate Review of State Judgments

By conventional account, the Supreme Court's appellate jurisdiction to review state court judgments formed the key feature of the Madisonian Compromise.[40] Article III contemplates that the Court will have appellate jurisdiction, but does not tie that jurisdiction to the kind of court that decided a matter below. Instead, Article III specifies only the "cases" or "controversies" on which the Court can rule. Since state courts, as well as inferior federal courts, may initially decide many of those matters, Article III permits the Court to review both state and federal court decisions. Recall that Congress might never have created inferior federal courts and thus might have left state courts alone to handle all the trial-level work in cases in which Article III envisioned the Supreme Court would have appellate jurisdiction. The Supremacy Clause explicitly binds "the Judges in every State" to respect federal law as the supreme Law of the Land." That clause contemplates, accordingly, both that state courts will have occasion to pass on federal questions and that their decisions will be subject to the discipline of a hierarchical appellate authority located in the "one supreme Court" the Constitution makes mandatory.[41]

---

36. This is true even when a state or the federal government sues in *parens partriae*, advancing the welfare of its citizens, as well as its own quasi-sovereign interests. E.g., *Alfred L. Snapp & Son v. Puerto Rico*, 458 U.S. 592 (1982) (a suit by Puerto Rico on behalf of its farm workers); *Pasadena City Bd. of Ed. v. Spangler*, 427 U.S. 424 (1976) (a school desegregation case brought by the federal government).

37. In *Louisiana v. Mississippi*, 488 U.S. 990 (1988), the Court denied Louisiana's motion for leave to file a boundary dispute action against Mississippi . Justice White's dissent revealed that the Court probably hoped that the dispute between the two states would be resolved in a pending district court action involving private parties, in which Louisiana had already filed a third-party complaint against Mississippi. Later, however, the Court held that, in light of § 1251, the district court lacked jurisdiction to determine that third-party claim. *Mississippi v. Louisiana*, 506 U.S. 73 (1992). For a time, it appeared that Louisiana would have no forum at all for its claim against Mississippi. But in the end the Court relented and granted a second motion for leave to file an original action. *Louisiana v. Mississippi*, 510 U.S. 941 (1993).

38. E.g., *New Jersey v. New York*, 118 S.Ct. 1726 (1998) (reviewing a master's scandalous and unnatural conclusion that most of Ellis Island is in Jersey).

39. See *Maryland v. Louisiana*, 451 U.S. 725, 765 (1981) (Rehnquist, J., dissenting).

40. See Chapter II, notes 12-13, 19-20 and accompanying text.

41. See Chapter IV, text accompanying note 1; Chapter II, text accompanying notes 46-47, 52 (discussing Hamilton's explanation in the Federalist Papers).

Congress provided for the Court's review of state court judgments in § 25 of the Judiciary Act of 1789.[42] The Court, for its part, quickly shouldered responsibility for superintending state courts and laid any constitutional objections to rest in three great cases from Virginia. The treaties that concluded the Revolutionary War guaranteed that land in America held by British loyalists would not be confiscated. Nevertheless, Virginia enacted a statute specifying that British land in the rich Northern Neck region should be seized and sold. In *Fairfax's Devisee v. Hunter's Lessee*,[43] the plaintiff, Hunter, claimed to have purchased some of that land from the state of Virginia. The defendant, Martin, claimed that he had inherited the same land from his uncle, Lord Fairfax, and that, in light of the treaties, Virginia could not lawfully sell it to Hunter.[44] The Virginia Court of Appeals upheld Hunter's claim on the theory that, as a matter of state law, he had obtained title to the parcel before the treaties became effective.[45] The Supreme Court reversed that judgment in an opinion by Justice Story, who concluded that Hunter's title had not been established before the treaties took effect and that Martin's federal claim under the treaties must therefore prevail.[46]

On remand, the Virginia Court of Appeals issued an order denying that the Supreme Court had appellate jurisdiction to review Virginia court judgments and declaring that the provision in the Judiciary Act of 1789 authorizing that jurisdiction was unconstitutional. In a famous separate opinion, Judge Cabell insisted

---

42. See Chapter II, text accompanying note 61.

43. 11 U.S. (7 Cranch) 603 (1812).

44. The odd style of the case derived from the common law procedure in ejectment. In order to test his title to the land, Hunter formally alleged that he had leased the property to a fictitious person, that the person had entered the land, and that he had been ousted by Martin. That allowed Hunter's fictitious lessee to sue Martin for interference with the lease, which, in turn, put Hunter's original authority to lease the property in issue. Martin was allowed to defend his own claim only if he first admitted the fictitious lease, entry, and ouster. Actually, the case was even more fictitious than the ejectment action required it to be. Hunter was only nominally involved. The true moving party was the state of Virginia, which wanted to confirm its authority to seize land held by British loyalists. Martin's role was also marginal. He had contracted to sell the land to a group of Virginians that included John Marshall. That group actually pressed the federal treaty claim against the opposing state claim that Virginia had sold the land pursuant to state statute. Marshall represented his group in some early proceedings in state court. His personal involvement probably explains why he did not participate in the Supreme Court's ultimate disposition.

45. Spencer Roane, John Marshall's arch rival in Virginia, wrote the state court's opinion.

46. The Supreme Court apparently understood that it had appellate jurisdiction to consider the case pursuant to the Judiciary Act of 1789, because the Virginia Court of Appeals had rejected Martin's federal treaty claim in favor of Hunter's state law claim. See Chapter II, text accompanying note 61. In order to reach the federal claim that Martin advanced, however, Justice Story first had to reject the state court's determination that, as a matter of state property law, Hunter had obtained title to the land before the treaties took effect. Story expressly reexamined the state court's treatment of that question and reached the opposite conclusion. *Fairfax's Devisee*, 11 U.S. at 622. Matasar and Bruch contend that *Fairfax's Devisee* proceeded from a premise that would not hold today—namely, that the Court had jurisdiction to second-guess the state court regarding an issue of state law. Richard A. Matasar & Gregory S. Bruch, *Procedural Common Law, Federal Jurisdictional Policy, and Abandonment of the Adequate and Independent State Grounds Doctrine*, 86 Colum. L. Rev. 1291, 1297-98 (1986); see notes 80-98 and accompanying text. It is more likely that Justice Story found it necessary to review the state court's treatment of the state law issue to prevent the state court from frustrating Martin's federal claim by manipulating an antecedent matter of state law. See text accompanying note 105.

that the Constitution recognized that both state and federal courts would handle federal question cases, but had "provided no umpire" if the two court systems should disagree. According to Cabell, the Supremacy Clause did not require state courts to accept judgments from the Supreme Court, but rather instructed them to enforce federal law as they themselves understood it and thus *barred* them from endorsing a Supreme Court decision with which they disagreed.[47] In his view, the Supreme Court had direct appellate jurisdiction only over inferior federal courts. If a single referee was essential to achieve uniformity, Congress could provide for the removal of federal question litigation to those courts and, ultimately, to the Supreme Court.[48]

The *Fairfax* litigation then went back to the Supreme Court. Again writing for the Court in *Martin v. Hunter's Lessee*,[49] Justice Story rejected the arguments advanced by Judge Cabell and confirmed that state court judgments *are* subject to Supreme Court review. Perhaps to avoid further conflict with the Virginia Court of Appeals, however, Story declined to issue another order to that court, but, instead, simply entered judgment for Martin.[50] Thereafter, the Court equally dismissed objections to its appellate jurisdiction in state criminal cases. In *Cohens v. Virginia*,[51] Chief Justice Marshall recognized that a criminal appeal is arguably different from a civil appeal inasmuch as the state is a formal party and, at that, a party *defendant* when a convict seeks review of a conviction. The presence of the state as a party, in turn, invites the argument that the Court's jurisdiction can only be original rather than appellate,[52] as well as the argument that federal jurisdiction is barred by the eleventh amendment.[53] Marshall rejected both contentions—the first on the ground that original jurisdiction need not be exclusive, the second on the theory that a criminal action is originally initiated *by* the state in state court.[54]

The Virginia cases were essential to the constitutional framework that is now so familiar. State courts act on the basis of the power they are granted by state law, and they enjoy equal and parallel status with the inferior federal courts. They are nonetheless part of a single national system of jurisprudence and must conform their judgments to the Supreme Court's ultimate authority for that system.[55] The Court's modern functions are clear enough: to maintain the accuracy,

---

47. *Hunter v. Martin*, 18 Va. 1, 9-11 (1815).

48. See Chapter VI, notes 116-48 and accompanying text (discussing the removal mechanism).

49. 14 U.S. (1 Wheat.) 304 (1816).

50. Id. at 362. When the Court reverses state court judgments today, it invariably remands for proceedings "not inconsistent" with its opinion. That disposition not only avoids the indelicacy of ordering state courts to take action, but also allows state courts the flexibility to reach other issues that may still justify a different result—for example, some previously unexamined state law question. See note 71 and accompanying text (explaining that state courts may decide state law issues even when the Supreme Court accepts appellate jurisdiction of cases to address federal questions).

51. 19 U.S. (6 Wheat.) 264 (1821).

52. See notes 1-7 and accompanying text.

53. See Chapter X, text accompanying notes 46-47.

54. See Chapter X, notes 64-65 and accompanying text.

55. Liebman and Ryan find it important that Justice Story explicitly rejected a further argument—that the Judiciary Act authorized the Supreme Court only to determine the meaning of the treaties in the abstract, but not to reexamine the state court's application of those treaties (properly understood) to the facts of the particular case. That understanding would have reduced the Court's effective appellate jurisdiction to rare cases that can be re-

uniformity, and supremacy of federal law. The Court can be successful in those responsibilities only if it can subject state courts to a hierarchical discipline.[56]

C. Federal Questions

Just as the Supreme Court's constitutional decisions confirm and sustain a unitary federal system, modern statutes regarding the Court's jurisdiction equally support that same framework. The Judiciary of 1789 conferred appellate jurisdiction on the Court to review "final" judgments by a state's "highest" court, but only if the party advancing a federal theory *lost* below. That arrangement allowed the Court to insist that federal law was held supreme, but it denied the Court authority to ensure as well that federal law was accurately and uniformly interpreted. Beginning in 1914, Congress eliminated those older features of appellate jurisdiction. Today, pursuant to 28 U.S.C. § 1257,[57] the Supreme Court has appellate jurisdiction to review a state court judgment irrespective of the outcome below, if: (1) a substantial federal question was presented to the highest state court that could determine the federal question; and (2) that court issued a final judgment.[58]

1. The Preservation Requirement

Litigants who wish to invoke the Supreme Court's appellate jurisdiction must first present a federal question to the highest state court with jurisdiction to consider it. In so doing, they must make the state court aware of the federal character of the question.[59] The Court has explained this requirement both as a construction of § 1257 and as a sound rule of judicial policy.[60] If parties were free to withhold a federal claim from the state courts and press it for the first time at the Supreme Court level, familiar structural arrangements would be compromised. State courts would have no opportunity to fulfill their duty and responsibility to address federal issues, and the Supreme Court would be unable to exercise genuine *appellate* review of the state courts' work.[61] The Court occasionally enter-

---

solved by determining "pure" legal questions alone and would have deprived the Court of the ability to ensure that state court judgments in actual cases are correct. James S. Liebman & William F. Ryan, *"Some Effectual Power": The Quantity and Quality of Decisionmaking Required of Article III Courts*, 98 Colum. L. Rev. 696, 798 (1998).

56. See Chapter IV, notes 95-96 and accompanying text (discussing Professor Hart's "essential function" thesis).

57. But see notes 97-98, 127-28 and accompanying text (explaining that state courts can insulate their judgments by resting them on adequate state grounds of decision).

58. The Supreme Court can protect its ability to exercise jurisdiction by issuing any "necessary" or "appropriate" writs. See 28 U.S.C. § 1651; *Ex parte Republic of Peru*, 318 U.S. 578 (1943).

59. *New York Central & H.R. Co. v. New York*, 186 U.S. 269 (1902).

60. E.g., *Cardinale v. Louisiana*, 394 U.S. 437 (1969). The highest court requirement is specified by § 1257, but the Supreme Court would undoubtedly have adopted it in the absence of statute.

61. The highest state court is typically the tribunal of last resort in the relevant state, even if that court has discretion to decline jurisdiction (tracking in that respect the Supreme Court's own discretionary control of its docket). E.g., *Costarelli v. Massachusetts*, 421 U.S.

tains issues that were not preserved in state court, perhaps on the theory that it is appropriate to overlook a party's default in order to correct "plain error."[62] Yet in the main, the Court adheres to the preservation requirement.

2. The Final Judgment Requirement

The Supreme Court's appellate jurisdiction equally depends on a final judgment by the highest state court below. For more than a century following the 1789 Act, the Court took the term "final" literally and thus disclaimed appellate jurisdiction if anything remained to be decided by the state courts in order to conclude the parties' dispute. Today, the Court construes § 1257 to allow considerable room for judgment. The shift undoubtedly reflects the Court's attempt to police state court determinations of federal law in an effective way. If the finality rule were more rigid, the Court might have no jurisdiction to examine federal claims at the time and in the posture best suited to maintaining the accuracy, uniformity, and supremacy of federal law.

Flexibility comes at a price. Chief Justice Rehnquist has argued that a strict finality rule would serve structural values.[63] When the Court adheres to the finality requirement and disclaims jurisdiction to review a state court judgment, the Court avoids confronting the state court unnecessarily and thus threatening harmonious relations within the federal system. In other contexts, the Court insists that inferior federal courts should avoid unnecessary interference with state courts.[64] In this context, too, Chief Justice Rehnquist contends that the Court itself should show similar restraint and thus should not reach out to decide federal questions that might be left for the time being, or indefinitely, with the state courts.[65]

---

193 (1975); see notes 182-90 and accompanying text; but see Chapter XII, note 83 (explaining that the exhaustion doctrine in the context of federal habeas corpus does *not* demand that litigants seek discretionary review in the highest state court). The rationale is that there is no final state judgment to which the Supreme Court's appellate jurisdiction can properly attach until the state court of last resort has had an opportunity to rule on a question. The highest state court can be an inferior state tribunal, even a trial-level court, if in the particular circumstances there is no further avenue for review in the state court system. E.g., *Thompson v. Louisville*, 362 U.S. 199 (1960). If a party does not raise a question in the highest state court, but that court nonetheless addresses the question on its own, the preservation requirement does not bar Supreme Court review. In that event, there is an authoritative state court judgment for the Court to examine, and the party's procedural default is inconsequential. *Adams v. Robertson*, 520 U.S. 83 (1997) (explaining that the Court has jurisdiction if a federal question was either addressed by or was properly presented to the court below).

62. Professor Spann argues that the Court has at least that much jurisdiction. Girardeau Spann, *Functional Analysis of the Plain-Error Rule*, 71 Gtn. L.J. 945 (1983).

63. *Cox Broadcasting Corp. v. Cohn*, 420 U.S. 469, 503-05 (1975) (Rehnquist, J., dissenting). See also *Radio Station WOW v. Johnson*, 326 U.S. 120, 123 (1945) (opinion of Frankfurter, J.); *Hudson Dist. v. Eli Lilly*, 377 U.S. 386, 397 (1964) (Harlan, J., dissenting).

64. In *Cohn*, Rehnquist referred explicitly to the abstention doctrine associated with *Younger v. Harris*, 401 U.S. 37 (1971); see Chapter XI, notes 132-281 and accompanying text.

65. The Chief Justice also contends that a flexible rule is administratively burdensome in that it requires the Court to anticipate the way it is likely to decide a federal question on the merits and to take that potential decision into account as it determines whether to ad-

The full Court resists Chief Justice Rehnquist's invitation to borrow from doctrines and practices designed to mitigate the lower federal courts' conflicts with state courts. The Court's own appellate jurisdiction to review state judgments for error stands on a different footing. That appellate jurisdiction must be exercised efficiently (to conserve the Court's scarce resources), and also in a timely way (to ensure that the Court performs its functions as the system's ultimate referee). Moreover, the Court must reconcile the final judgment requirement with the adequate state ground doctrine, which typically bars the Court from examining state court decisions that rest exclusively on state law grounds.[66] If the Court concludes that it has no current appellate jurisdiction to review a state court determination of a federal question (because the state court judgment is not yet final), it may happen that later, after pending state court proceedings have been completed, the Court will equally have no appellate jurisdiction (because the state courts ultimately resolve the parties' dispute on state law grounds alone). The Court can easily be caught in the middle between the final judgment requirement, on the one side, and the adequate state ground doctrine, on the other.

The Court responds to these difficulties by striking a balance. The Court retains and respects the final judgment requirement in the run of cases, but recognizes a variety of exceptions. In the leading case, *Cox Broadcasting Corp. v. Cohn*,[67] Justice White organized those exceptions under four headings: (1) cases in which the state proceedings yet to be undertaken are so *contingent* on an existing decision regarding a federal question that the result of those proceedings is preordained and it would be wasteful to delay Supreme Court review; (2) cases in which the state proceedings yet to be undertaken are so *independent* of an existing decision regarding a federal question that the federal question will survive for Supreme Court consideration, irrespective of the outcome of the further proceedings in state court; (3) cases in which the state proceedings yet to be undertaken will *insulate* a federal question from the Supreme Court's jurisdiction; and (4) cases in which further proceedings in state court *may* shield a federal question from Supreme Court review, depending on the outcome, and in which an immediate decision by the Supreme Court may both preclude those proceedings and avoid the erosion of important federal policies.

State proceedings that are controlled by a state court decision on a federal question. In some cases, the highest state court decides a federal question, and the only remaining issues are so dependent on that disposition that it is wasteful for the Supreme Court to postpone consideration of the federal question until the state court proceedings are complete. Justice White cited as illustrations cases in which criminal defendants lose on federal issues in the state appellate courts and then are scheduled for trials they cannot possibly win. In *Mills v. Alabama*,[68] for example, the Alabama Supreme Court rejected a criminal defendant's argument that an indictment violated the first amendment and remanded the case for trial. The Supreme Court assumed immediate jurisdiction to examine the state

---

dress the issue in the current posture of a case. *Cohn*, 420 U.S. at 501-08 (dissenting opinion). See note 76.

66. See notes 97-98 and accompanying text.
67. 420 U.S. 469 (1975).
68. 384 U.S. 214 (1966).

supreme court's decision. The defendant had no other defense and would plainly be convicted. At that point, he would appeal again, presenting the same federal question for the Court's attention. If, however, the Court sustained his first amendment claim with the case in its current posture, there would be no need to conduct a state trial.[69]

State proceedings that are independent of a state court decision on a federal question. In some instances, the highest state court renders a decision on a federal question and orders a trial on other issues that are so separate from the federal question that they cannot affect the state court's disposition of that issue. It will remain for review by the Supreme Court, no matter what happens in further state proceedings. Justice White offered as illustrations cases in which criminal defendants prevail on some grounds, but not on others. In *Brady v. Maryland*,[70] the Maryland Court of Appeals sustained a criminal defendant's claim that the prosecution had withheld exculpating evidence in violation of due process and remanded the case for an adjustment in his sentence. The Supreme Court assumed immediate jurisdiction to consider the state court's decision. The sentencing adjustment still to come in state court could have no effect on that judgment, and there was no point in postponing review of the federal issue.[71]

State proceedings that will insulate a federal question from Supreme Court jurisdiction. In some cases, the highest state court renders a decision on a federal question that will elude review in the Supreme Court if state proceedings yet to be undertaken proceed, irrespective of the outcome. Justice White gave as illustrations criminal cases in which the highest state court initially decides a federal question in the defendant's favor and remands for trial on that basis. In that kind of case, the dispute will ultimately be resolved exclusively on state law grounds, foreclosing the Supreme Court's appellate jurisdiction later. Ordinarily, the Court regards the prospect of avoiding federal questions as cause for restraint. Yet in cases in this third category, the Court's failure to act in the current posture of a case cannot avoid a federal question entirely. The Supreme Court itself will not pass on it, but the state court below already has. In *California v. Stewart*,[72] the

---

69. See also *Duquesne Light Co. v. Barasch*, 488 U.S. 299 (1989). In that case, the Pennsylvania Supreme Court rejected a power company's claim that its property would be taken unconstitutionally if it were not allowed to raise rates to recoup losses on a nuclear power plant. The state court remanded the matter to the public utilities commission, which had yet to compute the rates the company would be permitted to charge (without consideration of the losses the company insisted must constitutionally be taken into account). The Supreme Court held that the state court's decision on the federal "takings" claim was immediately reviewable. Nothing the public utility commission had yet to do could affect that decision. If the state court was wrong, the commission was about to undertake an expensive and time-consuming computation that would have to be revisited later.

70. 373 U.S. 83 (1963).

71. In *Radio Station WOW,* the Nebraska Supreme Court rejected a radio station's claim that its federal license would be impaired if it were required to transfer assets and remanded the case for computation of those assets with the expectation that they would be assigned to another company. The Supreme Court assumed immediate jurisdiction to examine the state supreme court's decision on the federal license issue. The outcome of the proceedings still planned in state court was not controlled by the state supreme court's decision on the station's federal claim. But nothing the state courts might decide regarding the value of the assets could affect that decision. Accordingly, the Court found it appropriate to consider it immediately. 326 U.S. at 127.

72. 384 U.S. 436 (1966) (consolidated with *Miranda v. Arizona*).

California Supreme Court reversed a criminal defendant's conviction on the ground that his confession had been obtained in violation of the fourteenth amendment. The state court then remanded for a new trial. The Supreme Court accepted appellate jurisdiction immediately. If the defendant was convicted in the second trial, he might appeal on some other ground (but not the ground on which he had already succeeded); if he was acquitted, the prosecution would be unable to appeal. Either way, the previous state court decision regarding the admissibility of the confession under federal law would escape the Supreme Court's appellate jurisdiction.

State proceedings that may insulate a federal question from Supreme Court review. In a final set of cases, the highest state court reaches a decision on a federal question that *may* be insulated from the Supreme Court's review, depending on the outcome of further state proceedings. Justice White offered as illustrations cases in which the highest state court decides a first amendment question against the party asserting the federal claim.[73] In that kind of case, it is not certain that the dispute will be resolved on state law grounds, eliminating the Court's opportunity to examine the state court's existing decision on the federal question. The party advancing the free speech claim *may* yet prevail in state court on other grounds, but then again may not. The risk of losing jurisdiction to review a state court decision on the meaning of the first amendment is too great. If the Supreme Court postpones review in the expectation that it will be able to reach the federal issue after state court proceedings are complete, the state court's determination will remain in place to frustrate first amendment rights during the interim. In some circumstances, delay itself violates free speech.[74]

According to Justice White, the *Cohn* case fell into this last category. In that case, a state statute in Georgia made it a criminal offense to publish a rape victim's name. In apparent violation of that statute, a television station identified the victim in a celebrated local case. Her father sued the station in state court, contending that the station's violation of the statute could be the basis for liability in damages. The station responded that it was entitled under the first amendment to identify the victim and that the statute was unconstitutional. The Georgia Supreme Court rejected the station's first amendment defense, but held that a violation of the statute did not alone establish the plaintiff's right to compensation under state law. The court thus remanded the case for trial to determine whether the plaintiff could recover for an invasion of privacy under general state tort law. The station sought review in the Supreme Court. Justice White acknowledged that the state courts had more work to do in order to resolve the dispute: The trial on the plaintiff's state claim lay ahead. Yet since the state supreme court had said all it would ever say about the station's constitutional claim, that court's judgment on that issue was immediately reviewable.

To justify an exception from the final judgment rule, Justice White anticipated three scenarios. First, the station might be held liable under state tort law

---

73. See, e.g., *Miami Herald Pub. Co. v. Tornillo,* 418 U.S. 241 (1974).

74. See *Nat'l Socialist Party v. Skokie,* 432 U.S. 43, 44 (1977) (explaining that a restraint on expression is problematic even if it continues only until the merits of a first amendment question can be resolved); *Org. for a Better Austin v. Keefe,* 402 U.S. 415, 418 (1971) (concluding that a preliminary injunction was sufficiently final because it had been in effect for three years and plainly restricted expression).

and might, then, appeal again. In that event, the Georgia Supreme Court would only reaffirm its decision that a television station could be forced to pay damages for broadcasting a rape victim's name, the first amendment notwithstanding. At that point, the station might again seek review in the Supreme Court. But the federal issue would be in no better position for the Court's attention then than it was already. Second, the station might elude liability under state law. If that happened, the federal question would fall out of the case. The disappointed plaintiff might appeal, but not on a federal theory. In that event, the state supreme court's unreviewed decision sustaining the statute against constitutional attack would remain in place, indicating (perhaps erroneously) that a television station had no first amendment right to identify a rape victim.

Justice White found both those scenarios unacceptable. Under the one, the Court would only postpone an important first amendment question that it would decide later, anyway. Under the other, the Court would allow that question to escape review altogether and thereby leave an important free press question in "an uneasy and unsettled constitutional posture."[75] Accordingly, White preferred a third scenario. If the Court examined the station's first amendment claim in its current posture and sustained the station's position, the litigation would be at an end. That would not only vindicate the first amendment claim advanced by the television station in the instant case, but would also avoid leaving other stations in Georgia to operate in the "shadow" of the statute even though its validity was in "serious doubt." [76]

The Court has not limited cases in this last category to disputes over the first amendment.[77] Nor has the Court fully rebutted Chief Justice Rehnquist's contention that this last category of exceptions from the finality rule (if not the first three) is entirely "formless" and thus threatens to swallow the rule itself.[78] The fair inference may be that the decisions under this heading reflect a prudential sense that the final judgment rule can and should be relaxed on an *ad hoc* basis when immediate appellate jurisdiction is appropriate to ensure the accuracy, uniformity, and supremacy of federal law. Formally, however, the Court disclaims any "expansion of the exceptions stated in" *Cohn*.[79]

---

75. *Cohn*, 420 U.S. at 485-86, quoting *Tornillo*, 418 U.S. at 247 n.6.

76. Id. at 486. Justice White conceded that, in this, he necessarily anticipated the Court's view of the merits of the station's first amendment claim. See note 65. In *Cohn*, as in many other cases like it, the Court reserved judgment on the finality issue until it heard the parties' arguments on the merits and was in a position to know the result it would reach if it had jurisdiction. There may be a lesson in that familiar practice. Once the justices have invested time and resources in a case and are poised to render a decision on the merits, they are unlikely to withhold judgment for want of a final judgment below. If, at that point, the justices *do* wash their hands of a case, it is probably for another reason (stated or unstated).

77. See, e.g., *Goodyear Atomic Corp. v. Miller*, 486 U.S. 174 (1988) (exercising jurisdiction to protect the federal interest in safety standards at nuclear power plants); *Southland Corp. v. Keating*, 465 U.S. 1 (1984) (exercising jurisdiction to avoid interference with the arbitration of labor disputes).

78. *Cohn*, 420 U.S. at 505-08 (dissenting opinion).

79. *Jefferson v. City of Tarrant*, 118 S.Ct. 481, 487 (1997). See note 179 and accompanying text (discussing the parallel final judgment rule attending appellate review of federal court judgments).

D. State Questions

The Supreme Court has jurisdiction to review state court judgments for errors of federal (not state) law. This has been the pattern from the outset. Section 25 of the Judiciary Act of 1789 specified that the Court could exercise appellate jurisdiction only if a state court first decided a federal question and could reverse only for "error" with respect to that federal question.[80] The Reconstruction Congress introduced doubts in 1867, when it enacted new legislation: (1) retaining the requirement that the Court could consider only cases in which a state court had ruled on a federal claim, but (2) deleting the follow-on requirement that only an error touching the federal question could be the basis for reversal. That change suggested that Congress had altered the scope of the Court's work in a fundamental way. Where previously the Court had been limited to dispositive questions of *federal* law, it appeared that under the 1867 Act, the Court would also consider *state* law issues. In *Murdock v. City of Memphis*,[81] however, the Court rejected that construction of the 1867 legislation.

Murdock's ancestors entered an agreement with Memphis, under which they conveyed a parcel of waterfront property to the city with the understanding that it would be used by the United States Navy. The agreement specified that if the Navy failed to establish a depot on the site, the land would be held in trust for the grantors and their heirs. The city sold the land to the Navy, and the Navy, in turn, began constructing a depot as planned. Ten years later, however, the Navy abandoned the project. By act of Congress, the federal government conveyed the parcel back to the city for the city's "use and benefit." Murdock filed suit in state court, claiming that as a beneficiary of the trust he was entitled to the land under the terms of the original agreement. The city responded that, as a matter of state property law, the ten-year attempt to establish the depot satisfied the original agreement and defeated the trust, that the suit was barred by the state statute of limitations, and that, in any event, the statute under which the city had received the land back from the government independently cleared the city's title as a matter of federal law. The state court ruled for the city on all counts.

On appellate review in the Supreme Court, Murdock insisted that he, too, claimed the land under federal law on the theory that the statute conveying the land to the city actually confirmed the trust created by the original agreement. Justice Miller doubted the merit of that theory, but agreed that it was sufficiently federal in character to invoke the Court's appellate jurisdiction. Miller focused, then, on Murdock's further argument that, pursuant to the 1867 Act, the Court should consider not only that federal question, but also the state law questions on which he had lost in state court. Justice Miller acknowledged the difficulty that the 1867 Act had introduced by dropping the provision in the 1789 Act restricting the Court to federal issues. But he refused to read the 1867 Act actually

---

80. See Chapter II, text accompanying note 61. Recall that Congress has considerable authority with respect to the Court's appellate jurisdiction. See Chapter IV, notes 48-72 and accompanying text.

81. 87 U.S. (20 Wall.) 590 (1874).

to discard that requirement and, instead, effectively read it back into the statute governing the Court's appellate jurisdiction.

Murdock contended that the Court's constitutional jurisdiction extended to "cases" and "controversies," which necessarily included both federal and state issues.[82] If, then, the Court was restricted to considering only federal questions, it must be because Congress had established that limit by statute. The 1789 Act might well have done so, but the superseding 1867 Act did not. That argument had force. Yet it proved too much. Justice Miller declined to infer such a "radical and hazardous" change from legislative silence. Invoking a clear statement rule, he insisted that if Congress had "intended" to alter something that had been policy since the central government's "foundation," it would have done so explicitly. Miller inferred just the opposite from the 1867 Act's express preservation of the baseline requirement that the state court must have decided a federal question in order to trigger the Court's jurisdiction. If, on considering a case, the Court was to examine all manner of state issues, Miller found it implausible that Congress would have made the existence of a federal question crucial in the first place.[83]

Justice Miller added that general policy fortified his conclusion that the Court's jurisdiction was limited to federal issues. In the past, when Congress had thought that federal rights could be protected only by giving a federal court jurisdiction to decide related state law issues, Congress had conferred that kind of jurisdiction on the inferior federal courts.[84] Moreover, an expanded scope for the Court's appellate jurisdiction would be subject to abuse. Unscrupulous litigants might inject marginal federal issues into cases for the purpose of obtaining Supreme Court consideration of state law questions.[85] Finally, Justice Miller said it was not entirely clear, after all, that the Court had previously restricted itself to federal issues only because of the limitation in the 1789 Act and not on the basis of "general principles." By that, Miller plainly meant the Constitution. He explained in the end that by reading the 1867 Act still to restrict the Court's purview to federal issues, he avoided any need to decide whether the Act would have been constitutional if it had extended the Court's reach to state law issues as well.[86]

It is possible (though by no means clear) that the Reconstruction Congress meant the 1867 Act to reshape the Court's appellate jurisdiction in the radical manner that Justice Miller disclaimed. Miller's opinion in *Murdock*, like his opinion for the Court in the *Slaughterhouse Cases*[87] and other notorious decisions in the period, may have been part of a general effort on the part of a conservative Supreme Court to circumscribe, if not to frustrate entirely, the nationalist agenda then ascendant in Congress.[88] Nevertheless, Miller's result was

---

82. See Chapter VIII, text accompanying note 6 (discussing this point).

83. 87 U.S. at 619, 626, 630.

84. See Chapter VIII, notes 288-301 and accompanying text (discussing the district courts' supplemental jurisdiction pursuant to 28 U.S.C. § 1367).

85. 87 U.S. at 629. None of Justice Miller's points was unanswerable, but his arguments were powerful in cumulative effect. Congress made no effort in the wake of *Murdock* to enact clear language calling on the Court to second-guess state courts on state law issues.

86. 87 U.S. at 632-33.

87. 83 U.S. (16 Wall.) 36 (1872).

88. See William M. Wiecek, *Murdock v. Memphis: Section 25 of the 1789 Judiciary Act and Judicial Federalism*, in Origins of the Federal Judiciary: Essays on the Judiciary Act of 1789, at 223, 238-39 (Marcus ed. 1992); Chapter II, notes 70-75 and accompanying text (discussing Reconstruction).

pragmatic and, in retrospect, essential to foundational understandings of American constitutional law.

Justice Miller recognized that the decision in *Murdock* had important implications both for the Supreme Court's relationship to state courts and for the practical conduct of appeals. By his account, the Court had appellate jurisdiction to determine any federal issue that had been decided by the state court below and to affirm the state court judgment if it was correct. If, however, the Court concluded that the state court had reached an erroneous decision on a federal issue, the Court must determine whether there was a separate state law ground on which the state court's judgment could properly rest. If so, then the Court must still affirm, notwithstanding the state court's error with respect to the federal question that triggered appellate jurisdiction in the first instance. The Court could reverse a state court only if it both *found* federal error and *failed to find* an alternative state law ground for the state court's judgment.[89]

Subsequently, the Court went a significant step further. In *Eustis v. Bolles*,[90] Justice Shiras said that if a state court judgment rests independently on a determination of state law, the Court must wash its hands of the case altogether, disclaiming authority to examine even the state court's decision on a federal question. The proper disposition is neither to affirm nor to reverse on any basis, but to *dismiss* for want of jurisdiction to consider either federal or state law issues.[91] Together, *Murdock* and *Eustis* entail three ideas that play crucial roles in the modern framework: (1) the state courts' authority to determine questions of state law; (2) the Supreme Court's inability to exercise supplemental jurisdiction over state law claims; and (3) the adequate state ground limit on the Supreme Court's appellate jurisdiction.

State court authority. State courts are authoritative with respect to state law. This follows from the absence of any federal court with jurisdiction to review state interpretations of state law for error.[92] More fundamentally, it almost certainly has substantive footing in constitutional law.[93] Justice Miller found it unnecessary to hold in *Murdock* that the Constitution leaves state issues to the state courts. Yet if the Court *had* authority to reject state courts' views of local law (and thus to substitute its own ideas of better policy), the very existence of autonomous state law (as distinct from federal law) would be unintelligible. In this respect, Miller was surely right in *Murdock*. A change from the traditional

---

89. *Murdock*, 87 U.S. at 635 (majority opinion).

90. 150 U.S. 361 (1893).

91. Matasar and Bruch contend that *Murdock* unjustifiably refused to accept jurisdiction to decide state law issues conferred by the 1867 Act and that *Eustis* unjustifiably refused to accept even the jurisdiction to decide federal issues that *Murdock*, for its part, embraced. Matasar & Bruch, note 46, at 1319-20.

92. *Dorchy v. Kansas*, 264 U.S. 286, 291 (1924). Federal courts *do* determine state law questions in a variety of contexts. But they do not have authority actually to second-guess the state courts on their own local law and to override state court decisions they regard as erroneous. See Chapter VI, notes 150-55 and accompanying text (explaining that the inferior federal courts have no appellate jurisdiction to review state judgments for error regarding *federal* law).

93. But see *Fay v. Noia*, 372 U.S. 391, 466-67 (1963) (Harlan, J., dissenting) (contending that state court authority regarding state law issues is a constitutional mandate).

understanding on this point would have revolutionized the system, top to bottom.[94]

Supplemental jurisdiction. The inferior federal courts have jurisdiction to determine both federal and related state law questions in order to resolve cases within their original jurisdiction.[95] The Supreme Court, by contrast, is limited to dispositive federal issues, even though state law issues, too, must be determined before a case can be laid to rest. This proposition, too, can rest on the Court's interpretation of the 1867 Act and its modern iteration in § 1257. By statute, then, the Court is limited to federal issues and has no authority to determine state claims, however important they may be to the just and proper resolution of the entire dispute. Any constitutional basis for the Supreme Court's inability to exercise supplemental jurisdiction is problematic. If the Constitution *does* make the state courts authoritative with respect to state law, it surely must follow that the Supreme Court has no power to review state court decisions for "error" that, by hypothesis, cannot exist. Yet if a federal question "case" within the meaning of Article III encompasses both federal and state law issues, then it seems to follow that the Supreme Court, like the inferior federal courts, should be able to determine whatever state law issues demand resolution in order to dispose of the entire "case."[96]

The answer lies in the different structural arrangements in which inferior federal courts and the Supreme Court operate. When a federal district court entertains an action as an original matter, there is typically no previous state court decision on any state law issues in the case. It makes sense, then, that the district court should have jurisdiction to give those issues an initial determination—hoping that its decision matches what a state court would have done in its place. When the Supreme Court entertains a case on appellate review, however, there *is* a previous state court judgment on state issues already in place. It makes little sense, then, that the Supreme Court should have jurisdiction either to second-guess the state courts regarding their own law or, certainly, simply to rubber-stamp a state decision the Supreme Court has jurisdiction to *consider*, but not to *change*. This is why Congress has never enacted a statute contemplating that the Supreme Court should exercise appellate jurisdiction in diversity cases initially adjudicated in state court. Given that state law controls in cases of that kind, the only "error" the Supreme Court might detect would be state court mistakes regarding state law.

Independent and adequate state grounds. As a general matter, the Supreme Court cannot upset state court judgments that rest on independent and adequate state grounds. The Court's appellate jurisdiction hinges on a state court's resolution of a case on a federal basis. The Court can affirm or reverse only with respect to a decision of that kind. If, then, a state court judgment rests on a separate state law ground, the Supreme Court has no jurisdiction in the matter at

---

94. See Martha A. Field, *Sources of Law: The Scope of Federal Common Law*, 99 Harv. L. Rev. 881, 921 (1986).

95. See Chapter VIII, notes 288-301 and accompanying text.

96. In a famous *amicus curiae* brief in *Murdock*, Benjamin Curtis, himself a former associate justice, argued that an Article III "case" cannot mean one thing when a district court exercises original jurisdiction and something else when the Supreme Court entertains an appeal.

all—not to reexamine the state court's decision regarding state law, no more to reexamine the state court's decision regarding a question of federal law. This is *Eustis'* extension beyond *Murdock*. The great flexibility of modern practice in the Supreme Court permits the Court to manipulate the issues presented for decision and, in that way, to elude some of the rigidity of the *Eustis* doctrine.[97] In the main, however, that doctrine holds: A state ground of decision, both independent and adequate, defeats the Supreme Court's appellate jurisdiction.

Once again, the explanation for this understanding may be simply that the Court has construed the statutes governing its jurisdiction this way. And, once again, there is a constitutional argument. If a state court has properly disposed of a case by means of an interpretation of state law that the Supreme Court has no authority to question, the constitutional framework may contemplate that the Court should not presume to interfere, even to address a federal question. The Court itself occasionally suggests that if it were to reexamine a state court's judgment on a federal question in those circumstances, it would act in an (improper) advisory capacity: If the state judgment will remain in place (resting as it does on state law), the Supreme Court's review of the federal issue can make no difference in the outcome.[98]

E. Independent State Grounds

Within its field of operation, the doctrine of independent and adequate state grounds insulates state court determinations of federal law from Supreme Court oversight. Accordingly, the administration of the doctrine bears implications for the Court's function as the system's ultimate referee. Upon the whole, the Court retains ample appellate jurisdiction to maintain the accuracy, uniformity, and supremacy of federal law. There are exceptions, but they tend to prove this general rule.

1. Parallel State and Federal Issues

When litigants in state court advance parallel state and federal claims in the alternative, they can succeed on *either* theory. In that kind of case, the effect of

---

97. See notes 191-94 and accompanying text.

98. See, e.g., *Herb v. Pitcairn*, 324 U.S. 117, 125-26 (1945); *Noia*, 372 U.S. at 466-67 (Harlan, J., dissenting). See Chapter IX, notes 6-22 and accompanying text (discussing the ban on advisory opinions) Matasar and Bruch contend that if the parties continue to dispute a federal question, there is still a case or controversy sufficient to support the exercise of Article III judicial power. Matasar & Bruch, note 46, at 1301-05. By some accounts, *Eustis* is best understood as a matter of pragmatic judgment. By disclaiming appellate jurisdiction, the Court avoids grappling with difficult federal questions, eschews unnecessary confrontations with state courts, and reserves its time and resources for other matters. Thomas E. Baker, *The Ambiguous Independent and Adequate State Ground in Criminal Cases: Federalism Along a Mobius Strip*, 19 Ga. L. Rev. 799 (1985). That explanation is probably correct, but incomplete. The Court needs no hard jurisdictional bar to achieve those ends, but can recognize formal jurisdiction and simply decline to exercise it. See notes 182-90 and accompanying text.

the adequate state ground doctrine on the Court's core functions depends on which party prevails in state court and the theory that proves successful there. If the party advancing a federal claim wins on both federal and state theories, the Supreme Court has no jurisdiction to review the judgment. The state court decision on the state claim is authoritative and decisive. The judgment can rest on that ground alone, and it will make no difference if the Supreme Court finds fault with the state court's treatment of the federal issue. The Court's ability to ensure the accuracy and uniformity of federal law is compromised. Yet, by hypothesis, the state court has either construed federal law correctly or given it an overly generous interpretation. Accordingly, the Court's capacity to ensure the supremacy of federal law is unaffected.

A famous old case, *Fox Film Corp. v. Muller*,[99] is the most commonly cited illustration of this point. Fox sued Muller in state court to recover damages for breach of two contracts. Muller answered that the contracts were unenforceable, because they contained an arbitration clause that had previously been held invalid under federal antitrust law. Fox countered that the offending arbitration clause was severable and that the remaining portions of the contracts could be enforced. The state supreme court held for Muller. When Fox sought appellate review, Muller argued that the state court had decided only that the arbitration clause was inseverable and that, since severability was a matter of state law, the state court had decided no federal issue to which the Supreme Court's jurisdiction could attach. Fox argued, by contrast, that the state court had decided both that the arbitration clause was inseverable (as a matter of state law) and that the contracts were invalid (as a matter of federal law). Justice Sutherland assumed that the state court had decided both issues, but then disclaimed Supreme Court appellate jurisdiction. Since the contracts were unenforceable on the state ground alone, nothing the Court said about any federal issues in the case would change the result below. As Sutherland saw the matter, the Supreme Court lacked jurisdiction in light of the "settled rule" that when a state court judgment "rests upon two grounds, one of which is federal and the other nonfederal," the Court's appellate jurisdiction "fails" if the non-federal ground is "independent of the federal ground and adequate to support the judgment."[100]

If, by contrast, the party advancing a federal claim *loses* on both federal and state theories, the Supreme Court *does* have appellate jurisdiction to review the state court's decision on the federal issue. The state court's unfavorable determination of the state question counts as an authoritative interpretation of state law, immune from Supreme Court review. But the state court's judgment cannot rest on that ground alone. Now it *does* make a difference if the Supreme Court takes a different view of federal claim. The Court can reverse the state court's failure to give that claim its rightful scope. Accordingly, the Court's ability to ensure the accuracy, uniformity, and supremacy of federal law is preserved intact. In *Hurley*

---

99. 296 U.S. 207 (1935).

100. Id. at 210. Justice Sutherland recognized that the separability issue arose only because the arbitration clause had previously been invalidated on federal grounds and, accordingly, that there was a formal federal issue at the bottom of the case. Yet since Fox conceded that the arbitration clause violated federal law, Sutherland found that question "foreclosed" and no longer a "subject of controversy" for the state courts. Id. See note 109 (discussing an alternative analysis of *Fox*).

v. Irish-American Gay, Lesbian and Bisexual Group of Boston,[101] for example, GLIB sued the organizers of the St. Patrick's Day Parade in state court, contending that the organizers had violated the Massachusetts public accommodations statute by refusing to allow GLIB to participate. The organizers responded on both state and federal grounds: By their account, the parade was not a public accommodation within the meaning of the state statute, and, if it was, they were nonetheless entitled under the first amendment to exclude GLIB in order to avoid association with GLIB's message. The state supreme court ruled against the organizers on both issues. Writing for the Supreme Court, Justice Souter reached the first amendment claim and reversed.

If a litigant advancing a federal claim loses on that claim, but wins on a parallel state claim, the Supreme Court has no appellate jurisdiction. The state court's decision on the state issue is decisive. The judgment will not change, irrespective of what the Court might say regarding the state court's treatment of the federal claim. The state court's favorable judgment on the state law claim may insulate a mistaken interpretation of federal law from Supreme Court review. Yet the harm is comparatively modest. By hypothesis, the party who might have won on the basis of a federal claim succeeds on an alternative state law basis. The Court's capacity to ensure the accuracy, uniformity, and supremacy of federal law is affected only moderately. If, by contrast, the plaintiff wins on the federal claim, but loses on the state claim, the Supreme Court has jurisdiction to examine the state court's decision on the federal issue (at the behest of the defendant). The state court's decision on the state issue is authoritative as always, but it is not independently decisive. The plaintiff's victory depends, instead, on the state court's determination of the federal claim. If that determination is erroneous, the Supreme Court can correct it and thus make a difference in the way the dispute is settled—namely, by reversing the state court's overly expansive interpretation of federal law. Once again, then, the Court has appellate jurisdiction to ensure accuracy and uniformity, though that jurisdiction is unnecessary to ensure the supremacy of federal law.

In *Michigan v. Long,*[102] for example, a state criminal defendant asked the state courts to suppress evidence that he contended had been obtained in a search that violated both the fourth amendment and the corresponding provision of the state constitution. The state supreme court ruled in the defendant's favor. In the Supreme Court, Justice O'Connor recognized that if that judgment rested exclusively on the state constitutional provision, the Court had no jurisdiction to address either that issue or the fourth amendment question. If, however, the state court judgment rested on the defendant's fourth amendment claim, the Court *did* have jurisdiction. In *Long,* Justice O'Connor resolved the ambiguity in favor of the Court's jurisdiction, reexamined the state court's treatment of the fourth amendment issue, and reversed.[103]

---

101. 515 U.S. 557 (1995).

102. 463 U.S. 1032 (1983).

103. See notes 123-29 and accompanying text. Dissenting in *Long,* Justice Stevens argued that the Court should reserve its appellate jurisdiction for cases in which Supreme Court action is needed to *"vindicate"* federal law and should not review state court judgments that over-protect federal rights. Id. at 1068 (emphasis in original). Yet the Court does have jurisdiction to correct state court judgments that read federal rights too expansively— and uses that jurisdiction to maintain accuracy and uniformity. When the justices find it advisable to bypass a case in which a party prevailed below on the basis of an erroneously ex-

2. State and Federal Issues in Tandem

The analysis is different when state and federal issues are linked sequentially, so that a party must prevail on both state and federal questions in order to succeed. If the state court holds against a party on a threshold question of state law, that determination is authoritative. And, *ceteris paribus*, it is decisive. The state court will typically decline even to consider the further federal issue. In this situation, however, the Supreme Court has jurisdiction to look beneath the state court's resolution of the threshold state law issue and may, in the end, examine a federal question even though the state court declined (for state law reasons) to reach it. Since the state court's decision regarding the antecedent state issue forecloses consideration of the federal question, it is not entirely independent. It must be tested to ensure that it is not an insubstantial (or even manipulative or duplicitous) excuse for refusing to enforce the follow-on federal claim.

In some instances, the Supreme Court treats an analytically prior state law issue as part of a party's ultimate federal claim and, on that basis, assumes jurisdiction to determine whether the state court's decision on the state question enjoys "fair support."[104] In the *Fairfax* litigation, for example, the state law question whether Hunter had obtained title to the contested parcel before the treaties took effect was antecedent to the federal question whether the treaties, if they were in force, defeated Hunter's claim.[105] To succeed, the party claiming under the treaties (Martin) had to prevail both on the issue of state property law and on the further theory that the treaties established his title. The Virginia Court of Appeals resolved the threshold state law issue against Martin, and ordinarily that decision would have foreclosed Supreme Court appellate jurisdiction. Nevertheless, Justice Story reviewed the state court's determination of the state law issue, evidently to ensure that Martin's federal claim was not prejudiced by means of a manipulative decision on an antecedent question of state law.

---

pansive interpretation of federal law, the Court need not rely on the adequate state ground doctrine, but can simply decline review in its discretion. See notes 182-90 and accompanying text. Justice Stevens has also argued (consistently) that to forestall needless Supreme Court consideration of federal claims, state courts should address state law issues first and resolve cases on that basis when possible. In that way, too, litigants advancing federal claims in state court may prevail (on state law grounds), even though the Supreme Court, were it to consider the merits of their federal claims on direct review, would find them wanting. *Massachusetts v. Upton*, 466 U.S. 727, 735 (1984) (concurring opinion).

104. Professor Wechsler called this an exercise of "ancillary" jurisdiction. Herbert Wechsler, *The Appellate Jurisdiction of the Supreme Court: Reflections on the Law and Logistics of Direct Review*, 34 Wash. & Lee L. Rev. 1043, 1052 (1977). But see notes 95-96 and accompanying text. The Court also safeguards federal claims from ill-advised determinations of threshold state law issues by insisting that state grounds must be *adequate* to support the state court's judgment. The cases on adequate state grounds typically involve litigants who fail to comply with state procedural rules and, for that reason, forfeit the opportunity to press federal claims in state court. See note 139 and accompanying text. If a state court's jurisdictional explanation for failing to consider a federal claim is found wanting, it may not count as a "valid excuse." See Chapter VI, notes 89-90 and accompanying text.

105. See note 46.

Similarly, in *Creswill v. Grand Lodge Knights of Pythias*,[106] the Court reviewed the Georgia Supreme Court's findings of fact underlying its determination of an antecedent question of state law. The plaintiffs in *Creswill* operated a whites-only Knights of Pythias lodge in Georgia. They sued a competing lodge (said to be operated for the "negro" and "Asiatic races") in state court, seeking an injunction preventing that lodge from incorporating in Georgia under the "Knights of Pythias" name. The African Americans who operated the second lodge countered that they were entitled to use that title under an act of Congress, which had authorized the original formation of their group in the District of Columbia. The state court rested judgment for the segregationist lodge on the theory that the African American defendants had waited too long to incorporate in Georgia and thus were guilty of *laches* within the meaning of state law. In the Supreme Court, Chief Justice White explained that since the state court's decision on the *laches* issue threatened to defeat a claim of federal right, the Court had appellate jurisdiction to determine whether that decision had "fair support" in the factual record. Finding that the evidence actually showed that the African American lodge had *not* hidden its claim to use the "Knights of Pythias" name, White reversed the state court decision.[107]

In *Ward v. Bd. of County Comm. of Love County*,[108] local authorities contended that members of an Indian tribe had paid state taxes voluntarily and thus could not sue for a refund on the theory that the taxes violated federal law. The Supreme Court acknowledged that if the Indians had actually paid the taxes without objection, there was an independent state law basis on which the state court judgment against them could rest—namely, the absence of a state statute authorizing reimbursement for unlawful taxes willingly paid. The Court explained, however, that it would be unconstitutional for the state to deny a refund if the Indians had been coerced. To ensure that the state's asserted state ground was genuine, the Court conducted its own examination of the question. Finding no "fair or substantial" support for the state court judgment that the Indians had paid voluntarily, the Court concluded that they had, in fact, paid under compulsion. Accordingly, there was no state law ground that could insulate the state court judgment from review.[109]

---

106. 225 U.S. 246 (1912).

107. Id. at 261.

108. 253 U.S. 17 (1920).

109. Id. at 22-24. The *Fox* case may also fit under this heading. If the state court had decided that the invalid arbitration clause *was* severable, Muller might have argued that the remaining provisions in the contracts were nonetheless unenforceable because they, too, violated federal antitrust law, even with the admittedly invalid arbitration clause stripped out. If the state court had ruled against Muller on that argument, its judgment would have been reviewable in the Supreme Court. Arguably, then, the Supreme Court lacked jurisdiction in *Fox* not because the state court resolved that case on a state law ground, but rather because the state court resolved it on a state law ground *in Muller's favor*. Sutherland saw that point, but denied that the state law severability issue required appellate attention on the theory that it was analytically prior to a federal question. Sutherland *did* say that the state court's decision on severability was "not without fair support" and thus may have satisfied himself that, if the state and federal issues *were* linked sequentially, the state's disposition of the state issue was not duplicitous. Id. at 209. Yet he did not purport to see the case that way and, in fact, said explicitly that the issues were *not* arranged in tandem. Id. at 211.

3. Hybrid Cases

The independence requirement can be difficult to administer when state and federal issues are not arranged neatly either in parallel or in sequence, but are entangled with each other. Decisions in hard cases are not always anchored in clear and predictable rules, but typically turn on pragmatic judgment about the needs of the federal system.[110] Illustrations fall into three groups: (1) cases in which state and federal issues are so intertwined that they defy separation; (2) cases in which state law incorporates federal law; and (3) cases in which federal law incorporates state law.

State and federal law interwoven. In some instances, state and federal issues are so entangled that they resist the very delineation that the requirement of independence demands. If the Court were to disclaim appellate jurisdiction, federal claims would suffer for their close association with state issues over which state courts have plenary authority. Accordingly, the Court has consistently insisted that its jurisdiction is *not* defeated. In *Enterprise Irrigation Dist. v. Farmers Mutual Canal Co.*,[111] the Court said that its appellate jurisdiction is "plain" in any case in which a state court rests judgment on a state ground that is "so interwoven" with federal law that it is not "an independent matter."[112] These cases overlap with the cases on state and federal issues arranged sequentially. Here, too, the Court typically focuses on an issue the state court considered to be a matter of state law and determines whether the state court decision on that question has "fair support." The overlap is not surprising. In both instances, the practical question is whether the state court's treatment of local law enjoys enough support to defuse concerns that the state court has only concocted an ostensible state law excuse for frustrating the enforcement of federal law.[113]

In *Enterprise Irrigation* itself, the Court concluded that the Supreme Court of Nebraska had fairly applied the state law of estoppel to foreclose a federal due process claim. The Canal Company obtained permission from a state administrative agency to develop a waterway. After the Company completed the project, competitors for the water sued in state court, claiming that they had been given no opportunity to be heard in the administrative proceeding in which the Canal Company had been authorized to proceed. Justice Van Devanter said that the state court's decision on the state law estoppel theory was perfectly sound. The plaintiffs had stood idly by while the Canal Company invested resources in the project and only then had asserted their claims.

State law incorporation of federal law. Cases in which state law incorporates federal law are prime candidates for Supreme Court appellate jurisdiction.[114] Even though a state court's analysis is formally a matter of state law, the state court purports to elaborate federal law as the content of state law and, on

---

110. See Ronald J. Greene, *Hybrid State Law in the Federal Courts*, 83 Harv. L. Rev. 289 (1969).

111. 243 U.S. 157 (1917).

112. Id. at 164.

113. Justice Sutherland essentially made this point in *Fox* when he said that the rule in *Enterprise Irrigation* (regarding "interwoven" issues) did not "apply" *because* the issues did not appear in tandem. Id. at 210-11.

114. See Chapter VIII, notes 192-200 and accompanying text (discussing the debate over whether federal district courts have jurisdiction in similar circumstances).

that basis, reaches a judgment that implicates federal interests. In *State Tax Com-m'n v. Van Cott*,[115] Van Cott filed suit in state court contending that the salary he earned as a federal employee was exempt from state income tax, both because income from federal sources was immune under federal law and because the state income tax statute recognized a similar exemption. The state supreme court held for Van Cott, and the Tax Commission sought review. The Commission conceded that the judgment rested formally on the state court's interpretation of the state statute. But the Commission insisted that the state court had not exercised independent judgment, but rather had thought that it was compelled to read the statute to exempt Van Cott's income in light of prior Supreme Court precedents (upholding exemptions in similar cases on federal constitutional grounds). In the Supreme Court, Justice Black agreed. In effect, state law incorporated federal law. The state court's judgment, then, was sufficiently federal in nature to warrant appellate review.[116]

The Court also exercises appellate jurisdiction when state law is not compelled to incorporate federal law, but does so nonetheless. In *Delaware v. Prouse*,[117] the Court reviewed a state court decision on a question of state constitutional law, because it appeared that the state court essentially equated the rights-bearing provisions of the state constitution with the federal Bill of Rights. In cases like *Prouse*, the Court asserts appellate jurisdiction to prevent state courts from either deflating or inflating federal constitutional rights behind the cover of interpreting their own local constitutions.[118]

Federal law incorporation of state law. The Court equally asserts appellate jurisdiction to supervise the state courts in cases in which federal law embraces state law. Cases under this heading also implicate the risks associated state and federal issues arranged sequentially: State courts may resolve issues that are formally matters of state law in a way that frustrates federal rights. In *Indiana ex rel. Anderson v. Brand*,[119] a tenured teacher sued school authorities in state court, contending that they had breached her employment contract. The authorities answered that the state legislature had repealed the tenure statute on which her contract was based. The state courts held for the school officials. In the Supreme Court, Justice Roberts explained that while the state court's interpretation of state contract law was entitled to "great weight," the Supreme Court must necessarily decide independently whether the state had violated the Con-

---

115. 306 U.S. 511 (1939).

116. Justice Black also explained that the Court had just upset the precedents on which the Utah court had relied and wanted to give the state court the opportunity to reexamine its construction of state law, free of the weight those precedents had previously carried. 306 U.S. at 515. The Utah Supreme Court ultimately reaffirmed its decision in Van Cott's favor.

117. 440 U.S. 648 (1979).

118. In *Moore v. Chesapeake & Ohio Ry.*, 291 U.S. 205 (1934), the Court said it would have appellate jurisdiction to review a state court determination of state tort law, if that local tort law incorporated federal safety regulations. In both *Prouse* and *Moore*, the Court preserved its ability to superintend the state courts regarding federal issues, even when only state law questions were formally on the table. In *Moore*, moreover, the Court's assertion that it would have appellate jurisdiction if federal law ultimately figured in the resolution of the dispute made it easier for the Court to hold that the case, as it stood, did not "arise under" federal law for purposes of original jurisdiction in a federal district court. See Chapter VIII, notes 192-95 and accompanying text.

119. 303 U.S. 95 (1938).

tracts Clause. Otherwise, that clause would merge with state law entirely and become a "dead letter."[120] There are other instances in which state law concepts are essential ingredients of federal claims. The obvious illustrations are cases under the Due Process Clause in which some substantive interest created by state law forms the property interest that, in turn, triggers constitutional requirements. In those cases, too, the Supreme Court has jurisdiction to reexamine state court judgments regarding issues that are formally matters of state law, but plainly figure in the analysis of related federal claims.[121]

4. Ambiguous State Court Decisions

The independence requirement is all the more difficult to administer when state courts fail to explain the basis on which they rest decision. Over its history, the Court has dealt with ambiguous state court opinions in a variety of ways.[122] In *Michigan v. Long*,[123] however, the Court adopted a single approach. Justice O'Connor explained that when a state court judgment "fairly appears" to "rest primarily on federal law," or to be "interwoven" with federal law, "and when the adequacy and independence of any possible state law ground is not clear from the face of the opinion," the Court will "accept as the most reasonable explanation" that the state court "decided the case the way it did because it believed that federal law required it to do so."[124]

This formulation has two elements: (1) a default position; and (2) a means of defeating that default position. The default position is *not* that the Court will always presume a federal ground in any case of uncertainty. It first must "fairly appear" that a state court decision rests either on a federal ground or on a ground that is "interwoven" with federal law in the sense of the rule articulated in the hybrid cases.[125] In *Long* itself, the Michigan Supreme Court cited the state constitution twice, but otherwise relied entirely on federal decisions elaborating federal search and seizure principles. Accordingly, Justice O'Connor concluded that the state decision "fairly appear[ed]" to depend "primarily" on federal law.[126]

---

120. *Brand*, 303 U.S. at 100.

121. See *Phillips v. Washington Legal Foundation*, 118 S.Ct. 1925, 1930 (1998) (explaining that the Constitution "protects rather than creates property interests" but nonetheless insisting that a state cannot "sidestep" a "takings" claim by "disavowing traditional property interests long recognized under state law"); *Webb's Fabulous Pharmacies v. Beckwith*, 449 U.S. 155 (1980) (rejecting a state court's determination that funds deposited in a state bank account were the "property" of the county rather than the individuals who had contributed to the account).

122. E.g., *Philadelphia Newspapers v. Jerome*, 434 U.S. 241 (1978) (asking a state court for clarification); *South Dakota v. Neville*, 459 U.S. 553 (1983) (making the determination itself); *Durley v. Mayo*, 351 U.S. 277 (1956) (dismissing on the theory that the Court's jurisdiction could not be established because the basis of the decision below was unclear).

123. See notes 102-03 and accompanying text.

124. 463 U.S. at 1040-41.

125. Id. at 1038 n.4 (citing *Enterprise Irrigation*); see notes 111-13 and accompanying text.

126. Justice O'Connor underscored that the default position is implicated only if a state court decision appears to rest on federal law in three subsequent cases: *Harris v. Reed*, 489 U.S. 255 (1989), *Coleman v. Thompson*, 501 U.S. 722 (1991), and *Ylst v. Nunnemaker*, 501

The means by which the default position can be defeated is a clear statement rule: A state court can control the ground of its own decision. If it wishes
to rely entirely on state law, it need only make that intention "clear" by inserting a "plain statement" in its opinion that precedents regarding federal law are
being used only for "guidance" and "do not themselves compel" the result.[127]
If the state court "indicates clearly and expressly" that its decision "is alternatively based on bona fide separate, adequate, and independent grounds," the
Supreme Court will "not undertake to review the decision."[128] Justice O'Connor explained in *Long* that, in this, the Court means both to respect state
court autonomy and to avoid rendering "advisory" opinions on federal law.[129]

The approach announced in *Long* has been questioned in academic circles.[130] If the point is in part to demonstrate respect for state courts, a rule that
tells those courts that their decisions will be reviewed unless they write clear
opinions scarcely seems apposite. If the point is actually to discover whether
state court decisions depend on federal law, a rule that invites disclaimers of
federal grounds may be ineffective. State judges may not satisfy the Court's desire for clarity, especially when so few parties seek Supreme Court review in
any event. Moreover, the Court's effort to distinguish federal and state grounds
more accurately may backfire: State courts may routinely drop boilerplate disclaimers of federal grounds into every opinion and thus formally rest all their
decisions on state grounds—whether or not federal principles play a significant
role.[131]

The chief criticism of *Long* is that it places the Court in a position to correct
state court errors of federal law primarily when the state courts have given federal rights an overly generous interpretation. On the whole, the default position
controls in cases like *Long* itself, in which litigants advance parallel state and
federal claims and obtain a favorable judgment in state court.[132] In cases of that

---

U.S. 797 (1991). In those cases, the question was not whether state courts had decided federal questions in a prisoner's favor, so that the Supreme Court could exercise appellate jurisdiction at the behest of the prosecution (and thus be in a position to reverse the state courts
and *sustain* a criminal conviction). Instead, the question in *Harris*, *Coleman*, and *Ylst* was
whether state courts had decided federal claims *against* a prisoner, so that the prisoner could
petition a federal district court for a writ of habeas corpus (in hopes of *defeating* a criminal
conviction as the justification for detention). See Chapter XII, note 108 and accompanying
text. The Court was comfortable with invoking the default position in a case like *Long*,
where the effect was to ensure its own jurisdiction, but plainly less enthusiastic about doing
the same thing in cases like *Harris*, *Coleman*, and *Ylst*, where the effect would have been to
allow convicts access to the inferior federal courts.

127. 463 U.S. at 1041.
128. Id.
129. Id. See note 98 and accompanying text.
130. E.g., Matasar & Bruch, note 46, at 1368-69.
131. See James A. Gardner, *The Failed Discourse of State Constitutionalism*, 90 Mich.
L. Rev. 761, 803-04 (1992) (reporting that the New Hampshire Supreme Court has adopted
this very practice). If the Supreme Court presumes that a state court has rested its decision
on federal grounds, accepts jurisdiction, and reverses, the state court is free on remand to reinstate its earlier judgment by clarifying that it actually was based on state law. Justice Ginsburg thinks the result is an unseemly pattern of Supreme Court decisions on constitutional
issues that are not ultimately dispositive. *Arizona v. Evans*, 514 U.S. 1, 31-33 (1995) (dissenting opinion).
132. The Court did not employ the *Long* approach in *Capital Cities Media v. Toole*,
466 U.S. 378 (1984). Broadcasting companies sued in state court, seeking access to state

kind, the only way in which the Supreme Court can alter the resolution is to take appellate jurisdiction of the federal claim and reverse. That is what happened in *Long*. A federal claim that had been upheld in state court was ultimately defeated. Supreme Court appellate jurisdiction in a case like *Long* serves the accuracy and uniformity of federal law, but it is unnecessary to guard its supremacy.[133] When the Court overturns a state decision regarding a federal claim, the Court not only sustains countervailing state interests, but also vindicates values that have their own constitutional footing in federalism, state autonomy, and democratic decision-making.[134] That insight, however, may only underscore the ideological implications of the approach the Supreme Court takes to its own jurisdiction in *Long* and similar cases.[135]

F. Adequate State Grounds

State law grounds of decision can foreclose Supreme Court appellate jurisdiction only if they are both independent and adequate. The adequacy of a state law ground is a question of federal law for the Court to determine.[136] Both state substantive and procedural grounds can qualify.[137] State substantive grounds tend to be tested for adequacy when state and federal issues are linked sequentially.[138] Most of the cases in which the Supreme Court finds state law grounds inadequate involve procedural grounds.[139]

---

criminal proceedings. The Pennsylvania Supreme Court refused to issue a writ of prohibition that would have forced a trial court to open the proceedings more fully. It was unclear whether the state supreme court meant to reject the broadcasters' first amendment claims or, instead, merely found a writ of prohibition unavailable as a matter of state law. Since the state court wrote no opinion at all, its decision could not "fairly appear" to rest on the federal ground. Given *Long*, the Court might have been expected to dismiss for want of jurisdiction. Instead, the Court vacated the state judgment and remanded for clarification. The disposition in *Capital Cities* may represent an departure from *Long* in a case in which the Court was particularly concerned that a federal right might otherwise be violated. It seems more likely, however, that the Court regarded *Capital Cities* as a case in which state and federal issues were arranged in tandem. The Court therefore assumed responsibility to test the independence and sufficiency of any supposed threshold state ground, lest it frustrate a federal claim that depended upon it. See notes 104-09 and accompanying text.

133. See text accompanying note 103.

134. Professor Bator often made this point. See Paul M. Bator, *The State Courts and Federal Constitutional Litigation*, 22 Wm. & Mary L. Rev. 605, 633 (1981).

135. Professor Glennon argues that *Long* allows the Court "to rein in liberal state judges." Robert J. Glennon, *The Jurisdictional Legacy of the Civil Rights Movement*, 61 Tenn. L. Rev. 869, 902 (1994). Professor Wells sees *Long* as one of many instances in which procedural rules are employed to promote substantive values. Michael Wells, *The Impact of Substantive Interests on the Law of Federal Courts*, 30 Wm. & Mary L. Rev. 499, 523-530 (1989).

136. *Street v. New York*, 394 U.S. 576, 583 (1969).

137. The *Murdock* case illustrates a state substantive ground of decision. The state court's judgment in that case rested on a matter of local real property law. See notes 81-89 and accompanying text.

138. See notes 104-09 and accompanying text.

139. Professor Meltzer provides an extensive catalog of the precedents. Daniel J. Meltzer, *State Court Forfeitures of Federal Rights*, 99 Harv. L. Rev. 1128 (1986).

State procedural grounds typically promote efficiency. For example, a state "contemporaneous objection" rule requires litigants to object to evidence at the time it is offered, on pain of forfeiting any later opportunity to complain either to the trial court or to the state appellate courts.[140] A rule of that kind encourages litigants to focus the trial court's attention on a claim at the earliest opportunity and thus allows the court either to sustain the objection and avoid error in the first instance or to build a record that will facilitate an appellate court's review of the matter. In the absence of such a rule, litigants might deliberately invite error by withholding claims from the trial court with the intention of urging an appellate court to reverse on those grounds if the trial court's judgment on the merits is unfavorable.[141]

The interest in efficient litigation does not always justify a refusal to consider federal claims.[142] Moreover, state procedural rules can be manipulated to frustrate federal claims indirectly. State procedural issues are invariably linked with federal questions in sequence: A state court declines to reach a federal claim, because the party advancing that claim failed to comply with the applicable local rule for presenting the claim in state court. That alone means that the Supreme Court must calculate whether the state ground is sufficient to foreclose appellate jurisdiction of the underlying federal claim. Thus when state courts foreclose federal claims because of a litigant's procedural default, the Court must inquire into the bona fides of the state court's work.

The Court rarely finds state grounds actually to *be* inadequate. To do so is to confront state courts that have disposed of cases on grounds they regard as sufficient and to insist that federal law has been sacrificed without justification. The political and ideological implications of that kind of conflict counsel restraint. The Supreme Court employs a process model to determine whether to consider federal questions that state courts refuse to entertain because of procedural default.[143] The cases in point fall into three categories: (1) cases in which state procedural rules violate federal law; (2) cases in which state rules are inconsistently applied; and (3) cases in which state rules have too little rational basis to warrant foreclosing Supreme Court review of federal issues.[144]

---

140. Litigants who fail to comply with state procedural rules of this kind are often said to "waive" the claims in issue. That is a misnomer. A waiver is a knowing and deliberate act. State procedural rules typically cut off claims if they are not seasonably advanced, whether or not the parties concerned consciously decided to withhold them. If, then, litigants lose the opportunity to press claims because of procedural default, they *forfeit* those claims in service of the state's interests in efficient litigation.

141. *Henry v. Mississippi*, 379 U.S. 443, 450 (1965). Professor Resnik disputes the notion that litigants commonly "sandbag" the state courts in this way. She argues that it is unrealistic to think that litigants and their lawyers plot such "fantastically risk-prone" strategies, particularly in criminal cases. It is far more likely that if counsel fails to object to illegal evidence at the proper time, it is because of ignorance or neglect. Judith Resnik, *Tiers*, 57 So. Calif. L. Rev. 837, 896-98 (1984). Accord Meltzer, note 139, at 1196-99.

142. Justice Holmes' famous dictum makes (but plainly overstates) this point: "[T]he assertion of federal rights, when plainly and reasonably made, is not to be defeated under the name of local practice." *Davis v. Wechsler*, 263 U.S. 22, 24 (1923).

143. See Chapter I, notes 61-65 and accompanying text (discussing the process model).

144. Professor Glennon contends that many of these cases reflect the Warren Court's efforts to contend with state court racism during the civil rights movement of the 1960s. Glennon, note 135, at 885-902.

Rules that violate federal law. A state court's implementation of a state procedural rule cannot be adequate to forestall Supreme Court review if the state rule itself violates federal law, either in general or as the rule is applied in a particular instance. If the state procedural rule is invalid as a federal matter, the Court has appellate jurisdiction to consider *that* federal issue, quite apart from the federal claim the state court failed to reach.[145] In *Brinkderhoff-Faris Trust & Savings Co. v. Hill*,[146] for example, the state court below deprived a taxpayer of property without due process by arbitrarily denying him an opportunity to attack a state tax on equal protection grounds. The Supreme Court reversed on the basis of the due process violation and remanded the case to state court for consideration of the equal protection claim.[147]

Modern illustrations tend to be cases in which state courts apply facially valid procedural rules in a fundamentally unfair way. In *Reece v. Georgia*,[148] an African American defendant claimed that blacks had been excluded from the grand jury that indicted him (for raping a white woman). The Georgia Supreme Court refused to consider that claim, because the defendant had failed to comply with a local rule requiring challenges to a grand jury array to be filed prior to indictment. The defendant had been indicted only three days after his arrest and before counsel had been appointed to represent him. In those circumstances, the Supreme Court held that the state's failure to give the defendant a "reasonable opportunity" to comply with the rule violated due process. Accordingly, his failure to comply supplied no adequate state ground for the state court's decision.

Due process cases are notoriously fact-sensitive. For every case like *Reece*, in which the individual prevailed, there are dozens of counter-examples in which litigants were unsuccessful. In *Michel v. Louisiana*,[149] decided with *Reece*, the Court rejected very similar due process arguments by African American defendants in Louisiana. And in *Herndon v. Georgia*,[150] the Court disclaimed jurisdiction to consider an obvious first amendment claim, because the defendant (an African American organizer for the Communist Party) had not advanced that claim until a motion for rehearing in state court. There were powerful reasons to decide *Michel* and *Herndon* the other way. But the Court plainly hesitated to confront the state courts in racially charged circumstances.[151]

Rules that are inconsistently applied. State grounds of decision can be inadequate if state courts enforce rules inconsistently or spring novel rules on litigants in the eleventh hour, when it is too late to comply.[152] In *NAACP v. Alabama ex*

---

145. See Alfred Hill, *The Inadequate State Ground*, 65 Colum. L. Rev. 943, 944-45 (1965). This is true, at least, if the validity of the procedural rule under federal law is properly presented to the state courts and thus preserved for Supreme Court attention. See notes 59-62 and accompanying text.

146. 281 U.S. 673 (1930).

147. Id. at 682.

148. 350 U.S. 85 (1955).

149. 350 U.S. 91 (1955).

150. 295 U.S. 441 (1935).

151. Dissenting in *Herndon*, Justice Cardozo argued that the first amendment claim in that case had not become clear until the Georgia Supreme Court gave the statute a surprising construction in another case and that the defendant had then advanced his claim as soon as he reasonably could—in a motion for rehearing. 295 U.S. at 446-47 (dissenting opinion).

152. The selective enforcement of state law can violate the fourteenth amendment, as can the retroactive application of a forfeiture rule. Moreover, in cases under this heading,

rel. Patterson,[153] the NAACP was held in contempt for refusing to produce its membership list for inspection by state authorities and appealed on the theory that the forced disclosure of its members' names would violate the first amendment. The Alabama Supreme Court refused to consider that federal claim, because the NAACP might have avoided contempt by resisting the original order to disclose the membership list in an action for a writ of prohibition. The state court had never before insisted on any such extraordinary procedure. Accordingly, the Supreme Court held that the NAACP's failure to follow that course did not furnish an adequate state ground for the state court's decision.[154]

One proposed extension on the *Patterson* theme is doubtful. In *Sullivan v. Little Hunting Park*,[155] Justice Douglas suggested that if a state court has authority to waive a rule, but does not always exercise that authority, it follows that the rule is inconsistently applied. In *Sullivan*, the Virginia Court of Appeals held that civil rights plaintiffs in a race discrimination case had committed procedural default under state law by failing to give opposing counsel a copy of the trial transcript. It was conceded that the state court had discretionary power to waive that rule to avoid a miscarriage of justice, but had declined to do so in *Sullivan*. In a separate opinion, Justice Harlan explained that if a state court's ability to make *ad hoc* exceptions to local procedural rules rendered its enforcement of those rules inadequate to support its judgments, state courts might respond by enforcing procedural rules relentlessly, without exceptions for cases in which justice called for dispensation. That, of course, would be perverse — and nothing that Justice Douglas would have wished to bring about.[156]

Rules that lack sufficient basis. State grounds of decision can be inadequate if they depend on peculiarly rigid rules that serve only trivial state interests. In *Staub v. City of Baxley*,[157] the state court refused to consider a first amendment attack on a city ordinance, because the plaintiff had challenged the statute in its entirety rather that specifying each section of the ordinance she meant to condemn. That, according to the Supreme Court, was to demand "an arid ritual of meaningless form."[158] In *Shuttlesworth v. City of Birmingham*,[159] the Court took a similar view of a rule regarding the paper on which an appellate brief could be printed. And in *James v. Kentucky*,[160] the Court refused to credit a state procedural ground where the state courts had declined to consider a criminal defendant's federal claim, because he had asked for a jury "instruction" when he should have asked for an "admonition." Here, too, there are close cases. Yet there are precedents enough to establish that some state procedural rules are in-

---

state courts may be charged with violating the underlying federal rights they purport to avoid — by erecting bogus state law grounds of decision for the deliberate purpose of frustrating federal law. See Hill, note 145, at 958-59; *Williams v. Georgia*, 349 U.S. 375, 399 (1955) (Clark, J., dissenting).

153. 357 U.S. 449 (1958).

154. Accord *NAACP v. Alabama ex rel. Flowers*, 377 U.S. 288 (1964); *Barr v. City of Columbia*, 378 U.S. 146 (1964).

155. 396 U.S. 229 (1969).

156. See Hill, note 145, at 985-86 n.174.

157. 355 U.S. 313 (1958).

158. Id. at 320.

159. 376 U.S. 339 (1964).

160. 466 U.S. 341 (1984).

sufficient to foreclose Supreme Court appellate review, even if those rules are not so baseless that they themselves violate the fourteenth amendment.[161]

When the Supreme Court concludes that a state ground of decision itself violates federal law, the Court typically reverses on that basis and remands the case to the state courts for consideration of the underlying federal claim. When the Court concludes that a state ground is inadequate, though not in itself invalid, the Court has no authority to reverse, unless and until it reaches the federal question that the state court declined to consider. The Court hesitates to determine federal questions without a state court decision below. Accordingly, the Court occasionally contrives to channel cases back to state court in an informal way. The classic illustrations in point, *Henry v. Mississippi*[162] and *Williams v. Georgia*,[163] were sensitive individual liberty cases. Both involved African American defendants convicted in state court at a time when racial tensions ran high. The Court clearly meant to encourage the state courts to set state procedural niceties aside and determine the merits of the defendants' federal constitutional claims. In both instances, the Court failed.[164]

In *Henry*, the Court acknowledged that the defendant had failed to comply with a state contemporaneous objection rule. Nevertheless, the Court reversed and remanded in hopes the state court would consider his federal claim anyway—if the state court concluded that he had not *deliberately* withheld the claim during trial and that the state's interests in efficiency were served just as well when he offered the claim in a post-trial motion.[165] In *Williams*, the Court acknowledged the validity of a state rule requiring challenges to the jury venire to be filed before trial, but intimated that the state court had applied that rule inconsistently. There, too, the Court reversed and remanded in hopes that the state court would reach the merits of the prisoner's underlying claim. Academics debate whether *Henry* and *Williams* prove that the adequate state ground doctrine is more a body of *ad hoc* prudential judgments than it is legal doctrine at all.[166]

---

161. Justice Frankfurter wrote separately in *Staub* to argue that it *did* make sense to ask the plaintiff to attack each section of the ordinance in turn, in order to focus her federal claims in the interest of rigorous analysis.

162. 379 U.S. 443 (1965).

163. 349 U.S. 375 (1955).

164. The defendant in *Henry*, the president of the local NAACP chapter, was ultimately vindicated in a habeas corpus proceeding in federal court. *Henry v. Williams*, 299 F. Supp. 36 (N.D. Miss. 1969). The defendant in *Williams* was executed. See Del Dickson, *State Court Defiance and the Limits of Supreme Court Authority: Williams v. Georgia Revisited*, 103 Yale L.J. 1423 (1994).

165. In *Henry*, accordingly, the Court suggested that the state's procedural ground of decision might be adequate only if the defendant had actually *waived* his federal constitutional claim. See note 140; Field, note 94, at 966-67. That idea has not survived. See Meltzer, note 139, at 1145. The Warren Court established a waiver standard for cases in which criminal defendants failed to comply with state procedural rules and then sought to raise federal claims via applications for the federal writ of habeas corpus. That rule, too, failed to survive. See Chapter XII, notes 100-06 and accompanying text.

166. Professor Meltzer contends that the source of the adequacy doctrine is federal common law, which allows states to employ a variety of rules in different contexts, but fixes a baseline (which itself varies with the circumstances) beneath which the states cannot go. Accordingly, the Court can vacate and remand a case if it finds a state law ground to be inadequate as a matter of federal common law, because state courts are obligated to apply that law just as would a federal court. Their failure to do so is reversible error. Meltzer, note 139, at 1132-33; see Chapter VI, notes 94-95 and accompanying text. Professor Field argues that

G. Standards of Review

In general, the standards the Supreme Court employs in reviewing state court judgments correspond to the three steps in the adjudicative function.[167] The Court extends great deference to state court determinations of historical facts and typically accepts findings of that kind if they are supported by "substantial evidence."[168] This is true (as a generalization) even with respect to findings touching constitutional claims.[169] In essence, the Court applies to state court findings the standard of review that Rule 52(a) of the Federal Rules of Civil Procedure prescribes for federal appellate review of factual findings by federal district courts. Under Rule 52(a), "[f]indings of fact, whether based on oral or documentary evidence, shall not be set aside unless clearly erroneous."[170] The Court equally defers to the state courts' rational inferences from historical facts.[171] By contrast, the Court exercises entirely fresh, *de novo* judgment regarding state court interpretations of federal law,[172] as well as state court applications of law to the facts of particular cases (determinations of so-called "mixed" questions of law and fact).[173]

The Court's authority to see that abstract principles of federal law are properly applied in actual cases was central to the great *Martin* case.[174] Hunter argued that if the Court had power to review the Virginia court's judgment at all, its power was limited to deciding whether the state court had correctly interpreted the treaties and did not extend to deciding whether the state court had correctly determined Martin's particular claim under the treaties, properly interpreted. Justice Story rejected that argument, explaining that the Court had appellate jurisdiction to review the state court's "decision" below. That decision must necessarily include both the state court's articulation of the abstract law of the matter and its application of that law to the instant facts.[175]

---

when the Court refuses to accept a state ground as adequate, it is not (necessarily) because that ground *is* inconsistent with federal common law, but rather because it *would* be if the Court were to create federal law for the occasion. According to Field, the Court's power to do that enables the Court to decide, instead, to "bend existing state rules to make them consistent with federal interests." Field, note 94, at 969-70.

167. See Chapter I, text accompanying note 5.

168. *General Motors v. Washington*, 377 U.S. 436, 442 (1964). If the state courts fail to find the material facts, the Court typically hesitates to make the necessary findings itself on the basis of the record and thus remands for further fact-finding at the state level. E.g., *United Bldg. & Constr. Trades Council v. Mayor of Camden*, 465 U.S. 208 (1984).

169. Cf. Chapter V, note 42.

170. See *Hernandez v. New York*, 500 U.S. 352, 365 (1991); *Bose Corp. v. Consumers Union*, 466 U.S. 485, 499 (1984).

171. See *Hernandez*, 500 U.S. at 369 (deferring to a state court's inference that a prosecutor's explanation for striking Hispanic jurors was not pretextual).

172. Hill, note 145, at 945.

173. *Norris v. Alabama*, 294 U.S. 587, 590 (1935); *Fiske v. Kansas*, 274 U.S. 380, 385 (1927).

174. *Martin*, 14 U.S. (1 Wheat.) 304 (1816); see notes 49-56 and accompanying text.

175. 14 U.S. at 358-59. Liebman and Ryan contend that *Martin* and other familiar precedents establish that all Article III courts exercising the federal judicial power must have authority to decide the "whole" case. Liebman & Ryan, note 55, at 696.

These generalizations hold in large measure, but they can be misleading. The Court routinely departs from them in sensitive contexts—sometimes to safeguard federal rights, sometimes to foster harmonious relations with state courts. In free speech cases, for example, the historical facts are invariably crucial, and an unsympathetic state court can skew proper constitutional analysis by misrepresenting the events on which first amendment principles are brought to bear. The Court has explained, accordingly, that it will reexamine state court findings of historical fact in speech cases as a safeguard against that contingency.[176] In other cases, the Court hesitates to give even state court determinations of mixed questions the independent examination that conventional doctrine contemplates. In order to disclaim that kind of review, the Court sometimes characterizes issues that are quite plainly mixed as, instead, questions of historical fact, and on that basis invokes a highly deferential standard of review.[177]

H. Appellate Review of Federal Judgments

The Supreme Court has appellate jurisdiction to review judgments rendered by the inferior federal courts. Pursuant to 28 U.S.C. § 1254, the Court may review cases "in the courts of appeals," either at the instance of a party or by certification from the court of appeals itself.[178] The circuit courts, in turn, have appellate jurisdiction (pursuant to 28 U.S.C. § 1291) to review "final decisions" by the district courts.[179] In the vast majority of cases, accordingly, the Supreme Court's

---

176. *Bose*, 466 U.S. at 499; *Hurley v. Irish-American Gay, Lesbian and Bisexual Group of Boston*, 515 U.S. 557 (1995).

177. In habeas corpus cases, the Court candidly acknowledges that if the Court itself regards the state courts as the best decision-makers with respect to a question, it is inclined to resolve doubts about the nature of the question in favor of finding it to be one of historical fact—for the very purpose of routing it to the state courts. See Chapter XII, notes 137-38 and accompanying text.

178. The idea of certifying questions to the Court seems sensible enough in the abstract. A circuit court may genuinely need the Court's guidance on a point of federal law before disposing of a case in which that question figures. See Sup. Ct. R. 19 (prescribing the procedure for certification). In the modern era, however, the Court has virtually ceased accepting certified questions. See *Wisniewski v. United States*, 353 U.S. 901, 902 (1957) (declining to answer a question that had divided different panels of the same circuit court and instructing the circuit court itself to "reconcile its internal difficulties").

179. See notes 57-58, 63-79 and accompanying text (discussing the finality rule with respect to judgments in state court). The Court cites cases involving the final judgment requirements in § 1291 and § 1257 interchangeably, as though the finality question is the same, irrespective of whether the tribunal below was a federal or state court. In *Cohn*, however, Chief Justice Rehnquist argued that while efficiency may be the chief consideration with respect to the former, more sensitive federalism concerns are at stake with respect to the latter. See notes 63-65 and accompanying text. Implementation of the finality rule under § 1291 has generated a maze of exceptions. See, e.g., *Firestone Tire & Rubber Co. v. Risjord*, 449 U.S. 368 (1981) (elaborating the "collateral order rule"). The circuit courts have jurisdiction to consider interlocutory appeals in a range of circumstances described by 28 U.S.C. § 1292. See Chapter X, notes 124, 282 (noting the availability of early appellate review in eleventh amendment and official immunity cases); Chapter XI, notes 127-28 and accompanying text (discussing interlocutory appeals in abstention cases). There are proposals to jettison the general finality rule and the special rules for interlocutory appeals captured in § 1292 in favor of a policy allowing appeals in an appellate court's discretion. See, e.g.,

jurisdiction attaches to circuit court judgments that depend on final judgments at the district level. The Court also enjoys an informal supervisory power to superintend the procedures followed in the inferior federal courts.[180] Each of these features of the Court's appellate jurisdiction generates its own problems.[181]

I. Discretionary Review

With few exceptions, the Supreme Court has discretion both to decide what cases it will accept for appellate review and to prescribe the criteria it will use to make the choices it does.[182] The old Eighteenth Century writs of error under which litigants were entitled to appellate review as of right,[183] together with Twentieth Century rights of direct appeal,[184] are gone. They have been replaced by a modern statutory writ of *certiorari*, which borrows only one characteristic

---

Robert J. Martineau, *Defining Finality and Appealability by Court Rule: Right Problem, Wrong Solution*, 54 U. Pitt. L. Rev. 717 (1993); Thomas D. Rowe, Jr., *Defining Finality and Appealability by Court Rule: A Comment on Martineau's Right Problem, Wrong Solution*, 54 U. Pitt. L. Rev. 795 (1993); John C. Nagel, *Replacing the Crazy Quilt of Interlocutory Appeals Jurisprudence with Discretionary Review*, 44 Duke L.J. 200 (1994). The Supreme Court has authority pursuant to § 1292(e) to promulgate different rules for interlocutory appeals, but has failed to exercise that authority.

180. See Sara Beale, *Reconsidering Supervisory Power in Criminal Cases: Constitutional and Statutory Limits on the Authority of the Federal Courts*, 84 Colum. L. Rev. 1433 (1984).

181. A party may seek review either "before or after" judgment, but the Court rarely finds it appropriate to act in advance of the circuit courts. See Sup. Ct. Rule 11 (stating that the Court will grant *certiorari* prior to judgment at the circuit level only in cases of "imperative public importance"); *Clinton v. City of New York*, 118 S.Ct. 2091, 2111 (1998) (Scalia, J., concurring and dissenting) (finding it appropriate to consider the line-item veto case on an expedited basis). Pursuant to 28 U.S.C. § 2253, habeas corpus petitioners who wish to appeal from unfavorable district court decisions must obtain a certificate of appealability from a single judge or circuit justice. In a series of decisions culminating in *House v. Mayo*, 324 U.S. 42 (1945), the Supreme Court held that a "case" was not "in" a circuit court of appeals unless and until a judge issued such a certificate. Accordingly, the Court itself had no jurisdiction under § 1254 to review the denial of a prisoner's request for such a certificate—made to an individual judge. The Court overruled *House* (on this point), in *Hohn v. United States*, 118 S.Ct. 1969 (1998). According to *Hohn*, the denial of a request for a certificate by an individual federal judge is itself a "case" within the meaning of § 1254 and thus can be reviewed in the Supreme Court, provided the Court chooses to grant the prisoner's *certiorari* petition. Justice Kennedy explained that the rule in *Hohn* comports with the language of § 1254 and, not coincidentally, permits the Court to fulfill its "normal function of reviewing possible misapplications of law" without resorting to extraordinary means. Id. at 1977. In *House*, for example, the Court ultimately sustained its jurisdiction under the All-Writs Act. See note 185.

182. See, e.g., 28 U.S.C. § 1253 (providing for appeals as of right in the relatively few cases decided by three-judge panels at the district level); 28 U.S.C. § 2284 (providing for three-judge district court panels in legislative apportionment cases). Both § 1257 (governing review of state court judgments) and § 1254 (governing review of inferior federal court judgments) recognize that the Court "may" accept a case for appellate review.

183. See Chapter II, text accompanying note 61.

184. See Bennett Boskey & Eugene Gressman, *The Supreme Court Bids Farewell to Mandatory Appeals*, 121 F.R.D. 81 (1988).

feature of its common law forerunner: its discretionary nature.[185] Litigants who suffer disappointing judgments on federal claims in either a state court or an inferior federal court may petition the Supreme Court for a writ of *certiorari* pursuant to § 1257 or § 1254, respectively. The Court receives thousands of petitions every year, but selects only about one hundred for full dress treatment.

Rule 10 of the Court's rules explains that a petition will be granted only for "compelling reasons" and "rarely" when the error the petitioner asks the Court to review is a mistaken "factual" finding or a "misapplication of a properly stated rule of law." Rule 10 offers an inexhaustive list of the kinds of cases that may warrant review: (1) cases in which inferior federal courts or state courts are divided over an "important matter" of federal law; (2) cases in which a federal court or a state court has decided an important question that "has not been, but should be" settled by the Supreme Court; and (3) cases in which a federal court or a state court has decided an important question "in a way that conflicts with" Supreme Court precedent.[186] The Court thus discourages petitions from litigants who complain only that the court below reached an erroneous judgment. The point is to screen the mass of cases in which lower courts may have made mistakes for those involving questions of larger moment for the legal system as a whole. The first illustrative category indicates that the Court means to settle disagreements between other courts in aid of uniformity. The second indicates that the Court means to decide hard cases in aid of accuracy. And the third signals that the Court means to superintend recalcitrant lower courts in aid of supremacy.

The Supreme Court does not operate on the private rights model.[187] It does not resolve isolated disputes and elaborate federal law only as a necessary by-product. Instead, the Court operates on something approaching the public rights model.[188] The Court chiefly elaborates federal law, using particular disputes as vehicles for its law-declaration function.[189] By common account, the Court must proceed in this way if it is to have any practical chance to perform its referee function in a system that constantly generates questions, both profound and technical, that demand authoritative answers.[190]

---

185. At common law, courts issued the writ of *certiorari* to obtain the record of a case in an inferior court in order to assume responsibility for the matter. Since that writ was familiar, the drafters of the Evarts Act in 1891 borrowed it (or rather its name) when they concluded that at least some portion of the Supreme Court's appellate workload should no longer be mandatory. The statutory writ of *certiorari* prescribed by § 1257 and § 1254 must be distinguished from the common law writ itself in its modern form. The All-Writs Act (28 U.S.C. § 1651) authorizes the Court to issue the common law writ in a proper case.

186. This formulation does not track Rule 10's own internal organization, but it accurately reflects the rule's content in substance. Rule 10 also mentions cases in which a circuit court of appeals has "so far departed from the accepted and usual course of judicial proceedings, or sanctioned such a departure by a lower court, as to call for an exercise of" the Supreme Court's supervisory power. See note 180 and accompanying text.

187. See Chapter I, notes 50-60 and accompanying text.

188. See Chapter I, notes 66-78 and accompanying text.

189. But see Chapter IX, notes 6-22 and accompanying text (discussing advisory opinions).

190. This insight has obvious implications for the Court's operations. For a discussion, see Samuel Estreicher & John Sexton, Redefining the Supreme Court's Role 128-36 (1986). Chief Justice Rehnquist has explained that in many instances the issues the Court must decide are not glamorous constitutional questions, but more rudimentary questions of federal

Not only does the Court select cases as vehicles for law-declaration. It also selects issues within cases in order to tailor its review to the matters that warrant attention. Rule 14 instructs petitioners to state the questions their cases present "concisely," so that the justices can identify plausible choices with a minimum of effort. If a case is selected, the Court commonly proceeds on the basis of the questions the petitioner articulates and limits itself to a consideration of those issues and any subsidiary questions "fairly included."[191] Often, however, the Court selects only one or more of the questions the petitioner identifies and denies review with respect to the others.[192] Occasionally, the Court introduces additional questions the petitioner did not advance,[193] or jettisons the petitioner's questions and substitutes a question or questions of its own.[194] The parties to a case the Court selects for appellate review thus may find themselves developing issues of federal law that the justices themselves have unilaterally injected into the case to make it serve some wider public purpose.

The Court has become increasingly bureaucratic in order to cope with the workload this screening function entails. The clerk's office guides litigants who wish to file *certiorari* petitions and ensures that the petitions received are in proper order. Petitions are then channeled to a pool of law clerks, employed by individual justices. The clerks in the pool examine the petitions in turn, test them against the criteria in Rule 10, and write short memoranda recommending either that they be rejected or accepted. The justices themselves receive the memoranda in chambers, and they, together with their clerks, identify the cases they deem to be "certworthy." The Chief Justice prepares a "discuss list" of candidates, and the other justices add any additional cases that they wish the Court to review. Ultimately, the justices confer and make the final choices. Under the customary

---

statutory construction. The Court's answers to those questions are not accurate in an ultimate objective sense, but *are* authoritative and thus satisfying when only clarity is genuinely needed. William H. Rehnquist, *The Changing Role of the Supreme Court*, 14 Fla. St. U. L. Rev. 1, 11 (1986). If the justices initially select a case for review, but later conclude that it does not provide a good vehicle for clarifying the law, they can simply change their minds and dismiss the writ of *certiorari* as "improvidently granted." E.g., *Rogers v. United States*, 118 S.Ct. 673 (1998).

191. Sup. Ct. Rule 14(1)(a); e.g., *Bragdon v. Abbott*, 118 S.Ct. 2196, 2205 (1998).

192. In *Lindh v. Murphy*, 521 U.S. 320 (1997), the Court granted *certiorari* to decide whether a newly enacted statute, 28 U.S.C. § 2254(d)(1), applied to the pending case, but denied review with respect to the contingent question whether, if § 2254(d)(1) was applicable, the circuit court below had correctly applied it. In *Lindh*, then, the Court deliberately declined to consider whether the dispute at hand had been decided correctly and chose, instead, to pass only on an abstract question of law, antecedent to the dispute.

193. The classic illustration is the list of questions the Court asked the parties to brief and argue in *Brown v. Bd. of Ed.*, 345 U.S. 972 (1953). In *Garcia v. San Antonio Metro. Transit Auth.*, 468 U.S. 1213 (1984), the Court asked the parties to brief the question whether the previous decision in *Nat'l League of Cities v. Usery*, 426 U.S. 833 (1976), should be overruled. In *Wright v. West*, 502 U.S. 1021 (1991), the Court asked the parties to brief a question that had not arisen in the lower courts. See Chapter XII, notes 180-83 and accompanying text (discussing *West*).

194. In *Hohn*, the Court bypassed the petitioner's issues and granted *certiorari* only on the different question whether the Court had jurisdiction to remand the case for further proceedings at the circuit level. When the Court concluded that it had jurisdiction, it remanded without going further. 118 S.Ct. at 1978. See note 181. For a useful (though dated) discussion, see Scott H. Bice, *The Limited Grant of Certiorari and the Justification of Judicial Review*, 1975 Wis. L. Rev. 343.

"Rule of Four," the vote of four justices is sufficient to grant a writ of *certiorari* and thus to place a case on the Court's docket for consideration on the merits.[195]

The Court's refusal to accept a case for review leaves the lower court decision undisturbed and therefore usually makes that decision final. In that practical sense, a denial of *certiorari* has genuine significance. Yet it is not a judgment on the merits and approves neither the result below nor the analysis that produced that result. A *certiorari* denial has no value as precedent.[196] The justices may have all manner of reasons for declining review, or no particular reason at all. To avoid misunderstanding, they typically offer no public explanations.[197] Individual justices occasionally attach separate opinions, either concurring in the denial of *certiorari* or dissenting from that action. Those opinions can throw light on the Court's thinking, but they are not authoritative.[198] On occasion, the Court grants a writ of *certiorari* and affirms or reverses the judgment below with little or no explanation. The precedential value of summary dispositions can vary.[199]

The parties invariably prepare extensive briefs. Very often, other individuals and organizations file independent *amicus curiae* briefs that draw the Court's attention to problems and arguments the parties may not fully explore.[200] The Court hears oral argument *en banc*, and soon thereafter the justices meet *in cam-*

---

195. See John P. Stevens, *The Life Span of a Judge-Made Rule*, 58 N.Y.U. L. Rev. 1, 10-13 (1983). For a more detailed account of the *certiorari* process, see H.W. Perry, Jr., Deciding to Decide (1991). Professor Straus has examined the Court's operations from the perspective of an administrative lawyer and formed the impression that in an attempt to keep its workload within manageable limits, the Court has made itself remote from much of the country's legal business. Peter L. Strauss, *One Hundred Fifty Cases Per Year: Some Implications of the Supreme Court's Limited Resources for Judicial Review of Agency Action*, 87 Colum. L. Rev. 1093 (1987).

196. The classic citation for this point is Justice Frankfurter's opinion respecting the denial of *certiorari* in *Maryland v. Baltimore Radio Show*, 338 U.S. 912, 917-18 (1950). Professor Linzer argues that the "orthodox" view of *certiorari* denials is "oversimplified" and that one can often find "hints" that "most" of the justices are not "strongly dissatisfied" with the decision below. Peter Linzer, *The Meaning of Certiorari Denials*, 79 Colum. L. Rev. 1227, 1229 (1979).

197. See *Singleton v. Commissioners*, 439 U.S. 940 (1978) (opinion of Blackmun, J.) (contending that reasons should not be given).

198. Professor Linzer relies in some measure on indications gleaned from separate opinions. Linzer, note 196.

199. Typically, summary dispositions are accompanied by a *per curiam*, which explains the Court's thinking. Justice Marshall contended, however, that once the Court grants review in a case, it should take no definitive action before seeing the parties' briefs on the merits. *Montana v. Hall*, 481 U.S. 400, 410 (1987) (dissenting opinion). The Court employed the summary disposition device more commonly when it was obliged to consider cases on appeal and could not simply deny review to those it thought were not worthy of attention. The celebrated illustration is *Doe v. Commonwealth's Attorney*, 425 U.S. 901 (1976), in which the Court summarily affirmed a district court decision upholding the validity of a state sodomy statute. The Court has since proceeded on the assumption that statutes of that kind are constitutional, but there is no consensus that the disposition in *Doe* is genuine precedent for that proposition.

200. Not all *amici curiae* are ideologically motivated, but many repeat players certainly are. Their participation in cases before the Court underscores the significance of the Court's work for a wide range of social policies. See Gregg Ivers & Karen O'Connor, *Friends as Foes: The Amicus Curiae Participation and Effectiveness of the American Civil Liberties Union and Americans for Effective Law Enforcement in Criminal Cases, 1969-1982*, 9 Law & Policy 161 (1987).

era to vote. When the Chief Justice is in the majority, he assigns the Court's opinion to himself or to one of the associate justices in the majority. When the Chief Justice is in the minority, the senior associate justice in the majority makes the assignment. Individual justices may file separate concurring or dissenting opinions, expressing their personal views. The Court typically announces decisions in public session. The justice who prepared the Court's opinion may summarize the result and the supporting analysis. The written opinions in cases are distributed at the same time and promptly come under the scrutiny of the hosts of observers who look to the Supreme Court's opinions as the final, authoritative statement of federal law.[201]

---

201. When the Court grants *certiorari* in a case, it typically holds other cases presenting the same issue until it decides that case and then disposes of them summarily, typically by granting *certiorari*, vacating the judgment below, and remanding for reconsideration in light of the new decision. The "GVR" practice is meant to ensure even-handed treatment, lest a single case be selected from a stream of similar cases and resolved in one way, while others of like character are concluded in another way. The proper management of "GVR" matters has occasionally been controversial within the Court. See, e.g., *Thomas v. Amer. Homes Products*, 117 S.Ct. 282 (1996).

Chapter VIII

Federal Questions in Federal District Court

Litigants who wish to advance federal claims in federal court usually must invoke the original jurisdiction of a United States district court. Article III contemplates that district courts may determine federal questions in a variety of contexts. Party-based categories of jurisdiction may offer opportunities. Cases in which states are involved typically turn on federal law,[1] as do controversies to which the United States is a party.[2] Categories of jurisdiction identified by subject matter also usually implicate federal questions. Admiralty cases, for example, are almost always governed by federal statutes or federal common law.[3] The general class of cases "arising under" the "Constitution" or "Laws of the United States" is the most commodious source of federal question jurisdiction.[4]

A. Cases Arising Under Federal Law

The Supreme Court has always given the idea of a case arising under federal law a generous interpretation. In *Osborn v. Bank of United States*,[5] Chief Justice Marshall recognized that Article III specifies federal jurisdiction of *cases*, not *issues* within cases. Cases, in turn, often involve both questions of federal law and questions of state law, as well. If, then, a federal court is to adjudicate the "whole case," the court must be able to resolve both federal and state issues.[6]

In *Osborn*, the Bank of the United States sued officials of the state of Ohio in a federal circuit court, seeking an injunction requiring those officers to return money they had seized pursuant to an unconstitutional tax on the bank's assets.

---

1. See note 63 and accompanying text. Recall that inferior federal courts may have concurrent jurisdiction to determine the kinds of cases that Article III permits the Supreme Court to entertain as an original matter. See Chapter VII, note 3 and accompanying text.

2. See text accompanying note 61.

3. See note 63 and accompanying text.

4. See notes 5-31 and accompanying text.

5. 22 U.S. (9 Wheat.) 738 (1824).

6. Id. at 819-23. See Chapter VII, notes 82, 96 and accompanying text (discussing this idea in connection with the Supreme Court's appellate jurisdiction).

The statute creating the bank gave it authority to "sue and be sued" in "any Circuit Court of the United States." Chief Justice Marshall read that language to establish a circuit court's jurisdiction to entertain suits brought by or against the bank.[7] That construction of the statute, in turn, presented Marshall with the constitutional question whether cases involving the bank arose under federal law within the meaning of Article III.[8] The defendants argued that only the validity of the tax was a question of federal law, that other issues would surface in the case, and that Congress could not confer jurisdiction on the circuit court to consider those state law matters. Marshall responded that there was no *constitutional* barrier to the circuit court's adjudication of both federal and state issues. He gave two explanations.

First, it was enough that the bank's "right" would be "defeated by one construction [of federal law] and sustained by the opposite construction."[9] That initial explanation suggested that the circuit court's jurisdiction was comparatively narrow: A case had to turn on an actual question of federal law, and that federal question had to be apparent at the time the suit was initiated. Once the court assumed jurisdiction on the basis of such a federal issue, the court could consider any incidental state questions that emerged.[10] In *Osborn* itself, those contingencies were satisfied. The bank's claim against the Ohio defendants was a federal constitutional challenge to the tax, and that claim was clear at the outset of the litigation.[11]

---

7. It now appears that the explicit mention of suits in the federal circuit courts was crucial to Marshall's interpretation of the statute to confer jurisdiction on those courts. In *Amer. Nat'l Red Cross v. S.G.*, 505 U.S. 247 (1992), the Court read similar language in the congressional charter issued to the Red Cross to confer jurisdiction on the federal courts to entertain a state tort claim. If the statutes in *Osborn* and *Red Cross* had only established that the bank and the Red Cross could "sue and be sued" in *some* court, without specifying a *federal* court, they would not have been understood to do jurisdictional work. In truth, those statutes did not read like jurisdictional statutes at all. They did not address the federal courts and empower them forthrightly, but instead addressed the bank and the Red Cross and thus affected the courts only indirectly—by authorizing the bank and the Red Cross to sue *in* federal court. See notes 87-88 and accompanying text. Looking back, it seems perfectly clear that the statute in *Osborn* contemplated that the circuit courts would have jurisdiction to entertain suits by and against the bank, even if the language it used to accomplish that end left something to be desired. Moreover, Chief Justice Marshall plainly wanted to read the statute to create federal jurisdiction and was not in a mood to demand more clarity. It is questionable whether it was equally expedient to read the statute in *Red Cross* in the same way and thus to place ordinary state law claims in federal court merely because the Red Cross held a charter containing the familiar "sue and be sued" boilerplate. See *Red Cross*, 505 U.S. at 267-69 (Scalia, J., dissenting).

8. If Marshall had found no statutory jurisdiction for the bank's suit in *Osborn*, the constitutional question would not have arisen.

9. 22 U.S. at 822.

10. See notes 288-301 and accompanying text (explaining that this is the way supplemental jurisdiction works in modern federal district courts).

11. See notes 183-85 (discussing the well-pleaded complaint rule as an interpretation of statute: 28 U.S.C. § 1331). The bank's suit was actually in equity to enjoin a trespass and for the common law writ of replevin. That kind of action does not translate neatly into modern terms. It is possible that the federal issue would have emerged as the bank's response to the state's defense, in which case modern standards for invoking federal jurisdiction (by statute) would not have been satisfied. See notes 183-210 and accompanying text (describing the classic cases on the well-pleaded complaint rule).

Second, the suit by the bank arose under federal law for Article III purposes because a federal question formed an "ingredient" of the "original cause."[12] Congress had enacted a statute establishing the bank and giving it authority to file lawsuits. At the threshold of any suit, an opposing party might challenge either the bank's existence as a corporate entity or its capacity to sue (in any court). Those objections, if raised, would turn on federal law—namely, the bank's charter. Marshall did not mean that a suit by the bank would arise under federal law *only* if an opposing party *actually* injected federal issues into a case in some way. He insisted that questions about the bank's credentials *could* be raised in "every possible case," and that was enough to make every action in which the bank was a party a case arising under federal law.[13]

Marshall's second explanation suggested that the circuit court's jurisdiction could be much more expansive. If the mere possibility that the bank's charter might be challenged would suffice, then the nature of the bank's legal claim in a lawsuit would make no difference. Marshall explained, for example, that a suit by the bank on an ordinary state contract claim would arise under federal law, even if neither party actually raised any federal issue for decision.[14] Moreover, numerous other entities and organizations (apart from the bank) also depended on federal statutes for their existence and authority to conduct business. If any suit involving the bank arose under federal law, it appeared that a suit involving any federally chartered party would equally qualify.[15] Indeed, by Marshall's second account, the range of cases arising under federal law extended even further. If the *possibility* that a federal question would develop was sufficient, there was no self-evident reason why that question must go to the very existence of a federally incorporated institution or its capacity to sue. All manner of cases having nothing to do with federally incorporated entities would be cases arising under federal law for Article III purposes.[16]

---

12. 22 U.S. at 823.

13. Id. at 824.

14. In a companion case, the Court held that just such a case arose under federal law for Article III purposes. *Bank of United States v. Planters' Bank*, 22 U.S. (9 Wheat.) 904 (1824).

15. The Court took this very position in the *Pac. R.R. Removal Cases*, 115 U.S. 1 (1885), where private plaintiffs were allowed to sue federally chartered railroads in federal court, even though the plaintiffs' tort claims against the railroads turned entirely on state law. Federal courts no longer routinely have jurisdiction of actions merely because federally incorporated entities are involved, unless the United States owns more than half their stock. 28 U.S.C. § 1349. In none of the three early cases, *Osborn*, *Planters' Bank*, or the *Removal Cases*, did the Court suggest that the federally chartered corporations involved were arms of the United States, so that federal judicial power could rest independently on the provision in Article III for controversies to which the United States itself is a party. See *Lebron v. Nat'l R.R. Passenger Corp.*, 513 U.S. 374, 398-99 (1995) (discussing *Planters' Bank*).

16. Dissenting in *Osborn*, Justice Johnson put two hypotheticals that demonstrated, to his satisfaction, that Marshall had gone too far. First, under federal revenue statutes, certain contracts (themselves governed entirely by state law) had to be written on stamped paper (indicating that certain federal taxes had been paid). It was *possible*, according to Johnson, that a party to such a contract might raise some issue touching the required stamp and the taxes owed to the federal government. Second, the title to land in the territories could always be traced back to a patent issued by the government. It was *possible*, then, that a party to an ordinary real estate suit could raise some issue touching that original federal patent. By

Marshall may have conceived that Article III must be interpreted expansively in order to accommodate both inferior courts' original jurisdiction and the Supreme Court's appellate jurisdiction.[17] Article III describes only one category of cases arising under federal law. Thus Marshall may have assumed that any appellate jurisdiction the Supreme Court draws from that category can be no greater than the original jurisdiction that the inferior federal courts obtain from it. If, then, Article III allows the Supreme Court *appellate* jurisdiction to adjudicate cases in which federal issues emerge only after litigation is under way, it must follow that Article III also allows federal trial courts *original* jurisdiction to entertain cases in which federal issues may (but may not) actually surface. That analysis may be true to the text of Article III, but it is not logically compelled. Even if it is assumed that the Supreme Court must have plenary jurisdiction to examine dispositive federal questions that emerge in cases after they are filed, it does not follow that federal trial courts equally require such an expansive purview.[18] Cases in which federal issues are only potentially implicated can proceed in state court and reach the Supreme Court later, if and when federal questions actually appear and become dispositive.[19]

The idea that cases can arise under federal law when federal issues are only potentially implicated is but a step away from the theory of "protective jurisdiction."[20] Academicians who promote that theory invariably rely on Marshall's analysis in *Osborn* to supply the fulcrum on which protective jurisdiction turns: Article III does not demand that a federal question must actually be presented for decision in a case, but only that it *might* be presented—*if* Congress were to use

---

Marshall's account, then, ordinary contract and real property disputes were cases arising under federal law for Article III purposes. 22 U.S. at 874-76 (dissenting opinion). Marshall himself may have indicated some doubt about his interpretation of Article III when he rejected a third hypothetical. He agreed that a naturalized citizen, too, was a "mere creature of law," but he did not concede that, on that account, cases involving naturalized citizens arose under federal law simply because an opposing party might challenge their federally created credentials. According to Marshall, a naturalized citizen, unlike a federally chartered corporation, owed nothing further to Congress and possessed all the rights of native citizens. Id. at 827-28 (majority opinion). Marshall probably meant to say only that he could not envision any practical instance in which the means by which a party had become a citizen could figure as an antecedent ingredient in a lawsuit. In that respect, he resisted Justice Johnson's charge that there were no limits at all on the cases that could arise under federal law for constitutional purposes. It has been argued that Marshall meant that the potential federal ingredient must be essential to the claimant's lawsuit (like the capacity to sue at all or to form the contract over which suit is initiated) and that any other kind of potential federal issue (like a federal defense offered by the defendant) would not suffice. See Note, *The Outer Limits of "Arising Under"*, 54 N.Y.U. L. Rev. 978, 987-88 (1982).

17. Marshall may also have embraced Hamilton's view that the federal government's judicial power must be coterminous with its legislative power. See Chapter II, note 47. That line of argument would have led Marshall to give the courts' power under Article III a capacious reading in order to keep pace with Congress' powers under Article I.

18. See Paul J. Mishkin, *The Federal "Question" in the District Courts*, 53 Colum. L. Rev. 157, 163 (1953).

19. See Chapter VII, notes 95-96 and accompanying text (discussing the same idea in connection with the *Murdock* case).

20. See Chapter VI, notes 128-32 and accompanying text (discussing protective jurisdiction in connection with removal under 28 U.S.C. § 1442).

the legislative authority it has to create federal law for the occasion.[21] In a famous dissent in the *Lincoln Mills* case,[22] Justice Frankfurter urged the Court not to extend *Osborn* so far. Frankfurter insisted that the labor dispute in *Lincoln Mills* was controlled by state law. That meant (to Frankfurter) that there was no substantive federal law under which the case could arise for Article III purposes.[23] Frankfurter considered the possibility that Congress could create federal jurisdiction alone, without providing substantive federal law for the federal courts to apply. But he dismissed that idea, in part because it rested (illogically) on the "beguiling" syllogism that the "greater" power must include the "lesser."[24]

The modern Court has indicated doubts about the "ingredient" test in general[25] and protective jurisdiction in particular.[26] Yet the Court has not revisited the question whether a purely speculative federal question will satisfy Article III. In *Verlinden B.V. v. Central Bank of Nigeria*,[27] the Court upheld a provision of the Foreign Sovereign Immunities Act giving federal district courts jurisdiction over actions against foreign nations that, under the Act, cannot insist upon immunity. Chief Justice Burger explained that the Act both makes a federal court's jurisdiction contingent on a foreign nation's inability to claim immunity and establishes the standards for determining the immunity issue as a matter of federal law. The threshold (federal) question whether a nation is immune must therefore

---

21. There is a connection between protective jurisdiction and the idea that cases in which federally chartered corporations are parties arise under federal law. The point of conferring jurisdiction on federal courts in cases involving federally chartered corporations is to protect those entities from state court provincialism.

22. *Textile Workers Union v. Lincoln Mills*, 353 U.S. 448, 460-84 (1957); see notes 58-60 and accompanying text.

23. A federal statute by which Congress purports to establish federal court jurisdiction cannot itself supply the federal law under which a case can be said to arise. If it could, Congress would be able to bootstrap federal jurisdiction in every conceivable case, simply by enacting a federal statute conferring jurisdiction and relying on that federal statute to provide the federal law required. The law under which a case arises is the legal standard the court may be asked to apply *in* the case. Justice Frankfurter rejected Judge Wyzanski's suggestion that a statute giving federal courts jurisdiction to decide state law issues might be read to incorporate state law into federal law and, in that way, to generate a body of federal law under which cases might arise. *Lincoln Mills*, 353 U.S. at 472 (dissenting opinion); see *Textile Workers Union v. Amer. Thread Co.*, 113 F. Supp. 137, 140 (D. Mass. 1953). Nor is it persuasive to argue that *every* jurisdictional statute necessarily authorizes the federal courts to fashion a federal common law of decision, which then can supply the law under which cases arise for Article III purposes. See note 62 and accompanying text. There is also an argument that Article III itself prescribes the only valid forms of protective jurisdiction (e.g., diversity jurisdiction to safeguard out-of-state citizens from local prejudice) and forecloses others by negative implication.

24. *Lincoln Mills*, 353 U.S. at 473 (dissenting opinion); see Chapter I, notes 21-22 and accompanying text.

25. In a related context, Justice Souter has noted potential constitutional difficulty with a statute allowing the Attorney General to invoke federal jurisdiction by unilaterally injecting the United States into a case as a party. *Gutierrez de Martinez v. Lamagno*, 515 U.S. 417, 443-44 (1995) (dissenting opinion).

26. See Chapter VI, notes 131-32 and accompanying text (discussing the *Mesa* case on removal jurisdiction).

27. 461 U.S. 480 (1983).

be presented in every case—as a condition of the federal court's jurisdiction.[28] Accordingly, the Act validly confers jurisdiction in cases that arise under federal law for Article III purposes.[29]

Even if purely speculative federal issues will not satisfy Article III, the Article III definition of cases arising under federal law is quite broad. The scope of federal jurisdiction implicates sensitive political values. The more jurisdiction federal courts have, the more routinely they will compete for business with state courts and the more commonly they will come into conflict with the other branches of the central government. The less jurisdiction federal courts have, the less authority they will command to enforce federal law—often against assertions of power by the states and the other branches. The scope of jurisdiction also entails administrative considerations. Once federal courts are granted jurisdiction sufficient to perform their institutional role, more subtle adjustments may be warranted to manage the flow of cases. It is difficult to anticipate the many and varied problems that may arise at that stage, and a capacity to fine-tune jurisdictional arrangements can be essential. It would be cumbersome to make those adjustments as interpretations of the Constitution. Accordingly, the Court essentially paints Article III out of the picture. Congress makes the basic allocation of judicial power in the first instance.[30] Then, the Court can introduce refinements when it places an authoritative construction on the statutes that Congress enacts. In the end, there are few *constitutional* limits on the jurisdiction the federal courts *can* be given. But that only means that the jurisdiction the federal courts actually *have* is a non-constitutional question of statutory construction, imbued by the Court's sense of sound policy.[31]

---

28. Subject matter jurisdiction is the threshold issue in every case. By convention, the plaintiff must demonstrate the court's jurisdiction at the outset of the litigation. See *McNutt v. GMAC*, 298 U.S. 178, 182 (1936). The parties cannot establish subject matter jurisdiction by consent. *Sosna v. Iowa*, 419 U.S. 393, 398 (1975). A federal court cannot assume that it has jurisdiction in order to dispose of a case on another ground. *Steel Co. v. Citizens for a Better Environment*, 118 S.Ct. 1003, 1012-16 (1998). Nor may a federal court fail to explore any doubts about its jurisdiction. *Louisville & Nashville R.R. v. Mottley*, 211 U.S. 149, 152 (1908).

29. Chief Justice Burger chided the lower court for relying on precedents regarding jurisdiction under the statute that ordinarily confers jurisdiction on district courts in federal question cases: 28 U.S.C. § 1331. The issue in *Verlinden* was not whether the quite different non-constitutional standards for invoking jurisdiction under § 1331 were met. Clearly, they were not. The issue was, instead, whether Article III allowed Congress to establish a more capacious jurisdiction via the Foreign Sovereign Immunities Act. 461 U.S. at 494-97.

30. Professor Holt has explained that Article III left most features of the federal judiciary to Congress. Wythe Holt, *"Federal Courts as the Asylum to Federal Interests": Randolph's Report, the Benson Amendment, and the "Original Understanding" of the Federal Judiciary*, 36 Buffalo L. Rev. 341 (1987).

31. Dissenting in *Osborn*, Justice Johnson insisted that a case could arise under federal law for Article III purposes only if a federal question actually appeared at some point. If it appeared in the plaintiff's complaint, a federal court could consider the case as an original matter. If it did not, by Johnson's account, a federal trial court could not entertain the case initially. If, then, the plaintiff went to state court and the federal question emerged as the case progressed, a federal court could *then* exercise jurisdiction, either by removal or on appellate review of the state court's judgment. *Osborn*, 22 U.S. at 888-89. Working from John Marshall's more generous interpretation of Article III, Congress and the Court have limited district court original jurisdiction to cases in which a federal claim appears in the plaintiff's complaint—but as a matter of non-constitutional policy. See notes 166-210 and accompanying text.

B. Federal Common Law

The federal question that triggers federal jurisdiction need not be constitutional or statutory in character. It can be a matter of federal common law created by the federal courts themselves. In *Erie R.R. Co. v. Tompkins*,[32] Justice Brandeis declared that there is no "general" federal common law. But that epigram only disclaimed federal court authority to create a "general" common law to govern federal diversity actions involving citizens of different states.[33] In the wake of *Erie*, and pursuant to the Rules of Decision Act, federal courts typically apply state substantive law in diversity actions.[34] Nevertheless, federal courts also fashion federal rules of decision in some circumstances.[35]

When federal common law governs a case, it supplies the law under which the case arises for jurisdictional purposes.[36] Yet there is often serious doubt about whether federal common law *does* govern. The Supreme Court decided early on that there is no federal common law of crimes.[37] Federal criminal offenses are

---

32. 304 U.S. 64, 78 (1938).

33. 28 U.S.C. § 1332 (stating the scope of federal diversity jurisdiction today); see *Swift v. Tyson*, 41 U.S. (16 Pet.) 1 (1842) (articulating the understanding that *Erie* discarded— i.e., that "general" federal law controlled in diversity cases); John Hart Ely, *The Irrepressible Myth of Erie*, 87 Harv. L. Rev. 693 (1974) (providing a discussion).

34. See Chapter II, note 60 (explaining that the Rules of Decision Act derives from the Judiciary Act of 1789).

35. As Judge Friendly once explained, *Erie* and subsequent cases on federal common law produced "complementary concepts" that are "so beautifully simple, and so simply beautiful, that we must wonder why a century and a half were needed to discover them." While *Erie* put the federal courts out of the business of fashioning a large and unnecessary body of federal law for diversity cases, the new federal common law cases put the federal courts in the business of creating federal law where it is genuinely needed to promote federal interests. See Henry J. Friendly, *In Praise of Erie—and of the New Federal Common Law*, 39 N.Y.U. L. Rev. 383, 422 (1964). Under the Rules of Decision Act, the "laws of the several states...shall be regarded as rules of decision," but only "where they apply" and only where "the Constitution or treaties of the United States or Acts of Congress [do not] otherwise require or provide." Accordingly, even in post-*Erie* cases in which diversity jurisdiction is invoked pursuant to 28 U.S.C. § 1332, federal common law may control *if* that federal law applies and state law does not. E.g., *Boyle v. United Technologies Corp.*, 487 U.S. 500 (1988).

36. See *Illinois v. Milwaukee*, 406 U.S. 91, 99-100 (1972), *overruled on other gr'ds*, *Milwaukee v. Illinois*, 451 U.S. 304 (1981); accord *Nat'l Farmers Ins. Co. v. Crow Tribe*, 471 U.S. 845, 850 (1985). In the celebrated Supreme Court cases on federal common law, the jurisdictional statute in play was typically *not* § 1331. Until the Supreme Court announced its decision, it was not clear that federal law controlled and might have supplied the basis for jurisdiction as an "arising under" matter.

37. *United States v. Hudson & Goodwin*, 11 U.S. (7 Cranch) 32 (1812); *United States v. Coolidge*, 14 U.S. (1 Wheat.) 415 (1816). Justice Story evidently thought it was perfectly appropriate for federal courts to entertain common law prosecutions. The idea of common law crimes figured in Federalist arguments for an expansive national government generally. Nevertheless, the decision in *Hudson & Goodwin*, authored by Justice Johnson (the Court's Jeffersonian member), concluded the issue the other way. See Gary D. Rowe, *The Sound of Silence: United States v. Hudson & Goodwin, the Jeffersonian Ascendancy, and the Abolition of Federal Common Law Crimes*, 101 Yale L.J. 919 (1992); see generally Stewart Jay, *Origins of Federal Common Law: Part One*, 133 U. Pa. L. Rev. 1003 (1985); Stewart Jay, *Origins of Federal Common Law: Part Two*, 133 U. Pa. L. Rev. 1231 (1985).

"solely creatures of statute."[38] In the civil context, however, federal common law is alive and well. In any particular instance, the existence of controlling federal common law is itself a question of federal law: whether federal courts have the power and the duty to announce and enforce federal law of their own making in the class of cases to which the instant case belongs.[39]

Federal courts routinely exercise creative judgment when they interpret federal statutes, and it is useless to attempt any clear distinction between interpretation and independent law declaration. That realistic point conceded, the entire body of federal common law may arguably be explained away as so many instances of imaginative statutory interpretation, requiring no special explanation or justification as free-standing judge-made law.[40] Most authorities resist such a facile explanation, however. If courts genuinely derive the rule they apply to a case from some statutory text, they do not create federal common law at all; the function of forging federal common law begins only where the function of interpreting statutes ends.[41] Yet particularly at a time when the Supreme Court's preferred approach to statutory construction is primarily textual,[42] it is hard to think that when the Court strays significantly from the language of a statute, it is still engaged in the "alchemy of construction."[43]

Justice Jackson contended that there are practical reasons why federal courts must be able to fashion common law. Congress, he said, cannot be expected to enact "all-complete statutory codes" that address every contingency that may arise.[44] Accordingly, federal courts must have authority to fill the gaps that statutes necessarily leave open, in order to effectuate the policies that statutes are meant to promote.[45] Thus "wherever" federal courts must decide a federal question that "cannot be answered from federal statutes alone," they can "resort to all of the source materials of the common law" and select a legal principle they think appropriate.[46] Jackson's explanation is incomplete. The practical necessity

---

38. *Dowling v. United States*, 473 U.S. 207, 213 (1985). Professor Kahan argues that Congress can give the courts "criminal lawmaking power" to fill in the details of "open-textured" statutes and that Congress has essentially done that in certain contexts—for example, in the RICO statute. 18 U.S.C. § 1961, *et seq.* Dan M. Kahan, *Lenity and Federal Common Law Crimes*, 1994 Sup. Ct. Rev. 345.

39. *D'Oench, Duhme & Co. v. FDIC*, 315 U.S. 447 (1942).

40. Professor Westen and Professor Lehman advance this argument. See Peter Westen & Jeffrey S. Lehman, *Is There Life for Erie After the Death of Diversity?*, 78 Mich. L. Rev. 311, 332-33 (1980). Professor Field also thinks that a sufficient federal statutory basis of decision can typically be located. Martha A. Field, *Sources of Law: The Scope of Federal Common Law*, 99 Harv. L. Rev. 881, 887 (1986).

41. See Bradford R. Clark, *Federal Common Law: A Structural Reinterpretation*, 144 U. Pa. L. Rev. 1245, 1248 (1996).

42. See Chapter I, notes 24-36 and accompanying text.

43. *Lincoln Mills*, 353 U.S. at 462 (Frankfurter, J., dissenting).

44. *D'Oench*, 315 U.S. at 468-70 (concurring opinion).

45. Id. at 472. Accord *United States v. Little Lake Misere Land Co.*, 412 U.S. 580, 593 (1973).

46. *D'Oench*, 315 U.S. at 469. In these passages, Justice Jackson had in mind cases in which federal statutes reflect a clear federal policy, but fail to see to the details that must be addressed to promote that policy. In many instances, however, federal statutes leave gaps of a different order. They reach and control behavior in one context, but leave similar conduct in other contexts untouched. In cases of that kind, the Court must decide whether to fill in the latter gaps with federal common law (so that the same policy reaches similar behavior in similar contexts) or, instead, to infer from a statute's failure to specify that result an author-

of filling gaps in federal statutes may mute concerns that the courts are intruding upon Congress' legislative preserve. But the displacement of available state law demands independent explanation. It is not self-evident that when imperfect federal statutes need to be supplemented, federal courts must fashion rules of their own choosing. They may be able to locate corresponding state rules and feed them into the mix.[47]

State courts routinely create state common law, just as courts of general jurisdiction always have within the Anglo-American system. Federal courts are not courts of general jurisdiction in that traditional sense.[48] They are restricted to the jurisdiction that Article III permits Congress to confer upon them, and, in turn, by the specific jurisdictional statutes that Congress, in its wisdom, decides to enact.[49] State courts can assume that they are entitled to fashion any legal standards needed to resolve a dispute within their jurisdiction, so long as they respect any relevant statutes or constitutional provisions.[50] By most accounts, however, federal courts require greater justification when they take "molar" rather than "molecular" jumps.[51]

Congress may expressly delegate authority to the federal courts to create the law needed to resolve cases. The best illustration is Rule 501 of the Federal Rules

---

itative legislative pronouncement that the same policy does *not* apply across the board. The current Court's textualism may commonly suggest the latter course. In *Moragne v. States Marine Lines*, 398 U.S. 375 (1970), Congress enacted statutes permitting wrongful death actions after accidents on the high seas, but failed to enact a similar statute for accidents in waters within an individual state (but still subject to federal maritime law). The Court explained that the latter omission did not reflect deliberate policy but, instead, rested on historical anomalies. Accordingly, the Court held that as a matter of federal judge-fashioned maritime law, a longshoreman's widow could recover for his wrongful death, even though the accident had occurred in Florida waters. In *Dooley v. Korean Air Lines*, 118 S.Ct. 1890 (1998), however, the Court held that survivors could not rely on "general" maritime law to recover for a decedent's pre-death pain and suffering. The statute in point in *Dooley* did not provide for that kind of suit, and the Court inferred that Congress meant to foreclose recovery under more general law by implication. Judge Mikva and Professor Pfander argue that federal courts should revive the *Moragne* approach in a different context: Rather than borrow state filing periods for federal rights of action, the courts should substitute the uniform four-year period that Congress has prescribed for federal rights of action established since 1990. Abner J. Mikva & James E. Pfander, *On the Meaning of Congressional Silence: Using Federal Common Law to Fill the Gap in Congress's Residual Statute of Limitations*, 107 Yale L.J. 393 (1997).

47. See notes 67-75 and accompanying text.

48. See Chapter I, notes 48-49 and accompanying text (discussing the "interstitial" character of federal law and federal courts according to the Hart and Wechsler paradigm).

49. See Chapter IV, notes 19-20 and accompanying text. Just as a particular grant of jurisdiction has its positive, power-giving side, it equally has its negative, power-denying side—in the obvious sense that the power it confers has limits.

50. As a matter of practice, state courts probably approach disputes from the other direction—looking first for a controlling statute and turning to their own law-making authority only when necessary. In the modern world, legislation often eclipses judge-crafted common law, in both the federal and state systems.

51. *Southern Pac. R.R. v. Jensen*, 244 U.S. 205, 221 (1917) (Holmes, J., dissenting), quoted in Louise Weinberg, *Federal Common Law*, 83 Nw. U. L. Rev. 805, 806 (1989). Professor Weinberg argues that the federal courts' authority to create federal common law parallels Congress' power to enact legislation in the same context. She does recognize limits, however. She does not endorse federal common law crimes. See notes 37-38 and accompanying text.

of Evidence, which specifies that certain evidentiary privileges are governed by "common law" principles, "as interpreted by" the federal courts "in light of reason and experience."[52] In cases of express delegation, judicial law-making is non-controversial.[53] Even when federal courts act on what they regard as an *implicit* delegation of authority, they can be on solid ground. The federal common law the courts have developed in anti-trust cases is an example.[54] There are cases, however, in which judicial law-making evokes concern, because it threatens both to appropriate the legislative power of Congress (and thus to upset the separation of powers within the national government)[55] and to preempt state law (and thus to undermine the values associated with federalism).[56]

The Supreme Court precedents in point recognize three conditions that typically attend the creation of federal common law: (1) some kind of invitation from Congress or, at least, congressional acquiescence (typically a grant of jurisdiction); (2) a significant interest on the part of the federal government (typically a regulatory, proprietary, or sovereign interest); and (3) a demonstrable need for a uniform rule across the country (as opposed to inconsistent rules supplied by different states).[57]

---

52. The Federal Deposit Insurance Corporation Act also explicitly delegates law-making authority inasmuch as it provides that civil suits in which the FDIC is a party "shall be deemed to arise under the laws of the United States." *D'Oench*, 315 U.S. at 455 n.2. See also notes 280-87 and accompanying text (discussing federal common law elaborating ERISA).

53. Congress may also explicitly instruct federal courts to apply state law. For example, the Federal Tort Claims Act typically makes the United States liable for torts committed by its officers where the government, were it a private person, would be liable "in accordance with the law of the place where the act or omission occurred." 28 U.S.C. § 1346(b). In a curious old case, *United States v. Standard Oil Co.*, 332 U.S. 301 (1947), the Court faced the inverse of the situation contemplated by § 1346(b): a suit *by* the United States against a private company to recover damages for losing the services of an soldier who had been injured by a company truck. The Court held that federal law controlled that case, because the government's monetary assets were at stake. Yet the Court declined to fashion any federal common law for the occasion and, instead, invited Congress to enact a statute. That disposition defeated the government's claim for want of any basis for holding the company liable.

54. See, e.g., *Nat'l Soc'y of Prof. Engineers v. United States*, 435 U.S. 679, 688 (1978).

55. See Chapter I, notes 2-15 and accompanying text. Professor Redish contends that this is the principal concern raised by federal judicial law-making. He notes that the Rules of Decision Act does not mention federal common law, but, instead (by his account), directs federal courts *always* to apply state law, unless a federal statute, a treaty, or the Constitution specifies otherwise. See note 35. Thus when federal courts presume to create federal common law, they not only usurp Congress' legislative authority, but actually violate an extant congressional enactment. See Martin H. Redish, *Federal Common Law, Political Legitimacy, and the Interpretive Process: An "Institutionalist" Perspective*, 83 Nw. U. L. Rev. 761, 786-801 (1989). Professor Weinberg understands federal common law cases to be instances in which the Constitution precludes the application of state law. Louise Weinberg, *The Curious Notion that the Rules of Decision Act Blocks Supreme Federal Common Law*, 83 Nw. U. L. Rev. 860, 865-66 (1989). Professor Meltzer adds that cases in which federal common law controls may be instances in which no state rules "apply." Daniel J. Meltzer, *State Court Forfeitures of Federal Rights*, 99 Harv. L. Rev. 1128, 1168 n.194 (1986).

56. See Chapter I, notes 16-20, 48-49 and accompanying text. Professor Field regards this as the chief (but easily surmountable) difficulty with federal common law. Field, note 40, at 924-26, 931.

57. Academicians offer their own variations on these themes. See Donald L. Doernberg, *Juridical Chameleons in the "New Erie" Canal*, 1990 Utah L. Rev. 759; Alfred Hill, *The Law-Making Power of the Federal Courts: Constitutional Preemption*, 67 Colum. L. Rev.

Congressional invitation or acquiescence. At the very least, Congress' acquiescence in judicial law-making is crucial, and something approaching an affirmative invitation is typically present. In two classic cases, *Textile Workers Union v. Lincoln Mills*[58] and *Clearfield Trust Co. v. United States*,[59] the Supreme Court relied, in part, on congressional grants of jurisdiction. In *Lincoln Mills*, a union sued an employer in a federal district court, invoking the court's jurisdiction under § 301(a) of the Labor Management Relations Act to entertain suits to enforce labor agreements. Justice Douglas read § 301(a) not only to confer jurisdiction on the district court, but also to express a "federal policy that federal courts should enforce" labor agreements. In some instances, the LMRA "expressly" specified substantive law for the federal courts to apply. But in other instances, the Act was silent, leaving problems in "the penumbra of express statutory mandates." In those instances, the courts themselves must create "federal law" consistent with the "policy of our national labor laws."[60] In *Clearfield*, the federal government sued a bank in a federal district court, invoking the court's jurisdiction under the precursor of 28 U.S.C. § 1345 to entertain suits in which the United States was a party. The government contended that the bank was liable for the amount of a stolen government check. Justice Douglas said that the "rights and duties" of the United States regarding government checks were governed by "federal rather than local law." Since Congress had failed to enact substantive rules, it was "for the federal courts to fashion" their own rules "according to their own standards."[61]

The mere existence of jurisdiction is not in itself a sufficient basis for judicial law-making generally.[62] The Court has always understood that federal courts have authority to make up federal common law to apply to cases within their jurisdiction over admiralty cases and disputes between states.[63] But the Court has never taken the same view of judicial law-making authority in ordinary diversity or federal question cases. The very point of *Erie* is that diversity jurisdiction does not empower the federal courts to create federal common law.[64] Moreover, relying on a jurisdictional grant as the basis for federal common law creates an anomaly when cases controlled by that law are entertained in state court. State courts are ostensibly called upon to apply federal law and thus necessarily to contribute to its development. Yet *state* courts cannot rest their law-making authority on a grant of jurisdiction to the *federal* courts.

Federal interests. Federal judicial law-making is warranted only when significant federal interests are at stake. The government had regulatory interests in *Lincoln Mills* and proprietary interests in *Clearfield*. In *Boyle v. United Tech-*

1024 (1967); Thomas W. Merrill, *The Common Law Powers of Federal Courts*, 52 U. Chi. L. Rev. 1 (1985); *Symposium*, 12 Pace L. Rev. 227 (1992).

58. 353 U.S. 448 (1957).

59. 318 U.S. 363 (1943).

60. 353 U.S. at 455-57.

61. 318 U.S. at 366.

62. See *Texas Indus. v. Radcliff Materials*, 451 U.S. 630, 640 (1981) (disclaiming the proposition that jurisdiction-granting statutes typically authorize federal courts to create federal common law).

63. See *Moragne v. States Marine Lines*, 398 U.S. 375 (1970) (admiralty cases); *Kentucky v. Indiana*, 281 U.S. 163 (1930) (disputes between states).

64. See notes 32-34 and accompanying text; Alfred Hill, *The Erie Doctrine and the Constitution*, 53 Nw. U. L. Rev. 427 (1958).

nologies Corp.,[65] the government's sovereign interests were implicated. The father of a Marine Corps pilot who had died in a helicopter accident invoked a federal district court's diversity jurisdiction to determine a state tort claim against the manufacturer. The plaintiff contended that the manufacturer was liable for design defects in the helicopter, even though the design conformed to Marine Corps specifications. Justice Scalia said that if state tort law rendered the manufacturer liable for producing a helicopter that met Marine Corps standards, it was preempted by federal common law. He explained that the plaintiff would not have been able to hold the government responsible for his son's death on the theory that the Marine Corps had misdesigned the helicopter. Imposing liability on the manufacturer was different, but not sufficiently different to warrant a contrary result. By Scalia's account, the same "uniquely federal" interests implicated in a suit against the government were also implicated in a suit against a private company for actions taken pursuant to a contract with the government.[66]

The need for a uniform rule. When federal interests obtain in a case, there is often value in a uniform body of national rules of decision, which can be supplied by federal courts in the form of federal common law. Nevertheless, this third explanation for judicial law-making is qualified by a countervailing consideration, cutting back the other way: Federal courts may recognize their *authority* to create uniform federal rules, but nonetheless decline to *exercise* that authority. They may, instead, incorporate state law into federal common law. In that event, state law no longer operates as "an independent source of private rights."[67] But it does generate results, and those results can vary from state to state.

The question whether federal courts should borrow state law to fill in the content of federal common law calls for pragmatic judgment. Justice Douglas said in *Lincoln Mills* that in some circumstances the courts might resort to state law regarding labor contracts, provided state law was "compatible with the purpose of § 301" and would "best effectuate" federal policy.[68] And in *Clearfield*, he recognized that the federal courts might adopt state rules governing commercial paper. In that instance, however, he concluded that reliance on state law was "inappropriate" because it would subject the government's "rights and duties" to "exceptional uncertainty."[69]

Critics tend to accept the Court's judgment in *Lincoln Mills*, but to express more doubt regarding *Clearfield*.[70] The government plainly has an interest in consistent rules that will apply wherever it does business. Yet the states also have their own interests in vindicating the local commercial policies promoted by state law. If, in *Clearfield*, the Court had applied the law of Pennsylvania, private merchants in that state would have been able to rely on local commercial law, both in their transactions with other merchants and in their dealings with the govern-

---

65. 487 U.S. 500 (1988).
66. Id. at 505.
67. *Lincoln Mills*, 353 U.S. at 457.
68. Id.
69. *Clearfield*, 318 U.S. at 367.
70. At the time, it must be said, some observers doubted that the federal courts would be equal to the task set for them in *Lincoln Mills*. See, e.g., Alexander M. Bickel & Harry H. Wellington, *Legislative Purpose and the Judicial Process: The Lincoln Mills Case*, 71 Harv. L. Rev. 1, 22-23 (1957).

ment.[71] In more recent cases, the Court has acknowledged federal judicial authority to create federal law to govern commercial disputes, but has insisted that there must be stronger justification for actually imposing uniform national rules. In *Kamen v. Kemper Financial Svc.*,[72] the Court adopted a "presumption" in favor of incorporating state law into federal law, particularly in the commercial and corporate context.[73] And in *O'Melveny & Myers v. FDIC*,[74] the Court said that federal courts may properly fashion their own federal rules of decision only in those "few and restricted" instances in which the application of state law would conflict with an important federal policy.[75]

---

71. In light of *Clearfield*, federal common law controls the federal government's own "rights and duties" attending its commercial paper. It does not follow, however, that federal common law equally governs all cases involving government checks. In *Bank of America Nat'l Trust & Savings Ass'n v. Parnell*, 352 U.S. 29 (1956), a bank sued a private individual to recover the value of government securities said to be overdue. The Court applied federal common law to decide whether the bonds *were* overdue, but said that state law controlled the different question whether the defendant had accepted the bonds in good faith. The due dates of the bonds implicated the federal government's interests, but the defendant's good faith went only to the bank's private claim against him.

72. 500 U.S. 90, 98 (1991).

73. See *United States v. Kimball Foods*, 440 U.S. 715, 740 (1979) (choosing the "prudent course" of adopting "the readymade body of state law as the federal rule of decision").

74. 512 U.S. 79, 87 (1994). Professor Lund has criticized the *Kamen* and *O'Melveny* decisions for failing to appreciate the federal interests at stake. Paul Lund, *The Decline of Federal Common Law*, 76 B.U. L. Rev. 895 (1996). He contends that *O'Melveny* cannot be distinguished from *D'Oench*. See note 52.

75. Acting on this premise, the Court held in *Atherton v. FDIC*, 519 U.S. 213 (1997), that the standard of care to which managers at federally chartered banks are held is a matter of state law, albeit a federal statute establishes "gross negligence" as a federal floor (which controls in any state that would otherwise let bank managers get away with all manner of mayhem). If federal courts *lack* authority to create federal law, then any relevant state law controls of its own authority. E.g., *Wallis v. Pan Amer. Petroleum Corp.*, 384 U.S. 63 (1966) (holding that state law controlled in a dispute between private parties over a mineral lease issued by the federal government). The practical result is the same if the federal courts *have* authority to create federal law, but then incorporate or absorb state law as the content of that federal law. The Court has said, accordingly, that when state law provides the rule of decision, it is "only of theoretical interest whether the basis of that application" is the state's "own sovereign power" or "federal adoption" of a state's law. *O'Melveny*, 512 U.S. at 85. Nevertheless, the theoretical difference between the two bases for bringing state law into play can have practical implications. If state law governs of its own force, both state and federal courts will in future adhere to that state law, even as it changes over time according to new state statutes and authoritative judgments of the relevant state's highest court. If, however, state law governs only *because* it is incorporated by federal law, both state and federal courts will in future enforce that law *as federal law*—subject to authoritative exposition by the Supreme Court. See *Local 174 v. Lucas Flour Co.*, 369 U.S. 95, 102-03 (1962) (refusing to permit a state court to depart from the federal common law that controlled a case). In the latter event, the ability of state legislatures and state courts to alter course may be limited. Things can become conceptually murky when state courts enforce law that originally took shape as state law (over which state courts were authoritative), but that has become federal in nature (so that state court decisions are subject to appellate review in the Supreme Court). Professor Mishkin has explained that the "incorporation" phenomenon is even more complex. The federal courts may not embrace the entirety of a state's legal rules in a given field, but only a few rules or a single rule; they may select only one feature of a rule and neglect its details; they may ignore other complicating aspects of state rules (e.g., state choice of law rules); and they may incorporate only rules they find in some states, but not in others. See Paul J. Mishkin, *The Variousness of "Federal Law": Competence and Discretion in the Choice of National and State Rules for Decision*, 105 U. Pa. L. Rev. 797, 804-08 (1957).

Critics find *Boyle* more troubling still. In that case, the Court did not discard state law entirely in favor of a uniform body of federal judge-made rules. Instead, the Court held only that in a lawsuit generally controlled by state law, the defendant was entitled to a federal defense that state law otherwise denied. Bluntly stated, the Court injected federal common law into a state tort action only insofar as was essential to guarantee that a large manufacturing company could resist a products liability claim that would have been successful, but for the intervention of federal law that the Court itself manufactured.[76] This from a Court that typically limits its purview to the text of enacted statutes.[77] The body of judicial decisions and academic commentaries touching federal common law provides few occasions for ideological controversy. Yet *Boyle* may be evidence that in this context, too, the Court can excite criticism that its doctrinal innovations reflect unstated underlying values.[78]

C. Federal Rights of Action

Litigants who wish to invoke the federal courts' jurisdiction must have both a claim that is federal in character *and* authorization to vindicate that claim by means of a private lawsuit. In common parlance, an authorization to sue is called a "cause of action." That label can be confusing. The better designation is a "right of action"—a right to *litigate* a substantive claim. There is a difference between a claim and a right of action. The one is the plaintiff's argument that the defendant has violated some species of federal law (federal common law, a federal statute, or the Constitution). The other is a procedural vehicle for advancing

---

76. Dissenting in *Boyle,* Justice Brennan said that the justices had to assume for purposes of decision that if United Technologies had designed such a "death trap" for a commercial firm rather than for the Marine Corps, the pilot's father would have recovered on his state law claim. 487 U.S. at 515. Congress had previously failed to enact bills that would have insulated the company from liability. See Michael D. Green & Richard A. Matasar, *The Supreme Court and the Products Liability Crisis: Lessons From Boyle's Government Contractor Defense,* 63 So. Calif. L. Rev. 637, 669 (1990).

77. See Chapter I, notes 24-36 and accompanying text. Cf. Chapter VI, note 33 and accompanying text (discussing Justice Scalia's position in the *Tafflin* case).

78. Professor Weinberg, herself a strong proponent of federal common law, contends that the serious question today is not whether federal common law controls a case in general, but rather whether federal common law offers individual plaintiffs affirmative federal claims or, instead, gives corporations federal defenses that vanquish state tort law meant to protect consumers. Professor Weinberg faults Justice Scalia for promoting the "government contractor defense" while discounting the state policies served by products liability law. See Weinberg, note 51, at 848-49. Professor Lund, also a proponent of federal common law, juxtaposes Justice Scalia's opinion in *Boyle* with his quite different opinion for the Court in *O'Melveny.* See text accompanying notes 74-75. Lund regards *Boyle* as an instance in which the Court had every reason to allow state law to operate. See Lund, note 74, at 959-64. Professor Cass and Professor Gillette have traced out what they think are the incentives created by the government contractor defense established in *Boyle.* They contend that the implications are much more complex than the Court seems to appreciate. Ronald A. Cass & Clayton P. Gillette, *The Government Contractor Defense: Contractual Allocation of Public Risk,* 77 Va. L. Rev. 257 (1991).

such an argument in court.[79] The dichotomy between a claim, on the one hand, and a means of access to court for the enforcement of that claim, on the other, challenges the familiar maxim that there can be no "right" without a "remedy." That adage only recognizes that we typically depend on courts to give meaning to legal claims by bringing judicial power to bear on violators—ordering them to cease unlawful behavior or to pay damages for the injuries they have caused.[80]

---

79. Courts and commentators alike typically employ the term "cause of action" to refer to a private party's entitlement to sue for the enforcement of a federal legal standard (i.e., a federal statute, a rule of federal common law, or the Constitution)—that is, to refer to the "right of action" described in the text. When "cause of action" is used that way, it means a procedural vehicle that litigants can employ to advance a substantive claim that the defendant has violated the law. Sometimes, however, courts and commentators use the same "cause of action" phrase to refer to the plaintiff's legal claim itself—the violation of law the plaintiff charges the defendant with committing. Sometimes, courts and commentators use the "cause of action" formulation to capture both ideas at once, and sometimes it is frankly hard to know *what* they mean. The difficulty is in part historical. The "cause of action" formulation dates from the early Nineteenth Century. It figured prominently in the Field Code, adopted in New York in 1848. In that context, a "cause of action" was a plaintiff's primary "right" to demand some behavior from the defendant, such that the defendant's breach of the duty to behave in that way constituted a "wrong." See Robert G. Bone, *Mapping the Boundaries of a Dispute: Conceptions of Ideal Lawsuit Structure From the Field Code to the Federal Rules*, 89 Colum. L. Rev. 1, 28 (1989). Under the Field Code, a plaintiff's ability to complain to a court that the defendant had committed a breach of duty was a different matter—a "remedial right." Bone, at 12 n.21, 3-14, 28. When courts and commentators today refer to a "cause of action" as an entitlement to sue in some court to vindicate a substantive right, they are not using the "cause of action" rubric in the way it was employed in the Field Code. They are talking about something that the Field Code did not consider to be part of a "cause of action" at all. Then again, when courts and commentators use "cause of action" in more or less the way it was understood in the Field Code (i.e., to refer to a substantive claim), they invite misunderstanding—given the way in which others use the same language. In part, too, the difficulty is conceptual. In a common law system of the kind the states are understood to have, there are few occasions for separating plaintiffs' claims that they have been wronged from their authority to sue in court. Common law courts sit to enforce whatever claims a party may have; they recognize no independent question whether the party is authorized to ask them for help. Better said, a claim is necessarily enforceable in court; anything that is not judicially enforceable is not a claim the law recognizes at all. In that context, then, the two ideas (a substantive claim and the authority to take that claim to court) genuinely (or at least typically) merge into one, and use of the single "cause of action" label creates no great uncertainty. By contrast, federal legal claims are *not* invariably enforceable in court. Federal courts do *not* sit routinely to enforce whatever claims parties might wish to present to them (even when those claims are federal in character), and a party's authorization to sue *does* present an independent question. Accordingly, it is essential to differentiate between claims, on the one hand, and rights of action, on the other. There is no easy escape from this terminological tangle. One can only parse opinions and academic discussions carefully in order to identify precisely what is being described: a legal claim (i.e., an assertion that the defendant has violated the law), a right of action (i.e., an authorization to ask a court to redress that violation in some way), or some combination of the two.

80. Herein more confusing nomenclature. When this common adage is used with reference to state law and access to state court, its essential message is typically accurate. Within a framework in which courts enjoy a general authority to adjudicate any and all claims that come through the door, a realist may sensibly conclude that there is no point in differentiating a claim, a right of action to enforce that claim in a lawsuit, the court's subject matter jurisdiction to entertain the lawsuit, and the relief the court will award if the plaintiff is successful on the merits. To the realist, all that matters is what a court is prepared to *do* on the plaintiff's behalf. When the adage is used with reference to federal law and access to federal court, its message (about the realistic relationship between claims and judicial enforcement

On examination, the relationship between abstract legal claims and judicial enforcement machinery is more complex where federal courts are concerned.[81]

By conventional account, Congress has significant authority to prescribe the means by which federal common law rules and statutes will be implemented. Congress may authorize civil lawsuits as an effective, traditional means of forcing officials and citizens to comply with federal law. But a lawsuit is scarcely the only choice on the menu or, certainly, a necessary choice. In addition to private suits, or as an alternative, Congress may make violations of some federal statutes a crime and invite the executive branch to prosecute violators in criminal proceedings. Or Congress may turn enforcement responsibility over to an administrative agency.[82] In any given instance, Congress is largely free to select whatever enforcement devices it pleases and is equally free to foreclose others—including lawsuits by individuals who wish to file their own actions in court.[83]

Congressional authority to establish devices for implementing the Constitution stands on a different footing. The Supreme Court has historically been willing to assume some responsibility for constitutional enforcement itself, in service of the Court's independent duty to see that the Constitution is respected as the supreme law. Nevertheless, conventional understanding acknowledges Congress' general authority to make decisions regarding enforcement vehicles for constitutional, as well as statutory, law.[84] As a practical matter, then, litigants who want

---

of claims) can be obscured, and a different (misleading) message can emerge. In this context, the very distinctions the adage suggests can be ignored must, instead, be drawn with analytic rigor. The existence of a plaintiff's abstract claim that the defendant has violated federal law does not automatically entail either an authorization to advance that claim in a lawsuit or a federal court's jurisdiction to entertain such a suit. And the remedy a court may grant in the end is something else again. For clarity's sake, one might want to reserve the term "remedy" for use in describing the form of relief a court may award. But courts and commentators refuse to cooperate. They sometimes use that term to describe a right of action or *both* the right of action needed in a case *and* the form of relief a court may be persuaded to order. See Chapter VI, note 60; Chapter XI, note 37.

81. It is tempting to think that any claim that can be described as an individual substantive "right" to demand that defendants change their behavior or pay damages must necessarily entail a "right of action" to take defendants to court, and that difficulties arise only when a plaintiff wishes to sue in order to hold defendants accountable for violating a federal statute or constitutional provision that does not confer such an individual "right" on the plaintiff. See Chapter IX, notes 62-101, 208-18 and accompanying text (discussing how ideas of this kind play out in the context of "standing" doctrine). Yet there are instances in which plaintiffs have substantive federal rights, but no right of action to enforce those rights in a lawsuit. See notes 130, 158-65 and accompanying text.

82. See Chapter V, notes 36-44, 87-109 and accompanying text (discussing agency adjudication and its relationship to Article III courts). If Congress does employ an agency for enforcement purposes in the first instance, the agency's performance is typically open to judicial review later—either by some means established by the statute itself, see Chapter V, text accompanying notes 11-13, or by the means provided by the Administrative Procedure Act. See notes 91, 95-97 and accompanying text.

83. The classic precedent is *Cary v. Curtis*, 44 U.S. (3 How.) 236 (1845). See Henry M. Hart, Jr., *The Power of Congress to Limit the Jurisdiction of Federal Courts: An Exercise in Dialectic*, 66 Harv. L. Rev. 1362, 1366-69 (1953).

84. Professor Dellinger contends that congressional authority regarding rights of action to enforce the Constitution (as opposed to federal statutes) can be derived from congressional authority to prescribe the federal courts' jurisdiction. See Walter E. Dellinger, *Of Rights and Remedies: The Constitution as a Sword*, 85 Harv. L. Rev. 1532, 1546-47 (1972); Chapter IV, notes 19-20 and accompanying text.

to enforce federal substantive law in a lawsuit must demonstrate that Congress will allow the action and has not selected some alternative implementation scheme to the exclusion of litigation by private citizens.[85]

Congress often authorizes private lawsuits explicitly. In the *Osborn* case, for example, the same "sue and be sued" language that John Marshall read to confer jurisdiction on the federal circuit court also performed two other functions.[86] It clarified that the bank, a newly constructed creature of statute, was competent to conduct its own litigation with other parties, and it authorized the bank and its adversaries to file lawsuits to settle their differences. In *Lincoln Mills*, Justice Douglas declined to read a similar "sue and be sued" provision in § 301(b) of the LMRA to confer jurisdiction.[87] But he did read that provision both to establish unions as entities capable of litigating for themselves and to authorize them and their adversaries to litigate claims under labor contracts governed by federal common law.[88]

When Congress enacts explicit right-of-action statutes, it typically does so in connection with particular regulatory schemes. Congress initially establishes a legal standard that must be enforced by some means, and then, in further provisions of the same statute, Congress authorizes private enforcement lawsuits and confers jurisdiction on federal courts to entertain them.[89] There are, however,

---

85. See notes 158-65 and accompanying text (discussing alternatives to *Bivens* actions).

86. See note 7 and accompanying text.

87. Douglas had no need to rest on § 301(b) for jurisdictional purposes, since § 301(a) independently performed that function. See note 60 and accompanying text.

88. The bank in *Osborn* and the union in *Lincoln Mills* needed both kinds of help from Congress. The bank was created by statute and could be competent to engage in litigation only if Congress made that capacity one of the bank's statutory properties. The union was an unincorporated association that would not have had capacity to sue at common law. So the union, too, needed a statute in order to engage in litigation "as an entity." *Lincoln Mills*, 353 U.S. at 451. In addition, the bank, the union, and their adversaries needed authorization from Congress to file lawsuits advancing federal legal claims. A right of action to enforce a federal legal standard is essential and sometimes cannot be supplied by state law (particularly for purposes of suits that begin in federal court and do not reach the federal forum via removal). See notes 225-26 and accompanying text. On the other hand, state law does provide a party's right of action to enforce state law claims, in either federal or state court. Or, perhaps better said, state law typically builds a right of action into the state law claim itself. See note 79. When entities like the bank and the union sue on state law grounds, and equally when their adversaries sue them on state law grounds, the authority that Congress has granted for federal question litigation does not operate. In the *Planters' Bank* case, accordingly, the bank relied on its congressionally granted competency to sue, but not on its congressionally granted right of action. See note 14. In *Red Cross,* the private plaintiffs relied on state law both for their tort claims against the Red Cross and for their right to sue. They relied on the "sue and be sued" provision in the federal charter issued to the Red Cross to establish the status of the Red Cross as an entity competent to be sued in its own name and for the federal court's jurisdiction. See note 7.

89. The statute in *Testa v. Katt,* 330 U.S. 386 (1947), is an illustration. See Chapter VI, notes 39-47 and accompanying text. The Emergency Price Control Act involved in that case: (1) established maximum prices that manufacturers could charge for their products; (2) authorized buyers to sue sellers for overcharging; and (3) conferred jurisdiction on federal district courts "concurrently" with state courts to entertain suits to enforce federal price limits. In each instance, the Act performed functions essential to judicial enforcement. Initially, in (1), the Act created a federal legal standard. Next, in (2), the Act established buyers' right of action to file enforcement suits. Then, in (3), the Act conferred jurisdiction on the federal courts. In yet a fourth provision, the Act authorized courts to award triple damages and thus prescribed a "remedy." See note 80.

some free standing right-of-action statutes that serve more generally as procedural vehicles by which litigants can enforce federal law by means of private lawsuits. The Ku Klux Klan Act, 42 U.S.C. § 1983, is one,[90] the Administrative Procedure Act, 5 U.S.C. § 702, is another,[91] and the Declaratory Judgment Act, 28 U.S.C. § 2201, may be yet another.[92]

Pursuant to § 1983, a "party injured" can file "an action at law, suit in equity, or other proper proceeding for redress," naming as a defendant a "person" who, "under color of any statute, ordinance, regulation, custom, or usage of any State or Territory" subjects a "citizen" or "other person" to the "deprivation of any rights, privileges, or immunities secured by the Constitution and laws."[93] Modern decisions give that archaic language an authoritative interpretation. It neither establishes substantive rights nor confers jurisdiction on the federal courts. But it does supply a right of action to be employed by plaintiffs who wish to vindicate rights that have some independent source in the Constitution or other "laws" of the United States.[94]

Pursuant to § 702, a "person" can seek judicial review of actions taken by certain federal administrative agencies, if the litigant either suffers "legal wrong" or is "adversely affected or aggrieved by agency action within the meaning of a relevant statute." If, then, Congress chooses to employ an agency to implement a federal statute in the first instance (perhaps to the exclusion of private suits), private litigants may sometimes enforce the statute at one step removed—by suing the *agency* to ensure it does not violate the very statute it is charged to implement (or some provision of the Constitution). This right of action is not always available.[95] Yet when § 702 *is* available, it performs (with respect to suits alleging that federal agencies have violated federal law) the same function that § 1983 performs (with respect to suits alleging that state officials have violated certain federal rights). It neither creates substantive rights nor confers jurisdiction on the

---

90. See Chapter II, notes 73-74 and accompanying text.

91. See Chapter II, note 77 and accompanying text. This provision in the APA also confers "standing" to appear in an Article III court. See Chapter IX, notes 82-90, 183-84, 209 and accompanying text.

92. See Chapter II, note 76 and accompanying text.

93. See notes 125-34 and accompanying text. The text of § 1983 goes on to state that "in any action brought against a judicial officer for an act or omission taken in such officer's judicial capacity, injunctive relief shall not be granted unless a declaratory decree was violated or declaratory relief was unavailable." See Chapter X, note 254 and accompanying text.

94. Recall that § 1983 actions can be filed in state court. See Chapter VI, note 51 and accompanying text. Plaintiffs in § 1983 actions typically advance fourteenth amendment claims and invoke federal court jurisdiction under the general authority provided by 28 U.S.C. § 1331. See text accompanying note 168. By common account, the Reconstruction Congress enacted § 1983 for the very purpose of enforcing the then-recent fourteenth amendment. See *Monroe v. Pape*, 365 U.S. 167, 171 (1961). An independent provision enacted at the same time originally supplied federal courts with the jurisdiction required to entertain § 1983 actions, irrespective of the amount in controversy between the parties. See 28 U.S.C. § 1343(3); Chapter II, note 73 and accompanying text. When Congress eliminated the amount-in-controversy requirement from § 1331 in 1976, there was no longer any need for § 1343(3). That statute remains in place, but it is now superfluous.

95. Judicial review under § 702 is contingent on a body of statutes and decisions that comprise a healthy portion of administrative law. For example, the APA applies only to certain departments and agencies, 5 U.S.C. § 701, and judicial review is typically restricted to agency action that is "final" within the meaning of 5 U.S.C. § 704.

federal courts.[96] But it does provide a right of action for litigants whose interests fall "arguably within the zone of interests" protected by the statutes or constitutional provisions they contend federal agencies have violated.[97]

Pursuant to § 2201, a federal court "may" declare the "rights and other legal relations of any interested party seeking such declaration," if an "appropriate pleading" is filed in "a case of actual controversy" within the court's jurisdiction. That language, too, is opaque. According to the Supreme Court's decisions, § 2201 neither creates substantive rights nor confers subject matter jurisdiction.[98] At a minimum, it enables federal courts to grant a declaratory judgment as a remedy—that is, as a form of judicial relief different from an award of damages or an injunction.[99] There is an argument that it does *only* that and does *not* itself create a right of action to sue in the first instance. Note in this vein that § 2201 expressly licenses the federal courts and does not, in so many words, empower potential litigants. Moreover, § 2201 *authorizes* the federal courts to issue declaratory judgments, but does not *require* them to do so. The discretionary character of declaratory relief may presuppose that litigants must establish a right of action on some independent basis.[100]

There is also an argument that the Declaratory Judgment Act, like § 1983 and § 702 of the APA, authorizes private plaintiffs to go to court, so long as they seek only declaratory relief.[101] Since declaratory judgments have no immediate

---

96. *Califano v. Sanders*, 430 U.S. 99 (1977). Like § 1983 suits in federal court, actions pursuant to § 702 typically rely on § 1331 for subject matter jurisdiction.

97. *Clarke v. Secur. Indus. Ass'n*, 479 U.S. 388, 399-400 (1987); see Chapter IX, notes 183-96 and accompanying text (discussing the zone test).

98. See Chapter IX, notes 15-16 and accompanying text.

99. The next section following, 28 U.S.C. § 2202, authorizes federal courts to issue "[f]urther necessary or proper relief" against parties who defy an authoritative declaration of their rights and legal relations. Since § 2202 authorizes injunctions to enforce declaratory judgments, it blurs the distinction between the two forms of relief. See Chapter IX, notes 286-90 and accompanying text (discussing declaratory actions in place of actions for injunctions); Chapter XI, notes 139-41, 193-201 and accompanying text (discussing decisions to abstain from exercising jurisdiction in declaratory judgment cases).

100. Professor Monaghan reads § 2201 this way. Henry P. Monaghan, *Federal Statutory Review Under § 1983 and the APA*, 91 Colum. L. Rev. 233, 238 (1991). Since § 2201 is addressed only to federal courts, it evidently supplies no right of action for suits in state court. In that way, too, § 2201 differs from § 1983 and thus arguably appears not to authorize suits in the first instance, but only to permit a certain form of relief in suits that are authorized by some independent source. On the district courts' discretion regarding declaratory relief, see *Wilton v. Seven Falls Co.*, 515 U.S. 277 (1995); *Public Svc. Comm'n v. Wycoff*, 344 U.S. 237, 241 (1952); Chapter IX, notes 286-90 and accompanying text (discussing the relationship between the availability of declaratory relief and the ripeness doctrine).

101. In *Calderon v. Ashmus*, 118 S.Ct. 1694 (1998), the lower court permitted a class of prison inmates to rely on § 2201 to supply a right of action. The prisoners also cited § 1983, but there was some doubt whether their claim (regarding the appropriate filing period for planned habeas corpus actions) rested on "rights" that § 1983 might be used to vindicate. See notes 131-32 and accompanying text. The Supreme Court decided *Ashmus* on constitutional grounds and did not address the capacity of the Declaratory Judgment Act to provide the prisoners with the right of action they needed. See Chapter IX, note 16 (discussing other aspects of *Ashmus*). In *Golden State Transit Corp. v. City of Los Angeles*, 493 U.S. 103 (1989), the Court held that § 1983 established a right of action for a suit seeking damages for a violation of the National Labor Relations Act. Justice Kennedy dissented from that holding (on the theory that the NLRA contained no "rights" that a § 1983 action could enforce). But Kennedy suggested that the plaintiffs could sue for a declaratory judgment pursuant to § 2201. Having set § 1983 aside, Justice Kennedy may have meant that § 2201

coercive effect, they lend themselves to cases in which the parties have a genuine dispute regarding the law governing their relations, but will find it easy enough to reconcile their differences once a court announces where each party stands.[102] Declaratory judgments are also valuable when one party plans to behave in a way that will very likely prompt the other to take legal action. The classic illustrations are cases in which citizens wish to engage in behavior they believe to be constitutionally protected, but it appears that they will be prosecuted. In the absence of a declaratory judgment device, it would be necessary to take the planned action, suffer prosecution, and then advance the constitutional claim as a defense to the criminal charge. The Declaratory Judgment Act gives litigants the option of filing a pre-enforcement civil suit in which to litigate the constitutional claim affirmatively.[103]

1. Rights of Action Implied in Federal Statutes

When Congress does not explicitly authorize suits to enforce federal statutes, the Court sometimes finds a right of action nonetheless to be implied in the substantive statute to be enforced.[104] Early on, the Court made implied actions the

---

could supply an independent right of action, so long as the plaintiffs sought only declaratory relief. Id. at 119 (dissenting opinion). See notes 268-70 and accompanying text (revisiting the problem of finding a right of action in cases in which plaintiffs contend that federal statutes preempt state law).

102. See text accompanying note 261 (discussing *Franchise Tax Board* as an illustration).

103. According to Professor Borchard's colorful metaphor, a citizen should not be told that the only way to know a mushroom from a toadstool is to eat it. Edwin M. Borchard, Declaratory Judgments 967 (2d ed. 1941). Declaratory judgments are not well adapted to redress past violations. In *Steel Co. v. Citizens for a Better Environment*, 118 S.Ct. 1003 (1998), the plaintiffs notified a company that it was in violation of a federal statute inasmuch as it had not filed periodic reports on its use of toxic materials. The company promptly supplied the reports, albeit out of time. At that point, the plaintiffs filed suit in federal court, seeking a declaratory judgment that the company had violated the statute in the past. Justice Scalia responded that a declaratory judgment would do nothing to redress the injuries the plaintiffs insisted they had suffered because of the company's misbehavior. It would only restate a matter that was uncontested at the time of suit (that the defendant had previously violated the statute) and thus would be "worthless." Id. at 1018. See Chapter IX, notes 158-62 and accompanying text (discussing the plaintiffs' "standing" in *Steel*).

104. The existence of implied rights of action contributes to the terminological confusion that plagues these materials. The point is that litigants can derive both a legal claim and a procedural vehicle for advancing that claim in court from a single source: a statutory provision that, on its face, establishes only the former. In this context, accordingly, it is small wonder that courts and commentators may *say* that litigants have a "cause of action" and *mean* that they have *both* a legal claim and a right of action. See note 79. Nevertheless, the two ideas are distinguishable. If they were not, there would be no body of Supreme Court decisions on implied rights of action. Any statute creating a substantive legal standard that a defendant might violate would necessarily entail a right of action in some plaintiff to call the defendant to account for that violation in court. That is not the case. In its decisions on implied rights of action, the Supreme Court posits that a statute sets forth a legal standard that can be violated and then focuses on the different question whether a private plaintiff has a right of action to go to court to establish that a defendant has committed such a violation.

rule, not the exception. In *J.I. Case v. Borak*,[105] Justice Clark acknowledged that the Securities and Exchange Act empowered the SEC to enforce federal rules regarding proxy solicitations and made no express provision for private suits by stockholders. Yet since private lawsuits promised to promote the Act's purpose to protect investors, Justice Clark allowed stockholders to file private suits of their own as a supplement to the SEC's efforts. More recently, the Court has adopted precisely the opposite default position. Implied rights of action are now the exception, not the rule.[106]

In the 1970s, the Court discarded the *Borak* approach in favor of more *ad hoc* judgment. In *Cort v. Ash*,[107] Justice Brennan identified four factors bearing on whether private suits should be permitted in the absence of explicit congressional authorization: (1) whether the statute in question established benefits for a special class, the members of which might reasonably wish to file enforcement suits; (2) whether the legislative history indicated congressional "intent" one way or the other; (3) whether private suits were consistent with the statute's underlying purpose; and (4) whether the subject matter of private suits was traditionally the concern of state law, so that fashioning a federal right of action would be "inappropriate."[108] In light of those factors, Justice Brennan concluded in *Cort* that authority to file private suits was not implied in a federal statute making it a crime for corporations and labor unions to contribute to presidential campaigns.[109]

In subsequent cases, the Court gradually hardened its position. In *Cannon v. University of Chicago*,[110] Justice Stevens approved private suits to enforce Title IX of the Education Amendments of 1972, banning sex discrimination in federally funded educational programs. But he did so only because Title IX presented an "atypical" situation in which all the factors identified in *Cort* indicated that private suits were implied. Even at that, Stevens said that when Congress creates statutory rights and "intends" that private litigants should be able to file their own actions to enforce those rights, the "far better course" for Congress is "to specify as much" rather than leave the question for the courts to resolve.[111]

---

105. 377 U.S. 426 (1964). Professor Foy contends that courts have found rights of action implicit in legislative enactments since the formative period of English law and that the notion that courts might *not* enforce statutes in private litigation is an entirely modern idea. H. Miles Foy, III, *Some Reflections on Legislation, Adjudication, and Implied Private Actions in the State and Federal Courts*, 71 Cornell L. Rev. 501 (1986); see id. at 524, quoting Lord Coke: "[E]very Act of Parliament made against any injury, mischiefe, or grievance doth either expressly, or impliedly give a remedy to the party wronged, or grieved." But see note 79 (explaining that rights and rights of action go hand-in-hand in a common law system).

106. See Chapter I, notes 37-41 and accompanying text (discussing the implications of imposing clear statement rules).

107. 422 U.S. 66 (1975). See *Merrill, Lynch v. Curran*, 456 U.S. 353, 377 (1982) (explaining that in *Cort* the Court "unanimously decided to modify its approach to the question whether a federal statute includes a private right of action").

108. 422 U.S. at 78.

109. Id. at 79-85.

110. 441 U.S. 677 (1979).

111. Id. at 717. The Court has since elaborated on the right of action recognized in *Cannon. Gebser v. Lago Vista Ind. School Dist.*, 118 S.Ct. 1989 (1998).

Today, the Court treats the question whether private actions are implied by a statute as "basically one of statutory construction."[112] In *Thompson v. Thompson*,[113] Justice Marshall explained that the controlling question is still whether Congress "intended" to authorize private suits. Yet the Court focuses almost exclusively on the language of the statute under examination and infers legislative "intent" from that alone.[114] For his part, Justice Scalia has urged the Court to "get out of the business" of finding private rights of action implicit in legislative schemes and to insist, instead, that Congress must authorize lawsuits explicitly, if at all.[115] The difference between the full Court and Justice Scalia may bear wider jurisprudential implications. But in practice the Court usually reaches the same results that Scalia would produce on his own. The Court has only rarely approved implied rights of action since *Cannon*.[116]

The explanations for this turnabout are clear. The Court puts decisions like *Borak* (and even *Cort* and *Cannon*) in the same category with the classic federal common law cases, *Lincoln Mills* and *Clearfield*.[117] When the Court approves private rights of action to enforce statutes in the absence of express authorization, the Court itself fashions a species of federal law. When, however, the Court demands some demonstration of congressional "intent" that private suits should be available, the Court rests more comfortably on statutory construction. The considerations that attend judicial law-making in this context are the same considerations that attend judicial law-making elsewhere: (1) deference to Congress' primary responsibility to prescribe legislative policies and the way they will be implemented; and (2) deference to state

---

112. *Cannon*, 441 U.S. at 717 (Rehnquist, J., concurring).

113. 484 U.S. 174 (1988).

114. See Chapter I, note 28 and accompanying text. If litigants wish to enforce federal legal standards in suits against federal agencies, § 702 of the APA can take them part of the way toward the statutory authority they require—provided the conditions that trigger § 702 are met. See notes 95-97 and accompanying text. The Court explained in *Clarke* that § 702 expresses a "presumption" in favor of judicial review in the cases to which it applies. 479 U.S. at 398-99. That makes sense, particularly where agency enforcement precludes first order private enforcement suits and limits private litigants to attacks on the way the agency performs. If even suits against the agency were barred, federal courts would be carved out of the picture entirely. Recall, however, that § 702 authorizes private suits only on behalf of litigants whose interests arguably fall within the zone of interests protected by the statutes they seek to enforce. See text accompanying note 97; see also Chapter IX, note 196 and accompanying text (discussing the relationship between a search for an implied right of action and a determination of whether plaintiffs' interests satisfy the zone test).

115. *Thompson*, 484 U.S. at 188 (concurring opinion).

116. In *Morse v. Republican Party*, 517 U.S. 186 (1996), the Court held that § 10 of the Voting Rights Act of 1965 establishes a private right of action notwithstanding the Act's failure to say so explicitly. In that instance, however, the Court emphasized that, in 1965, Congress acted against the backdrop of decisions like *Borak*, under which implied private actions were the rule, not the exception. The Court acknowledged that the absence of an explicit textual authorization in a statute enacted today would be fatal to any argument that implied authority should nonetheless be found. Id. at 230. Even at that, four justices dissented in *Morse*. Professor Ashford had previously called attention to the difficulties of changing the Court's approach to implied actions and then applying the new approach "retroactively" to statutes enacted when implied actions were readily allowed. Robert H.A. Ashford, *Implied Causes of Action Under Federal Laws: Calling the Court Back to Borak*, 79 Nw. U. L. Rev. 227 (1984).

117. See notes 58-59 and accompanying text. See also *Bivens v. Six Unknown Named Agents*, 403 U.S. 388, 402 n. 4 (1971) (Harlan, J., concurring) (reading *Borak* this way).

court authority to adjudicate disputes that Congress does not assign to the federal judiciary.[118]

Deference to Congress. The Court now regards the authorization of private rights of action as a legislative function.[119] When Congress establishes enforcement schemes other than private lawsuits and fails affirmatively to provide for private suits as well, the Court draws the inference that the former occupy the field to the exclusion of the latter.[120] This approach has been questioned. When, following *Lincoln Mills* and *Clearfield*, federal courts create substantive federal law to provide rules of decision, they fashion legislative policies of their own choosing.[121] When, by contrast, federal courts approve private lawsuits to enforce statutes that Congress has enacted, they implement policies that Congress has articulated. The intrusion on congressional prerogatives is therefore diminished, except in circumstances in which private actions do not augment, but actually impede, other enforcement mechanisms.[122]

Deference to state courts. The Court also hesitates to find implied authority for private suits, lest federal courts be charged with enlarging their own power unilaterally.[123] This explanation, too, has limited force. When federal courts construe their jurisdiction narrowly to ensure that they do not overstep the bounds that Congress has established, the usual consequence is that judicial business is channeled into state court. In this context, however, that is not the case. When federal courts decline to find rights of action implied in federal statutes, they typically close not only their own doors, but the doors of state courts as well. If private litigants have no right of action to enforce a federal statute in federal court, they usually have no right of action to enforce the statute in state court, either.[124]

---

118. See text accompanying note 57.

119. In an influential dissent in *Cannon*, Justice Powell condemned the approach in *Cort* as an "open invitation" to the federal courts to "legislate" private actions that Congress has not authorized. 441 U.S. at 731.

120. See notes 158-65 and accompanying text (discussing statutory schemes that displace private suits to enforce the Constitution).

121. See note 43 and accompanying text. But see text accompanying note 60 (noting the Court's insistence in *Lincoln Mills* that courts could develop federal common law for labor contracts as an extension of national policy initially prescribed by Congress).

122. There is a rich literature exploring the extent to which private rights of action may complement (or hinder) the enforcement efforts of federal agencies. See, e.g., Frank Easterbrook, *Foreward: The Court and the Economic System*, 98 Harv. L. Rev. 4 (1984); Richard B. Stewart & Cass R. Sunstein, *Public Programs and Private Rights*, 95 Harv. L. Rev. 1193 (1982). Forcing individuals who have ostensibly meritorious claims to rely on public prosecutors and regulators to enforce federal statute law bears political implications. Professor Weinberg dismisses the Court's concerns about judicial law-making as baseless. Weinberg, note 51, at 841.

123. According to Justice Powell, the idea that federal courts may volunteer their services "runs contrary" to the general principle that the courts should not expand their own jurisdiction beyond what Congress prescribes. *Cannon*, 441 U.S. at 746-47 (dissenting opinion), citing *American Fire & Cas. Co. v. Finn*, 341 U.S. 6, 17 (1951). Recall that Congress fixes the federal courts' jurisdiction within the limits established by Article III. Chapter IV, notes 19-20 and accompanying text.

124. State law may incorporate a federal statute and thus make a violation of that statute actionable as a matter of state law. Yet an authoritative decision that Congress has precluded private litigation to enforce the statute will control even in that event. See notes 215, 228 and accompanying text. In some instances, the federal courts' failure to find a current right of action implied only postpones federal court adjudication until after a federal

The Court's insistence that Congress must express its "intent" to establish private rights of action creates some tension with its interpretations of § 1983.[125] In *Maine v. Thiboutot*,[126] the Court held that § 1983 can supply a right of action for the enforcement of federal statutes that have none of their own.[127] Justice Brennan acknowledged that § 1983 more commonly serves litigants who wish to advance fourteenth amendment claims. Yet it also creates a right of action on behalf of a party injured by a violation of the "laws" of the United States.[128] The Court held in *Golden State Transit Corp. v. City of Los Angeles*,[129] that if § 1983 *can* provide litigants with a right of action to enforce a federal statute, the default position is that such an action *is* available. Congress can choose otherwise only by making itself clear in one of two ways: (1) by prohibiting § 1983 actions expressly; or (2) by creating a "carefully tailored" alternative enforcement scheme with which § 1983 actions would be inconsistent.[130]

---

administrative agency has acted, when § 702 of the APA or some similar statute authorizes disappointed private litigants to challenge the agency's performance. See notes 91, 95-97 and accompanying text; Chapter V, text accompanying notes 11-13. In *Hilton v. South Carolina Pub. Ry. Comm'n*, 502 U.S. 197 (1991), the eleventh amendment barred a private action against the state in federal court, but the Court held that plaintiffs could nonetheless sue in state court. It was clear in that case, however, that the availability of a state court suit was a question of statutory construction. The state courts below held that the relevant federal statute (the Federal Employers Liability Act) did not authorize private suits (in any court). The Supreme Court disagreed. See Chapter VI, note 88 (discussing other aspects of *Hilton*).

125. And (perhaps) the Declaratory Judgment Act. See notes 101-03 and accompanying text. On the implications for actions pursuant to § 702 of the APA, see note 114.

126. 448 U.S. 1 (1980).

127. This idea (that § 1983 can provide a right of action to enforce a federal statute that itself establishes only the basis for a legal claim) underscores that legal claims and rights of action are not elements of a single phenomenon (and thus cannot be captured under a single "cause of action" label without risking confusion). See note 79.

128. See text accompanying note 93. Justice Brennan relied (uncharacteristically) on the textualism that is often reflected in opinions by more conservative members of the Court. See Chapter I, notes 24-36 and accompanying text. In dissent, Justice Powell insisted that Brennan had blinded himself to the "plain" meaning of § 1983 in its "historical context." 448 U.S. at 12. Powell contended that the Reconstruction Congress used the general term "laws" when it actually meant only to include equal rights legislation.

129. 493 U.S. 103 (1989).

130. Id. at 106-07. See *Livadas v. Bradshaw*, 512 U.S. 107, 133 (1994) (confirming that § 1983 suits are "presumptively available" in preemption cases). Litigants' entitlement to file § 1983 actions is not defeated by the mere existence of alternative means of protecting their rights. Congress must do something more to make it clear that § 1983 actions are unavailable. In *Middlesex County Sewerage Auth. v. Nat'l Sea Clammers Ass'n*, 453 U.S. 1 (1981), the Court found it sufficient that Congress had created a "comprehensive enforcement scheme" attended by its own procedural requirements — which litigants would bypass by "bringing suit directly under § 1983." Id. at 20. The plaintiffs in *Sea Clammers* failed to satisfy notification standards required under the express right-of-action provisions in two federal environmental protection statutes. In *Smith v. Robinson*, 468 U.S. 992 (1984), the Court found a similar scheme sufficient to foreclose § 1983 actions. In *Wright v. City of Roanoke*, 479 U.S. 418 (1987), the Court explained that the regulatory schemes in *Sea Clammers* and *Smith* left "no room" for § 1983 actions. In the absence of comprehensive statutory schemes of that kind, the Court will "not lightly conclude that Congress intended to preclude reliance on § 1983." Id. at 423-24. Cf. *Blessing v. Freestone*, 117 S.Ct. 1353 (1997) (noting that *Sea Clammers* and *Smith* are the only cases in which the Court has found § 1983 actions to be precluded in the absence of express language to that effect). Writing soon after *Thiboutot*, Professor Sunstein argued that § 1983 actions should be avail-

Nevertheless, § 1983 does not answer in the run of statutory cases. Plaintiffs must allege that they have suffered a deprivation of "rights, privileges, or immunities secured" by federal law. Thus § 1983 can provide a vehicle for vindicating only statutes that establish special "benefits" for individuals that can reasonably be considered individual "rights" and not for challenging any "violation of federal law."[131] A statute creates the necessary rights if it: (1) benefits individuals who may be § 1983 plaintiffs; (2) imposes a "binding obligation" in mandatory (not precatory) terms; and (3) is not so "vague and amorphous" that its enforcement would "strain judicial competence."[132] Plaintiffs must also claim that the defendant has acted under color of "state" (not federal) law.[133] Thus § 1983 is largely useful only when litigants wish to sue state and local officials or private parties working with them.[134]

2. Rights of Action Implied in the Constitution

In some instances, Congress explicitly authorizes private rights of action to enforce the Constitution. The best example is § 1983, which typically supplies a vehicle for suits to vindicate fourteenth amendment rights.[135] Yet no statute au-

---

able whenever they would not be inconsistent with another enforcement mechanism. Cass R. Sunstein, *Section 1983 and Private Enforcement of Federal Law*, 49 U. Chi. L. Rev. 394 (1982). At that time, however, the lower courts often found § 1983 actions foreclosed. See George D. Brown, *Whither Thiboutot? Section 1983, Private Enforcement, and the Damages Dilemma*, 33 DePaul L. Rev. 31, (1983) (also describing unsuccessful proposals to overrule *Thiboutot* by statute).

131. *Golden State*, 493 U.S. at 106.

132. *Blessing*, 117 S.Ct. at 1359, relying on *Golden State*, 493 U.S. at 106; *Wright*, 479 U.S. at 430; and *Wilder v. Virginia Hosp. Ass'n*, 496 U.S. 498, 509-11 (1990). In *Wright*, the Court allowed tenants in federally funded low income housing to file § 1983 actions claiming that they had been denied the benefits of rent ceilings established by federal statutes and administrative regulations. Cf. *Dennis v. Higgins*, 498 U.S. 439 (1991) (holding that private businesses had a sufficient "right" under the Commerce Clause to conduct their affairs free of state regulation). In *Pennhurst State School & Hosp. v. Halderman*, 451 U.S. 1 (1981), however, the Court held that the Developmentally Disabled Assistance and Bill of Rights Act created no such rights. In *Suter v. Artist M.*, 503 U.S. 347 (1992), the Court held that the Adoption Assistance and Child Welfare Act rendered no rights, either. In the wake of *Suter*, Congress enacted further legislation in an apparent attempt to make § 1983 actions available in that instance. See Brian D. Ledahl, *Congress Overruling the Courts: Legislative Changes to the Scope of § 1983*, 29 Colum. J. Law & Soc. Prob. 411 (1996). Justice Scalia has explained that newly enacted statutory rights are "automatically embraced within § 1983"—unless Congress specifies otherwise, explicitly or implicitly (as in *Sea Clammers* and *Smith*). *Blessing*, 117 S.Ct. at 1364 (concurring opinion). Yet Scalia maintains that the rights that new statutes actually "secure" within the meaning of § 1983 may be determined not according to "modern notions," but in light of the "understanding of § 1983 when it was enacted." Specifically, Justice Scalia suggests that individuals who advance claims arising from contracts between the federal government and a state are only third party beneficiaries of those contracts and thus may have no rights "secured" by federal law in the necessary sense. He recognizes, however, that the Court has found claims of that kind to be enforceable via § 1983. E.g., *Wright*, 479 U.S. at 430-32.

133. See text accompanying note 93.

134. See, e.g., *Edelman v. Jordan*, 415 U.S. 651 (1974) (ultimately holding that a § 1983 suit was barred by the eleventh amendment); see Chapter X, notes 167-74 and accompanying text. Plaintiffs can also rely on § 1983 to sue municipalities and counties in some circumstances. See Chapter X, notes 209-15 and accompanying text.

135. See notes 90, 93-94 and accompanying text.

thorizes constitutional suits against defendants acting under color of *federal law*.[136] Accordingly, authority for private lawsuits to enforce the Constitution against federal officers must be found elsewhere. The Supreme Court routinely finds private rights of action implied in constitutional provisions. Nevertheless, modern decisions reflect the same doubts and concerns that figure in the cases on private suits to enforce federal statutes. Following the pattern set in the statutory cases, the Court has lost any enthusiasm it once had for constitutional actions and, concomitantly, is now inclined to find private suits foreclosed by other enforcement mechanisms that Congress sets in place.

Private suits for injunctive relief do not typically evoke controversy, despite Congress' failure to authorize actions of that kind explicitly.[137] If federal courts were to turn away litigants who seek only to bring an end to a current violation of the Constitution, or to prevent some future violation, they would decline to enforce the basic law in the most vivid way. Suits for monetary damages have always been more troubling.[138] In cases of that kind, Congress can waive the federal government's sovereign immunity or, in some instances, can abrogate the constitutional immunity the states enjoy under the eleventh amendment.[139] Yet no statute actually *does* open the government or the states routinely to constituional suits for damages.[140] Accordingly, actions for compensatory relief typically attempt to saddle individual officers with personal liability. That prospect implicates additional considerations. The Supreme Court is reluctant to hold individual agents personally accountable for their behavior in the line of duty.[141]

The Court initially approached private actions for damages in *Bell v. Hood*.[142] The plaintiff in that case sued FBI agents in a federal district court, contending that they had violated his fourth amendment rights. The lower courts dismissed for lack of jurisdiction. Justice Black acknowledged that it was questionable whether the fourth amendment was enforceable in a private action for monetary relief. Yet he explained that whether or not such an action could be brought, the *question* whether it was available raised a substantial issue of federal law. Accordingly, the complaint could not fail for want of *jurisdiction*. Black reversed on that basis alone, leaving the right-of-action issue unresolved.[143]

---

136. The Federal Tort Claims Act does not authorize suits against federal officers on constitutional grounds, though it does subject the government to suit on parallel state tort claims arising from the same conduct. *Carlson v. Green*, 446 U.S. 14, 19-20 (1980).

137. See Alfred Hill, *Constitutional Remedies*, 69 Colum. L. Rev. 1109 (1969).

138. Academicians debate whether actions for damages were generally available prior to the Court's modern decisions. Professor Collins thinks so; Professor Dellinger thinks not. See Michael G. Collins, *"Economic Rights," Implied Constitutional Actions, and the Scope of Section 1983*, 77 Gtn. L.J. 1493, 1517-25 (1989); Dellinger, note 84, at 1542.

139. See Chapter X, notes 7-11 and accompanying text (discussing sovereign immunity).

140. The Federal Tort Claims Act waives the federal government's sovereign immunity for a wide range of suits, but not for constitutional actions. *FDIC v. Meyer*, 510 U.S. 471, 477-78 (1994).

141. See Chapter X, notes 245-92 and accompanying text (discussing the availability of official immunity).

142. 327 U.S. 678 (1946).

143. Id. at 684.

The Court returned to that question a quarter century later in *Bivens v. Six Unknown Named Agents*.[144] The plaintiff in *Bivens* also sought damages from federal agents for a violation of his fourth amendment rights. The agents responded on two levels. First, they contended that the fourth amendment established no federal right of privacy, but only fortified a right of privacy created by state law. By their account, the plaintiff had to sue them in state court on a state tort theory. Then, if they resisted liability on the ground that they acted within their federal authority, the plaintiff would be entitled to counter that they exceeded that authority by violating the fourth amendment. Second, the agents argued that if the fourth amendment did establish a constitutional right of privacy, it was for Congress, not the courts, to decide whether that right should be enforceable in private lawsuits for damages. Justice Brennan rejected the notion that the fourth amendment could come into play only to defeat a defense to a state law tort claim and, turning to the question left open in *Bell*, said that a right of action to enforce the fourth amendment affirmatively *does* exist, even though neither the fourth amendment itself nor any statute enacted by Congress expressly says as much.[145]

Justice Brennan's opinion in *Bivens* was perfectly clear in announcing the Court's result, less so in explaining the supporting rationale. Justice Harlan was more revealing in an important concurring opinion. Harlan, for his part, placed *Bivens* squarely within the body of decisions approving the creation of federal common law—stretching from *Lincoln Mills* and *Clearfield* through *Borak*.[146] Accepting that kind of judicial law-making responsibility, Harlan said the Court should ponder the same "range of policy considerations" that a legislature would examine if it were deciding whether to authorize suits by statute.[147] In that vein, Harlan explained that the plaintiff in *Bivens* could no longer benefit from an injunction. His rights had already been invaded; it was "damages or nothing."[148] Accordingly, Justice Harlan concluded that, on balance, a suit for damages should be allowed.[149]

---

144. 403 U.S. 388 (1971).

145. Id. at 395-97. Justice Brennan remanded the case to allow the lower courts to determine whether the agents were entitled to official immunity.

146. 403 U.S. at 403-04 (concurring opinion). See notes 58-59, 105 and accompanying text.

147. Id. at 407. Justice Harlan explained that he could not distinguish suits for damages from suits for injunctions. Plaintiffs needed a right of action to sue at all, for either kind of remedy. In the past, he said, the Court had permitted plaintiffs to sue for injunctive relief without difficulty, resting solely on the federal courts' subject matter jurisdiction or, at any rate, *sans* any separate source for a right of action. That being true, Harlan concluded that plaintiffs seeking damages could equally proceed in the absence of an authorizing statute. Id. at 405.

148. Id. at 409-10. Unless the plaintiff in *Bivens* could demonstrate a credible threat that he might be mistreated in the same way in the future, he lacked "standing" to seek injunctive or declaratory relief. See Chapter IX, notes 156-57 and accompanying text (discussing the *Lyons* case).

149. In dissent, Justice Black insisted that the creation of a right of action was a legislative function, that by enacting § 1983 Congress had established such a right of action for challenging the behavior of state officials, that Congress had plainly failed to enact an analog to § 1983 for suits against federal officials, and that the Court should not take it upon itself to "legislate" such a right of action into existence by judicial decision. 403 U.S. at 427-28. Both Justice Black and Justice Blackmun argued that the recognition of private actions in *Bivens* would burden federal court dockets. Id. at 430 (Blackmun, J., dissenting). That par-

Since *Bivens*, the Court has held that plaintiffs can file lawsuits seeking compensation for violations of other constitutional provisions. In *Davis v. Passman*[150] and *Carlson v. Green*,[151] Justice Brennan said that the Court presumes that private suits to enforce the Constitution are available to litigants who have no other "effective means" to protect their rights.[152] The Court's conservatives, who doubt the wisdom of *Bivens*, have abandoned a frontal assault on that decision and launched flank attacks.[153] In the wake of *Bivens*, *Davis*, and *Green*, three related questions bear consideration: (1) whether, in retrospect, *Bivens* must be regarded as an interpretation of the fourth amendment itself; (2) whether Congress can substitute other enforcement devices for private actions; and (3) whether, if so, alternative mechanisms must be the equal of private suits for compensatory relief.

The basis of the Bivens decision. Since the fourth amendment was the only positive law Justice Brennan discussed in *Bivens*, he may well have meant to rest his decision on that constitutional ground.[154] Yet Brennan expressly declined to decide whether a right of action for damages is "necessary" to enforce the fourth amendment. Congress had not attempted to negate private suits and thus had not presented the Court with the question whether a statute barring private actions

---

ticular argument was weak. It was conceded in *Bivens* that federal officers sued in state court on state tort theories would routinely remove the actions against them to federal court via 28 U.S.C. § 1442. See Chapter VI, notes 125-32 and accompanying text. That being true, allowing private suits that might be filed originally in federal court would not (necessarily) contribute to federal docket congestion. 403 U.S. at 391 n.4 (majority opinion).

150. 442 U.S. 228 (1979) (fifth amendment due process).

151. 446 U.S. 14 (1980) (eighth amendment).

152. *Davis*, 442 U.S. at 242. Professor Harrison argues that fourteenth amendment rights present a special case. The fourteenth amendment contains (in section five) a specific provision authorizing Congress to enforce its substantive provisions (collected in section one) by legislation. That, according to Harrison, suggests that section one cannot alone be the source of a right of action to sue (even for anticipatory declaratory or injunctive relief) and that affirmative enforcement suits require independent statutory authority. Since § 1983 often provides that statutory authority, the implications of Harrison's view are largely academic. But in instances in which § 1983 or some other statute is not available, Harrison insists that individuals with fourteenth amendment claims are relegated to older, common law means of getting those claims into court—e.g., advancing them in reply to a defendant's defense to a state tort action. See text accompanying notes 144-45. In the absence of a federal right-of-action statute, by Harrison's account, individuals who wish to challenge a state statute cannot sue for declaratory or injunctive relief, but must commit a violation and then defend against prosecution on fourteenth amendment grounds. John Harrison, *Jurisdiction, Congressional Power, and Constitutional Remedies*, 86 Gtn. L.J. 2513 (1998). But see Daniel J. Meltzer, *Congress, Courts, and Constitutional Remedies*, 86 Gtn. L.J. 2537, 2551 (1998) (criticizing Harrison's view as "radical").

153. Conservative justices have not hesitated to speak their minds. In *Davis*, Justice Powell insisted that the Court should not regard private actions as a constitutional imperative, but should decide in each instance whether such suits should be allowed as a matter of "principled discretion." 442 U.S. at 251 (dissenting opinion). In *Carlson*, then-Justice Rehnquist, for his part, openly urged the Court to overrule *Bivens* altogether. 446 U.S. at 31 (dissenting opinion).

154. Professor Bandes contends that *Bivens* at least *should* be understood as a constitutional decision. See Susan Bandes, *Reinventing Bivens: The Self-Executing Constitution*, 68 So. Calif. L. Rev. 289 (1995).

would be valid.[155] Moreover, Brennan said that there were "no special factors" in *Bivens* "counselling hesitation" to recognize private suits.[156] That suggested that he (like Harlan) meant only to balance the competing considerations in aid of a reasoned non-constitutional holding. It appears, then, that *Bivens* is a species of federal common law.[157]

Alternative enforcement mechanisms. Justice Brennan explained in *Bivens* that Congress had not only failed to disclaim private enforcement suits, but had established no other "remedy" to which plaintiffs might be "remitted."[158] That suggested that Congress might yet shoulder responsibility for prescribing enforcement machinery. More recent decisions hold that Congress can create alternative enforcement mechanisms that displace private lawsuits.[159] In *Bush v. Lucas*,[160] the Court held that a federal employee who wished to sue his superior for an alleged violation of the first amendment had to be satisfied with the administrative procedures available to him under the federal civil service system. In *Schweiker v. Chilicky*,[161] the Court held that private plaintiffs with due process claims were obliged to use the administrative procedures provided by the Social Security Act. And in *Chappell v. Wallace*[162] and *United States v. Stanley*,[163] the Court held that soldiers could not sue for alleged constitutional violations arising from their military service and must, instead, seek relief through military channels.

---

155. 403 U.S. at 397.

156. Id. at 396.

157. Professor Monaghan reads *Bivens* this way. See Henry P. Monaghan, *Foreword: Constitutional Common Law*, 89 Harv. L. Rev. 1, 24-25 (1975). Professor Meltzer argues that *Bivens* cannot be understood entirely as a constitutional decision, but may be regarded as constitutionally "inspired." Meltzer, note 55, at 1128. If, however, *Bivens* is an instance of federal common law-making apart from constitutional interpretation, it must presumably rest on the justifications that have traditionally been given for the creation of federal common law. See text accompanying note 57. Professor Dellinger understands Justice Harlan to have rested his position in *Bivens* on the proposition that federal courts can fashion common law under the implicit authority of the relevant jurisdictional statute: 28 U.S.C. § 1331. Dellinger, note 84, at 1542-43. The difficulty with that explanation is that a grant of jurisdiction to federal courts cannot (even implicitly) supply law-making authority to *state* courts handling *Bivens* cases. See text accompanying note 64; Daniel J. Meltzer, *Deterring Constitutional Violations by Law Enforcement Officers: Plaintiffs and Defendants as Private Attorneys General*, 88 Colum. L. Rev. 247, 295 (1988). Professor Grey acknowledges that *Bivens* must be considered federal common law and thus can be overridden by legislation. Yet since the efficacy of constitutional rights is implicated, she urges the Court to require a clear statement from Congress before reading legislation to displace *Bivens* actions. Betsy J. Grey, *Preemption of Bivens Claims: How Clearly Must Congress Speak?*, 70 Wash. U. L.Q. 1087 (1992).

158. 403 U.S. at 397.

159. Here again, it is clear that a legal claim (that a defendant has violated the fourth amendment) must be distinguished from a right of action (a private plaintiff's authorization to press that claim in court). When courts and commentators say that the question in a case is whether the plaintiff has a fourth amendment "cause of action," they *can* mean that the issue is whether the plaintiff has a plausible claim that the defendant has violated the fourth amendment. They can *also* mean that the question is whether Congress has displaced the right of action that the Court recognized in *Bivens*. See note 79 and accompanying text.

160. 462 U.S. 367 (1983).

161. 487 U.S. 412 (1988).

162. 462 U.S. 296 (1983).

163. 483 U.S. 669 (1987).

The quality of alternatives. In *Bivens* itself, Justice Brennan explained that Congress had created no other enforcement mechanism that would be "equally effective."[164] That suggested (but did not squarely hold) that any alternative enforcement arrangements that Congress fashions to displace private suits must offer plaintiffs everything they might derive from the private actions that the Court itself authorized in *Bivens.* On this point, too, the *Bush, Chilicky, Chappell*, and *Stanley* decisions render a clear answer. None of the alternatives approved in those cases was the equivalent of a private lawsuit for damages. The Court nonetheless allowed them all to eclipse the plaintiffs' ability to file actions in reliance on *Bivens.*[165]

D. Statutory Jurisdiction

Litigants who have federal claims and a right of action to advance those claims in *some* court must independently establish that a federal district court has jurisdiction to entertain their lawsuits.[166] Congress prescribes the district courts' jurisdiction by statute.[167] The principal jurisdictional statute for federal question cases is 28 U.S.C. § 1331, which confers power on district courts to adjudicate "all civil actions arising under the Constitution, laws, or treaties of the United States." The text of § 1331 tracks its parent provision in Article III.[168] Congress can extend jurisdiction to the Article III perimeter, and some members of the Reconstruction Congress that enacted § 1331 probably meant to do just

---

164. 403 U.S. at 397.

165. For critiques of these decisions, see Joan Steinman, *Backing Off Bivens and the Ramifications of this Retreat for the Vindication of First Amendment Rights*, 83 Mich. L. Rev. 269 (1984); Barry Kellman, *Judicial Abdication of Military Tort Accountability: But Who Is to Guard the Guards Themselves?*, 1989 Duke L.J. 1597. Professor Nichol argues that conceiving of *Bivens* as a common law idea invites Congress to dilute the protections that private suits can supply by offering the victims of unconstitutional behavior alternative enforcement devices that make, at best, poor substitutes. Gene R. Nichol, *Bivens, Chilicky, and Constitutional Damages Claims*, 75 Va. L. Rev. 1117 (1989). By most accounts, a constitutional question would arise if Congress were to deny constitutional rights some indispensable minimum measure of enforcement. See Dellinger, note 84, at 1547-49.

166. Recall that the question whether a plaintiff has a right of action to press a federal claim in a private lawsuit is separate and apart from the question whether a district court has jurisdiction to entertain such a lawsuit. See notes 142-43 and accompanying text (discussing the Court's treatment in *Bell v. Hood*). If that were not true, the decisions regarding the existence of a right of action would be decisions on federal court jurisdiction. They are not. The Court underscores this point when it *decides* that no right of action exists and, for that reason, expressly declines to address the different question whether a district court has jurisdiction, e.g., *Nat'l R.R. Passenger Corp. v. Nat'l Ass'n of R.R. Passengers*, 414 U.S. 453, 456 (1974), and equally when it *assumes* that a right of action *does* exist in order to dispose of a case on other grounds. E.g., *Northwest Airlines v. County of Kent*, 510 U.S. 355, 365 (1994). See notes 94, 96 (explaining that plaintiffs who rely on § 1983 and § 702 of the APA to supply them with a right of action independently look to § 1331 to establish a federal court's jurisdiction).

167. See Chapter IV, notes 19-20 and accompanying text.

168. See text accompanying note 4.

that.[169] But the Supreme Court has construed § 1331 actually to grant judicial power on a much smaller scale.[170]

In many of the classic cases in point, the Court formally construed jurisdictional statutes other than § 1331. Occasionally, the statute at work was 28 U.S.C. § 1338, which confers jurisdiction on district courts in patent infringement cases. Since the Court has always given § 1338 the same scope it has given § 1331, precedents established in cases involving § 1338 are equally applicable to § 1331.[171] In some of the most important cases, the plaintiff initially filed suit in state court, and it was the defendant who attempted to gain access to a federal district court by petitioning for removal pursuant 28 U.S.C. § 1441. Removal is available only if the plaintiff might have sued in federal court in the first instance. Accordingly, the practical question in § 1441 cases is whether, if the plaintiff had filed suit in federal court originally, the federal court would have had jurisdiction pursuant to § 1331.[172]

Removal cases lend an air of artificiality to the Court's analysis of § 1331. The Court finds itself asking whether plaintiffs have any genuine business in federal court, when the plaintiffs themselves have never argued that they *should* be entitled to invoke federal jurisdiction. By hypothesis, they sued in state court. Moreover, since removal cases begin in state court, it is often state law that authorizes the lawsuits the plaintiffs actually initiate. When the Court asks whether the plaintiffs might have started in a federal district court instead, the Court finds itself grappling with the proposition that *state* law might have supplied the right of action that litigants would have needed to enforce *federal* law in *federal* court. That idea may appear unexceptional; lots of removal cases presuppose it. Yet rights of action created by state law are not easily reconciled with the language the Court uses to describe § 1331 jurisdiction and modern cases that largely give Congress the responsibility to decide whether federal rights will be enforceable in private litigation.[173]

The foundational precedent on the meaning of § 1331 was a removal case: *Amer. Well Works Co. v. Layne & Bowler Co.*[174] American sued Layne in state court, alleging that Layne had injured American's manufacturing business by claiming that American was infringing Layne's patent and by threatening to sue American for infringement. Layne removed the suit to a federal district court on the theory that American might have placed it in federal court in the first in-

---

169. Ray Forrester, *The Nature of a Federal Question*, 16 Tulane L. Rev. 362 (1942); see notes 5-31 and accompanying text (discussing the outer boundaries of Article III judicial power).

170. See Chapter I, text accompanying note 23 (noting that the Court has made the elaboration of § 1331 its own preserve without any pretense of textualism).

171. Professor Cohen explains that since § 1331 and § 1338 are coextensive, the latter would be superfluous if it did not make federal jurisdiction exclusive when it is properly invoked. Amy B. Cohen, *"Arising Under" Jurisdiction and the Copyright Laws*, 44 Hastings L.J. 337, 350 & n.59 (1993). Pursuant to 28 U.S.C. § 1337, the district courts have jurisdiction of "any civil action or proceeding arising under any Act of Congress regulating commerce or protecting trade and commerce against restraints and monopolies." The Court has drawn no distinction between § 1331 and § 1337, either. *Franchise Tax Board v. Constr. Laborers Vacation Trust*, 463 U.S. 1, 8 n.7 (1983).

172. See Chapter VI, note 122 and accompanying text.

173. See text accompanying notes 214, 225-26, 259, 273.

174. 241 U.S. 257 (1916).

stance pursuant to § 1338. Justice Holmes held, however, that American's action could not have been filed originally in federal court, because it did not arise under federal law for purposes of § 1338 or, by extension, § 1331. According to Holmes, American's suit was essentially a tort action in the nature of trade libel, governed by state law. If Layne had done American any "wrong" at all, it was by doing injury to American's business, and whether Layne's behavior actually constituted such a "wrong" depended on state law.[175]

Justice Holmes might have said that a suit "arises under" the law that supplies a plaintiff's substantive claim against the defendant. Since, in *Well Works*, that law was state tort law, American could not have invoked federal jurisdiction in the first instance. In fact, Justice Holmes said that a suit "arises under the law that creates the *cause of action*."[176] That formulation has been the point of departure for interpreting § 1331 ever since. And it has created no small amount of confusion. The problem is this: The Holmes formulation can be taken to mean that a civil action arises *not* under the law that creates the plaintiff's substantive *claim*, but rather under the law that creates the plaintiff's *right of action*—the law that authorizes the plaintiff to file a lawsuit to enforce a claim. In most instances, substantive claims and procedural vehicles for enforcing those claims have a common source. Where that is true, the distinction between the two makes no practical difference. Nevertheless, it is essential to keep that distinction clear in order to understand the cases in which legal arguments and the authority to make those arguments in court derive from different sources.

There are certainly Supreme Court opinions and academic commentaries that understand the Holmes formulation to mean that a civil action arises under the law that establishes a litigant's authority to go to court. By that account, any case in which the Supreme Court has found § 1331 jurisdiction to exist in the absence of a federally created right of action must be regarded as an exception to Holmes—justified, if at all, on some less neat and tidy basis. On the whole, however, it makes more sense to understand the Holmes formulation to mean that a civil action arises under the law that creates the plaintiff's substantive claim—the law that governs the parties' primary behavior, the law the plaintiff insists the defendant has violated, the law that makes the defendant's behavior a legal "wrong," the law that a federal court will be asked to use as the rule of decision

---

175. The procedural framework in *Well Works* was convoluted, even by federal courts standards. Recall that a district court's jurisdiction under § 1338 is exclusive. See Chapter VI, note 20 and accompanying text. In *Well Works*, accordingly, Layne contended not merely that American *might* have sued in federal court, but that American had no other choice. The federal district court agreed with Layne that American's suit arose under federal patent law for purposes of § 1338 jurisdiction. Yet that court dismissed Layne's removal petition anyway, because (at the time) the removal statute, § 1441, allowed a case to reach federal court by means of removal only if the state court in which the case was originally filed had jurisdiction. According to the district court, the action might have been filed in federal court, and, indeed, could have been filed in no other court. But it could not reach the district court via removal. When Justice Holmes concluded that American's action could not have been brought in federal court at all and could only be handled in state court, he, too, decided that Layne's removal petition was without merit. Nevertheless, Holmes reversed the district court's order (dismissing Layne's petition on the basis of just the opposite conclusion regarding § 1338 jurisdiction), so that the district court could remand the case back to state court where it belonged. Congress has since amended § 1441, eliminating any requirement that the state court from which a case is removed must itself have jurisdiction.

176. Id. at 260 (emphasis added).

in a case in which it has jurisdiction. The exceptions, then, are cases in which the plaintiff's legal argument is federal in nature, but nonetheless fails to establish § 1331 jurisdiction for some other good and sufficient reason.[177]

The Court has fortified the Holmes test for § 1331 jurisdiction with two supplemental rules: (1) the rule that jurisdiction can rest on a complaint that advances a substantial federal claim, even if it is unlikely that the plaintiff can prevail on the merits; and (2) the rule that the federal nature of the claim that triggers jurisdiction must appear on the face of the complaint.

The rule that a substantial claim establishes jurisdiction. The Court held in *Bell v. Hood*[178] that a plaintiff can invoke a federal district court's jurisdiction under § 1331 by filing a complaint stating a substantial federal claim, even if the claim is most unlikely to succeed. If the plaintiff's claim is "wholly insubstantial and frivolous," it will not suffice for jurisdiction. Otherwise, jurisdiction is estab-

---

177. See notes 215-26 (discussing *Merrell Dow*). Holmes himself had no occasion to distinguish between a substantive claim and a right of action to enforce a claim. He had in mind state tort law, wherein those two ideas typically merge. See note 79. Moreover, Holmes could not anticipate modern decisions that isolate claims from the means by which they are implemented and so often foreclose private suits in favor of alternative enforcement mechanisms. See notes 79-165 and accompanying text. If Holmes had been thinking in modern terms, he would scarcely have proposed that a § 1983 action to enforce the fourteenth amendment is within a district court's § 1331 jurisdiction not because the fourteenth amendment is a federal constitutional provision, but because § 1983 is a federal statute. Of course, Congress typically authorizes private lawsuits only for the purpose of enforcing federal law. So if it *were* true that § 1983 actions arise under federal law because § 1983 is federal, the results in ordinary cases would not change. Still, the distinction between claims and rights of action cannot be ignored. Consider the implications of a federal statute purporting to authorize private suits to enforce some species of *state* law. If it is circular to argue that a federal jurisdictional statute can itself supply the federal law under which a case arises for Article III purposes (and it is), then it is also circular to argue that a federal right-of-action statute can supply the federal law under which a civil action arises for purposes of § 1331. See note 23. A federal right-of-action statute authorizing private suits to enforce state law would reproduce in this context the same constitutional questions that attend protective jurisdiction. See note 20 and accompanying text. Consider, finally, another removal case. In *City of Chicago v. Internat'l College of Surgeons*, 118 S.Ct. 523 (1997), Justice O'Connor explained that a complaint advancing fourteenth amendment claims arises under federal law for § 1331 purposes, even though the procedural vehicle in which those claims are presented is a creature of state law. Id. at 529. In that case, ICS originally pressed constitutional claims in an administrative review suit, authorized by state law and filed in state court. Nevertheless, the Court held that the defendants (state authorities) could remove the suit to federal court pursuant to § 1441—because ICS might have invoked federal jurisdiction under § 1331, if ICS had chosen to litigate in federal court in the first instance. The suit arose under federal law, because ICS's substantive fourteenth amendment claims were federal. There is language in Justice O'Connor's opinion suggesting that *Surgeons* was an *exception* to Holmes' general rule that the "cause of action" must be federal. Id. (conceding that the "cause of action" in *Surgeons* was created by state law but insisting that federal jurisdiction "might still" be established). The better (and far simpler) view is that, within the Holmes formulation, a "cause of action" means a substantive claim, not a procedural vehicle. See Chapter VI, notes 120-23 and accompanying text (discussing the connection between § 1441 and § 1331). Professor Oakley has identified even more ways in which commonly employed nomenclature creates confusion—and proposes to clarify matters by specifying more rigorously what a "cause of action" entails. See John B. Oakley, *Federal Jurisdiction and the Problem of the Litigative Unit: When Does What "Arise Under" Federal Law?*, 76 Tex. L. Rev. 1829, 1858 (1998).

178. 327 U.S. 678 (1946); see notes 142-43 and accompanying text.

lished at the threshold and, once settled, empowers the court to decide other issues—including whether the plaintiff genuinely has a winning argument. Recall
that the plaintiff in *Bell* contended that FBI agents had violated his fourth
amendment rights and that he was entitled to damages. Justice Black found that
complaint sufficient to establish jurisdiction, notwithstanding serious doubt (at
the time) that the plaintiff actually had the affirmative constitutional claim he asserted and a right of action to enforce that claim in a suit for damages.[179] Black
recognized that the plaintiff might have framed his complaint as an ordinary action in trespass, relying on the agents' violation of the Constitution to show that
their behavior was tortious as a matter of state law. In that event, the complaint
might not have established jurisdiction under § 1331.[180] Black explained, however, that the plaintiff was master of his pleading and could decide, if he wished,
to advance a forthright claim under the Constitution.[181] As long as that claim
was not wholly frivolous, it could survive a motion to dismiss for want of jurisdiction.[182]

---

179. Recall that until the *Bivens* decision, there was a body of professional opinion to
the effect that the fourth amendment established no constitutional right of privacy, but only
served to defeat defenses to state tort actions. See text accompanying notes 144-45.

180. Defendants move under Rule 12(b)(1) to dismiss complaints for want of jurisdiction and under Rule 12(b)(6) to dismiss for want of a claim for which relief can be granted.
This is ostensibly consistent with *Bell*—which channels arguments that claims cannot support jurisdiction because they are frivolous to disposition under Rule 12(b)(1), and routes
arguments that plaintiffs have no right of action to disposition under Rule 12(b)(6). Nevertheless, things may not always fall into place so neatly. In the *Bell* situation itself, the Court
later held (in *Bivens*) that private plaintiffs *do* have a right of action to enforce the fourth
amendment in suits for damages. See notes 144-45 and accompanying text. In other contexts, the Court may ultimately decide that a right of action does *not* exist. If, in circumstances of that kind, a plaintiff should file a subsequent complaint insisting upon the very
right of action the Court has just held not to exist, a district court might entertain a motion
to dismiss under Rule 12(b)(1). With an authoritative determination against the plaintiff on
the right-of-action question in place, a complaint that depends on such a right of action may
be regarded as frivolous and thus subject to dismissal for want of jurisdiction. See note
222(discussing this possibility in connection with the *Merrell Dow* case).

181. 327 U.S. at 681, citing *The Fair v. Kohler Die & Specialty Co.*, 228 U.S. 22, 25
(1913). Dissenting in *Bell*, Chief Justice Stone expressed concern that the jurisdictional
power of the federal courts should be contingent on the way plaintiffs draw their complaints. 327 U.S. at 685-86; see notes 274-87 and accompanying text (discussing federal preemption of state law); Chapter VI, note 122 (also discussing preemption).

182. Chief Justice Rehnquist has argued that *Bell* does not map onto Rule 12 at all well
and thus should be reexamined. *Yazoo County Indus. Develop. Corp. v. Suthoff*, 454 U.S.
1157 (1982) (dissenting from the denial of *certiorari*). By his account, *Bell* contemplates
triage in three tiers: first, a district court may dismiss frivolous complaints for want of jurisdiction; second, the court may dismiss non-frivolous complaints if they present no claim for
which relief can be granted; and, third, the court must handle complaints that cannot be dismissed more thoroughly—by summary judgment or trial. According to the Chief Justice,
Rule 12(b) contemplates only two tiers, both captured in Rule 12(b)(6): A district court simply screens all complaints for claims on which relief can be granted, dismissing those that do
not measure up and giving more thorough treatment to those that do. The Chief Justice lays
Rule 12(b)(1) aside. By his account, it is only because *Bell* made the substantiality of claims
a jurisdictional matter that anyone has thought that Rule 12(b)(1) handles that kind of issue.
But for *Bell*, Rule 12(b)(1) would not figure in § 1331 cases, but would cover dismissals for
lack of diversity or a sufficient amount in controversy. Apparently, Chief Justice Rehnquist
would abandon the basic holding in *Bell* (that non-frivolous claims establish jurisdiction in
the first instance) and would allow district courts to dismiss (on the merits) any claims they
regard as insubstantial.

The well-pleaded complaint rule. The substantial federal claim that triggers jurisdiction must appear on the face of a "well-pleaded" or "properly pleaded" complaint. The leading case in point is *Louisville & Nashville R.R. Co. v. Mottley*.[183] The Mottleys, husband and wife, had been involved in a rail accident. By way of settlement, the railroad gave them a contract under which they were entitled to travel by train free of charge. Congress later enacted a statute forbidding railroads to issue free passes. The railroad reneged on its contract with the Mottleys, citing the statute as justification. The Mottleys sued the railroad in federal court, seeking specific performance of the contract. They claimed that the new statute did not release the railroad from its duty to perform under the contract and that, if it did, it violated the fifth amendment. Justice Moody said that the Mottleys' claim against the railroad did not arise under federal law for purposes of § 1331. Their affirmative claim was for breach of contract, based entirely on state law. They could plead the facts and the law regarding that claim without mentioning the federal issues they expected the railroad to raise by way of defense.[184] To the extent the Mottleys anticipated those federal issues in their complaint, they introduced matters that were not "well-pleaded" or "properly pleaded" in support of their affirmative claim.[185]

The well-pleaded complaint rule is usually an efficient device for identifying cases that satisfy the Holmes test for § 1331 jurisdiction. Nevertheless, fair arguments abound regarding the classic cases. On first blush, the well-pleaded complaint rule appears to explain the result in *Well Works* itself. State tort law established both American's right to operate its enterprise free of interference from Layne and, as well, Layne's duty to forbear unfounded accusations and threats that injured American's business. Accordingly, American's claim could be articulated without reference to any federal matter. Anything American said in its complaint about the validity of Layne's patent anticipated a federal issue that would only emerge later, if at all, in Layne's answer to American's state law claim. It is quite possible to argue, however, that American's state trade libel claim necessarily entailed an allegation that Layne's statements were untrue. If so, American was required to allege that Layne's claim of patent infringement was false, which, of course, would have implicated a federal question.[186]

In *Shoshone Mining Co. v. Rutter*,[187] the Court held that an "adverse suit" filed by a miner in a federal district court in Idaho did not arise under federal law for purposes of § 1331 jurisdiction. In the late Nineteenth Century, Congress enacted a statute under which federal land offices issued patents allowing miners to extract minerals from federal lands. Under that statute, a miner who wished to take minerals from a site filed an application for a patent with the closest land office. The land office published a notice of the application and its intention to

---

183. 211 U.S. 149 (1908).

184. See note 237 (elaborating this point).

185. The well-pleaded complaint rule underscores that the law that must be federal in a § 1331 case is the law on which the plaintiff relies for a substantive claim, not the law that gives the plaintiff permission to use a lawsuit to press the claim. The purpose of a complaint is to allege the elements of a claim sufficiently to give the defendant notice, not to explain that Congress has authorized the suit. See note 177 and accompanying text.

186. See William Cohen, *The Broken Compass: The Requirement That a Case Arise "Directly" Under Federal Law*, 115 U. Pa. L. Rev. 890, 897 (1967).

187. 177 U.S. 505 (1900).

grant the miner a patent within a fixed period of time, if no competitor came forward. Another miner could challenge the applicant's entitlement to a patent by filing an "adverse claim" regarding the same site. Any miner who did so was obliged by the statute to commence an "adverse suit" in a "court of competent jurisdiction" to determine which of the two miners had the superior "right of possession." Under the federal statute, the court could make that determination on the basis of "local customs and rules of miners" or "the statute of limitations for mining claims of the state or territory" where the land was situated.[188]

Justice Brewer recognized that federal issues might be implicated in some adverse suits. But upon the whole, he thought federal law would have no role. The federal statute did not incorporate local customs or state statutes into federal substantive law. Instead, the statute contemplated that courts entertaining adverse suits would simply use local customs and state statutes to resolve the question of rightful possession on the basis of the facts. Typically, the only real issue would be which of the two miners had first marked the site in the customary manner. Certainly, it would be the rare case in which a court would be asked to decide any issue touching the federal statute that established the underlying scheme. Justice Brewer acknowledged that the federal statute "authorized" adverse suits, but he said that was not "in and of itself sufficient to vest jurisdiction" in a federal court. The law that had to be federal was not the law that allowed the adverse claimant to file suit, but the law that the court would apply *in* that suit: "A statute authorizing an action to establish a right is very different from one which creates a right to be established."[189]

It is debatable whether *Shoshone Mining* can be reconciled with the Holmes formulation and the well-pleaded complaint rule. On the one hand, that case does seem to fit. An adverse claimant's claim of possession depended (at least typically) on historical facts and local law. The well-pleaded complaint would (typically) have no occasion to recite any federal issue.[190] On the other hand, the federal statute not only authorized an adverse claimant to sue, but forced such a suit if the challenger had any hope of keeping the original applicant from securing a patent. It was that statute, moreover, that made local customs and state statutes applicable to adverse suits. The federal statute may not have incorporated local customs and state statutes into the fabric of federal law. But it did lend those customs and state statutes their authoritative force in the resolution of the rightful possession question, which, in turn, determined which of the two competing miners ultimately received a federal patent to take minerals from federal land. Arguably, then, an adverse claimant's claim did rely on federal law, and a well-pleaded complaint could say so.[191]

---

188. See *Blackburn v. Portland Gold Mining Co.*, 175 U.S. 571, 576-78 (1900) (quoting the federal statute in full).

189. *Shoshone Mining*, 177 U.S. at 510-13.

190. Professor Shapiro adds that it made sense in *Shoshone Mining* to bar federal jurisdiction in most adverse suits in order to ensure that miners could obtain the decisions they needed from nearby state courts and were not forced to travel significant distances through the wilderness to appear before a federal court. David L. Shapiro, *Jurisdiction and Discretion*, 60 N.Y.U. L. Rev. 543, 569-70 (1985).

191. Professor Doernberg finds *Shoshone Mining* inconsistent with *Well Works*. Donald L. Doernberg, *There's No Reason For It: It's Just Our Policy: Why the Well-Pleaded Com-*

In *Moore v. Chesapeake & Ohio Ry.*,[192] the Court held that a worker's suit against a railroad did not arise under federal law for purposes of § 1331. The plaintiff in that case alleged that he had been injured on the job and was due compensation under the state workers compensation law.[193] He contended that he could neither be found guilty of contributory negligence nor held to have assumed the risk, because the accident was the result of the railroad's violation of federal law. According to the plaintiff, the railroad had failed to maintain the equipment on which he was working at the time of the accident according to standards established by the Federal Safety Appliance Act. Under state law, the railroad could not set up contributory negligence or assumption of risk to avoid liability in any case in which the railroad had violated federal laws enacted to protect employee safety. Chief Justice Hughes said that the plaintiff's claim was based entirely on state workers compensation law.[194]

It is also debatable whether *Moore* corresponds to the Holmes formulation and the well-pleaded complaint rule. On the one hand, *Moore* does appear to fit, more neatly perhaps than *Shoshone Mining*. The plaintiff did not claim that he was entitled to recover solely because the railroad had violated federal law. He rested his affirmative claim on the state workers compensation statute. He could articulate that claim without mentioning federal law. The only federal question that could arise in the case would come in later — if the railroad attempted to avoid liability by asserting contributory negligence or assumption of risk. Even then, nothing federal would be implicated until the plaintiff responded that those defenses were unavailable, because the railroad had violated federal law. And even *then*, federal law would be involved only because state

---

plaint Rule Sabotages the Purposes of Federal Question Jurisdiction, 38 Hastings L.J. 597, 627 n. 139 (1987). But in taking that position Doernberg appears to assume that the Holmes formulation, articulated in *Well Works*, contemplates that a civil action arises under the law that creates the plaintiff's authority to sue. See note 177 and accompanying text. It is hard to fault *Shoshone Mining* for rejecting the argument that adverse suits arose under federal law merely because a federal statute authorized miners to take their claims to court, irrespective of the nature of their arguments for rightful possession. See Oakley, note 177, at 1841-42 n.63. In *Puerto Rico v. Russell*, 288 U.S. 476 (1933), Puerto Rico sued an association of companies in the Insular Court in San Juan, seeking to collect taxes levied on the companies' land. The companies attempted to remove the action to the United States District Court for Puerto Rico on the theory that the suit arose under federal law. The validity of the tax in question had been contested for years, and Congress had ultimately enacted a statute authorizing Puerto Rico to collect the monies that were due by means of a lawsuit (rather than by simply seizing property). Justice Stone explained that "even though [Puerto Rico] derived its authority to maintain the suit" from an "Act of Congress," the suit "did not arise under the laws of the United States within the meaning of the jurisdictional statutes." Puerto Rico's suit was to recover taxes levied by the Puerto Rican legislature, not to "enforce a right created by a law of the United States." The complaint raised no issue with respect to the federal authorizing statute: "Federal jurisdiction may be invoked to vindicate a right or privilege claimed under a federal statute. It may *not* be invoked where the right asserted is non-federal, merely because the plaintiff's right to sue is derived from federal law.... *The federal nature of the right to be established is decisive — not the source of the authority to establish it.*" Id. at 483 (emphasis added).

192. 291 U.S. 205 (1934).

193. The plaintiff also claimed the railroad was liable under the Federal Employers Liability Act, but the Court's treatment of that claim did not raise jurisdictional questions.

194. The only consequence of the holding in *Moore* was that the plaintiff's claim under state law could remain in federal court only as a diversity matter under 28 U.S.C. § 1332. That meant that venue was proper in Indiana rather than Kentucky.

law incorporated its standards for the limited purpose of restricting the rail-road's defenses. On the other hand, it was quite clear in *Moore* that the federal questions the plaintiff anticipated were likely to emerge and, when they did, the court adjudicating the case would have to consult the federal Act in order to resolve them.[195]

In *Smith v. Kansas City Title & Trust Co.*,[196] the Court held that a suit by a stockholder to enjoin company managers from purchasing federal bonds *was* a civil action arising under federal law for § 1331 purposes. The corporation's charter barred unlawful investments. The plaintiff claimed that the bonds in question were unlawful, because they were issued by federal land banks pursuant to statutes that Congress had no constitutional power to enact. Justice Day said that the only legal claim in the plaintiff's complaint was his constitutional attack on the federal statutes creating the land banks. State law thus incorporated federal law. Since the plaintiff's "right to relief" turned on a construction of federal statutes and the Constitution, the suit arose under federal law.[197]

Justice Holmes dissented in *Smith*. He insisted that the shareholder's only claim was that management was about to violate the corporation's charter. According to Holmes, any duties the charter imposed on management were matters of state law. Holmes acknowledged that state law incorporated federal law inasmuch as state law barred management from purchasing securities issued under an unconstitutional federal statute. But even then, according to Holmes, the plaintiff's claim still rested formally on state law: Federal law had "relevance and effect" only because state law "took it up." By Holmes' account, "[t]he mere adoption" of federal law by state law, where federal law had "no force *proprio vigore*," could not make the shareholder's lawsuit arise under federal law.[198]

The decision in *Smith* may be the most unruly of the classic precedents. On the one hand, *Smith* seems consistent with the well-pleaded complaint rule. To plead the claim that management was about to violate the corporate charter, the shareholder had to allege that management was poised to make an unlawful investment. And to plead that purchasing the federal bonds was unlawful, the shareholder had to describe the constitutional flaw he saw in them.[199] On the other hand, Holmes himself thought that *Smith* could not be squared with his previous opinion for the Court in *Well Works*. Holmes did not mention the well-pleaded complaint rule. Instead, he insisted that, under *Well Works*, all that mattered was the source of the plaintiff's claim. And in *Smith* the shareholder's claim was formally based on state law. As Holmes explained, the shareholder would have had no occasion to contend that the bonds violated federal law if state law had not conditioned management's authority to buy them on their validity.

---

195. See text accompanying note 209 (discussing the Court's explanation of *Moore* in the *Merrell Dow* case); Chapter VI, notes 3-36 and accompanying text (discussing state court jurisdiction to determine federal issues).

196. 255 U.S. 180 (1921).

197. See text accompanying note 209 (discussing the Court's explanation of *Smith* in *Merrell Dow*).

198. 255 U.S. at 214-15.

199. Professor Doernberg explains that the shareholder's complaint would have been dismissed for "insufficiency" if it had not pleaded the "illegality of the bonds." Doernberg, note 191, at 629 n.147.

The *Smith* case is sometimes depicted as an exception to the Holmes formulation, because the Court approved § 1331 jurisdiction even though state law created the shareholder's "cause of action"—namely, the shareholder's authority to sue. To be sure, *Smith* is the only precedent that comes to mind in which a plaintiff who looked to state law for a right of action was able to invoke § 1331 jurisdiction originally, instead of beginning in state court and reaching federal court by removal. But it is confusing to suggest that *Smith* conflicts with the Holmes formulation because state law provided the shareholder with a right of action. It makes far more sense to understand the Holmes formulation to mean that federal jurisdiction turns on the source of the substantive claim that a plaintiff asks a federal court to consider. Holmes himself objected to the decision in *Smith* on the ground that the shareholder's substantive claim was that management was about to violate *state* law.[200]

The Holmes formulation and the well-pleaded complaint rule screen cases fairly well. The Holmes test demands that the substantive question to be decided in a case must be federal.[201] The well-pleaded complaint rule ensures that district

---

200. *Smith*, 255 U.S. at 214 (dissenting opinion). See note 177 and accompanying text; notes 225-26 and accompanying text (discussing the *Merrell Dow* case). Professor Shapiro finds *Smith* hard to square with other classic precedents, but *not* because the plaintiff's right of action was created by state law. For example, Shapiro finds *Smith* inconsistent with *Shoshone Mining*: "In *Smith*, the presence of a federal ingredient made relevant by state law was sufficient to confer jurisdiction, but in *Shoshone*, a federally created claim that turned on issues of state law was not." Shapiro, note 190, at 570.

201. Thus a "civil action" arising under federal law for purposes of § 1331 cannot depend on the *possibility* that a federal issue *might* emerge. See notes 12-31 and accompanying text (discussing the broader scope accorded to Article III). In *Gully v. First Nat'l Bank*, 299 U.S. 109 (1936), state authorities sued a nationally chartered bank in state court to collect taxes. The bank attempted to remove the suit to federal court on the theory that the state had power to impose the taxes only because a federal statute allowed national banks to be taxed at the state level and the complaint might have been drawn to advance a federal claim for purposes of § 1331 jurisdiction. Justice Cardozo responded that the state tax officials' claim was wholly one of state law. It was true that the state relied on federal law for its authority to impose the tax in the first instance. But that matter of federal law was not actually implicated in the suit and thus could not establish § 1331 jurisdiction. Id. at 116. Cases involving real estate actions make the same point. Recall that Justice Johnson worried in *Osborn* that Marshall's "ingredient" test would make every lawsuit involving western lands a case arising under federal law for Article III purposes—because one of the parties might conceivably contest the original patent issued by the federal government. See note 16. The Court has always been sensitive to that argument in its interpretation of § 1331. On the whole, the Court has held that plaintiffs who trace their title to a grant by the federal government cannot, for that reason alone, invoke § 1331 jurisdiction when they sue others for possession or title. The old real property cases typically took the form of ejectment actions, in which plaintiffs were not required to plead the original source of their claims. See Chapter VII, note 44 (explaining the elements of ejectment in connection with the *Fairfax* litigation). That may explain *Shoshone Mining*, at least in part. Moreover, once land is conveyed into private hands, federal law has done its work. Thereafter, the rights and duties attending the land are governed by state law. The Court took a different view in the special circumstances presented in *Oneida Indian Nation v. County of Oneida*, 414 U.S. 661 (1974). In that case, Indian tribes successfully invoked federal jurisdiction on the ground that their claims to the land in question did not rest merely on an original transfer from the federal government, but on the government's continuing protection of the tribes' interests in possession. In *Louisville & Nashville R.R. Co. v. Rice*, 247 U.S. 201 (1918), the Court held that common carriers can invoke federal jurisdiction under § 1337 to resolve disputes over ordinary freight charges, because the Interstate Commerce Act obligates them to collect the fees authorized by that Act. The *Rice* decision is hard to square with *Gully* and the real property cases. See

courts can determine whether such a federal question exists simply be reading the complaint, without pausing to hear arguments about issues that might emerge at a later stage. The well-pleaded complaint rule's rigidity has been questioned. Justice Cardozo once warned (in dictum) that it can be hazardous to "define broadly and in the abstract" what constitutes an action arising under federal law: "What is needed is something of that common-sense accommodation of judgment to kaleidoscopic situations which characterizes the law in its treatment of problems of causation."[202] Yet a categorical rule is generally thought to be justified on pragmatic grounds. The threshold question of jurisdiction should be easy to settle *without* the exercise of judgment — so that suits in which federal courts have no power to act can be dispatched in favor of matters that the courts have authority to address.[203]

The well-pleaded complaint rule is plainly underinclusive inasmuch as it bars jurisdiction in cases in which federal issues will predominate.[204] But it does not

---

note 171 (noting that the Court generally reads § 1331 and § 1337 in the same way). Yet the Court has recently reaffirmed its old decision, albeit in a case in which the circuit court below had presumed to say that *Rice* was no longer sound. *Thurston Motor Lines v. Jordan K. Rand*, 460 U.S. 533 (1983).

202. *Gully*, 299 U.S. at 117. Professor Cohen argues that it would be better for district courts to make *ad hoc* discretionary judgments about whether cases warrant federal adjudication. Cohen, note 186. Professor Shapiro thinks discretion of that kind at the threshold of litigation in the district courts would be unmanageable. Shapiro argues, however, that the Supreme Court may sensibly create exceptions to the Holmes formulation and the well-pleaded complaint rule when those formulae either include a body of cases that need not be in federal court or exclude a body of cases that should be. Shapiro, note 190, at 588-89. If the Court's classic precedents in point cannot easily be reconciled, Shapiro thinks it is because the Court has exercised discretionary judgment at that level.

203. The American Law Institute endorses the well-pleaded complaint rule chiefly for this pragmatic reason. ALI, Study of the Division of Jurisdiction Between State and Federal Courts 170 (1969). Professor Chadbourn and Professor Levin once proposed that the rule should be relaxed enough to allow jurisdiction if the plaintiff anticipates a federal defense and the defendant readily concedes that the defense will be raised. James H. Chadbourn & A. Leo Levin, *Original Jurisdiction of Federal Questions*, 90 U. Pa. L. Rev. 639, 674 (1942). Professor Trautman also contended that a "general allegation" of a federal issue should be sufficient to establish jurisdiction until pre-trial procedure progresses to the point at which the actual existence of such a question can be ascertained. Herman L. Trautman, *Federal Right Jurisdiction and the Declaratory Remedy*, 7 Vand. L. Rev. 445, 460 (1954). Professor Mishkin concedes that jurisdiction must turn on the content of the complaint, for the necessary and sufficient reason that the district court has only the complaint to go on. Mishkin argues, however, that jurisdiction need not depend on what is "properly" pleaded to state the plaintiff's claim. Complaints in diversity actions independently allege diverse citizenship for jurisdictional purposes alone. Similar special jurisdictional pleading might be allowed in federal question cases. Mishkin, note 18, at 164. Professor Mishkin contends, moreover, that the well-pleaded complaint rule is not so neat and tidy as it may seem inasmuch as it depends on an unstated and contestable understanding of what counts as "proper" pleading. Id. at 176. None of the Court's cases identifies the body of pleading rules to which district courts are to refer, and in some instances the need to plead something of a federal nature can be debated. Recall in this connection that notice pleading is ordinarily sufficient in federal lawsuits. To the extent the well-pleaded complaint rule contemplates that plaintiffs will spell out the elements of their claims, it is in some tension with Rule 8. See Chapter IX, notes 144-46 and accompanying text (discussing the pleading standards that must be met to establish "standing").

204. The only issues dividing the parties in *Mottley* were federal in nature: whether the new statute abrogated the contract and, if it did, whether it was constitutional. See notes 183-85 and accompanying text. After the Supreme Court held that the Mottleys could not

ordinarily foreclose jurisdiction in the kinds of cases that are most important for federal courts to handle: cases in which plaintiffs advance forthright claims under the Constitution or federal statutes. In ordinary § 1983 actions, for example, plaintiffs can easily invoke a district court's jurisdiction under § 1331 by properly pleading the elements of federal fourteenth amendment claims.[205] On the whole, then, the well-pleaded complaint rule evokes no serious ideological objections.

This said, it must also be said that the Supreme Court is not entirely comfortable with hard, inflexible rules controlling § 1331 jurisdiction. In *Merrell Dow Pharmaceuticals v. Thompson*,[206] all the justices conceded that the precedents are not always easily explained and justified by reference to the Holmes formulation and the well-pleaded complaint rule. Writing for a five-member majority, Justice Stevens quoted Justice Cardozo's famous dictum, suggesting (perhaps) that greater flexibility is called for.[207] Stevens said that the cases can be reconciled by reference to the "nature" of the "federal interest" at stake in each instance.[208] The federal interests were modest in *Shoshone Mining* and *Moore*, where finding § 1331 jurisdiction would have drawn numerous mining and workers compensation claims into the federal district courts, there to be adjudicated primarily on the basis of state law. The federal interest in *Smith* was compelling by comparison. By approving § 1331 jurisdiction in that case, the Court allowed a federal district court to entertain a constitutional attack on the validity of a federal statute. Otherwise, the state courts in Missouri would have shouldered that responsibility.[209]

Dissenting in *Merrell Dow* for himself and three other justices, Justice Brennan disputed both Justice Stevens' account of the Court's precedents and the implications of that account for the well-pleaded complaint rule. Justice Brennan reserved his most biting criticism for Justice Stevens' suggestion that district

---

sue originally in federal court, they filed suit in state court. The railroad could not remove the action to federal court pursuant to § 1441, because (as the Supreme Court had just explained) the Mottleys could not have begun there originally. The federal issues promptly surfaced in the litigation in state court and proved to be decisive. The Supreme Court thus had appellate jurisdiction to examine the state courts' disposition of those questions. See Chapter VII, notes 40-79 and accompanying text (discussing the Supreme Court's appellate jurisdiction to review state court decisions on federal issues). Equally in *Moore*, Chief Justice Hughes conceded that if the case went to state court and the state court decision ultimately turned on federal issues, the Supreme Court would have appellate jurisdiction. *Moore*, 291 U.S. at 214; see notes 192-95; Chapter VII, notes 114-18 and accompanying text (discussing the Supreme Court's appellate jurisdiction in cases in which state law incorporates federal law).

205. See note 94 and accompanying text.

206. 478 U.S. 804 (1986).

207. See text accompanying note 202.

208. 478 U.S. at 814 n.12.

209. See Chapter VI, notes 3-36 and accompanying text (discussing concurrent jurisdiction of federal question cases in state court). The shareholder in *Smith* almost certainly lacked "standing" to sue federal authorities directly to challenge the validity of the land banks and their bonds. Paradoxically, the Supreme Court found § 1331 jurisdiction lacking in *Shoshone Mining* and *Moore* (which were traditional bi-polar disputes in which individuals pressed personal claims), but sustained § 1331 jurisdiction in *Smith* (which was plainly a creative device for testing the constitutionality of a statute that affected the entire country). See Chapter IX, notes 111-29 and accompanying text (discussing the insufficiency of generalized grievances to establish "standing").

courts must make case-by-case judgments on the relative importance of federal issues in order to ascertain whether they have § 1331 jurisdiction. That, according to Brennan, would abandon the relative certainty and efficiency of the well-pleaded complaint rule in favor of an "infinitely malleable" (and thus unmanageable) test for jurisdiction.[210] It is hard to think that Justice Stevens genuinely meant to say that district courts must evaluate the nature of federal questions in *every* case. It is more likely that, if the federal importance of issues is relevant at all, it is relevant only in cases like *Merrell Dow* itself—in which plaintiffs would have had to rely on *state* law to supply a right of action to enforce federal statutory standards.

E. Rights of Action Revisited

Justice Stevens explained at the outset of his majority opinion in *Merrell Dow* that he meant to reconcile two lines of Supreme Court precedent: the old line of decisions on § 1331 jurisdiction generally and the new line of decisions requiring Congress to specify that federal statutes can be enforced in private lawsuits.[211] The Court had not previously grappled with the intersection between those two lines of precedent. The *Merrell Dow* case presented both a need and an opportunity to do so.

The Thompsons were parents whose child had been born with deformities, allegedly because the mother had taken the drug Bendectin during pregnancy. They sued the manufacturer, Merrell Dow, in state court, advancing negligence and products liability claims in six separate counts. In their fourth count, the Thompsons alleged that the company had failed to put a proper warning label on the bottle and thus had "misbranded" the drug in violation of the federal Food, Drug, and Cosmetic Act. That count advanced the claim that, under state law, the company's violation of the FDCA constituted a rebuttable presumption of negligence. Merrell Dow removed the lawsuit to federal court under § 1441 on the theory that the claim in the fourth count arose under federal law. The district court held that it had jurisdiction, citing the *Smith* case as the controlling authority.[212] The court of appeals reversed on the jurisdictional question. In the Supreme Court, Justice Stevens affirmed the circuit's judgment that the case did not arise under federal law for § 1331 purposes, but on the strength of a different analysis.[213]

---

210. 478 U.S. at 821 n.1. Professor Doernberg thinks Brennan's argument is unanswerable. Doernberg, note 191, at 657-58.

211. See notes 110-22 and accompanying text. Recall that the question whether a plaintiff has a private right of action to go to court to argue that the defendant has violated a federal statute is different from the question whether a district court has jurisdiction to entertain such a suit. See note 166.

212. See notes 196-97 and accompanying text (discussing *Smith*). Having accepted jurisdiction, the district court granted Merrell Dow's motion to dismiss the case on *forum non conveniens* grounds.

213. The court of appeals held that to the extent the fourth count advanced a federal claim, it was not "necessary" to the Thompsons' lawsuit, because the jury could find the company negligent without also finding a violation of the FDCA. Justice Stevens rejected that analysis. 478 U.S. at 817 n.15. As long as there is one substantial federal question in a

The removal posture of the case was crucial. The Thompsons had never argued that the FDCA itself or any other federal statute gave them a right of action to enforce the FDCA in private litigation. Nor had they invoked § 1331 as the jurisdictional basis for an action in federal court. They had advanced state tort claims against the company in state court and had alleged a violation of the FDCA in their fourth count only in service of a state law claim of negligence. Nevertheless, given the way removal jurisdiction operates, Justice Stevens addressed the artificial question whether the Thompsons might have sued to enforce the FDCA in federal court in the first instance.[214]

Plaintiffs who sue in federal court must have a right of action to enforce a federal statute — wholly apart from whether the federal court in which they file suit has jurisdiction under § 1331. In *Merrell Dow*, Justice Stevens assumed for purposes of decision that Congress had enacted no statute creating a *federal* right of action to enforce the FDCA.[215] The question, then, was whether the Thompsons might have established federal jurisdiction under § 1331, relying on the FDCA to supply only a substantive federal claim and on *state* law to supply the required right of action to vindicate that claim in a private lawsuit. Justice Stevens answered that question in the negative: "[T]he congressional determination that there should be no federal remedy for the violation of this federal statute is tantamount to a congressional conclusion that the presence of a claimed violation of the statute as an element of a state cause of action is insufficiently 'substantial' to confer federal-question jurisdiction."[216]

This passage is frightfully, not to say willfully, ambiguous.[217] But on examination, it yields a measure of clarity. Certainly, Justice Stevens did not simply say that a civil action arises under the law that establishes a litigant's authority to sue and that, for want of a federal statute authorizing private suits to enforce the FDCA, the Thompsons would not have been able to invoke § 1331 jurisdiction. Instead, he acknowledged (at least implicitly) that the source of a right of action is not always determinative. It is *possible* that he meant to say that the Holmes formulation ordinarily makes federal jurisdiction contingent on the existence of a federal right of action, but that there are exceptions to that — *Smith* and at least some removal cases being illustrations.[218] Yet it

---

case, a district court has jurisdiction under § 1331, even though most of the other issues are matters of state law. See notes 288-301 and accompanying text (discussing supplemental jurisdiction).

214. See text accompanying notes 172-73.

215. The circuit court had so held, and both parties agreed on this point.

216. 478 U.S. at 814.

217. Justice Stevens used the label "federal remedy" to mean a federally created private right of action — i.e., congressional authority to sue to enforce the FDCA's labeling standards. He (apparently) used the label "state cause of action" to mean *both* a state tort claim (i.e., the plaintiffs' right under state law to demand that the company take reasonable care in the preparation and distribution of its products) *and* state law authority to take such a state tort claim to court. See notes 79-80 (discussing the confusion this terminology can generate).

218. See text accompanying note 200. The editors of the Hart and Wechsler casebook once suggested that, immediately prior to *Merrell Dow*, the prerequisites for § 1331 jurisdiction could be captured in three propositions: (A) "A case 'arises under' federal law for purposes of the general federal question statute if it is brought to enforce a right of action created by federal law"; (B) "A case also 'arises under' federal law for the same purposes if it is brought to enforce a right of action created by state law, if under orderly rules of pleading and proof the plaintiff, as part of his case in chief, must establish the correctness and applic-

would make more sense to understand him to mean that the Holmes formulation makes federal jurisdiction turn on the existence of a federal substantive claim and that there are exceptions to *that*: In cases in which litigants rely on a right of action created by state law, they cannot invoke § 1331 jurisdiction to litigate any non-frivolous federal claim, but only a claim that is "substantial" in the sense that important federal interests will be served if it is adjudicated in federal court.

In *Merrell Dow*, state tort law incorporated the labeling standards established by the FDCA. Accordingly, insofar as the state courts were concerned, the Thompsons had a state tort claim against Merrell Dow, because they alleged that the company had violated the FDCA. In addition, insofar as the state courts were concerned, the Thompsons were entitled to advance that claim in a lawsuit—in the same way that any other state tort claim could be vindicated in private litigation.[219] Justice Stevens had no difficulty with that. He did not propose that Congress had forbidden private suits to enforce the FDCA in *state* court.[220] Yet Stevens would not agree that, if the Thompsons had originally filed suit in federal court, they would have been able to invoke the district court's § 1331 jurisdiction on the theory that their substantive claim (negligence established by a violation of federal law) was federal in nature.

According to Justice Stevens, the Thompsons' claim that Merrell Dow acted negligently by violating the FDCA was not "substantial" and thus could not establish federal jurisdiction. Stevens did not refer to *Bell v. Hood*,[221] and that omission was telling. It is hard to think that the Thompsons' allegation that Merrell Dow had misbranded Bendectin was frivolous merely because they advanced that allegation in aid of a state negligence claim.[222] Instead, Justice Stevens asserted that jurisdiction under § 1331 depends on the "nature" of the "federal in-

---

ability of federal law in order to prevail"; and (C) "No case other than those described in Propositions A and B 'arises under' federal law within the meaning of the general federal question statute." The Federal Courts and the Federal System 995 (Bator, Meltzer, Mishkin & Shapiro eds. 1988). The editors apparently meant Proposition A to describe most cases and Proposition B to describe *Smith*. See notes 176-77 and accompanying text (discussing the possibility that a civil action "arises under" the law that creates the plaintiff's procedural vehicle for bringing suit). After *Merrell Dow*, the editors suggested that a fourth proposition might be necessary to complete the picture: (D) "The rules stated in propositions A and B shall not apply to [categories of] cases where the court concludes that considerations of judicial administration and the degree of federal concern justify a refusal to exercise federal jurisdiction." Id. at 1021 (asking rhetorically whether the words in brackets should be included).

219. See note 79 (explaining that any substantive claims that state law recognizes in the abstract are typically enforceable in private lawsuits).

220. Justice Stevens acknowledged that Ohio could authorize private litigants to enforce the FDCA in suits of the kind that the Thompsons filed in state court. Moreover, he recognized that the Supreme Court would have appellate jurisdiction to review state court judgments on FDCA issues. He relied on the Court's appellate jurisdiction to ensure accuracy and uniformity in the interpretation of the FDCA, despite the inability of federal district courts to entertain private suits in the first instance. 478 U.S. at 816 & n.4; see Chapter VII, notes 114-18 and accompanying text (discussing the Court's appellate jurisdiction to review a state court judgment in the kind of case that the Thompsons initiated in state court).

221. See notes 178-82 and accompanying text.

222. It is tempting to think that Justice Stevens meant to say that, assuming that Congress had created no right of action to enforce the FDCA, a lawsuit filed in federal court for that very purpose must be frivolous in the *Bell v. Hood* sense. See note 180. Yet that under-

terest at stake."[223] In *Merrell Dow*, Stevens saw little federal interest in allowing the Thompsons to litigate their state law negligence claim in federal court, even though that claim incorporated the FDCA's labeling requirements. In his view, Congress itself had disavowed any significant federal interest by failing to enact a federal statute authorizing private suits to enforce the FDCA.[224]

Recall that Justice Stevens' mission in *Merrell Dow* was to reconcile the Court's jurisdiction cases (including *Smith*) with its more recent decisions on the importance of a federal right of action.[225] It is typically only in the artificial context of a removal case that the question arises whether *state* law might supply the necessary right of action to advance a *federal* claim in *federal* court. Justice Stevens may have meant to say that state law can perform that function only when federal adjudication is warranted because of the special importance of the federal interests at stake. In all probability, that is precisely what he *did* mean to say. But he muffled his message in ambiguity.[226]

In dissent, Justice Brennan insisted that *Smith* was controlling.[227] The Thompsons' fourth count advanced a state law negligence claim that incorporated the federal labeling requirements established by the FDCA. Since that claim was not frivolous, it would have sufficed for § 1331 jurisdiction if the Thompsons had filed their suit in federal court. Justice Brennan acknowledged Stevens' desire to reconcile the Court's recent decisions on federally created rights of action. He, too, assumed for purposes of discussion that Congress had created no right of action to enforce the FDCA. Yet Brennan saw no basis in that for construing the jurisdictional statute, § 1331, to foreclose the Thompsons' (hypothetical) suit. He pointed out that the implementation mechanisms that Congress *had* created (civil suits by the Food and Drug Administration and criminal prosecutions) would ultimately reach the federal courts. To Brennan, then, it was "rather strange" that Justice Stevens should take Congress to disclaim enough federal in-

---

standing would be hard to square with Stevens' refusal to hold that Congress had preempted private suits authorized by state law.

223. See notes 206-09 and accompanying text.

224. For an elaboration, see Patti Alleva, *Prerogative Lost: The Trouble with Statutory Federal Question Doctrine After Merrell Dow*, 52 Ohio St. L.J. 1477, 1484, 1502 (1991).

225. See text accompanying note 211.

226. State law clearly *can* provide the procedural vehicle for enforcing constitutional claims in federal court. *Surgeons*, 118 S.Ct. at 529; see note 177. In constitutional cases, however, the Court typically finds rights of action either in statutes like § 1983 (which would have been available in *Surgeons*) or implied in the constitutional provisions involved. See notes 90, 93-94 and accompanying text (discussing § 1983); notes 144-52 and accompanying text (discussing rights of action implied in the Constitution). In cases in which the Court has considered whether suits begun in state court can be removed on the theory that they advance federal common law claims, the Court has not cleanly isolated the right-of-action issue from the question whether federal common law does genuinely control. See notes 284-87 and accompanying text.

227. *Merrell Dow*, 478 U.S. at 820. Justice Brennan insisted that *Smith's* "continuing vitality" was "beyond challenge" and reminded Justice Stevens that the Court had "reaffirmed" the holding in that case very recently—in Brennan's own opinion for a unanimous Court in *Franchise Tax Board v. Constr. Laborers Vacation Trust*, 463 U.S. 1 (1983); see notes 259-73 and accompanying text. Justice Stevens, for his part, did not purport to overrule *Smith*. Instead, he distinguished *Smith* on the ground that the constitutional issue in that case created a sufficient federal interest in federal court jurisdiction. See note 209 and accompanying text.

terest in the interpretation of the FDCA to warrant federal jurisdiction of the Thompsons' lawsuit.[228]

The import of *Merrell Dow* can be debated—and has been (exhaustively) in academic circles. The removal posture of the case seems central, and its bearing on § 1331 jurisdiction may be limited, in practice, to that special context.[229] Justice Stevens *did* indicate that (in at least some cases) district courts must determine whether admittedly federal claims warrant federal jurisdiction because of the substantial "nature" of the "federal interests" involved. Yet it seems clear (enough) that district courts are obliged to consider the importance of federal interests only when state law provides the plaintiff with a right of action. If that is what *Merrell Dow* means, it poses no threat to the well-pleaded complaint rule in the run of cases.[230]

F. Declaratory Judgment Actions

Litigants who seek declaratory relief pursuant to the Declaratory Judgment Act would seem to satisfy the well-pleaded complaint rule simply by drawing a complaint to request an authoritative decision on a federal issue.[231] It is not that simple. Instead, declaratory plaintiffs proceeding under § 2201 can invoke § 1331 jurisdiction only if the federal issue on which they want the court to rule would equally secure federal jurisdiction in a suit for a more traditional (coercive) form of relief, such as compensatory damages or an injunction. There are two schools of thought about how this works.

By one account, declaratory plaintiffs can establish federal jurisdiction only if they themselves might have invoked § 1331 by filing a well-pleaded complaint

---

228. Justice Brennan conceded that Congress' failure to create a federal right of action to enforce the FDCA might be understood to preclude private suits in state court. But he did not understand Justice Stevens to rest on that ground. In Brennan's view, then, Congress' apparent failure to preempt state lawsuits, coupled with its failure to establish a federal right of action, actually *strengthened* his own argument that the Thompsons might have sued in federal court in the first instance. For Congress had apparently left the possibility of such a suit open. *Merrell Dow*, 478 U.S. at 831-32 (dissenting opinion).

229. See note 287 (discussing *Merrell Dow* in connection with the characterization of claims in preemption cases).

230. Since *Merrell Dow*, the Court has insisted that the well-pleaded complaint rule must be scrupulously enforced. In *Oklahoma Tax Comm'n v. Graham*, 489 U.S. 838 (1989), the Court summarily reversed a circuit decision for failure to do so. The *Graham* case arose in a removal posture, but the Court did not mention *Merrell Dow*, the source of the plaintiff's right of action, or the relative importance of the federal interests involved. In another removal case, *Surgeons*, Justice O'Connor noted that ICS did not contend that its constitutional claims were so "insubstantial as not to establish federal jurisdiction." 118 S.Ct. at 531. See notes 177, 226. O'Connor cited *Merrell Dow* without elaboration. Professor Miller understands *Merrell Dow* to mean that district courts should make *ad hoc* appraisals of the importance of the federal interests at stake only in cases in which state law provides the right of action. He reports that most lower courts also take that view of *Merrell Dow*. Arthur R. Miller, *Artful Pleading: A Doctrine in Search of Definition*, 76 Tex. L. Rev. 1781, 1786-91 (1998).

231. See notes 98-103 and accompanying text (discussing the Declaratory Judgment Act).

seeking coercive relief. By this (conservative) account, the Declaratory Judgment Act does nothing to enhance litigants' ability to establish federal jurisdiction. It only allows them to seek (and authorizes federal courts to grant) declaratory relief—either alone or in company with traditional remedies. The point of reading § 2201 and § 1331 this way is clear: If plaintiffs could establish jurisdiction by requesting a declaration regarding an issue that would not appear in a complaint for a different form of relief, they would be able to circumnavigate the well-pleaded complaint rule, provided they request only a declaratory judgment.[232]

By another account, declaratory plaintiffs can establish federal jurisdiction if *either* they or the *declaratory defendant* might have established jurisdiction in a coercive action. By this second (more generous) account, declaratory plaintiffs need not advance federal claims themselves, but can establish jurisdiction on the basis of federal claims that the declaratory defendant might raise—if the declaratory defendant were to sue the declaratory plaintiff for damages or an injunction. The rationale for this second account is also clear: The Declaratory Judgment Act authorizes litigants to obtain clarity regarding their rights and legal relations, so that they can proceed with their lives without undertaking (or risking) coercive lawsuits. If parties differ over a federal issue, it should make no difference which of them initiates the legal proceeding in which that issue can be resolved.[233]

The competition between these two accounts has roots in *Skelly Oil v. Phillips Petroleum*.[234] Skelly contracted to sell natural gas to Phillips, so that Phillips, in turn, could supply it to a distributor, the Michigan-Wisconsin Pipeline Company. The contract contained a provision allowing Skelly to terminate if Michigan-Wisconsin failed to obtain a "certificate of public convenience and necessity" (authorizing Michigan-Wisconsin to operate its pipeline) from the Federal Power Commission by a date certain. The FPC issued a provisional certificate. Skelly found that insufficient and notified Phillips that the deal was off. Phillips then sued Skelly in federal district court, invoking jurisdiction under § 1331 and seeking a declaratory judgment that the provisional certificate was valid and that Skelly was not entitled to renege. That question was federal, according to Phillips, because the contract incorporated federal standards for a timely FPC certificate.

In the Supreme Court, Justice Frankfurter said that, even so, Phillips could not establish § 1331 jurisdiction. Insofar as Phillips was concerned, the action was for breach of contract, governed by state law. The federal issue (if any there

---

232. See notes 183-85 and accompanying text. While this account is true to the well-pleaded complaint rule, it does not necessarily serve the policies on which that rule rests. In the cases in which the well-pleaded complaint rule was fashioned, the point was to ensure that courts could easily determine their jurisdiction by looking only at the face of a complaint. In declaratory judgment cases, that purpose is served when plaintiffs identify the issues on which they seek clarity.

233. See *Developments in the Law: Declaratory Judgments, 1941-1949*, 62 Harv. L. Rev. 787, 802-03 (1949) (taking this view). Years ago, Professor Trautman argued that the most refreshing feature of the Declaratory Judgment Act was that it would permit a plaintiff to advance a federal issue that, under common law pleading standards geared to other forms of relief, would not have been introduced until the defendant answered and, perhaps, not before the plaintiff replied. See Trautman, note 203, at 463.

234. 339 U.S. 667 (1950).

was)[235] would be introduced only when (and if) Skelly filed an answer insisting that it was entitled to exploit the escape clause (on the theory that the certificate did not meet federal standards). Phillips had no affirmative federal claim of its own, but only wished to defeat Skelly's federal defense. Justice Frankfurter acknowledged that by requesting a declaratory judgment that Skelly's anticipated defense was invalid, Phillips had pled a federal issue. But Frankfurter insisted that Phillips could not establish § 1331 jurisdiction in a suit for declaratory relief, unless Phillips could equally establish jurisdiction in a suit for damages or an injunction. The Declaratory Judgment Act, he said, was "procedural only" and could do nothing to assist Phillips in establishing jurisdiction that Phillips would have been unable to achieve in a suit for a traditional remedy.[236]

Justice Frankfurter's opinion in *Skelly* embraced the first account of the Declaratory Judgment Act's effect on § 1331 jurisdiction—namely, the view that § 2201 has no effect at all. Frankfurter explained that the declaratory plaintiff (Phillips) could not establish federal jurisdiction to seek a declaratory judgment against the declaratory defendant (Skelly), because Phillips could not have invoked federal jurisdiction to sue Skelly for some other form of relief. If, for example, Phillips had sued Skelly for damages, the well-pleaded complaint rule would have prevented Phillips from injecting a federal issue into its complaint by anticipating Skelly's federal defense. Frankfurter insisted that the Declaratory Judgment Act could not help a plaintiff like Phillips gain access to federal court when, but for the Act, that plaintiff would have been relegated to state court.[237]

It is possible nonetheless to find support in *Skelly* for the second account of the way jurisdiction works in declaratory actions. If the point is only that the Declaratory Judgment Act does not expand the federal courts' jurisdiction pursuant to § 1331, it should make no difference which of the two parties (the declaratory plaintiff or the declaratory defendant) would have been able to establish jurisdiction in an action for coercive relief. So long as one of them could have satisfied the well-pleaded complaint rule in a traditional lawsuit against the other, the case should count as one that a federal court might have considered apart from the Declaratory Judgment Act. One might sensibly say that the Act does not expand the federal courts' traditional jurisdiction by permitting a declaratory plaintiff to anticipate a declaratory defendant's federal defense—in a case in which the declaratory defendant might have turned that defense into

---

235. Writing separately in *Skelly*, Chief Justice Vinson said he doubted that there was any federal question in the case at all. He was not convinced that the parties could manufacture federal jurisdiction under § 1331 by building a federal issue into a term in a private contract. 339 U.S. at 679.

236. Id. at 671 (majority opinion), quoting *Aetna Life Ins. v. Haworth*, 300 U.S. 227, 240 (1937). When, in *Haworth*, Chief Justice Hughes said that the Declaratory Judgment Act is "procedural only," he meant that the Act makes no attempt to authorize advisory opinions in violation of Article III. See Chapter IX, text accompanying note 16.

237. *Skelly*, 339 U.S. at 672: "Whatever federal claim Phillips may be able to urge would in any event be injected into the case only in anticipation of a defense to be asserted by petitioners [Skelly]." The traditional way of making this point is to ask whether the Mottleys might have established § 1331 jurisdiction in their suit against the railroad if they had sought a declaratory judgment that the new statute in that case did *not* give the railroad a valid basis for refusing to perform under the contract. See notes 183-85 and accompanying text (discussing the *Mottley* case). Given what Frankfurter said in *Skelly*, it seems most unlikely that he would have allowed that.

an affirmative claim in an action against the declaratory plaintiff for coercive relief.[238]

Justice Frankfurter did not pause to ask whether Skelly might have established federal jurisdiction in a coercive lawsuit against Phillips. If he had, he would presumably have considered an action for rescission—filed by Skelly to rid itself of a contract that (in Skelly's view) was null and void. In a complaint for that kind of relief, Skelly would presumably have alleged that it was entitled to rely on the escape clause, because the FPC certificate had not been obtained on time. That allegation would arguably have satisfied the well-pleaded complaint rule. If Justice Frankfurter had followed the argument out in this way and *still* held that Phillips could not establish federal jurisdiction for a declaratory action against Skelly, it would follow that he meant what he said in the opinion he actually wrote: Phillips was unsuccessful because Phillips itself could not have invoked federal jurisdiction in a coercive action against Skelly.

Alternatively, if Frankfurter had considered the possibility of a suit by Skelly, he might have said that Skelly could *not* establish federal jurisdiction in an action for rescission. After all, Skelly's formal claim would have been that the contract was invalid (an issue of state law), and Skelly would have pled a federal issue only as an element of that overarching state law theory. Following Holmes, Frankfurter might have said that so long as the formal shell of Skelly's claim was a matter of state law, the incorporation of a federal condition was inconsequential.[239] Thus a hypothetical action for rescission filed by Skelly would have arisen under state law and would not have been cognizable in federal court. If Justice Frankfurter had followed the argument out in this different way and *then* held that Phillips could not establish federal jurisdiction for a declaratory action against Skelly, it would (or might) follow that he *really* meant something that he did *not* say expressly: Jurisdiction did not exist in *Skelly* because the Declaratory Judgment Act could not expand the federal courts' jurisdiction in a much more fundamental way—namely, by drawing into federal court a dispute that *no one* would have been able to place there in a suit for a traditional remedy.

This last understanding of *Skelly* posits that litigants may have federal defenses that cannot be turned into affirmative federal claims that independently establish § 1331 jurisdiction: If Phillips had sued Skelly for breach of contract, Skelly would have had a federal theory to put forward as a basis for defeating liability. Yet if Skelly had sued Phillips for rescission, Skelly would not have been able to advance that same federal theory as an affirmative claim and, on that basis, to invoke federal jurisdiction. The idea is scarcely illogical. And it may help to sort out the confusing way that *Skelly* has been described in subsequent cases. Upon the whole, the modern Court is inclined to embrace the first account of the relationship between § 2201 and § 1331. But the Court has not squarely

---

238. Professor Monaghan admits the possibility that the Declaratory Judgment Act "permits party realignment and alteration in the timing of an otherwise proper federal court suit." Monaghan, note 100, at 240. Yet he warns that the existence of a right of action as a vehicle for suit remains an independent problem.

239. See text accompanying note 198 (discussing Justice Holmes' argument that there was no federal jurisdiction in the *Smith* case where state law incorporated federal legal standards).

rejected the second account and, in fact, may preserve that approach in its boiler-plate doctrinal statements.

1. Potential Defenses

In *Franchise Tax Board v. Constr. Laborers Vacation Trust*,[240] Justice Brennan said that *Skelly* has "come to stand for the proposition that 'if, but for the availability of the declaratory judgment procedure, the federal claim would arise only as a defense to a state created action, jurisdiction is lacking.'"[241] In *Textron Lycoming Reciprocating Engine Div. v. UAW*,[242] Justice Scalia said that, according to *Skelly*, "a declaratory action asserting a federal defense to a nonfederal claim [is] not a 'civil action'" within the meaning of § 1331.[243] And in *Public Svc. Comm'n v. Wycoff*,[244] Justice Jackson said that "where the complaint in an action for declaratory judgment seeks in essence to assert a defense to an impending or threatened state court action, *it is the character of the threatened action, and not of the defense*, which will determine whether there is federal-question jurisdiction in the District Court."[245]

Those statements are puzzling and potentially misleading. They create the erroneous impression that declaratory plaintiffs cannot establish § 1331 jurisdiction even under the first (conservative) account of jurisdiction in declaratory actions—that is, when declaratory plaintiffs themselves have affirmative federal claims that might also be properly pled to establish federal jurisdiction in a suit for damages or an injunction. Frankfurter said nothing like that in *Skelly*. His point was that Phillips had no federal claim at all, but only a state law contract claim. Frankfurter did not suggest that litigants who *do* have federal claims of their own are unable to file declaratory judgment actions in federal court, because, if they were sued by someone else on a state law theory, they would introduce those federal claims as defenses. One of the key objectives of the Declara-

---

240. 463 U.S. 1 (1983).

241. Id. at 16, quoting Federal Practice and Procedure § 2767, at 744-45 (Wright, Miller & Kane eds. 1983).

242. 118 S.Ct. 1626 (1998).

243. Id. at 1630.

244. 344 U.S. 237 (1952).

245. Id. at 248 (emphasis added). In *Franchise Tax Board*, the Court forthrightly delineated district court jurisdiction under § 1331. See notes 259-73 and accompanying text. In *Textron*, the Court formally addressed district court jurisdiction under § 301(a) of the LMRA. See notes 254-57 and accompanying text. In *Wycoff*, the Court purported to decide only that the plaintiff could not obtain declaratory relief. In that case, a private film company sued state regulatory authorities in federal court, seeking a declaratory judgment that its business constituted interstate commerce and was therefore exempt from state regulation. There was no hard evidence that state regulators planned any action against the company. Accordingly, Justice Jackson concluded that the company's federal action was either premature for purposes of obtaining discretionary declaratory relief or unripe in the constitutional sense. See notes 99-100 (noting that declaratory relief is discretionary); Chapter IX, notes 264-90 (discussing ripeness). Jackson's comment about jurisdiction may fairly be regarded as dicta—offered as part of his explanation of why declaratory relief was unavailable unless and until the company was actually at risk from state regulatory agents.

tory Judgment Act is to permit litigants who have federal claims to sue for clarity regarding those claims before they are named as defendants in suits filed by others (advancing either federal or state claims) and, in that posture, must turn their federal claims into defenses. Legions of cases demonstrate that litigants can secure § 1331 jurisdiction for anticipatory declaratory actions.[246]

The formulations in *Franchise Tax Board*, *Textron*, and *Wycoff* make sense, however, if they are understood as (inartful) attempts to say something else. The Court may mean that declaratory plaintiffs cannot establish federal jurisdiction if they depend on potential federal defenses that would be advanced by declaratory *defendants*. That reading reflects the first account of jurisdiction in declaratory judgment cases—namely, the understanding that declaratory plaintiffs must advance their own federal claims and cannot depend in any way on what declaratory defendants may say or do. It fits the opinion that Justice Frankfurter actually wrote in *Skelly*.

Then again, the Court may mean that declaratory plaintiffs cannot rely on a declaratory defendant's federal argument if it could arise *only* as a defense—and thus could not be turned into an affirmative claim that would establish federal jurisdiction in a coercive lawsuit *brought by the declaratory defendant*. If this is what the Court means, then it may follow that the second (comparatively generous) account of the way the Declaratory Judgment Act works is sustained: Declaratory plaintiffs cannot establish § 1331 jurisdiction in *every* case in which the declaratory defendant will raise a federal defense. But they can invoke § 1331 jurisdiction if they anticipate the kind of federal defense that, turned into an affirmative claim on behalf of the declaratory defendant, would establish jurisdiction in an action for coercive relief.

---

246. See note 103 and accompanying text. E.g., *Shaw v. Delta Airlines*, 463 U.S. 85 (1983); see notes 268-70 and accompanying text; *Steffel v. Thompson*, 415 U.S. 452 (1974); see Chapter IX, notes 288-90 and accompanying text. Then again, litigants need a right of action to do so. In *Steffel*, § 1983 answered on that account. The right-of-action issue in *Shaw* was problematic. See note 270. If litigants with federal claims do not sue first, but wait until an adversary sues them in state court for a violation of state law, they usually will not be able to remove the action brought against them to federal court. See Chapter VI, note 124 and accompanying text. But it is a mistake to conclude that litigants who would not be able to remove state law suits against them on the basis of their own federal defenses cannot turn their potential federal defenses into affirmative federal claims in prior, anticipatory declaratory judgment actions. That is precisely what litigants who have their own federal claims *can* do. It is, again, the very point of the Declaratory Judgment Act—a point that Justice Frankfurter appreciated and respected in *Skelly*. Justice Jackson did not suggest in *Wycoff* that the plaintiff company in that case was attempting to get round the removal statute. He did say that "federal courts will not seize litigation from state courts merely because one, normally a defendant, goes to federal court to begin his federal-law defense before the state court begins the case under state law." *Wycoff*, 344 U.S. at 248. But at that point he was explaining that the company would have an opportunity to mount its constitutional attack on state regulation if and when state authorities actually filed an enforcement action in state court and that the Supreme Court itself might review the state courts' disposition. It is possible that Jackson was groping toward ideas that the Supreme Court has more recently elaborated as abstention doctrines—under which federal courts decline to exercise jurisdiction when state court proceedings against the plaintiff are pending or about to begin. Anticipatory declaratory judgment actions figure significantly in the cases on abstention. See Chapter XI, notes 139-41, 193-98 and accompanying text.

2. Claims by Defendants

Some lower court patent cases hold that declaratory plaintiffs can anticipate federal claims that declaratory defendants might advance in coercive suits. In those cases, companies invoke federal jurisdiction pursuant to § 1338 (or § 1331)[247] to seek declaratory judgments of *non*-infringement. The Seventh Circuit decision in *Edelmann v. Triple-A Specialty*[248] is the leading illustration. Edelmann let it be known in the trade that Triple-A was infringing Edelmann's patent on a hydrometer. Triple-A sued Edelmann in federal court, seeking a declaration that Triple-A was *not* infringing Edelmann's patent. Edelmann objected to the district court's jurisdiction on the ground that the patent statutes created no substantive or litigation rights in alleged infringers and that Triple-A only wished to defeat Edelmann's potential federal claim of patent infringement.[249] The court conceded that, prior to the Declaratory Judgment Act, only patentees were able to invoke federal jurisdiction to sue alleged patent infringers and thus to vindicate their own federal patent claims. The court held, however, that § 2201 allows alleged infringers to sue patentees.

The Supreme Court has acknowledged *Edelmann*, but in a backhanded way. In *Franchise Tax Board*, Justice Brennan cited *Edelmann* as evidence that "[f]ederal courts have regularly taken original jurisdiction over declaratory judgment suits in which, if the declaratory judgment defendant brought a coercive action to enforce its rights, that suit would necessarily present a federal question."[250] But in *Textron*, Justice Scalia intimated that *Edelmann* may be limited to the patent context.[251] There may be special reasons why alleged patent infringers are able to invoke federal jurisdiction to obtain clarity regarding the charges against them. It is true that the federal patent laws confer no federal rights on alleged infringers. Yet it is a mistake to lump alleged infringers with litigants who have only state law claims to advance.[252] When alleged infringers sue patent holders, they invariably present quintessentially federal issues: whether the patent holder's

---

247. See text accompanying note 171.

248. 88 F.2d 852 (7th Cir.), *cert. denied*, 300 U.S. 680 (1937).

249. For a description of the federal rights created by the patent and copyright laws and their implications for federal court jurisdiction, see Judge Friendly's opinion in *T.B. Harms v. Eliscu*, 339 F.2d 823 (2d Cir. 1964).

250. *Franchise Tax Board*, 463 U.S. at 19; see notes 264-73 and accompanying text.

251. See notes 256-57 and accompanying text.

252. Professor Doernberg and Professor Mushlin think of *Edelmann* as the declaratory judgment analog of *Well Works*. See notes 174-76 and accompanying text. Donald L. Doernberg & Michael B. Mushlin, *The Trojan Horse: How the Declaratory Judgment Act Created a Cause of Action and Expanded Federal Jurisdiction While the Supreme Court Wasn't Looking*, 36 UCLA L. Rev. 529, 574-77 (1989). Recall that in *Well Works*, Justice Holmes held that an alleged patent infringer could not invoke federal jurisdiction for a suit against a patentee, because the alleged infringer's claim sounded in trade libel under state law. If there was a federal question in dispute in *Well Works*, it would only be introduced by the defendant patentee. In *Well Works*, however, the infringer was able to allege facts that arguably made out a claim under state law. Alleged infringers may not be able to do that in all cases controlled by *Edelmann*. A company may be accused of patent infringement (and thus have every reason to sue for a declaration of non-infringement), but not yet be able to allege that the patent holder has committed acts that injure the alleged infringer in a way that makes a state tort action available or feasible.

patent is valid and, if so, whether the alleged infringer has done anything to infringe that patent.[253]

In *Textron*, the UAW sued Textron in federal court, challenging the validity of a collective bargaining agreement. The union invoked the district court's jurisdiction under § 301(a) of the Labor Management Relations Act. [254] Justice Scalia explained that § 301(a) reaches only actions to enforce labor agreements, not actions challenging the validity of agreements in the absence of breach. Accordingly, the district court should have dismissed the action for want of jurisdiction. The UAW countered that its pursuit of a declaratory judgment altered the case. The union argued that it made no difference that its own claim rested on state contract law. The district court's jurisdiction to entertain its declaratory action could rest on the federal claim that Textron would have against the union in a coercive action for breach of the collective bargaining agreement. Justice Scalia rejected that argument as well.[255]

---

253. Moreover, there are equitable considerations. Companies accused of patent infringement immediately begin to accrue liability for damages. If they cannot sue their accusers to settle matters early, they may run up massive liability waiting for patentees to sue *them* for infringement. See Lisa A. Dolak, *Declaratory Judgment Jurisdiction in Patent Cases: Restoring the Balance Between the Patentee and the Accused Infringer*, 38 B.C. L. Rev. 903 (1997). Alleged patent infringers thus genuinely need the ability to take the initiative. See note 103 and accompanying text. The legislative history behind the Declaratory Judgment Act suggests that at least some proponents had alleged patent infringers in mind as potential beneficiaries of the declaratory judgment device. Doernberg & Mushlin, note 252, at 564.

254. See text accompanying note 60. In addition to § 301(a), the UAW also cited § 1331 (on the theory that the suit arose under federal common law). Justice Scalia declined to address that possibility because it was not within the question on which *certiorari* had been granted. See Chapter VII, text accompanying note 191 (explaining that this is the Court's normal practice). Scalia nonetheless discussed the case law pertaining to § 1331.

255. Justice Scalia said that the UAW's argument made assumptions that the Court could not indulge. The first was that "facts which were the *converse* of *Skelly Oil*—i.e., a declaratory complaint raising a *nonfederal* defense to an anticipated *federal* claim— *would* confer § 1331 jurisdiction." 118 S.Ct. at 1630 (emphasis in original). The union did contend that it could invoke federal jurisdiction on the basis of a federal coercive action that Textron might file. But it is hard to see why that argument depended on an assumption that the facts in *Textron* differed in a meaningful way from the facts in *Skelly*, far less that the fact patterns in the two cases were polar opposites. The relevant facts were actually similar. In both instances, a declaratory plaintiff hoped to establish federal jurisdiction by anticipating a federal claim that the declaratory defendant might advance. The UAW argued (as any prudent litigant would) that its position was consistent with *Skelly*. But the union placed primary reliance on the Supreme Court's suggestion (in *Franchise Tax Board*) that cases like *Edelmann* are sound and that (*Skelly* notwithstanding) declaratory plaintiffs *can* invoke federal jurisdiction on the basis of federal claims that lie only in the mouth of the defendant. Justice Scalia correctly observed that the union's position arguably conflicted with the well-pleaded complaint rule. But that only underscored that the union hoped to succeed where Phillips had failed. Professor Collins has pointed out that Scalia's comparison of *Skelly* and *Textron* overlooked the telling distinction between the two cases. Phillips was in a position to identify an extant federal defense that Skelly would almost certainly raise. The UAW was *not* in a position to allege an existing federal defense on the part of Textron. The UAW had not violated the collective bargaining agreement, so Textron had no complaint at all, federal or otherwise. In that (important) sense, the union's declaratory judgment action could name no federal issue on which the parties were in dispute. But see note 257 (describing Justice Breyer's argument that Textron might have a justiciable federal claim if the union threatened breach and Textron came to the brink of filing an action).

Justice Scalia insisted that neither the UAW nor the Solicitor General (who appeared as *amicus* in *Textron*) could point to a decision by the Supreme Court or "any other federal court" upholding federal jurisdiction "on the basis of the anticipated claim against which the declaratory-judgment plaintiff presents a nonfederal defense." He acknowledged that *Franchise Tax Board* had observed "with seeming approval" that jurisdiction had been established on that very basis in cases like *Edelmann*. Justice Scalia explained, "*however*," that the "cases brought forward to support" that understanding were suits by alleged patent infringers to declare a patent invalid, "*which of course themselves raise a federal question*."[256] Scalia thus suggested that patent cases like *Edelmann* do not stand for the general proposition that declaratory plaintiffs who themselves have only a *state* law claim can invoke federal jurisdiction on the strength of a federal claim that the declaratory defendant may advance.[257]

In light of *Textron*, the first (conservative) account of §2201 and §1331 now appears ascendant. That account sharply restricts the utility of declaratory judgment actions. Plaintiffs can obtain §1331 jurisdiction if they want clarity regarding their own affirmative federal claims—claims that would appear on the face of a well-pleaded complaint in a suit for a traditional form of relief. But plaintiffs cannot test the validity of federal counterclaims that opposing parties may raise. That understanding of *Skelly* and, more broadly, the relationship between the Declaratory Judgment Act and §1331, is controversial in academic circles.[258] Yet even the *Franchise Tax Board* case, which cited *Edelmann* with apparent approval, arguably fortifies the view that declaratory plaintiffs must be

---

256. 118 S.Ct. at 1630 n.4 (emphasis added). Justice Scalia did not purport actually to decide that jurisdiction cannot be established on the basis of an anticipated claim by the declaratory defendant. He said only that it is "not clear" that jurisdiction can be established in that way and that it "can be argued" that declaratory plaintiffs who anticipate federal claims by the defendant are no more entitled to invoke federal jurisdiction than are plaintiffs in ordinary actions who allege only state law claims and anticipate federal defenses—namely, plaintiffs who are routinely foreclosed under the well-pleaded complaint rule. 118 S.Ct. at 1630.

257. Writing separately in *Textron*, Justice Breyer suggested a middle ground. By his account, a declaratory plaintiff can establish jurisdiction on the basis of the declaratory defendant's federal claim, but only when the declaratory defendant's coercive action advancing that federal claim against the declaratory plaintiff is imminent—in the sense that it already counts as an "actual" case or controversy. *Textron*, 118 S.Ct. at 1632 (concurring opinion). Breyer noted that the Declaratory Judgment Act specifically authorizes federal courts to declare "the rights and other legal relations of any interested party." See text accompanying note 98. So a federal court having jurisdiction of a declaratory defendant's federal claim can equally issue an authoritative declaration regarding a declaratory plaintiff's state law defense to that claim. By Breyer's account, it makes no difference that the declaratory plaintiff's state claim does not itself establish jurisdiction; it still can be adjudicated in a declaratory judgment action—once jurisdiction has been established via the declaratory defendant's federal claim. Justice Breyer drew support for this view from *Franchise Tax Board's* reference to *Edelmann*. His approach is appealing inasmuch as it would allow a party like the union in *Textron* to file suit in federal court without committing a breach that invites the employer to sue for coercive relief. See note 103 and accompanying text (explaining that declaratory judgment actions typically allow litigants to force litigation without putting themselves at risk of suit for violating the very legal standards on which they need clarity).

258. Professor Trautman decried *Skelly* as "unnecessary and unfortunate in an area of the law" that was "already unnecessarily complex." Trautman, note 203, at 468. The American Law Institute has proposed that *Skelly* be overruled by statute. ALI Study, note 203, at 171. Professor Doernberg and Professor Mushlin contend that the legislative history indi-

advancing their own affirmative federal claims, irrespective of the remedy they seek.

In *Franchise Tax Board*, construction companies in California established CLVT to hold funds for their employees' annual vacations. CLVT qualified as an "employee benefit plan" within the meaning of the federal Employee Retirement Income Security Act (ERISA) and thus was subject to extensive federal regulation. The Tax Board was the California agency with responsibility for collecting state taxes. If the Tax Board could not collect from taxpayers directly, it was authorized under state law to collect indirectly—by requiring a trust fund like CLVT to pay over funds held for the benefit of delinquents. On finding that CLVT was holding funds on behalf of three delinquent individuals, the Board directed CLVT to transmit to the Board an amount equal to those employees' outstanding tax bills. CLVT asked the United States Department of Labor whether it could comply. The Labor Department advised CLVT that ERISA preempted the tax laws of California and barred CLVT from surrendering trust monies to the Tax Board. On the basis of that opinion, CLVT declined to forward the funds.

The Tax Board sued CLVT in state court, advancing two claims. First, the Board claimed that CLVT was obliged under state law to transmit the requested funds. Second, the Board sought a declaratory judgment that ERISA did not preempt the Board's state law authority to collect the taxes and that CLVT had a legal duty under state law to comply. CLVT removed the case to a federal district court. In the Supreme Court, the question was whether the district court would have had jurisdiction under § 1331, if the Board had originally filed suit in federal court.[259] Writing for a unanimous Court, Justice Brennan said that neither of the Board's claims would have sufficed.

Brennan disposed of the first claim summarily. That was solely a state tax collection claim that stood entirely on state law and could be articulated in the Board's complaint without mention of any federal issue. Accordingly, it would not have satisfied either the Holmes test for § 1331 jurisdiction or the well-pleaded complaint rule.[260] Brennan found the second claim more difficult. He recognized that the case presented a classic occasion for a declaratory judgment action. The only genuine issue on which the parties disagreed was whether ERISA preempted the Board's efforts to reach funds that CLVT held in trust. Once that federal issue was resolved, they would easily settle their accounts accordingly.[261] Nevertheless, Brennan found *Skelly* controlling. The Board's request for a declaratory judgment on the federal preemption question would not have established § 1331 jurisdiction. The Board advanced no affirmative claim that federal law *did* preempt state law, but rather hoped to show that federal law did *not* preempt state law—so that the *defendant's* federal preemption claim would be defeated. If the Board had not sought a declaratory judgment, but some other form of relief, there would have been no occasion to mention CLVT's federal preemption defense in the complaint.[262]

cates a purpose to allow jurisdiction in some of the very instances in which *Skelly* finds it wanting. Doernberg & Mushlin, note 252, at 547-73.

259. See text accompanying notes 172-73.
260. See notes 176, 183-85 and accompanying text.
261. See text accompanying note 102.
262. This was clear enough from Justice Brennan's treatment of the Board's first claim under state law for the taxes the Board insisted were due. That was the only claim for coercive relief that the Board might have advanced.

Justice Brennan recognized that *Skelly* had interpreted the federal Declaratory Judgment Act, while the Tax Board had sued under the California state declaratory judgment statute. As a formal matter, then, state pleading rules governed the issues on which the Board could seek a judgment—pleading rules that might not contain an analogue of *Skelly*. Yet Brennan nonetheless relied on *Skelly* for what he regarded as a pragmatic reason. If he conceded that the Board might have invoked § 1331 jurisdiction for a suit authorized by a state declaratory judgment statute to which *Skelly* did not apply, he would invite the Board (and future plaintiffs, as well) to elude *Skelly* routinely, simply by relying on state declaratory judgment statutes with more liberal pleading standards rather than § 2201. In this, Justice Brennan was apparently haunted by the threat that troubled Justice Stevens in *Merrell Dow*—namely, the specter of plaintiffs litigating federal issues in federal court on the basis of an authority provided by state law.[263] Justice Brennan dealt with the issue differently. He held, in essence, that the state declaratory judgment statute could not supply what the federal Act, given *Skelly*, denied.

Justice Brennan acknowledged *Edelmann* by name.[264] If he saw any tension between that case and *Skelly*, he said nothing about it. Nor did he suggest that patent cases are governed by a special rule.[265] Instead, he treated *Edelmann* as yet another precedent ostensibly bearing on § 1331 jurisdiction. Accordingly, he considered whether the Tax Board would have been able invoke § 1331 jurisdiction in the first instance on the theory that CLVT might have done so in a suit for coercive relief against the Board.[266]

It appeared that CLVT might well have established jurisdiction to sue the Board for an injunction—by advancing an affirmative federal claim that ERISA preempted the Board's state law authority. Justice Brennan referred to prior cases in point.[267] He might also have relied on another case, decided on the very day that he delivered his opinion in *Franchise Tax Board*. In *Shaw v. Delta Airlines*,[268] Justice Blackmun held that Delta could invoke federal jurisdiction in a suit for injunctive and declaratory relief against New York authorities who threatened to force the airline to comply with state statutes preempted by ERISA.[269] In addition, Justice Brennan recognized that special provisions in

---

263. See text accompanying notes 215-16, 225-26.

264. 463 U.S. at 19 n.19.

265. But see text accompanying notes 256-57 (discussing Justice Scalia's reference to this part of *Franchise Tax Board* in his opinion for the Court in *Textron*).

266. See text accompanying notes 247-49. Justice Brennan quoted Justice Jackson's dictum in *Wycoff* and explained that *Edelmann* is consistent with it. 463 U.S. at 16 n.14, 19 n.19; see text accompanying note 245. That is true enough, but the point only underscores the tension between *Edelmann* and Frankfurter's opinion in *Skelly*. See text accompanying note 237.

267. On this point, Justice Brennan cited *Lake Carriers' Ass'n v. MacMullan*, 406 U.S. 498 (1972), and three other cases indicating that parties who are subject to federal regulation can sue state officials for an injunction against state regulations that conflict with their federal obligations and that, since they can sue for injunctive relief, they can equally sue for declaratory relief. 463 U.S. at 20 n.20.

268. 463 U.S. 85 (1983).

269. Unlike *Shaw*, *Franchise Tax Board* involved an attempt to evade state taxes. Justice Brennan declined to say whether the Tax Injunction Act would have precluded a suit by CLVT. 463 U.S. at 20 n.21. See Chapter XI, note 36 and accompanying text (discussing the Tax Injunction Act).

ERISA would have covered a suit by CLVT. One section, § 502(a)(3), authorized any "participant, beneficiary, or fiduciary" subject to ERISA to file "a civil action" seeking an injunction against any defendant who violated ERISA's substantive provisions. Another section, § 502(e)(1), conferred jurisdiction on federal district courts to entertain suits filed under the authority provided in § 502(a)(3).[270]

Justice Brennan concluded, however, that CLVT's apparent ability to establish federal jurisdiction to sue the Board could not translate into an ability on the part of the Board to establish federal jurisdiction for a declaratory action against CLVT. Brennan, like Justice Stevens in *Merrell Dow*, quoted Justice Cardozo's warning that jurisdictional issues require judgment.[271] In this instance, he said there were two reasons why, in good judgment, he could not say that the Board might have sued in federal court in the first instance. First, state tax authorities would not be "significantly prejudiced" if they were unable to invoke the jurisdiction of the federal courts in order to collect state taxes. They could easily take that peculiarly local business to state court. Second, the special provisions in ERISA plainly addressed only suits *by* institutions like CLVT and did not provide for suits *against* them. Brennan said he could not fairly read those sections of ERISA to empower a litigant like the Tax Board indirectly via the analysis in *Edelmann*.

Both Justice Brennan's reasons for distinguishing *Edelmann* have appeal, though both equally have weaknesses. By common account, the result he reached in the end was sensible. The case was, after all, a tax collection proceeding by state authorities who had never wanted to be in federal court in the first place. In general, matters of that kind are best left to the state courts.[272] If litigants like

---

270. Since *Shaw*, too, was an ERISA case, Justice Blackmun might have relied on these special provisions both for the airline's right of action and for the district court's jurisdiction. He did not. Instead, he relied on *Mottley*, *Smith*, and other cases indicating that litigants can establish federal jurisdiction under § 1331 if they advance affirmative federal claims in their complaints. See notes 183-85, 196-97 and accompanying text. Blackmun did not explain where the litigants in those cases found their rights of action. Nor did he explain where, apart from § 502(a)(3), the airline in *Shaw* might have found authority to sue. Given the Court's modern decisions requiring litigants to show wherein Congress has given them permission to enforce federal statutes via private litigation, that was a significant omission. Today, given *Merrell Dow*, Blackmun's failure to address the right-of-action question is even more problematic. See notes 211-26 and accompanying text (discussing the connection drawn in *Merrell Dow* between the existence of a federal right of action and § 1331 jurisdiction). In *Shaw* itself, the airline sought both injunctive and declaratory relief. If the Declaratory Judgment Act is an independent right-of-action statute, then § 2201 could answer in that case with respect to the latter remedy. See notes 101-03 and accompanying text. It has also been suggested that Justice Blackmun meant to recognize a right of action implied in the Supremacy Clause, serving litigants who wish to advance affirmative federal preemption claims. The Federal Courts and the Federal System 947-48 (Fallon, Meltzer & Shapiro eds. 1996). Justice Blackmun referred obliquely to *Ex parte Young*, 209 U.S. 123 (1908), which again begged the right-of-action question. See Chapter X, notes 161-65 and accompanying text. Professor Monaghan insists that *Shaw* "seems wrong" if it purports to hold that "any federal immunity holder" can have "automatic access to federal courts for declaratory and injunctive relief." Monaghan, note 100, at 241-42.

271. See text accompanying note 202.

272. Even if Justice Brennan did not formally rely on the Tax Injunction Act, he reached a result that seems in keeping with the general policy of that Act. See note 269 (noting Brennan's failure to decide whether the Tax Injunction Act bars declaratory suits to avoid state taxes).

CLVT wish to air their federal preemption claims in federal court, they typically can do so by filing their own lawsuits before state officials initiate litigation in state court. Once again, the removal posture of a case infused it with intellectual difficulty that would not have been presented in an ordinary § 1331 case filed originally in a federal district court.[273]

G. Preemption

Arguments that federal law preempts state law are commonly adjudicated in state court. Plaintiffs are masters of the theories they wish to litigate and choose to advance state law claims in the first instance. Defendants then argue federal preemption in defense, but cannot remove on that basis. In some instances, however, federal law occupies the entire field in which disputes arise, displacing any state law that would otherwise operate. When that is true, plaintiffs are not free to characterize their claims as state law matters. By hypothesis, there *is* no state law, but only superseding federal law.[274] Plaintiffs' claims are therefore necessarily federal in nature. It follows *ceteris paribus* that they might have filed suit in federal court in the first instance, invoking jurisdiction under § 1331. Accordingly, defendants are entitled to remove.[275]

The Supreme Court hesitates to find "complete" preemption and invariably demands a clear statement of congressional "intent" to displace state law entirely.[276] In *Avco v. Aero Lodge*,[277] an employer sued a union in state court for an injunction against a labor strike. The union removed the suit to federal court on the theory that § 301 of the Labor Management Relations Act preempted state law regarding labor contracts and occupied the field with federal common law. Accordingly, the employer had no state law contract action against the union,

---

273. See text accompanying notes 172-73.

274. In the instances in which the Court has found federal preemption to have this effect, the content of the federal law that displaces state law is largely federal common law — fashioned by the federal courts. Recall that when federal common law governs at all, it governs irrespective of whether a case is handled in federal or state court. See note 75.

275. See Comment, *Federal Preemption, Removal Jurisdiction, and the Well-Pleaded Complaint Rule*, 51 U. Chi. L. Rev. 634, 664-65 (1984). By contrast, if defendants merely have ordinary issue or claim preclusion defenses to state claims filed in state court, they cannot remove — even if those defenses are anchored in federal law. *Rivet v. Regions Bank*, 118 S.Ct. 921 (1998). In *Rivet*, the Court disclaimed a notorious footnote in *Federated Dep't Stores v. Moitie*, 452 U.S. 394, 397 n.2 (1981), which had suggested that a defendant could remove on the strength of an argument that a plaintiff's state claim was precluded by a federal judgment in a prior action. Justice Ginsburg explained that while a claim preclusion defense to a state claim may be federal in character, it can no more be the basis for removal than other federal defenses. It is only when the defendant shows that the *plaintiff's* claim is necessarily federal (because it is completely preempted by federal law) that removal is available. For a discussion of the problems the footnote in *Moitie* had created, see Miller, note 230, at 1800-18.

276. E.g., *Pilot Life Ins. Co. v. Dedeaux*, 481 U.S. 41, 55-57 (1987). In this instance, the Court has consulted legislative history much more than usual. See, e.g., id. at 46, 55; see Chapter I, notes 24-36 (discussing the Court's typical preference for resting judgment on the text of a statute rather than on background materials).

277. 390 U.S. 557 (1968).

but only a federal common law claim—which would have justified federal jurisdiction if the employer had sued in federal court in the first instance. Justice Douglas agreed. Given *Lincoln Mills*, an action to enforce a general labor contract
was governed by federal substantive law, wherever the plaintiff chose to file it.[278]
In *Caterpillar v. Williams*,[279] however, Justice Brennan explained that *Avco* meant
only that § 301 federalized claims under a collective bargaining agreement. State
law remained available to individual employees suing to enforce personal employment contracts. Those employees could characterize their claims as state law
matters and thus avoid removal.

The cases on ERISA follow a similar (uneven) pattern. In *Metropolitan Life
Ins. Co. v. Taylor*,[280] Justice O'Connor explained that ERISA displaced state law
with respect to the kinds of claims about which Congress was primarily concerned: suits *by* "participants, beneficiaries, and fiduciaries."[281] Accordingly, an
employee no longer had any state claims to advance regarding the way her demand for benefits had been handled by Metropolitan (an employee benefit plan
within the meaning of the Act). Those claims had been federalized. Since the employee might have filed suit in federal court in the first instance, Metropolitan
was entitled to remove. In *Franchise Tax Board*,[282] however, Justice Brennan held
that ERISA did not displace state law with respect to claims about which Congress was *not* primarily concerned: suits by other parties (like the Tax Board)
against "participants, beneficiaries, and fiduciaries" (like CLVT). Accordingly,
the Tax Board's claims had not been federalized, and CLVT could not remove.[283]

Justice Brennan fortified his conclusion in *Franchise Tax Board* with a separate argument. In *Avco*, the LMRA not only displaced state substantive law, but
also provided the plaintiff in that case with a federal right of action to vindicate
its federalized claim in the courts.[284] In *Franchise Tax Board*, by contrast, ERISA
did not provide litigants like the Board with a federal right of action. Brennan
took that as further evidence that Congress had not meant ERISA to federalize
the claims the Board wished to advance. Later, in *Caterpillar*,[285] Justice Brennan
explained that Congress can manifest a purpose to preempt formerly state law
claims without ensuring that plaintiffs can obtain the same "remedy" in federal
court that they might have obtained from the state courts.[286] In *Franchise Tax*

---

278. Douglas recognized that the Norris-LaGuardia Act would bar the federal court to
which the action was removed from issuing the injunction that the employer had hoped to
win from the state courts. But he explained that the "nature of the relief" that the federal
court might award after it adjudicated a suit could not affect the court's jurisdiction to adjudicate in the first instance. Jurisdiction, he said, depended entirely on the federal nature of
the employer's claim, coupled with the defendant's choice to remove. 390 U.S. at 560.

279. 482 U.S. 386 (1987).

280. 481 U.S. 58 (1987).

281. See text accompanying note 270.

282. See notes 259-73 and accompanying text.

283. For discussions, see Mary P. Twitchell, *Characterizing Federal Claims: Preemption,
Removal, and the Arising-Under Jurisdiction of the Federal Courts*, 54 Geo. Wash. L. Rev.
812, 840-70 (1986); Note, *Understanding Preemption Removal Under ERISA § 502*, 72
N.Y.U. L. Rev. 578 (1997).

284. Recall the Court's holding in *Lincoln Mills* that § 301(b) creates a federal right of
action for suits the federal courts have jurisdiction to entertain pursuant to § 301(a) and in
which they apply federal common law. See text accompanying note 88.

285. See note 279 and accompanying text.

286. *Caterpillar*, 482 U.S. at 391 n.4.

Board, then, Brennan regarded Congress' failure to provide the Board with a *right of action* as probative evidence that Congress did not mean to federalize the Board's claims. But in *Caterpillar*, he said that Congress' failure to ensure that a plaintiff might obtain a particular form of *relief* lacked the same significance in determining the congressional design.[287]

H. Supplemental Jurisdiction

A federal district court's jurisdiction to adjudicate a "civil action" under § 1331 depends on the existence of a substantial federal claim. The scope of that jurisdiction, once established, extends further. Pursuant to 28 U.S.C. § 1367(a), the court has "supplemental" jurisdiction[288] over "all other claims that are so related" to the federal claim "that they form part of the same case or controversy under Article III."[289] In *City of Chicago v. Internat'l College of Surgeons*,[290] Justice O'Conner said that a "case" within the meaning of Article III (and, by extension, supplemental jurisdiction under § 1367) extends to state claims that "derive from a common nucleus of operative fact."[291]

---

287. See note 80 (discussing the difference between rights of action and remedies). In light of *Merrell Dow*, this may make a certain amount of sense. The absence of a federally created right of action may rob a federal court of jurisdiction, even though the substantive claim at bar is plainly federal. See notes 211-26 and accompanying text. Yet one would not have expected to hear this from Justice Brennan, given his dissent in *Merrell Dow*. See notes 227-28 and accompanying text. Professor Hirshman has written a searching history and analysis of the interplay between the right-of-action cases and federal jurisdiction—up to and including *Franchise Tax Board*. Linda R. Hirshman, *Whose Law Is It, Anyway? A Reconsideration of Federal Question Jurisdiction Over Cases of Mixed State and Federal Law*, 60 Ind. L.J. 17 (1984).

288. This comparatively new statute substitutes the term "supplemental" jurisdiction for more traditional terminology. The shift was deliberate. Previous nomenclature could be confusing. Typically, courts referred to the exercise of jurisdiction over additional claims as "pendent" jurisdiction, and to the exercise of jurisdiction over additional parties as "ancillary" jurisdiction. Occasionally, however, courts used the label "pendent" jurisdiction to identify either additional claims or additional parties introduced by the plaintiff, and "ancillary" jurisdiction to identify additional claims or parties introduced by the defendant. Under § 1367, one label covers all variations on the same theme: power to consider matters that are related to cases over which a federal court has jurisdiction but would not otherwise fall within the court's authority to address. This said, it must also be said that § 1367 does not occupy the field, but only codifies "much of the common-law doctrine of ancillary jurisdiction" that courts otherwise enjoy. *Peacock v. Thomas*, 516 U.S. 349, 354 n.5 (1996). Given the sweep of supplemental jurisdiction under § 1367, it is hard to know what occasion federal district courts might have to rest on a residual basis of power to *decide* issues. More often, they may rely on extra-§ 1367 authority to *forego* decisions on state claims in their discretion. See note 301 and accompanying text.

289. This general rule, established by § 1367(a), is subject to exceptions, identified by § 1367(b), for claims advanced in certain diversity actions. In this context, the Court's ordinary test for identifying Article III cases will not answer. See text accompanying note 12. By hypothesis, federal courts can identify the state claims over which they are asked to exercise supplemental jurisdiction.

290. 118 S.Ct. 523 (1997); see note 177.

291. Id. at 529, quoting *United Mine Workers v. Gibbs*, 383 U.S. 715, 725 (1966). Professor Matasar argues that this definition neglects the more expansive definitions of a case envisioned by the civil rules on joinder of claims and parties. Richard A. Matasar, *Rediscov-*

In *Surgeons*, the Commission on Chicago Historical and Architectural Landmarks designated a building owned by ICS as an historical landmark. ICS sought judicial review of the Commission's action in state court. In that suit, ICS argued both that the Commission should have allowed ICS an exemption on the basis of economic hardship and that the landmarks ordinance on which the Commission relied violated the fourteenth amendment. The Commission removed the case to federal court on the theory that ICS might have filed its action there pursuant to § 1331.[292] Justice O'Connor agreed that the fourteenth amendment claim would have triggered § 1331 jurisdiction and that removal was therefore proper.[293] Moreover, she explained that § 1367(a) extended the federal court's jurisdiction to ICS's state claim that the Commission had reached an erroneous decision. Justice O'Connor recognized that the state claim was a peculiarly local matter. To determine it, a federal court would have to review the Commission's record, giving deference to the Commission's expertise and judgment. Yet since § 1367(a) explicitly refers to "all" other claims within a constitutional "case," Justice O'Connor refused to make any exceptions.[294]

---

ering *"One Constitutional Case": Procedural Rules and the Rejection of the Gibbs Test for Supplemental Jurisdiction*, 71 Calif. L. Rev. 1399 (1983). For an exhaustive discussion, see Susan Bandes, *The Idea of a Case*, 42 Stan. L. Rev. 227 (1990).

292. See text accompanying note 172.

293. Justice O'Connor was persuaded that § 1367 applies to § 1441 cases. *Surgeons*, 118 S.Ct. at 530. See id. at 535 (Ginsburg, J., dissenting) (expressing agreement on the point). See Joan Steinman, *Supplemental Jurisdiction in § 1441 Removed Cases: An Unsurveyed Frontier of Congress' Handiwork*, 35 Ariz. L. Rev. 305 (1993). But see John B. Oakley, *Prospectus for the American Law Institute's Federal Judicial Code Revision Project*, 31 U.C. Davis L. Rev. 855 (1998) (reporting that the ALI recommends restricting § 1367 to original jurisdiction cases).

294. 118 S.Ct. at 531. Justice O'Connor acknowledged *Chicago R.I. & P.R. Co. v. Stude*, 346 U.S. 574 (1954), in which the Court held that a case requiring a district court to consider state issues previously determined by a state administrative agency would not qualify as an original diversity action, but would contemplate impermissible appellate jurisdiction. See Chapter VI, notes 149-55 and accompanying text. Yet she explained that under § 1367, it was enough that ICS's federal claims would have established a "civil action" for purposes of § 1331. Professor Woolhandler and Professor Collins read *Surgeons* to avoid either endorsing or overruling *Stude*. When the Court accepts a case in which *Stude* figures more directly, they urge the Court to jettison that case. Their survey of historical materials persuades them that it is not at all out of character or troubling for federal courts to determine state law issues that call for some measure of deference to state agencies. Ann Woolhandler & Michael G. Collins, *Judicial Federalism and the Administrative States* (forthcoming). Justice O'Connor was plainly sensitive in *Surgeons* to the history behind the enactment of § 1367 in 1991. In *Finley v. United States*, 490 U.S. 545 (1989), a widow sued the United States in federal court, claiming that the FAA was responsible for the death of her husband and children in an airline accident. That claim was within the federal court's exclusive jurisdiction under the Federal Tort Claims Act. The plaintiff also included a state tort claim against a private company, alleging that the company had negligently positioned the power lines with which the plane had collided. Justice Scalia said that the federal court had no supplemental jurisdiction over the latter claim. He acknowledged that Article III would allow Congress to extend supplemental jurisdiction to claims against additional parties. Yet he declined to reach that result without more explicit guidance from Congress. The following year, Congress provided that very guidance in the form of § 1367. In *Surgeons*, accordingly, the justices acquiesced in a clear statement responding to *Finley*. For discussions of *Finley* and § 1367, see Denis F. McLaughlin, *The Federal Supplemental Jurisdiction Statute—A Constitutional and Statutory Analysis*, 24 Ariz. St. L.J. 849 (1992); Richard D. Freer, *Compounding Confusion and Hampering Diversity: Life After Finley and the Supplemental Jurisdiction Statute*, 40 Emory L.J. 445 (1991); *Essays, Compounding or Creating Confusion*

Chief Justice Marshall recognized in *Osborn* that some measure of supplemental jurisdiction is a practical necessity if federal courts are to adjudicate the "whole case."[295] In other instances, the Court has identified three additional reasons for extending a federal court's reach beyond the claims that originally trigger jurisdiction. In *Hurn v. Oursler*,[296] the Court recognized that supplemental jurisdiction is necessary in some cases to avoid a multiplicity of suits regarding the same subject matter. If a plaintiff has both federal and state claims to advance, and the federal claim must be filed in federal court because it is within the federal court's exclusive jurisdiction, the federal court must have supplemental jurisdiction to determine the state claim as well. Otherwise, the plaintiff will be forced to press the state law claim in a separate lawsuit in state court. In *United Mine Workers v. Gibbs*,[297] the Court recognized that similar, though less severe, difficulties arise when federal jurisdiction of a federal claim is not exclusive. In that event, supplemental jurisdiction in federal court is not essential to avoid more than one suit; the plaintiff is free to take both federal and state claims to state court. Yet if that is the result, the plaintiff will be denied the very promise that § 1331 holds out—namely, the ability to advance federal claims in federal court. Finally, in *Siler v. Louisville & Nashville R.R. Co.*,[298] the Court explained that supplemental jurisdiction provides federal courts with the opportunity to avoid federal constitutional issues by resolving disputes on state law grounds.

The federal question that triggers § 1331 jurisdiction must be substantial. Recall that, in *Bell v. Hood*,[299] the Court indicated that any non-frivolous claim will do. The Court recognizes that plaintiffs may be tempted to inject questionable federal claims into their complaints in hopes of obtaining federal jurisdiction over related state law issues.[300] In the main, however, the check on that kind of strategic behavior is not a demanding test for determining whether a federal court has power to consider state issues. It is, instead, the district court's discretion to forego the *exercise* of that power. Pursuant to § 1367(c), district courts may decline to exercise supplemental jurisdiction over a state claim if: (1) the claim "raises a novel or complex issue of State law;" (2) the claim "substantially predominates" over the federal claim that triggered jurisdiction in the first place; (3) the claim that triggered jurisdiction is dismissed, leaving only state claims in the case; or (4) in "exceptional circumstances," there are "other compelling rea-

---

About Supplemental Jurisdiction? A Reply to Professor Freer, 40 Emory L.J. 943 (1991) (Rowe, Burbank & Mengler).

295. *Osborn*, 22 U.S. at 822; see text accompanying note 6.

296. 289 U.S. 238 (1933). In *Hurn*, the Court linked supplemental jurisdiction to the law of preclusion—by permitting federal courts to determine state claims that were part of the plaintiff's "cause of action" and thus would ordinarily be foreclosed in future litigation between the two parties. This is one instance in which the Supreme Court has acknowledged the confusion that surrounds the "cause of action" formulation. The *Hurn* approach to supplemental jurisdiction has been discarded in favor of the approach codified in § 1367(a).

297. 383 U.S. 715 (1966).

298. 213 U.S. 175 (1909). But see Chapter X, notes 184-87 and accompanying text (discussing the way the *Pennhurst* decision regarding the eleventh amendment can affect this feature of supplemental jurisdiction in some instances).

299. 327 U.S. 678 (1946); see notes 142-43, 178-82 and accompanying text.

300. See *Hagans v. Lavine*, 415 U.S. 528, 552 (1974) (Powell, J., dissenting) (insisting that federal claims must have more than a "glimmer of merit" to justify exercising supplemental jurisdiction over state law claims). But see *Surgeons*, 118 S.Ct. at 531 (referring to *Merrell Dow* on this point); see note 230.

sons for declining jurisdiction." Even this list of open-ended standards is not exhaustive. In *Surgeons*, Justice O'Connor read § 1367(c) to reflect the considerations that the Court itself had previously identified: "[A] federal court should consider and weigh in each case, and at every stage of the litigation, the values of judicial economy, convenience, fairness, and comity."[301]

---

301. 118 S.Ct. at 534, quoting *Carnegie-Mellon v. Cohill*, 484 U.S. 343, 350 (1988). The statute of limitations is tolled for any state claim that a party seeks to litigate in federal court while the court decides whether to exercise supplemental jurisdiction over that claim.

Chapter IX

Justiciability

Litigants who seek adjudication in federal court must satisfy a series of doctrines that, taken together, establish the conditions under which a matter is "justiciable" in an Article III tribunal. These justiciability doctrines bear their own names. Yet they illustrate not different ideas, but different circumstances in which the Supreme Court recognizes and elaborates the same operative themes. In the main, the justiciability doctrines reflect and foster structural values: the separation of powers and federalism. They differentiate the judiciary's role from the legislative and executive responsibilities of Congress and the President and screen some matters out of federal court and into the hands of local authorities and state courts.[1] To some lesser extent, the justiciability doctrines serve functional objectives. They ensure that federal courts consider legal questions in a posture that promotes effective adjudicative methodology. Sound judicial process, in turn, produces workable decisions not only for the litigants at bar, but also for others whose interests may be affected and for the public at large.[2]

---

1. State courts need not employ the justiciability doctrines that govern access to the federal courts. *Internat'l Primate Protection League v. Administrators of Tulane Ed. Fund*, 500 U.S. 72, 78 n.4 (1991). Accordingly, when a federal court declines to entertain a suit for want of justiciability, a state court may be open to receive it. State courts often have their own justiciability doctrines that close their doors as well. In that event, issues are denied adjudication in any court at all. This is not an occasion when state courts are obliged to entertain federal claims. If a question is non-justiciable in federal court, it is by hypothesis a matter that can be resolved without adjudication of any kind. State courts thus have a valid excuse for withholding the state forum. See Chapter VI, notes 89-90 and accompanying text. The Supreme Court has developed standing doctrine primarily as a check on the behavior of the inferior Article III courts. The Court itself performs unique referee functions that call for greater flexibility. See Chapter VII, text accompanying notes 187-90. Nevertheless, standing doctrine formally governs the exercise of federal judicial power at all levels, and what the Court specifies regarding the lower courts' purview equally applies to the Court's own preserve. The Court sometimes defuses the resulting tension when it can open its own doors to litigants without, at the same time, opening the doors of the district courts. In *ASARCO v. Kadish*, 490 U.S. 605 (1989), the Court held that it can accept a case on appellate review from a state court even if the matter would not have been justiciable in a federal district court for want of a plaintiff with standing. The interests of the parties in the outcome of the appeal suffice for the injury required. In cases like *ASARCO*, accordingly, the justiciability doctrines that channel litigation to state court in the first instance do not foreclose federal adjudication later in the Supreme Court. Professor Fletcher and Professor Varat have proposed that state courts should be required to observe federal justiciability standards. William A. Fletcher, *The "Case or Controversy" Requirement in State Court Adjudication of Federal Questions*, 78 Calif. L. Rev. 263 (1990); Jonathan D. Varat, *Variable Justiciability and the Duke Power Case*, 58 Tex. L. Rev. 273 (1980).

2. To the extent the justiciability doctrines discourage federal litigation, they have the *effect* of conserving federal judicial resources. It is unlikely, however, that the Supreme Court

247

Roughly speaking, the justiciability doctrines govern *what* matters are susceptible to determination in federal court, *who* can invoke federal judicial power, and *when* federal court action is timely.[3] Some of the most basic doctrines go to *what* matters are justiciable in the sense that they disclaim duties the federal courts cannot perform: Federal courts cannot issue "advisory" opinions, render judgments that are not "final" within the judicial branch, or resolve "political" questions. The doctrine of "standing" originally identified *who* may sue in an Article III court and continues to address that question today. The doctrines of "ripeness" and "mootness" govern *when* issues can be considered. It is dangerous, however, to take generalizations of this kind very far. For example, in the context of standing, the Court has made it perfectly clear that *who* is entitled to be in an Article III tribunal is *not* the whole of the matter at all.[4] All the justiciability doctrines serve the same master: the Supreme Court's sense of the federal judiciary's role in relation to the other branches of the central government and the states. The Court commonly cites decisions rendered under the various justiciability doctrines interchangeably and thus underscores the cross-currents running between them.

In recent years, standing has become the central focus. Other justiciability doctrines spin off from standing and the ideas that standing entails. Standing doctrine, in turn, is the product of a profound struggle in this century between competing conceptions of the federal courts, conceptions that are roughly captured in the private rights model of adjudication and its rival, the public rights model.[5] That struggle has obvious political and ideological significance. And it is not yet at an end. Standing doctrine is therefore unruly, even incoherent, and by some accounts manipulable. The key to understanding is an appreciation of the jurisprudential backdrop and the monumental difficulties the Supreme Court faces in fashioning intellectual order out of so much conflicting material.

A. Basic Doctrines

1. Advisory Opinions

Federal courts cannot offer opinions that are merely advisory in the sense that they have no decisive consequences. The classic illustration came early. In 1793, President Washington asked his Secretary of State (Jefferson) to seek advice from the Supreme Court regarding the interpretation of treaties with European nations. When Jefferson wrote to the justices, however, they declined to act as consultants. In a famous letter addressed to Washington himself, the justices said there were "strong arguments" against the "propriety" of "deciding" ques-

---

tailors the justiciability doctrines for the *purpose* of controlling federal docket congestion. See Chapter II, text accompanying note 106.

3. See Henry P. Monaghan, *Constitutional Adjudication: The Who and When*, 82 Yale L.J. 1363 (1973).

4. See notes 99-100 and accompanying text.

5. See Chapter I, notes 50-60, 66-78 and accompanying text.

tions "extrajudicially"—namely, the "lines of separation drawn by the Constitution between the three departments of the government."[6]

By conventional account, judicial advice on legal questions outside the context of an actual lawsuit does not constitute *judicial* action at all, but is, instead, a species of executive or legislative behavior beyond the judicial purview. Justice Frankfurter explained, accordingly, that Article III bars advisory opinions insofar as it limits the exercise of judicial power to "cases" or "controversies" and thus restricts federal courts to the resolution of actual disputes pursuant to the private rights model.[7] When a federal court is asked merely to express its opinion on a matter in the abstract, it has no genuine case or controversy to determine and thus has no justification for taking action *as a court*.[8]

The ban on advisory opinions also reflects pragmatic methodological considerations.[9] By resisting involvement in the formulation of legal positions in the first instance, federal courts make themselves available to consider problems afresh at a later time, when it is essential to do so in order to resolve an actual case. Courts deliver better answers when issues are presented by self-interested advocates in the context of a discrete fact pattern. When they determine questions in the abstract, they are more likely to make mistakes or to announce sweeping principles that must be abandoned later when it appears that a more variegated approach is required.[10]

Concerns about advisory opinions figured in the formulation of the Declaratory Judgment Act.[11] In *Willing v. Chicago Aud. Ass'n*,[12] Justice Brandeis warned that "the power conferred upon the federal judiciary" did not extend to awarding a "declaratory judgment" that merely clarified a legal issue. That suggested that the Court would find a general statute empowering the federal courts to issue declaratory judgments to be an invalid attempt to authorize advisory opin-

---

6. See Correspondence of the Justices, August 8, 1793, reprt'd in The Federal Courts and the Federal System 93 (Fallon, Meltzer & Shapiro eds. 1996). The justices called attention to the specific provision in Article II authorizing the President to "require the Opinion, in writing, of the principal Officer in each of the Executive Departments, upon any Subject relating to the Duties of their respective Offices." U.S. Const. art. II, § 2, cl.1. That implied that Washington was limited to seeking advice from within the executive branch. The justices may actually have resisted any general role as advisors to the President in order to husband their resources and establish their independence within the new national scheme. Chief Justice Jay had previously prepared (but may not have sent) a letter to Washington challenging the constitutionality of forcing the justices to "ride circuit." Russell Wheeler, *Extrajudicial Activities of the Early Supreme Court*, 1973 Sup. Ct. Rev. 123, 148. See Chapter II, note 53 and accompanying text.

7. See Felix Frankfurter, *A Note on Advisory Opinions*, 37 Harv. L. Rev. 1002 (1924).

8. In this instance, an interpretation placed on the Constitution's text serves the structural values associated with the separation principle. See Chapter I, text accompanying note 14. Professor Pushaw contends that the private rights model befits Article III "controversies" defined by the identity of the parties. But he argues that the founding generation regarded "cases" implicating federal questions as occasions for elaborating the law, apart from any immediate need to do so in order to resolve disputes. Robert J. Pushaw, Jr., *Article III's Case/Controversy Distinction and the Dual Functions of Federal Courts*, 69 Notre Dame L. Rev. 447 (1994). See Chapter II, note 26 (noting alternative understandings).

9. See Chapter I, notes 50-60 and accompanying text (discussing traditional adjudication under the private rights model).

10. See notes 176-82 and accompanying text (discussing this rationale in connection with the first amendment overbreadth doctrine).

11. See Chapter II, note 76 and accompanying text.

12. 277 U.S. 274 (1928).

*Fed Crt can grant decl judgment only in actual case/controversy
(i.e. where a lawsuit would be for damages or injunction)*

ions. Soon thereafter, however, the Court accepted appellate jurisdiction in *Nashville, C. & St. L. Ry. v. Wallace*,[13] in which the plaintiff had sued in state court for a declaratory judgment (authorized by state law) that a state tax violated the Constitution. In *Wallace*, Justice Stone explained that since the plaintiff might have sought injunctive relief, his decision to seek only a declaration of his rights did not deprive the matter of its character as an Article III "case."[14]

Encouraged by *Wallace*, Congress enacted the Declaratory Judgment Act, 28 U.S.C. § 2201, which enables federal courts to issue declaratory judgments "in a case of actual controversy." The Supreme Court upheld the new Act in *Aetna Life Ins. Co. v. Haworth*.[15] Chief Justice Hughes was satisfied that Congress had made no attempt to authorize advisory opinions, because § 2201 limits declaratory judgments to "cases" on which the federal courts are entitled to rule. In a famous line, Hughes said that the "operation" of the Declaratory Judgment Act is "procedural only" in that it provides "remedies" and defines "procedure" for suits that, by hypothesis, satisfy the constitutional requirements for federal adjudication.[16]

Concerns about advisory opinions also surfaced in *Muskrat v. United States*.[17] In that case, Cherokee Indians complained that Congress had unconstitutionally restricted their ability to sell certain land. Congress responded by en-

---

13. 288 U.S. 249 (1933).

14. Id. at 264.

15. 300 U.S. 227 (1937).

16. Id. at 240. But see Chapter XI, note 200 (discussing Chief Justice Rehnquist's suggestion that declaratory judgments may not be entitled to preclusive effect). For a discussion of the functions of modern declaratory actions, see Chapter VIII, notes 101-03 and accompanying text. Litigants can use § 2201 to obtain authoritative declarations that entirely resolve a current case or controversy. They cannot use it to obtain clarity regarding particular *issues* that will be presented in a future case or controversy. In *Calderon v. Ashmus*, 118 S.Ct. 1694 (1998), a class of California prison inmates filed suit in federal court, citing both § 2201 and § 1983 as authority. The prisoners alleged that they planned to file individual habeas corpus actions attacking their criminal convictions (and death sentences) in federal district court. Pursuant to 28 U.S.C. § 2263 (then recently enacted), California could insist that petitions of that kind be filed within 180 days after the completion of direct review in state court—*if* California satisfied certain requirements to "qualify" for the 180-day filing period. Otherwise, the prisoners had a year in which to launch their habeas corpus actions. State officials publicly declared that California had done what was necessary to invoke the 180-day filing period. The prisoners in *Ashmus* took the position that California did not qualify and, accordingly, that they had twice that long to prepare their petitions. They alleged that they were in the very kind of dilemma that the Declaratory Judgment Act was meant to address. They needed clarity regarding their procedural rights in order to plan their future behavior. Without an authoritative declaration that California did *not* qualify, the prisoners would be forced to act within 180 days rather than run the risk that their position would ultimately be rejected. In the Supreme Court, Chief Justice Rehnquist said that the prisoners' class action was not an Article III case or controversy. Individual prisoners would have (individual) cases when they filed their own habeas corpus actions and, at that time, would be entitled to a judgment regarding the correct filing period. But the prisoners' anticipatory class action sought a judgment regarding a "collateral legal issue governing certain aspects" of those future cases. The class action did not itself constitute a case or controversy, because it could not entirely resolve the "underlying" disputes between the prisoners and their keepers (i.e., the validity of the prisoners' detention). Id. at 1699. The result, of course, was that prisoners in California were forced to file individual habeas corpus actions within 180 days, irrespective of whether California was legally entitled to demand that they proceed so quickly. No one would deliberately file later in order to litigate the issue and obtain an authoritative judgment.

17. 219 U.S. 346 (1911).

acting a special statute authorizing the Cherokees to file suit in federal court to obtain a judicial determination of the validity of what Congress had done. When the Cherokees initiated an action, the Court ruled that it did not qualify as a justiciable case or controversy: The suit did not constitute a genuine effort to enforce the Cherokees' constitutional rights, but was instead an artificial device for obtaining a judicial opinion on an abstract question of constitutional law. The federal government was not really an adverse party, and other private citizens who had a stake in the matter were not involved. The modern Court occasionally cites *Muskrat* for the general proposition that a justiciable case demands actual parties with demonstrable opposing positions.[18]

The prohibition on advisory opinions is well settled. It nonetheless bears critical examination. In related contexts, proponents of the private rights model insist that federal judicial power tracks the authority that "Colonial courts and the courts of Westminster" exercised "when the Constitution was framed."[19] The evidence suggests, however, that courts in England did not find advisory opinions to be "extrajudicial" at all.[20] The constitutional justifications for the prohibition on federal advisory opinions are also open to question. Originalists find little evidence in point. James Madison's statement that federal courts would determine only "cases of a Judiciary Nature" begged the question.[21] The Supreme Court pays lip service to the ban on advisory opinions. Yet in its own work, the Court routinely addresses abstract legal questions when it manipulates the issues presented in appellate cases in order to isolate the matters on which it wishes to rule.[22]

---

18. E.g., *Moore v. Charlotte-Mecklenburg Bd. of Ed.*, 402 U.S. 47, 48 (1971); see *Steel Co. v. Citizens for a Better Environment*, 118 S.Ct. 1003, 1016 (1998) (citing *Muskrat* in support of a holding that federal courts cannot assume "hypothetically" that an Article III case or controversy exists in order to dispose of a matter on other grounds). In other instances, however, the Court is more willing to allow Congress to establish mechanisms for obtaining clarity. In *South Carolina v. Katzenbach*, 383 U.S. 301 (1966), for example, the Court approved § 5 of the Voting Rights Act of 1965, which authorizes states to seek declaratory judgments regarding the effect of changes in local voting rules on the ability of racial minorities to participate in elections. But see *Texas v. United States*, 118 S.Ct. 1257 (1998) (holding that an attempt by Texas to obtain a declaratory judgment that a new state statute would not dilute minority voting power was not yet ripe for adjudication); see notes 264-90 and accompanying text (discussing the ripeness doctrine). Collusive suits are different. In *United States v. Johnson*, 319 U.S. 302 (1943), the Court refused to consider an action filed by a plaintiff who had been recruited by the defendant to file a lawsuit that the defendant could control.

19. *Joint Anti-Fascist Refugee Committee v. McGrath*, 341 U.S. 123, 150 (1951) (Frankfurter, J., concurring).

20. See Chapter II, notes 1-3 and accompanying text; Stewart Jay, *Servants of Monarchs and Lords: The Advisory Role of Early English Judges*, 38 Am. J. Legal Hist. 117 (1994).

21. See Chapter II, text accompanying note 24. Recall that Madison himself championed the council of revision idea. According to conventional wisdom, the delegates rejected that proposal on the theory that the justices should not participate in the legislative function. See Chapter II, text accompanying notes 9, 21.

22. See Chapter VII, text accompanying notes 187-94. Professor Lee notes that the Court expresses concerns about the "advisory" aspects of opinions in circumstances in which the Court does not mean that judicial action would violate Article III. The ban on advisory opinions, then, may actually entail generalized prudential concerns about the exercise of federal judicial power. See Evan Tsen Lee, *Deconstitutionalizing Justiciability: The Example of Mootness*, 105 Harv. L. Rev. 603, 644-49 (1992).

2. Finality

Just as federal courts are barred from issuing advisory opinions on abstract questions, they are equally barred from determining actual disputes if their orders are not final, but rather are subject to review in the executive or legislative branches. The working idea is much the same in both instances. If judicial opinions are not binding on the other branches, either because they are merely advisory (and thus can be ignored) or because they are not final (and thus can be overturned), they are not independently *judicial* in character. Instead, they are in service of the executive and legislative authorities whose decisions will actually control.[23] When courts render determinations that are not final, they invade the preserves of the other branches by doing preliminary executive or legislative work *for* officials who bear ultimate decision-making responsibility. Those executive or legislative officers, in turn, invade the preserve of the judiciary by presuming to reexamine court decisions rather than accepting them as authoritative pronouncements of law.[24]

The classic illustration is *Hayburn's Case*.[25] In 1792, Congress enacted the Invalid Pensions Act, which established pensions for veterans disabled in the Revolutionary War. To be eligible, applicants had to show that they had served honorably and that they had suffered wounds in the fighting. At the time, Congress had no experience with administrative agencies and turned to the federal circuit courts to receive applications, apply the criteria, and forward recommendations to the Secretary of War. The Secretary could either accept or reject the courts' recommendations. If he decided that a circuit court had made a mistake, he reported his decision to Congress. Thus the Secretary and Congress retained authority to make final decisions awarding or denying benefits.

When a circuit court in Pennsylvania declined to entertain a claim under the Act, Attorney General Randolph asked the Supreme Court to issue a writ of mandamus requiring that court to cooperate. Initially, the Court balked at Randolph's request, advanced without reference to any particular applicant and without any explicit authorizing statute. Randolph withdrew as Attorney General and reappeared as private counsel to William Hayburn, the applicant whose claim the circuit court had refused to consider.[26] At that point, the Court took

---

23. See *Chicago & Southern Air Lines v. Waterman*, 333 U.S. 103, 113-14 (1948) (making the connection expressly).

24. See Chapter I, notes 2-15 and accompanying text (discussing the separation principle).

25. 2 U.S. (2 Dall.) 408 (1792).

26. Professor Bloch suggests various reasons why the Court may have thought that Randolph needed to involve an individual claimant. The Court may have been concerned that if the Attorney General acted on behalf of the federal government alone in seeking a writ of mandamus running to a federal court, there would be no Article III case or controversy, because the United States would appear on both sides of the litigation—in its executive and judicial forms, respectively. The Court may also have been worried that the United States lacked standing to complain that the circuit court had refused to process benefits claims. The government could not lose money if the statute was not enforced, but would have to pay benefits if the writ issued and the circuit court was forced to approve at least some claims. See notes 57-203 and accompanying text. The Court may also have doubted that mandamus was the proper remedy. See Susan Low Bloch, *The Early Role of the Attorney General in Our Constitutional Scheme: In the Beginning There Was Pragmatism*, 1989 Duke L.J. 561, 599-600. Marcus and Teir contend (primarily on the basis of Justice Iredell's notes) that the Court would have allowed Randolph to act without involving Hayburn, if

the matter under advisement. Congress promptly amended the Act to eliminate the circuit courts' role. The Supreme Court, accordingly, never rendered an authoritative judgment on whether the Act imposed unconstitutional duties on the federal judiciary. Three circuit courts *did* address the issue. Since Supreme Court justices staffed those courts, their discussions were plainly significant.[27] All three declined to make preliminary determinations that the Secretary of War and Congress were free to reject.[28]

The authority to be gleaned from *Hayburn's Case* can be questioned. The precise issues that troubled the justices are unclear. Nevertheless, it is settled today that Congress cannot assign federal courts the duty to enter judgments that are subject to executive or legislative revision.[29] By a parity of reasoning, Congress cannot force courts to reopen judgments that they consider to be closed. The Supreme Court said as much in *Plaut v. Spendthrift Farm*.[30] Previously, the Court had held that suits under the Securities and Exchange Act must be filed within a year after the discovery of a claim.[31] On the basis of that decision, lower courts dismissed a number of actions that had been filed too late. Ostensibly to avoid injustice, Congress enacted a statute authorizing the courts to reopen those cases. Writing for the Court in *Plaut*, Justice Scalia held the statute invalid inas-

---

Randolph had first obtained Washington's express approval. Maeva Marcus & Robert Teir, *Hayburn's Case: A Misinterpretation of Precedent*, 1988 Wis. L. Rev. 527. The concerns that Professor Bloch identifies would not trouble the Court today. See, e.g., *United States v. Nixon*, 418 U.S. 683, 696-97 (1974) (rejecting President Nixon's argument that the Watergate special prosecutor's subpoena of the famous "Nixon tapes" presented a non-justiciable intrabranch dispute); *Tutun v. United States*, 270 U.S. 568, 577 (1926) (holding that an individual's uncontested application for naturalization constituted a "case" on which a federal court could act — because the federal government was at least a "possible adverse party"). See generally Michael Herz, *United States v. United States: When Can the Federal Government Sue Itself?*, 32 Wm. & Mary L. Rev. 893 (1991). The Attorney General now routinely litigates federal questions in federal court, though typically in circumstances in which some statute appears to authorize suit. See Larry W. Yackle, *A Worthy Champion for Fourteenth Amendment Rights: The United States in Parens Patriae*, 92 Nw. U. L. Rev. 111 (1997).

27. See Chapter II, note 53 and accompanying text (explaining that the early circuit courts had no judges of their own and depended on Supreme Court justices "riding circuit"). None of the circuit courts issued an opinion. All expressed their views in letters to President Washington. It may be that the justices hoped to impress on Washington personally their objections to circuit-riding. If the Act had been approved, they would have had to travel to sit in circuit courts all the more often in order to handle the increased caseload. See note 6. All six of the justices agreed that the duties imposed on the circuit courts were not judicial in nature and that the Act was, to that extent, invalid. See Bloch, note 26, at 591-92.

28. In one of the cases, the justices said that Congress could appoint them as individuals to make the necessary determinations as special commissioners (not as Article III judges). That maneuver was plainly meant to defuse the immediate constitutional question. Yet it raised another: the question whether Article III judges can be assigned extra-Article III duties to be performed in an executive capacity. See Chapter IV, notes 41-47 and accompanying text.

29. *Chicago & Southern Air Lines v. Waterman*, 333 U.S. 103, 113-14 (1948). In *Seminole Tribe v. Florida*, 519 U.S. 44 (1996), Justice Stevens argued that an obscure provision of the Indian Gaming Act violates this principle. Under that Act, a federal court is expected to name a mediator to help a state negotiate with an Indian tribe planning a gambling casino. If the parties decline to embrace a mediator's proposal, they have recourse not to the court, but to the Secretary of the Interior. See Chapter X, notes 92-99 and accompanying text (discussing other aspects of *Seminole Tribe*).

30. 514 U.S. 211 (1995).

31. *Lampf, Pleva v. Gilbertson*, 501 U.S. 350 (1991).

much as it attempted to upset Article III court judgments that were already final.[32]

3. Political Questions

Federal courts cannot entertain questions that are "political" and thus properly to be answered by the politically accountable (executive and legislative) branches of the government. This idea, too, sounds in the separation of powers and the private rights model for judicial action. The precedents in point began with *Marbury v. Madison*,[33] where Chief Justice Marshall recognized that federal courts have no authority to "inquire" how the President decides matters the Constitution assigns to his "discretion."[34] By some accounts, Marshall meant that when the President (or Congress) has constitutionally anchored discretion, there are no judicially enforceable standards to be met. The branch of the government that enjoys discretion simply makes (and is entitled to make) whatever decision it chooses, without fear that the courts may find it erroneous. Formally, a decision of that kind cannot *be* erroneous and therefore is not susceptible to judicial review. [35]

The Supreme Court is of two minds about political questions. On the one hand, the Court sometimes takes *Marbury* itself as the guide and suggests that to find a question political is simply to render a judicial decision that the Constitution assigns the question to one of the political branches. This approach deprives the political question doctrine of any genuine function as an explanation for *failing* to exercise judicial power. While the Court declines to grapple with the question on its own terms, the Court nonetheless renders an authoritative decision on the meaning of the Constitution—namely, that the decision reached by another branch of the government is (necessarily) correct.[36] On the other hand, the Court

---

32. Justice Scalia explained that Congress can affect the results in pending cases in a variety of other ways—by, for example, adjusting the applicable substantive law or by waiving defenses. See Chapter IV, note 82 and accompanying text.

33. 5 U.S. (1 Cranch) 137 (1803). See Chapter I, notes 54-58 and accompanying text.

34. *Marbury*, 5 U.S. at 170.

35. The ban on advisory opinions bars federal courts from deciding *legal* issues abstracted from *disputes*. See text accompanying notes 7-8. Complementing that idea, the ban on political questions bars federal courts from resolving *disputes* implicating issues that are not *legal*—because they are not susceptible to authoritative judicial orders that the other branches are bound to respect. The Constitution rarely leaves matters to the unbridled discretion of the President or Congress, but typically circumscribes their power with legal restraints that the courts can enforce. In *Marbury*, for example, Chief Justice Marshall said that Marbury's entitlement to his commission was not a political issue in the constitutional sense. Neither Jefferson nor Madison had any general Article II power to decide in his discretion whether to deliver the commission. Marbury claimed a legal right to delivery, and Marshall acknowledged that there was some federal *law* on which Marbury could rely—law that the Court would have been able to enforce if it had possessed the necessary jurisdiction. See Chapter I, text accompanying note 56.

36. This first approach has wide support in the academic literature. See, e.g., Herbert Wechsler, Principles, Politics and Fundamental Law 11-14 (1961). Professor Henkin argues that most of the Court's political question cases are actually instances in which the Court has made this kind of threshold constitutional determination and that others can be explained as occasions on which the Court has hesitated to award equitable relief. Louis Henkin, *Is There a Political Question Doctrine?*, 85 Yale L.J. 597 (1976). Professor Scharpf proposes a third theme—namely, that some questions would present intractable logistical

also sometimes suggests that the identification of a question as political is *not* it-self an interpretation of the Constitution, but is, instead, a matter of pragmatic judgment. According to this second approach, the political question doctrine is a prudential device for avoiding sensitive questions, particularly in volatile circum-stances in which workable judicial solutions are difficult to deliver.[37]

Both approaches figure in the classic political question cases, often reinforc-ing each other but nonetheless creating a measure of intellectual tension. In *Luther v. Borden*,[38] Chief Justice Taney said that the Constitution gave Congress the authority to decide whether to accept the credentials of individuals who claimed to be the elected representatives and senators from Rhode Island. It fol-lowed that Congress equally had the authority to decide whether those officers represented the lawful government of that state. Taney acknowledged that the Guarantee Clause obliged "the United States" to "guarantee to every State" a "Republican Form of Government."[39] But he said that a claim under that clause raised a political issue to the extent it asked the courts to review Congress' deci-sion to receive the representatives and senators who were already seated. In some respects, Taney appeared to rest the decision in *Luther* on an interpretation of the Constitution. Yet he also noted the difficulties that would follow if rival po-litical camps could draw the federal courts into local struggles for power.[40]

---

and other functional difficulties. See Fritz W. Scharpf, *Judicial Review and the Political Question: A Functional Analysis*, 75 Yale L.J. 517 (1966).

37. This approach is typically associated with Professor Bickel, who argued that the courts must calibrate the exercise of judicial power, so that they do not compromise their le-gitimacy by assuming responsibilities they are not equipped to meet or issuing orders they cannot enforce. To Bickel, a pragmatic political question doctrine should work together with other discretionary doctrines (not themselves prescribed by the Constitution, though fully consistent with it) to ensure proper judicial restraint in a variety of delicate circumstances. See Alexander Bickel, The Least Dangerous Branch 125-26 (1962); Alexander Bickel, *Fore-word: The Passive Virtues*, 75 Harv. L. Rev. 40 (1962). See generally David L. Shapiro, *Ju-risdiction and Discretion*, 60 N.Y.U. L. Rev. 543 (1985). The discretionary features of the political question doctrine have received a good deal of academic attention, most of it criti-cal. Professor Redish contends that any element of the doctrine that cannot be set down to judicial interpretation of the Constitution should be discarded. Martin H. Redish, *Judicial Review and the Political Question*, 79 Nw. U. L. Rev. 1031 (1984). Accord Erwin Chemerinsky, *Cases Under the Guarantee Clause Should be Justiciable*, 65 U. Colo. L. Rev. 849 (1994); Louise Weinberg, *Political Questions and the Guarantee Clause*, 65 U. Colo. L. Rev. 887 (1994); Michael Tigar, *Judicial Power, the "Political Question Doctrine," and For-eign Relations*, 17 UCLA L. Rev. 1135 (1970). Professor Nagel suggests (or perhaps laments) that academics' impatience with the political question doctrine reflects a growing consensus that adjudication has merged with policy-making and that it therefore makes no sense to continue the pretense that courts can reserve their authority for "principled" duties. Robert F. Nagel, *Political Law, Legalistic Politics: A Recent History of the Political Ques-tion Doctrine*, 56 U. Chi. L. Rev. 643, 658 (1989). Professor Mulhern contends that the stubborn persistence of the political question doctrine should prompt academicians to ac-knowledge that courts share responsibility for interpreting the Constitution with the other branches of the government. J. Peter Mulhern, *In Defense of the Political Question Doc-trine*, 137 U. Pa. L. Rev. 97 (1988).

38. 48 U.S. (7 How.) 1 (1849).

39. U.S. Const. art. IV, § 4.

40. The *Luther* case arose in connection with the unsettled affairs in Rhode Island in the wake of Dorr's Rebellion. Academicians debate the precise issues presented in the case, as well as the decisive elements of Taney's opinion for the Court. See William Wiecek, The Guarantee Clause of the United States Constitution (1972); Arthur Bonfield, *The Guarantee Clause of Article IV, Section 4: A Study in Constitutional Desuetude*, 46 Minn. L. Rev. 513

The Warren Court attempted to reconcile the two approaches within a single formula. In *Baker v. Carr*,[41] Justice Brennan explained that the political question doctrine contemplates a "case-by-case inquiry." Courts determine whether a question is political in light of six factors: (1) a "textually demonstrable constitutional commitment of the issue to a coordinate political department;" (2) a "lack of judicially discoverable and manageable standards for resolving it;" (3) the "impossibility of deciding without an initial policy determination of a kind clearly for nonjudicial discretion;" (4) the "impossibility of a court's undertaking independent resolution without expressing lack of the respect due coordinate branches of government;" (5) "an unusual need for unquestioning adherence to a political decision already made;" and (6) "the potentiality of embarrassment from multifarious pronouncements by various departments on one question."[42] The first factor reflects the *Marbury* approach to political questions. The other five, together with Brennan's introductory reference to "case-by-case" inquiries, reflect the pragmatic approach.

Invoking the six-part formulation in *Baker* itself, Justice Brennan concluded that an equal protection attack on the apportionment of the Tennessee state legislature did *not* raise a political question. He distinguished *Luther* on two grounds. First, while the Constitution assigned Congress the authority to decide whether representatives and senators actually represented valid state governments, the Constitution did not assign to Congress (or the President) the authority to decide whether state legislatures were validly apportioned. Second, the Equal Protection Clause implicated in *Baker* offered "judicially manageable" standards that the Guarantee Clause did not. Brennan's reasoning has been questioned.[43] But it freed the Court to find apportionment cases justiciable and thus to be in a position three years later to announce the famous "one-person, one-vote" standard in *Reynolds v. Sims*.[44] Justice Brennan and the other justices in the *Baker* majority plainly saw a compelling need to prescribe constitutional standards for apportionment cases, because incumbents would rarely be willing

---

(1962). Both approaches to the political question doctrine also figured in famous cases in the middle third of this century: *Colegrove v. Green*, 328 U.S. 549 (1946) (holding that a Guarantee Clause claim regarding the apportionment of congressional districts in Illinois was non-justiciable); *Coleman v. Miller*, 307 U.S. 433 (1939) (holding that a claim regarding a state's ratification of a proposed constitutional amendment was also political). Foreign affairs cases provide an obvious occasion for finding issues to be political. See, e.g., *Banco Nat'l de Cuba v. Sabbatino*, 376 U.S. 398 (1964) (declining to recognize an exception to the "act of state doctrine" because of the possibility of interfering with the executive's conduct of foreign affairs). But it would be misleading to suggest that *any* issue touching foreign relations is for that reason alone non-justiciable. Compare *Goldwater v. Carter*, 444 U.S. 996 (1979) (Rehnquist, J., concurring) (arguing that a challenge to the President's decision to terminate a treaty presented a political question), with *Japan Whaling Ass'n v. Amer. Cetacean Society*, 478 U.S. 221 (1986) (holding that an attack on the failure of the Secretary of Commerce to certify that the Japanese whaling fleet jeopardized international agreements *was* justiciable). Cf. *Gilligan v. Morgan*, 413 U.S. 1 (1973) (holding that an attack on the way the national guard is trained raises a political question for Congress). See generally Thomas Franck, Political Questions/Judicial Answers: Does the Rule of Law Apply to Foreign Affairs (1992); Louis Henkin, Foreign Affairs and the Constitution (1972).

41. 369 U.S. 186 (1962).
42. Id. at 217.
43. Justice Frankfurter argued in dissent that the plaintiffs were advancing "a Guarantee Clause claim masquerading under a different label." Id. at 297 (dissenting opinion).
44. 377 U.S. 533 (1964).

to change even plainly unrepresentative systems in fear that reforms would favor their opponents. The *Baker* decision thus illustrates the Court's willingness to decide thorny questions that the justices might prefer to leave to politics, when it appears that political bodies are paralyzed and cannot effectively respond.[45]

The Court also applied the six-part formula in *Powell v. McCormack*.[46] In that instance, Adam Clayton Powell asked the federal courts to review the House of Representatives' refusal to seat him as his district's representative. The House had found Powell "unqualified" because he had been accused of stealing public funds and other unseemly behavior. Chief Justice Warren recognized that the Constitution made the House "the Judge of the Elections, Returns and Qualifications of its own Members."[47] But he insisted that the Constitution also specified what those "Qualifications" were: candidates need only be twenty-five years of age, citizens of the United States, and residents of their districts.[48] The Constitution assigned the House the authority to apply those three standards, not to introduce additional qualifications that members must meet. If the House had found Powell unqualified for failing one of the three prescribed tests, an objection from Powell might have raised a political question. But the attempt to hold Powell to *different* standards presented a justiciable issue that federal courts could consider.

The Court continues to invoke the *Baker* formulation in political question cases, but plainly gives decisive weight to the first of the six elements. In *Nixon v. United States*,[49] Chief Justice Rehnquist explained that "in the first instance" courts must "interpret the text" of the pertinent constitutional provision and "determine whether and to what extent the issue is textually committed" to another branch. Courts must also consider whether the question is subject to "judicially manageable standards." But that inquiry is "not completely separate." The absence of manageable standards "may strengthen the conclusion that there is a textually demonstrable commitment to a coordinate branch."[50] The *Marbury* approach thus appears to be on the ascendant, the prudential approach on the decline.[51] This is in keeping with the Court's emphasis on textualism, albeit the text in this instance is the Constitution itself.[52]

In *Nixon*, a former federal district judge sought judicial review of his impeachment conviction in the Senate. He complained that the Senate had dele-

---

45. See Louis Pollak, *Judicial Power and "the Politics of the People"*, 72 Yale L.J. 81, 88 (1962). Justice Frankfurter argued that if state legislatures were unrepresentative, it was for an "informed, civically militant electorate" to force incumbents to make reforms, despite their personal interests. *Baker*, 369 U.S. at 270 (dissenting opinion).

46. 395 U.S. 486 (1969).

47. U.S. Const. art. I, § 5, cl.1

48. U.S. Const. art. I, § 2, cl.2.

49. 506 U.S. 224 (1993).

50. Id. at 228-29.

51. Justice Souter explicitly adopted the prudential approach in *Nixon*, but in a lone concurring opinion that no other justice joined. Id. at 252.

52. See Chapter I, notes 24-36 and accompanying text. This emphasis on constitutional text does not (necessarily) signal enthusiasm for deciding politically sensitive issues. The Court found the question in *Nixon* to be non-justiciable. Moreover, the Court often relies on other justiciability doctrines, particularly standing doctrine, to avoid questions it wishes to sidestep, at least for the moment. See note 129 (standing); note 295 and accompanying text (mootness).

gated responsibility for collecting evidence against him to a committee and had convicted him on the basis of the committee's report in violation of the constitutional requirement that the Senate "shall have the sole Power to try all Impeachments."[53] Chief Justice Rehnquist found the validity of the Senate's procedure to present a political question. He rested primarily on an interpretation of the relevant text, concluding that by giving the Senate the "sole" power to try impeachment cases, the Constitution committed the question "whether an individual should be acquitted or convicted" to the Senate exclusively, without possibility of judicial review.[54] Rehnquist said that the other elements of the *Baker* formulation fortified that conclusion: The term "try" lacks "sufficient precision to afford any judicially manageable standard of review" for examining the Senate's work;[55] judicial review of impeachment convictions would produce unsettlement; and, if a claim were found to be meritorious, it would be difficult to fashion appropriate relief.[56]

B. Standing: Background

Federal courts can entertain only suits advanced by parties who have "standing."[57] Some features of standing doctrine are constitutional prerequisites to the exercise of federal judicial power: Litigants must demonstrate: (1) "injury in fact" that is (2) "fairly traceable to" and thus "caused [by]" the defendant's al-

---

53. U.S. Const. art. I, § 3, cl.6.

54. 506 U.S. at 231. The Chief Justice fortified his interpretation of constitutional text both with references to the (thin) history behind the text and with inferences from structure—namely, the general scheme the Constitution contemplates for channeling impeachment decisions to the House (for charges) and then to the Senate (for trials), with no provision for judicial involvement. Id. at 236. See Chapter III, text accompanying notes 34-37. Professor Brown has questioned Rehnquist's "assumption" that judicial review of the procedure by which the Senate acts would necessarily be the equivalent of judicial review of a Senate "decision on the merits." Rebecca L. Brown, *When Political Questions Affect Individual Rights: The Other Nixon v. United States*, 1993 Sup. Ct. Rev. 125, 130-31.

55. 506 U.S. at 230. Rehnquist concluded that since the Constitution prescribes other, comparatively specific requirements for Senate trials (e.g., a two-thirds majority vote for conviction), the "Framers" did not "intend" that the courts should construe the ambiguous term "try" to demand that other procedures be followed. Id. Concurring in the judgment in *Nixon*, Justice White said it was "not without irony" that the Court should disclaim an ability to identify standards for "procedural justice." Id. at 248. Professor Weinberg suggests that the Chief Justice "cannot have been wearing a very straight face" when he advanced that argument. For "if courts do not know whether or not a case has been tried, nobody knows." Weinberg, note 37, at 915.

56. With respect to these points, the Chief Justice set aside the particular case at bar (involving the impeachment of a district judge) and anticipated, instead, the more troubling case of a presidential impeachment. If the President were not removed from office by a Senate conviction alone, but could seek judicial review of the Senate's action, the country might be thrown into dangerous uncertainty while time-consuming judicial proceedings progressed. And if the courts should find the President's claims of mistreatment meritorious, the indelicacy of a judicial order for his reinstatement would be self-evident. These questions are less troubling in the context of judicial impeachments, where other measures may be available. See Chapter III, notes 41-46 and accompanying text.

57. The term "standing" is derived from the Latin phrase "*locus standii*" (a place to stand), used in England to describe one's capacity to "stand" before Parliament to address a bill.

legedly unlawful behavior and (3) "likely [to] be redressed by a favorable decision" and an award of the "requested relief."[58] Other aspects of standing doctrine are "prudential" in nature—not themselves constitutionally required, but
operating in service of constitutional themes.

Standing is formally an issue in every instance in which Article III courts exercise judicial power, irrespective of the subject matter or the identity of the parties. In many instances, standing is readily apparent. Private citizens who invoke
diversity jurisdiction for suits against other private citizens on state law claims
easily meet applicable standing requirements. They advance their own legal rights
(created and made actionable by state law), the defendants they name appear to
be the responsible wrongdoers, and if their claims prove to be meritorious, they
can be awarded some conventional remedy. Private citizens who invoke federal
question jurisdiction may find standing more difficult to achieve, particularly if
they name government officials as defendants. The federal statutes or constitutional provisions they wish to enforce may (or may not) establish personal legal
rights of the kind the courts entertain with comfort. Congress may (or may not)
provide them with a right of action to enforce those statutes or constitutional
provisions in private lawsuits in federal court.[59]

The conceptual underpinnings of standing doctrine have developed as a reflection of, and a reaction to, the evolution of the modern administrative state.
The Supreme Court has permitted Congress to fashion extensive federal regulatory law and to establish federal agencies to administer it. Yet the Court has also
struggled to locate and defend a proper place for the federal judiciary in the resulting structure.[60] The Court's judgment regarding the federal courts' proper
role has shifted over time. Typically, the problems that arise follow a pattern:
Congress first enacts a federal statute that prescribes certain behavior but does
not create personal legal rights. Next, Congress establishes federal administrative
machinery to enforce the new regulatory law, subject to some form of judicial review at the behest of a designated class of private citizens. Then, private plaintiffs
contend that they are within the class of private litigants entitled to sue the
agency concerned in federal court to ensure that the agency conforms to the federal statute it is charged to implement. Not every controversial standing decision
follows this pattern. But the standing doctrine the Supreme Court applies in all
cases is intelligible only if its origins in cases of this kind are understood and kept
in mind.

The idea that litigants need standing to challenge governmental power shares
a common history with the idea that the sovereign is immune from suit.[61] In early
England, the king was the *source* of law and by hypothesis could not *violate* it.
The courts were the king's alter ego. What they did, they did in his name. It fol-

---

58. *Allen v. Wright*, 468 U.S. 737, 751 (1984); *Lujan v. Defenders of Wildlife*, 504 U.S.
555, 560-61 (1992).

59. See Chapter VIII, notes 79-165 and accompanying text.

60. See Chapter V, notes 9-13, 36-44 and accompanying text (discussing administrative
agencies).

61. Professor Vining provides the account summarized in the text. Joseph Vining, Legal
Identity 20-27 (1978). Professor Jaffe offered a similar account. Louis L. Jaffe, *Suits Against
Governments and Officers: Sovereign Immunity*, 77 Harv. L. Rev. 1 (1963). See Chapter X,
notes 7-11 and accompanying text (discussing the federal government's sovereign immunity).

lowed that the king was not subject to suit. He could not (acting through his own judges) find himself guilty of violating his own law, such that his victim was entitled to judicial relief. The same was true for the king's agents, who enjoyed his immunity from suit so long as they acted on his authority. In time, however, English courts adopted a fictitious means of eluding royal immunity. They split the king's men into two persons, the one sovereign (and still insulated from suit as was the king himself), the other private (and subject to suit in the same way that other Englishmen were held to account). The courts declared that agents were acting in their private capacity whenever they violated the rights of others. It thus became possible, after all, for private plaintiffs to force the king's agents (and through them the king himself) to conform to the developing common law of England.

In this country, suits challenging official action took essentially the same form: actions by private citizens (claiming a breach of private common law rights) against government officials (treated as private citizens who had violated the private rights of others).[62] In federal question suits against governmental authorities, just as in ordinary cases involving private plaintiffs and defendants, the courts' primary function was to resolve disputes over plaintiffs' assertions of private rights.[63] The private rights model of adjudication predominated in the federal courts until the Progressive Era, when it came under pressure from suits reflecting the public rights model.[64]

New kinds of federal regulatory statutes and corresponding administrative agencies generated new forms of litigation. Both the subjects of regulation (chiefly industrial corporations) and its beneficiaries (primarily workers, consumers, and competitors) sought access to the courts to vindicate their interests. Corporations typically *resisted* regulation, contending either that government officials had exceeded any lawful authority the new statutes gave them or, if they had not, that the regulatory statutes regulators enforced were unconstitutional. Workers, consumers, and competitors typically *exploited* regulation, contending that government officials had lawful authority, but failed to use it properly. Corporations advanced their own private rights. Workers, consumers, and competitors, by contrast, went to court to obtain benefits that would flow from forcing government agents to comply with federal statutes. If rights were at stake, they

---

62. E.g., *Perkins v. Lukens Steel Co.*, 310 U.S. 113 (1940) (determining the Secretary of Labor's amenability to suit on the basis of common law rules applicable to private agents and principals).

63. See Chapter I, notes 50-60 and accompanying text.

64. See Chapter I, notes 66-78 and accompanying text. Professor Sunstein develops this history and its significance. See Cass R. Sunstein, *Standing and the Privatization of Public Law*, 88 Colum. L. Rev. 1432 (1988). See also Lee A. Albert, *Standing to Challenge Administrative Action: An Inadequate Surrogate for Claim for Relief*, 83 Yale L.J. 425 (1974); Richard B. Stewart, *The Reformation of American Administrative Law*, 88 Harv. L. Rev. 1669, 1679-80, 1717-18 (1975). The notion that only litigants asserting personal rights could seek judicial relief was not monolithic, either in England or in America. Recall that colonial courts did not limit themselves to supplicants of that description. See Chapter II, notes 1-3 and accompanying text. Moreover, both English and American courts issued common law writs on behalf of citizens who advanced no rights of their own, but wished only to force government officials to conform their behavior to law. See Raoul Berger, *Standing to Sue in Public Actions: Is it a Constitutional Requirement?*, 78 Yale. L.J. 816 (1969); Louis L. Jaffe, *Standing to Secure Judicial Review: Public Actions*, 74 Harv. L. Rev. 1265 (1961).

were not personal, *private* rights, but *public* rights: the rights of Americans at large to demand that governmental officials conduct themselves according to law.[65]

Academics gave the plaintiffs in the new public rights cases a name. Professor Hohfeld had previously developed a symmetrical conceptual framework in which one party's right was set opposite an opposing party's correlative duty to respect that right. Professor Jaffee argued that the plaintiffs in cases that fit the traditional, private rights model were "Hohfeldian" in the sense that they sought to litigate some question regarding their own legal rights. The plaintiffs in the new public rights cases were "non-Hohfeldian." They had enough interest in litigation to give them an incentive to sue, but they did not advance legal rights to demand that government officials perform duties owed to them personally.[66]

The Supreme Court initially reacted negatively to non-Hohfeldian plaintiffs. Conservative and progressive justices alike maintained that litigants had standing to appear in federal court only to enforce their own legal rights in the traditional way.[67] Early signals of the Court's commitment to the private rights model came

---

65. The nomenclature here is conventional, but problematic. The law of standing typically draws a crucial distinction between litigants who have personal *rights* that they wish to enforce in federal litigation and litigants who have only personal *interests*, but wish to vindicate someone else's rights or to enforce a federal legal standard that begets no personal rights in anyone. Nevertheless, courts and commentators refer interchangeably to litigation to enforce "public rights" and litigation in the "public interest." See Chapter I, note 70; see also Chapter V, notes 63-75 (discussing the "public rights" label in connection with adjudication by administrative agencies and legislative courts).

66. Louis L. Jaffe, *The Citizen as Litigant in Public Actions: The Non-Hohfeldian or Ideological Plaintiff*, 116 U. Pa. L. Rev. 1033 (1968); see Wesley N. Hohfeld, *Some Fundamental Legal Conceptions as Applied in Judicial Reasoning*, 23 Yale L.J. 16 (1913). Professor Jaffe explained that it would only confuse analysis to say that plaintiffs who are given authority to sue must, for that reason alone, be understood to have a "legally protected interest" or, in Jaffe's lexicon, a "right," to the treatment they demand. Id. at 1033-34. Jaffe recognized only two kinds of litigants: Hohfeldian plaintiffs who assert legal rights for standing purposes, on the one hand, and non-Hohfeldian plaintiffs who assert no such rights, on the other. He drew no (clear and working) distinction *within* the non-Hohfeldian category between plaintiffs who assert some personal interest that distinguishes them from the crowd and plaintiffs who are entirely fungible with all others in "large, indeterminate groups" and who sue entirely for ideological reasons. Professor Fallon also appears to treat non-Hohfeldian litigants as an indivisible class. As he describes them, they claim no "injuries" that are "easily definable in terms of personal, financial loss or other harms actionable at common law," nor a breach of "a legal duty running personally to them." Instead, they "aspire to secure the enforcement of legal principles that touch others as directly as themselves and that are valued for moral or political reasons independent of economic interests." Richard H. Fallon, Jr., *Of Justiciability, Remedies, and Public Law Litigation: Notes on the Jurisprudence of Lyons*, 59 N.Y.U. L. Rev. 1, 4 (1984). See notes 183-203 and accompanying text (discussing the way the zone test allows some litigants who assert no rights to sue but nonetheless excludes purely ideological plaintiffs).

67. The Court had used the term "standing" on numerous occasions, but had never before elaborated a doctrine of that name as a significant barrier to litigants' access to the federal courts. See Louis L. Jaffe, *Standing to Secure Judicial Review: Private Actions*, 75 Harv. L. Rev. 255, 256 (1961); Steven L. Winter, *The Metaphor of Standing and the Problem of Self-Governance*, 40 Stan. L. Rev. 1371, 1376 & n.26 (1988). Frankfurter and Landis did not mention standing in their treatise on the federal courts. Felix Frankfurter & James Landis, The Business of the Supreme Court: A Study in the Federal Judicial System (1928).

in Justice Brandeis' reservations about declaratory judgment actions in *Willing*[68] and in the Court's refusal to entertain a taxpayer suit challenging a federal statute in *Frothingham v. Mellon.*[69] In the ensuing years, Justice Frankfurter became the chief architect of standing doctrine. He recognized that private rights flowed not only from the common law, but also from statutes and the Constitution, and that standing doctrine must acknowledge that litigants asserting statutory and constitutional rights could have access to the federal courts. Frankfurter insisted, however, that plaintiffs must advance *rights* of some character. By his account, litigants could not sue in federal court to advance just *any* interests they might have in seeing government officials comply with federal law, but only to press "*legal* interests": *private legal rights* anchored in the common law, a statute, or the Constitution.[70]

Beginning in the 1930s, Congress countered the Court's standing doctrine with a different kind of legislation.[71] In § 402(b) of the Communications Act of 1934, for example, Congress authorized anyone "aggrieved" by the actions of the Federal Communications Commission to seek review in the courts. That provision (and others like it in statutes touching other agencies) did not purport to create a *substantive* right that, in turn, could be the basis for litigant standing (to enforce the right) in a federal lawsuit. Instead, it created a *litigation* right. It simply authorized a class of people (persons "aggrieved" by agency action) to take their complaints to court. Judge Frank captured the idea in yet another metaphor still in use today. He noted that Congress commonly authorized the Attorney General to litigate on behalf of the public.[72] According to Frank, Congress could equally appoint non-Hohfeldian "aggrieved" persons as "private attorneys gen-

---

68. *Willing v. Chicago Aud. Ass'n*, 277 U.S. 274 (1928); see note 12 and accompanying text.

69. 262 U.S. 447 (1923); see text accompanying note 106. Professor Sunstein has explained that conservative justices were content to allow only corporations resisting regulation to sue and that Justice Brandeis cooperated because he thought suits by beneficiaries threatened the development of an enlightened administrative state that would displace the common law system. Sunstein, note 64, at 1437-38. Professor Winter has described Brandeis' influence in *Frothingham* and related cases. Winter, note 67, at 1376-79. Neither *Willing* nor *Frothingham* mentioned standing explicitly, but both those early cases demonstrated the Court's concerns about novel forms of litigation that departed from the traditional model.

70. See *Joint Anti-Fascist Refugee Comm. v. McGrath*, 341 U.S. 123, 152 (1951) (concurring opinion) (emphasis added); accord *Coleman*, 307 U.S. at 460 (opinion of Frankfurter, J.). Professor Pushaw has traced Frankfurter's contributions in detail. See Robert J. Pushaw, Jr., *Justiciability and Separation of Powers: A Neo-Federalist Approach*, 81 Cornell L. Rev. 393, 458-63 (1996). Here again, conventional jargon can be confusing. When Justice Frankfurter referred to "legally protected interests," he meant legal *rights*. He did not mean personal *interests* that would be served indirectly if the courts forced government agents to obey the law. See note 66 (discussing Professor Jaffe's explanation); Administrative Law: Cases and Materials 305-06 (Cass, Diver & Beermann eds. 1994). For a different account of the nature and origins of standing doctrine, see Maxwell L. Stearns, *Standing Back from the Forest: Justiciability and Social Choice*, 83 Calif. L. Rev. 1309 (1995) (offering a public choice perspective on standing doctrine); Maxwell L. Stearns, *Standing and Social Choice: Historical Evidence*, 144 U. Pa. L. Rev. 309 (1995) (offering a revisionist explanation of the Court's decisions).

71. See Sunstein, note 64, at 1438-43.

72. See note 26.

eral" and empower them to sue in federal court to ensure, on behalf of the public, that federal regulators complied with federal law.[73]

The Supreme Court essentially adopted that view of the matter in *FCC v. Sanders Bros. Radio Station*.[74] In that case, the FCC awarded a license to the Telegraph Herald in Dubuque, authorizing that company to establish a new radio station in an area in which Sanders already operated a station. Sanders sought judicial review of the FCC's decision on the theory that it was "aggrieved" inasmuch as the new station would compete with Sanders' existing business. Sanders had no private *right* to be free of competition, derived from the common law, the Communications Act, or the Constitution.[75] Justice Roberts nevertheless sustained Sanders' standing on the basis of § 402(b). That provision, he explained, reflected a decision by Congress that litigants like Sanders, who were "injured" by the FCC's actions, had a sufficient "interest" to bring any errors of law the FCC might commit to the attention of the courts. Roberts confirmed in *Sanders* that Congress had "power" to "confer such standing" on private litigants.[76] In *Scripps-Howard Radio v. FCC*,[77] Justice Frankfurter himself conceded that, pursuant to § 402(b), litigants who had no personal rights of their own nonetheless had standing "as representatives of the public interest."[78]

In some minds, actions by private attorneys general who claimed no invasion of their own rights came perilously close to requests for advisory opinions.[79]

---

73. *Assoc. Indus. v. Ickes*, 134 F.2d 694, 704 (2d Cir.), *vacated on other gr'ds*, 320 U.S. 707 (1943).

74. 309 U.S. 470 (1940).

75. Id. at 475. See *Tennessee Elec. Power Co. v. TVA*, 306 U.S. 118, 137-38 (1939).

76. 309 U.S. at 477.

77. 316 U.S. 4 (1942).

78. Id. at 14. The question in *Scripps-Howard* was whether a radio station that claimed only a competitive interest (but no legal rights) could obtain a stay of an FCC order granting a license to another station, pending the court's review of whether the FCC had followed applicable legal standards. Justice Frankfurter held that the reviewing court could grant such a stay. The Communications Act cases, *Sanders* and *Scripps-Howard*, put the standing issue graphically. The primary substantive legal standard the Act required the FCC to follow in deciding whether to issue licenses was whether the "public convenience, interest, or necessity" would be served. 47 U.S.C. § 307(a). The plaintiff in *Sanders* contended on the merits that the Commission had not developed sufficient evidence to warrant the conclusion that granting a license to the Telegraph Herald met that standard. The plaintiff in *Scripps-Howard* claimed that the FCC had awarded a license to a competitor in violation of its own rules (and due process). The Commission held no hearing in which the plaintiff might have shown that it was not in the "public interest" to introduce a new station into the area. Professor Jaffe explained that *Sanders* and *Scripps-Howard* recognized standing in non-Hohfeldian plaintiffs. Those cases explicitly denied that the plaintiffs had a "substantive right to be free of competition" but nonetheless allowed them to sue. Jaffe insisted that it would be circular to say that, since the plaintiffs in *Sanders* and *Scripps-Howard* had standing, they must necessarily have had a substantive "right" under the Communications Act to be treated in the way they demanded. If the kind of substantive right that had always sufficed for standing was merely a right to "have the law enforced," then, to Jaffe, the requirement of a "right" for standing was "meaningless." In *Sanders* and *Scripps-Howard*, the plaintiffs obtained standing without asserting any rights at all, but then were able simply to ask the courts to enforce the law. Jaffe, note 66, at 1035-36.

79. See, e.g., Albert, note 64, at 478; notes 6-22 and accompanying text (discussing the ban on advisory opinions).

Moreover, the public interest that private litigants proposed to vindicate was not monolithic. Private attorneys general might press only their own narrow perspectives and fail adequately to represent the interests of others with different points of view.[80] Nevertheless, the Court struck a tacit bargain with Congress and the public rights suits that Congress wished to authorize: Congress would be permitted to decide, on a case-by-case basis, whether the country would be well served by allowing private litigants to challenge agency action under specified federal statutes. Yet in the absence of a special standing provision like § 402(b) authorizing suits with respect to a particular agency's performance, litigants would still be required to advance their own legal rights.[81]

APA

In 1946, Congress enacted the Administrative Procedure Act and, concomitantly, the general provision on judicial review now codified in 5 U.S.C. § 702 — which authorized review of the actions of most federal agencies.[82] That provision authorized a "person" to seek judicial review if he or she either suffered a "legal wrong" because of agency action or was "adversely affected or aggrieved by agency action within the meaning of a relevant statute." By some accounts, § 702 merely codified the existing state of affairs. The reference to a "legal wrong" reflected the traditional rights-based model: One suffered a legal *wrong* when a legal *right* was violated. The reference to persons affected or aggrieved within the meaning of a relevant statute referred to litigants whom Congress had independently authorized to challenge actions by certain agencies. Accordingly, a "relevant" statute was a provision like § 402(b) of the Communications Act — a statute authorizing private litigants who claimed no rights of their own to sue on behalf of the public to ensure that a particular agency complied with the law.[83] In *Ass'n of Data Processing Svc. Orgs. v. Camp*,[84] however, the Court read § 702 in an entirely different way.[85]

In *Data Processing*, the Comptroller of the Currency ruled that banks could provide data processing services to their customers. The plaintiffs were independent data processing companies, who challenged that ruling on the ground that it violated the Bank Services Corporation Act, which limited banks to "bank services." The plaintiffs did not claim that the Act gave them any substantive right to be free of competition. Like the competing radio station in *Sanders*, they claimed only that they suffered economic harm from the Comptroller's ruling, because it allowed banks to enter their market. Justice Douglas acknowledged that, in the main, the Court had previously held that only plaintiffs who claimed an invasion of a "legal right" had standing to sue in federal court. The *Sanders* case was an exception that could be explained on the basis of § 402(b), which

---

80. Id. at 481. See note 169 and accompanying text (discussing this point in connection with third-party claims).

81. See *Perkins*, 310 U.S. at 125.

82. See Chapter II, note 77 and accompanying text.

83. See, e.g., Louis L. Jaffe, Judicial Control of Administrative Action 528-30 (1965); Richard B. Stewart, *Standing for Solidarity*, 88 Yale L.J. 1559, 1569 (1979). Justice Scalia once read § 702 this way. See Antonin Scalia, *The Doctrine of Standing as an Essential Element of the Separation of Powers*, 17 Suffolk L. Rev. 881, 887-88 (1983). He now recognizes that the Court has rejected it. See *Lujan v. Nat'l Wildlife Fed.*, 497 U.S. 871, 883 (1990) (opinion for the Court).

84. 397 U.S. 150, 153 (1970).

85. For a discussion of § 702's function as a right-of-action statute, see Chapter VIII, notes 91, 95-97 and accompanying text.

was inapplicable to the case at hand.[86] Douglas nonetheless held, in effect, that the conception of standing the Court had embraced in *Sanders* was not limited to that case, but was transferable to all standing cases.

By Douglas' account, the plaintiffs in *Data Processing* had standing to attack the Comptroller's ruling because: (1) they suffered "injury in fact" resulting from the Comptroller's ruling, and (2) their interests were "arguably" within the "zone of interests... protected or regulated by the statute or constitutional guarantee" they wished to enforce.[87] The plaintiffs had to demonstrate injury as a constitutional prerequisite for standing. Without that, they had no actual dispute with the Comptroller, no case or controversy within the meaning of Article III. The plaintiffs needed an interest that was "arguably" within the zone of interests protected by the Bank Services Corporation Act in order to satisfy an additional non-constitutional requirement for standing that Congress had created in § 702 — namely, that they must be "adversely affected" or "aggrieved" within the meaning of that Act.[88] It was clear enough that the Act limited banks to "banking" primarily to safeguard accounts.[89] Justice Douglas was satisfied, however, that the competitive interests of the data processing companies were also "arguably" covered.[90]

In effect, Justice Douglas read § 702 of the Administrative Procedure Act to do for all litigants seeking to challenge the actions of all agencies (covered by the APA) what Justice Roberts had read § 402(b) of the Communications Act to do for litigants seeking to challenge actions of one agency (the FCC).[91] But Douglas did more than that. He repudiated the rights-based conception of standing that had formed the previous baseline and replaced it with a new harm-based conception. Douglas did not deny that litigants who could assert legal rights could establish standing.[92] But he insisted that litigants were not generally *required* to advance rights. They were, instead, generally able to establish standing on the basis of "injury" to an "interest." Frankfurter's "legal interest" test [that is, the rights-based test] went not to the question of standing, but "to the merits" of litigants' legal claims.[93] The new harm-based approach was not merely an interpretation of § 702, limited to attacks

---

86. 397 U.S. at 153 n.1.

87. Id. at 152-53.

88. Professor Davis had previously argued that the reference to anyone "adversely affected" dispensed with any non-constitutional standing requirement and authorized anyone with injury in fact to sue. 3 Kenneth C. Davis, Administrative Law Treatise § 22.06, at 232 (1958).

89. The legislative history suggests that some members of Congress were concerned that if banks extended their operations to other activities, they might put their reserves at risk and compromise the safety of savings and checking accounts.

90. Having settled the standing question, Justice Douglas turned to (and rejected) the Comptroller's argument that Congress had absolutely precluded judicial review of his ruling by statute. 397 U.S. at 157; see Chapter IV, notes 83-89 and accompanying text.

91. Effectively, this is to say, *Data Processing* understood that Congress had decided against appraising the advisability of private suits with respect to each agency in turn, which would have produced a series of provisions like § 402(b) of the Communications Act. Instead, Congress had deputized private attorneys general *en masse* to litigate with all manner of agencies. See Administrative Law, note 70, at 310.

92. The "legal wrong" language in § 702 reaffirmed that, for Congress' part, litigants with rights to enforce had standing to attack agency action.

93. 397 U.S. at 153-54. See notes 251-63 and accompanying text (discussing the link between standing and the merits of litigants' legal claims).

on federal agency action. It was a comprehensive reconceptualization of standing, applicable in every context in which the standing question might arise.

The *Data Processing* decision accommodated the very public rights litigation that the Court had previously discouraged. By adopting a harm-based conception of standing, the Court made it possible for would-be litigants to achieve standing on the basis of observable, value-neutral *facts*, without any necessary reference to *law*.[94] That allowed non-Hohfeldian private attorneys general to gain access to the federal courts. The Warren Court regarded standing as a threshold requirement serving only to ensure that litigants have a "personal stake in the outcome" of a lawsuit to create an incentive to supply effective advocacy.[95] A harm-based framework serves that purpose inasmuch as it selects for litigants who will gain personally from the lawsuits they wish to undertake.

By some accounts, however, the Warren Court's attempt to distinguish between interests and rights has impeded the very public rights lawsuits the Court meant to nurture.[96] On reflection, what counts as injury brought about by a violation of law may depend on the law that is said to have been violated. If some consequential injuries seem obvious (a punch in the nose, for example), it is not because the fact of physical harm is analytically independent of the law governing assaults. It is because the relevant legal norms are so deeply rooted in the common law backdrop of American culture that their acceptance is universal and essentially unconscious. Accordingly, when the Warren Court assumed that injuries can be identified apart from the law, the Court condemned standing doctrine to consider *as* injuries only non-controversial harms of the sort the common law understood. That, in turn, means comparatively tangible burdens imposed on particular individuals.

Paradoxically, by this account, the Warren Court's harm-based conception of standing actually reinforces the rights-based conception of standing that *Data Processing* hoped to discard.[97] As the Court searches for a context in which to determine what qualifies as an interest, the Court falls back into reflexive reliance on common law understandings. Moreover, the resulting ersatz rights-based standing doctrine is more virulent than the original article. Since it purports not to rely on law at all, it discourages any open examination of interests in light of modern statutes. Those statutes, were they consulted, would invite a more expansive understanding of human interests that can be injured. Congress rarely attempts to protect identifiable individuals from harm, but rather fashions general

---

94. Professor Nichol explains that "injury in fact" is to be "distinguished, one supposes, from injury protected by law." Gene R. Nichol, Jr., *Rethinking Standing*, 72 Calif. L. Rev. 68, 74 (1984).

95. *Flast v. Cohen*, 392 U.S. 83, 101 (1968); see notes 107-10 and accompanying text. Justice Douglas said in *Data Processing* that the constitutional prerequisites of standing serve only this functional purpose. 397 U.S. at 151-52, citing *Flast*.

96. For elaborations of this thesis, see Albert, note 64; William A. Fletcher, *The Structure of Standing*, 98 Yale L.J. 221 (1988); Cass R. Sunstein, *Standing Injuries*, 1993 Sup. Ct. Rev. 37.

97. See Sunstein, note 64, at 1432-33; note 135 (describing Sunstein's proposed approach). Professor Nichol also argues that the current Court's approach to injuries is unjustifiably wedded to common law thinking and that the Court would do better to open its mind to the collective public rights that federal law entails. Gene R. Nichol, Jr., *Justice Scalia, Standing, and Public Law Litigation*, 42 Duke L.J. 1141, 1156-60 (1993). See notes 226-50 (discussing recent signals from the Supreme Court in this vein).

regulatory schemes to achieve systemic improvements for society as a whole: safer factories and cleaner water. When regulatory statutes are violated, they produce harms. But those harms are not the discrete personal injuries that the Court's standing doctrine appears to contemplate, but more diffuse deprivations of the generalized benefits that Congress means to generate. Injuries to interests of that kind might be easier to identify and appreciate if the Court were to focus attention directly on the statutes enacted to protect them.[98]

The Warren Court also failed to perpetuate its understanding of the reason for requiring litigants to have a personal interest in litigation. The Rehnquist Court rejects the notion that the "injury" requirement only ensures effective advocacy and insists, instead, that standing doctrine screens out litigants whose lawsuits would have federal courts interfere unduly with the other branches of the national government or the states.[99] The Court has explained that "the law of Article III standing is built on a single basic idea—the idea of separation of powers."[100] A disputed case is essential, then, not merely to sharpen legal issues for adjudication, but to confine the courts' law-making function to traditional disputes and to divert broader issues of public law and policy to the political arena. The Rehnquist Court has preserved the harm-based framework for standing that

---

98. See note 135 and accompanying text (discussing illustrations). The point is not that law is the exclusive source of value, but rather that law both reflects and projects value in a subtle, often unconscious way. Stated in a mild form, this argument may be insightful, but not startling. Stated in a strong form, it can be controversial. Professor Albert has argued, for example, that it would have been "inconceivable" to recognize environmental damage and even anti-competitive interests if Congress had not enacted legislation protecting interests of that kind. Albert, note 64, at 491.

99. Justice Scalia has acknowledged that if effective advocacy were the issue, the Supreme Court would not *reject*, but would *prefer*, ideologically committed organizational advocates, which promise to build a more convincing case than would a single, isolated individual. See Scalia, note 83, at 891. Professor Bandes argues that by allowing only litigants with personal injuries to sue, the Court actually invites plaintiffs with "trivial or tenuous" contentions into the federal courts to "argue the important constitutional claims of absentees." Susan Bandes, *The Idea of a Case*, 42 Stan. L. Rev. 227, 299 (1990). To avoid dismissal on standing grounds, ideological litigants must locate surrogates who can allege sufficient personal injury. Thus the Court's insistence that plaintiffs who suffer personal harm must be involved may actually (and perversely) demand precisely what the justices ostensibly wish to discourage—lawsuits that have the appearance of traditional private disputes, but are actually contrived to satisfy the Court's standing rules. Professor Tushnet argues that civil rights attorneys typically find it strategically advantageous to recruit individual clients and would do so without the spur that standing doctrine provides. Mark V. Tushnet, *The Sociology of Article III: A Response to Professor Brilmayer*, 93 Harv. L. Rev. 1698, 1713 (1980). Professor Brilmayer contends that, if that is so, then Tushnet and others should not object to the Court's extant doctrine. Lea Brilmayer, *A Reply*, 93 Harv. L. Rev. 1727 (1980).

100. *Allen v. Wright*, 468 U.S. 737, 752 (1984); see notes 125-29, 142-43, 151-52 and accompanying text. Justice O'Connor began her important opinion for the Court in *Allen* with a quotation from Judge Robert Bork: "All of the doctrines that cluster about Article III—not only standing but mootness, ripeness, political question, and the like—relate in part, and in different though overlapping ways, to an idea, which is more than an intuition but less than a rigorous and explicit theory, about the constitutional and prudential limits to the powers of an unelected, unrepresentative judiciary in our kind of government." *Vander Jagt v. O'Neil*, 699 F.2d 1166, 1178-79 (D.C. Cir. 1983) (Bork, J., concurring). According to the Warren Court, standing had nothing to do with the separation of powers. See *Flast*, 392 U.S. at 100; note 95. The Court has since repudiated that position expressly. See, e.g., *Spencer v. Kemna*, 118 S.Ct. 978, 985 (1998); *Lewis v. Casey*, 518 U.S. 343, 353 n.3 (1996).

Data Processing established. Yet to make that framework serve as the basis for allocating power among the three branches, the Court limits injuries to discrete personal harms, tightly linked to equally discrete violations of law. That, in turn, confirms the suspicion that the rights-based conception of standing is still dominant, hiding behind the formal requirement of injuries to interests.[101]

C. Standing: Constitutional Prerequisites

1. Injury in Fact

Litigants must allege that they have suffered, are suffering, or will "imminently" suffer "injury in fact." Stated in this way (as a *factual* matter), the injury requirement appears to demand only that litigants truthfully allege some nontrivial harm. When Justice Douglas initially coined the "injury in fact" formulation in *Data Processing*, that is precisely what he meant.[102] The current Court continues to insist that the injury required for standing is *de facto* harm and that (at the constitutional level) standing "in no way depends on the merits" of litigants' claims that "particular conduct is illegal."[103] Yet not every factual harm will do. The Court draws distinctions within the category of factual injuries, labeling some injuries "judicially cognizable,"[104] while finding others to be inadequate. Judicially cognizable injuries are typically (though not always) "particularized" and "personal" to the plaintiffs at bar.[105] As the Court searches for injuries of that nature, it gropes backward to the rights-based conception of standing that preceded *Data Processing*. The Court is uncomfortable with deploying federal judicial power in service of citizens who wish only to realize the benefits that modern regulatory legislation produces for society at large.

Decisions regarding the injury requirement can be organized in three categories: (1) cases in which the Court finds it sufficient that taxpayers allege economic harm when the government spends money from the public treasury; (2) cases in which the Court finds it insufficient that litigants assert "generalized grievances" shared by the public at large; and (3) cases in which the Court finds personal injuries sufficient only by characterizing them in a way that necessarily

---

101. E.g., Nichol, note 97, at 1156-60. Numerous academics critique the Court's insistence on the private rights model as the constitutional baseline for standing. Professor Bandes argues that it would be more consistent with the Constitution to adopt the public rights model and thus to see the federal courts' primary function as the elaboration of constitutional law. Bandes, note 99. Professor Doernberg argues that reliance on the private rights model makes standing unjustifiably individualistic, so that federal courts are unable to enforce collective rights. Donald L. Doernberg, *"We the People": John Locke, Collective Constitutional Rights, and Standing to Challenge Government Action*, 73 Calif. L. Rev. 52 (1985). Professor Winter also finds the Court's framework to be overly individualistic. See Winter, note 67.

102. See note 94 and accompanying text. But see notes 96-98 and accompanying text (discussing the arguable links between what is perceived as factual harm and the surrounding legal environment).

103. *Warth v. Seldin*, 422 U.S. 490, 500 (1975).

104. *Allen*, 468 U.S. at 752.

105. *Raines v. Byrd*, 117 S.Ct. 2312, 2317 (1997).

implicates the content of the legal claims litigants wish to advance, despite the harm-based conception of standing the Court purports to employ.

Taxpayer cases. In *Frothingham v. Mellon*,[106] a federal taxpayer challenged a statute under which the government funded medical services. She contended that the statute violated the Commerce Clause and due process. Justice Sutherland recognized that the plaintiff had an economic interest in the money held by the treasury. But that interest was "minute and indeterminate." Moreover, the effect of any particular expenditure was "remote, fluctuating and uncertain." Accordingly, Sutherland refused to allow the plaintiff to proceed. In *Flast v. Cohen*,[107] by contrast, the Warren Court held that federal taxpayers *did* have standing to attack a federal spending measure, ostensibly on the basis of their remote pecuniary interest in the state of the national treasury. The *Flast* decision roughly coincided with *Data Processing* and thus reflected the Court's nascent idea that standing should turn on the existence of factual injury, even the modest factual injury that any federal taxpayer might suffer from a disbursement of federal funds.

The Court distinguished *Frothingham* in *Flast*, but on grounds that were not of constitutional moment. The plaintiffs in *Flast* argued that a federal statutory scheme funneled public funds to parochial schools in violation of the Establishment Clause and that they were therefore being taxed to support religion. Chief Justice Warren explained that the plaintiffs had standing, because they demonstrated *both* a nexus between their status (as taxpayers who contributed to the public fisc) and the kind of legislative enactment they wished to challenge (a spending measure that disbursed public money) *and* a nexus between their status (as taxpayers) and the constitutional provision they contended the statute violated (the Establishment Clause—the chief purpose of which is to prohibit taxation for religious ends). By establishing the first nexus, the plaintiffs in *Flast* satisfied the (constitutional) "injury" requirement for standing; by establishing the second, they met a further non-constitutional standing requirement that the Court created for the occasion. The plaintiff in *Frothingham*, too, met the constitutional injury test, but failed the second, prudential standard.[108]

The decision in *Flast* illustrates the Warren Court's effort to break the hold that the rights-based conception of standing then had on access to the federal courts.[109] Specifically, Chief Justice Warren plainly meant to allow litigants to advance claims under the Establishment Clause where, previously, that provision of

---

106. 262 U.S. 447 (1923).

107. 392 U.S. 83 (1968).

108. Professor Davis explained at the time that despite some ambiguity in the *Flast* opinion, the Court regarded the injury in that case to be the admittedly "trifling" economic harm that taxpayers suffer when the government spends public money. See Kenneth C. Davis, *Standing: Taxpayers and Others*, 35 U. Chi. L. Rev. 601, 609-12 (1968). See also *Doremus v. Bd. of Ed.*, 342 U.S. 429, 434-35 (1952) (explaining that state taxpayers can establish standing when they press "good-faith pocketbook" actions). See notes 199-201 and accompanying text (explaining that the second nexus that Chief Justice Warren described in *Flast* was actually the zone test that the Court would soon announce in *Data Processing*). Mrs. Frothingham could not connect her status as a taxpayer (i.e., her economic interest in the treasury) to the Commerce Clause and due process claims she wished to advance, because those constitutional provisions are not especially conceived as limits on federal spending.

109. See notes 70-81 and accompanying text (describing the state of standing doctrine at the time).

the Constitution had largely gone without judicial enforcement. To that end, he articulated a formula for taxpayer standing that neatly fit the Establishment Clause cases he wished to make justiciable. Insofar as the constitutional element of that formula went, however, Warren was satisfied with a kind of injury that has not been sufficient in any other context since. The plaintiffs in *Flast* alleged no peculiar harm that distinguished them from any other taxpayers. Accordingly, *Flast* is the one instance in which litigants established the constitutionally required factual injury on the basis of harms they shared with the public at large.[110]

Generalized grievances. Apart from cases controlled by *Flast*, factual injuries will suffice for standing only if they are concrete, particularized, and personal to plaintiffs themselves. Injuries are insufficient if they are "generalized grievances" to be addressed in the political arena, not in the courts. In *FEC v. Akins*,[111] Justice Breyer explained that generalized grievances have two properties. They are: (1) "widely shared" with large numbers of other people; and (2) by nature, "abstract and indefinite."[112]

In *Akins*, the Federal Election Commission determined that the American Israel Public Affairs Committee was not a "political committee" within the meaning of the Federal Election Campaign Act and thus was not required to disclose its list of contributors. The plaintiffs were voters who alleged that they suffered

---

110. Taxpayer-litigants must also establish a nexus between their status as taxpayers and the statute or constitutional provision they wish to enforce. That further requirement does nothing to ensure that their injuries are more personal. It does mean, however, that *Flast* has little doctrinal significance for cases in which taxpayers challenge spending measures on grounds other than the Establishment clause. In a concurring opinion in *Flast*, Justice Stewart took a position more in keeping with rights-based standing doctrine that, in 1968, was formally still viable. He argued that taxpayers have a constitutional *right* under the Establishment Clause to be free from taxation for religious purposes and that they therefore have standing, on the strength of that *right*, to challenge federal payments to parochial schools. 392 U.S. at 114; see text accompanying note 70. That view has won a measure of support in the academic community. See note 209. In *Valley Forge Christian College v. Americans United for Separation of Church and State*, 454 U.S. 464, 482 (1982), however, the Court denied that the Establishment Clause confers on all taxpayers a "shared individuated" constitutional right to be free of taxation for religious purposes. The taxpayer-plaintiffs in *Valley Forge* claimed that a federal agency had given a private sectarian college a parcel of public property in violation of the Establishment Clause. Chief Justice Rehnquist restricted *Flast* to taxpayer attacks on federal statutes (rather than actions by federal agencies), and to attacks on statutes enacted pursuant to the spending power (rather than dispositions of federal property under U.S. Const. art. IV, § 3, cl.2). Professor Fletcher has suggested that it would "dignify" *Valley Forge* to treat it as "anything more than an intellectually disingenuous way to undercut *Flast*." See Fletcher, note 96, at 268. The Court has left *Flast* in place to control the class of cases for which the analysis in that decision was tailored—namely, taxpayer suits challenging federal disbursements on Establishment Clause grounds. On reflection, *Flast* may remain intact only because the current Court acknowledges the need for federal adjudication of Establishment Clause attacks on spending measures and sees no viable alternative to taxpayer suits as a means to that end.
111. 118 S.Ct. 1777 (1998).
112. Justice Breyer acknowledged that the Court has sometimes "styled" the ban on "generalized grievances" as a non-constitutional prudential standing rule, e.g., *Allen*, 468 U.S. at 751, and sometimes has treated it as a limit on the factual injuries that meet constitutional standards for standing. The latter position has prevailed most recently. E.g., *Lujan*, 504 U.S. at 560; *United States v. Hays*, 515 U.S. 737, 742 (1995).

factual harm in that they needed the contributor list in order to evaluate candidates that AIPAC supported and to track and publicize AIPAC's political influence. The plaintiffs sued the FEC, contending that AIPAC *was* a "political committee" and must disclose the information the Act required from organizations of that character. Justice Breyer acknowledged that the plaintiffs' interest in the AIPAC's contributor list was widely shared by voters at large. Yet that interest was not so abstract that it constituted a generalized grievance. Accordingly, the plaintiffs satisfied the constitutional injury requirement.[113]

The best illustrations of grievances meeting both parts of the *Akins* test for generalized grievances are cases in which plaintiffs assert a genuine, but commonly shared, psychological or ideological interest in seeing that government officers comply with the law. In *Schlesinger v. Reservists Committee to Stop the War*,[114] the Court refused to allow citizen-plaintiffs standing to challenge members of Congress who held military commissions in alleged violation of the Incompatibility Clause.[115] And in *United States v. Richardson*,[116] the Court similarly denied taxpayer-plaintiffs standing to attack Congress' failure to publish the CIA's budget in alleged violation of the Statement of Account Clause.[117] The injuries implicated in *Reservists* and *Richardson* existed in a factual sense. But those factual injuries would not suffice, because they were both widely shared and abstract.[118]

Environmental cases also help to define what counts as a generalized grievance. In *Sierra Club v. Morton*,[119] the club charged that the United States Forest Service's approval of a ski resort in the Mineral King Valley violated federal environmental statutes. The club alleged that it would be harmed if the project proceeded, because it had an interest in conserving the nation's natural resources. The Court held that the club's concerns for the environment were too generalized to be cognizable, but that some of the club's members might be able to assert sufficient injury as individuals, provided they sincerely alleged that they used the particular area to be developed and personally stood to suffer the loss of its pris-

---

113. In dissent, Justice Scalia argued that the Court's analysis of generalized grievances allowed any voter to challenge the FEC's administration of the Act and thus to force the FEC to undertake proceedings against organizations like AIPAC even when the FEC itself thought there was no basis for doing so. Scalia insisted that Breyer gave insufficient attention to cases demanding that injuries be "particularized" and, as a result, invited the courts to interfere with the executive's responsibility to enforce federal law. In truth, Justice Breyer's elaboration of generalized grievances *was* more generous to plaintiffs than might have been expected in light of other decisions in recent years. Nevertheless, the two-part test for generalized grievances now appears to be controlling.

114. 418 U.S. 208 (1974).

115. U.S. Const. art. I, § 6, cl.2.

116. 418 U.S. 166 (1974).

117. U.S. Const. art. I, § 9, cl.7.

118. Chief Justice Burger acknowledged in *Richardson* that if the taxpayers in that case had no standing, it might well be that no one did. That was not disturbing, he said, because it only suggested that the question itself might be political. 418 U.S. at 179. See notes 33-56 and accompanying text. Burger thus suggested that standing doctrine and the political question doctrine can reinforce each other as independent, but related, explanations for routing delicate issues to the political branches. Professor Bandes argues, by contrast, that the Chief Justice merely shored up "one dubious assumption" about the federal courts' role "with another." Bandes, note 99, at 268.

119. 405 U.S. 727 (1972).

tine beauty if the resort was constructed. The difficulty in *Sierra Club*, then, was that the club itself was not "among" those would-be litigants suffering special injury.[120]

In *Lujan v. Defenders of Wildlife*,[121] environmentalists sued to force the Secretary of the Interior to consult with other agency heads regarding the effect of overseas construction projects on endangered species. The plaintiffs alleged that they had previously visited sites where endangered animals (crocodiles in Egypt, elephants and leopards in Sri Lanka) were at risk from the effects of development and intended to return in hopes of actually seeing those creatures in their natural habitat. Justice Scalia acknowledged that the "desire" to "observe an animal species, even for purely aesthetic purposes" was "undeniably" an interest, an injury to which could establish standing in a proper case. He concluded, however, that the plaintiffs in *Lujan* had failed to allege sufficiently personal injuries of that kind, because they, like the club in *Sierra Club*, had not shown themselves to be "among the injured." Their previous visits to Egypt and Sri Lanka "prove[d] nothing," and their professed "intent" to return was speculative in the absence of "concrete plans."[122]

Once the Court specifies what is required in cases like *Sierra Club* and *Lujan*, plaintiffs may be able to compensate and comply. On remand in *Sierra Club* itself, individual members of the club alleged that they used the valley for recreational purposes and thus suffered the kind of personal injury that the Supreme Court had found wanting in the club itself. The district court agreed.[123] In *United*

---

120. Id. at 735. An organization can establish standing on the basis of injuries it suffers *as* an organization. In *Havens Realty Corp. v. Coleman*, 455 U.S. 363 (1982), the Court found it sufficient that a group advocating open housing alleged that it had been forced to expend additional resources to assist its clients because of the defendant's practice of steering racial minorities into segregated areas. An organization can also litigate on behalf of its members if: (1) the members themselves have standing to sue; (2) the interests the suit seeks to protect are "germane" to the organization's purposes; and (3) the litigation does not require that individual members participate in order to develop either the merits of the claim or the form of appropriate relief. *Hunt v. Washington State Apple Adv. Comm'n*, 432 U.S. 333, 343 (1977). See *UAW v. Brock*, 477 U.S. 274, 290 (1986) (rejecting the argument that members should be required to advance common claims in class actions). Units of government may have standing to advance both their own sovereign or quasi-sovereign interests and the claims of citizens. See *Alfred L. Snapp & Son v. Puerto Rico*, 458 U.S. 592 (1982). For a discussion of *parens patriae* litigation, see Ann Woolhandler & Michael G. Collins, *State Standing*, 81 Va. L. Rev. 387 (1995).

121. 504 U.S. 555 (1992).

122. Id. at 562-64. The plaintiffs advanced other, more creative interests peculiar to environmental litigation. But Justice Scalia dismissed those contentions summarily. Professor Carlson has suggested various ways in which environmental concerns are unique (and Scalia's analysis shallow). Ann E. Carlson, *Standing for the Environment*, 45 UCLA L. Rev. 937 (1998). Justice Scalia said in *Lujan* that the constitutional "injury in fact" test requires an "invasion of a legally-protected interest." Id. at 555. That phrase suggested the rights-based conception of standing that prevailed prior to *Data Processing*. See text accompanying note 70; note 66 (discussing Professor Jaffe's analysis). It is hard to think that Justice Scalia intended to convey that meaning, given that he went immediately on to the conventional question whether the plaintiffs suffered factual harm. Writing for the Court in *Steel Co. v. Citizens for a Better Environment*, 118 S.Ct. 1003 (1998), Justice Scalia stated the constitutional requirement as "concrete injury in fact." Id. at 1018.

123. *Sierra Club v. Morton*, 348 F. Supp. 219 (N.D. Calif. 1972). In a concurring opinion in *Lujan*, Justice Kennedy suggested that the plaintiffs in that case might yet be able to allege sufficient injury if they purchased airline tickets or even if they merely announced a

States v. SCRAP,[124] members of an organization called Students Challenging Regulatory Agency Procedures (SCRAP) contended that the Interstate Commerce Commission had taken action that diminished their enjoyment of the parks in Washington, D.C. Since the students alleged that they visited the parks that would be affected, the Court held that they had asserted personal injury in fact for standing purposes.

The Court has declined to find sufficient injuries in other leading cases and, in so doing, has solidified the understanding that generalized grievances cannot ordinarily be the basis for standing. In *Allen v. Wright*,[125] African American children challenged IRS standards for determining whether private schools were entitled to tax exempt status. They alleged that the standards did not screen out schools that refused to admit black students and thus effectively allowed segregationist academies to receive favorable tax treatment in violation of federal statutes and the Due Process Clause. Justice O'Connor understood the plaintiffs to allege two kinds of injury. First, they contended that they suffered harm "by the mere fact of Government financial aid to discriminatory private schools." Second, they argued that the tax exemptions the IRS had granted to segregationist schools made those private schools more attractive to white students and thus "impaired" the plaintiffs' ability to attend desegregated public schools.

Justice O'Connor rejected the plaintiffs' first contention out of hand. To the extent the children advanced an interest in seeing the IRS comply with federal law, their injury was no more "judicially cognizable" than the injuries in *Reservists* and *Richardson*. Citizens, she explained, "have no standing to complain simply that their government is violating the law." The children in *Allen* came no closer to the mark to the extent they alleged "stigmatic injury" or "denigration" from government complicity in racial discrimination. Injuries of that kind were not cognizable, because the children themselves "were not personally subject to the challenged discrimination." By contrast, Justice O'Connor found the *Allen* plaintiffs' second contention sufficient to establish injury for standing purposes. Their interest in attending desegregated public schools was "concrete" by contrast to their interest in government compliance with federal anti-discrimination law, because it was an interest they could claim as their own and did not share with the public at large.[126]

The difference between the injuries Justice O'Connor found inadequate in *Allen* and the injury she found sufficient is the difference between generalized grievances and a more personal harm. O'Connor resisted the notion that any African American citizen who is offended by race discrimination can, on that basis alone, allege the injury necessary to challenge that discrimination in federal court.[127] She insisted that only African Americans who suffer personal injuries that distinguish them from others can make the required showing.[128] That inter-

---

"date certain" on which they would return to the sites they had previously visited. 504 U.S. at 579.

124. 412 U.S. 669 (1973).

125. 468 U.S. 737 (1984).

126. Id. at 754-56.

127. Justice O'Connor explained that if "stigmatic injury" were enough, it would follow that an African American in Hawaii could challenge an IRS tax exemption granted to a private school in Maine. Id. at 771 n.3.

128. If, for example, the children in *Allen* had alleged that they had been denied admission to private schools on racial grounds in violation of federal law, they plainly would have

pretation of the injury requirement did not seriously diminish the sheer number of litigants in *Allen*. O'Connor recognized that the plaintiffs represented millions of children who could allege the very kind of injury she found to be cognizable. But her refusal to credit generalized grievances for standing purposes made the important doctrinal point.[129]

The characterization of injuries. In other instances, the Court has adjusted the harm-based conception of standing in another way—by consulting the legal claims that litigants wish to pursue in order to characterize the injuries they allege for standing purposes. In *Regents of the University of California v. Bakke*,[130] an unsuccessful white applicant for admission to medical school challenged the school's affirmative action program under which seats in the entering class were set aside for minority candidates. On first blush, it appeared that the plaintiff could show no personal injury. His ideological objection to race-based admissions policies was a generalized grievance that would not suffice, and he could not demonstrate that the personal disappointment he had suffered in being denied admission was related to the affirmative action program about which he complained. Justice Powell nevertheless sustained standing in *Bakke* by recharacterizing the plaintiff's injury: Because of his race, he had not been considered for one of the sixteen places reserved for minority candidates. He had suffered per-

---

suffered judicially cognizable injury and thus would have had standing to challenge their exclusion. E.g., *Runyan v. McCrary*, 427 U.S. 160 (1976).

129. In *Raines v. Byrd*, 117 S.Ct. 2312 (1997), the Court found injuries to be insufficient because they were shared with a few hundred others. Members of Congress complained that the Line Item Veto Act authorized the President to cancel spending measures and thus to dilute the effect of their votes for those bills. Chief Justice Rehnquist explained that the plaintiffs suffered no judicially cognizable injuries and thus lacked standing. They could not allege that they would be denied an opportunity to vote on any particular bill. Nor could they claim that their votes would be discounted and that a bill they supported would fail only because their participation in the legislative process was entirely nullified. They were affected by the Act in precisely the same way that other members of the House and Senate were affected. Of course, by denying standing to the plaintiffs in *Raines*, the Court only postponed an examination of the Act's validity. At some point, the President would cancel a particular spending measure, and the "putative beneficiaries" of that provision would then suffer a "cognizable injury" that would allow them to sue for judicial relief. Id. at 2325 (Souter, J., concurring). The Chief Justice did not suggest in *Raines* that the validity of the Act presented a non-justiciable political question. See notes 33-56 and accompanying text. It did not. The result in *Raines* illustrates, however, that by declining to entertain generalized grievances under the heading of standing doctrine, the courts can avoid politically sensitive controversies—at least for the moment. See note 52. In the next Term, when plaintiffs who could show economic injury from the President's actual use of the new statute filed suit, the Court found the law invalid—but on a sharply divided vote. *Clinton v. City of New York*, 118 S.Ct. 2091 (1998). For a speculative essay on why the justices may have wished to postpone treatment of the new law (and why they chose standing doctrine as a means to that end), see Neal Devins & Michael A. Fitts, *The Triumph of Timing: Raines v. Byrd and the Modern Supreme Court's Attempt to Control Constitutional Confrontations*, 86 Gtn. L.J. 351 (1997). Professor Nichol argues that the Court would do better to adopt a presumption that generalized grievances will not suffice and then allow some interests of that kind to establish standing when there is a "special need for intervention" by the courts. Gene R. Nichol, Jr., *Injury and the Disintegration of Article III*, 74 Calif. L. Rev. 1915, 1944 (1986).

130. 438 U.S. 265 (1978).

sonal harm not by being denied admission, but by being denied the opportunity to compete for all the seats in the class on a racially neutral basis.[131]

In *Northeastern Florida Chapter of Ass'n Gen. Contractors v. Jacksonville*,[132] white contractors attacked a local program reserving a percentage of the city's construction contracts for minority businesses. The plaintiffs in *Jacksonville* could not demonstrate that they had actually lost contracts because of the set-aside program for minorities and thus appeared to lack the injury required for standing. Writing for the Court, however, Justice Thomas characterized their injury as the denial of an opportunity to compete for city jobs on a racially neutral basis. Citing *Bakke*, Thomas explained that since the plaintiffs claimed that the city had established a scheme for distributing contracts that made it harder for them to succeed, they did not have to show that they would have obtained contracts if the scheme had not existed. The required injury could be found in the "denial of equal treatment" under a racially discriminatory program.[133]

Both *Bakke* and *Jacksonville* can be explained as cases in which the plaintiffs established standing by forthrightly asserting legal rights and thus had no need to contend that they were entitled to proceed on the basis of factual injury, apart from rights.[134] In both instances, the plaintiffs contended that the actions of the defendants violated their constitutional right to equal protection of the laws. Yet neither Justice Powell in *Bakke* nor Justice Thomas in *Jacksonville* explained his analysis in that way. Instead, both located the plaintiffs' injuries within the harm-

---

131. Id. at 281 n.14.

132. 508 U.S. 656 (1993).

133. Id. at 666. Professor Ely argues that the Court's decisions approving standing in racial gerrymandering cases can be explained in a similar way. See, e.g., *Shaw v. Reno*, 509 U.S. 630 (1993); *Miller v. Johnson*, 515 U.S. 900 (1995). In those cases, white voters challenged apportionment plans that placed them in congressional districts that had deliberately been drawn to ensure that African American voters would hold a majority. The Court sustained standing in each instance. In *Miller*, Justice Kennedy said that the plaintiffs had sufficient injury, because they suffered the stigma of being treated according to racial stereotypes and because their moral worth as citizens had been challenged. 515 U.S. at 911-12, 915. Injuries of that kind would appear to be generalized grievances: widely shared harms, abstract in nature. See text accompanying note 112 (discussing the definition of generalized grievances); text accompanying notes 125-29 (discussing the *Allen* case). Professor Ely contends, however, that the Court should simply have recharacterized the plaintiffs' injuries. By his account, when white voters are placed in districts in which African American voters are in the majority, it is for the very purpose of ensuring that African Americans will be able to elect African American representatives if they wish, while white "filler people" will be unable to elect white representatives. As distasteful as racial bloc voting may be, Ely argues that white voters have a legitimate interest in "a meaningful shot at helping to elect a representative" of their own race. Accordingly, filler people are personally harmed for standing purpose when they are deprived of that opportunity. John Hart Ely, *Standing to Challenge Pro-Minority Gerrymanders*, 111 Harv. L. Rev. 576, 594 (1997). For a critique of Ely's analysis, see Samuel Issacharoff & Pamela S. Karlan, *Standing and Misunderstanding in Voting Rights Law*, 111 Harv. L. Rev. 2276 (1998). Professor Dow argues the since state legislatures are overwhelmingly white, white voters who object to apportionment schemes that prevent them from helping to elect white representatives should be relegated to political remedies. David R. Dow, *The Equal Protection Clause and the Legislative Redistricting Cases—Some Notes Concerning the Standing of White Plaintiffs*, 81 Minn. L. Rev. 1123 (1997).

134. See text accompanying note 92 (explaining that allegations of the invasion of legal rights perform the same function within standing doctrine as allegations of factual harm).

based framework in *Data Processing*. That was problematic. In both cases, it was possible to characterize the plaintiffs' injuries as a denial of an opportunity to compete only by reference to the content of their legal theories—namely, their constitutional claims to be treated as equals. By some accounts, *Bakke* and *Jacksonville* implicitly conceded that the injury requirement is not, after all, entirely separate from the legal theories that litigants wish to advance.[135]

2. Causation

Litigants seeking access to federal court must show a "causal connection" between their injuries and the defendant's allegedly unlawful behavior.[136] This second constitutional prerequisite for standing is sensible enough, even logically implied. Yet it can be unpredictable.

In some instances, the Court is surprisingly easy to please. In the *SCRAP* case,[137] for example, the Court accepted the plaintiffs' allegation that the ICC's conduct injured their recreational activities. By the plaintiffs' account, the ICC failed to prepare an environmental impact statement before deciding to maintain a surcharge on railroad freight rates, the surcharge would keep freight rates high,

---

135. But see note 141 (discussing the *Warth* case). Writing for the Court in the second line-item veto case, *Clinton v. City of New York*, Justice Stevens cited *Jacksonville* for the proposition that parties who are denied a "benefit" in a "bargaining process" may be injured for standing purposes. 118 S.Ct. at 2101 n.22; see note 129. Dissenting in that case, Justice Scalia insisted that a "mere detriment to one's 'bargaining position'" is insufficient and that only a "demonstrated" loss of the bargain itself will do. According to Scalia, *Jacksonville* depends entirely on the right to equal protection and stands only for the proposition that the "denial of equal treatment" qualifies as "injury." 118 S.Ct. at 2112 (dissenting opinion). Professor Sunstein contends that the injuries in some or most of the Court's other standing cases might also have been recharacterized in a way that would have rendered them more likely to suffice for standing purposes. In *Allen*, see text accompanying notes 125-29, the African American plaintiffs might have been understood to complain of a deprivation of "the opportunity to have a desegregation process unaffected by unlawful incentives for white flight." And in *Lujan*, see text accompanying notes 121-22, the environmentalist plaintiffs might have been understood to complain of a deprivation of their "opportunity to see certain endangered species." Sunstein, note 96, at 50-51. Sunstein acknowledges that if the Court had recharacterized injuries in the manner he suggests, it would necessarily have had to refer to the legal claims that the plaintiffs concerned wished to advance—namely, claims to certain opportunities said to be conferred by the statutes and constitutional provisions in issue. But in his mind, that is inevitable. See notes 96-98 and accompanying text. Sunstein argues that by formulating the injuries in *Bakke* and *Jacksonville* in light of the legal claims the plaintiffs asserted in those cases, the Court indicated that it is coming to recognize that injuries are best understood against the backdrop provided by law. That, in Sunstein's view, should produce a more generous environment for public rights litigation: The Court may find novel injuries suggested by modern regulatory schemes where it would not have identified them previously. See also notes 226-50 (discussing recent signals from the Court). Professor Spann takes a different view. He regards *Bakke* and *Jacksonville* as illustrations of a "racially suspicious" tendency to deny standing to racial minorities who attack programmatic patterns of mistreatment, but to grant standing to groups of whites who wish to challenge affirmative action programs. Girardeau A. Spann, *Color-Coded Standing*, 80 Cornell L. Rev. 1422, 1423 (1995).

136. *Lujan*, 504 U.S. at 560.

137. See note 124 and accompanying text.

the cost of shipping refuse away would escalate, less refuse would be removed, recyclable bottles and cans would accumulate in public areas, and, accordingly, the plaintiffs' enjoyment of those facilities would be diminished. In *Duke Power Co. v. Carolina Envt'l Study Group*,[138] the Court accepted an equally tenuous causal chain. The plaintiffs in that case argued that the Price-Anderson Act, which limited power company liability in the case of nuclear accident, violated due process. They alleged injury to their use and enjoyment of a lake near their homes: The Act encouraged the power company to construct a nuclear facility on the lake, the plant would emit particles and heat, the lake water would be affected, and, in the end, the plaintiffs' enjoyment of the lake would be compromised.

In other instances, the Court has found causal connections insufficiently clear and definite. Typically, the Court faults causal chains that are contingent on the behavior of intermediate actors. In *Simon v. Eastern Kentucky Welfare Rights Org.*,[139] a group of low income people challenged an IRS decision no longer to require hospitals to provide free care to indigents in order to secure tax exempt status. The plaintiffs plainly alleged judicially cognizable injury: the loss of medical care. But the Court was not convinced that their injury was caused by the IRS action. The plaintiffs insisted that the IRS ruling would eliminate the hospitals' incentive to treat them and that the hospitals would respond by cutting costs they no longer were required to bear. Justice Powell responded that it was "speculative" whether the hospitals would react to the new IRS ruling in the way the plaintiffs predicted.

In *Warth v. Seldin*,[140] numerous individuals and organizations, alleging a variety of injuries, attacked a city zoning ordinance on the ground that it effectively precluded the construction of low income housing for racial minorities. Justice Powell concluded that all the plaintiffs lacked standing, some of them for want of a causal connection between the ordinance and their injuries. Three individuals, for example, alleged that they wished to relocate to the town, but could not do so because they could afford to live only in a low income project: The ordinance made it difficult for companies to build low income projects, it was for that reason that no suitable projects had been built, and, accordingly, the ordinance was the cause of their difficulties. Powell faulted that causal chain, because it depended on contractors who were willing to build low income housing, but were frustrated by the ordinance. The plaintiffs had not demonstrated that there *were* any such contractors waiting in the wings. Accordingly, they had not shown that the ordinance caused their injuries.[141]

---

138. 438 U.S. 59, 74 (1978).

139. 426 U.S. 26 (1976).

140. 422 U.S. 490 (1975).

141. The plaintiffs identified two unsuccessful proposals for housing projects in recent years, but failed to show that those projects, had they been built, would have supplied the plaintiffs with apartments they could afford. Even if the ordinance had frustrated those projects, and even if some low income people had suffered injury in the process, the three particular plaintiffs in *Warth* had not demonstrated that they themselves would have been among the injured. See text accompanying note 120. Professor Sager argues that it should have been unnecessary for the plaintiffs to show that the ordinance actually deprived them of the "ultimate benefit" of affordable housing and that it should have sufficed that the ordinance forestalled an "intermediate" state of affairs in which the plaintiffs' chances of securing housing would be improved. Lawrence G. Sager, *Insular Majorities Unabated: Warth v. Seldin and City of Eastlake v. Forest City Enterprises, Inc.*, 91 Harv. L. Rev. 1373, 1385-

The African American children in *Allen v. Wright*[142] also failed to establish causation. By their account, the IRS was employing standards that allowed private segregationist schools to obtain tax exemptions, those schools thus received subsidies that allowed them to operate as havens for white flight from public schools, the resulting exodus from public schools handicapped desegregation efforts, and, in the end, the plaintiffs lost the chance to receive a desegregated public education. According to Justice O'Connor, "the line of causation" between the award of tax exemptions to private schools and the injuries of which the plaintiffs complained was "attenuated." The unpredictable intermediate actors in *Allen* were private schools and the parents of white children. The plaintiffs had not demonstrated that enough private schools were receiving improper tax exemptions to make any "appreciable difference" to the attempts by public schools in the plaintiffs' communities to desegregate. Nor had the plaintiffs established that improper tax exemptions actually affected either the admissions policies of the private schools concerned or the decisions of white parents to enroll their children in those schools. Accordingly, it was not clear (enough) that, if the IRS had actually granted tax exemptions to segregationist private academies in violation of federal law, it made any difference to the public schools the plaintiffs attended.[143]

The Court's decisions on causation have been questioned. Plainly, the Court sets aside modern conventions of "notice pleading" in favor of much more exacting pleading standards.[144] Arguably, the Court examines fact-specific complaints inconsistently. In *SCRAP* and *Duke Power*, the Court accepted the plaintiffs' allegations that the companies concerned would respond to economic incentives in a predictable self-interested way. Yet in *Simon*, *Warth*, and *Allen*, the Court

---

86 (1978). See notes 130-35 and accompanying text (describing the way in which injuries can sometimes be recharacterized as lost opportunities). Consider in this vein that *Warth* was decided in 1975. It was not until *Washington v. Davis*, 426 U.S. 229 (1976), that the Court announced its novel formula for handling equal protection challenges to rules and practices that are race-neutral on their face, but impose burdens disproportionately on racial minorities. Then, a year after *Davis*, the Court concluded in *Village of Arlington Heights v. Metro. Hous. Develop. Corp.*, 429 U.S. 252 (1977), that plaintiffs attacking exclusionary zoning practices like those in *Warth* had established a sufficient causal chain and thus had standing to obtain an adjudication of their claim on the merits. The plaintiffs in *Arlington Heights* did connect themselves to a particular low income housing project they insisted was stalled by the ordinance in that case, and the Court distinguished *Warth* on that basis. Nevertheless, it seems inescapable that the Court may have wanted to avoid the substantive claim in *Warth* until the justices had settled on an analysis to fit it and that, once they announced such an analysis in *Davis*, they were more willing to revisit the issues in *Warth* in a new case (*Arlington Heights*) which then could serve as a vehicle for elaborating the *Davis* approach.

142. *See notes 125-29 and accompanying text.*

143. 468 U.S. at 757-59.

144. Dissenting in *Allen*, Justice Stevens complained that Justice O'Connor was applying intricate pleading rules "that would have gladdened the heart of Baron Parke." Id. at 785 n.2, quoting Abram Chayes, *The Role of the Judge in Public Law Litigation*, 89 Harv. L. Rev. 1281, 1305 (1976). In a separate dissent in *Allen*, Justice Brennan unsuccessfully urged the Court to remand the case so that the plaintiffs might amend their complaint in light of the Court's exacting pleading requirements. 468 U.S. at 775 n.6. Cf. *Havens*, 455 U.S. at 377-78 (following that course).

found allegations of that kind to be speculative.[145] The procedural posture of a case may offer a partial explanation in some instances, but not in all.[146]

The apparent inconsistency in the cases may reflect the Court's level of enthusiasm for adjudicating the claims that plaintiffs seek to advance. The Court may be generous to plaintiffs attempting to construct causal chains when it wants to reach the merits and needs to approve the plaintiffs' standing in order to do so. But the Court may be more demanding when it wishes to avoid the merits and thus needs a door-closing device that forecloses adjudication. In *Duke Power*, for example, the Court plainly wanted to reach the merits of the plaintiffs' challenge to the Price-Anderson Act in order to reverse the lower court's decision declaring that statute unconstitutional. In other instances, perhaps including *Warth*, *Simon*, and *Allen*, the Court may have been less anxious to grapple with the merits of the plaintiffs' substantive claims.[147]

By other accounts, the Court's cases regarding causation are actually decisions on the merits.[148] That is invariably true when, to satisfy the threshold requirement for standing, plaintiffs allege not only factual injury, but an invasion of a positive legal right. In cases of that kind, causation necessarily merges with the merits—namely, whether the defendant has, indeed, violated the plaintiffs' legal rights. Even in cases in which plaintiffs allege only injuries for standing purposes, causation approaches the merits. The same allegations plaintiffs offer to establish a causal connection between their injuries and the defendant's action are often equally crucial to their legal claims that the defendant's action is unlaw-

---

145. On this point, Justice Stevens said that the causation analysis in *Allen* required only a "restatement of elementary economics" of the kind the Court acknowledges in other contexts. 468 U.S. at 788 (dissenting opinion), citing *Regan v. Taxation With Representation*, 461 U.S. 540 (1983). Professor Nichol describes the allegation in *Allen* as "simple: tax exempt status makes private schools economically more attractive." Gene R. Nichol, Jr., *Abusing Standing: A Comment on Allen v. Wright*, 133 U. Pa. L. Rev. 635, 639 n. 26 (1985).

146. In *SCRAP*, for example, the sufficiency of the plaintiffs' allegations regarding standing was determined in the context of the ICC's motion to dismiss under Rule 12(b). In that posture, the Court assumed both that the allegations in the complaint were true and that general allegations embraced more specific assertions. If, by contrast, the defendant files a motion for summary judgment pursuant to Rule 56, plaintiffs may be required to produce affidavits or other evidence in support of allegations going to causation. See, e.g., *Lujan v. Nat'l Wildlife Fed.*, 497 U.S. 871, 889 (1990). This may explain the Court's generous examination of the complaint in *SCRAP*. But it does not defuse the tension between *SCRAP* and other cases in this line. *Simon* was handled in a Rule 56 posture. But both *Warth* and *Allen* were Rule 12 cases, albeit the motion in *Warth* was considered in light of "extensive supportive materials." 422 U.S. at 497. In retrospect, *SCRAP* probably should be dismissed as a sport.

147. Professor Nichol contends that the justices' views regarding the claims plaintiffs seek to advance "will likely affect the standing determination as long as judges with strong feelings about substantive claims decide jurisdictional issues." Nichol, note 145, at 650. Professor Sager contends that *Warth* rests on the premise that federal courts should leave zoning matters to state courts. Sager, note 141, at 1391. Professor Logan argues that causation is too fluid to be considered a constitutional mandate and would better be treated as a prudential consideration. David A. Logan, *Standing to Sue: A Proposed Separation of Powers Analysis*, 1984 Wis. L. Rev. 37, 82.

148. Professor Tushnet takes this view. Mark V. Tushnet, *The New Law of Standing: A Plea for Abandonment*, 62 Cornell L. Rev. 663 (1977).

ful. In *Allen*, for example, Justice O'Connor said that the plaintiffs had not al-leged an adequate causal chain in part because it was unclear that the IRS per-mitted enough ineligible private schools to receive tax exemptions to compromise efforts to desegregate the public schools the paintiffs attended. Yet that incorpo-rated the very legal claim the plaintiffs advanced—namely, the claim that the IRS was allowing private segregationist academies to obtain tax exemptions to which they were not lawfully entitled.[149]

3. Redressability

The Supreme Court originally equated the causation requirement with the prospect of effective judicial relief. Chief Justice Burger explained that the only question was whether the injury asserted for standing purposes "fairly" could be "traced" to the defendant, so that if a court found a plaintiff's claim to be meri-torious, the court could coerce the defendant to do something that redressed the plaintiff's injury.[150] Today, however, the Court treats "redressability" as a third constitutional prerequisite for standing. Justice O'Connor explained in *Allen* that "[t]o the extent there is a difference" between causation and redressability, it is that causation links the defendant's allegedly unlawful behavior to the plain-tiff's injury, while redressability links the plaintiff's injury to the relief the plain-tiff asks a court to award if it finds a claim to be meritorious.[151] That distinction granted, the Court nonetheless typically collapses its search for causal connec-tions into its evaluation of the likelihood of effective judicial relief.

In *Allen*, Justice O'Connor purported to rest her result on the ground that the plaintiffs had failed to demonstrate causation. They had not established that their judicially cognizable injury was "fairly traceable to the assertedly unlawful conduct of the IRS." O'Connor explained, however, that the causal linkage broke down, because it was unclear "whether withdrawal of a tax exemption from any particu-lar school would lead the school to change its policies." That, of course, went not to the causation question (whether existing IRS rules allowed private schools to obtain tax exemptions they did not deserve, effectively subsidized white flight from public schools, and thus caused the paintiffs to lose their chance for desegregated public education), but rather to the redressability question (whether, if the plaintiffs were successful on the merits, a court could remedy the plaintiffs' injury by forcing the IRS to use more effective standards that would deny tax exemptions to unde-serving private schools, create an incentive for those schools to admit black stu-dents in order to obtain lawful exemptions, eliminate private schools as a haven for white flight, and thus make it easier for public schools to desegregate).[152]

---

149. See text accompanying note 125. Professor Nichol has noted the overlap between causation and the merits of the claim in *Allen*. Nichol, note 145, at 640 n. 27.

150. *Duke Power*, 438 U.S. at 74. See also *Warth*, 422 U.S. at 505 (explaining that plaintiffs must allege that their injuries are the "consequence" of the defendant's actions "or" that the relief they seek will "remove the harm").

151. 468 U.S. at 753 n.19; see notes 125-29, 142-43 and accompanying text.

152. 468 U.S. at 753, 758. This same pattern is often repeated. In *Linda R.S. v. Richard D.*, 410 U.S. 614 (1973), the mother of an illegitimate child claimed that the child's father was not making support payments because officials pressed prosecutions only against the delinquent fathers of legitimate children. Justice Marshall said that the plaintiff had failed to

Occasionally, the Court treats redressability in isolation from causation. In the *Lujan* case,[153] Justice Scalia said that redressability would present a problem for the plaintiffs even if they formed definite plans to visit sites where construction projects threatened endangered species and thus established sufficient personal injury. If they succeeded on the merits of their claim, the only relief they could win was an order requiring the Secretary to consult with the federal agencies involved in those projects. Since those agencies were not themselves defendants, however, the court could not order *them* to consult with the Secretary. Moreover, even if all the government's arms agreed to consider the effects of the projects on endangered animals, the plaintiffs had not shown that officials in Egypt and Sri Lanka would pay any heed. They might disturb the animals' habitats, whether or not their American sponsors approved.[154]

In other instances, the Court has explained that the redressability requirement makes access to the federal courts contingent on the kind of relief that litigants desire. When plaintiffs have suffered harm in the past and seek backward-looking remedies in the nature of compensatory damages, redressability is rarely problematic. When, by contrast, plaintiffs seek forward-looking declaratory or injunctive relief, redressability can present a constitutional bar. This is true even in cases in which plaintiffs assert that their own legal rights have been violated (not merely that they suffer factual injury).[155]

The leading illustration is *City of Los Angeles v. Lyons*.[156] The plaintiff in that case alleged that the Los Angeles police used life-threatening "choke holds" to subdue suspects, that sixteen people had lost their lives in that way, and that he himself had been strangled into unconsciousness. Contending that the choke holds were unconstitutional, he sued the police both for compensatory damages and for an injunction barring use of the holds in the future. In the Supreme Court, Justice White acknowledged the plaintiff had standing to sue for compen-

---

allege a "sufficient nexus between her injury and the government action" she wished to challenge, in part because the only relief a court could award was an order requiring the defendants to prosecute cases involving illegitimate children. That might result in a prosecution of the father of the plaintiff's child, perhaps even in his incarceration. But it would not ensure that she would receive the support payments she was due.

153. See notes 121-22 and accompanying text.

154. Private litigants who wish to press claims against government and its officers often must shoot at a moving target. See Chapter X (discussing suits against government and its agents). Thus the ability of federal officers to defeat litigants' standing to sue any one of their number on redressability grounds may be only one piece of a larger puzzle. Justice Scalia's conclusion regarding redressability in *Lujan* received only plurality support.

155. See Chapter X, notes 245-92 and accompanying text (explaining that defendant officers may be immune from suit for compensatory relief). To the extent this feature of standing doctrine prefers actions for damages to suits for injunctions, it is in some tension with the Court's historical willingness to entertain private suits against government officers for injunctive relief and its comparative hesitancy over suits for compensatory damages. See Chapter VIII, text accompanying notes 137-38. Injunctions are appealing inasmuch as they force officials to comply with the law. On the other hand, in the context of standing, the Court insists that litigants' desire merely to see the law enforced is insufficient. See text accompanying notes 114-18, 126. Damage awards may deter misconduct. But monetary penalties are primarily tailored to compensate for losses already incurred and affect the future only indirectly. See Daniel J. Meltzer, *Deterring Constitutional Violations by Law Enforcement Officials: Plaintiffs and Defendants as Private Attorneys General*, 88 Colum. L. Rev. 247 (1988).

156. 461 U.S. 95 (1983).

satory damages, but held that he did not have standing to sue for injunctive relief. An injunction could only protect the plaintiff from being subjected to a choke hold on some future occasion. But he could not plausibly allege either that he would be arrested again or that, if he were, the police would restrain him in the same way. Justice White therefore concluded that the plaintiff lacked constitutional standing to seek the particular form of relief he requested.[157]

In *Steel Co. v. Citizens for a Better Environment*,[158] the plaintiffs were environmentalists who collected and distributed information about the use of hazardous materials. They notified a private company that it had failed to file reports regarding its use of toxic chemicals, as required by the Emergency Planning and Community Right-to-Know Act. The company filed the overdue reports, and the Environmental Protection Agency declined to take punitive action. The plaintiffs then sued the company, alleging that their "right to know" about the use of toxic substances and their "interests" in protecting the environment were "adversely affected" by the company's failure to supply information in a timely way. The plaintiffs alleged that the effects of the company's default lingered after the company submitted tardy reports, because the plaintiffs needed a steady flow of current data to fuel their public education campaign. Justice Scalia assumed for purposes of decision that the plaintiffs had alleged cognizable injury in fact for standing purposes.[159] He concluded, however, that they lacked standing because their injuries were not redressable.

Justice Scalia took each of the plaintiffs' requests for relief in turn. He agreed that they might win a declaratory judgment that the defendant had filed the re-

---

157. The *Lyons* analysis is not airtight. In *Kolender v. Lawson*, 461 U.S. 352 (1983), the plaintiff alleged that he had been arrested under a vague statute on fifteen occasions within a period of two years. That record established a "credible threat" that he would be arrested again and thus established his standing to seek injunctive relief. Id. at 355 n.3. See note 290 and accompanying text (discussing the need for a similar "credible threat" to sue for declaratory relief). Justice White also said in *Lyons* that, apart from Article III standing difficulties, the plaintiff could not meet the non-constitutional standards for obtaining injunctive relief. Professor Fallon argues that to the extent the Court was primarily concerned with the nature of the relief the plaintiff sought, it would have done better to decide the case on that non-constitutional basis. See Fallon, note 66, at 8.

158. 118 S.Ct. 1003 (1998).

159. Id. at 1017-18. Justice Scalia said that the Court had never decided whether "being deprived of the information" that the Act required companies to report was a "concrete" injury for standing purposes. He noted, however, that some of the plaintiffs in *Steel* resided in the community in which the company operated and that they did not merely allege that they had the kind of interest in the information that anyone might claim, but insisted that they had a "particular plan" for using it. Id. at 1017-18. See text accompanying notes 67-70 (discussing the Court's early misgivings about recognizing standing in the beneficiaries of regulatory programs); notes 111-29 and accompanying text (discussing the inadequacy of generalized grievances for standing purposes). In the *Akins* case, the Court held that plaintiffs suffered concrete factual injury when they were deprived of information they insisted a political committee was obligated by law to divulge. See notes 111-13 and accompanying text. Justice Breyer recognized that the plaintiffs in that case might never get the information they wanted, even if they were correct that the statute required it to be made available. The agency involved, the Federal Election Commission, had authority to waive that requirement in its discretion. Nevertheless, Justice Breyer swept aside any concerns regarding either causation or redressability on the ground that the plaintiffs were entitled to an authoritative judicial statement of the law as the basis for the agency's exercise of discretion. *Akins*, 118 S.Ct. at 1786-87.

quired reports after they were due. But since that violation of the Act was uncontested, such a declaration would be "worthless."[160] He also agreed that the plaintiffs might obtain an order requiring the company to pay a fine for failing to file the reports on time. He conceded that if the plaintiffs themselves were in line to receive that money, its recovery might redress their injuries as "a sort of compensation." But it was clear from the Act that any monetary payments the defaulting company might be ordered to make would go to the federal treasury, not to the plaintiffs.[161] Finally, Justice Scalia acknowledged that the plaintiffs had requested an order authorizing them to inspect the company's records and premises to ensure that the company complied with the Act. Citing *Lyons*, however, he said an injunctive order of that kind would not be available, because the district court would not assume that the company's misbehavior in the past demonstrated a sufficient likelihood of misbehavior in the future.[162]

D. Standing: Non-Constitutional Prerequisites

Some features of standing doctrine are not constitutional imperatives, but rest on a different, non-constitutional footing. Two implications attend the prudential nature of these ideas. First, the Court explicitly claims more discretion when it describes and applies non-constitutional rules of "self-restraint" than it claims when it elaborates standing rules it ascribes to the separation principle and Article III.[163] Second, Congress can establish or eliminate prudential standing rules by statute.[164] This second implication makes the significant operational point. When the Court declares that the injury, causation, and redressability features of standing doctrine are constitutional mandates, it claims for itself the authority to elaborate those ideas as constitutional law, not subject to statutory override or adjustment. When, however, the Court characterizes a feature of

---

160. See notes 11-16 and accompanying text (discussing the argument that declaratory judgments are advisory opinions).

161. See note 245 (discussing bounty schemes).

162. *Steel*, 118 S.Ct. at 1018-19. Justice Scalia also rejected the argument that the plaintiffs might recoup the money they had spent in pressing the lawsuit. Even if they obtained a reimbursement order, it would not redress the injuries that were said to have justified the suit originally. Certainly, he said, the prospect of being reimbursed for the costs of litigation could not independently establish injury for standing purposes. If that were true, plaintiffs would be able to manufacture injury in fact routinely, merely by investing funds in the very lawsuits they needed injury to launch in the first instance. See *Diamond v. Charles*, 476 U.S. 54, 70-71 (1986) (holding that an intervenor's interest in avoiding attorney fees was insufficient to maintain standing to appeal from an unfavorable judgment).

163. *Craig v. Boren*, 429 U.S. 190, 193 (1976). This distinction can be misleading. Obviously, the Court is responsible for the injury, causation, and redressability elements of standing, just as it is responsible for the non-constitutional aspects. Moreover, when the Court articulates and employs non-constitutional doctrines, it typically brings to bear the same considerations that drive its elaboration of the constitutional elements.

164. See, e.g., *United Food & Commercial Workers Union v. Brown Group*, 517 U.S. 544 (1996) (holding that Congress could legislatively eliminate a prudential feature of the Court's doctrine regarding "organizational standing").

standing doctrine as prudential, it opens standing doctrine in that respect to statutory alteration. The Court thus differentiates its own authority from that of Congress by placing various elements of standing doctrine in one category or the other.[165]

1. Third Party Claims

Once litigants satisfy the constitutional prerequisites for standing and gain a foothold in federal court, they usually can advance only the legal claims they themselves have against the defendant. The progenitor precedent for this basic idea is *Yazoo & Mississippi Valley R.R. v. Jackson Vinegar Co.*[166] In that case, the railroad attacked the constitutionality of a state statute not only as it had been applied in the case at bar, but also as it might be applied in other readily foreseeable contexts. The Supreme Court limited its consideration of the railroad's claim to the circumstances in which the state courts had enforced the statute below. The principle derived from *Yazoo* is that litigants must be content to press the claims they have at present and cannot ask the federal courts to anticipate claims that might arise from a different pattern of facts.[167]

Extrapolating from *Yazoo*, the Court typically insists that litigants are equally barred from advancing legal claims that belong to a third party—someone who does not formally appear on either of the two sides in the case at hand. Even though litigants have by hypothesis initiated an Article III "case" on which federal judicial power can be exercised, it still is intuitively sensible that, within that case, they should not be claiming that someone else's rights have been violated.[168] If individuals whose rights are actually at stake are not complaining, the Court hesitates to anticipate the claims they *might* one day advance on their own

---

165. See Nichol, note 97, at 1160; notes 204-50 and accompanying text (discussing congressional power).

166. 226 U.S. 217 (1912).

167. The railroad in *Yazoo* argued that a Mississippi statute violated due process inasmuch as it imposed a $25 fine on the railroad if it failed to settle any claim for lost or damaged freight within a fixed period. In the particular case at bar, the railroad had suffered such a fine for missing the deadline with respect to a legitimate claim. The Court sustained the statute on that basis. The railroad contended that the statute would also authorize a fine in the case of an extravagant claim that the railroad could not be expected to settle. The Court refused to consider that argument, because a case of that order had not yet arisen. Id. at 219-20.

168. It may be misleading to regard this rule as an aspect of standing doctrine. By hypothesis, litigants who are in federal court in the first instance have met the constitutional prerequisites for standing. The question, then, is not whether the litigants have any business in an Article III court, but whether the business they concededly have can include advancing claims on behalf of others. Nevertheless, the prohibition on third-party claims is commonly regarded as a feature of prudential standing doctrine. See Henry P. Monaghan, *Third Party Standing*, 84 Colum. L. Rev. 277, 278 n.6 (1984). The usual prohibition on third-party claims applies both to plaintiffs and to defendants. Of course, defendants have constitutional standing inasmuch as they suffer injury simply from being named in a lawsuit (and will suffer still more injury if they are found liable). The arguments they can advance by way of defense, however, implicate other prudential considerations. In the leading case, *Barrows v. Jackson*, 346 U.S. 249 (1953), the plaintiff sued a white property holder for selling her land to an African American buyer in violation of a racially restrictive covenant. The Court wrestled with the question whether the defendant should be permitted to answer that the

behalf, merely because there are litigants in court who currently seek an adjudication of those claims for their own purposes.[169]

In some circumstances, however, these rationales for the general rule against third-party claims do not hold, and the Supreme Court, accordingly, allows exceptions: (1) cases in which litigants are specially positioned to advocate *jus tertii* on behalf of other people; and (2) cases in which litigants attack statutes for overbreadth in violation of the first amendment.

Jus tertii cases. Litigants can advance legal claims that belong to others if two factors counsel an exception from the general rule against third-party arguments. First, the absent parties must face obstacles to proceeding on their own behalf. In that event, it cannot be assumed that the absent parties have failed to file suit because they consider the rights at stake unimportant. The obstacle need not prevent the absent parties from litigating altogether. In some instances, the Court has found it sufficient that they would engage significant personal costs if they were to file their own suits. In the leading case, *Singleton v. Wulff*,[170] the Court allowed physicians to advance the rights of their patients to obtain abortions. Justice Blackmun explained that female patients might have sued on their own behalf, but, in order to do so, would have risked exposing their private decisions regarding procreation.[171] In *Craig v. Boren*,[172] Justice Brennan permitted a liquor store proprietor to press the rights of her teenage male customers.

---

covenant violated the equal protection rights of the buyer. The Court concluded that the defendant *could* advance that argument.

169. Litigants who assert the rights of others may generate unfavorable results that will frustrate those whose rights are actually affected, if and when they proceed on their own behalf. Professor Brilmayer defends the body of constitutional and non-constitutional standing rules to the extent they discourage representative litigation that may compromise the interests and rights of those who are said to be represented. Lea Brilmayer, *The Jurisprudence of Article III: Perspectives on the "Case or Controversy" Requirement*, 93 Harv. L. Rev. 297 (1979).

170. 428 U.S. 106 (1976).

171. Justice Blackmun also said that any individual's claim might be rendered moot before a decision could be rendered. That legal impediment was only "technical," however, inasmuch as the Court had previously held that women could typically avoid dismissal on mootness grounds. Id. at 117. See note 300 and accompanying text (discussing the mootness doctrine in abortion cases).

172. 429 U.S. 190 (1976). In *Powers v. Ohio*, 499 U.S. 400 (1991), the Court held that a white criminal defendant can advance the equal protection claims of blacks who were excluded from the jury. The Court reasoned that individual veniremen have little incentive to shoulder the burdens of litigation to press their own claims in that context. See *Campbell v. Louisiana*, 118 S.Ct. 1419 (1998) (relying on *Powers* in a case involving racially discriminatory exclusions of blacks from grand juries). In *Miller v. Albright*, 118 S.Ct. 1428 (1998), the daughter of an American serviceman advanced her alleged father's equal protection claim against a federal statute requiring men (but not women) to take special measures to ensure that their illegitimate children born overseas become American citizens. The full Court passed on the merits of the claim and purported not to address the plaintiff's standing as an interested third party. Justice Breyer wrote a concurring opinion explaining that the father faced obstacles to suit on his own behalf. Justice O'Connor contended, however, that *Powers* had "articulated the contours of third-party standing in more greater detail" (since *Craig*) and established that the absent party must face genuinely "daunting" hurdles, not present in *Miller*. Justice Scalia (citing *Craig*) said in his own opinion concurring in the judgment that the doctrine on this point "is in need of what may charitably be called clarification." Id. at 1447 n.1.

Second (and in addition), litigants who wish to advance the claims of others must bear some relationship to the absent parties. If, for example, the litigants at bar hold a position of trust with respect to the other parties, or have some contractual relationship to those parties, it may follow that the litigants can supply effective advocacy. Their own interest in vindicating the rights of others is more concrete, their willingness and capacity to press those rights vigorously more certain. On this point, too, the Court is often generous to would-be litigants. The bartender's intimate and supportive relationship with her regulars in *Craig* was one thing, the physician's fleeting ministrations to his patients in *Wulff* quite another.[173]

It may be that the exceptions have virtually swallowed the general rule against *jus tertii* standing. The Court makes *ad hoc* judgments on whether claims should be heard and very often concludes that they should.[174] That flexibility, in turn, may reflect the Court's recognition that the classic rationales for the baseline rule against third-party claims underestimate the burdens of modern litigation. Ordinary citizens may fail to press their own claims chiefly because they find lawsuits daunting. It may be appropriate, then, to allow litigants who have constitutional standing (and thus have a sufficient stake in the outcome to ensure effective advocacy) to litigate issues, even though they do not themselves share the legal claims they seek to advance.[175]

---

173. In fact, the Court described the plaintiff in *Craig* as a "licensed vendor of 3.2% beer." See also *United States Dep't of Labor v. Triplett*, 494 U.S. 715 (1990) (permitting an attorney to advance the claims of his clients); *Maryland v. Joseph H. Munson Co.*, 467 U.S. 947 (1984) (allowing a professional fund raiser to press claims belonging his sources).

174. The *Craig* case may illustrate. In that case, Justice Brennan set aside the usual rule against third-party claims not because the parties whose rights were at stake faced special obstacles or because the plaintiff bore them a special relationship, but because the lower court had already passed on the merits. The defendant had raised no objection, and there was no reason to think that the issues would be presented more fully if the Court waited until teenage boys sued on their own behalf. A teenage boy had appeared as a plaintiff in *Craig* in the lower courts. But he had reached the age of 21 before the case arrived in the Supreme Court, and his personal claim was moot. See notes 291-305 and accompanying text (discussing the mootness doctrine). In some instances, however, the Court is especially suspicious of third-party claims. See, e.g., *Whitmore v. Arkansas*, 495 U.S. 149 (1990) (refusing to allow one death row inmate to press a constitutional claim on behalf of another who declined to proceed for himself). For a realistic appraisal of the consequences of cases like *Whitmore*, see Ann Althouse, *Standing, In Fluffy Slippers*, 77 Va. L. Rev. 1177 (1991).

175. Professor Sedler argues that most of the decisions in question can (and should) be understood as determinations that the litigants at bar were not asserting third-party claims at all, but their own personal rights. Sedler contends that the litigants in those cases themselves had rights to engage in activities with others and that those personal rights were put at risk when the other parties suffered some invalid burden. Professor Sedler explains *Craig*, for example, as a case in which a state statute that denied equal protection to the liquor store proprietor's male customers equally interfered with the proprietor's "liberty" and "property." Robert A. Sedler, *The Assertion of Constitutional Jus Tertii: A Substantive Approach*, 70 Calif. L. Rev. 1308, 1333 (1982). Professor Monaghan offers a similar general theory, which generates a similar revisionist explanation for *Craig*. Monaghan, note 168, at 300. In some instances, however, Sedler and Monaghan disagree. For example, Professor Sedler contends that the physicians in *Wulff* could assert their own constitutional right to receive fees for performing abortions in common with dispensing other medical services. Professor Monaghan, by contrast, argues that a litigant has a personal right to advance only if the statute or other action under attack constitutes a "more direct and meaningful interference" with an "interactive transaction" involving the litigant and the absent party. Monaghan, note 168, at 307. Monaghan finds that missing from *Wulff*.

Overbreadth cases. In ordinary *jus tertii* cases, the litigants at bar seek to advance claims that belong to identified (or at least identifiable) third parties. In a related class of free speech cases, litigants press claims that belong to hypothetical third parties. In keeping with the *Yazoo* principle, litigants who challenge a federal or state statute typically can argue only that the statute is invalid as applied in the circumstances of their own case.[176] The Supreme Court recognizes an exception, however, in some instances in which litigants claim that statutes violate freedom of speech protected by the first amendment.[177] No exception is necessary so long as litigants argue only that a statute violates their own first amendment rights, as the statute has been *applied* in the particular case at hand. An exception is necessary, however, if litigants argue that a statute is overbroad *on its face* and *would* violate the rights of *others* if it were applied in different circumstances.[178]

The Court allows an exception from the *Yazoo* principle for first amendment overbreadth cases, because the very existence of an overbroad statute can have a "chilling effect" on free speech.[179] If the statute *appears* to penalize expression

---

176. In *United States v. Salerno*, 481 U.S. 739 (1987), the Court said that a plaintiff attacking a statute on its face "must establish that no set of circumstances exists under which the Act would be valid." Id. at 745. Professor Dorf contends that, if that passage is taken literally, facial attacks should be virtually non-existent. Litigants who show that a statute cannot constitutionally be applied in the circumstances of their cases succeed on that basis and have no occasion to argue as well that the statute cannot be applied in other circumstances. Litigants who fail to demonstrate that the statute is invalid as applied lose on both counts. By showing that the statute can operate constitutionally in at least one instance, they disable themselves (under *Salerno*) from attacking the statute on its face, i.e., as it might apply in other circumstances. Michael C. Dorf, *Facial Challenges to State and Federal Statutes*, 46 Stan. L. Rev. 235, 239 (1994).

177. The Court's enthusiasm for this exception is not so strong now as it once was. In *Broadrick v. Oklahoma*, 413 U.S. 601 (1973), for example, the Court held that in cases in which "conduct" as well as expression is involved, statutes can be attacked on their face only if they are "substantially" overbroad. Cf. *Joseph H. Munson*, 467 U.S. at 978 (Rehnquist, J., dissenting) (expressing general doubts about permitting facial attacks on statutes). The Court does continue to apply the analysis. E.g., *City of Los Angeles v. Jews for Jesus*, 482 U.S. 569 (1987) (invalidating a blanket prohibition on "First Amendment activities" at the Los Angeles airport).

178. Statutes are often both overbroad (because they purport to reach protected expression) and vague (because they fail to specify the behavior they reach and thus may condemn protected speech). Yet a statute can be overbroad, even though it is perfectly clear. Overbreadth is a first amendment doctrine concerned with the chilling effect a statute may have on expression; vagueness is a due process doctrine concerned with fair notice of what a statute means.

179. See Note, *The First Amendment Overbreadth Doctrine*, 83 Harv. L. Rev. 844, 852-58 (1970). Professor Dorf argues that statutes should be subject to challenge for overbreadth not only if they affect free speech, but also if they affect other constitutional rights to engage in "primary conduct." He recognizes, however, that few constitutional rights are of that order. Dorf, note 176 at 264-65. See *Planned Parenthood v. Casey*, 505 U.S. 833 (1992) (entertaining a facial attack on an abortion regulation affecting the substantive right to procure an abortion without undue burdens); *Kolender v. Lawson*, 461 U.S 352 (1983) (allowing a litigant to whom a statute could plainly apply to attack the statute on its face for vagueness—on behalf of other potential defendants). Professor Fallon thinks overbreadth analysis has been limited to speech cases in the main because of the special values associated with expression. Richard H. Fallon, Jr., *Making Sense of Overbreadth*, 100 Yale L.J. 853 (1991). Cf. *Janklow v. Planned Parenthood*, 517 U.S. 1174 (1996) (Scalia, J., dissenting from the denial of *certiorari*) (urging the Court to reconsider whether abortion regulations are subject to facial challenge).

that is actually protected, it may discourage would-be speakers who will censor themselves rather than risk prosecution.[180] A statute that is invalid on its face cannot be applied in any circumstances—including cases in which a more narrowly drawn statute might be invoked to punish an individual's expressive behavior.[181] Accordingly, litigants whose own conduct might be penalized under a valid statute nonetheless escape punishment by establishing that the actual statute brought to bear on them is overbroad with respect to other, hypothetical speakers.[182]

2. The Zone Test

Litigants who satisfy the constitutional prerequisites for standing sometimes must satisfy a second non-constitutional rule. They must show that the injuries

---

180. In *Coates v. City of Cincinnati*, 402 U.S. 611 (1971), the Court held that a city ordinance that made it an offense for three or more people to assemble in public in a manner "annoying to persons passing by" was plainly overbroad. Justice Stewart said there was no need to investigate the "details of the conduct found to be annoying" in the particular case at hand, because it was "the ordinance on its face" that set "the standard of conduct" and warned "against transgression." Id. at 616. See also *Gooding v. Wilson*, 405 U.S. 518 (1972) (invalidating a statute that made it an offense to use "opprobrious words"). Professor Fallon has explained that some overbroad statutes may threaten a greater chilling effect on speech than others. Fallon, note 179.

181. Professor Monaghan argues that the overbreadth cases should be understood not as instances in which the Court allows an exception to the usual prohibition on third-party claims, but rather as instances in which the Court recognizes "first party" claims on behalf of litigants advancing overbreadth arguments. According to Monaghan, a litigant "always" has a "right to be judged in accordance with a constitutionally valid rule of law." Henry P. Monaghan, *Overbreadth*, 1981 Sup. Ct. Rev. 1, 3. By his account, a statute that makes it an offense to whistle is facially invalid and thus cannot be constitutionally invoked even against a defendant who disrupts a courtroom proceeding by whistling. Henry P. Monaghan, *Harmless Error and the Valid Rule Requirement*, 1989 Sup. Ct. Rev. 195, 196.

182. Courts can save statutes that are overbroad or vague as written by giving them an authoritative narrowing construction. See *Osborne v. Ohio*, 495 U.S. 103 (1990). If a statute as written is flawed only for overbreadth, a court can give it a saving construction after an individual has been charged and still, perhaps, apply the statute (in its new form) to that defendant. By hypothesis in an overbreadth case, the individual's attack on the statute's facial validity is in service of the rights of other speakers not before the court. Once the court eliminates the chilling effect on those speakers by construing the statute narrowly, the individual litigant no longer has a first amendment objection to the court's application of the statute to the case at bar. Id. at 115. In one famous case, *Shuttlesworth v. City of Birmingham*, 394 U.S. 147 (1969), the Court refused to allow the Alabama Supreme Court to cure overbreadth on appeal and, on that basis, to affirm the convictions of civil rights demonstrators. But *Shuttlesworth* was almost certainly a creature of its civil rights context. If a statute as written is vague, a court cannot repair the damage to individuals after they have been charged. The gravamen of the evil in a vagueness case is lack of fair notice, which cannot be remedied by construing a statute narrowly after defendants have had to guess at its meaning as written. Id. at 155. It is not always necessary to invalidate an overbroad statute in its entirety. Sometimes, courts can sever offending features and leave the rest in place. State courts are authoritative with respect to state statutes. See Chapter VII, notes 92-94 and accompanying text. Accordingly, the federal courts' ability to save overbroad statues in that way is more limited with respect to state statutes than it is with respect to federal statutes. But see *Brockett v. Spokane Arcades*, 472 U.S. 491 (1985) (holding that the overbroad features of a state statute could be stripped out on the authority of a severability clause).

they have suffered, or are about to suffer, implicate interests that are "arguably within the zone of interests" protected or regulated by the statute or constitutional provision they seek to enforce. The Court initially announced this zone test in *Data Processing* as a non-constitutional requirement for standing that Congress had fashioned for litigants proceeding under the authority of § 702 of the Administrative Procedure Act.[183] The zone test unquestionably counts as a prudential barrier to standing; Justice Douglas might have read § 702 to dispense with any standing requirement beyond the constitutional prerequisites.[184] In retrospect, however, it seems plain that Douglas meant the zone test as a litigant-friendly alternative to a competing interpretation of § 702 that would have been considerably less generous.[185] In 1970, the zone test was far more important for the cases it allowed into the federal courts than it was for the cases it excluded. For the most part, that remains true today.

The leading illustrations are cases like *Nat'l Credit Union Admin. v. First National Bank*,[186] in which commercial firms assert economic interests in the way federal agencies regulate their competitors. Under § 109 of the National Credit Union Act, credit unions can serve only customers who are connected by a common occupational bond or who reside in a defined geographic area. The NCUA interpreted § 109 to allow credit unions to serve multiple unrelated groups of customers, so long as the customers in each group shared a common bond. That interpretation permitted credit unions to expand their customer base and thus to compete with banks for depositors—causing banks economic injury in fact. In *First National Bank*, Justice Thomas held that banks had standing to challenge the NCUA's interpretation, because their competitive interests were arguably within the zone of interests protected by § 109.

Justice Thomas conceded that neither the text of § 109 nor its legislative history indicated that Congress had enacted § 109 with the specific "intent" or "purpose" to protect banks from competition. He acknowledged that the legislative history showed, instead, that Congress meant to ensure that credit unions would have a "cooperative nature" and would provide discrete groups of customers with a safe place to put their money and a ready pool of funds from which to borrow. Thomas insisted, however, that litigants can satisfy the zone test even though there is no "evidence" that Congress intended that they should benefit from the statute they wish to enforce. Litigants have an interest that is "arguably" within the zone if there is a "link" between that interest and the interests that a statute was actually enacted to serve. Thomas found such a connection in *First National Bank*. The immediate objective of § 109 was to limit the customers (and thus the markets) that credit unions could reach. That was also the banks' immediate objective. Therein an "unmistakeable" link. It made no difference that Congress' *reason* for limiting credit union markets (the creation of a

---

183. See text accompanying note 82.
184. This is what Justice Brennan would have done. In an opinion concurring in the result in *Data Processing*, Brennan insisted that Douglas should have approved the plaintiffs' standing on the basis of their economic injuries alone, without reference to the zone test as an additional non-constitutional requirement, and then should have gone immediately to the preclusion question. Brennan agreed that no statute precluded review of the Comptroller's ruling. *Data Processing*, 397 U.S. at 159.
185. See notes 82-95 and accompanying text.
186. 118 S.Ct. 927 (1998).

cooperative atmosphere) was not the banks' reason (the profit motive).[187] Other decisions in recent years reflect a similarly generous understanding of the zone test.[188]

The zone test bears a family resemblance to the rule against third-party claims. Roughly speaking, litigants whose own interests are *not* within the zone are foreclosed, because they are attempting to litigate on behalf of other people whose interests *are* within the zone.[189] Yet the two ideas are not identical. The zone test concerns the factual *injuries* sufficient to establish standing for access to

---

187. Id. at 933, 935, 936 & n.7. In dissent, Justice O'Connor charged Justice Thomas with eviscerating the zone test entirely, thus allowing any litigant who satisfies the constitutional prerequisites for standing to challenge agency action under § 702. According to O'-Connor, Thomas would permit anyone with an interest in enforcing a statute to do so, whether or not that interest corresponds to the interests that Congress enacted the statute to promote. For her part, O'Connor contended that the zone test requires "*some* indication in the statute, beyond the mere fact that its enforcement has the effect of incidentally benefiting the plaintiff, from which one can draw an inference that the plaintiff's injury arguably falls within the zone of interests sought to be protected by that statute." Id. at 947 (emphasis in original). In response, Justice Thomas said that he (and thus the majority) differed with Justice O'Connor not over the content of the zone test, but only over its application in the case at bar. He insisted that there *was* at least *some* indication in § 109 that the banks were arguably within the zone, because both Congress and the banks wished to limit the business that credit unions could undertake. The banks were "more than merely incidental beneficiaries of § 109's effects on competition." Id. at 936 n.7 (majority opinion). Despite Justice O'-Connor's rhetoric, *First National Bank* plainly did not eviscerate the zone test entirely. The alignment of the justices makes this clear. Not only Justice Thomas himself, but other conservative members of the Court who joined his opinion (Chief Justice Rehnquist and Justice Scalia) typically are inclined to *deny* access to the federal courts on standing grounds. Justice O'Connor, too, often finds standing to be a significant hurdle. But in *First National Bank* she was joined by more liberal justices, who typically are inclined to allow litigants access to the federal forum (e.g., Justice Stevens and Justice Breyer). In *Akins*, for example, Justice Breyer said that voters who wanted information about a political committee satisfied the zone test, because he could find nothing in the relevant statute to suggest that Congress meant to "exclude" their interests from the zone of interests protected by that statute. *Akins*, 118 S.Ct. at 1784; see notes 111-13 and accompanying text. Here again, the substance of the case at bar may be telling. In *First National Bank*, Justice Thomas allowed banks into federal court to attack the way a federal agency was regulating their competitors and then, on the merits, sided with the banks against the agency.

188. In *Clarke v. Secur. Indus. Ass'n*, 479 U.S. 388 (1987), Justice White said that § 702 expresses a "presumption" in favor of judicial review in the cases to which it applies and that the zone test is not "especially demanding." Id. at 399. In *Clarke*, accordingly, White said that securities dealers who competed with banks had interests that were within the zone of interests protected by the McFadden Act's limits on branch banking. Accordingly, they could challenge a ruling by the Comptroller of the Currency allowing banks to establish offices outside their home states. In *Lujan v. Nat'l Wildlife Fed.*, 497 U.S. 871 (1990), the Court said that environmentalists' interests were within the zone of interests protected by the Federal Land Policy and Management Act's specifications for opening public land to development. The plaintiffs' difficulty in that case was not the zone test, but their failure to allege sufficient personal use of particular areas to capitalize on the Court's willingness to consider their interests to be arguably protected by the FLPMA. Litigants do fall short on occasion. In *Air Courier Conf. v. Amer. Postal Workers Union*, 498 U.S. 517 (1991), the Court held that the interests of postal workers in retaining jobs did not fall within the zone of interests protected by the Postal Reorganization Act's provisions on maintaining the Postal Service's monopoly, because those provisions were meant to ensure the Service's financial security, not to protect its work force. Cf. *Bennett v. Spear*, 117 S.Ct. 1154 (1997); notes 214-18 and accompanying text.

189. See Laurence H. Tribe, American Constitutional Law 144-45 (1988).

federal court in the first instance. The ban on third-party claims concerns the *violations of law* that litigants assert once they are inside the door.[190] Recall that the crucial (though controversial) point of *Data Processing* was to distinguish the threshold matter of standing, on the one hand, from the further question of the legal claims to be adjudicated, on the other. The constitutional prerequisites for standing comport with that rationale inasmuch as they rest standing on the nature of personal injuries rather than on the content of legal claims. The zone test compromises the point inasmuch as it requires an examination of the statute or constitutional provision litigants wish to enforce in order to determine whether their interests are within the zone of interests protected. Nevertheless, the zone test does *not* obliterate the distinction entirely by collapsing the *interests* litigants must allege for standing into the *violations of law* that litigants assert the defendant committed when causing injury to those interests.[191]

The zone test also overlaps with the analysis the Court employs to determine whether litigants have a private right of action.[192] Of course, § 702 expressly authorizes *some* private litigants to enforce federal legal standards in court—and not only in court, but in federal court. This is to say, § 702 both creates a right of action for, and confers standing on, litigants whose interests are within the zone.[193] Yet the right of action that § 702 confers extends only to private litigants whose interests pass the zone test. Accordingly, this free standing procedural vehicle demands more interpretive work than right-of-action provisions typically found within substantive statutes.[194] Courts cannot examine § 702 alone, but must press on to identify the particular private litigants whose interests fall within the zone of interests protected by the statutes they wish to enforce.[195] That exercise invites the kind of analysis the Supreme Court once used in searching for *implied* rights of action. Since it is enough that litigants' interests are even arguably within the zone, it is not essential that they be expressly identified as the targets or beneficiaries of the statutes they claim the defendant has violated.[196]

---

190. *Duke Power*, 438 U.S. at 80-81.

191. See text accompanying notes 92-94. Justice Powell explained in *Warth* that the "source" of a plaintiff's claim to relief can have "critical importance" with respect to prudential standing rules. 422 U.S. at 500. Then again, the causation requirement does sometimes approach the merits. See notes 148-49 and accompanying text. The zone test illustrates how it is possible (and, indeed, quite common) to draw distinctions between groups of non-Hohfeldian plaintiffs. Plaintiffs need not assert legal rights to pass the zone test; they need only have interests that are within the zone. So they are plainly non-Hohfeldian. Yet they do have interests that distinguish them from the public at large— sometimes economic interests that were not actionable at common law. Certainly, they do not (necessarily) proceed solely for ideological purposes. But see note 66 (discussing different assessments).

192. *Clarke*, 479 U.S. at 399.

193. See Chapter VIII, notes 91, 95-97 and accompanying text.

194. See note 212 (noting illustrations).

195. In this sense, § 702 is like § 1983. Both are free standing right-of-action provisions that require an examination of the underlying statutes or constitutional provisions litigants seek to enforce in order to determine whether the particular litigants at bar are eligible to proceed. In § 702 cases, would-be litigants must advance interests that fall within the zone of interests protected by the statutes or constitutional provisions they claim the defendant has violated. In § 1983 cases, would-be litigants must allege a violation of (someone's) "rights" under color of state law. See Chapter VIII, notes 131-34 and accompanying text.

196. In *Clarke*, Justice White said that it is much easier for litigants to show that their interests fall within the zone of interests protected by a statute for purposes of § 702 than it is for litigants to show, under "conditions that make the APA inapplicable," that they

The zone test primarily controls cases arising under the APA, in which litigants rely on § 702 for authority to challenge actions taken by federal agencies.[197] Nevertheless, the Court has occasionally utilized the zone test outside the context of § 702 and has indicated that it is a feature of general prudential standing doctrine.[198] The Court invoked essentially the same idea as early as *Flast v. Cohen.*[199] Recall that Chief Justice Warren said that taxpayers have standing to challenge federal spending measures because they can demonstrate both a nexus between their status as taxpayers and the expenditures they attack and a nexus between their status and the constitutional provision they contend is violated—the Establishment Clause being a limitation on spending. The first nexus states the constitutional prerequisite for standing: injury caused by the enactment under attack.[200] The second is the zone test traveling under another name: injury to in-

---

nonetheless have a right of action implied from the statute involved. 479 U.S. at 400 n.16. The zone test is a "guide for deciding whether...a particular plaintiff should be heard to complain of a particular agency decision." Litigants will fail the zone test only if their interests are "so marginally related to or inconsistent with the purposes implicit in the statute that it cannot be assumed that Congress intended to permit the suit." Id. at 399. The question under the zone test is whether a "particular" plaintiff should be heard to complain that an agency has violated the law. Similarly, the question under the old approach to implied actions to enforce statutes (as well as the current analysis of implied actions to enforce constitutional provisions) is whether a "particular" plaintiff is "a member of the class of litigants that may, as a matter of law, appropriately invoke the power of the courts." *Davis v. Passman,* 442 U.S. 228, 239 n.18 (1979). In neither context, then, does the Court purport to decide that *all* private litigants (who have constitutional standing) are entitled to enforce federal statutes or constitutional provisions by means of private lawsuits. Nevertheless, in the implied action cases, anyone who possesses constitutional standing can typically go forward. For if a statute or constitutional provision is enforceable via private litigation, there is typically no reason why anyone should be foreclosed. In the zone test cases, that is not so. The very point of the zone test is to distinguish between classes of would-be private litigants and to authorize only some to sue. Then again, Congress can supersede the zone test by prescribing alternative definitions of the litigants authorized to sue or even by permitting anyone with constitutional standing to proceed. See notes 214-16 and accompanying text.

197. See *Clarke,* 479 U.S. at 400 & n.16.

198. See *Bennett,* 117 S.Ct. at 1161. In two other cases, the Court consulted the zone test, but easily found it to be satisfied. In *Boston Stock Exchange v. State Tax Comm'n,* 429 U.S. 318 (1977), taxpayers sued state authorities in state court, contending that a state tax violated the Commerce Clause. Justice White explained (in a footnote) that the plaintiffs had "standing under the two-part test" in *Data Processing.* Id. at 320-21 n.3. White said that since the taxpayers were asserting "their right under the Commerce Clause to engage in interstate commerce free of discriminatory taxes...they [were] arguably within the zone of interests" protected by the prohibition against discriminatory taxation established by the Commerce Clause. Id. In *Dennis v. Higgins,* 498 U.S. 439 (1991), Justice White cited the footnote in *Boston Stock Exchange* in aid of a holding that private businesses have a "right" to be free of discriminatory taxes that is enforceable in a § 1983 action. Id. at 449. See Chapter VIII, note 132. The assertion of a *legal right* is sufficient for standing wholly apart from the zone test. See text accompanying notes 92-94. Moreover, the Supreme Court can exercise appellate jurisdiction in cases arising from state court, even though the plaintiffs would not have been able to sue in a federal district court for want of standing. See note 1. In other cases, the Court has listed the zone test along with the ban on third-party claims and thus apparently as a "prudential standing requirement of general application." *Bennett,* 117 S.Ct. at 1161; *Allen,* 468 U.S. at 751; *Valley Forge,* 454 U.S. at 474-75.

199. See notes 107-08 and accompanying text.

200. See notes 102-35 and accompanying text.

terests that are within the zone of interests protected by the statute or constitutional provision said to be violated.[201] In other cases, the Court has disclaimed the zone test apart from § 702. In *Duke Power*,[202] Chief Justice Burger acknowledged that the plaintiffs' interest in the lake was not connected to their due process claim. But he confined the second nexus requirement in *Flast* (that is, the zone test) to taxpayer suits and thus held that the plaintiffs in *Duke Power* had standing without satisfying that test.[203]

E. Standing: Congressional Power

Congress has significant, but not plenary, authority to confer standing on would-be litigants. Initially, Congress can simply create positive legal rights in private citizens. An allegation of a violation of a legal right serves in place of an allegation of factual injury. This has been true since *Marbury v. Madison*.[204] To take a modern example, § 804 of the Fair Housing Act makes it unlawful "[t]o refuse to sell or rent" a dwelling to "any person because of race, color, religion, sex, or national origin" or to "represent to any person because of race, color, religion, sex, or national origin, that any dwelling is not available" for sale or rent when, in fact, the dwelling is available.[205] When litigants claim an invasion of the rights established by § 804, they clearly allege the kind of personal stake that other litigants establish by alleging injury. In *Havens Realty Corp. v. Coleman*,[206] two "testers," one African American and one white, contended that a real estate broker had violated § 804 by falsely telling the black tester that apartments were *not* available, while truthfully telling the white tester that they *were*. Justice Brennan interpreted § 804 to confer on "all 'persons' a *legal right* to truthful information about available housing." Accordingly, the African American tester satisfied

---

201. See Fallon, note 66, at 20; Nichol, note 94, at 96. In *Invest. Co. Inst. v. Camp*, 401 U.S. 617 (1971), decided just after *Data Processing*, investment companies attacked a ruling by the Comptroller of the Currency allowing banks to offer investment accounts. In a *per curiam*, the Court went directly to whether the ruling violated the Glass-Steagall Act's protections of competitors and, holding that it did, explained that there could be "no real question" that the plaintiffs' interests fell within the zone for standing purposes. Id. at 621. That disposition has been criticized for dodging the zone test. See Note, *A Defense of the "Zone of Interests" Standing Test*, 1983 Duke L.J. 447, 453. Yet if a litigant advances a legal right under a statute, it *does* follow that the litigant has standing—provided the litigant demonstrates causation and seeks a remedy that satisfies the redressability requirement. See text accompanying notes 92-94, 155-62 and accompanying text.

202. See note 138 and accompanying text.

203. The plaintiffs also alleged that they would suffer injuries to their lives and property if a nuclear accident occurred. The Chief Justice said that those injuries *were* connected to their due process claim. 438 U.S. at 78 n.23. Yet since he did not rely on injuries of that kind in satisfaction of the constitutional requirements for standing in *Duke Power*, he could not recruit them to service with respect to the zone test, either. Id. at 78-79.

204. 5 U.S. (1 Cranch) 137 (1803). See notes 70, 92-94 and accompanying text (discussing the sufficiency of legal rights for standing purposes); Chapter I, text accompanying note 56 (discussing *Marbury*).

205. 42 U.S.C. § 3604.

206. 455 U.S. 363 (1982).

the constitutional requirements for standing, because she claimed that the broker had violated her statutory right to the truth.[207]

Litigants who advance legal rights must also have a procedural vehicle: a right of action to vindicate their substantive rights by means of private lawsuits.[208] In cases where it apples, §702 of the APA performs that function. In cases in which litigants seek to enforce legal rights created by §804, adjacent provisions of the Fair Housing Act, §810 and §812, independently authorize private lawsuits. Those provisions specify that the rights established by §804 "may be enforced by civil actions in appropriate United States district courts."[209] Other statutes authorize litigants to file lawsuits in *some* forum, but do not confer standing to proceed in federal court. The most familiar illustration is §1983.[210]

Congress can also deputize non-Hohfeldian private citizens to litigate as private attorneys general, seeking judicial enforcement of the law in the public interest.[211] This is the authority that has attracted primary attention. It contemplates

---

207. Id. at 373 (emphasis added). Litigants who advance legal rights must also show causation and redressability. The former merges with the merits, but the latter may be problematic. See notes 155-62 and accompanying text.

208. See Chapter VIII, notes 79-134 and accompanying text (discussing rights of action).

209. *Gladstone, Realtors v. Village of Bellwood*, 441 U.S. 91, 94 n.1 (1979). See 42 U.S.C. §§3610, 3612. Since §810 and §812 explicitly authorize litigants to proceed in federal court, they (like §702) perform double duty: they both create a right of action to sue in *some* court *and* confer standing to sue in an Article III court. See text accompanying note 193. Some academics have proposed that the question whether litigants have standing should be reconceptualized as the question whether they have a right of action to sue in federal court. See, e.g., Albert, note 64; David P. Currie, *Misunderstanding Standing*, 1981 Sup. Ct. Rev. 41; Erwin Chemerinsky, *A Unified Approach to Justiciability*, 22 Conn. L. Rev. 677 (1990). Professor Sunstein and Professor Fletcher have elaborated that fundamental idea. In cases in which litigants seek to enforce federal statutes, Sunstein and Fletcher would collapse all the features of standing into the single question whether Congress has authorized the suit. They would depart dramatically from the conceptual framework the Court now employs inasmuch as they would discard the search for factual injury and concentrate, instead, on the instructions that Congress supplies regarding the judicial enforcement of its enactments. In practical effect, however, Sunstein and Fletcher suspect that their alternative approach would reproduce the results the Court has reached in many of its principal decisions on standing. See Cass R. Sunstein, *What's Standing After Lujan? Of Citizen Suits, "Injuries," and Article III*, 91 Mich. L. Rev. 163 (1992); Sunstein, note 64; Fletcher, note 96. In cases in which litigants seek to enforce the Constitution, Sunstein and Fletcher would let the particular provision in question be the source of both the right to be enforced and the authority for litigation. For example, Professor Fletcher endorses the position that Justice Stewart took regarding the Establishment Clause claim in *Flast*—namely, that taxpayers have standing to enforce the Establishment Clause because that clause itself gives taxpayers a judicially enforceable right to be free of taxation for religious purposes. See note 110.

210. *O'Shea v. Littleton*, 414 U.S. 488, 493-94 n.2 (1974) (confirming that §1983 does not address standing). See Chapter VI, notes 48-53 and accompanying text (discussing §1983 suits in state court). This is why, in §1983 cases like *Wulff* and *Craig*, see notes 170-72 and accompanying text, the Court invoked its own prudential standing rules without reference to anything Congress might have said with respect to standing. As a matter of statutory construction, the Court did not understand §1983 to deal with standing at all. Academicians who urge the Court to make the existence of a right of action central in standing cases sometimes argue that §1983 should be understood to have implications for standing, after all. E.g., Currie, note 209, at 45; Sunstein, note 96, at 46.

211. *Data Processing*, 397 U.S. at 154. Accord *Bennett*, 117 S.Ct. at 1162.

that Congress need not create substantive legal rights in anyone, but can limit it-self to conferring standing by creating rights of action to sue in federal court. Congress commonly establishes federal rights of action in connection with partic-ular statutory schemes and, in so doing, defines the class of authorized private lit-igants in the way Congress sees fit.[212] In § 702 of the APA, Congress has autho-rized suits by anyone whose interests are arguably within the zone of interests protected by any statutes that litigants wish to enforce.[213] Occasionally, Congress is more expansive still, empowering non-Hohfeldian litigants without specifying that they must be connected in any way to the statutes they insist have been vio-lated.

In *Bennett v. Spear*,[214] Justice Scalia explained that standing provisions of this last kind not only disclaim congressionally created non-constitutional stand-ing rules like the zone test, but also sweep aside any prudential standing require-ments that the courts would ordinarily invoke. Accordingly, the Court applies a clear statement rule to ensure that any particular standing statute genuinely means to be so generous.[215] If, however, Congress uses language that is suffi-ciently clear, Congress can eliminate all non-constitutional barriers and thus con-fer standing on "everyman" (who satisfies the constitutional prerequisites).[216]

In *Bennett*, ranchers contended that the Fish and Wildlife Service and the Bu-reau of Reclamation failed to comply with the Endangered Species Act in devel-oping a plan to keep the water levels in two reservoirs relatively high to protect an endangered species of sucker fish. According to the ranchers, the plan allowed too little water to escape for their commercial and recreational use. The circuit court below ruled that the ranchers' interests were not within the zone of inter-ests protected by the ESA. After all, the ranchers hoped to defeat the Act's pur-pose to safeguard the fish. Justice Scalia rejected that judgment with respect to some of the ranchers' claims on the ground that their economic interests *were* "arguably" within the zone of interests protected by the specific provisions of the ESA they contended the agencies had violated. With respect to other claims, Jus-tice Scalia said that it made no difference whether the ranchers satisfied the zone test, because Congress had superseded that test. The special "citizen standing" provision in the ESA[217] eliminated all non-constitutional limits that would other-wise have applied. Since the ranchers' economic injury satisfied the constitutional requirements for standing, they were free to contest what they viewed as a viola-tion of the Act, even though they were antagonistic to its primary objectives.[218]

Congress cannot dispense with injury, causation, and redressability. In the *Lujan* case,[219] Justice Scalia explained that those requirements are constitutional

---

212. See, e.g., 7 U.S.C. § 2305(c) (authorizing a person "injured in his business or prop-erty" to sue to enforce fair trade statutes); 15 U.S.C. § 298(b) (authorizing "competitors, customers, or subsequent purchasers" to sue to enforce gold and silver standards).

213. See notes 82-87, 183-96 and accompanying text.

214. 117 S.Ct. at 1162.

215. See Chapter I, notes 37-41 and accompanying text.

216. *Bennett*, 117 S.Ct. at 1163.

217. 16 U.S.C. § 1540(g).

218. 117 S.Ct. at 1162-63. The ranchers did not contest the EPA's determination that the fish were genuinely endangered, despite compelling evidence that the birth rate of suck-ers can be computed by the minute.

219. See notes 121-22 and accompanying text.

conditions that Congress is not free to waive. Congress may conclude that any-one willing to undertake the burdens of suit will serve well enough. But the con-stitutional aspects of standing doctrine do not merely ensure effective advocacy. They elaborate the separation of powers.[220] In *Lujan*, accordingly, Justice Scalia read the "citizen standing" provision in the Endangered Species Act to leave the constitutional prerequisites intact.[221]

By some accounts, Congress should be able to go further. Dissenting in *Flast*, Justice Harlan said that, for his part, Congress can confer standing on anyone it pleases, even litigants who allege no factual injury.[222] For if the underlying issue is the separation of powers, Congress can consent to an exercise of judicial power when it sees no threat to its own sphere.[223] Justice White may have agreed. In a brief concurring opinion in *Trafficante v. Metro. Life Ins. Co.*,[224] he said that he would have had "great difficulty" concluding that the plaintiffs presented a "case or controversy," if § 810 of the Fair Housing Act had not granted them au-thority to "sue in court."[225]

Despite *Lujan*, Congress may be able to affect the injuries and causal connec-tions required for standing. If Congress has authority of this kind, the scope of that authority is undeveloped. Justice Scalia insisted that the holding in *Lujan* was consistent with Justice Powell's statement in *Warth* that the injury required by Article III "may exist solely by virtue of statute"[226] and with Justice Mar-shall's dictum in *Linda R.S. v. Richard D.*[227] that "Congress may enact statutes creating legal rights, the invasion of which creates standing, even though no in-jury would exist without the statute."[228] Scalia explained, however, that in the cases on which Powell and Marshall relied, Congress had elevated "to the status of legally cognizable injuries concrete, de facto injuries that were previously inad-

---

220. See notes 99-100 and accompanying text.

221. By some accounts, the Court has deliberately denominated injury, causation, and redressability *as* constitutional requirements for the very *purpose* of insulating those features of standing doctrine from congressional adjustment. See note 165 and accompanying text.

222. See *Flast*, 392 U.S. at 131 (dissenting opinion).

223. The Court has said in other contexts that a "governmental unit whose domain is...narrowed" cannot consent to a breach of the separation of powers principle as elabo-rated by the Court. *New York v. United States*, 505 U.S. 144, 182 (1992). In a case like *Lujan*, moreover, it is not Congress' sphere, but that of the executive, that may be at risk. According to Justice Scalia, the injury requirement operated in *Lujan* to keep the courts from interfering with executive branch efforts to see that the laws were "faithfully exe-cuted." 504 U.S. at 577, quoting U.S. Const. art. II, § 3. It is one thing for Congress to waive separation of powers concerns with respect to lawsuits challenging federal statutes. It is arguably another for Congress to do so with respect to attacks on the way officials in the executive branch are implementing statutes they are assigned to enforce. Professor Sunstein contends that the President's authority to administer statutes is actually a *duty* and that Congress should be able to authorize private litigants to sue to enforce that duty in the courts. Sunstein, *What's Standing*, note 209, at 212. Krent and Shenkman insist that Con-gress cannot appoint private attorneys general who eclipse the executive branch entirely. Harold J. Krent & Ethan G. Shenkman, *Of Citizen Suits and Citizen Sunstein*, 91 Mich. L. Rev. 1793 (1993).

224. 409 U.S. 205 (1972).

225. Id. at 212; see note 241 and accompanying text.

226. 422 U.S. at 500; see notes 140-41 and accompanying text.

227. 410 U.S. 614 (1973); see note 152.

228. 410 U.S. at 617 n.3.

equate in law."[229] Borrowing a line from *Sierra Club*, Justice Scalia distinguished between federal statutes that broaden "the categories of injury that may be alleged in support of standing," on the one hand, and statutes that abandon "the requirement that the party seeking review must himself have suffered an injury," on the other.[230] These passages in *Lujan* are problematic. The difficulty lies in the *Linda R.S.* dictum, which mixes *legal rights* with *injuries*. Since *Data Processing*, the Court has distinguished between those two ideas. The injury feature of constitutional standing is conventionally understood to turn on factual circumstances, which would seem to be beyond Congress' power to affect by statute.[231] There are at least three ways to resolve the ambiguity.

Initially, *Linda R.S.* may only confirm that Congress can enact statutes establishing positive legal *rights* and that litigants who claim a violation of those rights satisfy the threshold constitutional requirement for standing without resorting to an allegation of factual *injury*.[232] Then, to harmonize that older proposition with the harm-based conception of standing, *Linda R.S.* simply has it that a violation of a legal right counts as injury. Justice Brennan read the *Linda R.S.* dictum this way in *Havens*.[233] The point is not that a violation of a legal right is entirely dependent on factual circumstances. The point is that a violation of a legal right (dependent on law as well as facts) does the same *work* that injury in fact performs within standing doctrine. In *Havens*, Justice Brennan drew a sharp distinction between the black tester (who had been given false information and thus had standing on the basis of a violation of her legal rights under § 804) and the white tester (who had received accurate information and thus could not claim that his legal right to truthful information had been violated). Justice Brennan said that the white tester might obtain standing on the basis of an *injury* to his *interest* in living in an integrated community. But that was a different allegation that would have to be developed on remand.[234]

Alternatively, *Linda R.S.* may confirm that Congress can enact statutes specifying non-constitutional standing rules that displace any prudential rules that the Court would otherwise apply. As Justice Scalia noted in *Lujan*, the two cases that Justice Marshall cited in *Linda R.S.* involved statutes of that kind. In *Hardin v. Kentucky Utilities Co.*,[235] a private utility company contended that the Tennessee Valley Authority had unlawfully sold electricity outside a prescribed area. Justice Black held that the company's economic interest in avoiding competition met the requirements for standing, because the statute the company charged the TVA with violating reflected "a legislative purpose to protect a competitive interest."[236] In *Data Processing*, Justice Douglas said that "no explicit statutory provision" had been "necessary to confer standing" in *Hardin*, because the plaintiff company was "within the class of persons that the statutory provision was de-

---

229. 504 U.S. at 578.
230. Id., quoting *Sierra Club*, 405 U.S. at 738; see notes 119-20 and accompanying text.
231. See note 94 and accompanying text; but see notes 96-98 and accompanying text.
232. See note 204 and accompanying text.
233. 441 U.S. at 373-74. Professor Fallon understands *Linda R.S.* this way. To test congressional power with respect to standing, Fallon posits the creation of what he calls, interchangeably, statutory "rights" or "legal interests." Fallon, note 66, at 19, 49.
234. 441 U.S. at 374-77.
235. 390 U.S. 1 (1968).
236. Id. at 6.

signed to protect." Douglas thus read *Hardin* to mean that the utility company needed no "specific" standing statute authorizing aggrieved citizens to sue the TVA in particular. The company was entitled to rely on the general standing provision in § 702 of the APA, which authorized the company to sue the TVA, provided the company's interests were within the zone of interests protected by the statute limiting the TVA's service area.[237]

In the other case, *Trafficante*,[238] tenants of an apartment building contended that the landlord discouraged African American applicants from renting rooms in violation of § 804 of the Fair Housing Act.[239] They did not argue that the landlord had violated their legal rights under § 804, but they insisted that they nonetheless had standing because they suffered factual injury: They were deprived of the benefits of living in a racially integrated building. Justice Douglas read one of the attendant standing provisions in the Act (§ 810) to eliminate any non-constitutional standing limits that otherwise would apply.[240] That left only the question whether the plaintiffs' interest in integrated housing supplied injury in fact for constitutional standing purposes. Douglas held that it did. Justice White then added his concurring opinion, in which he suggested that § 810 was sufficient in itself to satisfy Article III, even if the plaintiffs' alleged injury would not otherwise have sufficed.[241]

In *Lujan*, Justice Scalia suggested a third meaning for *Linda R.S.*, *Hardin*, and *Trafficante*. Recall what he said: Congress can identify "concrete, defacto injuries" that "previously" were "inadequate in law" and can elevate those injuries to "legally cognizable" status.[242] On first blush, this third account is difficult to follow. The injuries in those cases were *not* previously thought "inadequate in law" to qualify as factual injuries for constitutional standing purposes. Both the interest in avoiding competition and the interest in living in integrated housing existed prior to the creation of the TVA and the enactment of § 804. Those inter-

---

237. *Data Processing*, 397 U.S. at 155; see notes 183-203 and accompanying text (discussing the zone test). Alternatively, Justice Black may have conceived that the statute in *Hardin* gave the competing utility company a *legal right* to be free of competition from the TVA. If that is what he meant, *Hardin* did nothing new, but only applied the Court's then-familiar rights-based conception of standing. See text accompanying notes 67-81 (explaining standing doctrine just prior to *Data Processing*).

238. See note 224 and accompanying text.

239. See text accompanying note 205.

240. See text accompanying notes 208-09.

241. See text accompanying note 225. White's tone suggested not that he would cheerfully have gone further than Douglas, but rather that he joined Douglas only grudgingly. Nevertheless, White said that § 810 was crucial to his conclusion that Article III standing existed. He therefore necessarily contemplated a role for Congress that Douglas did not broach. Douglas noted legislative history suggesting that some members of Congress were concerned about the kind of interest the plaintiffs alleged. But that part of his opinion went not to whether the plaintiffs had injuries at all, but to whether the standing provision, § 810, was actually so sweeping as its language suggested. Douglas did not propose that § 810 made the plaintiffs' allegations sufficient for Article III standing. He said that § 810 eliminated any non-constitutional limits and that no constitutional question was presented because the plaintiffs had alleged *factual* injury "with particularity." 409 U.S. at 211 (majority opinion).

242. See text accompanying note 229.

ests were personal to the plaintiffs in *Hardin* and *Trafficante* and thus were "cognizable" without reference to any law that Congress created.[243] The plaintiffs in those cases needed a statute not to establish factual injuries to genuine interests, but to escape the Court's rights-based conception of standing, under which *injuries* to *interests*, however concrete, would not suffice.[244]

The important question now is not what Justice Marshall meant to say in *Linda R.S.*, nor what *Hardin* and *Trafficante* were about, but rather what the modern Court will allow Congress to do. Despite the disposition in *Lujan*, Congress may yet be able to identify some injuries that would otherwise be insufficient for Article III standing and give them that status by statute. According to Justice Scalia, however, there is a caveat: The injuries so identified must be "concrete" and "de facto."[245] That suggests a continuing attachment to common law thinking about the nature of adjudication.

Writing separately in *Lujan*, Justice Kennedy appeared to be open to lawsuits more consonant with public rights litigation. He agreed that there must be an "outer limit" on congressional power "to confer rights of action" and that Article III requires litigants to show that they suffer injury in a "concrete and personal way." He suggested, however, that "[a]s government policies and programs become more complex," the Court should be "sensitive to the articulation of new rights of action that do not have clear analogues in our common-law tradition."[246] According to Kennedy, Congress can "define injuries and articulate chains of causation that will give rise to a case or controversy where none existed before." But Congress must "at the very least identify the injury it seeks to vindi-

---

243. Recall that the Court recognized as early as *Sanders* that competitors suffer factual injury. See notes 74-76 and accompanying text.

244. See note 70 and accompanying text. To argue that the interests in *Hardin* and *Trafficante* depended on positive law would be to take an extravagant position regarding the extent to which law drives human values. See note 98. Federal anti-race discrimination legislation is a splendid thing, to be sure. But some of us understood that blacks and whites alike suffer harm from racial segregation well before Congress started writing statutes about it.

245. Scalia gave no examples. It has been suggested that he might allow Congress to declare that what is commonly regarded as an interest is, instead, a positive legal right. In *Lujan* itself, for example, Congress might have vested title to endangered animals in all Americans and invited citizens at large to enforce their new proprietary rights in federal court. Alternatively, Justice Scalia implied that Congress might manufacture a sufficient personal stake in the outcome of cases by offering to reward litigants who are successful. He mentioned that possibility again in the *Steel* case. See text accompanying note 161. Professor Sunstein thinks Justice Scalia would approve a bounty scheme, as does Professor Nichol. See Sunstein, note 209, at 232-33; Nichol, note 97, at 1165. Under *qui tam* arrangements, the government deputizes private citizens to sue other private citizens to recoup funds due the government and then gives anyone who is successful a share of the proceeds as a reward. The revival of that idea in the False Claims Act of 1986 has ignited an academic debate over whether *qui tam* schemes can survive the Court's modern standing doctrine. Compare Evan Caminker, *The Constitutionality of Qui Tam Actions*, 99 Yale L.J. 341 (1989) (arguing that suits envisioned by the 1986 Act can be sustained), with James T. Blanch, *The Constitutionality of the False Claims Act's Qui Tam Provision*, 16 Harv. J. Law & Pub. Policy 701 (1993) (arguing the contrary). Writing separately in *Steel*, Justice Stevens endorsed the idea that payments to plaintiffs would satisfy Article III and, in so doing, explicitly said that *qui tam* arrangements would meet constitutional requirements. *Steel*, 118 S.Ct. at 1030 (concurring opinion).

246. 504 U.S. at 580 (Kennedy, J., concurring) (joined by Souter, J.).

cate and relate the injury to the class of persons entitled to bring suit," rather than authorizing "anyone" to proceed.[247]

These tentative statements bear scrutiny. At least some of the justices may be coming to doubt that the constitutional prerequisites for standing can rest entirely on matters of fact, divorced from law. Conceivably, that could lead them to revive Justice Frankfurter's position that only litigants who advance legal rights can establish standing in the constitutional sense.[248] Critics of the harm-based conception of standing would find that result perverse.[249] They hope, instead, that the Court will ultimately regard the link between injuries and law as a reason for being more, not less, hospitable to suits within the model of public rights. Thus the Court may entertain arguments that Congress has identified and illuminated genuine human interests that were not previously appreciated as interests at all, and even that Congress has developed a satisfying account of the way in which unlawful conduct injures interests of that kind.[250]

F. Standing and the Merits

In cases in which litigants establish standing by asserting that the defendant has violated their legal rights, the showing they make at the standing stage is a preview of the presentation they will make of their legal claims on the merits. In cases in which litigants establish standing by showing that the defendant has caused them factual injury, that is not (necessarily) so. The relationship between the showing that injured litigants make at the standing stage and the presentation they make on the merits is more complex. There is always some overlap. The causation and redressability features of harm-based standing doctrine contemplate some attention to the violations of law that litigants contend are responsible for their injuries.[251] Prudential standing doctrines invariably implicate the merits of legal claims more directly.[252] Yet the very point of the harm-based

---

247. Id. Justice Breyer's opinion for the Court in *Akins* also contains hints in this direction. See notes 111-13 and accompanying text. Breyer was clear that the plaintiffs in that case alleged "genuine 'injury in fact'" flowing from their deprivation of information that could be of use to them. *Akins*, 118 S.Ct. at 1784. That injury existed wholly apart from the Federal Election Campaign Act, which allegedly established a legal duty in AIPAC to divulge the information the plaintiffs desired. Nevertheless, Justice Breyer emphasized that the Act required the information to be disclosed and appeared to link that point to his holding that the plaintiffs' alleged harm was sufficiently concrete to satisfy the Article III requirement of "specific injury." Id., quoting *Havens*, 455 U.S. at 373-74; see notes 206-07 and accompanying text.

248. See note 70 and accompanying text.

249. See notes 96-101, 135, 209 and accompanying text.

250. See notes 96-98 and accompanying (describing thinking along these lines). Krent and Shenkman argue that Justice Kennedy meant to say that Congress must be clear about both the litigants it wishes to empower and the injuries it seeks to protect—in order to ensure that Congress carefully weighs the risks of permitting unelected private citizens effectively to represent the public. See Krent & Shenkman, note 223, at 1822-23.

251. See notes 148-49 and accompanying text.

252. See notes 189-91 and accompanying text (discussing the zone test).

framework is to separate standing from the merits in order to enable non-Ho-hfeldian private attorneys general to litigate legal issues on behalf of the public.[253]

The working premise is that litigants who achieve standing on the basis of injuries are in a position to succeed on the merits if they can establish that the defendant has violated, is violating, or will imminently violate the law. That violation of law need not constitute a breach of any legal duty the defendant owes to the plaintiffs personally; it need not be conceived as a violation of their personal legal rights. It can be, and often is, simply a violation of some federal statute or constitutional provision specifying the way in which the defendant must behave. The *Bennett* case[254] provides an example. The ranchers in that case satisfied the requirements for harm-based standing and were therefore entitled to press a variety of legal claims against the defendant agencies. One of those claims was that in implementing various provisions of the Endangered Species Act, the Service and the Bureau had acted "arbitrarily and capriciously" or "otherwise not in accordance with law."[255] A claim of that kind could not usefully be understood as a claim that the agencies had violated the ranchers' personal legal rights. It was simply a claim that the Service and the Bureau had violated the law (in a way that harmed the ranchers who on the basis of that harm had standing to sue to enforce the law).

This proposition, solid as it is, nonetheless can be obscured in some cases. Recall that in *Data Processing*, Justice Douglas said that the competitor companies had standing under § 702 inasmuch as they suffered injury and their interests were arguably within the zone of interests protected by the Bank Services Corporation Act.[256] In a final paragraph, he said that whether anything in that Act gave the plaintiffs a "legal interest" that "protect[ed] them against violations," and whether the actions of the Comptroller "did in fact violate" the Act, were questions that went to "the merits" and thus remained to be resolved in the lower courts.[257] That final paragraph implied that Douglas' analysis of standing did not vanquish Frankfurter's "legal interest" requirement after all, but merely shifted attention to that requirement to a later stage of the proceedings, when litigants would still be expected to demonstrate that their own legal rights were violated.[258] Having obtained standing on the basis of *interests* with which the

---

253. See notes 92-94 and accompanying text. In cases in which litigants advance procedural rights with respect to agency action, they rely on injuries to interests in order to establish their eligibility to claim a *legal right* to procedure—e.g., a right to participate in a hearing. See *Lujan*, 504 U.S. at 573 nn.7-8; see notes 121-22 and accompanying text.

254. See notes 214-18 and accompanying text.

255. 5 U.S.C. § 706.

256. See text accompanying notes 88-90.

257. 397 U.S. at 158. Justice Douglas himself placed quotation marks around the phrase "legal interest." Justice Brennan left essentially the same impression. He said that once the plaintiffs established standing on the basis of "injury in fact," the inquiry would proceed to "the merits—to whether the specific legal interest claimed" by the plaintiffs was "protected by the statute" and "whether the protested agency action invaded that interest." *Barlow v. Collins*, 397 U.S. 159, 175 (1970) (dissenting opinion). Cf. *Invest. Co. Inst.*, 401 U.S. at 620 (reading *Data Processing* to mean that the question whether Congress has actually "prohibited" competition of which plaintiffs complain is a "question for the merits").

258. See text accompanying notes 70, 86-90 (discussing the "legal interest" test and Douglas' rejection of it in *Data Processing*).

statute was arguably *concerned*, they could succeed on the merits only by demonstrating personal legal *rights* that the statute actually *established*.[259]

It would not be illogical to treat the relationship between harm-based standing and the merits in that way. Standing might be understood as a rule of pleading, which screens out litigants who have so little interest that they do not warrant judicial attention at all, but then devotes judicial resources only to litigants who attempt to establish a violation of their own legal rights. Yet if that were all that the harm-based conception of standing meant, it would not be so important as, in fact, it is.[260]

Litigants who obtain standing on the basis of injuries to interests invariably attempt to convince the court to interpret federal law to their advantage. In so doing, they commonly contend that the purpose of a statute or constitutional provision is in some wise to protect the kinds of interests they themselves have. There is a genuine sense, then, in which litigants within the harm-based conception of standing *do* often press their own interests at the merits stage. In *Bennett*, for example, the ranchers contended that one of the ways in which the Service and the Bureau had violated the ESA was in failing to take account of the economic injuries the ranchers would suffer.[261] And in the *Steel* case, the plaintiffs argued that the company had violated their "right to know" the information the company had concealed.[262] Nevertheless, there is no formal requirement that litigants must contrive to couch a legal claim that the defendant has violated the *law* as a claim that the defendant has violated their individual *legal rights*.[263]

---

259. See The Federal Courts and the Federal System 176 (Fallon, Meltzer & Shapiro eds. 1996).

260. Professor Stewart argues that the "considerations that a litigant may advance on the merits should normally be no broader or narrower than those that the litigant may assert to secure standing." Otherwise, litigants with special concerns of their own may misrepresent the interests of others. Conflicts of interest, in turn, can produce poor decisions. See Stewart, note 83, at 1573 n.62. See also notes 79-80, 169 and accompanying text (discussing similar arguments by other academics regarding third-party claims). The conventional answer is that Congress addresses concerns of that kind when it decides to authorize private attorneys general and establishes the criteria they must meet to qualify as the public's champions. See note 91 and accompanying text (discussing the congressional judgment ascribed to the statutory zone test).

261. *Bennett*, 117 S.Ct. at 1160 (describing the ranchers' third claim); see notes 214-18, 254 and accompanying text.

262. See notes 158-59 and accompanying text.

263. In *Sierra Club*, the Court said that the radio station cases, *Sanders* and *Scripps-Howard*, establish that litigants who achieve standing on the basis of some cognizable injury are then in a position simply to contend that an agency "has failed to comply with its statutory mandate." 405 U.S. at 737; see notes 119-20 and accompanying text (discussing the *Sierra Club* case); notes 74-78 and accompanying text (discussing *Sanders* and *Scripps-Howard*). In *First National Bank*, the Court upset an agency interpretation of a federal regulatory statute—at the behest of competitor banks who barely passed the zone test, far less asserted any legal rights with respect to the agency's action. See notes 186-87 and accompanying text. In *TVA v. Hill*, 437 U.S. 153 (1978), biologists and other individuals who used the Little Tennessee Valley area where the Tellico Dam was being built sued the TVA for violating the Endangered Species Act by destroying the snail darter's habitat. The plaintiffs had the benefit of the "citizen standing" provision in the ESA, but they asserted no personal legal rights under the Act. The Court forthrightly addressed the question whether the very act of constructing the dam violated the Act and held that the plaintiffs were entitled to a permanent injunction against further work on the project. Of course, Congress may establish special statutory limits on the private actions that litigants can bring. In *Bennett*, for example, Justice Scalia examined the intricacies of the ESA and the APA to determine which

G. Ripeness

Federal courts can entertain claims only if they are "ripe" for adjudication. Claims are ripe when they are presented for decision in the context of an extant case or controversy within the meaning of Article III.[264] As a formal matter, accordingly, the ripeness doctrine adds nothing to the constitutional prerequisites for standing, but only focuses attention on whether the harm that litigants allege is sufficiently "imminent" to create the injury that standing requires.[265]

In the leading case, *United Public Workers v. Mitchell*,[266] federal employees challenged a provision of the Hatch Act barring them from taking an "active part" in political campaigns. The Civil Service Commission had already charged one of the plaintiffs with engaging in prohibited activity and had prepared an order for his dismissal. Justice Reed found that plaintiff's first amendment claim ripe for consideration. Reed explained, however, that the claims advanced by the other plaintiffs were premature. Those plaintiffs alleged in a general way that they wished to engage in the kinds of activities the Act condemned and that they feared that they, too, would be charged and potentially lose their jobs. But they did not detail the precise activities they had in mind. Without more specificity, Justice Reed said it was speculative whether those plaintiffs would actually do anything that the Commission would regard as a violation of the Act so as to prompt any disciplinary action against them. Alternatively, Reed might have rested the decision in *Mitchell* on conventional standing doctrine: The plaintiffs failed satisfactorily to allege that the Commission was causing them any current or imminent injury by frustrating actual plans for political activities.[267]

1. Relevant Considerations

In practice, the Court identifies four considerations regarding ripeness that do not always track the constitutional features of standing: (1) whether the legal claims that litigants advance especially warrant early judicial attention; (2) whether the issues and factual circumstances will be sharper at a later time; (3)

---

provisions permitted the ranchers to advance their various claims. And in some instances litigants may have difficulty identifying particular remedies that will redress their injuries in the constitutional sense. See notes 155-62 and accompanying text.

264. *Babbitt v. Farm Workers*, 442 U.S. 289, 297 (1979).

265. See text accompanying note 102 (noting that "imminent" injury is necessary for standing). Professor Nichol contends that the ripeness doctrine should be (and often is) more flexible than rules governing standing and that it is unwise to regard ripeness as an Article III requirement. See Gene R. Nichol, Jr., *Ripeness and the Constitution*, 54 U. Chi. L. Rev. 153 (1987). Professor Pushaw points out that ripeness *is* distinguishable from other constitutional requirements in that federal adjudication may be available once the factual and legal issues have matured. Pushaw, note 70, at 493.

266. 330 U.S. 75 (1947).

267. Dissenting in the *Duke Power* case, Justice Stevens insisted that the prospect of a nuclear accident was so remote that the plaintiffs' due process attack on the Price-Anderson Act could not be ripe for adjudication. *Duke Power*, 438 U.S. at 102-03; see note 138 and accompanying text. In response, Chief Justice Burger explained that his conclusion that the plaintiffs had standing equally meant that their claim was ripe. Id. at 81 (majority opinion).

whether the postponement of adjudication will avoid interference with the work of other non-judicial authorities; and (4) whether the postponement of adjudication will visit hardships on the parties.

Claims that warrant early attention. In some instances, litigants advance claims that can be determined on legal grounds alone, without attention to factual circumstances. In cases of that kind, there is little to be gained from delay. First amendment overbreadth claims fit this description.[268] Since the litigants at bar attack overbroad statutes on their face, without regard to the circumstances in which the statutes have been applied, it is feasible to adjudicate the merits in a comparatively abstract way. In *Adler v. Bd. of Ed.*,[269] for example, the Court allowed public school teachers to challenge the infamous Feinberg Law in New York, under which teachers were to be dismissed if they belonged to organizations advocating the overthrow of the government. Only Justice Frankfurter argued that the plaintiffs' overbreadth claim in *Adler* was not ripe, but that was because Frankfurter alone thought the validity of the Feinberg Law depended on the way it was applied in practice.[270]

Postponement in aid of a better record. Courts invariably prefer to examine legal issues on the basis of a fully developed factual record, which supplies both the need for adjudication and the wherewithal for sound decisions.[271] If, then, litigants present issues in a contingent posture, there may be a good deal to gain by delaying judicial action until the circumstances become more concrete. In some instances, unexpected events may defuse the parties' dispute and make it unnecessary to adjudicate at all.[272] In other instances, events will make the factual basis for decision more definite. In *Mitchell*, for example, it was not clear that the plaintiffs would follow through with any plans to become involved in political activities or, if they did, that the Commission would decide to invoke the Act against them. If, by contrast, the plaintiffs were ultimately charged with a violation, there would be a definite description of their conduct to work with in determining whether their first amendment claims were meritorious.[273]

---

268. See notes 176-82 and accompanying text.

269. 342 U.S. 485 (1952).

270. Id. at 504 (dissenting opinion). See Scharpf, note 36, at 532. The plaintiffs in *Mitchell* also attacked the Hatch Act on its face. It seems clear, however, that the Court regarded that claim as frivolous and thought that only a particularly egregious application of the Act could violate the first amendment. See *United States Civil Service Comm'n v. Nat'l Ass'n of Letter Carriers*, 413 U.S. 548 (1973) (rejecting an overbreadth attack on one provision of the Act).

271. See notes 7-10, 95 and accompanying text; Chapter I, notes 50-53 and accompanying text.

272. E.g., *Texas v. United States*, 118 S.Ct. 1257, 1260 (1998) (finding a matter not to be ripe because it was "too speculative whether the problem" the plaintiff presented would "ever need solving"). See notes 291-305 and accompanying text (discussing mootness).

273. See *Babbitt*, 442 U.S. at 300 (explaining that delay for purposes of developing a better record is appropriate even when there is no serious doubt that a rule will be enforced). Cases in which litigants wish to challenge criminal statutes also illustrate. Until individuals make a definite record of the behavior in which they want to engage, and until prosecuting officers make it clear that that behavior is subject to prosecution, courts may hesitate to find claims to be ripe. E.g., *Poe v. Ullman*, 367 U.S. 497 (1961). Nevertheless, the Supreme Court has allowed litigants to seek anticipatory relief against the enforcement of criminal statutes, so long as the prospect of prosecution is not entirely speculative. In *Pierce v. Society of Sisters*, 268 U.S. 510 (1925), the Court found it sufficient that local authorities had declared that they would prosecute parents who failed to send their children to public school in defiance of a state statute. By most accounts, the decisions in point are inconsis-

Postponement to avoid interference with other authorities. Courts attempt to avoid premature consideration of legal claims that might frustrate the performance of other bodies. In *Abbott Laboratories v. Gardner*,[274] Justice Harlan explained that declining adjudication on ripeness grounds keeps courts from becoming entangled in "abstract disagreements" with administrative agencies and concomitantly protects agencies from "judicial interference" before they have "formalized" their own decisions and brought them to bear on individuals.[275] Harlan identified two factors that govern judgment: the "fitness of the issues for judicial decision" and the "hardship to the parties" if adjudication is deferred. In *Abbott Labs* itself, the plaintiffs were drug companies who challenged a regulation requiring them to identify the drugs they sold by their generic names. Justice Harlan concluded that the question whether the regulation was valid was ripe for adjudication, because it was a purely legal issue that was "fit" for immediate consideration and because postponing review would work a hardship on the companies. If they chose to comply with the regulation in the short term, they would have to revise all their advertising literature; if they chose to defy it, they would risk prosecution.[276]

Early adjudication to avoid hardship. Courts generally take into account the costs to the litigants if judicial action is deferred—not just in cases in which federal agencies are involved. When this consideration predominates, it is hard to think that ripeness doctrine is entirely a creature of Article III. The convenience of the parties is irrelevant to the character of their dispute as a constitutional case or controversy. In *Duke Power*,[277] Chief Justice Burger placed concerns for the parties under the heading of the "*prudential considerations* embodied in the ripeness doctrine." In that vein, he said that prudence argued for immediate attention to the plaintiffs' claim. Delay would undermine the Price-Anderson Act's

---

tent, and the results may best be explained on other grounds. The Court plainly did not want to address the merits of the prohibition on contraceptives in *Poe*. In *Epperson v. Arkansas*, 393 U.S. 97 (1968), by contrast, the Court was eager to invalidate the notorious "Monkey Law" and thus found the question ripe even though no one stood to be prosecuted. Of course, when prosecution is likely, litigants suffer hardship if they are unable to gain access to federal court and must endure criminal charges and trials in order to advance their claims in state court. See Chapter VIII, notes 101-03 and accompanying text (discussing the availability of a declaratory judgment action in these circumstances).

274. 387 U.S. 136 (1967).

275. Id. at 148. Judicial review of actions taken by federal administrative agencies is governed by federal statutes and judicial decisions meant to discourage premature judicial consideration of intermediate agency behavior. The ripeness doctrine complements that body of law.

276. 387 U.S. at 149, 153. In practice, the ripeness doctrine tends to allow the subjects of regulation (like the drug companies in *Abbott Labs*) to attack agency rulings before they go into effect, but to force the beneficiaries of regulation to await an appellate form of judicial review later. The subjects of regulation typically must alter their behavior in response to a ruling as long as it is in place. Beneficiaries typically suffer no significant harm until an agency acts upon them personally in some manner. In *Ohio Forestry Ass'n v. Sierra Club*, 118 S.Ct. 1665 (1998), for example, the Court held that the Sierra Club's challenge to a Forest Service logging plan was not ripe for adjudication. The plan was a precondition to logging that would injure club members, but it did not, in itself, actually authorize timber to be harvested. Before anyone could begin cutting trees, the Service would have to take additional procedural steps in proceedings in which the club could participate. And then any final decision to permit cutting would be subject to the ordinary appellate review process.

277. See note 138 and accompanying text.

purpose to reassure the nuclear power industry and would foreclose any relief to which the plaintiffs might be entitled if the Act was unconstitutional. The only point of deferring judgment to a later time would be to await a nuclear disaster, after which it would become clear whether Congress had set aside sufficient funds to cover potential losses. That scenario was a bit drastic.[278]

2. Ripeness and Remedies

The ripeness doctrine overlaps not only with the constitutional aspects of standing, but also with the equitable and discretionary considerations attending the availability of injunctive and declaratory relief. In *O'Shea v. Littleton*[279] and *Rizzo v. Goode*,[280] residents of Cairo, Illinois and Philadelphia filed class actions against local authorities alleging that the police in those cities systematically enforced the law in a racially discriminatory manner. The plaintiffs alleged that African Americans were singled out for arrest, subjected to excessive bonds, and otherwise mistreated because of their race. In both instances, the Supreme Court found the issues not to be ripe, because the supporting allegations were vague and speculative.

In *O'Shea*, Justice White added that the constitutional question whether the plaintiffs' claims were ripe for adjudication "shade[d] into" the non-constitutional question whether the plaintiffs could be awarded injunctive relief. The plaintiffs had not established that they were personally threatened with "substantial and immediate irreparable injury" in circumstances in which equitable relief was necessary because there were no "adequate remedies at law." Their allegations were speculative, and if they themselves ultimately suffered the kind of race discrimination they anticipated, they would be able to press their constitutional claims in the course of the state legal proceedings against them. Moreover, any injunction the district court issued would apply to uncertain future events in an attempt to preempt unlawful race discrimination of unknown nature and proportions. An injunction of that kind, White said, would draw the federal district court into an "ongoing federal audit of state criminal proceedings."[281]

The decisions in *O'Shea* and *Rizzo* illustrate the Supreme Court's growing concerns in the 1970s about federal public rights litigation.[282] In cases involving segregation in public schools, racially discriminatory voting schemes, and poor conditions in state mental hospitals and prisons, federal district courts had issued elaborate injunctive decrees forcing state officials to reform the way they managed state functions and institutions. Equitable relief of that kind put pressure on federalism.[283] The Court responded by recruiting the ripeness doctrine, coupled with limits on equitable relief, to discourage litiga-

---

278. *Duke Power*, 438 U.S. at 81-82 (emphasis added).
279. 414 U.S. 488 (1974).
280. 423 U.S. 362 (1976).
281. 414 U.S. at 500.
282. See Chapter I, note 77 and accompanying text.
283. See Chapter I, notes 16-20 and accompanying text.

tion that, in the Court's view, had veered too far from the traditional private rights model of adjudication. Having linked Article III justiciability doctrines to the availability of equitable relief in class action cases like *O'Shea* and *Rizzo*, the Court carried that theme over to more traditional lawsuits. In the choke hold case, *Lyons*,[284] Justice White also found it premature to consider a single plaintiff's suit for an injunction, because the plaintiff's allegations about the future were speculative.[285]

Cases in which litigants seek declaratory relief sometimes follow a similar pattern. A declaratory judgment is not an equitable remedy. Accordingly, the classic conditions for injunctions are inapplicable.[286] Nevertheless, federal courts have discretion regarding declaratory relief, and, in practice, they exercise that discretion with ripeness in mind.[287] In *Steffel v. Thompson*,[288] the plaintiff alleged that local police officers had warned him that if he continued to distribute leaflets protesting the Vietnam War, he would be arrested and prosecuted for criminal trespass. The plaintiff left the scene, but soon thereafter filed an action in federal court, seeking a declaratory judgment that he was entitled to pass out the leaflets and that a prosecution for trespass would violate the first amendment.[289] He alleged that he wished to resume distributing handbills at the same location, but feared that, if he did so, he would be arrested. The prosecutor named as defendant stipulated that the plaintiff's concern was warranted. Justice Brennan acknowledged that the anticipatory nature of the suit raised questions about both ripeness and discretion to award declaratory relief.

Justice Brennan concluded that the plaintiff in *Steffel* could proceed. With respect to ripeness, Brennan explained that the risk of future prosecution created current harm: The plaintiff wanted to continue distributing leaflets, but he could not do so without bearing serious costs. His plans were concrete, the threat of prosecution real. Accordingly, his claim was ripe for judicial determination. With respect to declaratory relief, Brennan explained that one of the central purposes of the Declaratory Judgment Act was to furnish litigants with a mechanism for enforcing their federal rights without subjecting themselves to the costs and embarrassments of a criminal prosecution. A declaration that would provide clarity to both sides was, then, appropriate.[290]

---

284. See notes 156-57 and accompanying text.

285. Professor Fallon contends that the Court reacted in *Lyons* to the remedial difficulties that had been presented in the large class action cases, *O'Shea* and *Rizzo*. In *Lyons*, however, an injunction would not have disrupted local police functions on anything like the same scale. See Fallon, note 66, at 44.

286. *Zwickler v. Koota*, 389 U.S. 241, 254 (1967).

287. See Chapter VIII, note 100 and accompanying text.

288. 415 U.S. 452 (1974).

289. See Chapter XI, notes 193-95 and accompanying text (discussing the abstention issues in *Steffel*).

290. See Chapter VIII, note 103 and accompanying text. Even so, since the Vietnam War had wound down while the litigation in *Steffel* proceeded, Justice Brennan remanded for a current determination whether the petitioner retained an active interest in distributing the handbills. In *Ellis v. Dyson*, 421 U.S. 426 (1975), the Court explained that declaratory actions of the kind *Steffel* approved depend on the existence of a "credible threat" that the plaintiff will be prosecuted. Id. at 434-35.

H. Mootness

Federal courts cannot consider claims after the disputes in which they arose have been resolved by other means and are now "moot." The mootness doctrine mirrors the ripeness doctrine. Ripeness is concerned that federal adjudication not come too soon, while mootness is concerned that it not come too late. Like ripeness, mootness is formally a feature of the Article III requirement that federal judicial power can operate only upon a case or controversy.[291] Mootness is routinely linked to standing: The Supreme Court holds a case to be moot when, at some point during the litigation, something occurs to eliminate the injury on which a litigant relies for standing. Mootness is equally linked to the ban on advisory opinions: When a dispute has disappeared, nothing a federal court says or does will have any practical effect on the parties' positions.[292]

In *DeFunis v. Odegaard*,[293] the Court initially granted review to consider a constitutional attack on a race-conscious admissions program at the University of Washington Law School. By the time the case was ready for decision, the plaintiff had been admitted to the school and was in his last year of study. School authorities assured the Court that they had no intention of preventing the plaintiff's graduation, irrespective of the outcome of the lawsuit. At that point, the Court issued a *per curiam* finding the matter moot. The injury the plaintiff had alleged no longer sustained his standing to sue for the relief he had sought two years earlier: an injunction requiring that he be admitted to the entering class.[294]

Like the ripeness doctrine, the mootness doctrine is fluid in operation. It is hard, then, to accept the notion that mootness is truly a constitutional doctrine—particularly in a case like *DeFunis*, in which the parties had labored to present an important federal question in a concrete posture for decision. By common account, the Court often employs mootness as a means of avoiding is-

---

291. *Spencer*, 118 S.Ct. at 983.

292. The Court has embraced Professor Monaghan's assessment: Mootness is "standing set in a time frame." *Arizonans for Official English v. Arizona*, 117 S.Ct. 1055, 1069 n.22 (1997), quoting Monaghan, note 3, at 1384. It is not essential that the same injury that originally established standing must remain in place throughout the litigation, but only that some injury must always be present to preserve the plaintiff's personal stake in the outcome. In criminal cases, for example, federal courts can entertain attacks on convictions after the convicts concerned have served their sentences. Criminal convictions typically carry collateral legal consequences: convicts are not permitted to join certain professions, engage in certain businesses, or obtain certain licenses. Those disabilities constitute continuing harms. They are so common that the Court presumes they exist and that, because of them, cases involving criminal convictions are not typically moot. See *Sibron v. New York*, 392 U.S. 40, 55 (1968). But see *Spencer*, 118 S.Ct. at 984-85 (disparaging *Sibron* and declining to adopt a similar presumption that revocations of parole have collateral consequences). Cf. *Dove v. United States*, 423 U.S. 325 (1976) (holding that a convict's death moots an appeal).

293. 416 U.S. 312 (1974).

294. Mootness, like redressability, attends to the nature of the relief a plaintiff seeks. A case is moot, accordingly, if the relief sought is either unavailable or ineffective to remedy the plaintiff's complaint. Professor Fallon has suggested that the *Lyons* choke hold case might well have been handled as a matter of mootness. See Fallon, note 66, at 24-28. It is questionable whether a shift in labels would have made any difference.

sues it is not yet ready to decide.[295] In other instances, moreover, the Court recognizes special exceptions that rescue issues from mootness on pragmatic grounds: (1) cases in which the defendant voluntarily ceases the behavior under attack but is free to resume it in the future; (2) cases in which plaintiffs advance claims that exist only for a short time but by their nature are likely to recur; and (3) cases in which plaintiffs represent a class of litigants with similar claims.

Voluntary cessation. In some instances, cases become moot because the defendant voluntarily ceases to behave in the way the plaintiff contends is unlawful. Unilateral action of that kind can eliminate the dispute between the parties and, concomitantly, the justification for federal adjudication. This occurs, of course, only when the plaintiff seeks declaratory or injunctive relief looking to the future — the kind of relief that is unnecessary if the defendant has already decided to do what an injunction would require. The Supreme Court is suspicious, however, that defendants may use the mootness doctrine strategically, changing their behavior just long enough to win dismissal on mootness grounds. Accordingly, the Court typically does not allow voluntary cessation to render a case moot if the defendant acts only in response to litigation.[296] In general, the Court demands solid assurances that defendants will not resume the conduct to which plaintiffs object.[297]

Short-term disputes. Many short-lived disputes become moot before a final judgment can be rendered and thus are denied federal adjudication. In one class of short-term disputes, however, the Supreme Court recognizes an exception to the mootness doctrine: disputes that promise to recur periodically, only to be mooted in each instance. When an interest has ceased to exist, but is "capable of repetition yet evading review," a federal court can adjudicate, mootness notwithstanding.[298] It is not enough that others may suffer the same kind of injury in the future. The "capable of repetition" exception to mootness is available only if the plaintiff in the lawsuit at hand is likely to be in the same position again.[299] The best illustration is an attack on an abortion regulation. On the theory that "[p]regnancy often comes more than once to the same woman," the Court allows a single plaintiff to press a lawsuit of that kind, even after her pregnancy is terminated.[300]

Class actions. Class action lawsuits can also avoid mootness. In form, either the named plaintiff or the class must have a justiciable claim at every stage of the

---

295. Chief Justice Rehnquist has said that, for his part, mootness is a prudential device for orchestrating the exercise of judicial power and not a constitutional prohibition. *Honig v. Doe*, 484 U.S. 305, 331 (1988) (concurring opinion). Professor Lee develops that thesis and, in particular, attacks the received wisdom that to decide an issue that is moot by conventional standards would be to render an advisory opinion. See Lee, note 22; see notes 6-22 (discussing advisory opinions).

296. E.g., *United States v. W.T. Grant Co.*, 345 U.S. 629, 632 (1953).

297. In *City of Mesquite v. Aladdin's Castle*, 455 U.S. 283 (1982), the Court declined to hold that an attack on a city ordinance was moot, even though the ordinance had been repealed after a lower court held it invalid. Local authorities made it clear that they would reenact the ordinance if it was approved by the Supreme Court.

298. *Southern Pac. Terminal Co. v. ICC*, 219 U.S. 498, 515 (1911).

299. *Weinstein v. Bradford*, 423 U.S. 147, 149 (1975).

300. *Roe v. Wade*, 410 U.S. 113, 125 (1973). See Comment, *A Search for Principles of Mootness in the Federal Courts: Part One — The Continuing Impact Doctrines*, 54 Tex. L. Rev. 1289 (1976).

proceedings, from the filing of the complaint through final judgment. In practice, litigants can rely on fictional "relation back" devices to fill in gaps when they appear. If a named plaintiff's claim survives until the class is certified, the class becomes the plaintiff and the entire lawsuit can proceed, even if the named plaintiff's claim later becomes moot. In cases of that kind, the named plaintiff carries the case until it is handed off to the full class.[301] In some circumstances, the lawsuit can proceed even if the named plaintiff's claim becomes moot *before* the trial court certifies the class. If the named plaintiff's claim is so "inherently transitory" that it disappears before the court can rule on a motion to certify the class, the court's later order certifying the class relates back to the time the request for certification was filed. The actual gap between the time the named plaintiff's claim becomes moot and the time the class is certified is filled in by means of the "relation back" doctrine.[302] Finally, if the trial court *declines* to certify the class as requested and the named plaintiff's claim becomes moot, the matter *still* can proceed in order to give the appellate courts an opportunity to review the trial court's determination of the certification question.[303] The named plaintiff retains a sufficient interest in the motion for class certification to sustain the matter as an Article III case. If the trial court's determination is reversed on appeal and certification is ultimately granted, that certification order, too, relates back and saves the lawsuit from mootness.[304]

The Court's decisions regarding mootness, particularly the decisions involving class actions, are plainly more generous to litigants than are the Court's parallel decisions on standing. By some accounts, greater flexibility is warranted in this context, because the civil rules governing class actions are sharper tools for managing class litigation than is Article III.[305]

---

301. *Franks v. Bowman Trans. Co.*, 424 U.S. 747 (1976). The only remaining issue is whether the named plaintiff whose personal claim is moot continues to be a proper representative of the class. See *Kremens v. Bartley*, 431 U.S. 119 (1977).

302. *Gerstein v. Pugh*, 420 U.S. 103 (1975).

303. *United States Parole Comm'n v. Geraghty*, 445 U.S. 388 (1980).

304. Id. at 404; but see id. at 405-07 (warning that the named plaintiff's representative status may be questioned independently).

305. Professor Greenstein provides a discussion. See Richard K. Greenstein, *Bridging the Mootness Gap in Federal Court Class Actions*, 35 Stan. L. Rev. 897 (1983).

Chapter X

Suits Against Government

Lawsuits by or against government or government agents constitute the lion's share of federal question litigation in federal court. Suits *by* government are typically conducted by executive officers or agencies, acting under statutory authority either to protect government's sovereign and proprietary interests[1] or to seek judicial enforcement of statutes, regulations, or administrative rulings.[2] Actions of that kind occasionally raise important questions.[3] On the whole, however, private suits *against* government or government agents form the corpus on which federal courts doctrine operates. The Supreme Court keeps the law governing litigation with the federal government (and its agents) on a parallel track with the law governing litigation with the states (and their agents)—subject to statutes that Congress adds to the mix.[4] In both instances, the starting place is sovereign immunity.[5] Private litigants who satisfy the justiciability doctrines, and who demonstrate both a right of action to vindicate their federal claims in court and a federal district court's jurisdiction to entertain those claims, still may be thwarted if the party they name as defendant is immune from suit.[6]

---

1. The Attorney General typically has authority to litigate on behalf of the federal government. 28 U.S.C. § 516. Other agencies have authority to do so within their own fields. See *FDIC v. Meyer*, 510 U.S. 471, 475 (1994) (discussing the "sue and be sued" authority that Congress sometimes confers on federal agencies); Chapter VIII, note 7 and accompanying text (discussing the same boilerplate authority given to some federally chartered entities). Barring special statutory exception, the district courts have jurisdiction to entertain all suits "commenced by the United States, or by any agency or officer thereof expressly authorized to sue by Act of Congress." 28 U.S.C. § 1345. For a general treatment of suits by states, see Ann Woolhandler & Michael G. Collins, *State Standing*, 81 Va. L. Rev. 387 (1995).

2. See Chapter V, text accompanying notes 11-13 (discussing enforcement actions by federal administrative agencies).

3. See Henry P. Monaghan, *The Protective Power of the Presidency*, 93 Colum. L. Rev. 1 (1993); Woolhandler & Collins, note 1; Larry W. Yackle, *A Worthy Champion for Fourteenth Amendment Rights: The United States in Parens Patriae*, 92 Nw. U. L. Rev. 111 (1997).

4. See notes 38-44 and accompanying text.

5. See Chapter IX, notes 61-64 and accompanying text (discussing the link between sovereign immunity and standing doctrine).

6. Here again, conventional jargon can be confusing. Courts and commentators occasionally *say* that a federal court lacks "jurisdiction" in a case when they *mean* that the suit is barred by sovereign immunity. In his professorial days, Justice Scalia once attached an addendum to an article on sovereign immunity in order to plead for greater clarity on the use of the "jurisdiction" label. Antonin Scalia, *Sovereign Immunity and Nonstatutory Review of Federal Administrative Action: Some Conclusions from the Public Lands Cases*, 68 Mich. L. Rev. 867, 920 (1970). The practical lesson is only this: If litigants are to be successful with litigation in federal court, all the prerequisites must be in place: a federal claim, a right of action, subject matter jurisdiction, justiciability, an available form of relief, and, now, a defen-

A. Suits Against the Federal Government

The Constitution does not explicitly establish the federal government's sovereign immunity. By contrast, Article III includes controversies "to which the United States shall be a Party" within the federal judicial power.[7] Nevertheless, the Supreme Court has always recognized that the central government cannot be sued in its own name without its consent.[8] Apart from the historical account,[9] the Court explains the government's immunity on pragmatic grounds: Private suits for damages would divert public resources into the pockets of individual plaintiffs and away from the uses that government has chosen by democratic means.[10] Private suits for injunctive orders requiring the government to alter its behavior would stop the government "in its tracks," frustrating the administration of the public's business.[11]

1. Officer Suits

Despite the federal government's sovereign immunity, private litigants often can challenge actions taken on the government's behalf—by suing federal officers rather than the government itself.[12] The cases in point fall into two categories: (1) cases in which private litigants mean to impose personal liability on government agents as individuals; and (2) cases in which private litigants sue government agents only as a legal fiction in order to obtain relief against the government by indirection.

Suits to impose personal liability. The government's sovereign immunity is not implicated when private litigants sue government agents in a genuine attempt to impose personal liability on the agents themselves. Typically, plaintiffs claim that federal officers have violated the plaintiffs' rights under state tort law or the Constitution.[13] Liability depends on the circumstances. Behavior that would ordinarily count as an assault or a violation of the fourth amendment may have been perfectly lawful if, at the time, the officers were subduing a violent suspect. In some circumstances, officers can defeat personal liability on the basis of their own *official* immunity.[14] But they cannot assert the federal government's *sovereign* immunity. If plaintiffs are ultimately successful, they obtain compensatory

---

dant who lacks immunity. Litigants may often draw more than one item on the shopping list from a single source. Yet it is crucial that every item on the list be separately accounted for.

7. See Chapter IV, text accompanying note 4.

8. See *Cohens v. Virginia*, 19 U.S. (6 Wheat.) 264, 411-12 (1812) (dictum).

9. See Chapter IX, notes 61-64 and accompanying text.

10. *Dugan v. Rank*, 372 U.S. 609, 621 (1963). Professor Cramton has described and evaluated these rationales. Roger C. Cramton, *Nonstatutory Review of Federal Administrative Action: The Need for Statutory Reform of Sovereign Immunity, Subject Matter Jurisdiction, and Parties Defendant*, 68 Mich. L. Rev. 387, 396-97 (1970).

11. *Larson v. Domestic & Foreign Commerce Corp.*, 337 U.S. 682, 704 (1949).

12. See Chapter IX, text accompanying notes 62-63.

13. See *Little v. Barreme*, 6 U.S. (2 Cranch) 170 (1804) (holding a naval officer personally liable for trespass committed under color of official authority); Chapter VIII, notes 135-65 and accompanying text (discussing private suits against federal officers to vindicate federal constitutional rights).

14. See notes 245-92 and accompanying text.

damages to be paid out of the pockets of the officers concerned. The federal government is not liable as the defendants' employer on the theory of *respondeat superior*.[15]

Suits to affect the government. The federal government's sovereign immunity is sometimes (but not always) implicated when private litigants sue government officers in an attempt to reach the government indirectly.[16] John Marshall suggested in the *Osborn* case that plaintiffs can *always* elude the government's sovereign immunity, so long as they do not name the government itself as a formal defendant party of record—irrespective of what plaintiffs actually hope to gain from litigation.[17] That view no longer holds.[18] The Court looks beyond the formal pleadings to determine whether a suit is actually against the federal government.

Actions for common law writs are prototypical officer suits, neatly avoiding the government's sovereign immunity. Recall that Chief Justice Marshall said in *Marbury v. Madison* that, in a case of proper jurisdiction, a federal court might have issued the writ of mandamus to require the Secretary of State to deliver Marbury's commission.[19] Actions for injunctive relief against federal officers can also evade the government's immunity, provided plaintiffs advance *constitutional* claims.[20] When defendant officers comply with writs and injunctions, they do not act as individuals, but rather on behalf of the government. Nevertheless, they cannot set up the government's sovereign immunity.[21] In the leading case, *United States v. Lee*,[22] the Court held that a private citizen could sue federal officers in an ejectment action in order to regain possession of real estate. At the time, the

---

✳15. The federal government can indemnify federal officers and typically does.

16. On the use of fictional officer suits to elude sovereign immunity, see Kenneth C. Davis, *Suing the Government by Falsely Pretending to Sue an Officer*, 29 U. Chi. L. Rev. 435 (1962); Louis L. Jaffe, *Suits Against Governments and Officers: Sovereign Immunity*, 77 Harv. L. Rev. 1 (1963).

17. *Osborn v. Bank of United States*, 22 U.S. (9 Wheat.) 738, 856-57 (1824) (actually referring to a state's immunity under the eleventh amendment); see text accompanying note 66; Chapter VIII, notes 5-19 and accompanying text (discussing other aspects of *Osborn*).

18. See *In re Ayers*, 123 U.S. 443, 487 (1887) (also an eleventh amendment decision); notes 131-33 and accompanying text.

19. 5 U.S. (1 Cranch) 137, 173 (1803); see Chapter I, text accompanying note 56. Mandamus remains the most useful of the common law writs. Today, pursuant to 28 U.S.C. § 1361, federal district courts have original jurisdiction to entertain "any action in the nature of mandamus to compel an officer or employee of the United States or any agency thereof to perform a duty owed to the plaintiff." See Clark Byse & Joseph V. Fiocca, *Section 1361 of the Mandamus and Venue Act of 1962 and "Nonstatutory" Judicial Review of Federal Administrative Action*, 81 Harv. L. Rev. 308 (1967).

20. E.g., *Shields v. Utah Idaho Central R.R.*, 305 U.S. 177, 183-84 (1938).

21. See, e.g., *Heckler v. Ringer*, 466 U.S. 602 (1984) (allowing a suit against the Secretary of Health and Human Services); *Minnesota v. Hitchcock*, 185 U.S. 373 (1902) (permitting a suit against the Secretary of the Interior). See also Chapter XII, notes 34-40 and accompanying text (discussing petitions for the writ of habeas corpus running to federal officers). The writs of mandamus and habeas corpus are provided for by independent statute. Other common law writs may be issued pursuant to the All-Writs Act, 28 U.S.C. § 1651, which authorizes federal courts to issue "all writs necessary or appropriate in aid of their respective jurisdictions and agreeable to the usages and principles of law." None of the statutes regarding writs purports to waive the government's sovereign immunity. Each presupposes that petitions for writs running to individual federal officers do not implicate that immunity. See *Seminole Tribe v. Florida*, 517 U.S. 144, 177-78 (1996) (Souter, J., dissenting) (actually referring to state sovereign immunity under the eleventh amendment).

22. 106 U.S. 196 (1882).

plaintiff in *Lee* was unable to seek compensatory damages in the Court of Claims.[23] If the Court had also barred his suit to eject government agents from the land, he would have been deprived of his property without just compensation.[24]

In the middle of this century, the Court found officer suits ineffective to avoid sovereign immunity when plaintiffs advanced *nonconstitutional* tort or contract claims.[25] In *Larson v. Domestic & Foreign Commerce Corp.*,[26] for example, a private company contracted to buy coal from the War Assets Administration. Thereafter, the agency canceled the contract. The company sued Larson, the chief administrator, for an injunction ordering him to deliver the coal.[27] Chief Justice Vinson allowed Larson to assert the government's immunity and, on that basis, to defeat the company's suit. Vinson assumed that Larson had violated the contract and that if he had been an agent for a private seller, the company would have been entitled to an injunction. As it was, however, Vinson said that Larson had acted within his statutory authority to superintend sales of government coal. That made Larson's action "inescapably the action of the United States" and the company's effort to enjoin Larson "an effort to enjoin the United States."[28] Chief Justice Vinson distinguished *Lee* on the theory that the plaintiff in that case alleged a violation of the Constitution and had no other way to vindicate his claim.[29] In *Larson*, by contrast, there was no claim that Larson had "taken" the company's property unconstitutionally, and the company might have sought compensation in the Court of Claims.[30]

---

23. See note 39 and accompanying text (discussing the Tucker Act of 1887).

24. In *Lee*, Robert E. Lee's son initially filed the ejectment action in state court, claiming that federal agents had seized the Lee family estate pursuant to an unlawful tax foreclosure. The agents removed the suit to federal court, then moved to dismiss on sovereign immunity grounds. Recall that federal agents can remove, provided they assert federal defenses. 28 U.S.C. § 1442; see Chapter VI, notes 125-32 and accompanying text. Justice Miller acknowledged that, in truth, Lee meant to challenge the government's actions. The idea that Lee was suing only the officers as individuals was a legal fiction. If he obtained a judicial order requiring the agents to return the land, he would receive everything that he might have gained if he had been able to sue the government as a corporate entity. Yet Justice Miller found that fiction acceptable for the very reason that it *did* avoid the government's sovereign immunity. He explained that if the government was dissatisfied with the way its interests were treated in a suit against its agents, the government was free to initiate litigation on its own behalf. Ordinarily, the government is not bound by a judgment imposing personal liability on its officers. See *Carr v. United States*, 98 U.S. 433 (1878). The government *is* bound, however, if it takes an active role in litigation. E.g., *Montana v. United States*, 440 U.S. 147 (1979).

25. See generally *Developments in the Law: Remedies Against the United States and its Officers*, 70 Harv. L. Rev. 827, 831-32, 854-61 (1957).

26. 337 U.S. 682, 693 (1949).

27. The company invoked the district court's jurisdiction on the theory that it had already obtained title to the coal pursuant to the contract and thus had a federal claim to delivery (resting on the federal contract).

28. *Larson*, 337 U.S. at 703.

29. See text accompanying notes 23-24.

30. *Larson*, 337 U.S. at 703 n.27. Justice Frankfurter insisted in dissent that *Lee* and other cases stood for the general proposition that sovereign immunity would not defeat a suit naming a federal agent and alleging a common law tort. 337 U.S. at 722. Justice Douglas concurred on the theory that the Court's decision was limited to cases involving government property. Id. at 705.

The analysis in *Larson* threatened to vanquish officer suits entirely, except in cases in which federal agents acted beyond their statutory authority or violated federal constitutional rights. By Vinson's account, federal officers could routinely assert the government's sovereign immunity when they were sued regarding actions taken in their official capacity.[31] In subsequent cases, the Court took *Larson* just that far. In *Malone v. Bowdoin*,[32] the Court said that ejectment actions against federal agents could not be maintained in the absence of a constitutional claim. And in *Hawaii v. Gordon*,[33] the Court said that suits that "nominally" sought injunctive relief against government officers would be treated as suits against the sovereign itself if, in fact, they would "operate" against the government.[34] Academics criticized *Larson* and its progeny and, in time, Congress responded by enacting statutes that superseded those decisions by waiving the government's immunity in most instances.[35]

2. Waivers of Immunity

Congress can waive the federal government's sovereign immunity, thus permitting suits that would otherwise be barred. The Supreme Court occasionally

---

31. Professor Byse has explained that, in this, Vinson's analysis in *Larson* proved too much. If federal agents could set up the government's immunity to defeat any suit challenging their official behavior, then the "officer suit" device would no longer allow private litigants to challenge governmental action indirectly. Any suit attacking the conduct of government agents *qua* agents (other than constitutional actions) would constitute an action against the government itself. If courts are to review officer behavior, it must be possible for government agents to have official "authority" to make "erroneous as well as correct determinations." Clark Byse, *Proposed Reforms in Federal "Nonstatutory" Judicial Review: Sovereign Immunity, Indispensable Parties, Mandamus*, 75 Harv. L. Rev. 1479, 1491 (1962). The Court has worked this through in cases involving the eleventh and fourteenth amendments. See notes 137-51 and accompanying text. In a notorious footnote in *Larson*, Chief Justice Vinson only added to the confusion. He said that a suit "may fail, as one against the sovereign, even if it is claimed that the officer being sued has acted unconstitutionally or beyond his statutory powers, if the relief requested can not be granted by merely ordering the cessation of the conduct complained of but will require affirmative action by the sovereign or the disposition of unquestionably sovereign property." 337 U.S. at 691 n.11. On the one hand, the footnote confirmed that officer suits would remain available in some instances. On the other, it suggested that suits could be maintained only for negative (as opposed to affirmative) injunctive relief— even when litigants pressed constitutional claims. It is true that negative injunctions that require officers to cease unlawful behavior have a much longer history than do affirmative injunctions that command them to take prescribed action in the future. Yet the Court has allowed officer suits for both kinds of injunctions in cases involving the states, the eleventh amendment notwithstanding. See notes 150-51 and accompanying text.

32. 369 U.S. 643, 646-47 (1962).

33. 373 U.S. 57, 58 (1963).

34. Conventional wisdom has it that *Larson* and its progeny would control today (unless overruled), but for subsequent statutory revisions. Professor Pfander argues, however, that those cases neglected the first amendment right to "petition" the government for redress of grievances. By Pfander's account, that right extends to petitions directed to the courts and thus establishes a constitutional basis for suits against the government that sovereign immunity cannot deny. James E. Pfander, *Sovereign Immunity and the Right to Petition: Toward a First Amendment Right to Pursue Judicial Claims Against the Government*, 91 Nw. U. L. Rev. 899 (1997).

35. For criticisms of *Larson*, see Byse, note 31; Cramton, note 10; Davis, note 16; Jaffe, note 16; Scalia, note 6.

insists that Congress must use exacting language in waiver statutes.[36] Yet on the whole, the Court has read the statutes in point to be sufficiently clear.[37] In direct response to *Larson*, *Malone*, and *Gordon*, Congress inserted a general waiver of immunity for suits challenging agency action into § 702 of the Administrative Procedure Act: "An action in a court of the United States seeking relief other than money damages and stating a claim that an agency or officer or employee thereof acted or failed to act in an official capacity or under color of legal authority shall not be dismissed nor relief therein denied on the ground that it is against the United States." The APA now states explicitly that the United States "may be named as a defendant" in such an action and that a "judgment or decree may be entered against the federal government itself.[38]

The Tucker Act, first enacted in 1887, waives the government's immunity respecting certain claims for monetary relief: constitutional "takings" claims, claims under federal statutes, and most federal contract claims.[39] The Tucker Act expressly excludes tort actions. But the Federal Tort Claims Act, first enacted in 1946, waives the government's immunity for a wide range of suits in which private plaintiffs claim tortious injury at the hands of federal employees.[40] The FTCA covers negligence claims and some intentional torts.[41] It excludes claims that federal employees failed properly to perform a "discretionary function,"[42] most claims by military personnel,[43] and constitutional claims of the character that can be the basis for implied actions under the *Bivens* decision.[44]

---

36. E.g., *Lane v. Pena*, 518 U.S. 187, 192 (1996); *Library of Congress v. Shaw*, 478 U.S. 310, 318 (1986).

37. E.g., *Henderson v. United States*, 517 U.S. 654 (1996); *United States v. Mitchell*, 463 U.S. 206 (1983). In *FDIC v. Meyer*, 510 U.S. 471 (1994), the Court construed the conventional "sue and be sued" formulation in the statute creating the FDIC as a sufficient waiver. See Chapter VIII, notes 86-88 and accompanying text (noting other functions ascribed to the "sue and be sued" phrase).

38. This language, added in 1976, follows immediately the language in § 702 authorizing private suits and conferring standing on "aggrieved" parties who pass the zone test. See Chapter VIII, notes 95-97 and accompanying text; Chapter IX, notes 82-95 and accompanying text. For background, see Cramton, note 10. If *Larson* were to arise today, § 702 would produce a different result. Another statute, codified at 28 U.S.C. § 1346(f), waives the government's immunity for purposes of suits to quiet title to real estate. That statute would now produce a different result in *Malone*.

39. 28 U.S.C. § 1346 (a) (2). The Court of Federal Claims (a legislative court) has jurisdiction over most Tucker Act suits for monetary relief, subject to appellate review in the Court of Appeals for the Federal Circuit (an Article III court). See Chapter II, text accompanying note 80; Chapter V, note 21. Plaintiffs who seek injunctive or declaratory relief on constitutional grounds can sue federal officers in a district court. *Eastern Enterprises v. Apfel*, 118 S.Ct. 2131 (1998).

40. 28 U.S.C. § 1346 (b), §§ 2671-80. Recall that the FTCA largely incorporates state tort law to provide rules of decision. See Chapter VIII, note 53.

41. See Jack Boger, Mark Gitenstein & Paul Verkuil, *The Federal Tort Claims Act Intentional Torts Amendment: An Interpretative Analysis*, 54 N. Car. L. Rev. 497 (1976).

42. See *Berkovitz v. United States*, 486 U.S. 531 (1988) (reviewing the precedents in point).

43. See *Feres v. United States*, 340 U.S. 135 (1950); cf. *United States v. Johnson*, 481 U.S. 681 (1987) (expressing dissatisfaction with the "*Feres* doctrine" but declining to discard it).

44. *Bivens v. Six Unknown Named Agents*, 403 U.S. 388 (1971); see Chapter VIII, notes 144-65 and accompanying text. The district courts have exclusive jurisdiction of FTCA cases.

B. Suits Against a State

The Constitution does not explicitly establish the states' sovereign immunity any more than that of the federal government. Here, too, Article III itself appears to contemplate suits in which the states are parties, with no specification that the states can only be plaintiffs or defendants by their own consent.[45] Nevertheless, the Supreme Court has held that Article III was *meant* to respect state sovereign immunity. If that was not clear from the outset, then it became clear when the eleventh amendment was adopted.

1. The Eleventh Amendment

Neither Article III nor the eleventh amendment refers expressly to sovereign immunity. Article III affirmatively prescribes the federal judicial power. The eleventh amendment, in turn, prescribes the way in which that power is to be understood: "The Judicial Power of the United States *shall not be construed* to extend to any suit in law or equity, commenced or prosecuted *against* one of the United States *by Citizens of another State*, or *by Citizens or Subjects of any Foreign State*."[46] Nevertheless, Article III and the eleventh amendment constitutionalize the states' immunity from suit in federal court. That immunity operates even when citizens sue their own states on federal constitutional grounds.[47]

Roughly speaking, the Court interprets the eleventh amendment to prescribe an immunity for the states that conforms to the immunity that the federal government enjoys. Yet both the theoretical explanations and the practical effects are different. As a theoretical matter, the Court's decisions regarding the federal government's immunity adjust the relationship between the federal judiciary and Congress and thus reflect the values associated with the separation principle. The Court's decisions regarding the states' eleventh amendment immunity adjust the relationship between the federal judiciary and the states and thus reflect the values associated with federalism.[48] As a practical matter, the Court's decisions re-

---

45. See Chapter IV, text accompanying note 4.

46. U.S. Const. amend. XI (emphasis added).

47. See *Hans v. Louisiana*, 134 U.S. 1 (1890); notes 69-71 and accompanying text. Neither Article III nor the eleventh amendment immunizes a state against suit in the courts of another state. *Nevada v. Hall*, 440 U.S. 410 (1979).

48. See, e.g., *Pennhurst State School & Hosp. v. Halderman*, 465 U.S. 89, 106 (1984) (referring to the "principles of federalism that underlie the Eleventh Amendment"); but see notes 86-107 and accompanying text (discussing Congress' power to abrogate the states' eleventh amendment immunity by statute). There are parallels between the Court's decisions elaborating the eleventh amendment as a check on federal judicial power and its decisions elaborating federalism (and perhaps the tenth amendment) as a check on federal legislative power. See *Atascadero State Hosp. v. Scanlon*, 473 U.S. 234, 303 (1985) (Blackmun, J., dissenting) (stating that the two bodies of case law "spring from the same soil"); George D. Brown, *State Sovereignty Under the Burger Court—How the Eleventh Amendment Survived the Death of the Tenth: Some Broader Implications of Atascadero State Hospital v. Scanlon*, 74 Gtn. L.J. 363 (1985); Chapter VI, note 80 and accompanying text (discussing the tenth amendment in connection with Congress' authority to compel state courts to adjudicate federal claims). Professor Massey contends that the scope of the immunity that states

garding the federal government's immunity are largely inconsequential. Congress commonly waives the government's immunity.[49] By contrast, the Court's decisions regarding the eleventh amendment are typically decisive. The states *can* waive their immunity from suit in federal court, but they often choose to insist upon it.[50]

Sovereign immunity was an established feature of English law at the time the Constitution was written and ratified.[51] The Constitutional Convention nonetheless placed suits involving the states as parties on the Article III menu, ostensibly indicating that the states would not have immunity from suit in the Supreme Court or in any inferior federal courts that Congress might create. Recall that some Anti-Federalists took exception.[52] In response, both Madison and Hamilton gave assurances that Article III would not empower federal courts to entertain suits against the states without their consent.[53] Some ratifying conventions were dissatisfied and proposed amendments that would have made state sovereign immunity explicit.[54] Madison declined to include such an amendment in the group of amendments he drafted for consideration in the first congressional session.[55]

Two years later, in *Chisholm v. Georgia*,[56] the Supreme Court held that it could consider a contract action by a citizen of South Carolina against the state of Georgia. Chisholm represented the estate of a merchant who had sold military hardware to Georgia in 1777, but had never received payment. He filed suit in the Supreme Court itself, invoking the Court's original jurisdiction under the Judiciary Act of 1789 to adjudicate "all controversies of a civil nature" involving a state as a party.[57] The justices issued *seriatim* opinions. Justice Blair and Justice Cushing said that the Court's power rested on the provision in Article III extending the federal judicial power to controversies "between a State and Citizens of another State," together with the further provision that the Supreme Court had

---

derive from the eleventh amendment can best be determined by elaborating the tenth amendment. Calvin R. Massey, *State Sovereignty and the Tenth and Eleventh Amendments*, 56 U. Chi. L. Rev. 61 (1989).

49. See notes 36-44 and accompanying text.

50. See notes 119-26 and accompanying text.

51. Judge Gibbons contends that sovereign immunity existed at the time, but was relatively unimportant. He notes that the original charter in the Massachusetts Bay Colony expressly disavowed the idea as early as 1620. John J. Gibbons, *The Eleventh Amendment and State Sovereign Immunity: A Reinterpretation*, 83 Colum. L. Rev. 1889, 1896 (1983).

52. See Chapter II, text accompanying note 33.

53. Madison expressed this view to the Virginia convention. Hamilton said essentially the same thing in Federalist 81, addressed to the New York convention. See Chapter II, text accompanying note 49. Judge Gibbons argues that a close reading of both Madison and Hamilton reveals more ambiguity than is conventionally recognized. He contends, for example, that Hamilton may actually have meant to say only that private citizens would have no *right of action* to sue an unconsenting state in federal court, not that a state would be *immune* from suit. Gibbons, note 51, at 1911.

54. The New York convention offered such an amendment.

55. Chapter II, text accompanying note 35.

56. 2 U.S. (2 Dall.) 419 (1793).

57. 1 Stat. 73, 80; see Chapter II, text accompanying note 55. Everyone concerned recognized that the occasion was momentous. Attorney General Randolph appeared as counsel to Chisholm in order to make the case for federal judicial power; the state of Georgia refused to appear at all in order to underscore its contrary position.

original jurisdiction in cases "in which a State shall be a Party."[58] Chief Justice Jay and Justice Wilson acknowledged Georgia's claim of immunity, but rejected it out of hand. By their account, Article III discarded the "feudal" doctrine of sovereign immunity. Justice Iredell dissented, primarily on the theory that the Judiciary Act did not confer *statutory* jurisdiction to handle the case.[59]

By all accounts, the decision in *Chisholm* precipitated the eleventh amendment. Yet historians differ over the best understanding of what happened immediately following that case and in later years.[60] The Supreme Court has embraced this version of the events: *Chisholm* produced a "shock of surprise."[61] Scarcely anyone was prepared for the Court's holding that Article III obliterated the states' immunity with respect to suits in federal court.[62] Several members of Congress immediately proposed constitutional amendments to overturn the Court's decision. The preoccupation with *Chisholm* accounts for the eleventh amendment's otherwise curious language. Recall that it neither affirmatively establishes state sovereign immunity nor bars suits against states in every instance. Instead, by its express terms, it declares that the federal judicial power shall not be "construed" to reach a suit against a state by citizens of "another" state or citizens of a foreign nation.[63] That language tracks the circumstances in *Chisholm*.

The Court avoided an elaboration of the eleventh amendment for many years. John Marshall made very little of it. In *Cohens v. Virginia*,[64] he said that the eleventh amendment was concerned only with original jurisdiction in an Article III court. Accordingly, it did not apply to a case reaching the Supreme Court on appellate review of a state court judgment—even though, at that point, the state was no longer the moving party, but was defending the decision below.[65] In

---

58. See Chapter IV, text accompanying note 4. Recall that the Supreme Court's original jurisdiction is self-executing and thus requires no confirming statutory basis. See Chapter VII, note 10 and accompanying text.

59. Given the self-executing nature of the Supreme Court's original jurisdiction, and the similarity between the language of the Judiciary Act provision and the language of Article III, it is difficult to find Iredell's analysis persuasive. Professor Orth argues that Iredell clutched at a statutory ground for denying jurisdiction in hopes of avoiding a confrontation over the larger question of constitutional power. John V. Orth, *The Truth About Justice Iredell's Dissent in Chisholm v. Georgia*, 73 N. Car. L. Rev. 255, 267-68 (1994).

60. See notes 75-76 and accompanying text.

61. *Principality of Monaco v. Mississippi*, 292 U.S. 313, 325 (1934).

62. I Charles Warren, The Supreme Court in United States History 91-96 (1935).

63. See text accompanying note 46. Professor Pfander contends that the "shall not be construed" phraseology reflects an attempt to adopt an "explanatory" or "declaratory" provision, which would explain that, contra *Chisholm*, states could be sued in federal court only with respect to debts they incurred after the new Constitution was adopted and not for debts held over from the pre-Constitution period. James E. Pfander, *History and State Suability: An "Explanatory" Account of the Eleventh Amendment*, 83 Cornell L. Rev. 1269, 1276-79 (1998). See Clyde Jacobs, The Eleventh Amendment and Sovereign Immunity 68-69 (1972) (suggesting a variety of explanations for the "shall not be construed" formulation). See also note 80.

64. 19 U.S. (6 Wheat.) 264, 411-12 (1821).

65. The petitioner in *Cohens* was a citizen of Virginia, the state in which he had been convicted and thus the state that opposed him in the Supreme Court. Since the eleventh amendment refers expressly only to suits by citizens of "another" state, it was possible to hold, on that basis alone, that the eleventh amendment was inapplicable. Marshall did not rely on that narrow ground. Moreover, he reaffirmed *Cohens* in *Worcester v. Georgia*, 31 U.S. (6 Pet.) 515 (1832), in which the defendant was a citizen of Vermont. The *Cohens* rule

the *Osborn* case, Marshall offered the short-lived thesis that, even in original ju-risdiction cases, the eleventh amendment was implicated only if a state was for-mally named as the defendant.[66] Historians debate the implications of other cases.[67] The Nineteenth Century decision that mattered most was *Hans v. Louisiana*.[68]

In *Hans*, the state of Louisiana sold bonds promising a high rate of interest. Later, the state adopted an amendment to the state constitution that effectively reduced the return on those bonds. One of the bondholders, himself a citizen of Louisiana, sued the state in a federal circuit court, claiming that the change in state law amounted to an unconstitutional impairment of contract.[69] The plain-tiff contended that the eleventh amendment was limited to "diversity" actions against a state by citizens of "another" state.[70] Accordingly, it did not bar his suit against his own state. Chief Justice Bradley refused to take the eleventh amend-ment's language literally. Bradley said it would have made no sense for Congress to promulgate an amendment that barred only suits by citizens of other states, but left a state vulnerable to suits by its own citizens. The idea must have been to correct the *Chisholm* decision in a more fundamental way—by reaffirming state immunity from suit as a general matter. According to Bradley, Article III had never been meant to deny the states' immunity, and the eleventh amendment merely confirmed that understanding. Rejecting arguments to the contrary, the modern Court has frequently reaffirmed Bradley's interpretation.[71]

2. Alternative Interpretations

The Supreme Court's interpretation of the eleventh amendment in *Hans* has generated a rich academic literature, almost all of it critical. Alternative interpre-tations fall into four groups: (1) diversity theories; (2) conspiracy theories; (3) common law theories; and (4) forum-allocation theories.

Diversity theories. Many academicians contend that the text of the eleventh amendment *should* be taken literally. By this account, the eleventh amendment

---

survives today, despite its apparent conflict with the large body of eleventh amendment rules barring lower federal courts from entertaining actions against the states as an original mat-ter. See *McKesson Corp. v. Div. of Alcoholic Beverages & Tobacco*, 496 U.S. 18, 26-28 (1990); Chapter VI, note 73. Professor Jackson has examined the analytical difficulties that *Cohens* presents. She argues that the best resolution is to read the eleventh amendment not to be implicated in federal question cases. Vicki C. Jackson, *The Supreme Court, the Eleventh Amendment, and State Sovereign Immunity*, 98 Yale L.J. 1, 39 (1988).

66. See note 17 and accompanying text.
67. See Gibbons, note 51, at 1959-78.
68. 134 U.S. 1 (1890).
69. U.S. Const. art. I, § 10, cl.1. The decision in *Hans* was prefigured by other bond cases. See *Louisiana v. Jumel*, 107 U.S. 711 (1883) (holding that out-of-state bondholders could not avoid the eleventh amendment by naming state officers as defendants); *Virginia Coupon Cases*, 114 U.S. 269, 337-38 (1885) (Bradley, J., dissenting) (insisting that the eleventh amendment barred federal question suits as well as contract actions). For a discus-sion of those (and related) decisions with particular attention to the availability of suits in *state* court, see Ann Woolhandler, *The Common Law Origins of Constitutionally Compelled Remedies*, 107 Yale L.J. 77 (1997).
70. See text accompanying note 46.
71. See text accompanying note 96.

does not address sovereign immunity at all, but merely amends Article III by deleting from the federal judicial power two kinds of diversity actions: (1) suits by citizens of one state against another state; and (2) suits by citizens of a foreign nation against a state.[72] In its strong form, the diversity interpretation insists that the eleventh amendment is exclusively concerned with lawsuits that would otherwise be within the federal judicial power because of the identity of the parties. Accordingly, the eleventh amendment does not apply to suits against a state resting on Article III's provisions for cases identified by subject matter — most importantly, the provision for cases arising under federal law.[73] In its weak form, the diversity theory has it that the eleventh amendment bars all suits in the two categories it mentions, irrespective of the Article III basis they would otherwise have. Accordingly, the eleventh amendment *does* apply to federal question suits against a state, if they are filed by citizens of other states or foreign nations.[74]

Conspiracy theories. Other academics reach the same practical result as the academicians who promote the diversity theory: The eleventh amendment bars federal suits against the states only in the two instances it expressly mentions and *not* in federal question cases. But conspiracy theory proponents offer a different explanation for that result. Key public figures manipulated both the original adoption of the eleventh amendment and its interpretation in *Hans* for near-term tactical purposes.

By this account, *Chisholm* was not the surprise the Court pretends it was. Instead, Madison, Hamilton, Jefferson, and Jay intended that the federal courts would entertain suits against the states. If they misrepresented that reality to the ratifying conventions, they did so as a political strategy. In particular, those key figures had in mind suits by Tories and British nationalists seeking to collect on Revolutionary War debts. The treaties that ended the war committed the United States to honoring claims of that kind. When proposals to overrule *Chisholm* surfaced, Madison and the others contrived to limit the eleventh amendment to

---

72. Professor Fletcher is the principal proponent of this view. See William A. Fletcher, *A Historical Interpretation of the Eleventh Amendment: A Narrow Construction of an Affirmative Grant of Jurisdiction Rather than a Prohibition Against Jurisdiction*, 35 Stan. L. Rev. 1033 (1983). For a critique, see William P. Marshall, *The Diversity Theory of the Eleventh Amendment: A Critical Evaluation*, 102 Harv. L. Rev. 1372 (1989). For Professor Fletcher's response, see William A. Fletcher, *The Diversity Explanation of the Eleventh Amendment: A Reply to Critics*, 56 U. Chi. L. Rev. 1261 (1989). See generally *Exchange on the Eleventh Amendment*, 57 U. Chi. L. Rev. 117 (1990) (Massey, Marshall, Marshall & Fletcher).

73. E.g., Akhil R. Amar, *Of Sovereignty and Federalism*, 96 Yale L.J. 1425, 1473 (1987); Gibbons, note 51, at 2004. Apart from federal question cases, there are other categories of jurisdiction in Article III that do not depend on party status. For an analysis of the eleventh amendment's application to admiralty cases, see David J. Bederman, *Admiralty and the Eleventh Amendment*, 72 Notre Dame L. Rev. 935 (1997).

74. E.g., Lawrence C. Marshall, *Fighting the Words of the Eleventh Amendment*, 102 Harv. L. Rev. 1342, 1368 (1989). Professor Sherry has pointed out that, at the time *Hans* was decided, the Court did not distinguish clearly between diversity actions and federal question suits. Under *Swift v. Tyson*, 41 U.S. 1 (1842), federal common law controlled the former. See Chapter VIII, note 33 and accompanying text. According to Sherry, the Court may have failed fully to appreciate the significance of extending the eleventh amendment to federal question claims. For that reason, Sherry thinks it should be relatively easy to overrule *Hans* on the ground that subsequent developments have undermined its intellectual footing. Suzanna Sherry, *The Eleventh Amendment and Stare Decisis: Overruling Hans v. Louisiana*, 57 U. Chi. L. Rev. 1260 (1990).

diversity actions in order to preserve the federal courts' authority to entertain federal claims based on the treaties.[75] Thereafter, they avoided a confrontation regarding the eleventh amendment's application to federal question cases by channeling treaty cases to an international commission.[76]

Similar political machinations explain what happened a hundred years later in connection with a different set of public finance cases culminating in *Hans*.[77] The bonds that Louisiana and other states issued were actually used by Reconstruction governments in the former Confederacy to run up heavy debts. When opponents of those governments regained power, they took any steps they could to avoid paying unfair interest. The change in state law in *Hans* was only one of several devices to that end—all of them vulnerable to attack as violations of the Contract Clause. In order to be successful in repudiating bonds, the new southern leaders needed cooperation from the courts. State courts collaborated, but federal courts posed a genuine threat. It was essential, then, that the Supreme Court should read the eleventh amendment as a blanket prohibition on suits against a state, even if the plaintiffs were citizens of the defendant state and even if they claimed that the repudiation of their bonds violated federal law. That is the interpretation that *Hans* supplied.[78]

Common law theories. Still other academicians contend that the eleventh amendment does not constitutionalize state sovereign immunity, but only establishes that the Constitution itself is neutral on the question. If the states enjoyed immunity in their own courts prior to the Constitution, it can only have been because immunity existed at that time as a species of common law, carried over from England.[79] In *Chisholm*, the Supreme Court misread Article III to eliminate

---

75. Judge Gibbons argues that *Chisholm* was far less important than other cases pending at the time, which advanced *federal* treaty claims against state defendants. Gibbons, note 51, at 1916-26.

76. Id. at 1939-40. Professor Pfander argues that *Chisholm* was a shock, but not for the reason the Supreme Court gives. In his view, members of Congress were surprised not that the Court took jurisdiction of any case in which a state was named as an unconsenting defendant, but that the Court entertained a case in which the plaintiff meant to hold a state to account for an obligation that preexisted the Constitution. See Pfander, note 63, at 1278.

77. Professor Orth develops this account. John V. Orth, The Judicial Power of the United States: The Eleventh Amendment in American History (1987). For a critique, see Michael G. Collins, *The Conspiracy Theory of the Eleventh Amendment*, 88 Colum. L. Rev. 212 (1988).

78. Historians who paint this picture of events contend that the Compromise of 1877 figured mightily in the mix. After the election of 1876, the electoral college was deadlocked between Hayes (the Republican candidate) and Tilden (the Democrat). The House of Representatives appointed a commission to determine which of the two should receive twenty contested electoral votes. The commission included five members of the Supreme Court, among them Justice Bradley, who prepared the commission report giving those votes to Hayes. When some Democrats in Congress attempted to override the commission's decision, key southern Democrats declined to cooperate. Professor Orth contends that they were pacified by tacit commitments from Republicans in Congress to bring an end to Reconstruction and from the Court to foreclose debt collection cases in the federal courts. When Justice Bradley wrote the Court's opinion in *Hans*, according to Orth, he effectively delivered on that political promise. Orth, note 77, at 79.

79. Professor Field has advanced this argument. Martha A. Field, *The Eleventh Amendment and Other Sovereign Immunity Doctrines*, 126 U. Pa. L. Rev. 515 (1978); Martha A. Field, *The Eleventh Amendment and Other Sovereign Immunity Doctrines: Congressional Imposition of Suit Upon the States*, 126 U. Pa. L. Rev. 1203 (1978). See Chapter IX, notes 61-64 and accompanying text.

that immunity. Then, when the eleventh amendment corrected *Chisholm*, it restored the *status quo ante*—namely, the states' immunity as a matter of non-constitutional law. Of course, Congress can change non-constitutional law by statute. By this account, the Court may honor the states' immunity from suit in the absence of statute, but the Court should sustain legislation that Congress enacts to abrogate that immunity in the exercise of a legislative power delegated to Congress by Article I.[80]

Forum-allocation theories. Finally, some academics contend that the eleventh amendment forms part of a larger constitutional design, which allows the states to choose the courts in which they will answer federal claims.[81] In its strong form, the forum-allocation theory has it that the states are constitutionally obligated to open themselves to suit in one place or the other. If they are unwilling to waive their eleventh amendment immunity from suit in federal court, they cannot resist suit in state court on the basis of sovereign immunity.[82] In its weak form, the forum-allocation theory has it that Congress can override state assertions of immunity. Whether or not Congress can or does abrogate the states' eleventh amendment immunity, Congress can always force the states to answer federal claims in their own courts.[83] This last interpretation draws support from language in some of the Supreme Court's recent eleventh amendment decisions[84] and from precedents suggesting that state courts are constitutionally obliged to entertain federal claims, particularly constitutional "takings" and due process claims.[85]

3. Abrogation by Congress

In the 1980s, it appeared that the Supreme Court might be moved to do one of two things: either to abandon *Hans* entirely or to permit Congress to abrogate

---

80. Professor Tribe argues that since the eleventh amendment prescribes the way in which the federal judicial power is to be "construed," it addresses only the courts and not Congress. Laurence H. Tribe, *Intergovernmental Immunities in Litigation, Taxation, and Regulation: Separation of Powers Issues in Controversies About Federalism*, 89 Harv. L. Rev. 682, 694 (1976). But see note 63. Professor Jackson argues that the Supreme Court itself should overrule *Hans* and adopt a diversity theory of the eleventh amendment. If the Court were to do that, she contends that state sovereign immunity might continue to function—but as a non-constitutional feature of the federal law of remedies. Jackson, note 65, at 72.

81. Professor Vazquez has elaborated this approach. Carlos M. Vazquez, *What Is Eleventh Amendment Immunity?*, 106 Yale L.J. 1683 (1997).

82. Professor Monaghan offers this view. Henry P. Monaghan, *The Sovereign Immunity "Exception"*, 110 Harv. L. Rev. 102, 125 (1996).

83. See Vazquez, note 81, at 1690-93.

84. Concurring in *Employees v. Dep't of Pub. Health*, 411 U.S. 279 (1973), Justice Marshall said that state courts have an "independent constitutional obligation" to entertain federal *statutory* claims that the state declines to answer in federal court on the basis of eleventh amendment immunity. Id. at 298. In *Atascadero*, Justice Powell explained that an eleventh amendment bar to federal court adjudication of a federal statutory claim would not deprive the plaintiffs of any judicial forum at all—because the state courts would "enforce the supreme law of the land." 473 U.S. at 240 n.2.

85. See Chapter VI, notes 54-73 and accompanying text (discussing the *Reich* and *McKesson* cases).

the immunity recognized in *Hans* by statute.[86] Many academics preferred the former course, but recognized that the latter might be more appealing to the justices.[87] If the Court were to overrule *Hans*, it would assume judicial authority to alter the balance of federal and state power. It would also upset arrangements built up around the *Hans* baseline for nearly a century. If the Court were to hand the matter over to Congress, it would not only shift responsibility to the political branch. It would permit Congress to decide on a case-by-case basis whether the success of a regulatory program depended on making the states themselves subject to suit in federal court.[88] Justice Brennan and Justice Stevens pressed their colleagues to overrule *Hans* in favor of a diversity theory.[89] Failing that, Brennan and Stevens contended that Congress had power to abrogate the states' immunity by statute. They succeeded on the second front for a brief period. Writing for a plurality in *Pennsylvania v. Union Gas Co.*,[90] Justice Brennan held that Congress could override the states' immunity as an exercise of its power to regulate commerce.[91]

Seven years later, the Court overruled *Union Gas* in *Seminole Tribe v. Florida*.[92] The Indian Gaming Act entitled an Indian tribe to operate a gambling facility under a compact with the state in which the facility was located. The state was obliged to negotiate with the tribe in order to arrive at an arrangement agreeable to both. If the state failed to negotiate, the Act authorized the tribe to file an action in federal district court. Relying on that provision, the Seminole Tribe sued the state of Florida and its governor, seeking an order requiring the state to negotiate an agreement for gambling activities the tribe wished to conduct in that state. Writing for a five-member majority, Chief Justice Rehnquist first construed the Act as a clear attempt by Congress to authorize the tribe to

---

86. Writing in that period, Professor Althouse urged the Court to decide what to do in light of the modern federal interests at stake (rather than contested historical accounts). Ann Althouse, *When to Believe a Legal Fiction: Federal Interests and the Eleventh Amendment*, 40 Hastings L.J. 1123 (1989). See also Carol F. Lee, *Sovereign Immunity and the Eleventh Amendment: The Uses of History*, 18 Urban Lawyer 519, 549 (1986) (arguing that the justices' appraisal of historical materials was guided by their own "substantive values"). Professor Shreve suggested that the Court should shift its focus away from the eleventh amendment to Article III and the constitutional structure generally, thus to work out the appropriate balance between the federal judiciary and the states in a more comprehensive policy-driven manner. Gene R. Shreve, *Letting Go of the Eleventh Amendment*, 64 Ind. L.J. 601 (1989).
87. E.g., Vicki C. Jackson, *One Hundred Years of Folly: The Eleventh Amendment and the 1988 Term*, 64 So. Calif. L. Rev. 51, 103 (1990).
88. E.g., John Nowak, *The Scope of Congressional Power to Create Causes of Action Against State Government and the History of the Eleventh and Fourteenth Amendments*, 75 Colum. L. Rev. 1413 (1975). See also Brown, note 48, at 394.
89. See, e.g., *Welch v. Texas Dep't of Highways*, 483 U.S. 468, 496 (1987) (Brennan, J., dissenting) (joined by Marshall, Blackmun & Stevens, J.J.); *Atascadero*, 473 U.S. at 301-02 (Brennan, J., dissenting) (joined by Marshall, Blackmun & Stevens, J.J.).
90. 491 U.S. 1 (1989).
91. Concurring in *Union Gas*, Justice Stevens explained that, in his view, the eleventh amendment constitutionalizes sovereign immunity in the two kinds of cases it mentions explicitly and that, as to those cases, Congress has no power to abrogate the states' immunity. According to Stevens, however, the kind of immunity recognized in *Hans* for other kinds of cases (i.e., federal question suits by citizens against their own states) is entirely a matter of non-constitutional law that Congress can override when it exercises any of its enumerated powers. Id. at 23-24.
92. 517 U.S. 44 (1996).

sue a state in federal court without the state's consent.[93] That construction of the Act led him to the further question whether Congress had power to abrogate Florida's immunity from such a suit. Congress had enacted the Indian Gaming Act on the basis of its power to regulate commerce.[94] The Chief Justice found that power to be insufficient and thus invalidated the Act insofar as it attempted to deprive the state of immunity.[95]

Chief Justice Rehnquist dismissed the diversity, conspiracy, and common law theories. According to the Chief Justice, diversity theories depend on "blind deference" to the eleventh amendment's text. Conspiracy theories conflict with the Court's own "shock" thesis. Common law theories miss the point of the error in *Chisholm*. It is not that *Chisholm* misunderstood Article III to deny state immunity and that the eleventh amendment establishes that Article III is neutral. The point is that Article III itself recognizes state immunity, and the eleventh amendment makes that clear. Between them, Article III and the eleventh amendment establish a constitutional immunity that Congress must (ordinarily) respect.[96]

Chief Justice Rehnquist had no occasion to address forum-allocation theories directly.[97] After *Seminole Tribe*, the validity of those theories might be tested in two ways. First, the tribe might file a similar suit in the appropriate Florida state court. If the strong form of the forum-allocation theory is valid, neither the governor nor the state itself should be able to set up sovereign immunity to defeat such an action.[98] Second, Congress might amend the Indian Gaming Act to prescribe enforcement suits in state court. If the weak form of the forum-allocation

---

93. See note 104 and accompanying text (explaining that abrogation requires a clear statement from Congress).

94. In fact, Congress purported to act pursuant to its power to regulate commerce "with the Indian Tribes" rather than its power to regulate commerce "among the several States." U.S. Const. art. I, § 8, cl.3. The Chief Justice attached no significance to that point. For background on the sovereignty of Indian tribes, see Judith Resnik, *Dependent Sovereigns: Indian Tribes, States, and the Federal Courts*, 56 U. Chi. L. Rev. 671 (1989).

95. The state also objected that the Act "commandeered" the state in violation of the principle of federalism reflected in the tenth amendment. See Chapter VI, note 81 and accompanying text. The Chief Justice did not reach that argument. Professor Monaghan suggests that the eleventh amendment analysis the Chief Justice offered was so weak that even the tenth amendment might have provided a "more secure foundation" for his result. Monaghan, note 82, at 119.

96. Justice Souter filed a dissent in *Seminole Tribe*, in which he rehearsed the alternative interpretations of the eleventh amendment. 517 U.S. at 100 (joined by Ginsburg & Breyer, J.J.). Chief Justice Rehnquist said Souter's analysis was "cobbled together from law review articles" and Souter's "own version of historical events." Rehnquist preferred to rest on the Court's case law—namely, the precedent set by *Hans*. Id. at 68 (majority opinion). Justice Stevens filed a separate dissent reiterating his previous position. Id. at 76; see note 91.

97. Professor Vazquez has isolated lines in Chief Justice Rehnquist's opinion that appear to reject the forum-allocation interpretation—if they are taken both literally and out of context. Vazquez, note 81, at 1714-22. For example, the Chief Justice dismissed any concern that plaintiffs with federal claims might be left without any judicial forum at all in part on the ground that the Supreme Court itself can review a state court's judgment on a federal issue in a case "where a State has consented to suit." 517 U.S. at 71 n.4. That suggested that a suit against a state in state court also depends on the state's consent and, in turn, that a state might refuse to open itself to suit in either court system.

98. See text accompanying note 82; Chapter VI, notes 48-53 and accompanying text (discussing the *Howlett* case).

theory is valid, there again neither the governor nor the state should be able to rely on sovereign immunity. [99]

In *Seminole Tribe*, the Chief Justice said only that Congress cannot abrogate the states' immunity as an exercise of its power under the Commerce Clause. By contrast, the Court has held that Congress *can* abrogate the states' immunity when it acts pursuant to its independent power under section five of the fourteenth amendment to enforce that amendment's substantive provisions by "appropriate legislation." Writing for the Court in *Fitzpatrick v. Bitzer*,[100] then-Justice Rehnquist explained that Congress' power to enforce the fourteenth amendment differs from its power to regulate commerce in two crucial respects: (1) the power to enforce the fourteenth amendment was added to the Constitution *after* the eleventh amendment was in place and thus can be read to make a prospective change regarding state sovereignty; and (2) the fourteenth amendment's substantive provisions (the Equal Protection and Due Process Clauses) are expressly "directed at the States" and thus invite enforcement legislation that also reaches the states themselves.[101]

To ensure that Congress genuinely "intends" to abrogate state immunity, the Court has recruited a familiar device to service: Congress must make "its intention unmistakably clear in the language of the statute."[102] The justices often disagree over whether a statute is specific enough to satisfy the clear statement rule. Occasionally, the Court is willing to consult legislative history.[103] In the main, however, the Court insists upon exacting language in the text of an enacted statute.[104] In *Quern v. Jordan*,[105] the Court held that § 1983 is not sufficiently

---

99. See text accompanying note 83. Two other strategies come to mind. Congress might condition federal funds or the states' authority to police Indian gaming operations on the states' willingness to consent to suit in federal court. See Kit Kinports, *Implied Waiver After Seminole Tribe*, 82 Minn. L. Rev. 793 (1998); notes 125-26 and accompanying text. Alternatively, Congress might turn enforcement of the Act over to the Attorney General, proceeding on behalf of the federal government—which can sue states in federal court without concern for the eleventh amendment. See notes 110-12 and accompanying text. See Jonathan Siegel, *The Hidden Source of Congress's Power to Abrogate State Sovereign Immunity*, 73 Tex. L. Rev. 539 (1995) (offering a more ambitious account of what Congress might do to exploit the federal government's exemption from the eleventh amendment).

100. 427 U.S. 445 (1976).

101. Id. at 453.

102. *Atascadero*, 473 U.S. at 242 (declining to find the Rehabilitation Act of 1973 to be sufficiently clear). Justice Kennedy explained in *Hilton v. South Carolina Pub. Ry. Comm'n*, 502 U.S. 197 (1991), that the requirement of a clear statement to effect an abrogation of the eleventh amendment is itself a feature of the eleventh amendment and thus has the status of constitutional law.

103. E.g., *Hutto v. Finney*, 437 U.S. 678 (1978).

104. E.g., *Dellmuth v. Muth*, 491 U.S. 223 (1989). Writing for the Court in *Dellmuth*, Justice Kennedy disclaimed legislative history entirely. He said that Congress need not mention the eleventh amendment by name, but he plainly indicated that, if Congress genuinely wishes to be successful, it must list the states themselves as potential defendants. Id. at 230. See Chapter I, notes 24-41 (describing the Court's modern attention to the text of statutes).

105. 440 U.S. 332 (1979). By all accounts, § 1983 is anchored in section five of the fourteenth amendment and thus *could* abrogate state immunity if it were clear enough on the point. See Chapter II, notes 73-75 and accompanying text; Chapter VIII, notes 90, 93-94 and accompanying text.

clear and thus does not abrogate state immunity in the manner approved in *Fitz-patrick*.

Taken together, *Seminole Tribe* and *Fitzpatrick* work a practical compromise. Those decisions leave *Hans* in place and thus reject any suggestion that the Court itself should reinterpret the Constitution to allow suits against the states in federal court. Yet they permit Congress to abrogate the states' immunity. By contrast to what some academics have urged, however, Congress is limited to legislation that can be justified under the special power granted by section five.[106] On the one hand, the resulting compromise may be dissatisfying inasmuch as it preserves state sovereign immunity in a wide variety of circumstances and denies Congress the power to make adjustments. On the other hand, the compromise arguably makes some sense inasmuch as it allows Congress the power to act in precisely the cases in which state immunity can be most problematic: when states threaten to violate federal civil rights laws enacted pursuant to section five. In *Fitzpatrick*, for example, the Court permitted Congress to subject the states to suit in federal court when private litigants allege a violation of the Civil Rights Act of 1964.[107]

4. Categorical Exceptions

Given the baseline established by *Hans*, plaintiffs may not name the state itself as a formal defendant.[108] Nor may plaintiffs name state agencies, departments, and boards.[109] There are, however, four instances in which the eleventh

---

106. Prior to *Seminole Tribe* and *Fitzpatrick*, it was typically unnecessary to ascertain the precise constitutional power on which federal statutes could be said to rest. Today, however, it is crucial to identify whether section five power accounts for a statute in order to know whether Congress can subject the states to suit in federal court without their consent. In *Fitzpatrick*, the Court held that Congress had relied on section five to extend the Civil Rights Act's anti-discrimination provisions to state employers. Cf. *City of Boerne v. Flores*, 117 S.Ct. 2157 (1997) (elaborating the scope of section five power).

107. In many instances, the constitutional power on which Congress proceeds may be debatable. Some statutes now in place plainly rest on powers other than section five, but nonetheless purport to authorize suits against states in federal court. And in at least some instances, Congress has made federal jurisdiction exclusive. For illustrations, see *Seminole Tribe*, 517 U.S. at 77 n.1 (Stevens, J., dissenting); Martha A. Field, *The Seminole Case, Federalism, and the Indian Commerce Clause*, 29 Ariz. St. L.J. 3, 15-16 (1997); H. Stephen Harris & Michael P. Kenny, *Eleventh Amendment Jurisprudence After Atascadero: The Coming Clash With Antitrust, Copyright, and Other Causes of Action Over which the Federal Courts have Exclusive Jurisdiction*, 37 Emory L.J. 645 (1988).

108. *Alabama v. Pugh*, 438 U.S. 781 (1978).

109. *Ford Motor Co. v. Dep't of Treasury*, 323 U.S. 459 (1945). Questions occasionally arise over whether particular bodies count as the state for these purposes. See, e.g., *Regents of the University of California v. Doe*, 519 U.S. 425 (1997) (declining to examine lower court decisions holding that a state university enjoys the state's immunity). For discussions, see John R. Pagan, *Eleventh Amendment Analysis*, 39 Ark. L. Rev. 447 (1986); Note, *Clothing State Governmental Entities with Sovereign Immunity: Disarray in the Eleventh Amendment Arm-of-State Doctrine*, 92 Colum. L. Rev. 1243 (1992). See notes 127-51 and accompanying text (explaining that plaintiffs can often reach state agencies by suing their individual officers).

amendment has no effect: (1) suits by the United States; (2) suits by other states; (3) suits against political subdivisions of a state; and (4) suits against most multi-state entities.

Suits by the United States. The Court held in *United States v. Texas*[110] that the eleventh amendment does not bar a suit by the federal government against an individual state. That result may be inferred from the constitutional structure, which must contemplate some means of resolving disputes between the national government and autonomous states. If the federal government were unable to sue a state in federal court, it would have only two unappealing options: suing in state court (an unpromising possibility)[111] or exerting military force (an even less desirable course).[112]

Suits by other states. The Court explained in *Kansas v. Colorado*[113] that the eleventh amendment does not prevent one state from suing another state in federal court. Much the same rationale obtains. It would make little sense to insist that either state must submit to adjudication by the courts operated by the other, less to leave disputing states with no ostensibly neutral tribunal in which settle their accounts.[114]

Suits against political subdivisions. The Court held in *Lincoln County v. Luning*[115] that the eleventh amendment protects only the states themselves and not cities and counties. The rationale the Court gave for this (important) exception is formalistic. Historically, cities and counties were not thought to be sovereign themselves, but to have only the status and authority granted to them by their (sovereign) states.[116]

---

110. 143 U.S. 621 (1892). In *Texas*, the federal government invoked the Supreme Court's original jurisdiction. See Chapter VII, notes 25-27 and accompanying text.

111. Recall what Hamilton had to say about this. See Chapter II, text accompanying note 48.

112. But see *Principality of Monaco v. Mississippi*, 292 U.S. 313 (1934) (holding that the eleventh amendment prevents a foreign nation from suing a state in federal court). The Court said in *Texas* that the states implicitly consented to suits by the federal government when they joined the union. 143 U.S. at 646. To the extent that argument is only a restatement of the point that suits by the government are implicit in the constitutional structure, it does no great harm. To the extent it is meant to state genuine history, it suffers from a certain temporal embarrassment. After all, most of the states joined the union after the eleventh amendment was in place.

113. 206 U.S. 46 (1907).

114. Recall that the Supreme Court has exclusive jurisdiction of controversies between two states. See Chapter VII, notes 21, 37 and accompanying text. Cf. *Nevada v. Hall*, 440 U.S. 410 (1979)(holding that a state can be sued by the citizens of a sister state in the courts of that sister state).

115. 133 U.S. 529 (1890).

116. Id. at 530. Given the modern development of home rule, cities and counties now enjoy many of the attributes traditionally associated with sovereignty. Some critics argue, accordingly, that *Luning* is anomalous. For a defense of *Luning's* result (but not its analysis), see Melvyn R. Durchslag, *Should Political Subdivisions be Accorded Eleventh Amendment Immunity?*, 43 DePaul L. Rev. 577 (1994). Professor Durchslag acknowledges that cities and counties qualify as the state for purposes of the fourteenth amendment. But, in his view, it does not follow that they must equally count as the state for purposes of the eleventh amendment. If cities and counties were exempt from the fourteenth amendment, states could frustrate the individual rights that amendment protects simply by delegating authority to political subdivisions. Other constitutional references to a state cannot plausibly include cities and counties. Diversity jurisdiction surely does not exist simply because a citizen of Boston

Suits against multi-state entities. The Court held in *Hess v. Port Auth.*[117] that multi-state organizations are not typically entitled to eleventh amendment immunity. The idea is that the eleventh amendment reflects the status and dignity of the states as constituent elements of the federal union. Multi-state entities do not enjoy that status. They are not extensions of the states involved, but exist only by agreement between those states and Congress. When they are subjected to suit in federal court, no particular state's autonomy is threatened.[118]

5. Waivers of Immunity

The states can waive the immunity they enjoy under Article III and the eleventh amendment in two ways: (1) explicit consent; or (2) constructive consent.

Explicit consent. A state may consent to suit in federal court by clearly stating its intent. The Supreme Court will not assume that a state's attorney is entitled to waive a state's immunity in the absence of clear legislative authorization.[119] The Court will find waiver in a legislative act only if consent is stated in "the most express language or by such overwhelming implication from the text" that there can be "no room for any other reasonable construction."[120] A statute that waives immunity against suit in state court does not waive immunity against suit in federal court.[121] The rationale for tipping the scales *against* waiver in this context is that "constructive consent is not a doctrine commonly associated with the surrender of constitutional rights."[122] The existence of consent is jurisdictional and thus need not be raised at trial.[123] Yet if state's attorneys let the matter go too long, they may be charged with default and any eleventh amendment objection to federal adjudication may be lost.[124]

---

sues a citizen of Cambridge (even if Ronald Reagan *did* think he was in a foreign country whenever he visited Harvard). According to Durchslag, the analogy to the term "state" in the tenth amendment provides more food for thought. See *Nat'l League of Cities v. Usery*, 426 U.S. 833, 855 n.20 (1976) (holding that cities and counties *do* count as the state for purposes of the tenth amendment—whatever those purposes may be); note 48 (noting the parallels between the tenth and eleventh amendments).

117. 513 U.S. 30 (1994).

118. The Court said in *Hess* that the eleventh amendment might be implicated if a multi-state entity were deliberately "structured" to be entitled to the immunity that the member states enjoy. The key will be whether the member states concerned are liable for the multi-state organization's debts. 513 U.S. at 44-45. But see id. at 61-62 (O'Connor, J., dissenting) (arguing that a state's liability for a multi-state entity's debts should be sufficient but not necessary to bring the eleventh amendment into play).

119. *Ford Motor Co.*, 323 U.S. at 468.

120. *Port Auth. v. Feeney*, 495 U.S. 299, 305-06 (1990) (finding a state statute to be sufficiently clear).

121. *Ry. Co. v. Whitton's Adm'r*, 80 U.S. (13 Wall.) 270 (1871).

122. *Edelman v. Jordan*, 415 U.S. 651, 673 (1974). Compare Chapter XII, notes 104-24 and accompanying text (discussing decisions in the habeas corpus context in which the Court routinely visits a forfeiture on individuals who fail to raise constitutional claims seasonably).

123. *Edelman*, 415 U.S. at 678 (noting that the issue had been raised at the circuit level and that the circuit court had treated it as properly presented).

124. See *Blessing v. Freestone*, 117 S.Ct. 1353, 1359 n.3 (1997) (declining to consider an eleventh amendment issue that state's attorneys had neither preserved below nor presented in the petition for *certiorari*). In *Wisconsin Dep't of Corrections v. Schacht*, 118 S.Ct.

Constructive consent. Despite the Court's concerns about constructive waiver, the states can be charged with constructive consent if they engage in conduct that Congress permits only on the condition that the states open themselves to suit in federal court. Here again, the Court employs a doctrine of clear statement. In cases on express waiver, the Court demands that the *states* themselves must be explicit. In this context, as in the context of congressional abrogation of eleventh amendment immunity under section five, the Court demands that *Congress* must be explicit. The rationale is that states are entitled to know that the actions they take will make them subject to suit in federal court. If Congress is not clear, the states cannot be held to have knowingly waived their immunity. In *Employees v. Dep't of Pub. Health*,[125] for example, the Court held that the state of Missouri was immune from suit over alleged violations of the Fair Labor Standards Act. Congress had extended that Act to cover state employees, but had not made it sufficiently clear that a state would surrender its immunity by continuing to employ workers entitled to protection under that statute.[126]

2047 (1998), a prison inmate sued both state officials and the state itself in state court. The defendants removed the action to federal court and promptly raised an eleventh amendment objection to the federal court's ability to entertain the claims against the state itself. In the Supreme Court, Justice Breyer said that a state's "proper" assertion of an eleventh amendment bar "after removal" means that the federal court "cannot hear the barred claim." Yet the federal court does not similarly lose jurisdiction over claims against state officers, not similarly barred. Id. at 2054. In a concurring opinion, Justice Kennedy contended that the Court had "neither reached nor considered" the argument that by giving its "express consent" to removal, the state had "waived" its eleventh amendment immunity. For his part, Justice Kennedy indicated that waiver should be found, so that a state cannot consent to federal jurisdiction on removal and then "turn around and say" that the eleventh amendment bars that very jurisdiction. Id. at 2055 (concurring opinion). Kennedy suggested that the Court should adopt a rule similar to the rule governing objections to personal jurisdiction: If a state does not invoke eleventh amendment immunity in a timely fashion, that immunity should be forfeited. Otherwise, according to Kennedy, a state may have an unfair advantage. It can proceed to judgment without facing a genuine risk of an unfavorable outcome, because it can always raise the eleventh amendment in (How did he put it?) the eleventh hour. A district court's denial of a state's motion to dismiss on the basis of eleventh amendment immunity is immediately appealable. *Puerto Rico Aqueduct & Sewer Auth. v. Metcalf*, 506 U.S. 139, 147 (1993); see Chapter VII, note 179 (noting that this is an exception to the final judgment rule).

    125. 411 U.S. 279 (1973).

    126. The Court acknowledged that the Act could be enforced by other means, including suits by the Secretary of Labor. Id. at 285-86; see text accompanying notes 110-12 (explaining that suits by the federal government are not subject to the eleventh amendment). One would not expect the Court to hold that a state constructively consents to suit in federal court simply by conducting ordinary affairs (like employing state workers). The constructive consent theory contemplates an occasion for making a genuine choice, either to surrender immunity or to forego activities that a state might plausibly abandon in order to preserve immunity. The Court held in *Parden v. Terminal Ry.*, 377 U.S. 184 (1964), that a state constructively consented to suit in federal court by maintaining a public railroad after Congress enacted the Federal Employers Liability Act, which subjected "every" railroad to suit in federal court. In *Employees*, the court distinguished *Parden* on the ground that operating a railroad was proprietary in nature—the kind of thing a state might choose to abandon if retaining it meant the surrender of immunity from suit in federal court. In *Welch v. Texas Dep't of Highways*, 483 U.S. 468 (1987), moreover, the Court disapproved anything in *Parden* suggesting that constructive consent can be found without "unmistakably clear" language in the text of a relevant federal statute.

C. Officer Suits

Private litigants can often employ officer suits to avoid the states' immunity under Article III and the eleventh amendment.[127] Recall that suits against federal officers do not implicate the federal government's sovereign immunity if litigants genuinely mean to impose personal liability on the officers themselves.[128] The same is true of suits against state officers seeking compensatory damages out of the officers' own pockets.[129] Officer suits can also affect the states themselves, albeit indirectly.

1. Suits for Injunctive Relief

At the time that *Hans v. Louisiana* was decided, the Supreme Court threatened to do, with respect to suits against state officers, what it would later do, in *Larson* and its progeny, with respect to suits against federal officers.[130] In another state bond case, *In re Ayers*,[131] the plaintiffs attempted to obtain full value for their bonds by surrendering them to the state of Virginia as tax payments. The Virginia legislature enacted a statute authorizing state officers to proceed against the bondholders for cash. Some of the bondholders sued the state attorney general in federal court, seeking an injunction against those proceedings on the theory that they amounted to an unconstitutional impairment of the bond contracts.[132] Justice Matthews held that the suit against the attorney general was barred by the eleventh amendment. That suit, according to the Court, was in actuality an action to enforce the plaintiffs' contract with the state. The attorney general might be held personally liable for any torts he committed and thus might be forced to compensate his victims out of his own pocket. But he could not be held to account for breach of a contractual obligation that the state had undertaken and thus be made to deliver on the state's commitments.[133]

Ten years later, however, the Court adopted a different view in *Ex parte Young*,[134] one of the most important decisions the Court has ever rendered regarding the federal courts. In that case, shareholders sued the state attorney general in Minnesota, seeking an injunction against enforcement of railroad freight rates. They insisted that the rates were confiscatory and thus violated the fourteenth amendment.[135] In *Young*, by contrast to *Ayers*, the Court held that the

---

127. See text accompanying note 12 (discussing suits against federal officers).

128. See notes 13-15 and accompanying text.

129. But see notes 245-92 and accompanying text (discussing official immunity).

130. See notes 26-35 and accompanying text (discussing *Larson*).

131. 123 U.S. 443 (1887).

132. The federal court issued an injunction, and when the attorney general failed to comply with it, the court held him in contempt and placed him in custody. The attorney general then petitioned the Supreme Court for a writ of habeas corpus, and the Court considered the matter in that posture.

133. See Woolhandler, note 69 (providing an exhaustive discussion of the bond cases in the period).

134. 209 U.S. 123 (1908).

135. In *Young*, too, the state attorney general put the eleventh amendment issue before the Supreme Court in a petition for a writ of habeas corpus that would free him from deten-

eleventh amendment did *not* bar the plaintiffs' access to federal court. Justice Peckham acknowledged that the state itself was immune. But since the attorney general was charged with violating the Constitution, he was stripped of any authority the state might give him and could not set up the state's immunity to defeat the action against him personally. Justice Peckham distinguished *Ayers* on the theory that the plaintiffs in that case had attempted to enforce a contract with the state and thus to reach the state treasury. By most accounts, however, that distinction did not ring true. For in *Young*, too, the plaintiffs sued a state officer only as an indirect means of affecting the state itself.[136]

It is easy to misunderstand *Ex parte Young*. Justice Peckham invoked the familiar fiction that an officer suit is not a suit against the state itself, even when the idea is to reach the state indirectly — through its agents.[137] That, in itself, is confusing enough. Peckham confused matters still more. He said that if the attorney general's conduct violated due process, he could claim no state authority for his behavior and must have *acted* as a private citizen. That will not do. It calls to mind Chief Justice Vinson's troubling analysis in *Larson*.[138] The Constitution addresses only *governmental* action. If, in order to elude the eleventh amendment in *Young*, Justice Peckham had to deny that the attorney general acted for the state, then the entire case should have collapsed for want of a substantive claim that the *state* had done anything to violate the fourteenth amendment. Whatever Peckham may have *said* in *Young*, that case cannot mean that the eleventh amendment permits suits against state officers for violations of the fourteenth amendment only *because* those officers do not act for the state. For if officers do not act for the state, they cannot violate the fourteenth amendment at all. Properly framed, *Ex parte Young* stands for a different proposition: When state officers are charged with violating federal law, they cannot set up the state's eleventh amendment immunity to defeat the issuance of prospective injunctive relief.[139]

The Court made this clear in *Home Telephone & Telegraph v. Los Angeles*.[140] In that case, Chief Justice White explained that state and local officers do *act* for the state when they perform their official duties, even if it turns out that their behavior *violates* state law. The telephone company sued city officials in federal court, seeking an injunction against rates the company insisted were in vi-

---

tion for contempt of a district court injunction. See note 132 (describing the similar procedural path that the suit in *Ayers* took to the Court).

136. Dissenting in *Young*, Justice Harlan insisted that the plaintiffs had sued the attorney general only because he *was* the attorney general and thus meant, by enjoining his behavior on the state's behalf, to affect the state itself. 209 U.S. at 174.

137. Some observers insist that the officer suits recognized in *Young* do not really depend on a fiction, but rather have a solid historical foundation in the law of sovereign immunity. See Chapter IX, notes 61-64 and accompanying text. It may be that no fiction is required to maintain that plaintiffs can obtain compensation out of officers' own pockets. In cases of that kind, the state is neither sued nor held liable. Yet a fiction *is* required to maintain that plaintiffs are not suing the state itself when they name state officers for the very purpose of obtaining injunctive orders that those officers will follow as they perform their official duties for the state. See Eric H. Zagrans, *Under Color of What Law: A Reconstructed Model of Section 1983 Liability*, 71 Va. L. Rev. 499, 563 n.338 (1985).

138. See note 31 and accompanying text.

139. See notes 152-53 and accompanying text.

140. 227 U.S. 278 (1913).

olation of due process.[141] The officials responded that if the company was right that the rates violated due process, then they had no authority to enforce those rates and thus did not act for the state when they did so. The state constitution also barred confiscatory rates. The officers conceded that if the state constitution *allowed* the rates about which the company complained, the company *could* charge them with acting for the state. But to do that, the company would first have to sue them in state court and obtain an authoritative determination that their enforcement of the rates conformed to state law. Only then would the company be in a position to argue that the defendant officials acted for the state; only then would the company be able to advance a fourteenth amendment claim. Chief Justice White held, however, that the officers acted for the state in the fourteenth amendment "state action" sense, because they exercised "state power." The state "clothed" them with official authority, and that was sufficient for fourteenth amendment purposes.[142]

Chief Justice White acknowledged that a previous case, *Barney v. City of New York*,[143] had suggested that "state action" for fourteenth amendment purposes must necessarily be anchored in state positive law—e.g., a statute or state constitutional provision. But White rejected that notion out of hand. Later, in a concurring opinion in *Snowden v. Hughes*,[144] Justice Frankfurter suggested that *Barney* should be revived. Otherwise, the actions of a "policeman on the beat would be state action for purposes of suit in a federal court."[145] It may have seemed to Frankfurter that a police officer who violates state positive law cannot be said to act for the state in the fourteenth amendment sense. But that is precisely what *Home Telephone* held, and it is precisely what the Court has held ever since. To do otherwise would be to rob the fourteenth amendment of capacity to check state executive officers who abuse their authority. As Justice Souter has explained that if "compliance with state law authority were a defense" to an officer suit under *Ex parte Young*, "there would be precious few *Young* suits."[146]

Frankfurter's approach would have routed cases out of federal court and into state court. Consider the scenario he envisioned: Plaintiffs who complain that state officers are violating the fourteenth amendment would first sue in state court and, in that forum, would try to establish that the officers' conduct *conforms* to state law. If successful, the plaintiffs would then be able to contend that the state law that authorizes that behavior must itself violate the fourteenth amendment. It is scarcely sensible to think that plaintiffs would file lawsuits in state court to argue that state officers are *not* violating state law. If it were necessary for plaintiffs to go to state court at all, they would naturally contend that defendant officers are *violating* state law. Moreover, lest plaintiffs fall victim to preclusion, they would also advance their fourteenth amend-

---

141. The eleventh amendment was not implicated, because the defendants were city officials. See notes 115-16 and accompanying text. Those officers were, however, "state" officials for purposes of the fourteenth amendment.

142. 227 U.S. at 288-89.

143. 193 U.S. 430 (1904).

144. 321 U.S. 1 (1944).

145. Id. at 16.

146. *Idaho v. Coeur d'Alene Tribe*, 117 S.Ct. 2028, 2054 (1997) (dissenting opinion).

ment claims in state court.[147] If the state courts were to hold for the plaintiffs on state law grounds, the fourteenth amendment issues would not be reached. If the state courts were to determine fourteenth amendment claims, their judgments would be reviewable in the Supreme Court, but would probably be entitled to preclusive effect in an inferior federal court.[148] In the end, plaintiffs would be channeled out of federal court and into state court for the adjudication of fourteenth amendment claims that do not challenge formal state enactments.

That is precisely what Justice Frankfurter thought *should* happen.[149] But the full Court plainly rejected his point of view. Instead, *Ex parte Young* and *Home Telephone* neatly reconcile the eleventh and fourteenth amendments in a way that permits officer suits for injunctive relief in federal court. According to *Young*, state officers performing official state functions cannot use the state's eleventh immunity to fend off suits challenging their behavior on the state's behalf. According to *Home Telephone*, state officers nonetheless act for the state for purposes of the fourteenth amendment, even if their behavior violates state law. Private citizens may therefore seek injunctive or declaratory relief from current or future violations of federal law at the hands of state officials, without pausing to consider, much less to litigate, whether state officers have also violated state law.[150] But for *Young* and *Home Telephone*, the large body of modern civil rights and civil liberties litigation in federal court would not exist.[151]

Modern pleading practice contemplates that officer suits will routinely be employed to produce changes in the way a state behaves, operating through its agents. When plaintiffs sue a state official seeking injunctive or declaratory orders that will, in fact, cause the officer to take action for the state, they *can* name the defendant officer in a "personal" or "individual" capacity. That would be in keeping with the fiction that the officer can be held to account as an ordinary citizen. Nevertheless, plaintiffs can (and more commonly do) name a state officer in an "official" capacity. That formulation reflects the reality of what is afoot: The action is not against the officer personally, but against the "office" the officer

---

147. See Chapter VI, notes 169-73 and accompanying text (discussing the Full Faith and Credit Statute's incorporation of the state law of claim preclusion).

148. See Chapter VI, notes 166-68 and accompanying text (discussing issue preclusion in cases of this kind).

149. See notes 144-46 and accompanying text.

150. For example, *Ex parte Young* explains why state prisoners need not be concerned about the eleventh amendment when they petition the federal courts for a writ of habeas corpus running to the wardens of state penitentiaries (but effectively challenging their convictions in state court). See *Seminole Tribe*, 517 U.S. at 178 (Souter, J., dissenting).

151. The Court did not have civil rights and civil liberties cases in mind in 1908. By all accounts, *Ex parte Young* was of a piece with *Lochner v. New York*, 198 U.S. 45 (1905). The Court needed a means of circumventing the eleventh amendment in order to enforce economic due process claims in the federal forum. See Michael G. Collins, *Economic Rights, Implied Constitutional Actions and the Scope of Section 1983*, 77 Gtn. L.J. 1493, 1494-95 (1989); Herbert Hovenkamp, *Judicial Restraint and Constitutional Federalism: The Supreme Court's Lopez and Seminole Tribe Decisions*, 96 Colum. L. Rev. 2213, 2246 (1996).

holds.[152] Relevant procedural rules encourage plaintiffs to name state officers in an official capacity in order to clarify their actual objectives.[153]

In a curious opinion announcing the Court's judgment in *Idaho v. Coeur d'Alene Tribe*,[154] Justice Kennedy suggested that *Ex parte Young* is not the routinely available device for eluding the eleventh amendment that it is generally supposed to be. The tribe sued Idaho officials in federal court, seeking a declaration that the tribe had rightful title to a parcel of real estate and an injunction barring the defendant officers from exercising any regulatory authority with respect to the land. Justice Kennedy marshaled a five-member majority to support his holding that the suit was barred by the eleventh amendment, *Ex parte Young* notwithstanding.[155] In the main, he explained that the suit was effectively an action to quiet title to the property and that it implicated "special sovereignty interests" in land, water, and regulatory authority that ordinary officer suits do not.[156]

Apart from that holding, Justice Kennedy offered a novel explanation of *Ex parte Young*. Joined in this only by Chief Justice Rehnquist, Kennedy said that plaintiffs' ability to advance officer suits under *Young* depends on a "careful balancing and accommodation of state interests" on a "case-by-case" basis. Courts, he said, must consider the availability of a lawsuit in state court, the nature of the federal claims to be considered, and any "special factors counselling hesitation."[157] The dissenters dismissed Kennedy's attempt to "redefine" the *Young*

---

152. *Brandon v. Holt*, 469 U.S. 464, 470-71 (1985); *Hutto v. Finney*, 437 U.S. 678, 693 (1978); see *Will v. Michigan Dep't of State Police*, 491 U.S. 58, 71 (1989. But see note 172 and accompanying text (discussing suits for compensatory relief).

153. Officers sued in their official capacity can be described by their official titles (rather than their personal names), and if they leave office while a lawsuit is pending, their successors in office are substituted as defendants by operation of law. Fed. R. Civ. P. 25(d). See *Hafer v. Melo*, 502 U.S. 21, 25 (1991); *Brandon*, 469 U.S. at 470-71.

154. 117 S.Ct. 2028 (1997).

155. Justices Stevens, Ginsburg, and Breyer joined Justice Souter's dissent both from the Court's holding and from its analysis. Id. at 2047 (dissenting opinion).

156. Id. at 2040 (plurality opinion). In *California v. Deep Sea Research*, 118 S.Ct. 1464 (1998), the Court cited *Coeur d'Alene* for the proposition that the eleventh amendment bars federal jurisdiction of "general title disputes relating to State property interests." Id. at 1472. The Court held, however, that the eleventh amendment does not affect suits in which federal courts exercise *in rem* jurisdiction over personal property not in the state's possession. In a concurring opinion, Justice Kennedy suggested that the eleventh amendment might be inapplicable to *any* suit involving *in rem* jurisdiction of personal items (like the sunken cargo in *Deep Sea Research*).

157. *Coeur d'Alene*, 117 S.Ct. at 2038-39, quoting *Bivens*, 403 U.S. at 396; see Chapter VIII, text accompanying note 156. While Justice Kennedy said that the "nature" of a plaintiff's claim should be a factor for consideration, he did not suggest that officer suits should be allowed in federal court only to advance constitutional (rather than federal statutory) claims. Even if a claim is statutory, it remains part of the supreme law, and its enforcement against state officers comports with the supremacy point of *Young*. Nevertheless, Professor Jackson argues that Kennedy's opinion in *Coeur d'Alene* and Chief Justice Rehnquist's opinion for the Court in *Seminole Tribe* illustrate a resurgence of the "federalist" perspective on the role of federal courts. Vicki C. Jackson, *Coeur d'Alene, Federal Courts and the Supremacy of Federal Law: The Competing Paradigms of Chief Justices Marshall and Rehnquist*, 15 Const. Comm. 301 (1998); see Chapter I, note 17 and accompanying text. In *Corey v. White*, 457 U.S. 85 (1982), the Court held that the eleventh amendment barred a federal interpleader action that, in form, alleged no violation of federal law of any kind, but

doctrine.[158] Justice O'Connor also disclaimed Kennedy's discussion of *Young* in a sharply worded concurring opinion, joined by Justice Scalia and Justice Thomas. By O'Connor's (controlling) account, *Young* continues to supply a means of avoiding the eleventh amendment when plaintiffs allege an "ongoing violation of federal law" and seek "prospective rather than retrospective" relief.[159] Accordingly, federal courts are not to determine the availability of an officer suit on the basis of an *ad hoc* examination of factors.[160]

An officer suit pursuant to *Ex parte Young* performs only one function: It evades the state's eleventh amendment immunity. Plaintiffs must independently satisfy the other requirements for obtaining federal adjudication of their claims on the merits.[161] For example, plaintiffs must have a right of action—that is, an entitlement to take their claims to court. In many instances, plaintiffs can rely on § 1983 for that purpose.[162] Recall, however, that if Congress establishes an alternative scheme for enforcing a federal statute and clearly leaves no room for a § 1983 action, plaintiffs must typically make do with that arrangement.[163] In *Seminole Tribe*, the Court initially read the Indian Gaming Act to prescribe suits

---

merely asked the federal court to decide which of two competing states was entitled to administer Howard Hughes' estate. Since *Corey* was a dispute between two states, the rule of decision was a matter of federal common law. Yet in the peculiar procedural posture of the case, neither side alleged that the other was actually *violating* that law.

158. 117 S.Ct. at 2048 (Souter, J., dissenting).

159. Id. at 2045-46 (O'Connor, J., concurring).

160. If it was Justice Kennedy's suggestion that courts must make *ad hoc* judgments about the availability of *Ex parte Young* that troubled the other justices, it may be that they would warm to a systematic attempt to define entire categories of cases in some rule-oriented way and to carve those categories out of *Young* at wholesale. For a discussion, see Eric B. Wolff, *Coeur d'Alene and Existential Categories for Sovereign Immunity Cases*, 86 Calif. L. Rev. 879 (1998).

161. See text accompanying note 6.

162. If § 1983 had been understood in 1908 in the way it is understood today, the suit in *Ex parte Young* would have been filed as a § 1983 action. At that time, however, § 1983 served only plaintiffs pressing personal liberty claims, and not the "property" claims the shareholders in *Young* meant to vindicate. E.g., *Holt v. Indiana Mfg. Co.*, 176 U.S. 68, 72 (1900) (limiting § 1983 to "civil rights" claims); see *Lynch v. Household Finance Corp.*, 405 U.S. 538 (1972) (surveying early attempts to distinguish "liberty" claims and "property" claims for purposes of § 1983). In any case, the Court did not rely on § 1983 (or any other statute) to supply a right of action in *Young*. The real explanation is probably that the Court attached no great significance to the "right of action" issue with which the justices are so vitally concerned today. See Chapter VIII, notes 79-145 and accompanying text. Some observers contend that the Court operated on the assumption that a right of action was implied in the fourteenth amendment. E.g., Daniel J. Meltzer, *The Seminole Decision and State Sovereign Immunity*, 1996 Sup. Ct. Rev. 1, 38; Monaghan, note 82, at 130-31. See Chapter VIII, note 150 and accompanying text (noting that the Court has found a right of action implied in the Due Process Clause of the fifth amendment). The existence of a right of action and the effect of the eleventh amendment are analytically distinct ideas. The Court in *Young* decided both questions in favor of the plaintiffs, but provided an explanation only for the latter. Whatever the Court may have been thinking in *Young*, Professor Harrison urges the current Court to hold that the fourteenth amendment only nullifies state action inconsistent with its substantive provisions, and that a right of action to advance a claim in court must have an independent source—e.g., a statute like §1983. John Harrison, *Jurisdiction, Congressional Power, and Constitutional Remedies*, 86 Gtn. L.J. 2513 (1998). See Chapter VIII, note 152. For a critique of Harrison, see Daniel J. Meltzer, *Congress, Courts, and Constitutional Remedies*, 86 Gtn. L.J. 2537, 2549-65 (1998).

163. See Chapter VIII, note 130 and accompanying text.

against the states as the mechanism for forcing state authorities to negotiate.[164] Chief Justice Rehnquist found suits of that kind to be barred by the eleventh amendment. Thereafter, he turned to the tribe's alternative theory that its suit could proceed as an officer suit against the governor. The Chief Justice rejected that argument as well: By specifying suits against the states themselves as the means by which the Act was to be enforced, Congress had foreclosed any right of action against state officers.[165]

2. Suits for Compensatory Relief

Plaintiffs can use officer suits to elude the state's eleventh amendment immunity only if they seek injunctive or declaratory orders that terminate or forestall a current or impending violation of federal law. Plaintiffs who sue state officers seeking relief with respect to a violation of their federal rights in the past are un-

---

164. See text accompanying note 93.

165. 517 U.S. at 75-76. The Chief Justice relied primarily on *Schweiker v. Chilicky*, 487 U.S. 412 (1988), one of the cases in which the Court had previously found *Bivens* actions foreclosed. See Chapter VIII, note 161 and accompanying text. Professor Meltzer contends that the Court should have held that in the absence of clear statutory language to the contrary, § 1983 provided a right of action to enforce the Act. Meltzer, note 162, at 39-40. Recall that § 1983 can supply a right of action to enforce a federal statute. See Chapter VIII, notes 127-28 and accompanying text. That default position may be overridden by legislation establishing an alternative enforcement mechanism. E.g., *Middlesex County Sewerage Auth. v. Nat'l Sea Clammers Ass'n*, 453 U.S. 1 (1981). According to Professor Currie, "*Seminole Tribe* was just another application of the *Sea Clammers* principle." David P. Currie, *Ex Parte Young After Seminole Tribe*, 72 N.Y.U. L. Rev. 547, 549 (1997) (citation omitted). Accord Monaghan, note 82, at 128-29. Recall, too, that § 1983 is limited to statutes that establish individual "rights" and cannot serve in cases in which plaintiffs wish only to redress violations of federal law. See Chapter VIII, notes 131-32 and accompanying text. The tribe did not purport to rely on § 1983. That may be the (admittedly formalistic) reason why the Chief Justice did not consider whether § 1983 might answer. In his opinion for the Court in *Seminole Tribe*, Chief Justice Rehnquist did not anticipate the revisionist appraisal of *Young* itself that he and Justice Kennedy later advanced (for themselves alone) in *Coeur d'Alene*. See notes 154-57 and accompanying text. Professor Jackson nonetheless argues that *Seminole Tribe* and *Coeur d'Alene* may be part of a larger agenda for "redrawing lines of federalism," which puts officer suits under *Young* at risk. Vicki C. Jackson, *Seminole Tribe, the Eleventh Amendment, and the Potential Evisceration of Ex parte Young*, 72 N.Y.U. L. Rev. 495, 530, 542 (1997). Jackson notes, for example, that if the Chief Justice meant in *Seminole Tribe* only to say that the Indian Gaming Act itself barred the tribe from filing a private suit against the governor, he should have said that at the end of his opinion—rather than declaring that since an officer suit was not available, the "suit" was "barred *by the Eleventh Amendment* and must be dismissed for lack of *jurisdiction*." 517 U.S. at 76 (emphasis added); Jackson, at 521. At that point, however, the Chief Justice may only have been summing up his conclusion regarding the tribe's instant lawsuit against the state itself. He may have meant either that the eleventh amendment established a jurisdictional bar to the suit against Florida, see note 6, or that the jurisdictional provision in the Indian Gaming Act (which contemplated a suit against the state) did not supply a jurisdictional basis for a suit against the governor. See also Chapter VIII, notes 211-30 (discussing the linkage between the existence of a right of action and the interpretation of adjacent jurisdictional statutes). In any case, it would seem that Congress could resolve the difficulty with respect to the Indian Gaming Act simply by enacting a right-of-action statute authorizing tribes to sue state officers. Wayne L. Baker, *Seminole Speaks to Sovereign Immunity and Ex Parte Young*, 71 St. John's L. Rev. 739 (1997).

derstood to sue the state itself—and the eleventh amendment establishes a bar. If, for example, plaintiffs seek compensatory damages to be paid from the state treasury, the state is the "real, substantial party in interest," even if individual state officers are the "nominal defendants."[166] In the leading modern case, *Edelman v. Jordan*,[167] private plaintiffs claimed that they had been denied federal monetary aid under a Social Security program administered by state officials in cooperation with the Department of HEW. They filed a § 1983 action in federal court, naming state officers as defendants and contending that those officers had denied the plaintiffs the payments to which they were entitled—in violation of HEW regulations and the fourteenth amendment. The plaintiffs sought a declaration that the defendants had acted unlawfully and an injunction requiring them to give the plaintiffs the money that had been wrongfully withheld from them. Then-Justice Rehnquist held that the action was barred by the eleventh amendment.

Justice Rehnquist explained that the plaintiffs' suit was not an attempt to hold the state officers individually liable for unpaid benefits and thus to seek compensation from those officers personally. Instead, the plaintiffs clearly meant to reach the state treasury. They hoped to hold the state itself accountable for a "monetary loss" resulting from a "past breach of a legal duty" by the state's agents. In that critical respect, the plaintiffs' action was more like *Ayers* than *Ex parte Young*.[168] Justice Rehnquist acknowledged that *Young* would permit plaintiffs to obtain forward-looking injunctive orders that might entail the expenditure of state funds in the future. But *Young* did not justify an injunction that would constitute, in effect, an award of compensatory damages against the state for failing to meet legal obligations in the past.

The distinction in *Edelman* between prospective and retrospective injunctions is hard to defend. State officers will inevitably spend state funds in order to comply with *any* injunctive order, even one that addresses only the future. So it would not answer to draw the line between injunctions that require expenditures and those that do not. The latter category would be a null set. In hard economic terms, however, there is little to choose between prospective and retrospective orders, both of which demand expenditures. Justice Rehnquist explained in *Edelman* that prospective orders are comparatively manageable inasmuch as the state has an opportunity to budget for any increased expenditures that must be made. Orders that require a state to make unplanned expenditures to compensate for past misdeeds are, by their nature, more likely to disrupt the state's current efforts to manage its own affairs.[169] Yet courts can always establish a future pay-

---

166. *Ford Motor Co.*, 323 U.S. at 464. Recall, however, that plaintiffs face no similar eleventh amendment barrier if they sue state officers for compensatory relief to be paid from the officers' own pockets. See notes 128, 191-203 and accompanying text.

167. 415 U.S. 651 (1974).

168. See text accompanying notes 131-33 (discussing *Ayers*).

169. 415 U.S. at 666 n.11. The circuit court below in *Edelman* had treated the plaintiffs' prayer for relief as a request for "equitable restitution." Justice Rehnquist rejected that characterization of the case. 415 U.S. at 668. It is not coincidental that Rehnquist offered a similar analysis of the effects on state budgets in his opinion for the Court in *Nat'l League of Cities v. Usery*, 426 U.S. 833 (1976). See note 48 (noting the parallels between the Court's decisions on congressional power and its decisions regarding the eleventh amendment). There is, however, a long tradition distinguishing (for immunity purposes) between actions sounding in contract and actions sounding in tort. See Jaffe, note 16, at 29.

ment schedule for compensatory damages, so that states can equally budget for making backward-looking compensatory payments. As a practical matter, *Edelman* puts a state that concededly violated federal law in the past in a better position than a state that is attempting to comply with federal law in the future.[170]

The distinction in *Edelman* is also hard to administer.[171] Yet it survives intact. Plaintiffs who sue state officials seeking compensation for violations of federal law in the past must look to the officers' themselves, not to the treasury of the state the officers serve. Pleading practice bears this out. If a plaintiff names a state officer in an official capacity, seeking backward-looking compensatory relief, the plaintiff will be understood to be seeking money from the state's treasury and thus to be suing the state. In that event, the plaintiff faces an eleventh amendment bar, unless Congress has abrogated the state's immunity or the state has consented to the suit.[172] Plaintiffs who hope to impose liability on individual officers must name those officers in an individual or personal capacity in order to signal that they do not hope to reach the state treasury. That will eliminate the eleventh amendment from the picture.[173] If a plaintiff sues an officer in the officer's individual capacity for compensation from the officer's personal assets and the officer leaves office before the matter is settled, the plaintiff must pursue the named defendant into private life. If a plaintiff names an officer in an individual capacity and the officer dies before execution on a judgment, the plaintiff must pursue the decedent's personal estate.[174]

---

170. The Court has explained that *Edelman* was not exclusively concerned with the effect on the state's budget, but saw that effect as evidence that the state was the real party in interest. *Corey*, 457 U.S. at 90-91. Cf. *Arizonans for Official English v. Arizona*, 117 S.Ct. 1055, 1070 n.24 (1997) (indicating that *Edelman* bars even a nominal award of damages if it is to be paid from the state treasury).

171. In *Quern v. Jordan*, 440 U.S. 332 (1979), the Court held that the district court could order the state officers in *Edelman* to spend state funds in order to notify the members of the plaintiff class that they could still seek payments via state administrative procedures. But in *Green v. Mansour*, 474 U.S. 64 (1985), the Court held that the eleventh amendment barred a suit for a declaratory judgment that state officials had violated federal law regarding AFDC benefits and an order requiring state officials to notify individuals of their entitlement to benefits. In *Green*, the state officers had already conformed to federal law and there was no prospective injunction to which a notification order could be attached. In *Milliken v. Bradley*, 433 U.S. 267 (1977), the Court found no eleventh amendment bar to an injunction requiring state officers to expend state funds to pay for remedial programs for students whose education suffered because they had been assigned to racially segregated schools. In *Hutto v. Finney*, 437 U.S. 678 (1978), the Court approved an award of attorneys fees "ancillary" to a prospective injunction regarding prison conditions. The fees compensated counsel for work in the past, but the Court treated them as tantamount to court costs. In *Papasan v. Allain*, 478 U.S. 265 (1986), the Court held that the eleventh amendment prevented children from obtaining funding for their schools on the theory that state officials had unlawfully administered public lands held in trust for the schools. The Court rejected the argument that the state officers were engaged in an ongoing breach of the trust, but, instead, read the complaint to seek redress for a violation of federal law in the past.

172. *Kentucky v. Graham*, 473 U.S. 159, 166 (1985) (explaining that a suit naming an officer of a governmental entity in an official capacity is "treated as a suit against the entity" in "all respects other than name"); *Will v. Michigan Dep't of State Police*, 491 U.S. 58, 71 (1989) (confirming the point).

173. *Hafer*, 502 U.S. at 30.

174. *Graham*, 473 U.S. at 166 n. 11. But see notes 245-92 and accompanying text (discussing official immunity). A state may voluntarily indemnify state officers who are held personally liable. Insurance typically has no affect on the eleventh amendment's reach. *Jackson*

3. Suits to Enforce State Law

When plaintiffs file officer suits advancing both federal claims and supplemental state claims for injunctive or declaratory relief, only the federal claims can have the benefit of *Ex parte Young*. In *Pennhurst State School & Hosp. v. Halderman*,[175] residents at a state hospital for the mentally ill sued state and county officials in federal court, contending that those officers were operating the institution in violation of a federal statute, relevant state statutes, and the fourteenth amendment. The district court sustained all three claims and issued an injunction requiring the defendant officers to make sweeping changes in the way the institution would be managed in the future. The circuit court affirmed, but only on the basis of the federal statutory claim. The Supreme Court overturned that judgment on the ground that the federal statute did not establish substantive federal rights in the plaintiffs.[176] On remand, the circuit court turned next to the plaintiffs' state claims in order to avoid the fourteenth amendment issue, if possible.[177] When the circuit reaffirmed its judgment on the basis of state law, the Supreme Court reversed yet again. Justice Powell explained that officer suits pursuant to *Ex parte Young* can be justified in order to "vindicate federal rights and hold state officials responsible to 'the supreme authority of the United States.'"[178] When, by contrast, plaintiffs seek to enforce state law, there is no such justification for denying a state's eleventh amendment immunity.[179]

The result in *Pennhurst* might have been predicted. The plaintiffs' suit was a public rights class action inviting the district court to issue a structural injunction

---

v. Georgia Dep't of Transp., 16 F.3d 1573 (11th Cir. 1994). Cf. *Regents of the University of California v. Doe*, 117 S.Ct. 900, 904 (1997) (stating that a state does not surrender its eleventh amendment immunity by purchasing insurance and thus making a private insurance company liable to pay judgments). Professor Jeffries finds *Edelman* analytically unsound, but thinks no great harm is done. Plaintiffs can impose personal liability on individual officers, and when that happens the state is likely to be "bound by conscience" to indemnify them. John C. Jeffries, Jr., *In Praise of the Eleventh Amendment and Section 1983*, 84 Va. L. Rev. 47, 61 (1998).

175. 465 U.S. 89 (1984).

176. See Chapter VIII, note 132.

177. See Chapter VIII, note 298 and accompanying text (discussing the *Siler* case).

178. *Pennhurst*, 465 U.S. at 105, quoting *Ex parte Young*, 209 U.S. at 160.

179. Justice Powell spent most of his opinion responding to a vigorous dissent by Justice Stevens. The two debated a welter of old decisions, particularly *Larson*, in hopes of fortifying their opposing positions. See notes 26-35 and accompanying text. Powell contended that *Larson* demonstrates that officer suits are not typically available to advance non-constitutional claims, unless agents act entirely *ultra vires* "without any authority whatever." Id. at 102 n.11, quoting *Larson*, 337 U.S. at 694. Stevens, for his part, insisted that *Larson* actually stands for the proposition that officers act *ultra vires* whenever they commit acts that are either unauthorized or forbidden by statute. Professor Shapiro faults Justice Powell for carrying the (erroneous) *Larson* decision a step further into even more error. By Shapiro's account, the only basis Justice Powell had for concluding that the defendants in *Pennhurst* had acted within their statutory authority was the lower court's decision that they could rely on qualified immunity to avoid personal liability for damages. See notes 266-92 and accompanying text. Justice Powell thus contrived to translate a form of personal immunity meant to safeguard individual officers' assets into a blanket governmental immunity from suit for injunctive relief. David L. Shapiro, *Wrong Turns: The Eleventh Amendment and the Pennhurst Case*, 98 Harv. L. Rev. 61, 75-76 (1984).

requiring far-reaching changes in the operation of a state institution.[180] The district court's injunctive order was comprehensive and contemplated the appointment of a special master to monitor its implementation over time. In the 1980s, that was precisely the kind of lawsuit the Court meant to discourage.[181] Nevertheless, the means by which the Court brought the district court to heel was surprising. Justice Powell might have focused on the scope of the relief below and set about curbing the district court's aggressive use of federal equitable remedies.[182] Instead, he located a federal constitutional bar to the lawsuit in the first instance. Historians debate whether *Pennhurst* had intellectual precursors. Prior to that case, the eleventh amendment had been concerned with the plaintiffs' choice of defendants and their requests for relief, not with the nature of their substantive claims.[183]

The decision in *Pennhurst* has implications for supplemental jurisdiction over state law claims.[184] By hypothesis, a district court has no constitutional power to entertain a state law claim for injunctive relief against state officers.[185] Accordingly, a plaintiff who wishes to advance both federal and state claims has

---

180. See Chapter I, notes 66-78 and accompanying text.

181. Professor Rudenstine and Professor Dwyer regard *Pennhurst* as primarily a response to what the Court considered to be overly aggressive "institutional" litigation. David Rudenstine, *Pennhurst and the Scope of Federal Judicial Power to Reform Social Institutions*, 6 Cardozo L. Rev. 71 (1984); John P. Dwyer, *Pendent Jurisdiction and the Eleventh Amendment*, 75 Calif. L. Rev. 129 (1987).

182. See Chapter IX, notes 279-85 and accompanying text (describing the Court's use of the ripeness doctrine to limit the availability of injunctive relief in class action civil rights cases).

183. Most academic treatments of *Pennhurst* are critical. E.g., Louise Weinberg, *The New Judicial Federalism: Where Are We Now?*, 19 Ga. L. Rev. 1075, 1078-79 (1985); George D. Brown, *Beyond Pennhurst—Protective Jurisdiction, the Eleventh Amendment, and the Power of Congress to Enlarge Federal Jurisdiction in Response to the Burger Court*, 71 Va. L. Rev. 343 (1985); Erwin Chemerinsky, *State Sovereignty and Federal Court Power: The Eleventh Amendment After Pennhurst v. Halderman*, 12 Hastings Const. L.Q. 643 (1985); Robert H. Smith, *Pennhurst v. Halderman: The Eleventh Amendment, Erie, and Pendent State Law Claims*, 34 Buffalo L. Rev. 227 (1985). Professor Jackson notes, however, that to the extent *Pennhurst* invokes the eleventh amendment because a federal claim is *not* at stake, that case has the virtue of drawing attention back to what Jackson regards as the eleventh amendment's proper purview—namely, suits that are in federal court on some basis other than the existence of federal question jurisdiction. Jackson, note 65, at 52. Professor Amar agrees, but finds the point only to underscore what Amar regards as the Court's erroneous decision in *Hans* that the eleventh amendment covers federal question cases. Amar, note 73, at 1476-77. Professor Althouse applauds *Pennhurst* for inviting state courts to police their own precincts. Ann Althouse, *How to Build a Separate Sphere: Federal Courts and State Power*, 100 Harv. L. Rev. 1485 (1987).

184. See Chapter VIII, note 298 and accompanying text.

185. Of course, *Pennhurst* does not affect *every* supplemental jurisdiction case, but only those in which plaintiffs sue state officers. Moreover, Justice Powell suggested in a footnote that the eleventh amendment bar recognized in *Pennhurst* affects only officer suits for injunctive relief, not suits for compensatory damages to be paid by individuals. 465 U.S. at 111 n.21. Accordingly, plaintiffs who sue state officers for damages on federal grounds can still attach supplemental claims (for damages) on state law theories. Justice Powell did not mention suits for declaratory relief, but it is hard to think that the eleventh amendment does not treat declaratory judgments like injunctions in this context. Professor Shapiro suggests that if declaratory relief can be granted, but no follow-on injunctions can issue, it is still likely that declaratory judgments themselves can have preclusive effect between the parties. Shapiro, note 179, at 82.

an option. The plaintiff can file a single action in state court (joining both federal and state claims), or the plaintiff can file two actions (one in federal court to advance federal claims and another in state court to press state claims). In the one scenario, the plaintiff surrenders the very thing that § 1367(a) appears to establish: an ability to litigate federal claims in federal court without sacrificing related state claims. In the other, the plaintiff preserves the federal forum for federal claims, but only at the cost of inefficiency. If the plaintiff chooses to sue in both courts at once, further questions arise. One court or the other may find it appropriate to stay its hand while the other proceeds.[186] If the state court completes its work first, the state judgment will be reviewable only in the Supreme Court and almost certainly will be entitled to preclusive effect in the federal district court in which the plaintiff's other action is pending.[187]

D. The Ku Klux Klan Act

Officer suits naming state agents as defendants typically rely on § 1983 for the right of action required. That is in keeping with § 1983's historical links with the fourteenth amendment and federal constitutional checks on state power.[188] The Supreme Court recognizes as much and has construed § 1983 to conform to the eleventh amendment environment in which § 1983 actions typically operate. Recall that § 1983 does not abrogate a state's eleventh amendment immunity.[189] Consistently, the Court has held that a state is not a "person" within the meaning of § 1983 and thus cannot be named as a defendant in a § 1983 action.[190]

---

186. See Chapter XI, notes 58, 77-78 and accompanying text (discussing the district courts' ability to abstain from deciding constitutional issues until uncertain questions of state law are resolved in state court); Keith Werhan, *Pullman Abstention After Pennhurst: A Comment on Judicial Federalism*, 27 Wm. & Mary L. Rev. 449 (1986).

187. See Chapter VI, notes 156-87 and accompanying text (discussing preclusion); Shapiro, note 179, at 80-81. Presumably, litigants cannot be faulted for failing to advance state claims in federal court in the teeth of an eleventh amendment bar. Yet they might well be expected to press federal claims in state court. Once either court actually determines an issue, the losing party may be foreclosed from attacking that determination in the other tribunal. The *Pennhurst* decision also frustrates *Siler*, inasmuch as it deprives federal courts of the opportunity to avoid federal questions by resting judgment on state law grounds.

188. See Chapter II, text accompanying notes 73-75; Chapter VIII, notes 90, 93-94 and accompanying text.

189. See note 105 and accompanying text.

190. *Will*, 491 U.S. at 71. The Court also held in *Ngiraingas v. Sanchez*, 495 U.S. 182 (1990), that a territory (in that case Guam) is not a person for § 1983 purposes. The Court said in *Will* that an officer sued in an official capacity for compensatory relief counts as the state and thus is not a person for § 1983 purposes. That comports with the understanding that suits of that kind are genuinely against the state itself. See note 152 and accompanying text. The Court made it clear, however, that an officer sued in an official capacity for injunctive relief *is* a person. Accordingly, § 1983 can supply the right of action required for modern suits of the kind the Court approved in *Ex parte Young*. *Will*, 491 U.S. at 71 n.10; see notes 134-39 and accompanying text. The § 1983 action in *Will* was filed in state court (where the eleventh amendment is inapplicable). Nevertheless, the Court plainly relied on eleventh amendment jurisprudence to arrive at its holding that a state cannot be a person for § 1983 purposes (in any court). In light of *Will*, plaintiffs cannot sue a state in a § 1983 action (in either state or federal court), even if the state consents. 491 U.S. at 85 (Brennan, J.,

The Court has also conformed § 1983 to *Home Telephone*.[191] In that case, the Court clarified an element of a substantive fourteenth amendment claim (the requirement that the action of which the plaintiff complains must be ascribable to the state). In this context, the task has been to explain an element of the right of action that § 1983 supplies for advancing substantive claims (often fourteenth amendment claims). By its terms, § 1983 authorizes lawsuits only against defendants who act under "color" of a state "statute, ordinance, regulation, custom or usage."[192] In *Monroe v. Pape*,[193] the plaintiffs filed a § 1983 action against Chicago police officers, contending that the officers had violated the plaintiffs' fourteenth amendment rights by breaking into their home and conducting an unreasonable search. The officers responded that they had not acted under color of state law for purposes of § 1983, because Illinois law did not authorize them to commit the acts of which the plaintiffs complained. Accordingly, the plaintiffs' proper course was to file suit in state court, seeking compensatory damages for the violation of their rights under state tort law.

In the Supreme Court, Justice Douglas said that the "color of law" requirement in § 1983 tracks the "state action" requirement in the fourteenth amendment, as elaborated in *Home Telephone*. Officers act under color of state law when they exercise the official authority in which they are "clothed," even if they actually *violate* state law.[194] There was no occasion, then, to fault the plaintiffs in *Monroe* for failing to sue the police in state court. Irrespective of whether the officers had violated state law, they had acted under color of that law and thus could be sued in a § 1983 action in federal court.[195] In that § 1983 action, the of-

---

dissenting) (lamenting this implication); *Arizonans for Official English*, 117 S.Ct. at 1069-70 (confirming it).

191. See notes 140-51 and accompanying text.

192. See Chapter VIII, text accompanying note 93.

193. 365 U.S. 167 (1961).

194. Justice Douglas relied on *United States v. Classic*, 313 U.S. 299 (1941); *Screws v. United States*, 325 U.S. 91 (1945); and *Williams v. United States*, 341 U.S. 97 (1951). In those cases, the Court construed other statutes from the Reconstruction era, which contain the same "color of law" language found in § 1983. In the main, defendants act under color of law (and thus are subject to suit via § 1983) if their behavior can be ascribed to the state (and thus counts as state action for purposes of the fourteenth amendment). That is what makes § 1983 the common right-of-action vehicle for fourteenth amendment claims. Most defendants in § 1983 suits are employees of state or local government. Conceptually, however, the "color of law" category is larger than the "state action" category. Otherwise, the Court would be unable to reach the fourteenth amendment "state action" question in a § 1983 action. Every case would be resolved on the basis of the analytically prior, non-constitutional question whether the defendant acted under color of law. As it is, the Court assumes (*sub silentio*) that a defendant's behavior was under color of law for § 1983 purposes and then focuses on whether that action was ascribable to the state for purposes of the fourteenth amendment. Some cases are easy, others more controversial. In *Lugar v. Edmondson*, 457 U.S. 922 (1982), Justice White mustered only a bare majority for a holding that the conduct of private parties is state action when they participate jointly with state officials in the seizure of disputed property. See Chapter XI, notes 243-44 and accompanying text (discussing the *Lugar* dissenters' disinclination to rely on that case in *Pennzoil v. Texaco*).

195. The Court has since held that § 1983 actions can be filed in both federal and state court. See Chapter VI, text accompanying note 52. In *Monroe*, however, the point was that the plaintiffs were entitled to choose the federal forum if they wished, relying on § 1983 for a right of action and on a separate statute, § 1343(3), for the district court's jurisdiction. Today, § 1983 actions invariably rest on § 1331 for subject matter jurisdiction in federal court. See Chapter VIII, note 94.

ficers could be held liable for violating the plaintiffs' federal rights — again, without regard to whether the officers had violated state law as well.[196] According to Justice Douglas, § 1983 provides plaintiffs with a right of action for vindicating federal rights that is "supplementary" to any action they might file in state court, pressing parallel state claims arising from the same episode.[197]

In dissent, Justice Frankfurter insisted that the "color of law" requirement in § 1983 should be understood to incorporate (in essence) the view that he previously took (without success) regarding "state action" for fourteenth amendment purposes.[198] In most instances, according to Frankfurter, state officers act under color of state law only if some species of positive state law authorizes their behavior. If plaintiffs wish to charge state officers with misusing their official positions to commit unauthorized acts, the proper course is to file suit in state court in order to allow those courts to enforce state tort law. By Frankfurter's account, an "unlawful intrusion by a policeman in Chicago" should entail no "different consequences" than an "unlawful intrusion by a hoodlum." Justice Frankfurter acknowledged that § 1983 authorizes suits against officers acting under color of "custom or usage" and that, in that way, appears not to require that they have explicit authority in a formal state statute. Yet he contended that any qualifying "custom or usage" must be so settled and systematic as to have the "cast of law."[199]

With respect to "state action" (for purposes of the fourteenth amendment), Justice Frankfurter insisted that *no* instance of officer behavior should count, unless and until a state court delivers an authoritative judgment that it *conforms* to state law. That arrangement would drive fourteenth amendment suits against abusive state executive officers into state court.[200] With respect to action under "color of law" (for purposes of § 1983), Frankfurter was less severe. On that account, he said it should be enough if plaintiffs can point to some state statute or clear systematic practice authorizing the officers' behavior. As a practical matter, however, Frankfurter's view of the "color of law" requirement would also channel plaintiffs into state court in cases in which they allege that executive officers have abused their official authority. That, in turn, would produce the same consequences that would have attended his interpretation of "state action."[201]

---

196. Recall that § 1983 supplies no substantive rights itself, but serves only as a procedural vehicle for pressing other rights (typically fourteenth amendment rights) in court.

197. 365 U.S. at 183. Douglas relied on legislative history indicating that Congress enacted § 1983 *because* the Ku Klux Klan, often acting in concert with local authorities, was abusing private citizens in the teeth of state statutes condemning Klan violence.

198. See notes 144-49 and accompanying text.

199. 365 U.S. at 236, 239 (dissenting opinion). Frankfurter thus insisted that the plaintiffs' suit in *Monroe* could not go forward on the basis of their general allegation that the defendant officers had violated the fourteenth amendment — ignoring unquestioned evidence that state law, too, condemned the same conduct. Frankfurter acknowledged, however, that the plaintiffs alleged that the officers acted in some respects on the basis of settled and systematic practices. He conceded that the § 1983 action might be allowed to proceed, limited to those particular allegations. Frankfurter's unsuccessful proposal for interpreting § 1983 thus tracked the interpretation the Court has given the civil rights removal statute, 28 U.S.C. § 1443. See Chapter VI, notes 133-48 and accompanying text.

200. Plaintiffs would retain only the ability to attack state statutes or constitutional provisions as themselves inconsistent with federal law.

201. Concurring in *Monroe*, Justice Harlan said he would have found the debate between Douglas and Frankfurter "close" if the Court had not previously adopted Justice Douglas' interpretation of the "color of law" formulation. See note 194. Yet on the merits

Justice Frankfurter plainly hoped to interpret § 1983 in a way that would divert litigation into state court. But in 1961, when *Monroe* was decided, the Warren Court just as plainly meant to open the federal courts for the adjudication of federal claims, particularly civil rights and civil liberties claims under the fourteenth amendment. By holding that § 1983 supplies the required right of action, the Court built upon the foundation laid in *Ex parte Young* and *Home Telephone* to erect a general framework for litigation of that kind. Prior to *Monroe*, § 1983 had largely been used only in officer suits seeking injunctive relief from ongoing violations of federal law. In *Monroe*, the Court recruited § 1983 to service as a vehicle for officer suits seeking compensatory relief for violations in the past.[202] Today, the availability of a § 1983 action in federal court is typically the *sine qua non* of a successful challenge to the actions of state officers.[203]

The text of § 1983 merely establishes a right of action and does not address ancillary questions that can arise. The Supreme Court fashions rules and procedures for § 1983 actions as a matter of federal common law, typically by borrowing from the law of tort and analogous state law rules.[204] Pursuant to 42 U.S.C.

---

of Frankfurter's position, Harlan said he could not be persuaded that the Reconstruction Congress that wrote § 1983 would have wished to force plaintiffs into state court in the absence of a formal enactment or settled practice authorizing officer behavior. The point of enacting § 1983 was not that state law formally permitted state officers to mistreat the citizenry, but that citizens were being mistreated despite the requirements of state law. 365 U.S. at 487. Professor Zagrans contends that Frankfurter had the better of the historical argument. Zagrans, note 137. Professor Winter sides with Douglas. Steven L. Winter, *The Meaning of "Under Color of" Law*, 91 Mich. L. Rev. 323 (1992). Dissenting in *Crawford-El v. Britton*, 118 S.Ct. 1584 (1998), Justice Scalia expressed sympathy for Frankfurter's position on the "color of law" question. Id. at 1603. Justice Thomas joined Scalia's attack on *Monroe's* analysis.

202. On the significance of *Monroe* in this respect, see Michael Wells, *Constitutional Torts, Common Law Tort, and Due Process of Law*, 72 Chicago-Kent L. Rev. 617, 620 (1997); Christina B. Whitman, *Emphasizing the Constitutional in Constitutional Torts*, 72 Chicago-Kent L. Rev. 661, 664-66 (1997). Professor Weinberg points out that the Court decided *Monroe* in the midst of its decisions applying the Bill of Rights to the states. She argues that *Monroe* supplied a means of enforcing those rights (most of them rights against abusive police behavior) in cases in which plaintiffs had already been harmed and wanted compensation for their injuries. Louise Weinberg, *The Monroe Mystery Solved: Beyond the "Unhappy History" Theory of Civil Rights Litigation*, 1991 B.Y.U. L. Rev. 737, 757.

203. For exhaustive treatments of § 1983, see Sheldon H. Nahmod, Civil Rights and Civil Liberties Litigation: The Law of Section 1983 (4th ed. 1997); *Developments in the Law: Section 1983 and Federalism*, 90 Harv. L. Rev. 1133 (1977). For an ideological assessment of § 1983 and its potential, see Jack M. Beermann, *A Critical Approach to Section 1983 With Special Attention to the Sources of Law*, 42 Stan. L. Rev. 51 (1989).

204. The Court occasionally relies upon 42 U.S.C. § 1988, which instructs federal courts to apply state law in § 1983 actions when federal law is "deficient." E.g., *Wilson v. Garcia*, 471 U.S. 261 (1985) (adopting a state statute of limitations); *Robertson v. Wegmann*, 436 U.S. 584, 594-95 (1978) (adopting a state rule of survivorship). But see *Felder v. Casey*, 487 U.S. 131 (1988) (rejecting a state notice requirement because it would routinely frustrate the enforcement of federal rights). For discussions of § 1988, see Seth F. Kreimer, *The Source of Law in Civil Rights Actions: Some Old Light on Section 1988*, 133 U. Pa. L. Rev. 601 (1985); Theodore Eisenberg, *State Law in Federal Civil Rights Cases: The Proper Scope of Section 1988*, 128 U. Pa. L. Rev. 499 (1980). Here again, the Court departs from the textualism that characterizes its construction of other statutes. See Harold S. Lewis, Jr. & Theodore Y. Blumoff, *Reshaping Section 1983's Asymmetry*, 140 U. Pa. L. Rev. 755, 760 (1992) (describing § 1983 as "almost entirely a judicial construct"); Chapter I, notes 24-36 and accompanying text (discussing the Court's usual emphasis on the text of statutes). Pro-

§ 1988, the losing party can be taxed for the winner's reasonable attorney fees.[205] Only successful plaintiffs can typically recover fees under § 1988.[206] Successful defendants can do so only if the actions against them are frivolous or vexatious.[207] Attorney fee awards raise no eleventh amendment questions in § 1983 actions in federal court.[208]

1. Suits Against Cities and Counties

While a state cannot be a "person" within the meaning of § 1983, a city or county can be. The Supreme Court held as much in *Monell v. Dep't of Social Svc.*[209] Recall that cities and counties have no eleventh amendment immunity from suit in federal court.[210] In *Monell*, Justice Brennan said that plaintiffs are free to name them as the nominal defendants in § 1983 actions (filed either in federal court or in state court) and to seek injunctions, declaratory judgments, or compensatory damages to be paid from the public treasury. Brennan explained, however, that cities and counties cannot be held liable for the misdeeds of their agents on the principle of *respondeat superior*. They are accountable only for actions traceable to a "law, statute, ordinance, regulation, custom, or usage" that can "fairly be said to represent official policy."[211]

---

fessor Beermann argues that the Court eschews a more textual approach to § 1983, because it would not serve the Court's "conservative agenda." Jack M. Beermann, *Common Law Elements of the Section 1983 Action*, 72 Chicago-Kent L. Rev. 695, 699 (1997). Professor Wells contends that § 1983 will not bear the meaning required of a workable right-of-action statute. He argues that the Court should set § 1983 aside, find a right of action implied in the Due Process Clause, and proceed to elaborate that right of action as a matter of constitutional tort law. Michael Wells, *The Past and the Future of Constitutional Torts: From Statutory Interpretation to Common Law Rules*, 19 Conn. L. Rev. 53 (1986). See note 162 (discussing the possibility of a right of action implied in the fourteenth amendment); Chapter VIII, notes 104-65 and accompanying text (discussing implied actions generally).

205. Liability for attorney fees under § 1988 follows liability on the merits. Accordingly, if state officers are held personally liable for damages, they must equally pay the plaintiffs' attorney fees. The state that employs them cannot be liable on the merits, because it has eleventh amendment immunity. Likewise, the state cannot be liable for attorney fees. *Graham*, 473 U.S. at 167-68.

206. *Maher v. Gagne*, 448 U.S. 122 (1980).

207. *Hughes v. Rowe*, 449 U.S. 5 (1980).

208. See note 170 (noting the *Hutto* case).

209. 436 U.S. 658 (1978). The Court took the other view in *Monroe*, but *Monell* squarely overruled *Monroe* on this point, relying on a reassessment of the relevant legislative history. Id. at 690. Cf. *Mt. Healthy City Bd. of Ed. v. Doyle*, 429 U.S. 274, 277-79 (1977) (noting but failing to decide the question whether a local school board can be subject to suit under § 1983).

210. See notes 115-16 and accompanying text.

211. 436 U.S. at 691, 694, quoting the text of § 1983. Justice Stevens dissented on this point. Professor Kramer and Professor Sykes contend that Stevens had the better of the argument. Larry Kramer & Alan O. Sykes, *Municipal Liability Under § 1983: A Legal and Economic Analysis*, 1987 Sup. Ct. Rev. 249, 261-62. The rule is not that a city or county can be liable only if a policy or custom itself violates the plaintiffs' federal rights. The rule is that a city or county can be liable only if there is a "direct causal link" between a policy or custom and the action of the employee that violates the plaintiffs federal rights, *City of Canton v. Harris*, 489 U.S. 378, 385 (1989), so that the policy or custom is the "moving force" behind the violation that occurs. *Bd. of County Comm'rs v. Brown*, 117 S.Ct. 1382, 1388 (1997). In *Harris*, accordingly, the Court said that the city would be liable for failing to train

The construction of § 1983 in *Monell* does not affect plaintiffs' ability to obtain injunctive or declaratory relief against city and county officers. Officer suits for prospective remedies do not depend on the liability of the parent authority. It does affect plaintiffs' ability to obtain compensatory relief from public coffers. On the one hand, it allows plaintiffs to sue cities and counties as corporate entities.[212] On the other hand, *Monell*'s construction of § 1983 does with respect to the liability of cities and counties what Justice Frankfurter tried (but failed) to do with respect to the liability of individual state officers: To obtain compensation, plaintiffs must tie a violation of their federal rights to a general policy or custom ascribable to the corporate body.[213] Legislative enactments will suffice. Customs that are so widespread as to have the force of law will also answer, even though they have not been formally approved. Isolated decisions by the governing bodies concerned will do, albeit those decisions are not framed as general rules.[214] The Court has had difficulty with cases in which individual city or county officers have authority to make general policy, and plaintiffs claim they have done so when making particular decisions.[215]

---

police officers if it were shown to maintain a policy of "deliberate indifference" to the federal rights of persons with whom poorly trained officers would come into contact. The Court remanded the case in order that the plaintiff could attempt to demonstrate such a policy. In the wake of that resounding victory, there was no noticeable upturn in the number of successful § 1983 actions grounded on a "failure to train" theory. Cf. *Brown*, 117 S.Ct. at 1401 (Breyer, J., dissenting) (urging the Court to reconsider *Monell*'s rejection of *respondeat superior* liability). Even if the city or county authorizes unconstitutional activity, there can be no corporate liability unless some officer actually commits a violation. *City of Los Angeles v. Heller*, 475 U.S. 796 (1986). For a discussion of the advantages and disadvantages of *respondeat superior* in § 1983 cases, see Lewis & Blumoff, note 204; Note, *Government Tort Liability*, 111 Harv. L. Rev. 2009 (1998).

212. Recall that a state cannot be named as a defendant in a § 1983 action at all and that the eleventh amendment bars officer suits that attempt to reach the state treasury. See notes 167-69 and accompanying text. In *McMillian v. Monroe County*, 520 U.S. 781 (1997), the Court held that, as a matter of state law, a sheriff acting in a law enforcement capacity was a state, not a county, officer. Accordingly, the plaintiffs' claim for compensatory relief could succeed only if it was repackaged as a suit to obtain damages from the sheriff personally.

213. See notes 198-99 and accompanying text. If the point is to deter violations of federal rights, there is a case to be made for visiting liability on officers personally. See Peter H. Schuck, Suing Government: Citizen Remedies for Official Wrongs 68 (1983). If, however, the point is compensation for victims, most commentators argue that it is important to reach the public treasury. E.g., Ronald A. Cass, *Damage Suits Against Public Officers*, 129 U. Pa. L. Rev. 1110 (1981); Jon O. Newman, *Suing the Lawbreakers: Proposals to Strengthen the Section 1983 Damage Remedy for Law Enforcers' Misconduct*, 87 Yale L.J. 447 (1978); Peter Schuck, *Municipal Liability Under Section 1983: Some Lessons from Tort Law and Organization Theory*, 77 Gtn. L.J. 1753 (1989). According to one (dated) study, police misconduct suits rarely produce compensation awards. *Project: Suing the Police in Federal Court*, 88 Yale L.J. 781 (1979).

214. E.g., *Owen v. City of Independence*, 445 U.S. 622 (1980) (holding a city liable for the city council's violation of due process in summarily dismissing an employee); *Newport v. Fact Concerts*, 453 U.S. 247 (1981) (holding a city responsible for the city council's violation of the first amendment in summarily canceling a concert).

215. Compare *Pembaur v. City of Cincinnati*, 475 U.S. 469 (1986) (holding a county liable for an authoritative decision by a prosecutor), with *City of St. Louis v. Praprotnik*, 485 U.S. 112 (1988) (declining to hold a city liable for the actions of two senior supervisors in dismissing a subordinate). In both *Pembaur* and *Praprotnik*, the Court took account of local law in making the determination whether the relevant officer enjoyed policy-making authority.

2. Constitutional Torts

The right of action established by § 1983 bears an uneasy relationship to the law of tort. In the groundwork case, *Monroe v. Pape*,[216] Justice Douglas declared that § 1983 "should be read against the background of tort liability that makes a man responsible for the natural consequences of his actions."[217] Plaintiffs who employ § 1983 must necessarily seek to vindicate some right secured by federal law. The content of a claim advanced in a § 1983 lawsuit is neither more nor less than the content of the federal right the plaintiff hopes to establish. Suits under § 1983 actions merely supply occasions for interpreting and applying federal constitutional and statutory rights on their own (federal) bottom.[218] Most Supreme Court decisions reflect this understanding. The Court elaborates the meaning of federal claims without suggesting that it makes any difference that plaintiffs present those claims in a § 1983 action rather than by some other means.[219]

In *Parratt v. Taylor*,[220] for example, a state prison inmate ordered a hobby kit from a mail order house. The kit was lost or stolen after its arrival at the institution. The prisoner filed a § 1983 action in federal court, contending that the defendants (the manager of the prison's hobby center and the warden) had deprived him of his property without due process of law. The prisoner did not explicitly allege that the defendants acted deliberately; his complaint could be read to complain only that they had been negligent. Then-Justice Rehnquist first decided what he regarded as a question of statutory interpretation: whether negligence would "support a claim for relief under § 1983." He found nothing in § 1983 to condition liability on "a particular state of mind" and thus relied on Justice Douglas' statement in *Monroe* that the ordinary "natural consequences" rule in tort law should apply.[221] That was a mistake. Later, in *Daniels v.*

---

216. See notes 193-97 and accompanying text. For discussions of these problems, see Susan Bandes, *Monell, Parratt, Daniels & Davidson: Distinguishing a Custom or Policy from a Random, Unauthorized Act*, 72 Iowa L. Rev. 101 (1986); Michael J. Gerhardt, *The Monell Legacy: Balancing Federalism Concerns and Municipal Accountability Under Section 1983*, 62 So. Calif. L. Rev. 539 (1989).

217. 365 U.S. at 187. Douglas offered this statement by way of distinguishing civil actions for damages under § 1983 from criminal prosecutions under 18 U.S.C. § 242, in which it is necessary for the prosecution to prove that a defendant acted "wilfully" and thus with a "specific intent to deprive a person of a federal right." *Monroe*, 365 U.S. at 187, quoting *Screws*, 325 U.S. at 103. Douglas did not mean that tort law determines the state of mind required for civil liability under § 1983. He meant that § 1983 does not require proof that a defendant was aware of the plaintiff's federal rights and subjectively intended to violate those rights.

218. Many provisions of the Constitution have roots in the common law, and the Supreme Court routinely consults common law materials in coming to an authoritative decision regarding their meaning. That, however, is only familiar interpretive methodology. It does not deny that the law being interpreted has an independent federal existence.

219. See *Baker v. McCollan*, 443 U.S. 137 (1979) (explaining that it is insufficient for plaintiffs in § 1983 actions to allege the elements of common law torts and that it is essential that they allege a violation of federal rights). Professor Whitman applauds this approach and discourages the notion that the common law of tort can provide a "useful model for constitutional decision-making." Whitman, note 202, at 661.

220. 451 U.S. 527 (1981).

221. See text accompanying note 217.

Williams,[222] Justice Rehnquist repudiated *Parratt* on this point. He explained that if a defendant's liability turns on a "state of mind," it is only because that mental state is an element of the claim that the plaintiff advances *in* a § 1983 action. Treating the "state of mind" issue in that way, Justice Rehnquist decided in *Daniels* that negligence cannot constitute a "deprivation" of property within the meaning of the Due Process Clause.[223]

Nevertheless, in cases in which plaintiffs seek compensatory damages (either from officers themselves or from a city or county), the Court often insists that § 1983 "creates a species of tort liability."[224] By referring to tort law, the Court may only mean to recognize that a defendant's behavior often constitutes both a violation of the plaintiff's federal rights for purposes of § 1983 and a common law wrong, compensable under state law.[225] Alternatively, the Court may mean to acknowledge that it consults tort principles when it chooses federal rules to govern various aspects of § 1983 litigation and liability, apart from the nature of the claims that plaintiffs' advance.[226] There are decisions, however, in which it is hard to isolate the Court's references to tort law from its articulation of the elements of plaintiffs' federal claims.[227] Those decisions have baffled the lower courts and spawned yet another body of academic literature.

---

222. 474 U.S. 327, 330 (1986).

223. See *Brown*, 117 S.Ct. at 1388-89 (confirming that § 1983 itself contains no "state-of-mind" requirement and that plaintiffs must establish only the "state of mind required to prove the underlying violation"); *Farmer v. Brennan*, 511 U.S. 825, 834 (1994) (explaining that the "deliberate indifference" state of mind necessary to a meritorious eighth amendment claim is a function of the eighth amendment itself). Professor Gildin points out that the defendant's state of mind may figure in the availability of qualified immunity. Gary S. Gildin, *The Standard of Culpability in Section 1983 and Bivens Actions: The Prima Facie Case, Qualified Immunity and the Constitution*, 11 Hofstra L. Rev. 557, 560 (1983); see notes 266-92 and accompanying text.

224. *Memphis Community School Dist. v. Stachura*, 477 U.S. 299, 305 (1986).

225. See notes 195-97 and accompanying text.

226. See *Carey v. Piphus*, 435 U.S. 247, 258 (1978) (explaining that "tort rules of damages" may typically be applied to § 1983 actions). Professor Jeffries has explored the difficulties of computing damages to compensate plaintiffs in § 1983 actions. E.g., John C. Jeffries, Jr., *Compensation for Constitutional Torts: Reflections on the Significance of Fault*, 88 Mich. L. Rev. 82 (1989); John C. Jeffries, Jr., *Damages for Constitutional Violations: The Relation of Risk to Injury in Constitutional Torts*, 75 Va. L. Rev. 1461 (1989). For a critique of Jeffries, see Sheldon H. Nahmod, *Constitutional Damages and Corrective Justice: A Different View*, 76 Va. L. Rev. 997 (1990).

227. In *Heck v. Humphrey*, 512 U.S. 477 (1994), a prison inmate filed a § 1983 action in federal court, contending that state law enforcement officers had conducted an unreasonable criminal investigation, destroyed evidence, and contrived to introduce inadmissible evidence at his trial—leading to his unconstitutional conviction. He sought compensatory damages, but no injunctive relief. Justice Scalia said that the prisoner was effectively challenging the validity of his conviction, even if he was not seeking immediate release from custody. Accordingly, he was attempting to employ § 1983 as a substitute for the more conventional vehicle for attacking criminal convictions—a petition for a writ of habeas corpus. The question, then, was whether the prisoner could proceed under § 1983 (on the theory that he was entitled to compensation for an invalid conviction) *before* he established that the conviction was invalid by the ordinary means (a habeas corpus action). One might have expected Justice Scalia to resolve that question as a matter of statutory construction, reconciling § 1983 with the statutes governing habeas corpus actions. Instead, he repeated the boilerplate that § 1983 "creates a species of tort liability" and insisted that he could decide whether there was a "bar" to the plaintiff's § 1983 action only by looking "first to the common law of torts." Turning to tort law, Scalia said that the "closest analogy" to the plain-

The overlap between § 1983 suits advancing federal claims and state tort actions has important implications for the allocation of business between federal and state courts. Critics charge that by linking § 1983 lawsuits to the common law of tort, the Court trivializes the federal rights that § 1983 exists to enforce and lays the groundwork for relegating those claims to state court.[228] The Court makes it appear that § 1983 lawsuits threaten to shift traditional state tort claims to federal court, as plaintiffs repackage their theories for recovery as federal claims in order to litigate them under the authority provided by § 1983.[229] Then, the Court justifies new limits on federal rights as a necessary response to that threat. The best illustrations are cases in which plaintiffs assert the most amorphous kind of constitutional claim: arbitrary action in violation of due process. Claims of that sort often absorb the kind of wrongful treatment that is conventionally redressed in tort. Ostensibly to discourage plaintiffs from using § 1983 to advance due process claims in federal court, the Supreme Court interprets due process itself in a way that channels litigants into state court.[230]

---

tiff's constitutional claim was an action for malicious prosecution. That kind of tort action contemplated that a plaintiff must first undermine the validity of a conviction by some other means and only thereafter seek compensatory damages. Importing that feature of the common law malicious prosecution tort into the plaintiff's instant § 1983 action, Scalia concluded that the § 1983 action was premature. The prisoner must first dislodge his conviction via habeas corpus proceedings or some comparable form of action. In dissent, Justice Souter (and three other justices) did not "object to referring to the common law" for guidance, but rather complained that Justice Scalia had allowed common law principles to override the first order of business: the proper construction of § 1983. Souter then went on to offer a different assessment of the way analogous common law actions should bear on the question at hand. Professor Beermann reads *Heck* to suggest that § 1983 plaintiffs must plead and prove the elements of common law torts, after all. Beermann, note 204, at 711-14. See Chapter XII, notes 248-53 and accompanying text (discussing *Heck's* relationship to habeas corpus).

228. Professor Eisenberg and Professor Schwab contend that the Court's decisions uniformly hope to limit access to the federal courts. Theodore Eisenberg & Stewart J. Schwab, *The Reality of Constitutional Tort Litigation*, 72 Cornell L. Rev. 641, 646-47 (1987). Professor Nahmod argues that by using the "rhetoric" of tort to describe § 1983 actions, the Court hopes to "marginalize" § 1983 litigation. Sheldon H. Nahmod, *Section 1983 Discourse: The Move From Constitution to Tort*, 77 Gtn. L.J. 1719, 1719-20 (1989). Justice Blackmun once said that the Court is "inclined to cut back on § 1983 in any way" it can, short of "ignoring the language of the statute" and existing precedent. Harry A. Blackmun, *Section 1983 and Federal Protection of Individual Rights—Will the Statute Remain Alive or Fade Away?*, 60 N.Y.U. L. Rev. 1, 23 (1985). For exhaustive treatments of the cases in point, see Constitutional Torts (Nahmod, Wells & Eaton eds. 1995); Christina B. Whitman, *Government Responsibility for Constitutional Torts*, 85 Mich. L. Rev. 225 (1986); Christina B. Whitman, *Constitutional Torts*, 79 Mich. L. Rev. 5 (1980).

229. E.g., Marshall S. Shapo, *Constitutional Tort: Monroe v. Pape and the Frontiers Beyond*, 60 Nw. U. L. Rev. 277, 323-24 (1965). The promise of attorney fees in § 1983 actions creates an additional incentive to characterize claims as federal in nature. See notes 205-08 and accompanying text. Since § 1983 actions can be filed in state court, however, plaintiffs who package their claims as alleged violations of federal rights primarily to obtain attorney fees may choose to remain in the state forum. Even then, however, the elaboration of the substantive content of federal rights can be skewed if litigants merely contrive to extend those rights to cover tortious behavior in order to be in a position to win attorney fees. For a discussion, see Stewart J. Schwab & Theodore Eisenberg, *Explaining Constitutional Tort Litigation: The Influence of the Attorney Fees Statute and the Government as Defendant*, 73 Cornell L. Rev. 719, 780 (1988) (reporting inconclusive results from an empirical study).

230. E.g., *Collins v. City of Harker Heights*, 503 U.S. 115, 127 (1992) (acknowledging the Court's reluctance to elaborate the scope of substantive due process "because guideposts for responsible decisionmaking in this uncharted area are scarce and open-ended"); *Paul v.*

In *Parratt*, Justice Rehnquist understood the prisoner to advance a *procedural* due process claim: His property had been taken without a hearing. Rehnquist agreed that due process mandated some kind of procedure before the state "finally" deprived the prisoner of his hobby kit. But in the circumstances in *Parratt*, it was useless to propose that a hearing should have been held before the hobby kit disappeared. Since the loss or theft of the kit was "tortious," it was a "random and unauthorized" act, not the sort of thing that the state might have anticipated. Accordingly, the Due Process Clause must be satisfied by process *after* the fact. That process, in turn, need not be supplied by the defendants themselves at the penitentiary. It could be offered later in state court, when the prisoner sued the defendants in tort.[231] Justice Rehnquist concluded, accordingly, that the prisoner had not "alleged a violation" of due process, because he had not challenged the adequacy of the process the state offered in the form of state judicial proceedings.[232]

The decision in *Parratt* rested on an interpretation of procedural due process. Justice Rehnquist posited a deprivation of property; the only question was when and how the state was obliged to provide the process that was due. Yet by holding that the state could satisfy due process by offering the plaintiff an opportu-

---

Davis, 424 U.S. 693, 701 (1976) (expressing concern that § 1983 could become a "font of tort law"); *Crawford-El*, 118 S.Ct. at 1603 (Scalia, J., dissenting) (insisting that the Court's interpretation of § 1983 in *Monroe* engages the Court in "a losing struggle to prevent the Constitution from degenerating into a general tort law"). Professor Wells acknowledges that the Court cannot very well hold that a state officer's every tortious act is a violation of the victim's constitutional rights. Tort law is subject to adjustment in the ordinary majoritarian manner. If it were constitutitionalized to any significant degree, the courts (and particularly the federal courts) would displace state legislatures in the formulation of social policy on a wide scale. Wells argues that the Court should nonetheless welcome the insight that substantive due process governs cases on the boundary of constitutional law and common law tort and should rationalize its cases under a general substantive due process heading. The Court should "pay attention" to tort law, but the Court should not regard tort law as a "source" of constitutional law and certainly should not adopt a rule simply *because* it has a basis in common law. Instead, by Wells' account, the Court should elaborate *constitutional* tort law in a way that vindicates constitutional rights. Michael Wells, *Constitutional Remedies, Section 1983 and the Common Law* (forthcoming); Wells, note 202, at 618. Professor Whitman argues that "torts is a distraction" and that, to the extent the Court allows itself to worry about moving matters that might be handled as state tort actions into federal court, the Court allows the law of torts to "drive thinking about constitutional substance." Whitman, note 202, at 661.

231. In the particular case at bar, Justice Rehnquist noted that Nebraska had established a special mechanism for adjudicating prisoner claims of the kind the plaintiff wished to advance in federal court. Professor Kupfer detects tension between *Parratt's* ready acceptance of state process and *Monroe's* emphasis on the value of a federal right of action. Susan G. Kupfer, *Restructuring the Monroe Doctrine: Current Litigation Under Section 1983*, 9 Hastings Const. L.Q. 463 (1982). See also Leon Friedman, *Parratt v. Taylor: Opening and Closing the Door on Section 1983*, 9 Hastings Const. L.Q. 545 (1982).

232. The assumed negligence of the defendants' behavior in *Parratt* was not critical to the characterization of that behavior as "random and unauthorized." In *Hudson v. Palmer*, 468 U.S. 517 (1984), the Court applied the same characterization to intentional (tortious) conduct. By insisting that the prisoner's procedural due process claim must acknowledge not only any process that the prison officials offered (or failed to offer), but also the process provided by state courts, Justice Rehnquist presupposed that all the arms of the state could help satisfy the claim. That put pressure on the *Ex parte Young* "officer suit" fiction on which he implicitly rested to avoid the eleventh amendment. See notes 137-39 and accompanying text. Perhaps he can be forgiven for leaving that particular stone unturned.

nity to sue in state court, Rehnquist effectively barred the prisoner (and others like him) from using § 1983 to press complaints in federal court. Any procedural due process claim was incomplete, unless and until the plaintiff gave the state courts an opportunity to examine the matter.[233] Justice Rehnquist did not hide the forum-allocation implications of the *Parratt* decision. He explained that any other interpretation would have allowed plaintiffs to turn ordinary tortious injuries into constitutional claims to be litigated in federal court in § 1983 actions.[234]

In *Zinermon v. Burch*,[235] the Court underscored that *Parratt* was a procedural due process decision. The plaintiff was found wandering the streets in a disoriented condition. He was taken to a state mental health facility, where he signed forms requesting "voluntary" admission. Under state law, the facility was entitled to accept voluntary patients only if they gave informed consent. There was no established procedure for determining whether a patient was capable of giving consent. Later, the plaintiff sued the staff members who admitted him in a § 1983 action in federal court. Justice Blackmun took the plaintiff's claim to be that he had been denied procedural due process inasmuch as the defendants had committed him without engaging any procedure for determining his ability to make an intelligent decision. Distinguishing *Parratt*, Blackmun held that claim to be complete and adjudicable in federal court.[236]

---

233. Even when a state erroneously deprives an individual of liberty or property, it does not necessarily follow that the state has violated the individual's right to procedural due process. *Martinez v. California*, 444 U.S. 277, 284 n.9 (1980).

234. 451 U.S. at 544. It is well to consider what Justice Rehnquist did *not* hold in *Parratt*. He did *not* deny that the defendant officers had acted under color of state law. Given *Monroe*, those officers clearly *had* acted under color of law for purposes of § 1983 and, given *Home Telephone*, they had equally acted for the state for purposes of the fourteenth amendment. See notes 193-97 and accompanying text. Nevertheless, Professor Alexander argues that Rehnquist actually departed from *Monroe* and *Home Telephone* and, in essence, held that state officers do not act for the state when they violate state law. Larry Alexander, *Constitutional Torts, the Supreme Court, and the Law of Noncontradiction: An Essay on Zinermon v. Burch*, 87 Nw. U. L. Rev. 576, 582 (1993). Justice Rehnquist did *not* hold that the prisoner in *Parratt* was required to exhaust state opportunities for adjudicating his claim before seeking federal adjudication. Litigants need not exhaust state procedures before filing § 1983 actions. *Patsy v. Bd. of Regents*, 457 U.S. 496 (1982); see Chapter XI, notes 48-52 and accompanying text. The point in *Parratt* was not, in any case, that the state courts of Nebraska should be given the first opportunity to resolve the prisoner's claim that he had not received the process he was due. It was that the plaintiff had not been denied that process, because he had never given the state an opportunity to provide it to him: He had not filed suit in state court after suffering the loss of his property. Finally, Justice Rehnquist did *not* hold that the federal court should have abstained from considering the prisoner's due process claim until the state courts resolved the question whether he had a meritorious state tort claim. See Chapter XI, notes 58, 77-78 and accompanying text. Rehnquist did not propose that consideration of the prisoner's procedural due process claim should be postponed. He addressed it squarely and decided it against the plaintiff—on the theory that the prisoner had not been *denied* process that he had never sought. Professor Fallon concedes that Justice Rehnquist did not rest on abstention, but argues that the *Parratt* decision would have made more sense if he had. Richard H. Fallon, Jr., *Some Confusions About Due Process, Judicial Review, and Constitutional Remedies*, 93 Colum. L. Rev. 309, 345 (1993).

235. 494 U.S. 113 (1990).

236. Professor Alexander faults Justice Blackmun for drawing the substance/process line in *Zinermon* and insists that, in doing so, Blackmun surrendered the opportunity that case presented to revisit (and overrule) *Parratt*. Alexander, note 234, at 587-88.

Justice Blackmun explained that when a plaintiff's claim is that state officers acted in a "random and unauthorized" manner, pre-deprivation process is unnecessary and post-deprivation process by means of a state tort lawsuit will suffice. That was *Parratt*. In *Zinermon*, however, the hospital staff members did not act in a "random and unauthorized" way. They followed instructions. The difficulty arose because those instructions were incomplete. The state might well have anticipated the need for some process to determine a voluntary patient's capacity to give consent before the patient was deprived of liberty. But the state had established no such process. The plaintiff therefore could allege a complete procedural due process claim in a § 1983 action without going to state court—namely, a claim that he had been denied the pre-deprivation process to which he was entitled.[237]

Plaintiffs whose procedural due process claims fall on the *Parratt* (rather than the *Zinermon*) side of the line must give the state courts an opportunity to supply the process that is due. The means by which the adequacy of that state process can be tested is problematic. A federal district court will typically be barred from entertaining a § 1983 action in which a plaintiff complains about procedural irregularities in state court.[238] The Supreme Court has appellate jurisdiction to examine any state court failure to provide due process. But, of course, that avenue is more theoretical than real. If the Court accepts a case for review, the standards the Court should apply are unclear. The precedents in point suggest that state process may be constitutionally adequate even if state procedures are truncated and perhaps even if state immunity doctrine bars compensatory relief.[239] If a state can provide the process that is due by summarily *dismissing* an action on the basis of sovereign immunity, then *Parratt's* interpretation of procedural due process is devastating to claims of that nature.[240]

---

237. In dissent, Justice O'Connor accepted Justice Blackmun's premise that both *Zinermon* and *Parratt* were procedural due process cases. But she insisted that Blackmun's opinion is unworkable, because it requires courts to decide at the threshold of every case whether a need for process might have been anticipated. O'Connor argued, instead, for a blanket rule that post-deprivation process is always sufficient when plaintiffs do not attack the adequacy of existing procedural arrangements, but complain that procedures were not put in place where the need for them might have been forecast.

238. See Chapter VI, notes 150-87 and accompanying text (discussing the *Rooker* doctrine and preclusion rules applicable pursuant to the Full Faith and Credit Statute). Professor Blum has suggested that if a plaintiff initially files a § 1983 action pressing a procedural due process claim, the federal court can hold that action in abeyance pending the plaintiff's pursuit of relief in state court. Later, if the plaintiff is dissatisfied with the process in state court and returns to federal court, the court can reinstate the action and review the adequacy of what the state courts did. Karen M. Blum, *Applying the Parratt/Hudson Doctrine: Defining the Scope of the Logan Established State Procedure Exception and Determining the Adequacy of State Postdeprivation Remedies*, 13 Hastings Const. L.Q. 695, 726-28 (1986). See Chapter XI, notes 83-89 and accompanying text (describing a similar procedure in state-question abstention cases).

239. See, e.g., *Daniels*, 474 U.S. 332, 342 (Stevens, J., concurring); see also *Albright v. Oliver*, 510 U.S. 266, 285-86 (1994) (Kennedy, J., concurring) (suggesting that a minimum of state process will suffice).

240. See Chapter VI, notes 54-67 and accompanying text. Then, too, if this is *Parratt's* end-product, there may be a conflict with the decisions requiring the states to provide compensation in due process "takings" cases. It is hard to think that the Court can hold that the states must give the well-heeled classes a judicial remedy for unlawful deprivations of real estate, but then can find it constitutionally satisfying for a state to refuse hospital patients any redress at all for deprivations of physical liberty. The Court relied on *Parratt* by analogy

The analysis of procedural due process claims in *Parratt* and *Zinermon* does not suffice in cases in which litigants advance *substantive* due process claims. In that instance, the constitutional violation is complete at the time of the defendant's initial conduct. No amount of procedure can make up for it. The Supreme Court elaborated on the substance/process distinction in *County of Sacramento v. Lewis*.[241] In that case, police officers in a squad car chased two teenage boys on a motorcycle at speeds in excess of a hundred miles per hour. When the motorcycle tipped over on a curve, the police were going too fast to stop and skidded over one of the boys, killing him on the spot. The decedent's parents filed a § 1983 action against the officers involved, claiming that their actions violated due process. In the Supreme Court, Justice Souter acknowledged that the parents did not contend that state procedures were inadequate in any way, but rather that the officers had abused their executive power. That claim was complete and adjudicable, wholly apart from the availability of state process.[242]

The Court is especially suspicious that substantive due process claims are only state tort claims dressed in federal clothing. In an apparent effort to delineate more clearly between state and federal theories, the Court declines to recognize substantive due process claims at all, if plaintiffs' contentions can fairly be recharacterized as claims under independent provisions of the Bill of Rights, incorporated by the fourteenth amendment.[243] In cases in which no provision of the Bill of Rights fits, the Court grapples with substantive due process theories on their own bottom. Yet the Court insists that only the most arbitrary and oppressive treatment can actually establish a violation. In *Lewis*, for example, Justice Souter explained that the plaintiffs could win only by showing that the officers' behavior "shock[ed] the conscience."[244]

---

in *Williamson County Regional Planning Comm'n v. Hamilton Bank*, 473 U.S. 172, 194-96 (1985), when it held that a "takings" claim is not mature until local condemnation proceedings are complete and the state has arguably failed to provide just compensation.

241. 118 S.Ct. 1708 (1998).

242. Several commentators argue that *Parratt*, too, was actually a substantive due process case. The prisoner in that instance did not want more process, but simply complained that he had been victimized arbitrarily. See, e.g., Fallon, note 234, at 343-44; Michael Wells & Thomas A. Eaton, *Substantive Due Process and the Scope of Constitutional Torts*, 18 Ga. L. Rev. 201, 215-23 (1984); Henry P. Monaghan, *State Law Wrongs, State Law Remedies, and the Fourteenth Amendment*, 86 Colum. L. Rev. 979, 984-86 (1986). The Court deliberately treated the claim as a matter of procedural due process. Otherwise, the Court's wholly procedural analysis would be unintelligible. In a concurring opinion in *Albright*, Justice Kennedy nonetheless said that *Parratt* would be rendered a "dead letter" if plaintiffs could demonstrate that a state tort action was not sufficient to respond to their substantive due process claims. 510 U.S. at 285. But see *Lewis*, 118 S.Ct. at 1721 (Kennedy, J, concurring) (acknowledging that "certain actions" are barred by substantive due process "no matter what procedures attend them").

243. E.g., *Albright*, 510 U.S. at 271-73; *Graham v. Connor*, 490 U.S. 386 (1989); see *Whitley v. Albers*, 475 U.S. 312 (1986) (finding a substantive due process claim essentially subsumed by an eighth amendment claim). Cases like *Albright* and *Connor* are a twist on the old "incorporation" cases, in which many of the justices hesitated to permit litigants to rely on provisions of the Bill of Rights and preferred that they proceed on the basis of due process alone. See *Adamson v. California*, 322 U.S. 46, 124 (1947) (Frankfurter, J., concurring). Now, the Court insists that litigants must press Bill of Rights claims rather than substantive due process claims.

244. 118 S.Ct. at 1717, relying explicitly on *Rochin v. California*, 342 U.S. 165 (1952). Professor Urbonya has reviewed the pre-*Lewis* lower court decisions puzzling out the elements of "excessive force" claims. See Kathryn R. Urbonya, *Establishing a Deprivation of a*

E. Official Immunity

In addition to *sovereign* immunity (which protects government itself), defendants in officer suits may be able to defeat lawsuits challenging their behavior on the basis of *official* immunity (which protects government agents). Official immunity doctrine is largely the same for both federal and state officers, as well as for officers serving cities and counties.[245] The official immunity issue typically arises when plaintiffs sue federal officers, relying on a right of action implied in a constitutional provision,[246] and when plaintiffs sue state and local officers, relying on § 1983 to supply the required right of action.[247] Implied actions and § 1983 actions are not generally subject to official immunity because of anything Congress has done.[248] The Supreme Court fashions official immunity doctrine as a species of judge-made federal law. To do so, the Court draws on two sources: (1) the immunities that governmental officers enjoyed in 1871, when § 1983 was enacted; and (2) the Court's own judgment regarding the nature and scope of the immunities that should be recognized today, in light of relevant policy considerations. Here again, the Court relies on tort law to elaborate federal rules for liability in lawsuits advancing constitutional claims.[249]

When officers assert that they are immune, the Supreme Court ascertains whether some similar form of immunity existed in 1871. If no such immunity was recognized at that time, the Court declines to recognize it today, even if there is a

---

Constitutional Right to Personal Security Under Section 1983: The Use of Unjustified Force by State Officials in Violation of the Fourth, Fifth, and Fourteenth Amendments, 51 Albany L. Rev. 171 (1987).

245. *Butz v. Economou*, 438 U.S. 478, 503-04 (1978).

246. See Chapter VIII, notes 135-53 and accompanying text.

247. See notes 162, 188 and accompanying text. Only government officers are entitled to official immunity. In *Wyatt v. Cole*, 504 U.S. 158 (1992), the plaintiff filed a § 1983 action against private citizens, contending that they had acted in concert with state officers (and thus under color of state law) but were not entitled to invoke official immunity. The Supreme Court agreed on the immunity point. Since the defendants were not state officers, they had no *official* immunity of any kind. The Court followed *Wyatt* in *Richardson v. McKnight*, 521 U.S. 399 (1997), where the defendants were prison guards employed by a private management firm. Justice Scalia and three other justices dissented in *Richardson* on the ground that the guards performed a function that was historically "public."

248. The one exception is the newly enacted prohibition on injunctive suits against judicial officers acting under color of state law. See note 254 and accompanying text. The Court generally assumes that § 1983 presupposes the immunities that existed at the time it was adopted. Writing before the 1996 amendment, Professor Matasar insisted that since § 1983 said nothing about immunities of any kind, the Court should infer that none was available. Richard A. Matasar, *Personal Immunities Under Section 1983: The Limits of the Court's Historical Analysis*, 40 Ark. L. Rev. 741, 771 (1987). Professor Wells contends that the Court should read § 1983 not to embrace the 1871 baseline, but to delegate to the Court itself an authority to fashion immunity rules that serve the purposes of § 1983 and the constitutional rights that § 1983 is typically employed to enforce. Wells, note 230.

249. See notes 216-19 and accompanying text. The Court explained in *Tower v. Glover*, 467 U.S. 914 (1984), that it has no "license" to establish immunities in § 1983 actions on the basis of its own views of "sound public policy" and that it will determine in every instance whether "§ 1983's history or purposes" contemplate an immunity. Id. at 920-24. But, in fact, the Court's actual analysis is driven by history and policy and draws nothing of significance from the statute itself.

plausible reason for doing so.[250] If an immunity did exist in 1871, the Court determines the governmental function that immunity protected and the extent to which potential liability might affect officers' performance of that function today. Cases in which official immunity operates fall into two categories: (1) cases in which officers have absolute immunity; and (2) cases in which they have qualified immunity.

1. Absolute Immunity

By the Supreme Court's account, officers performing legislative functions had absolute immunity in 1871. Legislative affairs were thought to be so sensitive that it was intolerable that legislators should be exposed to suit in any way. The Court takes the same view of the matter today. If legislators abuse their authority, disgruntled constituents can call them to account at the polls. Accordingly, officers are absolutely immune from suit with respect to legislative functions, irrespective of whether plaintiffs seek compensatory damages or prospective injunctive or declaratory relief.[251] Officers performing judicial functions are largely treated in the same way. They, too, were absolutely immune from suit for compensatory damages in 1871—ostensibly to ensure that they did not temper their judgments to forestall litigation and liability. The Court has held that officers performing judicial functions are equally immune from suit for monetary relief today.[252] Judges were not historically immune from suits for prospective relief.[253] But an amendment to § 1983, enacted in 1996, prohibits suits for injunctions against a "judicial" officer for "an act or omission taken in a judicial capacity," unless the officer first violates a declaratory judgment or declaratory relief is "unavailable."[254] By extension of the analysis regarding judges, the Supreme Court has held that officers performing prosecutorial functions, as well as jurors and witnesses, are also absolutely immune from liability for compensatory damages.[255]

---

250. In *Tower*, the Court held that public defenders have no official immunity from suit—because public defenders did not exist in 1871. 467 U.S. at 921.

251. *Eastland v. United States Servicemen's Fund*, 421 U.S. 491 (1975) (relying on the Speech and Debate Clause protecting members of Congress); *Supreme Court of Virginia v. Consumers' Union*, 446 U.S. 719, 732-33 (1980) (holding that judges performing legislative functions are entitled to legislative immunity); *Bogan v. Scott-Harris*, 118 S.Ct. 966 (1998) (holding that members of local legislative bodies also enjoy absolute immunity from liability for damages). See generally Robert Reinstein & Harvey Silverglate, *Legislative Privilege and the Separation of Powers*, 86 Harv. L. Rev. 1113 (1973).

252. *Pierson v. Ray*, 386 U.S. 547 (1967).

253. *Pulliam v. Allen*, 466 U.S. 522 (1984).

254. The 1996 amendment purports to overrule *Pulliam*, which had previously held that state judges are not immune from suits for prospective relief. An accompanying amendment to 42 U.S.C. § 1988 makes state judges immune from liability for attorney fees. For background, see Don Kates, *Immunity of State Judges Under the Federal Civil Rights Acts: Pierson v. Ray Reconsidered*, 65 Nw. U. L. Rev. 615 (1970).

255. *Imbler v. Pachtman*, 424 U.S. 409 (1976) (prosecutors); *Briscoe v. LaHue*, 460 U.S. 325 (1983) (jurors and witnesses). When public prosecutors prefer charges and conduct judicial proceedings, their functions are indistinguishable for these purposes from the functions of judges. See Note, *Delimiting the Scope of Prosecutorial Immunity from Section 1983 Damage Suits*, 52 N.Y.U. L. Rev. 173 (1977). The witnesses in *Briscoe* were police officers. That made it easier for the plaintiff to contend that they acted under color of state law for purposes of § 1983.

It is not enough that officers hold formal *titles* suggesting that they are entitled to absolute immunity. The behavior of which plaintiffs complain must genuinely fall within the governmental *function* to which absolute immunity attaches. The Court is inclined to be generous to legislators and judges. In *Tenney v. Brandhove*,[256] for example, the Court said that legislators acted in their legislative capacity in the conduct of a committee investigation of "un-American activities."[257] In *Stump v. Sparkman*,[258] the Court held that a judge acted in his judicial capacity when he summarily ordered a young woman to be sterilized without her knowledge.[259] According to *Stump*, judges surrender their absolute immunity only if they take action "in the clear absence of all jurisdiction."[260] The Court is less generous to prosecutors who extend their activities outside conventional bounds. In *Mitchell v. Forsyth*[261] and *Burns v. Reed*,[262] the Court held that prosecutors surrender their absolute immunity when they assume responsibility for directing police investigations.[263]

Absolute immunity is an affirmative defense. Plaintiffs are not obliged to anticipate that defense in an original complaint.[264] In most instances, however, defendants can and do insist upon immunity early in the process in order to avoid the burdens of discovery and trial. Typically, the availability of absolute immunity can be determined from the face of the complaint, and when that is so the matter can be resolved on the defendant's motion to dismiss for failure to state a claim for which relief can be granted.[265]

---

256. 341 U.S. 367 (1951).

257. Id. at 369.

258. 435 U.S. 349 (1978). The President is absolutely immune from suit for damages regarding activities within the scope of his duties, *Nixon v. Fitzgerald*, 457 U.S. 731 (1982), but not regarding private conduct occurring before he took office. *Clinton v. Jones*, 520 U.S. 681 (1997).

259. See Irene Rosenberg, *Stump v. Sparkman: The Doctrine of Judicial Impunity*, 64 Va. L. Rev. 833 (1978). But see *Mireles v. Waco*, 502 U.S. 9 (1991) (holding that a judge did not act in his judicial capacity when he ordered a public defender to be seized "with excessive force"); *Forrester v. White*, 484 U.S. 219 (1988) (holding that a judge did not act in a judicial capacity when he fired a probation officer). Occasionally, officers who are not denominated "judges" nonetheless perform judicial functions of a sort and thus claim absolute immunity—usually without success. E.g., *Antoine v. Byers & Anderson*, 508 U.S. 429 (1993) (holding that a court reporter did not act in a judicial capacity when preparing a trial transcript); *Cleavinger v. Saxner*, 474 U.S. 193 (1985) (holding that prison authorities did not act in a judicial capacity for these purposes when they presided at disciplinary proceedings).

260. Id. at 349, relying on *Bradley v. Fisher*, 80 U.S. 335, 351 (1871).

261. 472 U.S. 511 (1985).

262. 500 U.S. 478 (1991).

263. See also *Buckley v. Fitzsimmons*, 509 U.S. 259 (1993) (denying prosecutors absolute immunity with respect to statements made at a press conference).

264. *Gomez v. Toledo*, 446 U.S. 635, 639-41 (1980); *Connor*, 490 U.S. at 399 n.12. The Supreme Court has rejected attempts by lower courts to impose special pleading standards on plaintiffs in *Bivens* and § 1983 actions. *Leatherman v. Tarrant County Narcotics Unit*, 507 U.S. 163 (1993). While those "heightened" standards went to the specificity of plaintiffs' allegations regarding the merits of their claims, they were also meant to force plaintiffs to anticipate and defuse potential immunity defenses. Cf. *Crawford-El*, 118 S.Ct. at 1592-96 (declining to require plaintiffs to prove by "clear and convincing evidence" that defendants had the state of mind required for liability).

265. Fed. R. Civ. P. 12(b)(6). Professor Chen has explained that absolute immunity defenses tend to be relatively categorical and thus lend themselves to resolution on the plead-

2. Qualified Immunity

By the Supreme Court's account, officers performing executive functions had *qualified* official immunity in 1871—not a blanket shield against suit, but a contingent immunity from liability for money damages in some circumstances. Until recently, the Court held that qualified immunity had both objective and subjective elements: Officers could avoid liability if they neither knew nor should have known that they were violating federal law and thus acted in good faith and without malice.[266] Today, however, qualified immunity is an entirely objective matter. In *Harlow v. Fitzgerald*,[267] the Court held that officers "are shielded from liability from civil damages insofar as their conduct does not violate clearly established statutory or constitutional rights of which a reasonable person would have known."[268]

According to the Court, the task of fashioning qualified immunity doctrine for executive officers requires striking a balance between compensating plaintiffs whose rights have been violated, on the one hand, and promoting a range of "special federal policy concerns," on the other.[269] Those policy concerns are pragmatic. Officers performing executive functions occupy the spectrum from cabinet ministers to police officers on the beat.[270] In the main, they should not be faced with the "specter of damages liability for judgments calls made in a legally uncertain environment."[271] The threat of trials and liability in other than extraordinary circumstances might discourage competent people from accepting public employment or, having done so, from aggressively discharging their duties.[272] Particularly in cases involving law enforcement officers, public safety suffers if officers are over-deterred and thus fail to pursue and apprehend genuine suspects.[273] Moreover, when executive officers are forced to defend themselves at trial, "society as a whole" must bear the "expenses of litigation" and the "diversion of official energy from pressing public issues."[274]

Qualified immunity doctrine protects executive officers in two ways: (1) by defining "clearly established" law at a low level of generality; and (2) by encour-

---

ings. Alan K. Chen, *The Ultimate Standard: Qualified Immunity in the Age of Constitutional Balancing Tests*, 81 Iowa L. Rev. 261, 262 (1994).

266. See, e.g., *Wood v. Strickland*, 420 U.S. 308 (1975). See William Theis, *"Good Faith" as a Defense to Suits for Police Deprivations of Individual Rights*, 59 Minn. L. Rev. 991 (1975) (criticizing the subjective elements of the analysis in cases like *Wood*).

267. 457 U.S. 800 (1982).

268. Id. at 818. Professor Nahmod contends that *Harlow* marked a general retreat from the promise that *Bivens* suits and § 1983 actions would effectively enforce federal rights. Sheldon H. Nahmod, *Constitutional Wrongs Without Remedies: Executive Official Immunity*, 62 Wash. U. L.Q. 221 (1984). For a discussion of qualified immunity, see Kit Kinports, *Qualified Immunity in Section 1983 Cases: The Unanswered Questions*, 23 Ga. L. Rev. 597 (1989). For an early description of the lower courts' reception of *Harlow*, see Comment, *Harlow v. Fitzgerald: The Lower Courts Implement the New Standard for Qualified Immunity Under Section 1983*, 132 U. Pa. L. Rev. 901 (1984).

269. *Reynoldsville Casket Co. v. Hyde*, 514 U.S. 749, 758 (1995).

270. E.g., *Butz v. Economou*, 438 U.S. 478 (1978) (involving what passed for the Secretary of Agriculture in the Nixon Administration); *Malley v. Briggs*, 475 U.S. 335 (1986) (involving local police officers).

271. *Ryder v. United States*, 515 U.S. 177, 185 (1995).

272. *Harlow*, 457 U.S. at 814.

273. *Anderson v. Creighton*, 483 U.S. 635, 638 (1987).

274. *Harlow*, 457 U.S. at 814.

aging the resolution of the immunity issue at the summary judgment stage, so that officers are spared unwarranted legal proceedings as well as unwarranted liability.

The definition of "clearly established" law. The point of giving officers immunity unless they violate clearly established law is to ensure that they are not ordinarily held accountable for violating federal rights. The Court is perfectly forthright on this point: The idea is to insulate from liability all but "plainly incompetent" officers or those who "knowingly violate the law."[275] The key to the analysis is the level of generality at which the law must have been clear. For example, the fourth amendment bars "unreasonable" searches. If the "law" of a fourth amendment case is stated in those general terms, then that law has been "clearly established" since 1791.[276] In *Anderson v. Creighton*,[277] however, Justice Scalia explained that for qualified immunity purposes, the law that must have been clear is defined at a more "particularized" level—namely, the "reasonableness" of the kind of search that the officer conducted in the case at bar. Justice Scalia insisted that there need be no previous decision squarely holding that the "very action" the officer took was invalid. Yet the precedents must have made it "apparent" that what the officer did was unlawful.[278]

Early disposition. Like absolute immunity, qualified immunity is an affirmative defense that must be raised by the defendant at the proper time.[279] Unlike absolute immunity, qualified immunity typically demands attention to the circumstances of the defendant's behavior and thus rarely can be settled on a motion to

---

275. *Malley*, 475 U.S. at 341.

276. Or 1949, when the Court initially held that "arbitrary intrusions by the police" violate the fourteenth amendment. *Wolf v. Colorado*, 338 U.S. 25 (1949).

277. 483 U.S. 635 (1987).

278. Id. at 639-40. Officers are therefore immune from liability in the absence of precedent that, while not "on all fours," nevertheless puts them on notice that their conduct is unlawful. Officers in the field are charged with knowledge of that kind of precedent—and only that kind of precedent. Even then, liability is anchored in a "fiction"—the "fragile belief" that a "cop on the beat" appreciates the current state of constitutional law." Lewis & Blumoff, note 204, at 783. It is because individual police officers are treated generously that plaintiffs turn their sights on cities and counties in suits claiming local governmental liability for failing to train officers properly. Suits of that kind are possible, but only barely. See note 211. In *FDIC v. Meyer*, 510 U.S. 471 (1994), the Court expressed concern that if plaintiffs cannot hold federal officers personally liable, they will compensate by suing the federal agencies that employ them. To nip that possibility in the bud, Justice Thomas held that agencies are not subject to *Bivens* suits. Id. at 485. See Chapter VIII, notes 144-52 and accompanying text (discussing *Bivens*). Professor Urbonya argues that by defining "clearly established" law at a low level of generality, Justice Scalia abandoned *Harlow's* attempt to make qualified immunity turn on questions of law and substituted a fact-sensitive analysis that overlaps with the merits of fourth amendment claims in "excessive force" cases. Kathryn R. Urbonya, *Problematic Standards of Reasonableness: Qualified Immunity in Section 1983 Actions for a Police Officer's Use of Excessive Force*, 62 Temple L.Q. 61 (1989). Professor Rudovsky has elaborated the effect of *Anderson* on actual litigation. David Rudovsky, *The Qualified Immunity Doctrine in the Supreme Court: Judicial Activism and the Restriction of Constitutional Rights*, 138 U. Pa. L. Rev. 23 (1989). Professor Nourse contends that the "clear law" orientation in these and other cases suggests simplicity, but actually masks a welter of subtle jurisprudential questions touching the essential variability of law. Victoria F. Nourse, *Making Constitutional Doctrine in a Realist Age*, 145 U. Pa. L. Rev. 1401 (1997). See Chapter XII, notes 218-20 and accompanying text (discussing the "clearly established law" formulation in habeas corpus cases).

279. *Gomez*, 446 U.S. at 639-41; *Connor*, 490 U.S. at 399.

dismiss. Nevertheless, the Court held in *Hunter v. Bryant*[280] that qualified immunity *can* often be determined on a motion for summary judgment — and *should* be handled that way to spare the defendant officer any further unnecessary burdens. When an officer moves for summary judgment, the plaintiff must proffer evidence to demonstrate the existence of triable issues.[281] Inasmuch as the officer's immunity turns on whether particular conduct violated clearly established law, immunity issues may be resolved on the basis of an agreed-upon statement of facts and legal briefs regarding the precedents in existence at the time.[282]

Qualified immunity is structured to ensure that plaintiffs are compensated when executive officers abuse their authority by taking actions they should know are unlawful. The Court held in *Owen v. City of Independence*[283] that those purposes would not be served by according immunity to a city or county. The policies that justify sparing individual officers from liability do not obtain with respect to units of government.[284] Accordingly, cities and counties cannot assert qualified immunity from suits for damages, even if the officers whose behavior is in question *can* assert immunity to avoid personal liability.[285]

Qualified immunity can threaten the federal courts' ability to enforce federal law. Recall that plaintiffs who have suffered injury at the hands of executive officers often lack standing to seek injunctive or declaratory relief and must, accordingly, sue for retrospective relief in the form of compensatory damages.[286] If offi-

---

280. 502 U.S. 224 (1991).

281. See *Celotex Corp. v. Catrett*, 477 U.S. 317 (1986). Here again, the Supreme Court has refused to approve special pleading requirements meant to force plaintiffs to anticipate immunity defenses in the first instance. See note 264. Professor Chen contends that qualified immunity (as opposed to absolute immunity) is comparatively fact-sensitive and *cannot* typically be handled on motion for summary judgment. See Chen, note 265; Alan R. Chen, *The Burdens of Qualified Immunity: Summary Judgment and the Role of Facts in Constitutional Tort Law*, 47 Am. U. L. Rev. 1 (1997). In his view, the Court's decisions elaborating the content of the qualified immunity defense are in conflict with its apparent desire to minimize the costs of constitutional litigation by resolving cases at the summary judgment stage.

282. If a district court's decision on summary judgment rests entirely on a matter of law, it is immediately subject to appeal. *Mitchell v. Forsyth*, 472 U.S. 511 (1985). See Chapter VII, note 179 (discussing this rule in connection with the final judgment requirement). If it rests on a determination of fact, it is not. *Johnson v. Jones*, 515 U.S. 304 (1995). If an officer is unsuccessful on interlocutory appeal from a district court's denial of a motion to dismiss, the officer may file a motion for summary judgment and, if necessary, can take an interlocutory appeal from the district court's judgment on that. *Behrens v. Pelletier*, 516 U.S. 299 (1996). But see *Johnson v. Fankell*, 520 U.S. 911 (1997) (holding that the states are free to adopt different rules for interlocutory appeals on immunity issues for purposes of § 1983 actions in state court). The Court held in *Elder v. Holloway*, 510 U.S. 510 (1994), that an appellate court should take account of any precedents that existed at the time the officer acted, even if neither party presented those precedents to the district court below.

283. 445 U.S. 622 (1980).

284. See text accompanying notes 271-74.

285. The Court did not address absolute immunity in *Owen*, but by a parity of reasoning it would seem that cities and counties should be denied either form of immunity.

286. See Chapter IX, notes 155-57 and accompanying text. In *Ashcroft v. Mattis*, 431 U.S. 171 (1977), for example, police officers shot and killed a teenage boy. The boy's father sued both for damages and for a declaratory judgment that the state statutes authorizing the police to use deadly force were unconstitutional. The defendant officers successfully asserted immunity from liability for damages. The Supreme Court issued a *per curiam* explaining that the father could no longer maintain an Article III case or controversy. The boy was dead and thus beyond any threat of further deadly force, the father was due no compen-

cers can successfully defeat actions for damages on the basis of qualified immunity, plaintiffs who suffer a violation of their federal rights will be denied any judicial remedy at all. By contrast to cases in which plaintiffs lack standing, however, cases in which defendant officers have qualified immunity hold out the promise that the courts will determine the merits of their claims. The Supreme Court explained in *Siegert v. Gilley*[287] that the question whether a plaintiff's federal rights have been violated is analytically prior to the question whether a defendant officer is immune from suit. Accordingly, a court entertaining an officer suit for compensatory damages must determine in the first instance whether the plaintiff has alleged a violation of federal law.[288] That determination contributes to the corpus of federal law—even if the defendant officer at bar ultimately escapes liability.[289]

The Court usually insists that federal courts should avoid constitutional questions whenever possible.[290] Justice Souter explained in *Lewis*, however, that qualified immunity cases warrant a departure from that policy in order to ensure that federal courts clarify the standards of conduct that government officers are obliged to meet. If courts were to bypass the threshold question whether a plaintiff has alleged a violation of a federal right, and were to go immediately to the validity of an immunity defense, they would routinely leave the law in a state of uncertainty. Many cases, perhaps most, would be resolved on the ground that the plaintiff's right was not established clearly enough at the time of the episode. Precedents of that kind provide no clarity regarding the true content of federal rights and thus leave both citizens and public officials in doubt. The better course, accordingly, is "to determine the right before determining whether it was previously established with clarity."[291]

---

satory damages, and a declaratory judgment would be hypothetical. Professor Wells argues that society at large suffers if courts are unable to enforce the Constitution *either* in cases in which plaintiffs seek prospective relief *or* in cases in which they seek compensatory damages. By his account, qualified immunity doctrine places too much emphasis on concerns that officers may be over-deterred and too little on concerns that they may violate federal law. Wells thinks that common law immunity doctrine is a poor means of ensuring that executive officers are free to be aggressive and that it would be preferable to induce public employers to purchase insurance to indemnify officers who get out of line. Current law unjustifiably visits costs on the innocent victims of government's uninsured agents. Wells, note 230.

287. 500 U.S. 226 (1991). Accord *McCollan*, 443 U.S. at 140.

288. This does not mean that courts routinely undertake a thoroughgoing adjudication of claims on the merits before they turn to the availability of immunity, but only that they first decide whether a plaintiff's allegations, if true, would make out a meritorious claim. The idea is to screen for cases that warrant further proceedings—discovery and trial. *Siegert*, 500 U.S. at 232-33.

289. There is no doubt that litigants seeking compensatory damages have standing to sue in an Article III court, even if it turns out (after litigation) that they cannot actually win that relief. There would be a redressability issue only if the relief prisoners seek would not redress their injuries, even if they were to obtain it. See Chapter IX, notes 153-62 and accompanying text. Nor is there any doubt that a federal court can pass on the merits of a claim as an analytically anterior matter before turning to the further question whether compensatory relief can be granted. Federal judgments on the merits are not advisory merely because a particular form of relief is not forthcoming.

290. Chapter I, note 21.

291. 118 S.Ct. at 1714 n.5. Concurring in the judgment in *Lewis*, Justice Stevens proposed that when plaintiffs advance claims that are "both difficult and unresolved," it would be better for courts to address the immunity issue first and thus (perhaps) avoid "unneces-

In the end, qualified immunity doctrine is tailored to the values and policies obviously at stake when a private litigant sues an executive officer, seeking to establish a violation of federal law and to hold the officer personally liable. In order to achieve clarity regarding federal rights for the future, the court initially determines whether the plaintiff has alleged a violation of federal law. If so, the court turns to the further question whether the defendant can be held personally accountable. At that stage, the public's interest in effective and aggressive law enforcement is paramount. Executive officers are not steeped in current constitutional law and, in any event, they have neither the resources nor the time to resolve thorny legal questions before taking decisive action in the field. Accordingly, the court will hold an officer liable only for behavior that was so egregious that the officer must have known that it was unlawful.[292]

---

sary" constitutional adjudication. Id. at 1723. Speaking for the full Court, Justice Souter explicitly rejected that idea, because it would tend to leave federal law in perpetual uncertainty. Of course, suits for damages are not the only means of obtaining an adjudication of federal claims. In some instances, plaintiffs have standing to seek prospective declaratory or injunctive relief. Justice Souter found those vehicles insufficient. Id. at 1714 n.5.

    292. See text accompanying notes 275-78.

Chapter XI

Abstention

When the prerequisites for federal adjudication of federal claims are satisfied, federal district courts still may decline to *exercise* their power. Inferior federal courts have no discretion to turn business away *ad hoc*. That is a luxury reserved for the Supreme Court.[1] Yet the district courts do *abstain* in a variety of circumstances prescribed by a body of quasi-constitutional principles, statutes, and judge-made doctrines. Abstention is rooted in the preconditions for particular judicial remedies, particularly injunctions. Yet the law governing remedies does not fully account for the body of decisions under this heading. Abstention is another device for allocating authority and responsibility between federal and state courts. Into the bargain, abstention moderates the friction that inevitably develops between two sets of courts functioning together in a single judicial system. Federal courts abstain not only because the maxims of equity foreclose injunctive relief, but also because state courts are entitled to "comity"—the respect federal courts owe to tribunals of equal rank and authority within the overarching scheme.[2]

Recall that state courts typically have concurrent jurisdiction to determine federal question cases.[3] It is quite possible that the same parties can be involved in litigation in both state and federal court at the same time, perhaps quarreling over the same issues in both places. In principle, that prospect presents no difficulty, but follows as the natural implication of a bifurcated system.[4] State courts

---

1. See Chapter VII, notes 182-201 and accompanying text.
2. The term "comity" is borrowed from the law of nations. The Supreme Court explained "comity" in that context in *Hilton v. Guyot*, 159 U.S. 113, 163-64 (1895): "'Comity,' in the legal sense, is neither a matter of absolute obligation, on the one hand, nor of mere courtesy and good will, upon the other." It is "the recognition which one nation allows within its territory to the legislative, executive or judicial acts of another nation, having due regard both to international duty and convenience." Courts and commentators also use the comity idea in working out the relations between individual states. In that context, comity usually connotes something akin to reciprocity. See Larry Kramer, *Rethinking Choice of Law*, 90 Colum. L. Rev. 277 (1990); Louise Weinberg, *Against Comity*, 80 Gtn. L.J. 53 (1991). In the context of federal-state judicial relations, comity refers to the "proper respect" the federal courts accord to state functions and, in particular, state judicial functions. *Younger v. Harris*, 401 U.S. 37, 44 (1971); cf. *Calderon v. Thompson*, 118 S.Ct. 1489, 1499 (1998) (noting that comity is owed both to state courts and to state executive officers). Critics complain that the content of comity is "undefined" and that decisions anchored in comity are at best unpredictable and at worst unprincipled. See, e.g., Shirley M. Hufstedler, *Comity and the Constitution: The Changing Role of the Federal Judiciary*, 47 N.Y.U. L. Rev. 841, 867 (1972). Professor Wells argues, however, that it is the very "shapelessness" of comity that makes the idea so valuable to the Supreme Court. Michael Wells, *The Role of Comity in the Law of Federal Courts*, 60 N. Car. L. Rev. 59, 86 (1981).
3. See Chapter VI, notes 20-36 and accompanying text.
4. See *Kline v. Burke Constr. Co.*, 260 U.S. 226 (1922).

are constitutionally barred from interfering with proceedings in federal court.[5] Federal courts are not constitutionally barred from interfering with proceedings in state court. Yet federal courts generally have no cause either to enjoin parallel state proceedings or to stay their own hand. Instead, lawsuits can proceed in state and federal court on separate tracks.[6] Trial court errors can be corrected on direct review. Thereafter, the law of preclusion will determine whether there is anything left for the other set of courts to decide.[7] Nevertheless, there are competing considerations: the special value that may attach to federal adjudication of federal claims, the costs attending a multiplicity of suits, and the conflicts that simultaneous lawsuits often entail. Accordingly, both Congress and the Supreme Court have devised ways to channel business into state court in the first instance and to prevent federal courts from taking simultaneous parallel action. The task of allocating judicial responsibility is problematic. The statutes and rules in this context are both complex in themselves and riddled with exceptions into the bargain.

A. Statutory Limitations

1. The Anti-Injunction Act

The Anti-Injunction Act, 28 U.S.C. § 2283, bars a "court of the United States" from granting an injunction "to stay proceedings in a State court" except: (1) "as expressly authorized by Act of Congress;" (2) "where necessary in aid of its jurisdiction;" or (3) "to protect or effectuate its judgments." In *Atlantic Coast Line R.R. v. Brotherhood of Locomotive Engineers*,[8] Justice Black rejected the argument that § 2283 merely warns federal courts to take comity into account. Instead, § 2283 is a "clear-cut prohibition qualified only by specifically defined exceptions." Moreover, inasmuch as § 2283 "rests on the fundamental constitutional independence of the States and their courts," Justice Black insisted that the three exceptions "should not be enlarged by loose statutory construction." In *Atlantic Coast Line*, accordingly, he held that a union could not obtain a federal injunction that would keep an employer from maintaining an action in state court, even though the employer was seeking state court relief that would violate federal labor law. Black explained that although the injunction was addressed to one of the parties and not directly to the state court, it was nonetheless an injunction "to stay proceedings in State court" and thus was barred by § 2283.[9]

Despite Justice Black's rhetoric in *Atlantic Coast Line*, the Anti-Injunction Act has never functioned as a sweeping restraint on federal court authority to

---

5. See Chapter VI, notes 112-13 and accompanying text.

6. *Kline*, 260 U.S. at 230.

7. See Chapter VI, notes 150-87 and accompanying text (discussing the *Rooker/Feldman* doctrine and the preclusive effects of state judgments in subsequent federal proceedings).

8. 398 U.S. 281 (1970).

9. Id. at 287, 295. Justice Black noted that if the state court reached an erroneous judgment, the union could attack it in the state appellate courts and, if necessary, in the Supreme Court on *certiorari*. Id. at 296; see Chapter VII, notes 40-56 and accompanying text.

issue injunctions that interfere with state functions. The Act protects only state *judicial* proceedings and has no application to the hosts of cases involving state administrative action.[10] It protects judicial proceedings only if they are already pending when a federal court is asked to take action.[11] It has no effect in cases in which the federal government or a federal agency seeks an injunction.[12] Nor does it affect the ability of strangers to a pending state court action to obtain a federal injunction that affects the state court proceeding.[13]

When it was first enacted in 1793, the Anti-Injunction Act had nothing to do with circumscribing the authority of the inferior federal courts.[14] Later, when the Court came to regard it as a general limitation on federal court power, the Court read it to allow for exceptions in a range of circumstances in which the Court though injunctions were warranted.[15] In *Toucey v. United States*,[16] however, the

---

10. E.g., *Lynch v. Household Fin. Corp.*, 405 U.S. 538, 553 (1972) (finding § 2283 inapplicable to a prejudgment garnishment conducted by a deputy sheriff without judicial involvement)

11. *Dombrowski v. Pfister*, 380 U.S. 479, 485 n.2 (1965); see note 135.

12. *Leiter Minerals v. United States*, 352 U.S. 220, 225-26 (1957); *NLRB v. Nash-Finch Co.*, 404 U.S. 138, 144-46 (1971).

13. *Hale v. Bimco Trading*, 306 U.S. 375 (1939). The point of § 2283 is not that a federal court can never bar anyone from pursuing an action in state court, but that when two parties are already engaged in state court litigation, a federal court cannot lend one of them a hand by issuing an injunction that forces the other to desist. The mere existence of a state court lawsuit involving some parties does not prevent someone else from seeking federal injunctive relief, even if that relief will run to one of the parties to the current state proceeding and even if it bears on the issues the state court is considering. See *County of Imperial v. Munoz*, 449 U.S. 54 (1980) (explaining that federal courts can act only on behalf of genuine "strangers").

14. Professor Mayton has developed irresistible evidence that the language in the 1793 Act that later was to become the Anti-Injunction Act actually addressed only Supreme Court justices "riding circuit." See Chapter II, note 53 and accompanying text. By Mayton's account, the legislation enacted in 1793 *did* contain some restrictions on federal courts generally. See Chapter II, text accompanying notes 66-67. Yet in this particular instance Congress meant to *extend* the authority of individual justices. The All-Writs Act, now codified at 28 U.S.C. § 1651, authorized "courts" to issue common law writs, but failed to authorize individual circuit justices to do so. Congress thus inserted a provision in the 1793 Act giving circuit justices power to issue writs, but added as a proviso that they could not use their new authority to enjoin state proceedings. Then, in the middle of the Nineteenth Century, the Supreme Court picked the latter language out of context and treated it as a restriction on federal courts at large. *Peck v. Jenness*, 48 U.S. (7 How.) 612 (1849). That misconstruction was codified in 1874. William T. Mayton, *Ersatz Federalism Under the Anti-Injunction Statute*, 78 Colum. L. Rev. 330 (1978). If Mayton is right about the history behind the Anti-Injunction Act (and he almost certainly is), the Court's handling of the Act parallels its handling of the eleventh amendment. Both the statute and the constitutional amendment may have been misinterpreted early on. But the modern Court has its own reasons for leaving those mistakes in place. It is not merely that the Court hesitates to overrule old precedents. The Court thinks it is good policy that federal courts should not routinely enjoin state court proceedings and that the states should be immune from suit in federal court. Then again, the Court allows exceptions in each instance in hopes of striking an appropriate balance. See Chapter X, notes 106-07, 110-18, 150-51 (discussing the Court's eleventh amendment decisions).

15. For a discussion of illustrative cases, see Edgar N. Durfee & Robert L. Sloss, *Federal Injunction Against Proceedings in State Courts: The Life History of a Statute*, 30 Mich. L. Rev. 1145 (1932); Telford Taylor & Everett I. Willis, *The Power of Federal Courts to Enjoin Proceedings in State Courts*, 42 Yale L.J. 1169 (1933).

16. 314 U.S. 118 (1941).

Court changed its position. In that case, Justice Frankfurter read the Act to establish an unqualified prohibition on injunctions. Accordingly, he concluded that a federal district court could not prevent a party who had lost a case in federal court from filing a subsequent suit in state court in an attempt to relitigate the matter. Congress soon amended the Act not only to overrule *Toucey*, but also to incorporate some of the exceptions the Court had previously recognized. The exceptions now codified in § 2283 have not been narrowly construed in the way that Justice Black declared they should be. By some accounts, they have largely swallowed any general (statutory) rule barring federal injunctions against state court proceedings.

The exceptions to the bar on injunctions:

① **Expressly authorized injunctions.** In *Mitchum v. Foster*,[17] the Court held that § 1983 qualifies as an "Act of Congress" that "expressly" authorizes federal courts to issue injunctions that would otherwise be barred. Accordingly, when private plaintiffs file § 1983 actions in federal court, seeking injunctions against state judicial proceedings, § 2283 poses no barrier. In a single stroke, *Mitchum* eliminated the Anti-Injunction Act as a factor in the most sensitive instances: cases in which federal injunctions against state proceedings may be needed (to keep state officers from using state courts to violate federal rights), but in which state interests in state court litigation are high (because state authorities naturally wish to use their own courts to enforce state law). In *Atlantic Coast Line*, Justice Black insisted that the very point of § 2283 is that state courts are willing to respect federal rights and that if they make a mistake, they can be corrected on direct review. In *Mitchum*, Justice Stewart explained that the point of § 1983 is that "state officers" may be "antipathetic" to federal rights and that their "failings" may extend to state courts.[18]

Nothing in § 1983 "expressly" approves injunctions against state judicial proceedings. Justice Stewart explained, however, that § 1983 is an integral element of the body of legislation enacted by the Reconstruction Congress for the very purpose of "altering the relationship between the States and the Nation with respect to the protection of federally created rights." He said that § 1983 authorizes actions for federal equitable relief against state authorities and thus can be "given its intended scope" only if federal courts are able to stay state court proceedings.[19] At the same time, Stewart disclaimed any purpose to "question or

---

17. 407 U.S. 225 (1972).

18. *Atlantic Coast Line*, 398 U.S. at 296; *Mitchum*, 407 U.S. at 242. The two cases illustrate the internal debate over parity that is constantly waged within the Court. See Chapter I, notes 79-91 and accompanying text. Professor Fallon regards *Atlantic Coast Line* as a decision reflecting the federalist perspective on federal-state relations and *Mitchum* as an illustration of the nationalist perspective. Richard H. Fallon, Jr., *The Ideologies of Federal Courts Law*, 74 Va. L. Rev. 1141, 1165 n.92, 1166 n.93 (1988); see Chapter I, note 17 and accompanying text.

19. 407 U.S. at 242; see Chapter II, notes 73-75. Judge Wood once said that, according to *Mitchum*, "expressly authorized" actually means "implicitly authorized." Diane P. Wood, *Fine-Tuning Judicial Federalism: A Proposal for Reform of the Anti-Injunction Act*, 1990 B.Y.U. L. Rev. 289, 297, relying on David P. Currie, *The Federal Courts and the American Law Institute, Part II*, 36 U. Chi. L. Rev. 268, 322 (1969). Professor Nichol argues that *Mitchum* rests on "an essentially accurate vision" of the legislative "intent" behind § 1983. Gene R. Nichol, Jr., *Federalism, State Courts, and Section 1983*, 73 Va. L. Rev. 959, 1000 (1987). Professor Redish faults *Mitchum* for looking beyond the text of § 1983. Martin H. Redish, *The Anti-Injunction Statute Reconsidered*, 44 U. Chi. L. Rev. 717, 735 (1977). In *Vendo Co. v. Lektro-Vend Corp.*, 433 U.S. 623 (1977), the Court held that § 16 of the Clayton Act is

qualify" the conventional "principles of equity, comity, and federalism" that restrain federal courts when they are asked to interfere with litigation in state court. That disclaimer left the practical consequences of *Mitchum* in some doubt. Federal district courts entertaining § 1983 actions are not barred by § 2283 from issuing injunctions that short-circuit pending state court proceedings. Yet they are restricted by judicially fashioned limitations that typically have much the same effect.[20]

Injunctions in aid of jurisdiction. By common account, this second exception is meant to reconcile the Anti-Injunction Act with the All-Writs Act, 28 U.S.C. § 1651, which explicitly authorizes federal courts to issue writs "in aid of their respective jurisdictions."[21] A federal court must have jurisdiction on some independent basis. Then, pursuant to the additional authority provided by § 1651, and under this exception to § 2283, the court can issue orders that stay state proceedings "in aid of" that previously established jurisdiction.[22] This exception accommodates two kinds of cases in which the Supreme Court found injunctions warranted prior to *Toucey*: (1) cases in which lawsuits have been removed to federal court;[23] and (2) cases in which federal jurisdiction is *in rem* and thus depends on the federal court's possession or control of some physical object.[24] In the former cases, the state court from which a suit has been removed has lost jurisdiction by operation of law and thus poaches on the federal court's jurisdiction if it threatens to continue.[25] In the latter cases, the federal court's ability to deal with a "res" would be impaired if a state court were to assert jurisdiction over the same object.[26]

Injunctions to protect or effectuate judgments. The final exception in § 2283 covers cases in which a federal court initially reaches a judgment, but the losing party continues to press a parallel action in state court, hoping for a favorable judgment there. The party who prevailed in federal court may be content simply to insist upon preclusion in state court and to appeal from any unfavorable state court decision on the preclusion issue. Yet under this exception, a federal court can issue a preemptive federal injunction.[27]

---

not a statute expressly authorizing federal injunctions against state judicial proceedings. There was no majority opinion. For an appraisal of various justices' views, see Redish at 739-43.

20. 407 U.S. at 243; see notes 130-281 and accompanying text (discussing the judicially crafted doctrine the Court has developed to substitute for § 2283 in § 1983 actions).

21. See note 14.

22. In *Amalgamated Clothing Workers v. Richman Bros.*, 348 U.S. 511 (1955), the Court found this exception unavailable, because the federal court had no independent basis of jurisdiction "in aid of" which an injunctive order could operate.

23. E.g., *French v. Hay*, 89 U.S. (22 Wall.) 250 (1874).

24. E.g., *Kline v. Burke Constr. Co.*, 260 U.S. 226 (1922).

25. Professor Redish argues that federal injunctions may be warranted in removal cases on the independent ground that they are "expressly" authorized by the removal statute, 28 U.S.C. § 1441. He agrees that *in rem* cases fit under this heading, but insists that the "in aid of jurisdiction" exception should be broad enough to include many other cases in which state proceedings present a "substantial" threat to efficient federal adjudication. Redish, note 19, at 744, 753-60.

26. This second exception may also permit federal injunctions when state proceedings interfere with complex federal lawsuits, particularly lawsuits in the class action form. Steven M. Larimore, *Exploring the Interface Between Rule 23 Class Actions and the Anti-Injunction Act*, 18 Ga. L. Rev. 259 (1984).

27. The Supreme Court held in *Chick Kam Choo v. Exxon Corp.*, 486 U.S. 140 (1988), that the prevailing party in federal court can obtain a federal injunction against any further

By some accounts, Congress should amend the Act yet again, this time either establishing a single general standard to apply in every instance or specifying more carefully when federal injunctions are warranted and when they are barred.[28] By other accounts, the courts should make decisions on an *ad hoc* basis in light of relevant considerations.[29] Already, in light of *Mitchum*, § 2283 is largely limited to disputes between private litigants, many of which turn on state law and reach federal court on the basis of diversity jurisdiction. Those are scarcely cases in which federal injunctions would be appropriate, even apart from a special statute in point.[30] Meanwhile, various abstention doctrines fashioned by the Supreme Court largely prescribe the circumstances in which federal injunctive relief can be available in more politically volatile federal question cases.

2. Other Statutes

Other statutes bear on the federal courts' ability to issue injunctive relief regarding federal issues: (1) three-judge court statutes; (2) the Johnson Act; and (3) the Tax Injunction Act.

Three-judge court statutes. Congress sometimes specifies that only three-judge panels at the district court level have authority to issue injunctive relief, subject to direct appellate review in the Supreme Court.[31] Three-judge courts are notoriously unpopular within the judicial branch — for four related reasons: (1) they challenge the integrity and capacity of individual district judges; (2) they draw heavily on judicial resources; (3) they bypass the corrective function of the circuit courts of appeals; and (4) they burden the Supreme Court. When Congress provides for three-judge courts, it is usually to signal displeasure with what the courts are doing at the moment.[32] For example, only three-judge courts can

---

proceedings in state court seeking a different outcome on issues the federal court has already adjudicated. Professor Martinez argues that *Chick Kam Choo* also permits a federal court to enjoin state proceedings regarding issues that might have been, but were not, adjudicated in the prior federal proceeding. George A. Martinez, *The Anti-Injunction Act: Fending Off the New Attack on the Relitigation Exception*, 72 Neb. L. Rev. 643 (1993). In *Parsons Steel v. First Alabama Bank*, 474 U.S. 518 (1986), the Court explained that the federal court must act before the state proceeding itself comes to a close. For at that point the Full Faith and Credit Statute, 28 U.S.C. § 1738, instructs the federal court to give the state judgment the preclusive effect it would have in the courts of the state concerned. See Chapter VI, note 156 and accompanying text. Judge Wood has suggested that *Parsons* may create a perverse incentive. If the party that prevailed in federal court raises preclusion as a defense in state court and *loses* on that point, there is no recourse to the federal court that previously decided the issue. Accordingly, to be safe, a litigant may bypass any presentation of the preclusion issue in state court and go immediately to federal court for a federal injunction that stops the state proceeding in its tracks. Wood, note 19, at 305-06.

28. E.g., Currie, note 19, at 329 (proposing a single general standard); ALI, Study of the Division of Jurisdiction Between State and Federal Courts 51-52 (1969) (proposing a longer list of exceptions).

29. Judge Wood identifies the options, including repeal of § 2283. She proposes rewriting what are now statutory exceptions as a set of (more flexible) principles. Wood, note 19, at 318-20.

30. Mayton, note 14, at 355.

31. See 28 U.S.C. § 1253; Chapter VII, note 182.

32. Immediately following *Ex parte Young*, 209 U.S. 123 (1908); see Chapter X, notes 134-39 and accompanying text, Congress enacted statutes specifying that only three-judge

issue injunctions in suits attacking the constitutionality of legislative apportion-ment schemes[33] and injunctions requiring the release of convicts to reduce over-crowding in state penitentiaries.[34]

The Johnson Act. Pursuant to 28 U.S.C. § 1342, the district courts are gener-ally barred from issuing injunctions that "enjoin, suspend, or restrain" a state regulatory body's orders regarding utility rates. The Johnson Act insulates rate orders from federal interference on four conditions: (1) federal jurisdiction is based solely on diversity of citizenship or on the presence of a federal constitu-tional question; (2) the relevant order does not interfere with interstate com-merce; (3) the agency issued the order only after notice and a hearing; and (4) the utility company that is subject to the order has a "plain, speedy and efficient remedy" in state court. Each of the four conditions can generate litigation.[35]

The Tax Injunction Act. Pursuant to 28 U.S.C. § 1341, the district courts are barred from issuing injunctions that "enjoin, suspend or restrain" the enforce-ment of state taxes. The Tax Injunction Act specifies only one precondition: The taxpayer must have a "plain, speedy and efficient remedy" in state court. This Act, too, can generate litigation.[36]

B. Exhaustion of Non-Judicial Remedies

Some statutes require litigants to "exhaust" state non-judicial remedies be-fore filing lawsuits in federal court.[37] Exhaustion requirements are by nature rules of timing alone. They hold out the promise of federal adjudication at some point, but they postpone that adjudication until litigants have first taken their quarrels to state authorities. Exhaustion rules both respect state arrangements for

---

courts could enjoin state statutes. The concern then was that the federal courts would frus-trate economic regulation. See Chapter X, note 151. Those statutes were repealed in 1976.

33. 28 U.S.C. § 2284(a). For a discussion, see Napoleon B. Williams, Jr., *The New Three-Judge Courts of Reapportionment and Continuing Problems of Three-Judge-Court Procedure*, 65 Gtn. L.J. 971 (1977); Michael E. Solimine, *The Three-Judge District Court in Voting Rights Litigation*, 30 U. Mich. J. L. Ref. 79 (1996).

34. 18 U.S.C. § 3626(a)(3)(B). This provision was added in 1996. For a discussion of the larger bill and the political backdrop, see Mark V. Tushnet & Larry W. Yackle, *Symbolic Statutes and Real Laws: The Pathologies of the Antiterrorism and Effective Death Penalty Act and the Prison Litigation Reform Act*, 47 Duke L.J. 1 (1997).

35. For a discussion of the Johnson Act, see Federal Practice and Procedure: Jurisdic-tion, § 4236 (Wright, Miller & Cooper eds. 1988).

36. Recall, for example, the argument in *Franchise Tax Board v. Constr. Laborers Vaca-tion Trust*, 463 U.S. 1 (1983), that the Tax Injunction Act bars a fiduciary subject to ERISA from suing state tax authorities in federal court, seeking an injunction against a third-party assessment. See Chapter VIII, note 269. For a discussion of the Tax Injunction Act, see Fed-eral Practice and Procedure, note 35, at § 4237.

37. E.g., Title VII of the Civil Rights Act of 1964, 42 U.S.C. § 2000e-5(c) (requiring plaintiffs to exhaust state administrative procedures for resolving employment discrimina-tion claims before filing federal court actions under the Act); Civil Rights of Institutionalized Persons Act, 42 U.S.C. § 1997e (requiring state prison inmates to exhaust certain state ad-ministrative procedures for resolving claims about their treatment before filing § 1983 ac-tions). In this context, it is conventional to refer generally to state administrative arrange-ments for addressing complaints as "remedies." See Chapter VIII, note 80.

resolving disputes and reap the benefits of those procedures. If state non-judicial authorities give litigants the relief they want, there will be no need for federal court adjudication at all. If state non-judicial authorities do not satisfy litigants entirely, they still may develop the record in a way that makes later federal adjudication more efficient. Decisions by state non-judicial authorities are not ordinarily entitled to preclusive effect in federal court. If they were, the exhaustion requirement would cease to be merely a rule of timing. A scheme that compromises the capacity of the federal courts to adjudicate a dispute at some point cannot properly be called an exhaustion rule.[38]

The Supreme Court enforces exhaustion doctrines of its own creation in two instances: (1) when there are further opportunities for litigants to affect the state legislative policy they wish to attack in federal court; and (2) when there are state administrative procedures for resolving their difficulties without the need for litigation.[39]

Legislative remedies. A federal lawsuit is premature if it challenges state legislative action that is incomplete. Ordinarily, litigants attack enacted statutes, and there is no basis for suggesting that they are obliged to pursue political strategies

---

38. See note 152 (discussing this point in the context of the federal-question abstention doctrine). In *Kremer v. Chem. Constr. Corp.*, 456 U.S. 461 (1982), and *University of Tennessee v. Elliott*, 478 U.S. 788 (1986), the Court recognized that Title VII both requires litigants to exhaust state administrative remedies before filing federal employment discrimination actions and guarantees litigants who ultimately file federal lawsuits the opportunity for *de novo* adjudication in federal court. The litigant in *Kremer* engaged preclusion only because he went beyond state administrative procedures and sued for relief in state court — thus bringing the Full Faith and Credit Statute into play. The litigant in *Elliott* engaged preclusion only with respect to his voluntary presentation of *constitutional* claims to the state agency in that case. See Chapter VI, notes 180-85 and accompanying text. The Court typically requires litigants to exhaust *federal* administrative remedies and nevertheless gives preclusive effect to agency findings of fact. See *McKart v. United States*, 395 U.S. 167 (1961). To that extent, the Court departs from the conventional understanding that an exhaustion rule is exclusively a rule of timing.

39. Of course, there is no ordinary doctrine requiring litigants to exhaust state *judicial* opportunities to press federal claims. When litigants proceed in state court and attempt to revisit the same issues later in federal court, the Full Faith and Credit Statute typically instructs federal courts to give the previous state judgment the preclusive effect it would have under state law. See Chapter VI, notes 156-87 and accompanying text. But see Chapter XII, note 4 and accompanying text (noting that federal habeas corpus is an exception). The general rule that litigants must exhaust *federal* administrative remedies is meant to ensure that all the adjudicative institutions established by Congress (including both courts and agencies) function efficiently together. Chapter IX, notes 274-76 and accompanying text (discussing the related doctrine of ripeness). Yet the Court allows exceptions when non-judicial remedies do not promise fair and effective machinery or when they threaten undue delays. E.g., *McCarthy v. Madigan*, 503 U.S. 140 (1992) (declining to require a federal prison inmate to exhaust administrative remedies before filing a *Bivens* action against penal authorities). See Chapter VIII, notes 144-52 (discussing *Bivens*). Professor Power has reviewed the Court's cases and concluded that they form no coherent doctrine. Robert C. Power, *Help Is Sometimes Close at Hand: The Exhaustion Problem and the Ripeness Solution*, 1987 U. Ill. L. Rev. 547. In *Darby v. Cisneros*, 509 U.S. 137 (1993), the Court held that in cases controlled by the Administrative Procedure Act, litigants need exhaust only the remedies that Congress prescribes by statute and need not pursue additional administrative procedures that the Court itself might otherwise have required.

for persuading the legislature to change what it has already done. In some circumstances, however, states allocate legislative power in an unconventional way. In the leading case, *Prentis v. Atlantic Coast Line Co.*,[40] the state of Virginia authorized an administrative agency to make an initial legislative judgment regarding the maximum rates that railroads could charge, but then gave the Virginia Supreme Court authority to set the agency's rate order aside and substitute an order of its own making. Justice Holmes explained that an arrangement of that kind did not merely subject the agency's action to judicial review in state court. Instead, it conferred independent *legislative* power on the state supreme court. Accordingly, Holmes held that the railroad must complain to that court that the agency had fixed the rate too low and, in that way, allow all the state's legislative institutions to operate as planned. Thereafter, if the railroad was dissatisfied with the state court's legislative decision, the railroad would be free to attack that legislative action in a federal lawsuit.[41]

The *Prentis* doctrine is conventionally regarded as a rule of exhaustion. Yet it may be more accurate to regard it as a rule of finality. The idea is that, in some circumstances, local legislative action does not take its final authoritative form until private litigants press for an ultimate resolution. The means for doing that may have the look and feel of a lawsuit in state court. But in theory the state court performs a legislative function.[42] Unless the arrangement is unduly burdensome, private litigants may fairly be asked to play their role in the state legislative process before seeking genuine judicial relief in court.[43] The *Prentis* doctrine is analogous to the Court's decisions regarding claims that state authorities have taken property without giving just compensation. In order to be in a position to complain that the compensation the state has awarded is insufficient, litigants

---

40. 211 U.S. 210 (1908).

41. Holmes made it clear that the railroad's lawsuit in that instance would be filed in the appropriate federal trial court for the exercise of original jurisdiction. Since the state supreme court's action was legislative in nature, the railroad could not seek appellate review of its order directly in the Supreme Court of the United States. The Supreme Court reviews judgments by state courts (acting in a judicial capacity), not state legislatures (or state courts acting in a legislative capacity). See Chapter VII, notes 57-58 (discussing the scope of the Court's appellate jurisdiction of state court judgments).

42. In *Prentis*, Justice Holmes was confident that the state supreme court acted in a legislative capacity. In *Bacon v. Rutland R.R.*, 232 U.S. 134 (1914), by contrast, he concluded that the Vermont Supreme Court had only the conventional authority to review a utility rate order in a judicial capacity. Accordingly, the *Prentis* doctrine did not apply, and the railroad in *Bacon* was entitled to sue in federal court. If the railroad had sought judicial review in the Vermont Supreme Court, it would almost certainly have been unable to sue thereafter in a federal trial court. See Chapter VI, notes 149-87 (discussing the *Rooker/Feldman* doctrine and the preclusive effects of state court judgments). These cases place a premium on characterizing the nature of the state court's function as either judicial or legislative. See Chapter VI, notes 153-55, 182 and accompanying text (discussing the same problem with respect to *Rooker/Feldman* and § 1738). In *Oklahoma Packing Co. v. Oklahoma Gas & Elec. Co.*, 309 U.S. 4 (1940), the Court indicated that it may rely on a state court's own characterization of its function.

43. See *Pac. Tel. & Tel. Co. v. Kuykendall*, 265 U.S. 196 (1924) (permitting a federal court to act before a state court had completed a final leg of the state legislative process — because state law allowed no stay of the rates under attack while the company's arguments were heard in state court).

must advance their claims before all the state entities with authority to make adjustments in their favor.[44]

Administrative remedies. A federal lawsuit can also be premature if there is some workable administrative means for addressing the matter that has not yet been engaged. In *Fair Assessment in Real Estate Ass'n v. McNary*,[45] taxpayers contended that state officials had administered state taxes in violation of the fourteenth amendment. In hopes of eluding the Tax Injunction Act, the plaintiffs framed their suit in federal court as a § 1983 action, seeking compensatory damages for invalid assessments and penalties.[46] Then-Justice Rehnquist set § 1341 aside and rested judgment on a construction of § 1983. He found the prospect of disrupting tax collections intolerable and held, accordingly, that § 1983 would not allow taxpayers to bypass the state administrative remedies available to them.[47]

In *Patsy v. Bd. of Regents*,[48] the Court held that litigants need not exhaust state administrative remedies before filing § 1983 actions attacking other kinds of state action. Justice Marshall emphasized the historic purpose of § 1983 as a means of seeking prompt judicial redress for violations of federal law.[49] On the surface, *Patsy* operates in this context much in the way that *Mitchum v. Foster* operates in the context of the Anti-Injunction Act—exempting the most politi-

---

44. E.g., *Williamson County Regional Planning Comm'n v. Hamilton Bank*, 473 U.S. 172 (1985) (requiring a plaintiff to complete all available administrative procedures for obtaining a zoning adjustment). Professor Ryckman has explained that land use cases are peculiarly local and that zoning boards and planning commissions invariably offer developers the best chance of getting what they want. William E. Ryckman, Jr., *Land Use Litigation, Federal Jurisdiction, and the Abstention Doctrines*, 69 Calif. L. Rev. 377 (1981) (nonetheless detailing the way in which land use cases are affected by the various abstention doctrines). There is also a surface analogy to the *Parratt* and *Zinermon* cases, in which the Court finds some procedural due process claims incomplete if plaintiffs have not taken advantage of state tort lawsuits that might provide the process that is due. See Chapter X, note 240 (noting that the Court relied on *Parratt* in *Williamson*). There, however, the Court finds the process that state courts offer (in a judicial capacity) to be sufficient to satisfy constitutional standards. The *Parratt* and *Zinermon* cases are not, then, cases about postponing federal court adjudication of claims until state court means of redressing those claims have been exhausted. See Chapter X, note 234.
45. 454 U.S. 100 (1981).
46. See text accompanying note 36.
47. 454 U.S. at 113-15. In an important concurring opinion, Justice Brennan agreed that, if the exhaustion of state administrative remedies was required before taxpayers could file suit in state court, the same should be true if they wished, instead, to file suit in federal court. Id. at 117. Professor Bravemen argues that *McNary's* loose rationale cannot easily be limited to taxation cases and thus poses a threat to § 1983 actions in other kinds of cases. Daan Bravemen, *Fair Assessment and Federal Jurisdiction in Civil Rights Cases*, 45 U. Pitt. L. Rev. 351, 366-70 (1984). Bravemen notes, however, that the Court was divided over the proper analysis to be applied in *McNary* and that the decision in that case may not bear heavy precedential weight. The Court relied on *McNary* in *Nat'l Private Truck Council v. Oklahoma Tax Comm'n*, 515 U.S. 582 (1995) (holding that taxpayers cannot avoid the Tax Injunction Act by filing § 1983 actions in *state* court seeking injunctions against the collection of state taxes). In *Quackenbush v. Allstate Ins. Co.*, 517 U.S. 706 (1996), the Court characterized the *McNary* and *Nat'l Private Truck* cases as interpretations of § 1983.
48. 457 U.S. 496 (1982).
49. Justice Marshall also noted that Congress has enacted a special statute requiring state prison inmates to exhaust state administrative remedies. See note 37. Accordingly, it appears by negative inference that in the run of § 1983 actions, exhaustion is not required. 457 U.S. at 507-12.

cally sensitive cases from a rule that would otherwise burden would-be federal plaintiffs.[50] In practice, *Patsy* may be more potent than *Mitchum*. The Court has made up for *Mitchum* by fashioning its own doctrinal rules limiting § 1983 injunctive actions against state proceedings.[51] But the Court has not filled the gap that *Patsy* created in the exhaustion doctrine. Accordingly, plaintiffs who wish to file § 1983 actions can typically bypass state administrative remedies, if they wish.[52]

C. State-Question Abstention

Federal courts often have authority to determine state issues that are related to the federal questions that trigger jurisdiction pursuant to § 1331. Yet they may abstain from exercising their jurisdiction in order to give state courts an opportunity to pass on questions of state law. In *Railroad Comm'n of Texas v. Pullman Co.*,[53] the Texas Railroad Commission issued an order requiring all trains operated in Texas to be under the supervision of Pullman conductors rather than porters. At the time, Pullman conductors were invariably white; porters were invariably black. The railroad sued for an injunction in federal court, contending that the Commission's order both violated federal law (the Commerce Clause and the fourteenth amendment) and exceeded the Commission's authority under state law. The district court issued the injunction, but the Supreme Court held that the court should have abstained.

Justice Frankfurter initially relied on traditional equitable considerations. He said that the railroad had no "right" to injunctive relief, despite the merits of its claims, and that, instead, the request for an injunction was addressed to the "sound discretion" of the court.[54] In England, injunctions were typically awarded only by Chancery, and then only if there was no "adequate remedy" in the "law" courts and injunctive relief was essential to spare litigants "irreparable" harm, both "great and immediate."[55] Frankfurter recognized that the district court below had jurisdictional power to entertain the lawsuit and to award appropriate relief. He insisted, however, that the historical preconditions for equitable relief could do service in the cause of federalism: Federal district courts should withhold equitable relief for the purpose of avoiding needless friction with the states and state courts.[56]

---

50. See notes 17-20 and accompanying text.

51. See notes 130-281 and accompanying text.

52. Recall that litigants have an incentive to bypass state administrative agencies to avoid the preclusive effects of their determinations. See Chapter VI, notes 180-85 (discussing the *Elliott* decision).

53. 312 U.S. 496 (1941).

54. Id. at 500, quoting *Beal v. Missouri Pac. R.R.*, 312 U.S. 45, 50 (1941).

55. For a synopsis of the classic materials, see Donald H. Zeigler, *Rights Require Remedies: A New Approach to the Enforcement of Rights in the Federal Courts*, 38 Hastings L.J. 665, 667-71 (1987).

56. 312 U.S. at 500-01. Professor Fiss questions the Court's reliance on traditional preconditions for equitable relief to resolve federalism issues. By his account, it would be the purest accident if rules developed to govern the relations between Chancery and Common Pleas in medieval England should somehow manage to strike just the right balance between federal and state judicial authority in this country today. Owen Fiss, *Dombrowski*, 86 Yale

Next, Justice Frankfurter insisted that if the railroad's state claim was meritorious, the case should be resolved on that basis alone. In that event, the federal constitutional issues would not arise.[57] With respect to state issues, he explained that federal courts always run the risk that they may misconceive state law. Erroneous federal decisions regarding state law may dispose of particular cases. But in future cases, state courts can provide the really authoritative judgment. Frankfurter explained that federal court "forecasts" about state law can easily be displaced by later state court decisions and are therefore wasteful and potentially offensive to the states. Moreover, in the near term, erroneous federal rulings on state issues may interfere with "sensitive" state policies. If, then, the parties have "an easy and ample means" of obtaining an authoritative judgment from the state courts, federal courts should postpone their own work to allow the parties to seek that judgment.[58]

Over his career, Justice Frankfurter attempted to divert litigation into state court in a number of ways. It is important to understand the analytic differences between his tactics. There is a certain similarity between the abstention doctrine Frankfurter established in *Pullman* and the arguments he pressed (unsuccessfully) in *Snowden v. Hughes*[59] and *Monroe v. Pape*.[60] In *Snowden* and *Monroe*, Frankfurter argued (in the main) that plaintiffs with federal claims should be sent to state court in pursuit of authoritative decisions on whether state officers have taken action consistent with state law. By Frankfurter's (erroneous) account, state court decisions regarding state law have a crucial bearing on the plaintiffs' federal claims (the applicability of the fourteenth amendment and the availability of § 1983). In *Pullman*, by contrast, Frankfurter held that plaintiffs should be sent to state court in pursuit of authoritative state court decisions on independent (though related) state claims that, if successful, would obviate the need to determine their federal claims.[61]

State-question abstention has followed an uneven course since *Pullman*. In some ways, abstention under this heading has gained ground. Despite Justice Frankfurter's heavy reliance on equitable discretion, the Court has invoked *Pullman* abstention in actions "at law" for damages.[62] And despite Frankfurter's in-

---

L.J. 1103, 1107 (1977). In truth, according to Fiss, the Court does not simply apply equitable principles in abstention cases, but uses the language of equity to explain policy choices regarding the exercise of federal judicial power.

57. Recall the Court's policy of avoiding constitutional questions whenever possible. See Chapter I, note 21.

58. 312 U.S. at 499-501.

59. 321 U.S. 1 (1944).

60. 365 U.S. 167 (1961). See Chapter X, notes 144-46, 198-201 and accompanying text.

61. See also Chapter X, note 234 (explaining the difference between *Pullman* abstention and the Court's analysis of procedural due process in *Parratt*). Professor McManamon has traced Justice Frankfurter's many efforts to achieve similar practical ends. Mary Brigid McManamon, *Felix Frankfurter: The Architect of "Our Federalism"*, 27 Ga. L. Rev. 697 (1993).

62. E.g., *Clay v. Sun Ins. Office*, 363 U.S. 207 (1960); *Fornaris v. Ridge Tool Co.*, 400 U.S. 41 (1970). In *Quackenbush*, the Court emphasized that in cases like *Clay* and *Fornaris*, the effect of abstention was to postpone the exercise of federal jurisdiction. That, of course, is a core feature of state-question abstention generally. See note 58 and accompanying text. In *Quackenbush*, by contrast, abstention in an action for damages would have relinquished federal jurisdiction entirely. In that case, the plaintiff initially sued in state court, alleging breach of contract under state law. The defendant removed on the basis of diversity. The plaintiff then sought a remand order on the theory that the federal court should abstain. Writing for the Court, Justice O'Connor held that, in those circumstances, a remand on the basis of abstention was unwarranted. It would mean not merely delaying the federal court's

sistence that the principal point is to avoid needless adjudication of federal constitutional questions, the Court has invoked *Pullman* abstention in diversity cases in which no federal issues are implicated.[63] Moreover, the Court has held that § 1983 actions are not exempt from state-question abstention and, in fact, typically provide the occasion for abstention when there are federal constitutional claims to be deferred.[64] In other respects, state-question abstention has lost ground, primarily because of the costs it visits upon the parties.[65] Academicians debate the merits of the Court's work. By some accounts, state-question abstention is inconsistent with the separation of powers inasmuch as it defies Congress' primary authority to establish the federal courts' jurisdiction.[66] By other accounts, state-question abstention (properly orchestrated) is one of many defensible devices by which the courts determine when to exercise the jurisdiction that Congress confers.[67] By many accounts, state-question abstention is objectionable

---

exercise of jurisdiction, but rather dismissing the suit and remitting the matter to state court without recourse. Summarizing the precedents, O'Connor explained that in cases in which federal plaintiffs seek equitable or declaratory relief, the Court sometimes approves abstention orders that dismiss, rather than defer, the exercise of federal jurisdiction. But in cases in which federal plaintiffs seek relief that federal courts have no discretion to deny (e.g., compensatory damages), the Court approves only abstention orders that postpone the exercise of federal jurisdiction. Accepting that summary as defensible, Justice O'Connor concluded that a remand order in *Quackenbush* would amount to a dismissal and thus was impermissible. The form of abstention involved in *Quackenbush* was not state-question abstention under *Pullman*, but the kind of "administrative" abstention associated with *Burford v. Sun Oil Co.*, 319 U.S. 315 (1943); see notes 91-104 and accompanying text. But Justice O'Connor tailored her analysis to cover other forms of abstention, as well. After *Quackenbush*, federal courts that abstain from exercising jurisdiction over federal lawsuits for damages can only stay their own proceedings. They cannot relinquish jurisdiction altogether by issuing orders that operate as dismissals. The only exceptions are cases in which federal courts dismiss federal actions for *forum non conveniens*. Justice O'Connor singled cases like that out and explained that they are governed by other considerations that do not attend abstention in any of its forms. 517 U.S. at 722-23.

63. Both *Clay* and *Fornaris* were diversity cases. See note 62.

64. E.g., *Harrison v. NAACP*, 360 U.S. 167 (1959). The Court did not mention § 1983 in *Pullman* itself, which preceded *Monroe v. Pape* by twenty years. See Chapter X, notes 193-97 and accompanying text (discussing *Monroe*). Today, an action like the one in *Pullman* would be authorized by § 1983, albeit an attempt to obtain injunctive relief regarding a violation of state law would implicate the eleventh amendment, as interpreted in *Pennhurst State School & Hosp. v. Halderman*, 465 U.S. 89 (1984); see Chapter X, notes 175-87 and accompanying text.

65. See notes 79-82 and accompanying text.

66. Professor Redish presses this view. Martin H. Redish, *Abstention, Separation of Powers, and the Limits of the Judicial Function*, 94 Yale L.J. 71 (1984). Professor Wells thinks Redish pays insufficient attention to the Court's responsibility for elaborating the statutes that Congress enacts—particularly § 1983. Michael Wells, *Why Professor Redish is Wrong About Abstention*, 19 Ga. L. Rev. 1097 (1985).

67. Professor Shapiro promotes this position. David L. Shapiro, *Jurisdiction and Discretion*, 60 N.Y.U. L. Rev. 543 (1985). He argues that Congress cannot hope to "answer in gross" the many questions that arise regarding the prudent exercise of federal judicial power and that the courts are "functionally better adapted to engage in the necessary fine tuning." Id. at 574. Professor Friedman contends that the Supreme Court employs abstention as a means of deciding whether cases warrant federal court treatment at the *trial* level or can be handled sufficiently well on appellate review from state court judgments. Barry Friedman, *A Revisionist Theory of Abstention*, 88 Mich. L. Rev. 530, 533, 577-80 (1989). Professor Redish has responded to Shapiro and Wells. See Martin H. Redish, The Federal Courts in the Political Order 51-67 (1991).

inasmuch as it postpones (and can frustrate) litigants' access to the federal courts for the adjudication of federal constitutional claims.[68]

1. Prerequisites

Justice Frankfurter summed up the abstention doctrine associated with *Pullman* this way: When (1) a plaintiff in federal court asserts both federal constitutional and state law claims for equitable relief; (2) the resolution of the state claim might dispose of the matter without recourse to the constitutional claim; (3) the state question is unsettled, so that there is a serious chance that the federal court will fail to predict the way in which the state courts will ultimately decide it; and (4) the state courts offer an effective means of obtaining an authoritative judgment on the state issue—then the federal court should postpone a federal decision on either claim pending state court adjudication of the state claim.

Alternative federal and state claims. State-question abstention presupposes that plaintiffs advance both federal and state claims. Federal courts have no occasion to abstain on the theory that plaintiffs *might* have added supplemental state claims to their complaints. To rest abstention on claims that plaintiffs choose not to present would be to neglect plaintiffs' traditional ability to select their own theories.[69] Into the bargain, it would require federal courts to entertain arguments from defendants who wish to explore the corpus of state law in search of claims that plaintiffs have overlooked or deliberately eschewed.[70] At the same time, state-question abstention undermines supplemental jurisdiction. The principal point of § 1367 is to ensure that litigants with federal claims are able to ob-

---

68. See Martha A. Field, *Abstention in Constitutional Cases: The Scope of the Pullman Abstention Doctrine Today*, 122 U. Pa. L. Rev. 1071, 1095-96 (1974). Charles A. Wright, *The Abstention Doctrine Reconsidered*, 37 Tex. L. Rev. 815, 817-18 (1959).

69. See Chapter VIII, notes 181, 274 and accompanying text.

70. Some lower court decisions indulge defendants in this way. E.g., *Internat'l Brotherhood of Electrical Workers v. Public Svc. Comm'n*, 614 F.2d 206, 213 n.2 (9th Cir. 1980) (indicating that a plaintiff's failure to advance a state claim is not decisive). Yet there is no Supreme Court precedent for it. Chief Justice Burger once argued (unsuccessfully) that federal courts should abstain in cases in which plaintiffs raise federal constitutional claims but fail to add state constitutional claims of a similar order. *Wisconsin v. Constantineau*, 400 U.S. 433, 439 (1971) (dissenting opinion). Justice Blackmun concurred in *Pennzoil v. Texaco*, 481 U.S. 1 (1987), on the theory that abstention was justified for the reasons given in *Pullman*—even though the plaintiff (Texaco) had advanced no formal state law claim and the defendant (Pennzoil) had abandoned the argument that *Pullman* abstention was warranted. The parties had nonetheless briefed a variety of state law questions, and Blackmun thought it was appropriate to allow the state courts to examine those questions in hopes that Texaco's federal constitutional claim could be avoided. Id. at 27; see note 252. Professor Althouse argues that *Pennzoil* was not an appropriate case for *Pullman* abstention, because the state law issues were not susceptible to resolution in a way that would obviate the federal constitutional question. See note 249 (explaining that the only possibility was that the state courts might elaborate an obscure provision of the state constitution). Ann Althouse, *The Misguided Search for State Interest in Abstention Cases: Observations on the Occasion of Pennzoil v. Texaco*, 63 N.Y.U. L. Rev. 1051, 1072 (1988).

tain an adjudication of those claims in federal court without abandoning related state claims.[71] Yet when federal courts abstain in favor of state adjudication of state claims, that purpose is sacrificed to comity and federalism. Abstention discourages plaintiffs from invoking a federal district court's supplemental jurisdiction over related state law claims. If plaintiffs follow that course, they risk the postponement of their federal claims while they are obliged to litigate their state claims in state court.[72]

Avoidance of constitutional claims. State-question abstention chiefly hopes to make it unnecessary to grapple with federal constitutional claims.[73] The Court acted on this same principle in *Siler v. Louisville & Nashville R.R. Co.*[74] In *Siler*, however, the Court held only that a federal court should address potentially dispositive state issues before taking up federal constitutional questions. The *Pullman* decision goes a step further—channeling state questions into state court. The Court has said that abstention is warranted only if a plausible determination of a state law question will obviate federal constitutional issues.[75] But the Court has also found abstention appropriate if the state courts' treatment of state issues may improve the record on which federal constitutional issues will be adjudicated.[76]

Unsettled state law. State-question abstention is justified only when a state law claim is so unsettled that there is a serious risk that a federal district court will reach an erroneous judgment. The "relevant inquiry" is not whether there is a "bare, though unlikely, possibility" that the state courts "*might*" decide a state issue in a way that avoids a constitutional claim. The state law issue must be genuinely "uncertain" and "obviously susceptible" to a construction of that kind.[77] Abstention is not to be used as a thinly veiled invitation to the state courts to "rewrite" state statutes in order to forestall federal constitutional issues.[78]

---

71. See Chapter VIII, text accompanying notes 297-98.

72. Recall that supplemental jurisdiction is also compromised in cases in which the *Pennhurst* decision forecloses federal court consideration of state claims for injunctive relief. See Chapter X, notes 184-87 and accompanying text. *Pennhurst*, in turn, creates some tension with abstention under *Pullman*. If a plaintiff files suit in federal court advancing both a federal claim and a state claim barred by the eleventh amendment, the court may be obliged to dismiss the state claim for want of jurisdiction and thus may not be in a position to abstain in favor of state court consideration of that claim. See Keith Werhan, *Pullman Abstention After Pennhurst: A Comment on Judicial Federalism*, 27 Wm. & Mary L. Rev. 449, 487 (1986). See notes 83-89 and accompanying text (discussing the procedural scenarios).

73. Professor Bezanson contends that if abstention is warranted to avoid constitutional issues, it is equally justified to avoid non-constitutional federal questions. Randall P. Bezanson, *Abstention: The Supreme Court and Allocation of Judicial Power*, 27 Vand. L. Rev. 1107, 1112 (1974). The Court has not taken that view. See *Propper v. Clark*, 337 U.S. 472, 490 (1949).

74. 213 U.S. 175 (1909); see Chapter VIII, text accompanying note 298.

75. *Baggett v. Bullitt*, 377 U.S. 360, 375-77 (1964).

76. E.g., *Lake Carriers' Ass'n v. MacMullan*, 406 U.S. 498, 510-12 (1972); *Zwickler v. Koota*, 389 U.S. 241, 248-49 (1967). Professor Bezanson draws an analogy to the ripeness doctrine, which also postpones federal adjudication in part to achieve a better basis for judgment on constitutional claims. Bezanson, note 73, at 1118-19; see Chapter IX, notes 271-73.

77. *Hawaii Housing Auth. v. Midkiff*, 467 U.S. 229, 237 (1984) (emphasis in original).

78. *City of Houston v. Hill*, 482 U.S. 451, 470-71 (1987). It is insufficient that the state courts have never construed a statute and a federal court would have to do so on a clean slate. The statute must be unclear, and there must be a plausible construction of it that would avoid

State court machinery. State-question abstention depends on a reasonably efficient means for obtaining an authoritative state court judgment on the plaintiff's state claim. Plaintiffs who are diverted to state court usually must initiate entirely new lawsuits, typically in the form of actions for declaratory relief. Litigation of that kind can consume years before reaching final judgment.[79] Most states facilitate abstention by inviting federal courts to "certify" unsettled questions of state law to the state's highest court for expedited treatment. The Supreme Court encourages the district and circuit courts to exploit mechanisms of that kind.[80] Yet certification does not always answer.[81] The functional difficulty of obtaining authoritative state court judgments within a reasonable time

---

the federal constitutional issue, or at least place that question in a different posture. See *Brockett v. Spokane Arcades*, 472 U.S. 491 (1985). Cases involving ambiguous state constitutional provisions are problematic. Even though the text of such a provision may track the language of a parallel provision of the United States Constitution, the state courts may not (and perhaps should not) give it the same interpretation. And since state constitutional law is typically underdeveloped, there may be few state precedents on which to base a genuine prediction. In *Reetz v. Bozanich*, 397 U.S. 82 (1970), the Court found abstention warranted, because the state constitutional claim rested on peculiar provisions of the Alaska constitution that had never been addressed by the courts of that state. In *Examining Bd. of Engineers v. Flores de Otero*, 426 U.S. 572 (1976), the Court found abstention unjustified, because the state constitutional claim rested on a state analogue of the federal Equal Protection Clause. The Court explained in *Otero* that if abstention were warranted in every case in which a plaintiff advanced a claim based on a "broad and sweeping" state constitutional provision, state-question abstention would no longer be an exception to the exercise of federal jurisdiction, but would become the rule. Id. at 598. The Court said in *Harris County Comm'rs Court v. Moore*, 420 U.S. 77 (1975), that abstention is appropriate if a state claim rests on a state statute that is part of an integrated scheme of local statutes, regulations, and constitutional provisions that "as a whole calls for clarifying interpretation by the state courts." Id. at 84 n.8.

79. For discussions of the burdens and delays that state-question abstention entails, see Donald S. Chisum, *The Tensions of Judicial Federalism*, 33 Stan. L. Rev. 1161, 1179 (1981); Philip B. Kurland, *Toward a Co-operative Judicial Federalism: The Federal Court Abstention Doctrine*, 24 F.R.D. 481, 489 (1959).

80. E.g., *Bellotti v. Baird*, 428 U.S. 132, 151 (1976). Certification can "simplif[y]" abstention, *Planned Parenthood Ass'n v. Ashcroft*, 462 U.S. 476, 493 n.21 (1983), but does not alone *justify* abstention. *Hill*, 482 U.S. at 470-71. In *Arizonans for Official English v. Arizona*, 117 S.Ct. 1055 (1997), the Court suggested that the availability of certification should cut in favor of abstention in a case involving a "novel or unsettled question of state law." Id. at 1073.

81. Some certification schemes authorize state supreme courts to answer only questions from other appellate courts—not federal district courts. When state supreme courts can (and are willing to) respond, they necessarily do so without a trial and the usual development of the issues. For discussions of these and other functional shortcomings, see Paul A. LeBel, *Legal Positivism and Federalism: The Certification Experience*, 19 Ga. L. Rev. 999 (1985); Bruce M. Selya, *Certified Madness: Ask a Silly Question...*, 29 Suffolk U. L. Rev. 677 (1995); M. Bryan Schneider, *But Answer Came There None: The Michigan Supreme Court and the Certified Question of State Law*, 41 Wayne L. Rev. 273 (1995). The Chief Justice has warned that certification can be burdensome and time-consuming. *Lehman Bros. v. Schein*, 416 U.S. 386, 394-95 (1974) (concurring opinion). The American Law Institute has developed a model act in hopes of perfecting the mechanism. That model, too, has flaws. See Ira P. Robbins, *The Uniform Certification of Questions of Law Act: A Proposal for Reform*, 18 J. Legis. 127 (1992). For an endorsement of state certification schemes, see Bradford R. Clark, *Ascertaining the Laws of the Several States: Positivism and Judicial Federalism After Erie*, 145 U. Pa. L. Rev. 1459, 1544-64 (1997).

has always been and remains the principal flaw in the framework that Justice Frankfurter envisioned.[82]

2. Procedure

The point of state-question abstention pursuant to *Pullman* is not (necessarily) to relinquish responsibility for a case entirely, but to defer adjudication in order to avoid wrestling with the plaintiff's federal constitutional claim.[83] The federal court retains formal jurisdiction of the matter, but stays further federal proceedings while the plaintiff takes the state question to state court.[84] When the state courts entertain the state claim, they are entitled to know that the plaintiff also has a related federal constitutional claim. The federal environment in which a state claim is situated can affect its proper resolution. Accordingly, the plaintiff must apprise the state courts of both the state claim and the federal claim.[85] Having gone that far, the plaintiff may decide to abandon the federal forum altogether and commit both claims for resolution in state court. In that instance, the plaintiff will typically be bound by the state courts' ultimate decision on both claims, subject to Supreme Court appellate review if the federal claim is dispositive.[86] The federal district court in which the plaintiff originally filed suit will have no jurisdiction to review the state court judgment for error and will, instead, give that judgment the preclusive effect it would have in another state court.[87]

In *England v. Louisiana State Bd. of Med. Examiners*,[88] the Court held that a plaintiff who does *not* wish to commit both state and federal claims to the state courts need not do so. Justice Brennan explained that the plaintiff can alert the state courts to both issues, but reserve the right to return to the federal district court once the state courts have given the state law claim an authoritative interpretation. In that instance, the federal court's formal retention of jurisdiction permits that court to resume responsibility for the case. Thereafter, the litigation can

---

82. See David P. Currie, *The Federal Courts and the American Law Institute: Part II*, 36 U. Chi. L. Rev. 268, 317 (1969).

83. *Growe v. Emison*, 507 U.S. 25, 32 n.1 (1993).

84. The Supreme Court of Texas once refused to entertain a declaratory judgment action regarding an unsettled question of state law while the plaintiff's original lawsuit was formally pending in federal court. To satisfy that court, the Supreme Court said in the *Moore* case that a district court in Texas could formally dismiss an action in order to ensure that the plaintiff could gain access to the Texas state courts following the federal court's abstention. *Moore*, 420 U.S. at 88-89. The Court explained that the dismissal would be without prejudice to the plaintiff's return to federal court later, after the Texas courts had resolved the state law issue that triggered abstention. Other state courts are more cooperative, and formal dismissal is unnecessary.

85. *Gov't & Civic Employees Org. Comm. v. Windsor*, 353 U.S. 364 (1957).

86. See Chapter VII, notes 57-79. If a party fully commits all issues to the state courts, the federal district court's formal retention of jurisdiction is inconsequential, and the final judgment rendered in state court is subject to Supreme Court review in the ordinary manner. *NAACP v. Button*, 371 U.S. 415, 427 (1963).

87. See Chapter VI, notes 150-87 (discussing the *Rooker/Feldman* doctrine and the preclusive effects of state court judgments).

88. 375 U.S. 411 (1964).

continue through the federal judicial system in the ordinary course. By all accounts, the procedure described in *England* is awkward for both litigants and courts. Its only redeeming feature is that it protects the plaintiff's opportunity to advance federal claims in federal court, provided the plaintiff has the resources and stamina to make use of it.[89]

D. Special State Interests

Federal courts may abstain from exercising jurisdiction in three additional contexts, primarily (though not exclusively) identified by the special state interests at stake. District courts either postpone or relinquish jurisdiction if federal court action would: (1) disrupt coordinated arrangements under which state administrative agencies and courts regulate matters of peculiar complexity and local importance; (2) risk an erroneous judgment on a difficult issue of state law touching a state's sovereign interests; or (3) duplicate litigation already pending in state court in special circumstances warranting deference. By most accounts, the Supreme Court decisions under these headings articulate no reliable formulaic principles or rules. They are authoritative precedents not to be ignored. But, in truth, they represent no predictable abstention *doctrines* at all. When they are honored, it is often in the breach.[90]

1. State Administrative Interests

In *Burford v. Sun Oil Co.*,[91] the Court grappled with a scheme under which Texas regulated the East Texas Oil Field.[92] The Texas Railroad Commission had broad discretionary authority to maintain the proper balance between economically beneficial drilling in the near term, on the one hand, and safeguards for the future of the field, on the other. State trial courts in Austin had authority to work with the Commission to ensure that the oil field was supervised in an effective, geologically sound manner. The Commission issued an order permitting Burford to drill new wells. The Sun Oil Company filed suit in federal court, contending that the order violated both state law and the fourteenth amendment. The case did not

---

89. The American Law Institute has recommended that the *England* procedure should be discarded. According to the ALI, state-question abstention usually should be available only when the value of sending litigants to state court is so great that federal district courts are justified in surrendering jurisdiction entirely, leaving it to the Supreme Court to correct state court errors on direct review. Yet the ALI would eliminate state-question abstention in race discrimination cases like *Pullman*. ALI, Study of the Division of Jurisdiction Between State and Federal Courts 49-50, 282-86 (1969).

90. See notes 102-03, 111-17, 125-26 and accompanying text.

91. 319 U.S. 315 (1943).

92. The wells that a private operator drilled in that area drew oil not only from beneath the operator's own land, but from the extensive reservoir of oil beneath all the land in the field. Moreover, even a single well reduced the underground pressure throughout the field and thus made it more difficult and expensive to extract oil from other sites. Texas depended on the oil field to generate economic activity and tax revenues.

satisfy the criteria for state-question abstention. The company sought equitable relief with respect to federal and state claims, but there was no reason to regard the relevant state law as unsettled or to think that the state courts might resolve the state claim in a way that would make it unnecessary to reach the federal constitutional issue.[93] Nevertheless, the Supreme Court held that abstention was warranted.

Justice Black offered no doctrinal explanation, but rested, instead, on an extensive review of the facts. He emphasized the special nature of the administrative scheme in Texas and the expertise required for regulating such a vital and economically important local resource. Moreover, he said that the state courts authorized to review the Commission's decisions were "working partners" with the Commission, performing a function that was neither wholly legislative in the sense of the *Prentis* case,[94] nor wholly judicial, either. If the federal court were to involve itself in that scheme, it might disrupt the state's attempt to achieve uniform decisions on largely technical questions. Given those special circumstances, Black said that a "sound respect for the independence of state action" required a federal "equity court" to dismiss the oil company's federal lawsuit.[95]

The Supreme Court has relied on *Burford* to justify abstention in only one other case, decided nearly a half century ago.[96] Yet the Court has occasionally recalled *Burford* with apparent approval, albeit stating the message in the case only vaguely. In *NOPSI v. Council of New Orleans*,[97] the Court gave this account: So long as "timely and adequate state-court review is available," a federal court "sitting in equity must decline to interfere with" state administrative agencies when there are "difficult questions of state law bearing on policy problems of substantial public import whose importance transcends the result in the case then at bar" or when the "exercise of federal review" of state questions would be "disruptive of state efforts to establish a coherent policy with respect to a matter of substantial public concern."[98] Then again, the Court made it clear in *NOPSI*

---

93. Id. at 339-42 (Frankfurter, J., dissenting).

94. See notes 40-41 and accompanying text (discussing *Prentis*).

95. 319 U.S. at 334 (majority opinion). Professor Young has parsed Justice Black's "rambling" opinion for these and other points. Gordon G. Young, *Federal Court Abstention and State Administrative Law From Burford to Ankenbrandt: Fifty Years of Judicial Federalism Under Burford v. Sun Oil Co. and Kindred Doctrines*, 42 DePaul L. Rev. 859, 877-78 (1993).

96. In *Alabama Pub. Svc. Comm'n v. Southern Ry.*, 341 U.S. 341 (1951), state regulators denied the railroad's request to drop two intrastate routes. There was a procedure for seeking review of that order in state court. Like the oil company in *Burford*, the railroad filed suit in federal court, attacking the order on both state and fourteenth amendment grounds. Chief Justice Vinson said that intrastate railroad traffic was generally a matter of state concern and that since state law concentrated supervisory authority in a particular state court, the railroad must pursue relief from that court. Id. at 348. In *McNeese v. Bd. of Ed.*, 373 U.S. 668 (1963), the Court declined to invoke *Burford* in a school desegregation context. In that case, the Court said that *Burford* is limited to circumstances in which a federal issue is "entangled in a skein of state law" that "must be untangled before the federal case can proceed." Id. at 674.

97. 491 U.S. 350 (1989).

98. Id. at 361. Justice Scalia borrowed some of this language from *Colorado River Water Conservation Dist. v. United States*, 424 U.S. 800, 814 (1976), where the Court had previously used it to describe the abstention usually associated with the *Thibodaux* decision. See text accompanying notes 116-17.

that *Burford* does *not* require federal district courts to dismiss routine cases in which plaintiffs mount federal attacks on orders issued by state regulatory agencies.

In *NOPSI*, an electrical power company (NOPSI) agreed to contribute to the costs of constructing two nuclear plants. The price of electricity went down, the costs of building the plants went up, and construction was suspended. The Federal Energy Regulatory Commission (FERC) determined the losses that should be allocated to NOPSI. NOPSI then asked the local regulatory agency (the Council) to fix intrastate power rates at a level that would allow NOPSI to recoup the losses that FERC identified. The Council set the case for a hearing. NOPSI immediately filed suit in federal court, seeking a declaratory judgment that the Council was obliged to approve the requested rates and an injunction ordering the Council to do so. The district court dismissed that suit, relying on *Burford* abstention and the Johnson Act as alternative grounds.[99] The Council then initiated an investigation of NOPSI's involvement in the power plant deal. During the investigation, NOPSI filed a second federal lawsuit. The district court also dismissed that suit, invoking both *Burford* and the ripeness doctrine.[100] The Council ultimately issued an order establishing lower rates than NOPSI had requested. NOPSI then filed both a petition for review of the Council's order in state court and a third lawsuit in federal court. The district court dismissed the federal action, but the Supreme Court reversed.

NOPSI advanced no significant claims under state law. Nor did NOPSI contest the way in which the Council had weighed "state-law" factors in reaching its decision. Instead, in both its state and federal court actions, NOPSI primarily contended that the Council's rate order was preempted by federal law (because it conflicted with FERC's determination of NOPSI's share of the expenses associated with the new plants). Justice Scalia explained that there was nothing especially complex about the regulatory scheme in the case. Nor did the review proceeding in state court exhibit the special features the Court had found significant in *Burford*. NOPSI's federal preemption claim went to the validity of the rate order on its face and could be determined without going beyond the order's "four corners." Accordingly, the district court's adjudication of that claim would not disrupt the state agency's efforts to enforce local regulatory law in an accurate, uniform, and efficient manner.[101]

In the wake of *NOPSI*, the only safe (though admittedly narrow) formulation for *Burford* abstention must be gleaned from the facts of *Burford* itself: Abstention is warranted if the exercise of federal jurisdiction will seriously interfere with coordinated state regulatory schemes in which administrative agencies and state courts function as partners to bring technical expertise to bear on peculiarly complex and important local matters—involving at least some questions of state regulatory law.[102] If this is what *Burford* means, however, it may have been over-

---

99. See note 35 and accompanying text (discussing the Johnson Act).

100. See Chapter IX, notes 264-90 and accompanying text (discussing ripeness).

101. Id. at 361-63. The pendency of the parallel state court action did not, in itself, warrant abstention pursuant to *Burford* or any other abstention doctrine. See notes 258, 264 and accompanying text (discussing the Court's treatment of *Colorado River* abstention in *NOPSI*); notes 257-59 and accompanying text (discussing the Court's treatment of *Younger* abstention in *NOPSI*).

102. Professor Young has explored the lower court decisions elaborating *Burford*. Some adopt this narrow formulation, but others give *Burford* a much broader purview. Young,

taken by more recent developments. It is possible that the suit in *Burford* might have been filed pursuant to § 1983. Today, plaintiffs in § 1983 actions need not exhaust state administrative remedies.[103]

The abstention doctrine associated with *Burford* (if doctrine it is) differs from state-question abstention under *Pullman* in two important respects: (1) the point of *Burford* abstention is to avoid disrupting state affairs, not needless consideration of federal constitutional questions; and (2) the consequence of *Burford* abstention is relinquishment of federal responsibility for both state and federal claims, not postponement of federal adjudication.[104]

---

note 95, at 900-02. See also Julie A. Davies, *Pullman and Burford Abstention: Clarifying the Roles of State and Federal Courts in Constitutional Cases*, 20 U.C. Davis L. Rev. 1 (1986) (also reporting wide variations in lower court decisions). In *Ankenbrandt v. Richards*, 504 U.S. 689 (1992), the Court reaffirmed that federal district courts have no diversity jurisdiction to issue divorce, alimony, and child custody decrees. The Court noted that the district courts may also abstain in other kinds of domestic relations cases on the basis of *Burford*. Id. at 705-06. That suggested (but did not decide) that *Burford* abstention may yet extend beyond the factual setting in *Burford* itself. There is nothing to suggest, however, that *Burford* could sensibly be extended to the lengths that some lower courts have taken that case. For discussions of the jurisdictional rule in *Ankenbrandt*, see Naomi R. Cahn, *Family Law, Federalism, and the Federal Courts*, 79 Iowa L. Rev. 1073 (1994); Michael A. Stein, *The Domestic Relations Exception to Federal Jurisdiction: Rethinking an Unsettled Federal Courts Doctrine*, 36 B.C. L. Rev. 669 (1995). Professor Wells argues that *Burford* is addressed to business regulation cases, which no longer present serious federal constitutional questions and are thus best left to state law, enforced by state courts. Wells, note 2, at 77.

103. See notes 48-52 and accompanying text (discussing the *Patsy* case); Chapter VIII, notes 93-94, 125-34 (describing the prerequisites for a § 1983 action); but see Chapter VI, notes 180-85 and accompanying text (noting that litigants who choose to pursue relief in state administrative agencies may find that they cannot revisit factual issues in later litigation in federal court). Some academics find *Burford* unobjectionable, even desirable. E.g., Bezanson, note 73, at 1124; Calvin R. Massey, *Abstention and the Constitutional Limits of the Judicial Power of the United States*, 1991 B.Y.U. L. Rev. 811, 849. Others are critical. Professor Young argues that *Burford* is an artifact of the formative period of American administrative law and illustrates the Court's early efforts to accommodate both state and federal agencies. Young, note 95, at 886-94. Professor Woolhandler and Professor Collins contend that *Burford* reflects out-sized concerns that federal courts will be drawn into shaping state administrative law and, at that, will appear to be exercising a form of appellate review of state administrative orders. They argue that federal courts have historically handled similar kinds of matters and that the routine invocation of abstention in cases involving state administrative action is not only unnecessary, but in tension with the jurisdiction that Congress has conferred via § 1331 and § 1332. While diversity may not be popular in academic circles, it can be defended as a means of protecting out-of-state litigants from bias in local courts. And as long as diversity jurisdiction exists, Woolhandler and Collins argue that *Burford* abstention can be justified only when federal plaintiffs advance rudimentary claims that state agencies have acted arbitrarily in isolated instances. Ann Woolhandler & Michael G. Collins, *Judicial Federalism and the Administrative States* (forthcoming). Woolhandler and Collins contend that federal courts can mitigate any genuine interference with state administrative mechanisms by giving agency determinations the kind of (relaxed) review they enjoy as a matter of state law. See Chapter VIII, note 294 (discussing the *Surgeons* and *Stude* cases).

104. Justice Black explicitly approved the district court's dismissal of the action in *Burford*. But see note 62 (explaining that the Court has since limited *Burford* abstention to postponements in cases in which federal plaintiffs seek non-discretionary relief). Justice Frankfurter dissented in *Burford* and concurred on other grounds in *Southern Ry*. See note 96. In both instances, Frankfurter argued that abstention can be justified only to avoid needless constitutional adjudication and that, in any event, should only postpone the exercise of federal jurisdiction. Frankfurter insisted that abstention is not warranted merely because a

2. State Sovereign Interests

In *Louisiana Power & Light Co. v. City of Thibodaux*,[105] the city initiated an action in state court to condemn property owned by the company. The company removed the suit to federal court on the basis of diversity. The only dispute was over the city's authority to condemn land at all. The relevant state statute appeared to give the city the necessary power, but an opinion by the state attorney general denied it. There was no state court precedent regarding the statute's meaning. The Supreme Court upheld the district court's decision to abstain while the company pursued a declaratory judgment action in state court, seeking a definitive construction of the statute. Justice Frankfurter explained that the "special nature of eminent domain," together with the sensitivity of determining the relations between a state and one of its subdivisions, justified abstention. The case called for a determination of a question of state law that was "intimately involved with sovereign prerogative." Only the state courts could make that determination authoritatively. The attorney general's opinion clouded the issue, presenting a genuine risk that the federal court might reach an erroneous result. That, in turn, would produce needless friction with the state courts.[106]

The decision in *Thibodaux* shared some features with *Pullman*: It would have been hard to "forecast" the way the state courts would construe the statute, and the district court did not dismiss the federal suit, but held it on the docket pending resolution of the state suit.[107] Yet the chief rationales for abstention in *Pullman* were missing. The company did not seek an injunction, so the court could not rest its decision to abstain on equitable considerations. And there was no reason to think that the state courts might interpret the state statute in a way that would make it unnecessary to decide a federal constitutional question. Since the case was in federal court only on the basis of diversity, the federal court could be expected to decide state law questions, with or without significant guidance from state precedents.[108] The only special factors were the state's sovereign

---

federal district court may reach a decision on a state law question that differs from the decision that a state court would render. He denied that his analysis in *Pullman* implies that conclusion. By his account, the very point of federal diversity jurisdiction is that a comparatively neutral federal court is a better judge of state law than the courts of either interested state. *Burford*, 319 U.S. at 344-45 (dissenting opinion).

105. 360 U.S. 25 (1959).

106. Id. at 28.

107. Since *Thibodaux* was a diversity case in which the only immediately contested question was the proper construction of the state statute, it was not entirely clear why Justice Frankfurter found it important that the district court had merely stayed the federal action rather than dismissing it outright. For once the state courts settled the question whether the city had state law authority to condemn the property, there would be nothing left to decide. Frankfurter may have thought it essential for the federal court to keep the case formally on the federal docket to ensure that the state proceedings were handled efficiently. He may also have anticipated that, if the condemnation ultimately went forward, the company might contest the adequacy of the compensation—a federal matter. Recall that in the *Quackenbush* case, the Court held that abstention dismissals may be warranted when federal plaintiffs seek discretionary relief (e.g., injunctions or declaratory judgments), but not when plaintiffs seek compensatory relief to which they are entitled if they are successful on the merits. See note 62.

108. See *Meredith v. Winter Haven*, 320 U.S. 228, 234 (1943) (stating the general rule that abstention is inappropriate in a diversity case merely because the state law issues to be

interests in eminent domain and the authority delegated to a political subdivision. Justice Brennan dissented in *Thibodaux*. Then, in an opinion for the Court
in *Allegheny County v. Frank Mashuda Co.*,[109] decided on the same day, Brennan
disclaimed abstention in another eminent domain case that was distinguishable
from *Thibodaux* only on the most tenuous grounds.[110]

The Supreme Court has never relied on *Thibodaux* to justify abstention in
any other case.[111] Yet the Court has cited *Thibodaux* with apparent approval,
much in the way it has cited *Burford*.[112] In *Colorado River Water Conservation
Dist. v. United States*,[113] Justice Brennan said that *Thibodaux* calls for abstention
when a case presents "difficult questions of state law bearing on policy problems
of substantial public import whose importance transcends the result in the case
then at bar."[114] That formulation is far too broad to be accurate. Not only does it
reach beyond cases implicating special questions of sovereignty, but (taken literally) it covers a host of ordinary diversity actions in which federal courts may
wish to wash their hands of intricate state law questions.[115] In the *NOPSI* case,
Justice Scalia borrowed Brennan's description of *Thibodaux* to form part of his
account of *Burford*.[116] It may be, then, that the Court now regards *Thibodaux*
and *Burford* as illustrations of the same general idea.[117]

---

decided are difficult). See note 104 (discussing Justice Frankfurter's previous criticism of abstention in diversity cases). In *Thibodaux*, Frankfurter distinguished *Meredith* on the ground
that, in that case, the lower court had dismissed a federal lawsuit entirely rather than retaining jurisdiction pending litigation in state court. *Thibodaux*, 360 U.S. at 27 n.2.

109. 360 U.S. 185 (1959).

110. In *Mashuda*, Brennan essentially reiterated the arguments he had just made in dissent in *Thibodaux*. Frankfurter, for his part, joined Justice Clark's dissent in *Mashuda*—
which cited essentially the same grounds that Frankfurter had just given (for the Court) to
justify abstention in *Thibodaux*. Justice Stewart and Justice Whittaker saw the two cases differently. In *Thibodaux*, the key issue was the proper interpretation of a state statute; in
Mashuda, the chief question was whether property had been taken for a public use. Professor Friedman suggests that the two cases were distinguishable inasmuch as the question in
Mashuda was essentially one of "fact," making that diversity action the kind of matter that
Congress might sensibly have wished to channel to a comparatively neutral federal court.
Friedman, note 67, at 582-83. Recalling the *Thibodaux* and *Mashuda* cases in *Quacken-
bush*, Justice O'Connor explained the different results in those cases on a familiar ground: In
Thibodaux, the district court had only stayed federal proceedings, but in *Mashuda* the dis-
trict court had dismissed the federal action entirely. 517 U.S. at 720-21; see notes 62, 107.

111. There are, however, largely unexplained decisions that call *Thibodaux* to mind.
E.g., *Kaiser Steel Corp. v. W.S. Ranch Co.*, 391 U.S. 593 (1968) (ordering the lower court to
stay a federal diversity action pending a state declaratory judgment suit regarding water
rights under state law); *Lehman Bros. v. Schein*, 416 U.S. 386 (1974) (ordering the circuit
court handling a diversity suit to use a state certification scheme to obtain an answer to a
question of state law).

112. See text accompanying note 96-98.

113. 424 U.S. 800 (1976).

114. Id. at 814.

115. Professor Hickman argues that if abstention is justified at all in diversity cases, it
must be narrowly restricted. Kelly D. Hickman, *Federal Court Abstention in Diversity of
Citizenship Cases*, 62 So. Calif. L. Rev. 1237 (1989).

116. See note 98 and accompanying text.

117. But see James C. Rehnquist, *Taking Comity Seriously: How to Neutralize the Abstention Doctrine*, 46 Stan. L. Rev. 1049, 1083 (1994) (noting once again that *Burford* calls
for the dismissal of federal suits while *Thibodaux* calls only for postponement). Professor
Young argues that while the Court's literal descriptions suggest that *Thibodaux* abstention is
a "variety" of *Burford* abstention, it would make more sense to regard *Burford* as a subset

3. Parallel Litigation in State Court

In *Colorado River*,[118] the Court revisited the classic problem: parallel lawsuits involving the same parties and issues, proceeding simultaneously in federal and state court. Colorado maintained a special system of "water courts" to resolve disputes over water rights in each of seven districts. The federal government asserted water rights in areas located in some of those districts. The government had participated in state court suits in some districts, but was not involved in any of several such actions pending in District No. 7. To advance its claims to water in that district, the government filed suit in federal court, naming competing private water users as defendants and seeking a declaratory judgment. The defendants invoked the McCarran Amendment to join the government as a party to one of the actions already under way in state court and moved for dismissal of the government's federal suit in deference to the parallel proceedings in state court.[119] The district court agreed to dismiss the federal suit, and the Supreme Court affirmed.

Justice Brennan acknowledged that the pendency of an action in state court is "no bar to proceedings concerning the same matter" in federal court.[120] By contrast, federal courts ordinarily have an "unflagging" duty to exercise the jurisdiction that Congress gives them. Abstention is the "exception, not the rule."[121] Brennan summarized the cases in which the Court had found abstention appropriate in the past (including *Burford* and *Thibodaux*) and conceded that none of those cases called for abstention in the case at bar. Nevertheless, in the "particular" circumstances presented in *Colorado River*, Justice Brennan concluded that abstention was warranted in the interests of "[w]ise judicial administration, giving regard to conservation of judicial resources and comprehensive disposition of litigation."[122]

Justice Brennan offered no doctrinal formulation to account for abstention in *Colorado River*. Instead, he explained that several factors (no one of which was "necessarily determinative") counseled against the exercise of federal jurisdiction: The McCarran Amendment established a "clear federal policy" of avoiding

---

of *Thibodaux*. After all, *Burford* is typically linked to federal deference to state administrative agency proceedings, but *Thibodaux* is not. Young, note 95, at 874-75. Professor Woolhandler and Professor Collins critique *Burford* abstention for the reason that it appears to single out state administrative cases for special treatment. They note that the Court may have been moved by a similar impulse in *Thibodaux*, but they regard *Burford* as especially troubling in that respect. Woolhandler & Collins, note 103. In truth, the justices (or their law clerks) are probably passing along cut-and-paste boilerplate in heartless disregard for academics attempting to understand their results and rationales.

118. See note 113 and accompanying text.

119. The McCarran Amendment, 43 U.S.C. § 666, allows plaintiffs to make the United States a defendant in "any" suit "for the adjudication of rights to the use of water," provided that the government owns the relevant water. The Amendment waives the immunity the government would otherwise enjoy. See Chapter X, notes 8-11 and accompanying text.

120. 424 U.S. at 817, quoting *McClellan v. Garland*, 217 U.S. 268, 282 (1910); see note 4 and accompanying text.

121. 424 U.S. at 813.

122. Id. at 817, quoting *Kerotest Mfg. Co. v. C-O-Two Fire Equip. Co.*, 342 U.S. 180, 183 (1952). In *Kerotest*, the Court considered the question whether one federal court should stay its hand in deference to parallel litigation in another federal court.

"piecemeal adjudication of water rights." The state court action had been filed
first, and the government's action in federal court had not progressed beyond the
initial pleading stage. The federal action would be tried in Denver, some distance
from District No. 7, where most of the private defendants resided. And the government had previously been willing to participate in state court actions in other
districts.[123] The Court was divided in *Colorado River*. In dissent, Justice Stewart
dismissed as insubstantial all the factors that Justice Brennan mentioned.[124]

The Court has relied on *Colorado River* in more recent instances.[125] Yet in so
doing, the Court has consistently reiterated that *Colorado River*, like its cousins
(*Burford* and *Thibodaux*), illustrates an exception to the general rule that federal
courts are duty-bound to exercise the jurisdiction that Congress confers upon

---

123. 424 U.S. at 818-20.

124. Justice Stewart distinguished the cases indicating that a court may prudently stay
its own proceedings when another court has control of a "res" and an attempt to adjudicate
rights in the same "res" may produce conflict. Id. at 822-24; see notes 24-26 and accompanying text. Stewart insisted that neither the federal court nor the state courts in *Colorado
River* needed physical control of the water in Colorado streams in order to adjudicate disputes over rights to that water.

125. In *Arizona v. San Carlos Apache Tribe*, 463 U.S. 545 (1983), the Court followed
Colorado River in a factually similar water rights case in which the tribe (rather than the
federal government) was the plaintiff in federal court. In *Iowa Mut. Ins. Co. v. LaPlante*,
480 U.S. 9 (1987), the Court approved abstention in a diversity case in deference to pending
proceedings in an Indian tribal court. And in *Growe v. Emison*, 507 U.S. 25 (1993), the
Court relied on *Colorado River* in directing a three-judge district court to stay its hand in a
legislative apportionment case. The Court referred to *Colorado River* in the *NOPSI* case,
but primarily only for *Colorado River's* summary of *Burford*. See note 98 and accompanying text. In *Wilton v. Seven Falls Co.*, 515 U.S. 277 (1995), the Court upheld a district
court's decision to stay a federal diversity action filed by an insurance company seeking a declaratory judgment that it was not obliged to indemnify an oil company for its losses in litigation. Soon after the insurance company filed that suit, the oil company sued the insurance
company in state court, seeking to recover under the policy in the ordinary course. In the
Supreme Court, Justice O'Connor acknowledged that there were no exceptional circumstances of the kind that *Colorado River* requires. The lawsuit in state court would take up
the same (state law) issues, but that in itself was insufficient to warrant abstention — particularly in a case in which the state court lawsuit was filed *after* the suit in federal court. O'-
Connor sustained abstention, however, because federal declaratory relief is discretionary and
she could not say that the district court had abused its discretion by taking the parallel litigation in state court into account in deciding whether a declaratory remedy was warranted.
See Chapter VIII, notes 99-100 and accompanying text (noting that the Declaratory Judgment Act only *enables* federal courts to award declaratory relief). The analysis in *Wilton* is
problematic, given that the abstention doctrines generally rest on the threshold notion that
litigants have no absolute right to the relief they seek in federal court. See note 54 and accompanying text (noting Justice Frankfurter's discussion of the nature of equitable relief in
Pullman); note 140 and accompanying text (noting Justice Black's discussion of the nature
of declaratory relief in *Samuels*). One might have thought, accordingly, that the abstention
doctrines capture and specify the content of the federal courts' discretion in the cases to
which they apply, leaving federal courts with no reservoir of discretion to divest themselves
of cases that the abstention doctrines do not foreclose. As it turns out, it just is not that simple. The abstention doctrines do add a measure of clarity, but they do not occupy the field.
In *Wilton*, it must be said, the insurance company did not seek federal declaratory relief for
any of the classic reasons. See Chapter VIII, notes 102-03 and accompanying text. Moreover, the company advanced no federal claims, but invoked federal jurisdiction only to obtain federal adjudication of state claims on which the state courts were authoritative. If,
then, there was ever a case for approving a district court's decision to abstain in the absence
of exceptional circumstances, *Wilton* was that case.

them. The difficulty, once again, is that the Court's attempt to generalize its thinking produces a formulation that is far too elastic to be taken seriously—for example, the general notion that district courts have "discretion" to abstain in the name of "wise judicial administration." District court decisions to abstain are reviewable for abuse,[126] and the Court weights appellate review *against* abstention. A district court order refusing to abstain is not sufficiently final to be immediately appealable.[127] An order staying or dismissing an action *is* final and can be appealed.[128] Nevertheless, most academic commentary on *Colorado River* is critical.[129]

E. Federal-Question Abstention

In a final (and far more important) class of cases, federal courts entertaining § 1983 actions may abstain for the express purpose of permitting state courts to adjudicate federal claims (typically federal constitutional claims) in pending (or soon to be initiated) litigation in state court. On first blush, this last form of abstention is not surprising. The Anti-Injunction Act, § 2283, ordinarily bars federal courts from issuing injunctions that interfere with pending state proceedings.[130] Recall, however, that § 2283 is inapplicable to § 1983 actions. According to the *Mitchum* decision, federal courts must have authority to enjoin pending state proceedings in § 1983 cases in order to protect individual rights secured by federal law.[131] In this last class of cases, federal courts abstain nonetheless—in

Anti Inj Act not applic to §1983 ... tions

---

126. E.g., *Moses H. Cone Mem. Hosp. v. Mercury Constr. Corp.*, 460 U.S. 1 (1983) (holding that a district court had abused its discretion by declining a contract action).

127. *Gulfstream Aerospace Corp. v. Mayacamas Corp.* 485 U.S. 271 (1988).

128. *Moses H. Cone*, 460 U.S. at 8-13. See Chapter VII, note 179 and accompanying text (discussing the finality rule).

129. Professor Mullenix argues that abstention can be warranted by comity and federalism, but cannot be justified "for reasons of sound judicial administration." Accordingly, she thinks *Colorado River* should be discarded. Linda S. Mullenix, *A Branch Too Far: Pruning the Abstention Doctrine*, 75 Gtn. L.J. 99, 156 (1986). Professor Redish argues that *Colorado River* cannot be squared with Congress' power to establish the federal courts' jurisdiction. Redish, note 66, at 96-98. Professor Sonenshein agrees that *Colorado River* was unjustified at its inception, but contends that it can be revised to provide more guidance to the lower courts. David A. Sonenshein, *Abstention: The Crooked Course of Colorado River*, 59 Tulane L. Rev. 651 (1985). Professor Friedman finds *Colorado River* "anomalous," apart from other abstention decisions depending on comity and federalism. Friedman, note 67, at 592. Professor Bartels considers *Colorado River* to rest primarily on a construction of the McCarren Amendment and thus doubts that the case bears significance in other contexts— for example, the context of civil rights. Robert Bartels, *Avoiding a Comity of Errors: A Model for Adjudicating Federal Civil Rights Suits that "Interfere" with State Civil Proceedings*, 29 Stan. L. Rev. 27, 58 (1976). But see Rehnquist, note 117 (arguing that *Colorado River* is the one form of abstention that *can* be justified—provided it is reduced to a simple rule that the federal courts should routinely defer to *preexisting* state lawsuits that offer litigants an adequate opportunity to litigate their federal claims).

130. See text accompanying note 8.

131. See notes 17-19 and accompanying text.

obedience to doctrine that the Supreme Court has elaborated, apart from any statute.

In the leading case, *Younger v. Harris*,[132] John Harris was arrested for distributing leaflets advancing the Progressive Labor Party's agenda. He was charged under the California "syndicalism" statute, which made it a crime to advocate political change by violent means. Harris contended that the syndicalism law was invalid on its face for overbreadth.[133] The state courts rejected that argument and set the case for trial. Harris then filed a § 1983 suit in federal court, seeking an injunction against the state prosecution on the theory that it would violate his first amendment rights.[134] The district court issued the injunction, but the Supreme Court held that the district court should have abstained.[135]

Justice Black started where Justice Frankfurter had begun in *Pullman*, using traditional restraints on equitable relief to condition federal court orders affecting state court proceedings.[136] Black recalled that under a "basic doctrine of eq-

---

132. 401 U.S. 37 (1971).

133. See Chapter IX, notes 176-82 and accompanying text.

134. At the time *Younger* was before the Court, *Mitchum* had not yet been decided. See notes 17-20 and accompanying text. Since Harris was a defendant in a pending state criminal prosecution, Justice Black might have invoked the Anti-Injunction Act to condemn the district court's injunction or, in the alternative, might have explicitly anticipated the view the Court would ultimately take in *Mitchum*—namely, that § 2283 was inapplicable because Harris had filed his federal lawsuit under the authority of § 1983. Instead, Black rested the decision in *Younger* entirely on non-statutory grounds and explicitly declined to say whether § 2283 was otherwise controlling "in and of itself." Black relied on § 2283 only as evidence that Congress had always manifested a "desire to permit state courts to try state cases free from interference by federal courts." 401 U.S. at 43.

135. The lower courts in *Younger* relied on the Supreme Court's then-recent precedent in *Dombrowski v. Pfister*, 380 U.S. 479 (1965). In that case, the Court had approved an injunction against a prosecution under a virtually identical syndicalism statute in a Louisiana case. Writing for the Court, Justice Brennan said in *Dombrowski* that a defense to a charge under an overbroad statute would not be adequate. Prospective defendants suffered "irreparable harm" because of the "chilling effect" on their freedom of speech, which arose from the *threat* of prosecution. It would not do to hold that anyone who refused to be chilled could raise a free speech defense at trial. The point was to address and relieve the chilling effect on the less intrepid. The only effective mechanism for dealing effectively with an overbroad statute, according to Brennan, was an affirmative civil suit for injunctive or declaratory relief, in which the statute could be struck from the books entirely, not merely rendered ineffective as applied to an individual case. Id. at 488-89. By all accounts, *Younger* departed from *Dombrowski*. The violent shift between the two cases may be the most vivid illustration of the way the Court's approach to federal courts questions changed with the change in its membership. Between 1965 and 1971, the Warren Court's liberal majority was replaced by a more conservative cohort of Nixon appointees. See Chapter I, notes 77-78 and accompanying text. The Court was divided in *Dombrowski*, as it was later in *Younger*. In *Dombrowski*, Brennan wrote for a five-member Court (himself, Warren, Douglas, Goldberg, and White). Harlan and Clark dissented; Black and Stewart did not participate. During the interim between the two cases, Fortas and Marshall replaced Goldberg and Clark, and Burger and Blackmun replaced Warren and Fortas. Then, in *Younger*, Black wrote for only a plurality (himself, Burger, and Blackmun). Harlan and Stewart concurred to make a majority of five. Brennan also concurred (with Marshall and White), but only with respect to Black's discussion of injunctions (not declaratory judgments). See text accompanying note 195. Douglas dissented.

136. See notes 54-56 and accompanying text.

uity jurisprudence," courts should not "restrain a criminal prosecution" when the defendant has an "adequate remedy at law" and will suffer no "irreparable" injury if the injunction is denied.[137] He explained that Harris had an adequate remedy at law inasmuch as he was free to press his first amendment claim as a defense to the charge against him in state court. If the statute under which he was charged was overbroad as written, the state courts might well save it by giving it a narrow construction. Apart from equity, Justice Black relied on comity as an "even more vital" consideration. In turn, Black merged comity ("a proper respect for state functions") with "Our Federalism." Federal courts must strike a balance, neither according "blind deference" to the states nor interfering "unduly" with state activities. Ordinarily, he explained, federal injunctions against pending state criminal prosecutions tip that balance and should be denied.[138]

Justice Black took the same view of declaratory relief. Writing for the Court in a companion case, *Samuels v. Mackell*,[139] he acknowledged that declaratory judgments are not governed by the same equitable rules and traditions attending injunctions. But he insisted that declaratory relief is discretionary and that comity and federalism can inform that discretion.[140] By Black's account, federal declaratory judgments interfere with state criminal proceedings in virtually the same way as injunctions. He assumed that any de-

---

137. *Douglas v. City of Jeannette*, 319 U.S. 157, 162-65 (1943); see *Stefanelli v. Minard*, 342 U.S. 117 (1951) (holding that federal courts should not enjoin the use of illegally seized evidence in a state trial). Professor Soifer and Professor Macgill have shown that injunctions were historically much more readily available than Justice Black suggested. Aviam Soifer & H. C. Macgill, *The Younger Doctrine: Reconstructing Reconstruction*, 55 Tex. L. Rev. 1141, 1148-55 (1977). Professor Laycock takes a similar view. Douglas Laycock, *Federal Interference with State Prosecutions: The Cases that Dombrowski Forgot*, 46 U. Chi. L. Rev. 636 (1979).

138. 401 U.S. at 44-49. Justice Black had it that the phrase "Our Federalism" enjoys an old and venerable lineage in American jurisprudence. As a matter of fact, Justice Frankfurter introduced that phrase when he joined the Court in 1939. Michael G. Collins, *Whose Federalism?*, 9 Const. Comm. 75 (1992); see also note 61 and accompanying text. Since Justice Black relied on comity and federalism in *Younger*, as well as on equitable considerations, it is open to argue that the federal-question abstention doctrine he elaborated in that case reaches § 1983 suits for damages. The Supreme Court has never squarely decided the question. But see *Deakins v. Monaghan*, 484 U.S. 193, 205 (1988) (White, J., concurring) (giving a positive answer). In *McNary*, the Court cited *Younger* in partial support of its holding that § 1983 does not authorize a federal suit for damages arising from wrongful state taxation. See notes 45-47 and accompanying text. The core of the idea in *Younger* is that federal courts should not interfere with pending state prosecutions. Interference is perfectly obvious if federal courts presume to enjoin state proceedings, less so if federal courts merely exercise jurisdiction over legal actions involving the same parties and issues. Recall that another abstention case, *Colorado River*, purports to describe the circumstances in which federal courts should abstain in favor of parallel state proceedings in order to avoid a duplication of effort. See notes 118-29 and accompanying text. Parallel federal § 1983 suits for damages and state criminal prosecutions would not appear to meet the *Colorado River* standards (such as they are). Cf. *Heck v. Humphrey*, 512 U.S. 477 (1994) (interpreting § 1983 not to be available to most prison inmates seeking compensatory damages for unconstitutional criminal convictions); see Chapter XII, notes 248-53 and accompanying text (discussing *Heck* and related decisions).

139. 401 U.S. 66 (1971).

140. See Chapter VIII, notes 99-100 and accompanying text; Chapter IX, notes 286-90 and accompanying text.

claratory judgment that a district court rendered would be entitled to preclusive effect in state court. If the state courts declined to respect it, the district
court would have authority to issue an injunction after all, as a means of enforcing the declaratory judgment. Accordingly, federal courts should ordinarily
refuse to issue declaratory judgments regarding the validity of pending state
criminal prosecutions.[141]

The abstention doctrine associated with *Younger* and *Samuels* differs fundamentally from the abstention doctrine associated with *Pullman*.[142] Federal courts
do not *stay* federal § 1983 actions, forcing litigants to file *new* lawsuits in state
court in order to give the state courts an opportunity to determine potentially
dispositive issues of *state* law.[143] Under the *Younger* doctrine, federal courts *relinquish* federal jurisdiction entirely, forcing litigants to be satisfied with already
pending actions in state court, in which state courts will determine *federal*
claims.[144] When district courts conclude that *Younger* and *Samuels* bar federal injunctive or declaratory relief, they dismiss the § 1983 actions before them in
favor of pending state proceedings.[145] In *Huffman v. Pursue*,[146] the Court held
that state court proceedings are "pending" within the meaning of *Younger* and
Samuels not only while they are before state trials courts, but also over the
course of direct review within the state court system. Accordingly, litigants whose
federal § 1983 actions are dismissed must advance their federal theories both at

---

141. Justice Brennan concurred on this point in *Samuels*, but only because the indictment in that case had been filed before the federal suit was initiated. In a separate opinion in
yet another companion case, *Perez v. Ledesma*, 401 U.S. 82 (1971), Brennan distinguished
cases in which § 1983 plaintiffs seek declaratory relief in federal court *before* charges are
filed in state court. See notes 193-98 and accompanying text (discussing Brennan's subsequent opinion for the Court in *Steffel v. Thompson*).

142. This last abstention doctrine is also distinguishable from *Burford*, *Thibodaux*, and
Colorado River. See notes 91-129 and accompanying text. In *Thibodaux*, the Court approved a stay of federal litigation in favor of a state court determination of a doubtful question of state law. In *Burford* and *Colorado River*, the Court ordered abstention dismissals
knowing that the state courts would decide federal issues. But in neither of those cases was
that the point of abstention.

143. See notes 57-58, 73-76, 88-89 and accompanying text.

144. The Supreme Court also supervises the implementation of *Younger* and *Samuels*
differently from the way it superintends the application of *Pullman*. None of the abstention
doctrines purports to deny the federal courts' subject matter jurisdiction, but only to orchestrate the exercise of jurisdiction the federal courts are understood to enjoy. Accordingly, if
defendants in federal actions fail to request abstention, federal courts are not required to address the question *sua sponte*. In *Ohio Bureau of Employment Svc. v. Hodory*, 431 U.S. 471
(1977), the Court said that if state authorities do not invoke *Younger* abstention, and thus
"voluntarily" agree to litigate in federal court, the federal court may proceed. The "principles of comity do not demand that the federal court force the case back into the State's own
system." Id. at 480. The Court explained, however, that it would not quickly approve such a
waiver of *Pullman* abstention. In cases otherwise controlled by *Younger*, the consequence of
accepting a waiver is that a federal court (rather than a state court) will pass on a federal
claim for injunctive or declaratory relief. In cases subject to *Pullman*, by contrast, the consequence of accepting a waiver is that the federal court will forego the chance to avoid a federal constitutional question. But see *Pennzoil*, 481 U.S. at 11 n.9 (declining to rest on *Pullman* because the interested party had abandoned its argument for abstention on that basis);
note 252.

145. E.g., *Hicks v. Miranda*, 422 U.S. 332, 352 (1975).

146. 420 U.S. 592 (1975).

the trial court level in state court and (if they suffer defeat at that level) in the state appellate courts.[147]

Litigants whose federal theories are finally rejected in state court may seek appellate review in the Supreme Court, though that avenue for federal adjudication is more theoretical than real.[148] Litigants who suffer criminal conviction and are sentenced to imprisonment may be able to petition a federal court for a writ of habeas corpus.[149] In that indirect way, they may put federal claims about their treatment before an inferior federal court at a later time.[150] Apart from habeas corpus, however, there is no mechanism by which § 1983 plaintiffs whose actions are dismissed under *Younger* and *Samuels* can return to federal district court.[151] Inferior federal courts have no jurisdiction to review state court decisions directly, and, in the main, they are obliged to give state court judgments preclusive effect.[152]

---

147. In *Huffman*, state authorities filed a state court action against the proprietor of a motion picture theater, charging that the theater was exhibiting obscene films. As soon as the trial court issued an order barring further showings, the proprietor filed a federal § 1983 action attacking the state obscenity statute on first amendment grounds. Then-Justice Rehnquist said that the state court proceeding was still pending inasmuch as the proprietor had a right to appeal the trial court's order to higher state courts. It did not matter that, by seeking appellate review, the theater proprietor would no longer be responding to state charges brought by state officials in state court, but would become the moving party asking the state appellate courts to determine a federal issue.

148. See Chapter VII, notes 182-90 and accompanying text.

149. See Chapter XII, notes 41-71 and accompanying text.

150. Inasmuch as John Harris was at risk of a criminal conviction in state court and a potential sentence to confinement, the Court's decision in *Younger* did not (necessarily) mean that Harris would never have an opportunity to press his first amendment claim in a federal district court. If he landed in jail after conviction, he would be able to seek a federal writ of habeas corpus. In that rough sense, *Younger* itself *postponed* federal district court adjudication (for some individuals). See Harry T. Edwards, *The Changing Notion of "Our Federalism"*, 33 Wayne L. Rev. 1015, 1030-31 (1987). In *Huffman*, by contrast, the Court extended the *Younger* abstention doctrine to a *civil* proceeding in state court, which allowed for no punishment by imprisonment and, accordingly, no possibility of subsequent district court adjudication in habeas corpus. Cases like *Huffman* plainly establish that the consequence of federal-question abstention is not typically a deferral of federal district court adjudication, but a surrender of jurisdiction to state courts whose judgments will almost always be final. See Larry W. Yackle, *Explaining Habeas Corpus*, 60 N.Y.U. L. Rev. 991, 1045-46 (1985). Justice Rehnquist acknowledged as much in *Huffman* and discounted objections with the explanation that litigants are not always entitled to a federal trial-level tribunal for the determination of federal claims. *Huffman*, 420 U.S. at 605-06. For further discussion of *Younger's* application to civil proceedings, see notes 223-64 and accompanying text.

151. The federal-question abstention doctrine in *Younger* recognizes no analogue to *England*. See notes 88-89 and accompanying text.

152. See Chapter VI, notes 154-93 and accompanying text. Justice Rehnquist described the result in *Huffman* in an unfortunate way: The theater proprietor "must *exhaust* his state appellate remedies *before* seeking relief" in a federal district court "unless he can bring himself within one of the exceptions specified in *Younger*." *Huffman*, 420 U.S. at 608 (emphasis added). Clearly, Rehnquist did not mean to announce a genuine exhaustion doctrine—a rule of timing that merely postpones federal adjudication until the state courts have had an opportunity to pass on federal claims. See notes 37-38 and accompanying text. If, in *Huffman*, the state's highest court rejected the proprietor's first amendment claim, that judgment would probably be entitled to preclusive effect, pursuant to the Full Faith and Credit Statute. See Chapter VI, notes 162-93 and accompanying text. The proprietor might seek *certiorari* review in the Supreme Court, but he would not ordinarily be able to relitigate his federal claim in a federal district court. See *Ellis v. Dyson*, 421 U.S. 426, 437 (1975) (Pow-

The general rule that plaintiffs in federal § 1983 actions cannot obtain injunctions or declaratory judgments against pending state criminal prosecutions is consistent with the statutes governing removal. Recall that under 28 U.S.C. § 1441, defendants in state court cannot ordinarily remove the actions against them to federal court on the basis of a federal defense.[153] In both instances, the default position is that state court litigation, once under way, will be allowed to take its course without federal interference. Many observers propose that § 1441 should be amended to permit removal on the basis of a federal defense in *civil* litigation. But no one seriously contends that defendants in state *criminal* actions should be able to remove whenever they advance federal defenses.[154] Accordingly, if federal-question abstention were limited to the rule announced in *Younger*, this final category of abstention cases would be largely non-controversial. As it is, however, federal-question abstention is intensively controversial — not for what it was in *Younger* itself, but for what it has become in the years since.[155]

By some accounts, federal-question abstention conflicts with *Mitchum's* explanation of § 1983.[156] If the point of § 1983 is to empower federal courts to enforce federal rights that state courts may fail to respect, it is hard to justify curtailing federal judicial authority on the theory that state courts are, after all, perfectly reliable. Moreover, § 1983 states a national policy ascribable to Congress. Once the Supreme Court has given that statute an authoritative interpretation (as it did in *Mitchum*), the Court cannot easily fashion a limiting doctrine that denies federal courts the very remedial authority that Congress, by hypothesis, has decided they should have. To the extent federal-question abstention approaches the kind of blanket prohibition on injunctions in § 1983 cases that § 2283 would have imposed (absent *Mitchum*), this judicially created doctrine arguably undermines Congress' authority to prescribe the means by which federal rights will be enforced.[157]

---

ell, J., dissenting) (explaining the usual scenario). Justice Rehnquist indicated as much when he noted, in an aside, that he would have reached the same result if the time for filing an appeal in state court had expired. In that event, the proprietor would (ordinarily) have no recourse to *any* court. 420 U.S. at 611 n.22. But see Chapter VI, notes 180-85 and accompanying text (discussing exceptions to preclusion when state court procedures offer no opportunity for full and fair adjudication); Chapter VII, notes 137-66 and accompanying text (discussing the Supreme Court's authority to reach federal issues when state procedural grounds are inadequate to sustain a judgment disposing of a federal claim).

153. See Chapter VI, notes 119-24 and accompanying text; but see Chapter VI, notes 125-48 and accompanying text (discussing the limited circumstances in which defendants in state court *can* remove on the basis of a federal defense).

154. See Chapter VI, notes 144-45. Federal-question abstention recognizes exceptions for cases in which the process in state court is flawed. See notes 164-89 and accompanying text. Recall that the Court has not employed the process model to determine the availability of removal pursuant to § 1443. See Chapter VI, notes 142-45 and accompanying text. Accordingly, litigants can avoid federal-question abstention in circumstances in which they would not be able to remove the actions against them to federal court. Then again, since federal courts rarely conclude that state procedural machinery is inadequate, the distinction makes little practical difference.

155. See notes 255, 264, 279.

156. See notes 17-20 and accompanying text.

157. Professor Redish recognizes that at least some of the justices may think that *Mitchum* was wrongly decided and thus regard *Younger* and *Samuels* as consistent with congressional will, as expressed in the Anti-Injunction Act. In his opinion for the Court in

By other accounts, federal-question abstention is yet another illustration of the modern Court's commitment to the private rights model of adjudication.[158] Both *Younger* and *Samuels* contemplate that would-be federal § 1983 plaintiffs can just as easily vindicate their federal claims in state court. In some instances, that may be true. But it certainly is not true in all. Federal courts entertaining civil § 1983 actions for injunctive or declaratory relief are in a position to protect federal rights in a variety of ways. They can issue temporary orders that protect citizens from prosecution while federal claims are under consideration. If they conclude that federal claims are meritorious, they can grant permanent prospective relief that will safeguard citizens in the future. And they can issue orders on behalf of classes of plaintiffs, so that anyone whose federal rights are at stake can benefit. By contrast, state criminal courts have authority only to determine whether a state statute can validly be applied to a particular defendant.[159] Of course, litigants who want and need prospective relief for an entire class may be

---

Younger, Justice Black relied on § 2283 as evidence of Congress' general desire to free state court proceedings from federal interference. See note 134. If, however, the Court continues to endorse *Mitchum's* account of § 1983, Redish contends that *Younger* constitutes "judicial usurpation of legislative authority." Redish, note 66, at 88. See also Donald L. Doernberg, *"You Can Lead a Horse to Water..."*: The Supreme Court's Refusal to Allow the Exercise of Original Jurisdiction Conferred by Congress, 40 Case Western Res. L. Rev. 999, 1017 (1990) (describing *Younger* as the "clearest" of several examples of the Court's "abdication" of jurisdiction that Congress has prescribed); Nichol, note 19, at 992 (contending that "*Younger* largely takes away what *Mitchum* grants"). Professor Althouse suggests that the 1971 decision in *Younger* was essential to the 1972 decision in *Mitchum*. By her account, the Court was willing to release its grip on a statutory basis for curbing the district courts only after it had established an independent, judge-crafted basis for doing much the same thing. The Court may have preferred to rely on its own doctrine rather than a statute simply to achieve greater flexibility. Ann Althouse, *The Humble and the Treasonous: Judge-Made Jurisdiction Law*, 40 Case Western Res. L. Rev. 1035, 1043 (1990). Professor Beermann doubts that the separation principle can answer the sensitive ideological questions that abstention entails. Jack M. Beermann, *"Bad" Judicial Activism and Liberal Federal-Courts Doctrine: A Comment on Professor Doernberg and Professor Redish*, 40 Case Western Res. L. Rev. 1053 (1990). Professor Wells argues that it is unrealistic to draw any distinction between the creative statutory construction the Court undertakes in cases like *Mitchum* and the elaboration of doctrine the Court undertakes in cases like *Younger*. Wells, note 66; see also Michael Wells, *The Role of Comity in the Law of Federal Courts*, 60 N. Car. L. Rev. 59 (1981).

158. See Chapter I, notes 50-60 and accompanying text.

159. Under classic precedents, a remedy at law is "adequate" only if it is as "complete, practical and efficient as that which equity could afford." *Terrace v. Thompson*, 263 U.S. 197, 214 (1923). Professor Laycock argues that since state criminal prosecutions often cannot meet that standard, private litigants should be allowed to seek injunctive and declaratory relief in federal § 1983 actions in many more cases than the Court's abstention doctrine allows. Douglas Laycock, *Federal Interference with State Prosecutions: The Need for Prospective Relief*, 1977 Sup. Ct. Rev. 193. Professor Zeigler contends that private litigants need access to the federal courts via § 1983 class actions in order to achieve systemic reforms of state criminal process—the kinds of reforms that state courts are unlikely to undertake in the context of individual prosecutions. Donald H. Zeigler, *Federal Court Reform of State Criminal Justice Systems: A Reassessment of the Younger Doctrine from a Modern Perspective*, 19 U.C. Davis L. Rev. 31 (1985). The New York State Bar Association has published guidelines that federal district courts might follow in order to ensure that they abstain in class action cases only when the policies on which *Younger* rests will actually be promoted. For a discussion, see Georgene M. Vairo, *Making Younger Civil: The Consequences of Federal Court Deference to State Court Proceedings*, 58 Fordham L. Rev. 173 (1989).

able to obtain it via civil actions in *state* court.[160] But if it is once recognized that litigants must launch separate civil actions to achieve what they cannot accomplish by defending against isolated criminal charges, it would seem that they should be entitled to do so in federal court, if they wish.[161]

By still other accounts, federal-question abstention illustrates the current Court's general tendency to deny access to federal courts in a wide variety of circumstances in which individuals seek protection from the excesses of state officials. The Court insists upon parity between federal and state courts and, on that basis, justifies routing federal question business to the latter as a routine matter.[162] If this is what *Younger* and *Samuels* mean, this last form of abstention reflects an agenda with sensitive political implications: a general "devolution of power" to the states.[163]

1. The Process Model

There are exceptions to federal-question abstention. In *Younger*, Justice Black said that federal courts need not abstain in three kinds of cases: (1) cases in which the proceedings in state court constitute "bad faith and harassment;" (2) cases in which the state statute involved is not only arguable invalid on its face, but "flagrantly and patently violative of express constitutional prohibitions in every clause, sentence and paragraph, and in whatever manner and against whomever an effort might be made to apply it;" and (3) cases involving "other unusual situations calling for federal intervention."[164] The Court has assimilated those exceptions into the process model: Federal courts need not abstain if the process available in state court fails to offer an adequate opportunity for the adjudication of federal claims.[165]

Bad faith and harassment. This exception plainly goes to the integrity of the adjudicative process in state court. It encompasses prosecutions pressed without any genuine expectation that a valid conviction can be secured, but only to pun-

---

160. See Chapter VI, note 52 and accompanying text.

161. See *NOPSI*, 491 U.S. at 359, quoting *Willcox v. Consolidated Gas Co.*, 212 U.S. 19, 40 (1909): "The right of a party plaintiff to choose a Federal court where there is a choice cannot be properly denied."

162. See Chapter I, notes 79-91 and accompanying text. On this point, Professor Wells argues that the Court does not genuinely think that federal and state courts are fungible at all. By contrast, the Court recognizes that federal courts are more likely to find individual claims meritorious, while state courts are more likely to side with state officials. Capitalizing on the *absence* of parity, the Court uses abstention to achieve substantive results—by deliberating diverting cases into state court, where state interests are more likely to prevail. Wells himself deplores the illiberal results the Court appears to have in mind, but he contends that the use of forum-allocation rules is a legitimate means of achieving substantive ends without making overt changes in formal constitutional doctrine. Michael Wells, *Is Disparity a Problem?*, 22 Ga. L. Rev. 283, 326-27 (1988).

163. Soifer & Macgill, note 137, at 1141. See Louise Weinberg, *The New Judicial Federalism*, 29 Stan. L. Rev. 1191, 1203 (1977) (depicting *Younger* as an aspect of a "jurisdictional counterrevolution" in which an increasingly conservative Court has denied access to federal courts for the enforcement of federal rights); Zeigler, note 55, at 689 (arguing that *Younger* frustrates federal court vindication of federal rights and should be "abandoned").

164. 401 U.S. at 53-54.

165. See Chapter I, notes 61-65 and accompanying text.

ish individuals by subjecting them to burdensome and expensive legal proceedings.[166] The only illustrative precedent in the Supreme Court is *Dombrowski v. Pfister*,[167] decided before (and distinguished in) *Younger*. In *Dombrowski*, local prosecutors in Louisiana repeatedly charged civil rights workers with violating a facially overbroad statute, but routinely dismissed the charges on the eve of trial—just before the state courts would have had an opportunity to consider the defendants' first amendment claims.[168] The idea at work in this first exception, accordingly, is that federal courts can issue injunctions or declaratory judgments regarding pending state proceedings—when the procedural machinery at the state level is inadequate to protect federal rights.[169]

Flagrantly invalid state statutes. This second exception is obviously extremely narrow. The Court has never found a statute to fit it. If a statute were so obviously unconstitutional, the state courts would presumably recognize as much and refuse to enforce it—making federal injunctive relief unnecessary, even if it is available.[170] Moreover, if state prosecuting authorities or state courts were to enforce such a statute, their actions would very likely be in bad faith—collapsing this second exception into the first.[171] The point, again, is that abstention is unwarranted when pending state court proceedings offer no opportunity for full and fair adjudication.[172]

Other unusual circumstances. This final exception bears the marks of a catch-all category to cover circumstances that are difficult to anticipate. In fact, the Supreme Court has relied on it only once. In *Gibson v. Berryhill*,[173] the Court approved an injunction against a pending state license-revocation proceeding.[174] The licensing board was presumptively biased, because its members had a financial incentive to revoke the licenses of their competitors. The point of *Berryhill*, then, was once again that the process available at the state level was fundamen-

---

166. See *Kugler v. Helfant*, 421 U.S. 117, 126 n.6 (1975).

167. 380 U.S. 479 (1965).

168. While Justice Brennan discussed this aspect of the record in *Dombrowski*, he plainly relied on the related, but analytically distinct, ground that the plaintiffs advanced a first amendment overbreadth claim. See note 135. When Justice Black seized upon Brennan's reference to "bad faith and harassment," he did it as a deliberate device for limiting *Dombrowski* to that kind of case. See Fiss, note 56, at 1120. For a survey and analysis of lower court decisions, see C. Keith Wingate, *The Bad Faith-Harassment Exception to the Younger Doctrine: Exploring the Empty Universe*, 5 Rev. Litigation 123 (1986).

169. Professor Fiss makes this connection. See Fiss, note 56, at 1114-15.

170. Michael G. Collins, *The Right to Avoid Trial: Justifying Federal Court Intervention into Ongoing State Court Proceedings*, 66 N. Car. L. Rev. 49, 67 (1987).

171. Ralph V. Whitten, *Federal Declaratory and Injunctive Interference With State Court Proceedings: The Supreme Court and the Limits of Judicial Discretion*, 53 N. Car. L. Rev. 591, 618-19 (1975).

172. Justice Stevens has argued that if this exception to abstention is concerned with the adequacy of state process, it should allow a federal district court to act when § 1983 plaintiffs challenge the validity of the very state procedural machinery they will have to engage if the district court abstains. *Trainor v. Hernandez*, 431 U.S. 434, 469-70 (1977) (dissenting opinion); *Juidice v. Vail*, 430 U.S. 327, 339-41 (1977) (concurring opinion). The full Court has rejected Stevens' view. See, e.g., *Moore v. Sims*, 442 U.S. 415, 426-27 n.10 (1979).

173. 411 U.S. 564 (1973).

174. See *Kugler*, 421 U.S. at 125 n.4 (recalling *Berryhill* as a case in which the Court relied on the "extraordinary circumstances" exception).

tally flawed.[175] In this instance, the Court invokes the process model in its traditional formulation: Other unusual circumstances are limited to conditions that "render the state court incapable of fairly and fully adjudicating the federal issues before it."[176]

The Court elaborated the process orientation of the three *Younger* exceptions in *Moore v. Sims*. [177] State authorities assumed temporary custody of minor children thought to be the victims of parental abuse and initiated proceedings in state court, seeking judicial approval for placing the children with their grandparents. The parents employed a variety of state law devices for regaining custody of the children. The litigation in state court became confused, and the parents soon filed a § 1983 action in federal court, advancing federal constitutional arguments against the state statutory scheme under which the state authorities purported to act. The parents primarily contended that the state scheme violated procedural due process inasmuch as it authorized state officials to detain children for a considerable period of time without a hearing.[178] The district court issued a preliminary injunction barring state officers from proceeding any further in state court while the district court considered the parents' constitutional challenge. After trial, the district court found the state statutory scheme invalid on its face and issued a permanent injunction against its use. The Supreme Court reversed on the theory that the district court should have abstained.

Then-Justice Rehnquist acknowledged that *Moore* differed from *Younger*. When the parents filed their § 1983 suit, they were not defendants in any state court proceeding in which they might have advanced their claims against the state scheme as a defense. The only state proceeding pending at all was the action to deprive the parents of custody. That action turned on the "best interests" of particular children, quite apart from the constitutional validity of the general statutory scheme. Justice Rehnquist explained, however, that abstention was appropriate if the parents had the "opportunity" to "present" their other claims in that proceeding. It was unclear whether Texas procedure would allow the parents to do that. But Justice Rehnquist insisted that doubts should be resolved in favor of abstention. He rejected the district court's suggestion that abstention was unwarranted because the parents' claims were "broad and novel." According to Justice Rehnquist, the "breadth" of the parents' challenge to the state statutory scheme "militated in *favor* of abstention, not *against* it." If federal courts presumed to entertain claims of that kind, state courts would be denied the opportunity to give state statutes a "narrowing" construction that would "obviate" federal issues.[179]

---

175. Since the board itself was biased, it could not be relied upon to consider the validity of its own composition. The licensee had a right to appeal an adverse decision to the state courts, but he could not retain his license while that appeal was pending. Collins, note 170, at 70.

176. *Kugler*, 421 U.S. at 124-25.

177. 442 U.S. 415 (1979).

178. They also contended that the state failed to provide for guardians *ad litem* to represent children, authorized the severance of parental rights on the basis of a preponderance of the evidence (rather than "clear and convincing" proof), and permitted state officials to collect and disseminate data regarding *suspected* child abuse without an adequate judicial determination of *actual* mistreatment.

179. 442 U.S. at 425 (emphasis in original). See text accompanying note 138 (discussing Justice Black's reliance on the same point in *Younger*).

Taken literally, *Moore* contemplates that abstention is warranted in any instance in which federal § 1983 plaintiffs are involved in a state court proceeding into which they might inject the federal issues they wish to litigate in federal court.[180] The question is not whether the state proceeding necessarily implicates those federal issues, so that the state courts will pass on them in due course. Instead, the question is whether the state proceeding can be made to accommodate federal theories that otherwise would not be addressed. That, in turn, approaches the proposition that litigants are not, after all, entitled to choose a federal forum if they wish, but must put their federal claims before state courts — when those courts offer an adequate procedural opportunity to do so.[181] Recall, however, that the parents in *Moore* did not merely choose to file a § 1983 action in federal court at a time when they happened to be involved in related proceedings in state court. They sought and obtained an injunction against those state proceedings (and any other proceedings like them).[182]

The appearance of the process model at this juncture further delineates the practical effect of the Court's decision in *Mitchum* (exempting § 1983 actions from the Anti-Injunction Act).[183] If § 2283 were applicable, federal courts entertaining § 1983 actions would be barred from issuing injunctions that interfere with pending state court proceedings, subject to the other exceptions that § 2283 itself recognizes.[184] As it is, § 2283 is inapplicable, and the Court's own federal-question abstention doctrine fills the void. Under that doctrine, federal courts entertaining § 1983 suits are also (ordinarily) barred from issuing injunctions (and declaratory judgments) that interfere with pending state criminal proceedings.[185] But the exceptions are different. Federal-question abstention acknowledges not the exceptions listed in § 2283, but the different exceptions listed in *Younger* (which, in turn, boil down to cases in which state court process fails to provide an opportunity for adequate adjudication of federal claims).

Federal-question abstention assumes parity, proceeds on the private rights model, and recognizes exceptions in familiar circumstances: when the processes of adjudication in state court break down.[186] This form of abstention thus re-

---

180. In dissent, Justice Stevens contended that the pending child custody proceeding bore no more relation to the claims in the parents' federal § 1983 action than a pending traffic violation charge would have. *Moore*, 442 U.S. at 435-36.

181. Professor Marcus criticizes the Court's decisions on this ground and proposes a more complicated (but still workable) alternative. She would have federal district courts determine not whether there is some discernible bar to state court consideration of federal claims, but whether federal claims will "probably" be adjudicated in the state proceedings to which federal courts defer. Maria L. Marcus, *Wanted: A Federal Standard for Evaluating the Adequate State Forum*, 50 Md. L. Rev. 131 (1991).

182. Justice Rehnquist was also troubled by the scope of the district court's order in *Moore*. He wondered aloud whether the plaintiffs had standing to press all the claims the district court explored. 442 U.S. at 428-29. See Chapter IX, text accompanying notes 57-58 (noting the constitutional prerequisites of standing: injury, causation, and redressability).

183. See notes 17-20 and accompanying text.

184. See notes 21-27 and accompanying text.

185. But see notes 190-204 and accompanying text (discussing the inapplicability of federal-question abstention when no state proceeding is pending); cf. notes 223-73 and accompanying text (discussing the extension of federal-question abstention to civil proceedings in state court).

186. See Chapter I, notes 50-65, 79-91 and accompanying text.

strains federal judicial power while state court proceedings are *pending* in much the way that the Full Faith and Credit Statute restrains federal judicial power when state court proceedings are *complete*. Recall that under 28 U.S.C. § 1738, federal courts give state court judgments the preclusive effect they would have in state court. Ordinarily, federal claims that were, or might have been, advanced in state court are foreclosed thereafter. There is an exception, however, for circumstances in which litigants are denied an opportunity for "full and fair" adjudication in the initial state proceeding.[187] Here again, then, the Court achieves a certain symmetry. Positing that state court litigation is satisfying in the main, the Court generally insists that litigants must advance their federal claims in those courts and accept the outcomes the state courts render.[188] Yet recognizing that inadequate state procedures undermine the reliability of state judgments, the Court allows for exceptions (in both instances) on procedural grounds.[189]

2. Anticipatory Actions

In *Younger* and *Samuels*, the Supreme Court elaborated federal-question abstention for cases in which federal courts are asked to issue injunctions or declaratory judgments that interfere with state criminal proceedings that are already under way.[190] In cases of that kind, district courts always decline to intervene, unless the proceedings pending in state court fail to provide an opportunity for full and fair adjudication of federal claims. If no state proceedings are pending, district courts fall back on the general prerequisites for equitable and declaratory relief. Plaintiffs seeking injunctions must demonstrate irreparable harm for which there is no adequate remedy at law. Plaintiffs seeking declaratory

---

187. See Chapter VI, notes 175-79 and accompanying text. But see Chapter VI, notes 142-45 (noting that the process model does not control the availability of civil rights removal under § 1443).

188. Subject to the theoretical possibility of direct review in the Supreme Court and, in some instances, a petition for federal habeas corpus.

189. In this abstention context, however, the Court has not suggested that state processes are adequate if they comport with due process in the fourteenth amendment sense. See Chapter VI, note 178 and accompanying text (discussing the *Kremer* decision regarding "full and fair adjudication" in the preclusion context). Professor Bator endorsed the Court's process-oriented sense of the circumstances that warrant federal intervention. Paul M. Bator, *The State Courts and Federal Constitutional Litigation*, 22 Wm. & Mary L. Rev. 605, 626-27 (1981). Professor Collins is also sympathetic. Collins, note 170. Professor Rosenfeld prefers an analogy to the Tax Injunction Act's condition that the state courts must offer a "plain, speedy, and effective" means of addressing federal claims. S. Stephan Rosenfeld, *The Place of State Courts in the Era of Younger v. Harris*, 59 B.U. L. Rev. 597 (1979); see note 36 and accompanying text. For a review of lower court decisions, see Brian Stagner, *Avoiding Abstention: The Younger Exceptions*, 29 Texas Tech. L. Rev. 137 (1998). The Judiciary Act of 1789 included a provision barring federal courts of equity from entertaining suits for injunctions when there was a "plain, adequate, and complete" remedy at law. That section contemplated, however, that such a remedy at law would be found on the "law side" of a *federal* court—not in a state criminal proceeding. See *Guaranty Trust Co. v. York*, 326 U.S. 99 (1945). It was repealed in 1948 when Congress abandoned the old dichotomy between law and equity.

190. Justice Black explicitly declined to decide whether the same abstention doctrine applies in cases in which federal courts are asked to issue injunctions or declaratory judgments regarding prospective prosecutions. *Younger*, 401 U.S. at 41; *Samuels*, 401 U.S. at 73-74.

judgments must show a sufficient need for clarity to warrant discretionary relief.[191]

There are differences between § 1983 plaintiffs who ask federal courts to interfere with pending state prosecutions and § 1983 plaintiffs who ask federal
courts to protect them from prosecution in the future. Plaintiffs who are already
under indictment have an ostensibly adequate means of vindicating their federal
claims in state court: They can raise those claims as defenses to the pending state
prosecution. Federal injunctive or declaratory relief will disrupt ongoing state
processes. By contrast, plaintiffs who have not been indicted have no immediate
means of advancing their federal claims in state court. To obtain an adjudication
of those claims, they must launch new litigation in one set of courts or the other.
Together, § 1983 and § 1331 ostensibly entitle them to choose the federal courts,
if they wish. Federal courts will not (necessarily) disturb state processes simply
by exercising their jurisdiction—when no state court has taken, or has been
asked to take, any action with respect to the matter.[192]

There are also differences between § 1983 plaintiffs who ask federal courts to
interfere with state prosecutions regarding *past* behavior and § 1983 plaintiffs
who seek federal protection from prosecution for *future* behavior. Plaintiffs who
are charged or threatened with prosecution on the basis of past behavior have already placed themselves at risk. Plaintiffs who have not taken the same risks may
be shrinking violets by comparison, but they may also be more appealing candidates for federal litigation: They wish to conform their behavior to the law and
seek assurance that the behavior in which they want to engage *is* lawful. Accordingly, they ask federal courts to determine *ex ante* whether they are entitled to
carry out their plans and, if they are, either to enjoin state officials from prosecuting them or to declare that prosecution would violate their federal rights.

The Supreme Court has grappled with these distinctions in a series of cases.
In *Steffel v. Thompson*,[193] the Court held that the *Younger/Samuels* formulation
is inapplicable to cases that have the strongest purchase on federal court action:
cases in which § 1983 plaintiffs seek federal declaratory relief from the threat of
prosecution for planned conduct in the future.[194] Justice Brennan insisted that the

---

191. See text accompanying notes 54-55 (describing the traditional limits on equitable
relief); Chapter VIII, text accompanying notes 99-100 (discussing the discretionary character
of declaratory relief). It may be helpful to think of the federal-question abstention doctrine
in *Younger* and *Samuels* as a distillation of the traditional criteria for equitable and declaratory relief for purposes of cases in which certain state proceedings are pending. Yet the
Supreme Court sometimes insists upon flexibility beyond what the abstention doctrines entail. See note 125 (discussing the *Wilton* case). Moreover, *Younger* and *Samuels* surface in
other contexts, where their particular doctrinal features do not operate. When, for example,
the Court invokes *Younger* because district court action would disrupt state executive functions, there is no occasion for asking whether proceedings in state court are adequate to address plaintiffs' federal claims. See notes 274-81 and accompanying text.
192. See Chapter VIII, text accompanying notes 166-70.
193. 415 U.S. 452 (1974).
194. Recall that the plaintiff in *Steffel* had not been formally charged when he filed suit
in federal court, but it was clear that he would be arrested and prosecuted if he tried to distribute his leaflets again. See Chapter IX, notes 288-90 and accompanying text. In his earlier
opinion for the Court in *Dombrowski*, Justice Brennan had it that it is *most* important that
federal courts entertain actions challenging the facial validity of state statutes. See note 135.
In *Steffel*, however, he explained that even when federal § 1983 plaintiffs claim that a valid

state interests that explain abstention when state proceedings are pending do not hold when a state prosecution is not yet under way. Moreover, he said that the Declaratory Judgment Act is meant to provide a "milder alternative" to injunctions in anticipatory suits.[195]

The holding in *Steffel* is solid and reliable. Yet Brennan's two explanations are problematic. The first understates the disruptive effects of federal declaratory judgments that preempt prospective state prosecutions. The second overstates the distinction between declaratory judgments and injunctions. By emphasizing the virtues of declaratory actions, Justice Brennan left the impression that the result might have been different if Steffel had sought an injunction. That is unlikely. The point of the Declaratory Judgment Act is to make it *unnecessary* for district courts to issue injunctions in anticipatory actions, not to foreclose injunctive relief when it is warranted. Apart from *Steffel*, the Court has recognized that both declaratory judgments and injunctions can disrupt state proceedings.[196] And in numerous other cases, including *Ex parte Young*,[197] the Court has held that injunctions, too, can be granted when plaintiffs need protection from future state prosecutions.[198]

In the end, accordingly, neither anticipatory § 1983 suits for declaratory judgments nor anticipatory § 1983 suits for injunctions are governed by *Younger/Samuels*. Both are controlled, instead, by more general discretionary and equitable considerations.[199] Typically, plaintiffs request both forms of relief.

---

statute will be unconstitutionally applied to them, a federal court can act—so long as no prosecution is yet under way.

195. 415 U.S. at 467, quoting his own concurring opinion in *Perez*, 401 U.S. at 111.

196. See text accompanying notes 139-41 (discussing Justice Black's explanation in *Samuels*).

197. 209 U.S. 123 (1908); see Chapter X, notes 134-39 and accompanying text.

198. The shareholder plaintiffs in *Young* sought a federal injunction that would shield their railroad and its employees from future prosecution for charging higher rates than state law permitted. Justice Peckham said that a federal court would not "of course" interfere with a pending state prosecution, but could enjoin a future prosecution in exceptional circumstances warranting equitable relief. Id. at 162. Peckham explained that the railroad faced irreparable injury for which there was no adequate remedy at law. The only way to test the validity of the rates fixed by state law was to violate that law on one occasion and then challenge its constitutionality as a defense to a criminal charge. Since the penalties for even one violation were stiff, Peckham doubted that the railroad could find employees willing to put themselves at risk. If a cooperative employee could be found, the railroad would still have to engage lengthy state proceedings in an attempt to establish its constitutional claim. In the interim, it would have to comply with rate limits it insisted were confiscatory. And if the railroad ultimately established that those regulations were invalid, it might not be able to recover its lost revenues. Id. at 163-65. Recalling *Young* in *Idaho v. Coeur d'Alene Tribe*, 117 S.Ct. 2028 (1997), Justice Kennedy said that there was no available state court forum in that case at all. Id. at 2035; see Chapter X, notes 154-60 and accompanying text. That was an overstatement—as Justice Souter explained in dissent in *Coeur d'Alene*. 117 S.Ct. at 2056. The holding in *Young* was that it would have been exceptionally burdensome for the railroad to press its federal claims as a defense to a state criminal action. Accordingly, there was no adequate remedy at law, and a federal court could issue an injunction that would preempt prosecution. Professor Laycock contends that in the wake of *Young*, and despite cases like *Douglas*, see note 137, federal courts often issued injunctions to protect litigants from *future* prosecution. Laycock, note 159, at 197.

199. This is the understanding to be gleaned both from the precedents as a whole and from most explicit statements from the Court. E.g., *Ankenbrandt*, 504 U.S. at 705 (stating that the Court has "never applied the notions of comity so critical to *Younger's* 'Our Feder-

When district courts are satisfied that relief of some kind is in order, they turn to the further question whether declaratory relief alone will suffice (at least in the near term). The decisive factor is the extent to which a declaratory judgment will spare § 1983 plaintiffs the risks and burdens associated with prospective prosecution. Local authorities will often respect a federal declaration that prosecution would be unlawful. If prosecuting officers initiate state proceedings in the teeth of a federal declaration, the state courts will give the federal judgment preclusive effect.[200] If the state courts, too, refuse to respect a declaratory judgment, then, as a last resort, the federal district court can issue an injunction directing local prosecutors to desist.[201]

In some circumstances, immediate injunctive relief may be warranted.[202] In *Wooley v. Maynard*,[203] the plaintiff had been prosecuted on three occasions for obscuring the state's charmingly pastoral motto ("Live Free or Die") on the license plate of his car. He filed a § 1983 action in federal court, in which he contended that the state statute forcing him to display the motto violated his first amendment rights. Chief Justice Burger said that in those circumstances the district court could properly issue an injunction against future prosecutions. There was no indication in *Wooley* that a declaratory judgment alone would deter local authorities from initiating further actions against the plaintiff. He was at risk whenever he left his driveway.[204]

---

alism' when no state proceeding [is] pending"). There is, however, a body of opinion within the Court that *Younger* and *Samuels* should control anticipatory suits, as well. That minority sentiment occasionally appears in opinions for the full Court, written by individual members who continue to press their position. E.g., *Morales v. TWA*, 504 U.S. 374, 381 n.1 (1992) (indicating that *Younger* imposes "heightened requirements for an injunction to restrain an already-pending or an about-to-be-pending state criminal action") (opinion for the Court by Scalia, J.).

200. Concurring in *Steffel*, then-Justice Rehnquist suggested the novel theory that a federal declaratory judgment issued in a § 1983 suit might not be entitled to preclusive effect in subsequent proceedings in state court. *Steffel*, 415 U.S. at 479. By his account, a federal declaratory judgment is "simply a statement" that local authorities may "choose" either to accept or to ignore. Such a declaration of rights may well persuade local officials to drop their plans to prosecute, or it may persuade the state courts to dismiss any charges that are brought. But, according to Rehnquist, if a declaratory judgment has greater effect (as a "giant step toward . . . an injunction"), it ceases to be distinguishable from an injunction at all. Id. at 481-82. But see id. at 477 (White, J., concurring) (indicating that declaratory judgments should have the usual preclusive effect). Professor Shapiro contends that federal declaratory judgments are entitled to preclusive effect and would otherwise be unintelligible. David L. Shapiro, *State Courts and Federal Declaratory Judgments*, 74 Nw. U. L. Rev. 759, 764-65 (1979). See also Chapter IX, notes 11-16 (discussing the historical debate over whether declaratory judgments constitute unconstitutional advisory opinions). In the typical case, a federal declaratory judgment will not cover all the issues in a subsequent state prosecution. Yet it will often capture the crucial issue: the validity of an individual's federal defense to a charge laid on the basis of an anticipated set of facts.

201. Recall that federal district courts are authorized to issue injunctions to enforce previously issued declaratory judgments. See Chapter VIII, note 99.

202. E.g., *Bellotti v. Baird*, 443 U.S. 622, 651 (1979) (approving anticipatory injunctive relief without discussion); see *Zablocki v. Redhail*, 434 U.S. 374, 380 n.5 (1978) (explaining that *Younger* did not bar a district court from enjoining a prospective civil proceeding threatened by local authorities).

203. 430 U.S. 705 (1977).

204. Id. at 712. Chief Justice Burger explained that the plaintiff's three prior convictions in state court did not preclude federal court action, because the plaintiff sought no relief with respect to those convictions and requested only injunctive relief regarding future ex-

This does not mean that injunctions or declaratory judgments are routinely available. The prerequisites for both are demanding.[205] Recall, moreover, that those prerequisites shade into the requirements for standing and ripeness.[206] Plaintiffs must time their applications to the federal courts with care. If they proceed too soon (before state charges are imminent), they may find that their injuries are insufficiently concrete, their claims premature. If they proceed too late (when state charges are about to be laid), they may find that they have lost the race to court, that state authorities have managed to initiate state proceedings, and that federal-question abstention as articulated in *Younger/Samuels* is controlling.[207]

Plaintiffs who file anticipatory suits in federal court can sometimes obtain temporary orders that maintain the *status quo* while their requests for injunctive or declaratory relief are under consideration. In *Doran v. Salem Inn*,[208] the proprietors of two fashionable night spots filed a § 1983 action in federal court, contending that a city ordinance banning "topless" dancing violated their first amendment rights. They sought both injunctive and declaratory protection from prosecution under the ordinance. The district court issued a preliminary injunction barring local authorities from charging the taverns until the court could determine the merits of their claims and decide whether to issue declaratory or (permanent) injunctive relief. Thereafter, the tavern operators resumed the nude performances that would otherwise have put them at risk of prosecution. The Supreme Court sustained the district court's preliminary injunction.

Justice Rehnquist explained that since the tavern operators sought federal relief when no state prosecution was pending, their cases were not governed by *Younger/Samuels*.[209] He acknowledged that the conventional equitable standards for the issuance of a preliminary injunction are strict: Applicants must show that they will suffer irreparable harm while their claims are under review and that

---

posure. Id. at 711. That will not wash. The point of preclusion is that issues that were, or might have been, determined previously ordinarily cannot be revisited in subsequent litigation. Plainly, at least some issues of fact had been determined in the three prior prosecutions and, arguably, some key issues of law—namely, federal constitutional law. See David P. Currie, *Res Judicata: The Neglected Defense*, 45 U. Chi. L. Rev. 317, 334-46 (1978); see Chapter VI, notes 169-73 and accompanying text. Recall, however, that *Wooley* was decided three years before *Allen v. McCurry*, 449 U.S. 90 (1980), in which the Court squarely held that § 1983 actions are subject to the Full Faith and Credit Statute. See Chapter VI, notes 161-63 and accompanying text. Dissenting in *Wooley*, Justices White, Blackmun, and Rehnquist said nothing about preclusion, but insisted that local authorities should have been given a chance to comply with a declaratory judgment.

205. E.g., *Boyle v. Landry*, 401 U.S. 77 (1971) (holding that African Americans who had not been personally mistreated by the Chicago police could not allege irreparable injury for purposes of a suit contesting a pattern of racially charged police misconduct in the city).

206. See Chapter IX, notes 279-90 and accompanying text.

207. See notes 213-16 and accompanying text (explaining that litigants who file federal § 1983 actions just before state authorities file state charges may still be channeled into the after-filed proceedings in state court).

208. 422 U.S. 922 (1975).

209. Writing in 1975, Justice Rehnquist limited his account of this point to the plaintiffs' request for a declaratory judgment and explicitly noted that the Court had not yet decided whether *Younger/Samuels* applied to suits for an injunction against future prosecution. 422 U.S. at 930; see note 190 and accompanying text. Since then, the Court has made it clear that the *Younger/Samuels* doctrine controls only in cases in which state proceedings are under way (or soon will be). See notes 193-204 and accompanying text.

they are "likely to prevail on the merits."[210] In the circumstances of *Salem Inn*, however, he could not say that the district court had abused its discretion in finding those standards satisfied.[211] Without a federal order protecting them from prosecution in the near term, the tavern proprietors would have been forced to choose between violating the ordinance (and inviting prosecution), on the one hand, or complying with it (and losing business), on the other. By choosing the former course, they would have surrendered their attempt to obtain a federal adjudication of their claims; by choosing the latter, they would have jeopardized their livelihood.[212]

Plaintiffs cannot always escape *Younger/Samuels* abstention by filing § 1983 actions in federal court before state authorities formally initiate prosecutions in state court. In *Hicks v. Miranda*,[213] Justice White said it would "trivialize" the "principles" of *Younger/Samuels* to let the applicability of the federal-question abstention doctrine turn on the outcome of a race to the court house.[214] In *Hicks*, local authorities charged two employees of a movie theater with the criminal offense of purveying obscene material.[215] The theater owners then filed a § 1983 action in federal court, seeking a declaration that the state obscenity statute was unconstitutional and an injunction against its enforcement. Shortly thereafter, local officials added the owners as defendants in the criminal prosecution previously filed against their employees. At that time, the federal district court entertaining the owners' § 1983 action had received motions to dismiss and for summary judgment. But it had conducted no hearings and issued no orders. Justice White held that since the owners had been named in a state criminal prosecution "before any proceedings of substance on the merits" in their federal action, the case was controlled by *Younger/Samuels*.[216]

At first glance, *Hicks* appears to be in tension with *Salem Inn*.[217] In that case, the Court allowed federal § 1983 plaintiffs to obtain a preliminary injunction insulating them from prosecution in state court while their federal lawsuit was under consideration. It may seem, then, that if the plaintiffs in *Hicks* had obtained a near-term protective order of that kind, the local authorities would not have been able to short circuit their federal action by quickly filing state charges. In *Salem Inn*, however, the preliminary injunction protected the bar operators only from prosecution on the basis of *future* behavior.[218] In *Hicks*, the theater

---

210. 422 U.S. at 931.

211. The Supreme Court's appellate review of a district court's decision to grant preliminary relief is limited to deciding whether the district court's judgment constitutes an "abuse of discretion." Id. at 931-32.

212. See note 198 (discussing the similar considerations in *Ex parte Young*). Of course, whatever commercial value the nude dancing may have had, the taverns contended that their ability to express themselves would suffer. The Chief Justice warmed more easily to the argument that profits were at stake.

213. 422 U.S. 332 (1975).

214. Id. at 350.

215. State authorities also initiated a civil proceeding in which the owners were summoned to show why the film in question ("Deep Throat") was not obscene.

216. 422 U.S. at 349.

217. See notes 208-12 and accompanying text.

218. Justice Rehnquist explained in *Salem Inn* that a third tavern operator was not entitled to a preliminary injunction, because that operator had already defied state authorities

owners would have needed protection from prosecution for past behavior. The state officials in *Hicks* filed criminal charges against the theater owners after they were already in federal court. But the basis of those charges was the operators' prior exhibition of the movie. Nothing in *Salem Inn* suggests that citizens can violate state statutes and then thwart state prosecution by promptly filing federal § 1983 lawsuits and obtaining preliminary injunctions against prosecution in state court.[219]

The decision in *Hicks* plainly *is* in tension with *Steffel* and *Wooley*.[220] Those cases appear to make the formal initiation of state proceedings crucial to deciding whether federal court action is controlled by *Younger/Samuels* or by the traditional standards for injunctive and declaratory relief: If state court proceedings are pending, *Younger/Samuels* controls; if not, traditional standards govern. According to *Hicks*, however, the crucial question is not whether a federal § 1983 action is filed before the plaintiffs in that action are prosecuted in state court. Local prosecutors can *lose* the race to the court house and *still* rely on *Younger/Samuels* to defeat a federal § 1983 action filed previously by individuals who are more fleet afoot. According to *Hicks*, the dates on which federal and state proceedings are initiated are not conclusive. The decisive question is whether proceedings in the federal lawsuit have moved beyond the "embryonic" stage.[221]

It does seem formalistic to make the applicability of *Younger/Samuels* turn entirely on whether a federal § 1983 action is filed before or after an indictment

---

and violated the ordinance. Rehnquist thus made it clear that a federal district court cannot protect a litigant from future prosecution on the basis of past behavior. Professor Laycock contends that, even if the third operator was properly denied a preliminary injunction that would block prosecution for a past violation, that operator should have been entitled to a preliminary order protecting him from prosecution for future violations. With respect to future violations, the third operator was in the same position as the two operators who *did* obtain preliminary injunctions. Laycock, note 159, at 206-07.

219. If plaintiffs' federal claims turn out to be without merit, the preliminary injunctions that have shielded them from prosecution will be withdrawn, and they may face charges for offenses committed under its aegis. It seems unfair that anyone should suffer for behavior that was effectively sanctioned by federal order at the time it occurred. Yet it is conceptually difficult to contend that a federal court can immunize conduct that later, on more thorough consideration, is determined to be criminal. See *Edgar v. MITE Corp.*, 457 U.S. 624, 647 (1982) (Stevens, J., concurring) (indicating that federal courts cannot insulate private behavior to that extent).

220. The *Hicks* case is equally in tension with *Ex parte Young*. See notes 197-98 and accompanying text. Justice Peckham explained in *Young* that a federal court that "first" assumes jurisdiction to consider plaintiffs' federal claims retains authority, "to the exclusion of all other courts," until its duty is "fully performed." When a state official who is a defendant in a federal lawsuit subsequently initiates a state criminal prosecution regarding the "same right" that is in issue in federal court, the federal court "may enjoin" the state criminal action. *Young*, 209 U.S. at 161-62.

221. *Salem Inn*, 422 U.S. at 929. This different criterion is comparatively amorphous and thus more difficult for the lower courts to apply. The Supreme Court has offered little guidance on when proceedings in federal court have progressed far enough that after-filed state court proceedings can no longer trigger *Younger/Samuels*. The Court has declined to decide whether a temporary restraining order will suffice, but has explained that a preliminary injunction *does* count as a proceeding "of substance on the merits." *Midkiff*, 467 U.S. at 238. A temporary restraining order can be issued *ex parte*; a preliminary injunction can be issued only after the defendant has an opportunity to respond, typically in a hearing.

is returned in state court. Yet it makes important conceptual sense. By some accounts, *Hicks* allows federal-question abstention to undermine the statutory scheme by which Congress makes federal courts available to adjudicate federal claims. Plaintiffs who file federal lawsuits when no state court proceedings are pending do so on the authority they are given by § 1983, invoking the jurisdiction that federal courts are given by § 1331. Yet *Hicks* permits state officials to retrieve federal questions that have been properly presented to the federal courts, drag those questions into state court, and hold them there until the state courts render decisions that are effectively final.[222]

3. Civil Proceedings in State Court

Federal-question abstention is not limited to cases in which § 1983 plaintiffs seek injunctive or declaratory relief from *criminal* prosecutions pending in state court. Federal courts also abstain when § 1983 plaintiffs seek relief from some *civil* proceedings in which particularly important state interests are implicated. In *Huffman v. Pursue*,[223] then-Justice Rehnquist recognized that abstention in favor of civil actions cannot rest on the special equitable rule that Justice Black emphasized in *Younger*—namely, the rule that courts of equity ordinarily do not enjoin criminal prosecutions.[224] Rehnquist explained, however, that other considerations fortifying *Younger* (comity and federalism) are sometimes implicated "as much" with respect to civil actions as they are with respect to criminal actions. Federal court orders preempting civil proceedings: (1) prevent the state from "effectuating its substantive policies;" (2) frustrate the state's attempt to provide a "forum competent to vindicate any constitutional objections interposed against those policies;" (3) duplicate proceedings already under way in state court; and (4) cast doubt on the state courts' ability to enforce federal law.[225]

Those four consequences would appear to attend federal injunctive or declaratory relief with respect to *any* pending state proceedings. Yet Justice Rehnquist added two further points about *Huffman* that bear significant limiting potential. The state proceeding in that case was an action to abate a movie theater as a public nuisance. According to Justice Rehnquist, it was important that: (1) state officials were the moving parties in that proceeding; and (2) while state law regarded the proceeding as civil in nature, it was "more akin to a criminal prosecution than are most civil cases."[226] The same two conditions also obtained in *Moore v. Sims*,[227] where the Court invoked federal-question abstention in favor of child custody proceedings initiated by the responsible state authorities.[228]

---

222. Professor Fiss describes a state prosecutor's capacity under *Hicks* as a "reverse removal power." Fiss, note 56, at 1136.

223. 420 U.S. 592 (1975); see notes 146-47 and accompanying text.

224. See text accompanying note 137.

225. 420 U.S. at 604.

226. Id.

227. See notes 177-82 and accompanying text.

228. See also *Trainor v. Hernandez*, 431 U.S. 434 (1977) (holding that abstention was required in deference to a state civil action to recover state funds that had allegedly been obtained unlawfully).

The two limiting factors did *not* appear in two other cases: *Juidice v. Vail*[229] and *Pennzoil v. Texaco*.[230] In *Juidice*, a New York statute allowed private creditors who had won judgments against private debtors to obtain subpoenas requiring debtors to appear and divulge their assets. If debtors failed to comply, the state courts could hold them in contempt and jail or fine them in order to force them to cooperate. A class of debtors filed a federal § 1983 action, contending that the state scheme violated the fourteenth amendment. They named state judges who had issued contempt orders as defendants and sought an injunction ordering the judges to cease.[231] The district court distinguished *Huffman*, held the statute unconstitutional, and enjoined the judges from relying on it in the future. The Supreme Court held that the district court should have abstained.

Then-Justice Rehnquist acknowledged that the moving parties in state court were private creditors (rather than state officers) and that the state proceedings were ordinary loan-default matters (not civil enforcement actions akin to criminal prosecutions). He also acknowledged that the state's interest in enforcing its "contempt process" was less important than its interest in enforcing its criminal laws and, perhaps, less important than its interest in maintaining "quasi-criminal" proceedings like the nuisance action in *Huffman*. Nevertheless, the state's interest in its contempt process was "of sufficiently great import" to warrant abstention. The contempt power "lies at the core" of the state's administration of its courts.[232] The plaintiffs in the federal class action had been given an opportunity to present their federal objections both to the state trial courts that held them in contempt and to the state appellate courts. That was sufficient to dispose of any of the recognized exceptions to *Younger/Samuels*.[233]

In *Huffman*, *Moore*, and *Juidice*, the Court declined to hold that federal-question abstention obliges federal courts to defer to *all* civil proceedings pending in state court.[234] Obviously, *Younger* and *Samuels* cannot extend to ordinary private lawsuits in state court. Recall that the Court's judicially created abstention doctrine governs only when plaintiffs seek declaratory judgments or injunctions in federal § 1983 actions.[235] Plaintiffs must, then, name defendants who act "under color" of state law.[236] The defendants in § 1983 actions are almost always state officers, and plaintiffs almost always want relief from state proceedings in which those state officers are the moving parties. Plaintiffs ordinarily have no basis for filing a federal § 1983 action against state officials, seeking a federal order protecting them from pending state lawsuits brought by other private litigants (strangers to the § 1983 action). Without some basis for proceeding under

---

229. 430 U.S. 327 (1977).

230. 481 U.S. 1 (1987).

231. Two of the plaintiffs sought damages for past violations of their federal rights, but those claims were dismissed on the basis of the judges' immunity. Today, state judges might have immunity in a case like *Juidice*, even if plaintiffs request only injunctive relief—unless the judges concerned first refuse to comply with a declaratory judgment. See Chapter X, note 254 and accompanying text.

232. 430 U.S. at 335.

233. Id. at 337. See text accompanying note 165.

234. *Huffman*, 420 U.S. at 594; *Moore*, 442 U.S. at 423 n.8; *Juidice*, 430 U.S. at 236 n.13.

235. See text accompanying note 20.

236. See Chapter VIII, text accompanying note 93; Chapter X, notes 192-94 and accompanying text.

§ 1983 in federal court, plaintiffs will be denied the relief they seek against privately initiated proceedings in state court—not because federal courts invoke *Younger* and *Samuels*, but because (in the absence of a § 1983 action) the Anti-Injunction Act establishes an independent statutory bar.[237] If the Court's interpretation of § 1983 in *Mitchum* has any practical significance at all, federal-question abstention under *Younger* and *Samuels* cannot be coextensive with § 2283.[238] Yet the further the Court extends abstention into the domain of privately initiated state proceedings, the less likely it is that federal courts will have § 1983 actions before them in which they might issue injunctions or declaratory judgments against those proceedings. At some point, *Younger* and *Samuels* lose meaning, because § 1983 no longer provides a mechanism for avoiding § 2283. And at that point, the statute takes over.[239]

The contempt case, *Juidice*, was singular in this respect inasmuch as the plaintiffs in federal court directly challenged state officials (the judges) for using heavy handed tactics to help private loan companies collect their bad debts. If a federal injunction had been available in that case, it would have run to state judicial officers. That was a rare instance, then, in which a federal § 1983 action against state officials might have produced injunctive or declaratory relief affecting private litigation in state court. Moreover, it was a case in which a federal order would have interfered with state officials' performance of an important state function—namely, the exercise of the contempt power. So *Juidice* was *both* a case in which § 1983 was available to circumnavigate § 2283 *and* a case in which there was (by the Court's account) an important state interest justifying abstention in the absence of § 2283.[240]

The *Pennzoil* case was also extraordinary, but in a different way. In that case, a private plaintiff was able to file a federal § 1983 action against another private party. Pennzoil initially sued Texaco in state court in Texas, contending that Texaco had interfered with Pennzoil's contract with another oil company. The understandably incensed jury gave Pennzoil an award of damages that seemed, in all justice, to fit Texaco's offense rather well: $10 billion, give or take a billion. Under Texas law, Pennzoil was entitled to the assistance of local constables to collect. Texaco could avoid immediate execution of the judgment pending review in the state appellate courts, if Texaco would only be so good as to post a bond in the amount of the judgment. Texaco found a bond of that magnitude a bit steep to be covered out of petty cash. So Texaco filed something else: a § 1983 action against Pennzoil in a federal district court in New York.[241] In that federal lawsuit, Texaco claimed that the state judgment violated various provisions of the Constitution and two federal statutes, and that the sizeable bond

---

237. But see notes 21-27 and accompanying (discussing two other exceptions to § 2283).

238. See notes 17-20, 156-57 and accompanying text.

239. See text accompanying note 30 (explaining that there is little reason think that federal courts should routinely enjoin state court litigation between private parties).

240. See Althouse, note 70, at 1080.

241. Texaco contended that venue was proper in New York because its offices were there and it was there that it would file for bankruptcy if its § 1983 action proved unsuccessful. The (geographically challenged) district court contrived to find venue appropriate on the theory that Texaco's federal claims "arose" in lower Manhattan. 28 U.S.C. § 1391(b). Pennzoil did not object to venue and thus forfeited any argument in that respect. See 481 U.S. at 23-24 (Marshall, J., concurring in the judgment).

that Texas required for an appeal in state court violated the fourteenth amendment. The district court enjoined Pennzoil from attempting to enforce the existing Texas state judgment. In the Supreme Court, Justice Powell explained that the district court should have abstained in light of "the principles of federalism enunciated in" *Younger*.[242]

The first order of business was whether Texaco could properly rely on § 1983 to advance its claims in federal court. If not, the Anti-Injunction Act presumably foreclosed the district court's order. To proceed under § 1983, Texaco had to establish that Pennzoil acted under color of state law. In separate opinions concurring in the judgment, four justices said that Pennzoil *would* act under color of law as soon as it invoked the Texas scheme for enforcing the state judgment and thus began working in concert with the state constabulary.[243] Justice Powell passed over that fine point and went directly to whether the circumstances warranted abstention.[244] He conceded that the equitable basis of *Younger* would not answer. But he insisted that comity mandated abstention nonetheless. His explanation was circular: Comity "mandates" abstention when "certain" civil proceedings are pending in state court and the state's interests are "so important that exercise of federal judicial power would disregard the comity between the States and the National Government."[245]

Justice Powell rested primarily on *Juidice*. By his account, the state interest the Court had found sufficient to warrant abstention there (the interest in effectuating state court judgments via the contempt power) was equally implicated in *Pennzoil*. The district court's order barring Pennzoil from executing the state judgment interfered with the state's interest in "enforcing the orders and judgments" of its courts in cases pending before those courts.[246] Powell's reliance on *Juidice* has been questioned. By some accounts, *Juidice* attached importance not to the enforcement of state judgments by means of the contempt power, but rather to the contempt power itself—used by state courts in all manner of circumstances.[247] Recall, too, that the injunction in *Juidice* would have run directly to the state judges who exercised the contempt power and thus would plainly have interfered with the state's interest in the preservation of that power. By contrast, the district court's injunction in *Pennzoil* ran to a private company (Pennzoil) and affected the state's sovereign interests only indirectly.[248]

Justice Powell also said that abstention was required in order to avoid an unwarranted federal court determination of Texaco's federal constitutional questions. If Texaco pressed its claims in state court, those courts might construe the

---

242. 430 U.S. at 10.

243. E.g., id. at 30 n.1 (Stevens, J., concurring in the judgment) See Chapter X, note 194, discussing *Lugar v. Edmondson*, 457 U.S. 922 (1982).

244. Justice Powell dissented in *Lugar*, joined by then-Justice Rehnquist and Justice O'Connor (who joined Powell's opinion in *Pennzoil*).

245. 481 U.S. at 11.

246. Id. at 13-14.

247. Professor Althouse takes this view. Althouse, note 70, at 1080-81.

248. In fact, Texas filed an *amicus* brief in the district court, denying any interest at all in the matter. According to Professor Althouse, Justice Powell's opinion in *Pennzoil* "made a rather dramatic new extension of *Younger*, applying it to a case with no state official as defendant, where the state's interest was so insignificant that the state itself disclaimed it." Id. at 1082.

statute requiring such a significant bond in a way that would save it from constitutional attack.[249] Powell acknowledged that the avoidance of federal constitutional issues is typically the point of *Pullman* abstention.[250] But he explained
(fairly enough) that *Younger* abstention, too, allows state courts an opportunity
to find alternative state law grounds for resolving disputes, thus defusing federal
questions.[251] In this regard, Justice Powell declared that "the various types of abstention" are not "rigid pigeonholes into which federal courts must try to fit
cases," but rather "reflect a complex of considerations" for softening federal-
state relations.[252]

By now, Powell was plainly dissembling. He (and most of the other justices)
were convinced that Texaco's lawsuit did not belong in federal court, and he was
merely offering additional observations to fortify the conclusion that abstention
was appropriate. Other members of the Court groped for still other approaches
to the case, arguing among themselves over whether *Rooker/Feldman* should
control.[253] In the end, the result in *Pennzoil* was scarcely surprising, but its precedential significance is problematic. By some accounts, *Pennzoil* was unique—the
product of a silly judgment in state court, audacious forum-shopping, and the
complexities that invariably attend litigation over great sums of money.[254] Powell
himself disclaimed any doctrinal innovation. He insisted that *Pennzoil* involved

---

249. Justice Powell noted that the Texas courts might read the statute with the "open
courts" provision of the state constitution and conclude that it did not authorize a bond that
no litigant could afford. 481 U.S. at 11-12.
250. See notes 57-58, 73-76 and accompanying text.
251. 481 U.S. at 11-12; see notes 138, 179 and accompanying text.
252. 481 U.S. at 11 n.9. Writing separately, Justice Blackmun relied on *Pullman* forthrightly. That was a neat trick inasmuch as Texaco had advanced no supplemental state law
claims. See notes 69-72 and accompanying text. It appears that Blackmun reached for *Pullman* in order to avoid joining Justice Powell in what Blackmun regarded as a dangerous extension of *Younger*. 481 U.S. at 27-29 (Blackmun, J., concurring). Justice Powell declined to
rest formally on *Pullman*, because Pennzoil had not argued the point. That was also a neat
trick inasmuch as the Court had previously said that it would not permit the parties to control the application of *Pullman* abstention. See note 144. It is questionable whether Justice
Powell genuinely meant in *Pennzoil* to collapse all the abstention precedents into a single
multi-faceted idea. Professor Althouse thinks it is unlikely that Powell intended his
"offhanded comment" in a footnote to have "doctrine-shattering" implications. Althouse,
note 70, at 1072-73. It is true that some of the separate abstention "doctrines" are actually
only precedents with inexact implications for other cases. See text accompanying note 90. It
is also true that the federal-question abstention doctrine associated with *Younger* has developed well beyond its intellectual roots. Still, it is hard to think that it would advance analytic clarity to collect so many distant cousins under a single roof. In the *NOPSI* case, Justice
Scalia "acknowledge[d]" that the abstention doctrines are not "rigid pigeonholes," quoting
Powell. Yet he explained that the "policy considerations" supporting *Burford* abstention, as
well as *Younger*, are sufficiently "distinct" to justify "independent analysis." *NOPSI*, 491
U.S. at 359-60; see notes 97-101 and accompanying text.
253. See Chapter VI, notes 150-55 and accompanying text. Justice Marshall thought so.
481 U.S. at 24-25 (concurring opinion). Justice Scalia thought not—because the federal
court had not been asked actually to second-guess a previous state court decision on the
merits of Texaco's federal claims. Id. at 18 (concurring opinion). Justice Brennan and Justice
Stevens preferred to reach the merits rather than rest on any door-closing device. They
would have rejected Texaco's challenge to the bond scheme.
254. Justice Marshall offered something of this view, putting *Pennzoil* down as yet another illustration of Holmes' warning that "hard cases make bad law." Id. at 26 (concurring
opinion), quoting *Northern Secur. Co. v. United States*, 193 U.S. 197, 400 (1904) (Holmes,
J., dissenting).

the same state interest previously found to be important in *Juidice* and, once again, dropped a footnote setting aside the question whether *Younger* governs cases in which the states have no special interest in private litigation pending in state court.[255] At all events, *Pennzoil* offers a good case study of the intersections between § 1983, § 2283, the abstention doctrines, and related ideas (like *Rooker/Feldman*).[256]

The Supreme Court declined in *NOPSI* to advance federal-question abstention further into new territory.[257] Recall that NOPSI filed simultaneous suits in state and federal court, advancing the same federal preemption claim in both places. The district court relied primarily on *Burford* to dismiss the federal suit, but the circuit court invoked *Younger* as well. In the Supreme Court, Justice Scalia rejected the idea that federal courts have discretion to dismiss lawsuits simply because the parties are also litigating the same issues in state court. Recalling Justice Brennan's declaration in *Colorado River*, he said that federal courts have an "unflagging" obligation to decide cases within their jurisdiction, and he depicted *Younger* as only one of a "class of cases" in which federal courts withhold otherwise authorized equitable relief to avoid "undue interference with state proceedings."[258] Justice Scalia explained that the state court review proceeding in *NOPSI* was not of the "type" to which *Younger* was applicable. He acknowledged that the Court had applied *Younger* to civil actions in *Huffman, Juidice,* and *Pennzoil*. But he insisted that the Court had never suggested that *Younger* also applies to state court review of executive or legislative action. To press *Younger* that far, he said, would make a "mockery" of the understanding that abstention is the exception, not the rule.[259]

It would be a mistake to read *NOPSI* as a belated attempt to put the *Younger* genie back in the equity bottle.[260] Justice Scalia himself recognized that

---

255. 481 U.S. at 14 n.12. Professor Althouse regards *Pennzoil* as convincing evidence that the Court has lost sight of the thinking that generated *Younger* in the first place — namely, the assumption that state courts are (typically) ready, willing, and able to adjudicate federal claims effectively. As the Court has extended *Younger* to civil actions, the Court has used as a limiting "principle" the requirement that abstention is warranted only when states have especially important interests in the state court litigation in question. Yet it is when the state has a special interest, according to Althouse, that state courts may *not* offer the kind of disinterested adjudication that *Younger* presupposes. On the one hand, *Pennzoil* appears to be a surprising and troubling further extension of *Younger* into a context in which an especially important state interest is difficult to find. Yet on the other, *Pennzoil* may represent the strongest case for abstention — for the very reason that in the *absence* of an important state interest in the enforcement of a private judgment, the state courts are ostensibly neutral and thus constitute "trustworthy" tribunals for the adjudication of federal questions. Althouse, note 70, at 1087-88.

256. The Court has not elaborated on *Pennzoil* since that case was decided. Reviewing lower court decisions three years later, Professor Baker reported inclusive results. Thomas E. Baker, *"Our Federalism" in Pennzoil Co. v. Texaco, Inc. or How the Younger Doctrine Keeps Getting Older Not Better*, 9 Rev. Litigation 303 (1990).

257. See notes 97-101 and accompanying text (discussing *NOPSI*).

258. *NOPSI*, 491 U.S. at 359.

259. Id. at 368.

260. Professor Brown has suggested that Justice Scalia's rhetoric about the obligation to exercise jurisdiction "reads like a reprint of Professor Redish's article." George D. Brown, *When Federalism and Separation of Powers Collide — Rethinking Younger Abstention*, 59 Geo. Wash. L. Rev. 114, 150 (1990). See note 66 and accompanying text. At the same time, Scalia also cited Professor Shapiro's article — which takes a decidedly different set of positions. See note 67.

Justice Black rested in *Younger* "primarily" on comity and federalism.[261] Moreover, *NOPSI* offered no occasion for a thoroughgoing examination of *Younger*
and its progeny. NOPSI did not seek injunctive or declaratory relief against a
pending state court action filed by an opposing party. By contrast, NOPSI itself
filed suit in state court.[262] Accordingly, the *NOPSI* case was not about whether a
federal district court should entertain a § 1983 action seeking a federal court
order terminating a pending state court proceeding. It was about whether a federal court should allow a litigant to press a federal claim in both federal and state
court at the same time. Parallel lawsuits can create friction. That was true in
NOPSI, where state authorities were parties to NOPSI's suit in state court and
important state regulatory interests were implicated.[263] Justice Scalia recognized
that if the federal district court reached a judgment first, its disposition might
well affect (or even preempt) the parallel state court action. Yet neither *Younger*
nor any other precedent suggests that federal courts must (or can) decline jurisdiction on those grounds alone.[264]

4. State Administrative Proceedings

Federal-question abstention is also applicable in cases in which federal
§ 1983 plaintiffs seek injunctive or declaratory relief from proceedings pending
before state administrative agencies, provided those proceedings are *judicial* in
nature.[265] In *Middlesex County Ethics Comm. v. Garden State Bar Ass'n*,[266] an
attorney filed a federal § 1983 action, seeking an injunction against the enforcement of a bar association rule forbidding lawyers to make public statements
"prejudicial to the administration of justice." At the time, the lawyer was
charged with violating that rule, and his case was pending before a state ethics
committee impaneled under the auspices of the state supreme court. In those circumstances, Chief Justice Burger sustained the district court's decision to abstain.
Burger explained that the ethics committee proceeding satisfied the three conditions for triggering *Younger*: (1) it was judicial in nature; (2) it implicated an im-

---

261. *NOPSI*, 491 U.S. at 364; see note 138 and accompanying text.
262. Justice Scalia noted that NOPSI filed the state court action only because the district court had dismissed its prior federal actions and might well dismiss its third. 491 U.S.
at 357. By the time the case reached the Supreme Court, NOPSI's suit in state court had
been consolidated with an independent suit (by the Council) for a state declaratory judgment validating the rate order and with a third suit (against the Council) by a consumer
group hoping to prevent the Council from acceding to NOPSI's demands. Since NOPSI
sought no federal relief respecting those lawsuits, their existence did not trigger *Younger* abstention. Justice Scalia noted them in a footnote. 491 U.S. at 358 n.3.
263. See text accompanying note 226.
264. Whatever may be the scope of the abstention doctrine associated with *Colorado
River*, it plainly falls well short of a general rule that federal courts must defer to parallel litigation in state court in any and all circumstances. See note 121 and accompanying text.
Most academics doubt the wisdom of extending *Younger* abstention to ordinary civil cases
in state court. For a rare endorsement, see Howard B. Stravitz, *Younger Abstention Reaches
a Civil Maturity: Pennzoil Co. v. Texaco, Inc.*, 57 Fordham L. Rev. 997 (1989).
265. See Chapter VI, text accompanying note 182 (discussing the adjudicative functions
that state agencies sometimes perform); cf. Chapter V, text accompanying notes 1-2 (noting
that federal agencies commonly adjudicate claims).
266. 457 U.S. 423 (1982).

portant state interest; and (3) it provided the § 1983 plaintiff with an "adequate opportunity" to litigate his first amendment claim. Burger acknowledged that the committee itself might not supply the necessary adjudication. But he explained that, if the committee rejected the attorney's constitutional defense, he would be entitled to seek appellate review in the state courts, which *would* consider his claim.[267]

Federal-question abstention is *not* applicable if federal § 1983 plaintiffs seek relief from state administrative proceedings that are *legislative* in nature. The characterization a state places on a proceeding carries some weight.[268] Yet federal courts make their own independent appraisals. The question can be close in some instances, the difference between judicial and legislative action being elusive. On the whole, state agency proceedings are judicial in the relevant sense if they manifest the usual features of adjudication (the determination of historical facts, the identification of the proper legal standard, and the application of the standard to the facts). Agency proceedings are legislative when they undertake the formulation of substantive policy for the future.[269]

In a final effort to invoke *Younger* in *NOPSI*, the Council contended that the district court was obliged to abstain in favor of the Council's own administrative proceeding and that, in turn, the district court was equally obliged to abstain in favor of the state courts' review of the Council's order.[270] For the first point, the Council relied on *Middlesex*; for the second, the Council cited *Huffman*, albeit by analogy.[271] Justice Scalia rejected both parts of the Council's argument. Initially, he explained that the Council's proceeding was not "judicial in nature," but was essentially legislative. Accordingly, *Middlesex* did not control. That point raised another. Recalling the *Prentis* case, Justice Scalia conceded that the district court could not enjoin a state legislative process, either—while it was under way.[272] In *NOPSI*, however, the Council's legislative action had come to an

---

267. Id. at 433-36 & n.15. The decision in *Middlesex* was arguably narrow. The ethics committee was not an ordinary state administrative agency, but was formally an instrumentality of the state courts. Even Justice Brennan concurred in the Court's judgment—though he reaffirmed his view that *Younger* is "in general inapplicable to civil proceedings." Id. at 438. In *Ohio Civil Rights Comm'n v. Dayton Christian Schools*, 477 U.S. 619 (1986), however, the Court invoked *Younger* to foreclose federal interference with a state civil rights agency's investigation of a religious school. The Commission's orders were reviewable in state court, and it was in state court that the school would receive an opportunity to litigate its first amendment claims. But there was no other relationship between the state agency and the state courts. Then-Justice Rehnquist dismissed any apparent tension with the rule that § 1983 plaintiffs need not exhaust state administrative remedies. See notes 48-52 and accompanying text (discussing *Patsy*). The religious school was not required to initiate a proceeding before the Commission as a means of obtaining affirmative relief before filing a federal § 1983 action. The Commission had itself instituted an investigation of the school for alleged violations of its employees' rights.

268. In the *Dayton* case, the Court distinguished one precedent on the ground that state law indicated that the agency in that case did not act in a judicial capacity. *Dayton Christian Schools*, 477 U.S. at 627 n.2.

269. See Chapter I, notes 5, 52-53 and accompanying text.

270. See notes 257-59 and accompanying text.

271. See notes 146-47 and accompanying text (explaining that in the *Huffman* case the Court held that a state *judicial* proceeding is "pending" for purposes of *Younger* throughout the process of appellate review in higher state courts).

272. See notes 40-41 and accompanying text (discussing *Prentis*).

end before NOPSI filed its two lawsuits (attacking the Council's legislative product) in federal and state court. Unlike the state court in *Prentis* (which exercised
legislative authority), the state court in *NOPSI* was charged with the ordinary judicial responsibility to determine whether NOPSI's attack on the Council's order
was meritorious. Accordingly, the Council's analogy to *Huffman* was of no moment. Once the Council completed its legislative activity (by producing the
order), NOPSI was free to attack that order in state court, in federal court, or in
both courts at once.[273]

5. State Executive Activities

Federal-question abstention is also applicable in some cases in which federal
§ 1983 plaintiffs seek injunctive or declaratory relief with respect to certain kinds
of executive activity. Recall that in *O'Shea v. Littleton*[274] and *Rizzo v. Goode*,[275]
the Supreme Court held that federal district courts could not issue orders barring
the police in Chicago and Philadelphia from continuing a pattern of abusive behavior, typically targeting racial minorities. In the main, the Court held (in both
cases) that the plaintiffs' federal claims were not ripe for adjudication in an Article III court.[276] That ground was sufficient in itself (formally speaking) to dispose
of the two cases. Yet in both instances the Court went on to rely in the alternative on equitable considerations, comity, and federalism. And in so doing, the
Court explicitly invoked *Younger* and cases in the *Younger* line.

In *O'Shea*, Justice White said that *Younger* reaffirmed that federal courts
should not ordinarily restrain state criminal prosecutions. That idea, in turn, lead
to another: The need for a "proper balance" between "federal and state *courts*"
counsels restraint regarding injunctions against "state officers engaged in the *administration* of the State's criminal laws."[277] In *Rizzo*, then-Justice Rehnquist also
acknowledged that the "principles of federalism" elaborated in *Younger* and its
progeny were "initially expounded and perhaps entitled to the greatest weight" in
cases in which federal courts are asked to enjoin state criminal prosecutions. Yet
he, too, insisted that the same "principles" have "applicability where injunctive
relief is sought, *not* against the *judicial* branch of... state government, but against
those in charge of an *executive* branch of... state or local government."[278]

---

273. Since Justice Scalia held that the Council's own action was not judicial in nature
and thus did not bring *Younger* abstention into play, he had no occasion to decide whether
the Council's analogy to *Huffman* was sound. He only assumed the validity of that analogy
for purposes of analysis. 491 U.S. at 369. Concurring in the judgment, Justice Blackmun
was "not entirely persuaded" that the question was actually "open." Id. at 374-75 (concurring opinion). Recall that in *Dayton Christian Schools*, Justice Rehnquist said that the
school would have an opportunity to press its federal claim in state court, on judicial review
of the agency's action in that case. See note 267. Justice Scalia acknowledged in *NOPSI* that,
in that way, *Dayton Christian Schools* "suggested" that (by analogy to *Huffman*) a state administrative proceeding that is sufficiently judicial to invoke *Younger* remains pending while
the agency's order is reviewed in state court. 491 U.S. at 369 n.4 (majority opinion).
274. 414 U.S. 488 (1974).
275. 423 U.S. 362 (1976).
276. See Chapter IX, notes 279-81 and accompanying text.
277. *O'Shea*, 414 U.S. at 499 (emphasis added).
278. *Rizzo*, 423 U.S. at 380 (emphasis added).

These passages do not simply cite *Younger* and related abstention cases as illustrations of the way in which equitable restraint, comity, and federalism temper federal court action with respect to the states. They purport actually to extend at least the "principles" associated with *Younger* to entirely different precincts — federal court actions challenging state executive activities. It is hard to think that the idea in *Younger* can range so far afield and still retain any trace of its original character. By some accounts, *O'Shea* and *Rizzo* abandon any pretense that the Supreme Court is elaborating coherent doctrine governing abstention and essentially concede that *Younger* is a short-hand for a general refusal to entertain civil rights actions for the vindication of fourteenth amendment rights against state power.[279] All the same, *O'Shea* and *Rizzo* were decided in the middle 1970s, when the Court was taking aggressive steps to bring the expansive Warren Court period to a close.[280] More recent decisions touching *Younger* suggest that the Court may now be less intent on withholding federal judicial power in cases in which § 1983 and § 1331 authorize its use.[281]

---

279. E.g., H. Jefferson Powell, *The Compleat Jeffersonian: Justice Rehnquist and Federalism*, 91 Yale L.J. 1317, 1343-44 (1982); Soifer & Macgill, note 137, at 1215; Weinberg, note 163, at 1215-22.

280. See Chapter I, text accompanying note 77.

281. See notes 257-59 and accompanying text.

Chapter XII

Habeas Corpus

The writ of habeas corpus is the traditional Anglo-American vehicle for inquiring into the validity of personal detention. The writ takes its name, "you have the body," from the basic purpose it serves.[1] Historically, the writ has been an unusually efficient and expeditious device for ensuring that prisoners do not suffer deprivations of liberty without prompt judicial attention. In addition, the writ has been an instrument of governmental administration, both holding government to answer in independent courts and reconciling conflicts of jurisdiction between different courts competing for hegemony. The writ often figures in federal court battles with the executive and legislative branches of the national government and equally in confrontations between federal courts and the states. Habeas corpus cases thus invariably implicate the separation principle and federalism.[2]

A. Function and History of the Writ

Prisoners in state custody typically seek federal habeas corpus relief *after* state courts have had an opportunity to pass on their claims.[3] As a formal matter, applications for the federal writ are not subject to state preclusion rules under the Full Faith and Credit Statute.[4] On first blush, then, federal habeas appears to offer (on a deferred basis) what the federal-question abstention doctrine (and so many other doctrines, as well) usually deny at earlier stages — namely, a federal forum for the adjudication of federal claims. The writ occasionally functions in precisely that way. Nevertheless, modern habeas corpus is so tightly restricted that litigants who are unable to gain access to federal court before or during state proceedings are also typically foreclosed thereafter. Various statutes

---

1. II Pollock & Maitland, History of English Law 593 n.4 (1898).

2. Recall that some of the most famous cases in federal courts law originated as petitions for the writ of habeas corpus. In *Ex parte McCardle*, the Supreme Court maneuvered for position with respect to Congress. See Chapter IV, notes 54-72 and accompanying text. And in *Ex parte Young*, the Court grappled with the relationship between the federal judiciary and the states. See Chapter X, notes 134-39 and accompanying text.

3. See notes 72-95 and accompanying text (discussing the exhaustion doctrine).

4. *Kremer v. Chem. Constr. Corp.*, 456 U.S. 461, 485 n.27 (1982); see Chapter VI, note 164 and accompanying text.

and judge-made doctrines establish federal door-closing rules in the interests of comity.[5]

The origins of habeas corpus can be traced to the early central courts in England.[6] Initially, those courts issued the writ to obtain the presence of individuals so that matters in which they were involved could be adjudicated.[7] Later, the common law courts (King's Bench and Common Pleas) used the writ to draw litigation away from local manorial courts and to bring cases under the King's central authority.[8] Later still, those courts also relied on the writ in their competition with Chancery, which administered the King's equity.[9] Ultimately, they used the writ to challenge the King's own prerogatives.[10] In the Seventeenth Century, John Selden and Lord Coke fashioned habeas corpus into a procedural device for enforcing the thirty-ninth chapter of Magna Charta, which, by their (creative) account, barred the King from summarily sending Englishmen to the Tower of London. According to Selden and Coke, imprisonment at the King's command alone violated the "law of the land," which Coke abbreviated as "due process."[11] The English Habeas Corpus Act of 1679 established procedures for using the writ routinely to prevent the Crown from holding prisoners in jail for lengthy periods awaiting trial. Thereafter, Parliament occasionally denied the writ *ad hoc* in cases of "high treason." On the whole, however, habeas corpus continued to develop as the Great Writ of Liberty.[12]

American colonists laid claim to the writ of habeas corpus as one of the rights they were due as Englishmen. But historians have no clear picture of the writ's actual use in the colonial period.[13] It was not until after the Constitution was adopted that most states enacted American versions of the English Act of 1679. By some accounts, the paucity of earlier statutes actually demonstrates that habeas was well entrenched: The colonists may have thought the writ was so fundamental that it needed no codification in legislation or state constitutions.[14]

---

5. See notes 96-130 and accompanying text (discussing procedural default doctrine).

6. See 9 William S. Holdsworth, History of English Law 108-09 (4th ed. 1926); Daniel J. Meador, Habeas Corpus and Magna Carta 7-9 (1966).

7. Robert J. Sharpe, The Law of Habeas Corpus 2 n.1 (1976).

8. See Robert Walker, The Constitutional and Legal Development of Habeas Corpus as the Writ of Liberty 25 (1960) (linking the writ to the "centralization of judicial power in the hands of the royal courts").

9. Holdsworth, note 6, at 109-10.

10. In the typical scenario, Chancery issued injunctions forbidding would-be litigants to sue in the law courts and, if they failed to comply, ordered them imprisoned for contempt. Then, the law courts protected their own turf by issuing the writ of habeas corpus to discharge the prisoners and allow them to sue, after all.

11. Meador, note 6, at 14-20; Walker, note 8, at 24; William F. Duker, *The English Origins of the Writ of Habeas Corpus: A Peculiar Path to Fame*, 53 N.Y.U. L. Rev. 983, 1031-32 (1978).

12. Rollin C. Hurd, A Treatise on the Right of Personal Liberty and on the Writ of Habeas Corpus 122-27 (1858).

13. See Dallin H. Oaks, *Habeas Corpus in the States—1776-1865*, 32 U. Chi. L. Rev. 243 (1965); Neil McFeeley, *The Historical Development of Habeas Corpus*, 30 Sw. L.J. 585 (1976).

14. This was Professor Chafee's view. Zechariah Chafee, Jr., *The Most Important Human Right in the Constitution*, 32 B.U. L. Rev. 143, 146 (1952).

1. The Suspension Clause

The delegates to the Philadelphia Convention referred to the writ of habeas corpus in the text of the new Constitution, but only in the oblique Suspension Clause: "The Privilege of the Writ of Habeas Corpus shall not be suspended unless when in Cases of Rebellion or Invasion the public Safety may require it."[15] That language does not explicitly confer jurisdiction on federal courts to issue the writ. Instead, it presupposes that the writ already exists and addresses only the circumstances in which access to it can be suspended—presumably by Congress.[16] The records of the Convention, such as they are, provide little interpretive help. The delegates debated only whether to allow suspension in cases of emergency.[17]

By some accounts, the Suspension Clause amounts to very little. At most, it contemplates that *state* courts may have authority to issue the writ of habeas corpus and limits Congress' authority to interfere with that jurisdiction: Parliament had routinely suspended the writ in England in order to keep dissenters in prison, so the Convention put a provision in the new American Constitution that would prevent Congress from following that course.[18] By other accounts, the Suspension Clause means a great deal. It constitutes a self-executing source of *federal* judicial power, authorizing federal courts to issue the writ of habeas corpus in appropriate cases: The Suspension Clause may not obligate Congress to create inferior federal courts. But if Congress chooses to establish inferior courts, Congress cannot deny those courts power to entertain habeas corpus applications. To do so would be to suspend the writ.[19]

If it is once posited that the Suspension Clause has something to do with the authority of federal courts, further debates typically slide into quarrels about the scope of a federal court's purview in a habeas corpus case. Two questions are paramount: (1) whether the Suspension Clause is exclusively concerned with

---

15. U.S. Const. art. I, § 9, cl.2.

16. Note that the Suspension Clause is located in § 9 of Article I, where certain limitations on congressional power are collected. In 1861, President Lincoln purported to suspend the writ in order to permit union troops to administer martial law in civilian areas. Chief Justice Taney wrote an order in *Ex parte Merryman*, 17 F. Cas. 144 (1861), insisting that only Congress had that power. Military leaders ignored Taney's opinion at the time. Congress later defused the issue by enacting legislation ratifying Lincoln's action. See Martin S. Sheffer, *Presidential Power to Suspend Habeas Corpus: The Taney-Bates Dialogue and Ex parte Merryman*, 11 Okla. City U. L. Rev. 1 (1986).

17. Professor Freedman argues that the delegates in Philadelphia and at the ratifying conventions did not debate whether federal courts would have power to issue the writ, because there was widespread agreement that those courts *would* have that jurisdiction as a matter of course. Eric M. Freedman, *The Suspension Clause in the Ratification Debates*, 44 Buffalo L. Rev. 451 (1996).

18. William F. Duker, A Constitutional History of Habeas Corpus 126-56 (1980); Akhil R. Amar, *Of Sovereignty and Federalism*, 96 Yale L.J. 1425, 1509 (1987); Rex A. Collings, Jr., *Habeas Corpus for Convicts—Constitutional Right or Legislative Grace?*, 40 Calif. L. Rev. 335, 345 (1952). Professor Meltzer has pointed out that this interpretation of the Suspension Clause necessarily denies that *Tarble's Case* was a constitutional decision. Daniel J. Meltzer, *Congress, Courts, and Constitutional Remedies*, 86 Gtn. L.J. 2537, 2566-67 (1998). See Chapter VI, note 107 and accompanying text.

19. Francis Paschal, *The Constitution and Habeas Corpus*, 1970 Duke L.J. 605.

prisoners held in executive detention without trial or, instead, also addresses prisoners serving sentences after conviction; and (2) whether the Suspension Clause is exclusively concerned with prisoners held by federal authorities or, instead, also addresses prisoners in state custody. Originalists typically insist that the Suspension Clause guarantees the writ of habeas corpus only in the form in which it existed in England in 1787. Beginning from that premise, different originalists give different answers to these two key questions, depending on their reading of the relevant historical materials.[20] Meanwhile, non-originalists deny that the Suspension codifies the writ as it was fixed in 1787 and contend, by contrast, that it constitutionalizes a dynamic procedural device that was changing even then and has never ceased to evolve over time.[21] Non-originalists, too, disagree among themselves, but typically argue that the Suspension Clause can and should be understood to ensure federal court authority to entertain petitions from convicts in the custody of state, as well as federal, authorities.[22]

The Supreme Court has never given the Suspension Clause an authoritative interpretation. Chief Justice Marshall intimated in *Ex parte Bollman*[23] that federal court authority to issue the writ depends entirely on the jurisdictional statues that Congress enacts: "[T]he power to award the writ by any of the courts of the United States must be given by *written law*."[24] That suggested that the Suspension Clause has no independent significance and that Congress may give federal courts jurisdiction in habeas corpus cases or not, as Congress pleases—within the ordinary parameters established by Article III. Then again, Marshall's purpose in *Bollman* was to disclaim any common law authority to issue the writ. He

---

20. Justice Brennan once said that the writ *did* extend to convicts in 1787. *Fay v. Noia*, 372 U.S. 391, 403 (1963), citing the English precedent in *Bushell's Case*, 124 Eng. Rep. 1006 (1670). See also *McNally v. Hill*, 293 U.S. 131, 135 (1934) (explaining that the Suspension Clause "implicitly recognize[s]" the "use of the writ" by sentenced prisoners). According to Chief Justice Burger, however, courts in 1787 had no authority to issue the writ on behalf of petitioners held in jail under court order. In Burger's view, then, the Suspension Clause allows Congress to deny the writ to convicts, even if they claim to have been convicted and sentenced in violation of federal law. *Swain v. Pressley*, 430 U.S. 372, 386 (1977) (Burger, C.J., concurring). It is scarcely surprising that there is no abundance of early precedent regarding the availability of the writ for convicts. It was not until the 1830s that incarceration became a common means of punishing criminal offenders. Prior to that time, a criminal conviction and sentence typically terminated pre-trial detention, rendering habeas corpus no longer necessary. Marc M. Arkin, *The Ghost at the Banquet: Slavery, Federalism, and Habeas Corpus for State Prisoners*, 70 Tulane L. Rev. 1, 10-11 & n.40 (1995). The Court held in *Ex parte Dorr*, 44 U.S. (3 How.) 103 (1845), that the federal courts' habeas corpus jurisdiction did not (at that time) reach prisoners in state custody. But the Court did not mention the Suspension Clause in *Dorr*.

21. In a famous brief, Professor Freund once contended that "[w]e shall have to look to history for the essentials of the Great Writ, but not to one point in that history." Brief for Respondent, *United States v. Hayman*, 342 U.S. 205 (1952). For an illustration of a non-originalist interpretation of the Suspension Clause focusing on immigration cases, see Gerald L. Neuman, *Habeas Corpus, Executive Detention, and the Removal of Aliens*, 98 Colum. L. Rev. 961, 970 (1998).

22. Professor Steiker argues that the fourteenth amendment "constitutionalized" federal court responsibility to determine federal claims in criminal cases and thus imposed an obligation on Congress to extend habeas jurisdiction to applications from state convicts. Jordan Steiker, *Incorporating the Suspension Clause: Is There a Constitutional Right to Federal Habeas Corpus for State Prisoners?*, 92 Mich. L. Rev. 862 (1994).

23. 8 U.S. (4 Cranch) 75 (1807).

24. Id. at 94 (emphasis added). See Chapter IV, text accompanying notes 19-20.

did not mention the Suspension Clause. Accordingly, he did not specify that only a *statute* could supply the written law required (rather than the Suspension Clause itself). Moreover, Marshall *did* say this in *Bollman*: "[Congress] must have felt, with peculiar force, the *obligation* of providing efficient means by which this great *constitutional* privilege should receive life and activity; for if the means be not in existence, the privilege itself would be lost."[25]

Since Congress has generally provided for federal jurisdiction in habeas corpus cases, the Court has had few occasions to consider whether a restriction on that jurisdiction might be unconstitutional. The Judiciary Act of 1789 granted federal courts authority to entertain habeas corpus petitions from prisoners in federal custody.[26] Other statutes expanded that jurisdiction incrementally.[27] Then, during Reconstruction, the 1867 Act opened federal courts to petitions from state prisoners claiming to be deprived of their liberty in violation of federal law.[28] The derivative modern statute, 28 U.S.C. § 2241(a), (c)(3), describes the federal habeas corpus jurisdiction in the negative: "Writs of habeas corpus may be granted by the Supreme Court, any justice thereof, the district courts and any circuit judge within their respective jurisdictions." But the writ of habeas corpus "shall not extend to a prisoner" unless "[h]e is in custody in violation of the Constitution or laws or treaties of the United States."[29]

The Court occasionally relies on the Suspension Clause for leverage in reaching an appropriate construction of § 2241 and related statutes. In partial justification for reading statutory language to leave federal court authority intact, the Court explains that an alternative construction would raise Suspension Clause questions.[30] The precedents in point typically involve convicts attempting to attack their convictions. Sometimes, those convicts complain that they are held in

---

25. 8 U.S. at 95 (emphasis added). The issue in *Bollman* was whether the Supreme Court had authority to entertain an "original" habeas corpus petition. See Chapter IV, note 70.

26. See Chapter II, note 56 and accompanying text.

27. In 1833 and 1842, respectively, Congress gave federal courts power to issue the writ on behalf of federal officials and foreign nationals held in state custody. See Armistead M. Dobie, *Habeas Corpus in the Federal Courts*, 13 Va. L. Rev. 433, 442 (1927).

28. It has been argued that the 1867 Act was actually meant to make the writ available to emancipated slaves and indentured servants held in a state of peonage after the Civil War. See Lewis Mayers, *The Habeas Corpus Act of 1867: The Supreme Court as Legal Historian*, 33 U. Chi. L. Rev. 31 (1965). That account depends on thin evidence regarding the drafters' personal intentions. Those drafters promoted the bill to their colleagues as a means of extending the writ to state prisoners generally. See Larry W. Yackle, *Form and Function in the Administration of Justice: The Bill of Rights and Federal Habeas Corpus*, 23 U. Mich. J. L. Ref. 685, 695-98 (1990). Professor Forsythe contends that the "plain language" of the 1867 Act makes it clear that convicts would not be eligible petitioners. He fortifies that interpretation with other remnants of legislative history which, in his view, demonstrate that the proponents' floor speeches do not tell the full story. Clarke D. Forsythe, *The Historical Origins of Broad Federal Habeas Review Reconsidered*, 70 Notre Dame L. Rev. 1079, 1105-17 (1995).

29. Read literally, § 2241 confers jurisdiction on both the Supreme Court and its individual justices, on the district courts as corporate bodies, but then only on circuit judges individually. In practice, those distinctions make no difference. For a discussion, see Larry W. Yackle, Postconviction Remedies 80-84 (1981).

30. E.g., *Hayman*, 342 U.S. at 223. See Chapter I, note 21 (noting the avoidance principle generally).

state, not federal, custody.[31] The Court is clearly at pains to avoid grappling with the Suspension Clause and determining what, if anything, that clause adds to Article III. In *Felker v. Turpin*,[32] for example, Chief Justice Rehnquist assumed for purposes of analysis that the Suspension Clause "refers to the writ as it exists today, rather than as it existed in 1789."[33]

2. Challenges to Executive Detention

Habeas corpus is not limited to applicants who contend they are detained unlawfully in connection with criminal charges. Deprivations of liberty are rare apart from the criminal process, but not unknown. Illustrations include selective service cases in which petitioners face involuntary conscription into the military services and immigration cases in which petitioners face exclusion from the country or deportation. Congress occasionally enacts legislation curbing judicial review of induction decisions. Yet in the celebrated World War II case, *Estep v. United States*,[34] some of the justices explained that the usual means by which federal claims were adjudicated could be curtailed *because* disappointed inductees could still file applications for habeas corpus relief.[35]

Immigrants threatened with exclusion or deportation are also typically entitled to challenge their treatment in federal habeas corpus proceedings. The Court held as much in one of the early Chinese exclusion cases, *United States v. Jung Ah Lung*.[36] In the immigration context, however, the Court has sometimes permitted Congress to immunize executive actions from judicial examination. In the leading case, *Nishimura Ekiu v. United States*,[37] Justice Gray relied expressly on the theory that immigration cases implicate "public rights" that need not be subject to adjudication in the courts.[38] A provision of current law, 8 U.S.C. § 1252, authorizes immigration officials to deport aliens who have committed certain crimes and explicitly makes orders of that kind "final"—not subject "to review by any court." That provision apparently eliminates ordinary review mechanisms. Its effect on federal court jurisdiction to entertain habeas corpus petitions

---

31. E.g., *United States v. MacCollom*, 426 U.S. 317, 322-23 (1976) (mentioning but avoiding a Suspension Clause claim in a case involving a federal convict); *Jones v. Cunningham*, 371 U.S. 236, 238 (1963) (stating in a case involving a state convict that the habeas corpus statutes implement the "constitutional command that the writ of habeas corpus be made available"); see *Schlup v. Delo*, 513 U.S. 298, 343 (1995) (Scalia, J., dissenting) (referring to Congress' authority to curtail federal habeas corpus for state prisoners "within the very broad limits set by the Suspension Clause").

32. 518 U.S. 651 (1996); see Chapter IV, note 67 and accompanying text.

33. *Felker*, 518 U.S. at 664. The Court focused in *Felker* not on the Suspension Clause, but on the Article III implications of a statute that (arguably) deprived the Court itself of jurisdiction to supervise actions at the circuit level. Professor Fallon and Professor Cole contend that the Suspension Clause cannot be considered in isolation from Article III and due process. Richard H. Fallon, Jr., *Applying the Suspension Clause to Immigration Cases*, 98 Colum. L. Rev. 1068 (1998); David Cole, *Jurisdiction and Liberty: Habeas Corpus and Due Process as Limits on Congress's Control of Federal Jurisdiction*, 86 Gtn. L.J. 2481 (1998).

34. 327 U.S. 114 (1946).

35. Id. at 146 (Burton, J., dissenting).

36. 124 U.S. 621 (1888).

37. 142 U.S. 651 (1892).

38. See Chapter V, notes 63-75 and accompanying text (discussing *Murray's Lessee*).

is problematic, particularly in cases in which litigants advance constitutional claims.[39] Since § 1252 does not jettison habeas jurisdiction expressly, it may leave that jurisdiction in place. If it abrogates all judicial review, including habeas corpus, it may be unconstitutional.[40]

3. Challenges to Criminal Convictions

The most controversial habeas corpus cases involve prison inmates who have been convicted of criminal offenses and sentenced to incarceration or death. According to conventional theory, a habeas corpus proceeding is not part of the criminal prosecution undertaken by government prosecutors. A prisoner who files a petition initiates an original civil lawsuit, naming the custodian (usually the prison warden) as the respondent and hoping to show that the custodian has no lawful basis for depriving the prisoner of liberty. The federal court entertaining the petition is not (typically) concerned about whether the prisoner is guilty or innocent.[41] Nor does the federal court presume (formally) to second-guess the

---

39. See Chapter V, note 124 and accompanying text (linking public rights cases to federal statutory claims). But see Cole, note 33, at 2502 (arguing that due process requires that aliens in detention be given an opportunity to advance non-constitutional claims against their custody); Jonathan L. Hafetz, *The Untold Story of Noncriminal Habeas Corpus and the 1996 Immigration Acts*, 107 Yale L.J. 2509 (1998) (contending that habeas corpus was available in deportation cases at common law and that it would be unconstitutional for Congress to restrict federal courts to constitutional claims).

40. Compare *Williams v. INS*, 114 F.3d 82 (5th Cir. 1997) (holding that § 1252 does not abolish federal habeas corpus jurisdiction pursuant to § 2241), with *Magana-Pizano v. INS*, 152 F.3d 1213 (9th Cir. 1998) (holding that § 1252 violates the Suspension Clause to the extent it purports to deprive federal district courts of habeas corpus jurisdiction to determine constitutional claims). Professor Neuman and Professor Cole develop an elaborate argument that the Suspension Clause bars Congress from absolutely foreclosing habeas jurisdiction in immigration cases. Neuman, note 21; Cole, note 33. See Chapter IV, notes 83-89 (discussing the preclusion of judicial review generally). Professor Fallon contends that immigration cases illustrate the difficulties of assimilating the public rights tradition into a coherent modern framework. In his view, the argument that immigration cases simply *are* public rights cases and therefore can be determined without judicial involvement at all proves too much. To reconcile immigration cases with developed understandings in adjacent fields, the public rights idea should be reconceptualized as a recognition that Congress can specify the form that Article III court involvement should take. In many instances, according to Fallon, after-the-fact judicial review, via habeas corpus or some other procedural vehicle, is both necessary and sufficient to satisfy the Suspension Clause, Article III, and due process. See Fallon, note 33; Chapter V, notes 104-06 and accompanying text (noting that the existence of Article III court review is a factor affecting the validity of non-Article III adjudication in public rights cases). Professor Meltzer has doubts about the argument that aliens have a constitutional right of access to a federal court. But he thinks aliens probably do have a right of access to some court, perhaps a state court. Meltzer, note 18, at 2566-74.

41. *Noia*, 372 U.S. at 422-24. Since federal habeas courts have jurisdiction only to consider federal claims, it would be strange if they were expected to attend to fact-sensitive questions of criminal liability under state criminal law. Nevertheless, there is a body of opinion to the effect that federal habeas corpus requires some morally persuasive justification, and the idea that federal courts may detect mistaken convictions may fill that void. Thinking along these lines typically produces procedural rules for the conduct of habeas litigation that privilege legal claims linked in some way to actual innocence. See, e.g., notes 119-21, 139-40, 234 and accompanying text. Judge Friendly authored the most celebrated statement of the argument. Henry Friendly, *Is Innocence Irrelevant? Collateral Attack on Criminal Judg-*

court that conducted the criminal trial and imposed the sentence.[42] Instead, the federal court focuses exclusively on the validity of the prisoner's current detention. As a practical matter, however, the custodian invariably offers the conviction and sentence as the explanation for the prisoner's custody. And when the federal court evaluates that explanation, the court necessarily also examines federal issues that the sentencing court determined previously. In a real sense, then, federal habeas corpus is a device by which prisoners can ask federal courts to revisit prior judgments regarding federal claims.[43]

Congress occasionally adjusts this conceptual picture legislatively and, in so doing, recognizes what petitioners genuinely mean to accomplish. For example, Congress has largely eliminated the ability of *federal* convicts to attack their convictions and sentences collaterally under §2241 and substituted a motion procedure to perform the same function. Pursuant to 28 U.S.C. §2255, a federal prisoner who claims "the right to be released" from confinement under a sentence imposed in violation of federal law may "move the court which imposed" the sentence "to vacate, set aside or correct" it. A federal prisoner who is authorized to file a §2255 motion can petition for habeas corpus relief under §2241 only if a §2255 motion is "inadequate or ineffective to test the legality of his detention."[44] The Supreme Court sustained §2255 in *United States v. Hayman*.[45] Chief Justice Vinson assumed (but did not decide) that the Suspension Clause would bar Congress from abrogating the writ of habeas corpus, even in cases in which prisoners are serving sentences for criminal offenses. But he read §2255 to authorize an equally "independent and collateral inquiry into the validity" of federal custody. Since federal prisoners lost nothing in the switch from §2241 to §2255, there was no constitutional difficulty. Today, §2255 provides federal prisoners with a means of access to federal court that is "exactly commensurate" with the writ of habeas corpus that was previously available to them.[46] The only

---

ments, 38 U. Chi. L. Rev. 142 (1970). See note 58 (noting a proposal by Professor Hoffmann and Professor Stuntz to use a "colorable" showing of innocence in a different way).

42. *Coleman v. Thompson*, 501 U.S. 722, 730 (1991).

43. Federal district courts have no appellate jurisdiction to review state court judgments for error in the ordinary course. See Chapter VI, notes 149-55 and accompanying text (discussing the *Rooker/Feldman* doctrine). Nevertheless, habeas has an undeniable appellate flavor, and numerous academics contend that is it best understood as an appellate mechanism. E.g., Barry Friedman, *A Tale of Two Habeas*, 73 Minn. L. Rev. 247 (1988); Barry Friedman, *Pas De Deux: The Supreme Court and the Habeas Courts*, 66 So. Calif. L. Rev. 2467 (1993); James S. Liebman, *Apocalypse Next Time?: The Anachronistic Attack on Habeas Corpus/Direct Review Parity*, 92 Colum. L. Rev. 1997 (1992).

44. Cases in which a §2255 motion is inadequate in this sense are virtually non-existent. In *Triestman v. United States*, 124 F.3d 361 (2d Cir. 1997), the court held that §2255 was inadequate (and that a habeas corpus petition under §2241 was therefore available), because §2255 would not permit a prisoner to file a second application advancing a novel non-constitutional federal claim.

45. 342 U.S. 205 (1952).

46. *Hill v. United States*, 368 U.S. 424, 427 (1962). See also *Heflin v. United States*, 358 U.S. 415, 418 n.7 (1959) (stating that a §2255 proceeding is equally "an independent civil suit"). The characterizations of §2255 in *Hayman*, *Hill*, and *Heflin* are hard to reconcile with *United States v. Morgan*, 346 U.S. 502 (1954), where the Court said that a §2255 motion is of the "same general character" as a petition for a writ of coram nobis—which is traditionally understood to be a further step in a criminal case and *not* an independent civil proceeding. Id. at 505 n.4. The point, however, is that §2255 affords federal prisoners the

practical difference is that, previously, habeas corpus petitions under § 2241 were filed in a district court near the place of confinement, while § 2255 motions are filed in the sentencing court.[47]

It is debatable whether federal prisoners should be entitled to attack criminal judgments collaterally—by means of § 2255, habeas corpus, or any other vehicle. It is also debatable whether state prisoners should be entitled to petition federal district courts for habeas corpus relief from state criminal convictions and sentences. Federal habeas corpus following state criminal prosecutions appears to be inefficient, even redundant. Elsewhere, statutes and judge-crafted doctrines channel federal question litigation either to state court or to federal court, and proponents of federal adjudication are pressed to explain why a federal forum should be available. In this context, litigants who have once *been* to state court claim an entitlement to litigate *again* in federal court.

The explanation is historical and functional. Federal habeas corpus for state prisoners is largely the product of the Supreme Court's efforts in the middle decades of this century to improve the quality of state criminal justice. In the famous "incorporation" decisions, the Court read the fourteenth amendment to make the procedural safeguards prescribed in the Bill of Rights applicable to criminal cases tried in state court.[48] Simultaneously, the Court expanded the scope of federal habeas corpus so that federal courts could enforce those rights. The Court recognized that it could not police fifty state courts by exercising appellate jurisdiction alone and so turned to the lower federal courts as surrogates. On examination, then, the availability of federal habeas after state courts have completed their work is not anomalous. Habeas provides prisoners deprived of their liberty an opportunity to press any federal claims they may have in federal court at a time when federal adjudication can no longer interfere with ongoing proceedings in state court.[49]

---

same postconviction access to a federal judicial forum that was previously achieved by means of habeas corpus.

47. By all accounts, Congress created § 2255 motions primarily as a docket control measure. Previously, district courts located near major federal penitentiaries were swamped with § 2241 habeas corpus petitions. Moreover, those courts faced practical difficulties. The relevant files and records were in the sentencing court, and if a hearing was necessary the witnesses were typically near that court, as well. By rerouting prisoners to the sentencing court, Congress hoped to achieve greater efficiency in the adjudication of the same kinds of claims. See John J. Parker, *Limiting the Abuse of Habeas Corpus*, 8 F.R.D. 171 (1948). Prisoners convicted in the local courts of the District of Columbia are similarly barred from seeking federal habeas relief from district courts and must, instead, file postconviction motions in the courts in which they were sentenced. The Supreme Court sustained that scheme in *Swain v. Pressley*, 430 U.S. 372 (1977), relying heavily on an analogy to § 2255. The statute controlling District of Columbia cases tracks the language of § 2255 verbatim—and thus includes the (formally important) proviso that habeas corpus remains available if the motion remedy proves to be "inadequate or ineffective to test the legality" of a prisoner's detention. But see note 44.

48. See Kenneth Pye, *The Warren Court and Criminal Procedure*, 67 Mich. L. Rev. 249 (1968); Henry Friendly, *The Bill of Rights as a Code of Criminal Procedure*, 53 Calif. L. Rev. 929 (1965).

49. See generally William J. Brennan, Jr., *Federal Habeas Corpus and State Prisoners: An Exercise in Federalism*, 7 Utah L. Rev. 423 (1961); Robert M. Cover & T. Alexander Aleinikoff, *Dialectical Federalism: Habeas Corpus and the Court*, 86 Yale L.J. 1035 (1977); Daniel J. Meador, *The Impact of Federal Habeas Corpus on State Trial Procedures*, 52 Va.

By most accounts, the idea that federal habeas should be a sequel to state criminal proceedings began with Justice Holmes' great dissent in Leo Frank's case.[50] It took hold in Holmes' opinion for the Court in *Moore v. Dempsey*,[51] emerged fully developed in Justice Frankfurter's opinion in *Brown v. Allen*,[52] and then flowered in a trilogy of decisions in the Warren Court period—*Fay v. Noia*,[53] *Townsend v. Sain*,[54] and *Sanders v. United States*.[55] By the middle 1960s, habeas corpus had become the procedural analogue of the Warren Court's innovations in criminal procedure, providing the federal machinery for bringing new constitutional values to bear in concrete cases.[56] To political liberals, federal habeas corpus for state prisoners is the embodiment of all that was *right* about the Warren Court and the vision that Court offered of a meaningful system of American liberty, underwritten by independent Article III courts willing and able to check the coercive power of government. In habeas proceedings, federal courts can examine federal claims in isolation both from the individual's guilt or innocence and from state court procedural rules that can insulate violations of federal rights from judicial review, either in the state courts themselves or in the Supreme Court later.[57] To political conservatives, by contrast, federal habeas is the paradigm of all that was *wrong* with the Warren Court—namely, that Court's distrust of the states and state courts and its celebration of individual liberty at the expense of order and stability. In habeas corpus cases, accordingly, the familiar debates over federalism and parity surface yet again.[58]

L. Rev. 286 (1966); Larry W. Yackle, *The Habeas Hagioscope*, 66 So. Calif. L. Rev. 2331, 2337-2349 (1993).

50. *Frank v. Mangum*, 237 U.S. 309, 346 (1915): Habeas corpus "comes in from the outside, not in subordination to the proceedings, and although every form may have been preserved opens the inquiry whether they have been more than an empty shell."

51. 261 U.S. 86 (1923).

52. 344 U.S. 443, 506 (1953) (concurring opinion).

53. 372 U.S. 391 (1963).

54. 372 U.S. 293 (1963).

55. 373 U.S. 1 (1963).

56. For reviews of these developments, see Paul M. Bator, *Finality in Criminal Law and Federal Habeas Corpus for State Prisoners*, 76 Harv. L. Rev. 441 (1963); Henry M. Hart, Jr., *Foreword: The Time Chart of the Justices*, 73 Harv. L. Rev. 84 (1959); Gary Peller, *In Defense of Federal Habeas Corpus Relitigation*, 16 Harv. C.R.-C.L. L. Rev. 579 (1982); Keith G. Meyer & Larry W. Yackle, *Collateral Challenges to Criminal Convictions*, 21 Kan. L. Rev. 259 (1973); *Developments in the Law: Federal Habeas Corpus*, 83 Harv. L. Rev. 1038 (1970). Professor Woolhandler argues that most accounts of older cases fail to appreciate that the development of habeas corpus as a vehicle for enforcing federal rights was linked to the contemporaneous development of other devices for holding government agents responsible. Ann Woolhandler, *DeModeling Habeas*, 45 Stan. L. Rev. 575 (1993).

57. See Note, *Federal Habeas Corpus for State Prisoners: The Isolation Principle*, 39 N.Y.U. L. Rev. 78 (1964); Chapter VII, notes 140-41 and accompanying text (explaining that a criminal defendant's failure to comply with state procedural rules can result in a forfeiture of any later opportunity to advance a federal claim in state court and an adequate state ground of decision foreclosing Supreme Court appellate review).

58. See generally Chapter I, notes 16-20, 79-91 and accompanying text (reviewing the arguments touching federalism and parity). For an illustrative appraisal of federal habeas corpus when Edwin Meese was Attorney General, see U.S. Dep't of Justice, Report to the Attorney General: Federal Habeas Corpus Review of State Judgments (1988). For a critique of that report, see Yackle, note 28. Professor Bator was the Warren Court's principal critic. See Bator, note 56. He contended that habeas corpus should generally be governed by the process model. Prisoners convicted in state court should not be entitled to claim that the state courts reached an erroneous outcome regarding a federal issue, but only that the

Just as the Warren Court developed constitutional safeguards and habeas corpus in a creative way to advance that Court's civil liberties agenda, the justices who arrived in the 1970s exercised equally active imaginations in an effort to reestablish comparative discipline. Soon after the Court's membership changed, its decisions touching criminal procedure and habeas corpus also shifted—notwithstanding that "the statutory language authorizing" federal habeas "remained unchanged."[59] The Rehnquist Court has sometimes squarely overruled Warren Court precedents and sometimes forged its own novel doctrines to circumscribe the writ. In this rough sense, the Court's decisions regarding federal habeas corpus parallel its decisions regarding the Ku Klux Klan Act, § 1983, civil rights removal, immunity, and federal-question abstention. In each instance, the Court has fashioned extremely complex doctrines in a perpetual effort to strike the balance the justices think proper between federal judicial power and state prerogatives.

The controversy over habeas corpus is also fueled by the contemporaneous national debate over capital punishment. In some minds, habeas corpus serves only to postpone lawful executions. Habeas litigation in capital cases tends to be complex and time-consuming, both because prisoners' claims are typically chal-

---

process the state courts employed to arrive at a judgment was inadequate to ensure sound decision-making. For a critique of Bator's argument, see Larry W. Yackle, *Explaining Habeas Corpus*, 60 N.Y.U. L. Rev. 991, 1014-19 (1985). Professor Hoffmann and Professor Stuntz fault the Supreme Court and other commentators for regarding federal habeas corpus as an occasion for working through familiar federalism themes. By their account, the Warren Court decisions putting teeth in the fourteenth amendment revolutionized criminal procedure, rendering the rules for processing criminal cases almost entirely federal. In that light, Hoffmann and Stuntz argue that federal habeas should be understood as a stage in the criminal process, and the scope of the federal courts' purview should turn on the purposes of criminal prosecutions—ascertaining guilt, while respecting procedural rights. Hoffmann and Stuntz would have federal courts exercise an entirely independent and rigorous examination of any claims advanced by prisoners who make a colorable showing of innocence. But they would have federal courts defer to any "reasonable" state court decisions on claims by prisoners who fail to draw their guilt into question. Joseph L. Hoffmann & William J. Stuntz, *Habeas After the Revolution*, 1993 Sup. Ct. Rev. 65, 69. The success rate for habeas corpus actions in federal court is quite low (about 4%). That may be because most prisoners have no lawyers to marshal their claims and because there are so many procedural obstacles to an adjudication on the merits. See Richard Faust, Tina J. Rubenstein & Larry W. Yackle, *The Great Writ in Action: Empirical Light on the Federal Habeas Corpus Debate*, 18 N.Y.U. Rev. L. & Soc. Change 637, 660 (1991) (reporting data from New York City showing that "professional representation is the single best predictor of success in federal habeas corpus"). The data may also suggest that state courts usually catch federal errors and, consequently, that subsequent federal litigation may not be worth the candle. See Daniel J. Meltzer, *Habeas Corpus Jurisdiction: The Limits of Models*, 66 So. Calif. L. Rev. 2507, 2523-24 (1993) (contending that the low success rate is a factor to be considered). In death penalty cases, by contrast, the success rate is quite high (as high as 40%). See *Habeas Corpus Issues: Hearings before the Subcommittee on Civil and Constitutional Rights of the House Committee on the Judiciary*, 102d Cong., 1st Sess. 358 (1992) (statement of Larry W. Yackle) (reporting the results of a study by Professor Liebman). By one account, that rate has diminished (to about 15%) in recent years. Kent S. Scheidegger, *Habeas Corpus, Relitigation, and the Legislative Power*, 98 Colum. L. Rev. 888, 943 (1998). If fifteen percent of the death-sentenced prisoners who seek habeas corpus relief are successful on the merits, it would seem that previous litigation of the federal claims in those cases is not always what it should be.

59. *Wainwright v. Sykes*, 433 U.S. 72, 81 (1977).

lenging and because the habeas process has itself become increasingly complex (largely through the introduction of intricate doctrines ostensibly meant to keep federal courts from unduly interfering with state judgments).[60] Death penalty proponents are suspicious that their adversaries defend habeas corpus primarily to frustrate capital punishment by the back door. Many Supreme Court decisions illustrate the Court's attempts to accommodate the special demands that capital litigation places on the judicial system. Given the political implications, Congress, too, has responded. After debating a host of habeas corpus bills over a thirty-year period, Congress enacted the Antiterrorism and Effective Death Penalty Act of 1996.[61] Some provisions in the 1996 Act apply to all habeas corpus cases; some address only death penalty cases.[62] Some essentially endorse and fortify Supreme Court decisions curbing the writ; others impose additional restrictions.[63]

---

60. For an exhaustive treatment, see James S. Liebman & Randy Hertz, Federal Habeas Corpus Practice and Procedure (2d ed. 1994).

61. See Yackle, note 49 (discussing prior bills); Larry W. Yackle, *The Reagan Administration's Habeas Corpus Proposals*, 68 Iowa L. Rev. 609 (1983) (examining the Reagan Administration's initiative); Larry W. Yackle, *A Primer on the New Habeas Corpus Statute*, 44 Buffalo L. Rev. 381 (1996) (summarizing the 1996 Act); Marshall J. Hartman & Jeanette Nyden, *Habeas Corpus and the New Federalism After the Antiterrorism and Effective Death Penalty Act of 1996*, 30 John Marshall L. Rev. 337 (1997) (also providing a summary).

62. The Supreme Court held in *Lindh v. Murphy*, 521 U.S. 320 (1997), that the provisions of the 1996 Act addressed to both capital and non-capital cases (collected in amendments to the preexisting provisions in Chapter 153 of Title 28, United States Code) do not apply to cases already pending on the date of enactment, April 24, 1996. The provisions addressed exclusively to capital cases are collected in an optional chapter: Chapter 154 of Title 28, United States Code, 28 U.S.C. § 2261, *et seq.* Those provisions are applicable only to death penalty habeas corpus cases in states that trigger Chapter 154 by establishing a system for providing indigent death row prisoners with competent and properly compensated counsel in *state* postconviction proceedings. The optional framework was suggested by a committee of the Judicial Conference of the United States, appointed by Chief Justice Rehnquist and chaired by Justice Powell. Ad Hoc Committee Report and Proposal (1989), reprt'd in *Habeas Corpus Legislation: Hearings on H.R. 4737, H.R. 1090, H.R. 1953 & H.R. 3584 before the Subcommittee on Courts, Intellectual Property, and the Administration of Justice of the Committee on the Judiciary of the House of Representatives*, 101st Cong., 2d Sess. 45-68 (1990). The 1996 Act also incorporates some of the Powell Committee's other proposals, but by no means all. See *Symposium*, 19 Capital U. L. Rev. 599 (1990) (reviewing the Powell Committee's recommendations); Ronald J. Tabak & J. Mark Lane, *Judicial Activism and Legislative "Reform" of Federal Habeas Corpus: A Critical Analysis of Recent Developments and Current Proposals*, 55 Albany L. Rev. 1, 56-84 (1991) (offering a similar review). The Powell Committee's program was hotly debated within the Judicial Conference. Senior circuit judges insisted that it would limit the federal courts too much and would render the habeas process even more complex into the bargain. See Donald P. Lay, *The Writ of Habeas Corpus: A Complex Procedure for a Simple Process*, 77 Minn. L. Rev. 1015, 1048-63 (1993).

63. See Mark V. Tushnet & Larry W. Yackle, *Symbolic Statutes and Real Laws: The Pathologies of the Antiterrorism and Effective Death Penalty Act and the Prison Litigation Reform Act*, 47 Duke L.J. 1 (1997) (contending that some of the key provisions in the 1996 Act only reinforce changes that the Supreme Court had already instituted on its own). For a (tedious) section-by-section discussion of the 1996 Act and early returns from the lower courts, see Larry W. Yackle, *Developments in Habeas Corpus*, The Champion, Part I, Sept./Oct. 1997, at 14; Part II, Nov. 1997, at 16; Part III, Dec. 1997, at 16.

B. Prerequisites

1. The Custody Doctrine

Litigants who wish to invoke a federal district court's jurisdiction pursuant to § 2241 must claim they are in "custody" in violation of federal law.[64] Custody is a jurisdictional prerequisite, bearing a correlative relationship to the function of habeas corpus: to secure the release of a person suffering wrongful detention.[65] Applicants for the writ must be held in some form of custody from which they wish to be discharged.[66] As a practical matter, however, the custody requirement operates as a gate-keeping device, screening cases according to the nature of the individual interests at stake. All litigants in federal court must have some kind of concrete injury to establish standing.[67] The custody requirement further subdivides the field of litigants by identifying those who can have access to federal court after state court proceedings are complete, without facing state preclusion rules.[68]

The custody doctrine does not demand actual incarceration, but can be satisfied by constructive restraints on liberty. In selective service and immigration cases, for example, petitioners often suffer milder limits on their freedom and the threat of actual incarceration in the future.[69] In cases touching criminal prosecutions, it is enough if petitioners are subject to bail or parole conditions.[70] The

---

64. See text accompanying note 29.

65. *Maleng v. Cook*, 490 U.S. 488, 490-91 (1989).

66. The custody requirement is linked to the relief that federal courts can award if they conclude that prisoners' detention violates federal law. The federal courts have no authority to overturn convictions or to set aside sentences, but can only order custodians to release prisoners for want of a lawful basis for their detention. *Noia*, 372 U.S. at 431. Ordinarily, however, courts stay release orders to give prosecutors an opportunity to cure the deficiencies that the habeas corpus proceeding has uncovered—typically by conducting a new trial that does not repeat the federal errors that were committed previously. In some instances, moreover, prisoners win orders releasing them from some sentences, but still remain in prison serving other valid terms. See note 71. For a general discussion of the relief available in federal habeas proceedings, see Yackle, note 29, at 527-545.

67. See Chapter IX, notes 102-35 and accompanying text.

68. See note 4 and accompanying text. Custody is also a jurisdictional prerequisite for motions by federal convicts pursuant to § 2255. In the case of federal prisoners, however, the absence of custody is not fatal. The Court held in *Morgan* that federal convicts who have completed their sentences can file a petition for the writ of coram nobis in the sentencing court. *Morgan*, 346 U.S. at 512-13; see note 46. By means of that old writ, authorized by the All-Writs Act, 28 U.S.C. § 1651, federal convicts can advance the same claims that they would otherwise press in a § 2255 motion. State prisoners cannot follow suit. When a federal court entertains an application from a prisoner who was convicted and sentenced in state court, the court has no prior criminal jurisdiction to rely upon. Accordingly, the state prisoner must invoke an independent basis of jurisdiction under § 2241. That jurisdiction is contingent on custody.

69. See text accompanying notes 34-40.

70. *Hensley v. Municipal Court*, 411 U.S. 345 (1973) (bail); *Jones v. Cunningham*, 371 U.S. 236 (1963) (parole); see *Justices of Boston Municipal Court v. Lydon*, 466 U.S. 294 (1984) (finding that a prisoner released on personal recognizance after a preliminary bench trial was in custody for purposes of federal habeas).

flexibility of the custody idea is a function of the Supreme Court's desire (during the 1960s) to open federal habeas corpus to a wide range of petitioners, particularly convicts seeking, in effect, to attack their convictions and sentences collaterally. It takes time to get to federal court with a petition for habeas corpus relief. If the custody doctrine required physical detention, many would-be applicants would be foreclosed—having been released from that kind of restraint during the interim.[71]

2. The Exhaustion Doctrine

Pursuant to 28 U.S.C. § 2254(b), prisoners attacking custody in the hands of state officials ordinarily must exhaust state judicial opportunities to litigate federal claims before presenting those claims to a federal court in a petition for a writ of habeas corpus. The exhaustion of state procedures is not a formal jurisdictional prerequisite.[72] The statute enacted by Congress codifies the Supreme Court's holding in *Ex parte Royall*.[73] In that case, a criminal defendant filed a petition in federal court while he was awaiting trial in state court. Justice Harlan recognized that the district court had jurisdiction to entertain the petition. But in light of the comity owed to the state and its courts, Harlan said that the district court should have declined to exercise its jurisdiction while the state criminal prosecution was under way. Nevertheless, exhaustion is very much the rule, not the exception. Under other Supreme Court precedents, as well as § 2254(b), prisoners must seek relief in state court first, unless the state court opportunities that appear to be "available" are actually "ineffective" to protect federal rights.[74]

---

71. Federal courts determine whether prisoners are in custody for purposes of § 2241 at the time a petition is filed. Once jurisdiction attaches, it continues even though prisoners may be fully relieved of all restraints before a final judgment is entered. *Carafas v. LaVallee*, 391 U.S. 234 (1968). The only question is whether the matter will at some point be rendered moot, because the applicant no longer has enough interest to keep an Article III case or controversy alive. Typically, habeas actions do not become moot. The Court presumes that petitioners continue to suffer legal consequences from criminal convictions even after their sentences have been served. See Chapter IX, note 292. In this same vein, the Court accommodates habeas applications from prisoners who are sentenced to serve multiple terms of confinement. A petitioner may attack one of two concurrent sentences, even though the other (unchallenged) sentence will keep the petitioner in jail, whatever happens. Equally, a prisoner can challenge one of two consecutive sentences, even though the petitioner is not yet serving the sentence under attack. The Court aggregates consecutive sentences for purposes of ascertaining custody. *Peyton v. Rowe*, 391 U.S. 54 (1968); *Garlotte v. Fordice*, 515 U.S. 39 (1995). A prisoner who has been fully discharged after completing an isolated sentence is no longer in custody under that sentence and thus cannot attack the conviction that gave rise to it straightforwardly in a habeas action. *Maleng*, 490 U.S. at 492-93. If, however, the prisoner is subsequently sentenced to a new term that is enhanced on the basis of the previously completed sentence, the prisoner may be able to reach the older sentence indirectly—by attacking detention under the *new* sentence on the ground that the new sentence rests on an invalid prior conviction. The Court noted this possibility in *Maleng*, but declined to address it.

72. See *Bowen v. Johnston*, 306 U.S. 19, 27 (1939) (explaining that the exhaustion doctrine "is not one defining power but one which relates to the appropriate exercise of power").

73. 117 U.S. 241 (1886).

74. There are certainly cases in which it is so clear that the state courts are unwilling to consider prisoners' claims that there is no point in requiring prisoners to make the attempt.

The exhaustion doctrine has two objectives: (1) to avoid premature federal interference with state processes; and (2) to preserve the state courts' role in the making and enforcement of federal law.[75] To accomplish those ends, federal courts routinely dismiss premature federal petitions. A dismissal for want of exhaustion is without prejudice and thus merely postpones federal adjudication until the prisoner meets the exhaustion doctrine's requirements.[76] Then, when no state court opportunities for litigation remain, federal adjudication can proceed, *ceteris paribus*.[77] Here again, the point of habeas corpus is to provide a federal forum, but at a time when state proceedings are finished and federal adjudication is no longer disruptive.

The exhaustion doctrine typically prevents prisoners who are charged with criminal offenses from escaping into federal court to advance federal defenses and, instead, forces them to offer those defenses at trial and on appeal in state court. The exhaustion requirement thus complements the law of removal and the federal-question abstention doctrine.[78] Federal district courts usually decline to interfere with ongoing state prosecutions for several overlapping reasons: because there is no general statute authorizing removal on the basis of a federal defense, because federal injunctive or declaratory relief is inappropriate while pending state proceedings offer an adequate opportunity for litigating federal claims, *and* because a petition for habeas corpus is premature when ostensibly effective state court opportunities for litigation have yet to be exhausted. When federal courts *do* act, it is again for reasons that justify more than one form of federal intervention. Removal is almost never available.[79] But federal courts can issue in-

---

E.g., *Engle v. Isaac*, 456 U.S. 107, 125-26 n.28 (1982). Those cases do not establish that the exhaustion doctrine can be *avoided*, but rather illustrate the way the exhaustion doctrine can be *satisfied*. The point is not that prisoners are excused when state court litigation is unlikely to be successful, but that prisoners are obliged to pursue only state court opportunities that are genuinely open to be exhausted at the time a federal petition is filed.

75. For an account of the exhaustion doctrine's development, see Larry W. Yackle, *The Exhaustion Doctrine in Federal Habeas Corpus: An Argument for a Return to First Principles*, 44 Ohio St. L.J. 393 (1983).

76. *Slayton v. Smith*, 404 U.S. 53 (1971). One might have expected federal courts merely to stay their own work pending further litigation in state court rather than to dismiss outright. See Chapter XI, text accompanying note 84 (describing state-question abstention). But dismissals without prejudice have the same effect, as well as the virtue of leaving federal dockets uncluttered.

77. Recall that litigants who press claims in state court in the first instance and come away with an unfavorable judgment usually cannot try again in federal court. The Full Faith and Credit Statute instructs federal courts to give prior state judgments the preclusive effect they would have in another state court. See Chapter VI, notes 156-79 and accompanying text. Federal habeas corpus is an exception. See note 4 and accompanying text. Otherwise, the requirement that prisoners exhaust state judicial remedies *before* filing federal petitions would be unintelligible. See Chapter XI, text accompanying note 38 (explaining the nature of an exhaustion doctrine).

78. See Chapter VI, notes 133-48 and accompanying text (discussing civil rights removal); Chapter XI, notes 130-89 and accompanying text (discussing abstention with respect to state criminal prosecutions). For a discussion, see Michael G. Collins, *The Right to Avoid Trial: Justifying Federal Court Intervention into Ongoing State Court Proceedings*, 66 N. Car. L. Rev. 49 (1987).

79. Recall that the Court has given the civil rights removal statute, 28 U.S.C. § 1443(1), an extremely narrow interpretation. The idea is that transferring state criminal prosecutions to federal court would be far too disruptive and that, when necessary, federal courts can protect defendants from inadequate state process by issuing injunctive or habeas relief. See

junctive, declaratory, or habeas corpus relief on those (rare) occasions when the state court proceedings under way do not provide an adequate opportunity for vindicating federal rights.[80]

In many instances, prisoners must also engage any state postconviction procedures available after their convictions are affirmed on direct review.[81] Prisoners must identify their claims to the state courts in the proper procedural posture, so that those courts have a fair chance to address them.[82] If inferior state courts react negatively, prisoners must press on to the highest state court in which an appeal lies as a matter of right.[83] Then again, prisoners need not engage in redun-

---

Chapter VI, 142-48 and accompanying text. See Yackle, note 58, at 1019 (contending that prisoners' access to federal district courts *after* conviction by means of habeas corpus is best explained as a sensible trade-off for their inability to remove their prosecutions to federal court in the first instance on the basis of federal defenses).

80. If, for example, prisoners have claims that cannot be vindicated by raising them as defenses in state court, federal habeas corpus is available even in advance of trial. E.g., *Braden v. 30th Judicial Circuit Court*, 410 U.S. 484 (1973) (entertaining a pre-trial federal habeas corpus petition filed by a prisoner contending that state authorities had denied him a speedy trial by failing to schedule a trial at all); *Arizona v. Washington*, 434 U.S. 497 (1978) (entertaining a pre-trial habeas petition filed by a prisoner who claimed that a state trial would itself constitute double jeopardy). Then again, prisoners must first exhaust any pretrial procedures available in state court. *Braden*, 410 U.S. at 491.

81. Postconviction petitions and motions take various forms. Typically, they are filed in the trial court in which the conviction was obtained, seeking correction of fundamental errors that were not cured at trial or on direct review—including errors of constitutional moment. The need to engage state postconviction processes typically turns on the nature of the claims in question. Prisoners who advance claims that can be determined on the basis of the record made at trial can usually satisfy the exhaustion doctrine by presenting those claims to the appellate courts on direct review of a criminal conviction. Prisoners who press claims that can be determined only if the record is expanded typically must file postconviction petitions or motions that can prompt an evidentiary hearing. See Yackle, note 29, at 264-86. For a discussion of the postconviction procedures that states typically offer (and their shortcomings), see Larry W. Yackle, *The Misadventures of State Postconviction Remedies*, 16 N.Y.U. Rev. L. & Soc. Change 359 (1988). By some accounts, federal habeas corpus would be less important than it is if state postconviction procedures were more effective in identifying and correcting violations of federal rights in criminal cases. The 1996 Act ostensibly hopes to foster improvements by encouraging the states to provide indigent death row inmates with lawyers in state postconviction proceedings. In exchange, the Act offers states a variety of procedural advantages in the federal habeas corpus proceedings that come later—for example, a shorter filing period. See note 91. The *quid pro quo* framework in the Act was originally proposed by the Powell Committee. See note 62.

82. In *Picard v. Connor*, 404 U.S. 270 (1971), the Court said that prisoners need not cite "book and verse on the federal constitution," but *are* obligated to identify the "substance" of their federal claims for consideration in state court. Certainly, prisoners cannot satisfy the exhaustion doctrine by presenting the state courts with one claim and then advancing a "clearly distinct" claim in federal court. Id. at 276-78. For illustrations of the way the *Picard* principle is implemented, see *Anderson v. Harless*, 459 U.S. 4 (1982); *Duncan v. Henry*, 513 U.S. 364 (1995). Prisoners must employ ordinary state procedural vehicles for advancing federal claims and cannot comply with the exhaustion doctrine by filing exotic petitions and motions that the state courts are likely to dismiss on procedural grounds. E.g., *Pitchess v. Davis*, 421 U.S. 482 (1975) (finding it insufficient that a prisoner raised a federal claim in a pre-trial petition for a writ of prohibition in the California Supreme Court).

83. In many states, prisoners have no right of appeal to the state supreme court, but can only petition that court for review in its discretion. The state supreme court thus functions in much the way that the Supreme Court operates—accepting for review only cases that have larger significance. See Chapter VII, notes 182-201 (describing the Supreme Court's discretionary control of its docket). It would make little sense to require prisoners to petition a state

dant litigation. Once the highest state court has had an opportunity to pass on a claim and has failed to render a favorable judgment, the exhaustion doctrine is satisfied and federal habeas corpus need be postponed no longer.[84] Of course, prisoners cannot force state courts actually to address properly presented claims. The exhaustion doctrine is satisfied if the highest state court has a fair opportunity to reach the merits, even if the court declines to do so on procedural grounds or simply overlooks or disregards the claim without explanation.[85]

Prisoners sometimes file federal habeas corpus petitions containing multiple claims, some of which are ready for federal adjudication and some of which are not. The Supreme Court held in *Rose v. Lundy*[86] that district courts should dismiss "mixed" petitions in their entirety. The point is to encourage prisoners to exhaust state opportunities for litigating all their claims and then to aggregate those claims in a single federal petition. In effect, *Lundy* puts prisoners to a choice. On the one hand, they can accept dismissal of the entire petition, pursue available state court litigation opportunities for the claims that are premature, and then return to federal court when they have satisfied the exhaustion doctrine with respect to all claims. That option necessarily defers federal adjudication of the claims that are currently ready for consideration. On the other hand, prisoners can abandon any claims that are not yet cognizable and proceed with claims the state courts have already considered and rejected.[87]

---

supreme court in every instance in order to comply with the federal exhaustion doctrine. That would ignore state efforts to *discourage* petitions for discretionary review in routine cases. See *Buck v. Green*, 743 F.2d 1567 (11th Cir. 1984) (holding that prisoners in Georgia need not ordinarily seek *certiorari* review in the Georgia Supreme Court). While state prisoners may petition the Supreme Court of the United States for *certiorari* review, they need not do so in order to satisfy the exhaustion doctrine, which has only to do with *state* opportunities for litigation. The functional point is the same. The Supreme Court sensibly means to discourage *certiorari* petitions in routine cases. *County Court of Ulster County v. Allen*, 442 U.S. 140, 149-50 n.7 (1979). If a prisoner does file a *certiorari* petition in the Supreme Court and review is denied (as is usually the case), the Supreme Court's disposition has no effect on later habeas proceedings in a district court. *Brown v. Allen*, 344 U.S. at 488-97 (Frankfurter, J., concurring). If, however, the Supreme Court accepts a case for review and determines the merits of the prisoner's claim, that decision *does* foreclose a later habeas application to a district court. 28 U.S.C. § 2244(c); see Yackle, note 29, at 566-77.

84. It is typically sufficient if prisoners fairly exhaust one of several alternative procedures in state court. *Wade v. Mayo*, 334 U.S. 672, 678 (1948).

85. *Smith v. Digmon*, 434 U.S. 332 (1978). Pursuant to § 2264(a), a federal court entertaining a habeas corpus petition from a prisoner on death row can ordinarily consider only claims that were previously "raised" and "decided on the merits" in state court. That provision must presuppose that the state courts addressed and resolved properly presented claims. Otherwise, it would foreclose federal adjudication of a claim the state courts chose to ignore, even though it was fairly presented for decision. The Powell Committee, which provided the model for § 2264(a), recommended that federal courts should be limited to claims that were "actually presented and litigated" (not decided) in state court. See note 62.

86. 455 U.S. 509 (1982).

87. Writing for the Court in *Lundy*, Justice O'Connor said only that prisoners who strip premature claims out of their petitions run the "risk" that those claims will be foreclosed, if and when they are renewed in a subsequent habeas application. Id. at 520-21. The lower courts took that to be a gentle way of saying that any claims dropped from a current petition would be barred later. The Supreme Court has said nothing to the contrary since *Lundy*. See also notes 231-33 and accompanying text (noting that under § 2244(b)(1) a claim that was presented in a prior application "shall be dismissed" if it is submitted again in a subsequent petition).

Pursuant to § 2254(b)(2), federal district courts "may" ignore prisoners' failure to exhaust, provided the courts deny relief "on the merits." If federal courts were to do that routinely, they would deny state courts any opportunity to consider the claims in question and would therefore sacrifice the policies that explain the exhaustion doctrine in the first place. It is sensible to make that sacrifice only when claims are so frivolous that there is no chance that the state courts would sustain them. In cases of that kind, it would be wasteful to dismiss for want of exhaustion and condemn both prisoners and state courts to futile litigation. Accordingly, federal courts leapfrog over the exhaustion requirement and deny relief on the merits only when they are "convinced" that claims have "no merit" and that litigation in state court would be "useless."[88]

State authorities may waive the exhaustion doctrine and thus submit claims to federal adjudication before the state courts have had an opportunity to pass on them. Yet they cannot forfeit the state's interests through inattention. The Supreme Court explained in *Granberry v. Greer*[89] that states' attorneys have a duty to advise district courts about whether, in their view, prisoners have exhausted the state procedures open to them. In the run of cases, accordingly, the exhaustion issue should not be overlooked unintentionally. If states' attorneys nonetheless fail to raise an exhaustion doctrine objection, the state's prerogatives are preserved. Under § 2254(b)(3), states' attorneys can forego exhaustion only if they do so "expressly." A state will not otherwise be "deemed to have waived the exhaustion requirement or be estopped from reliance" on it.[90]

The exhaustion doctrine must be reconciled with the filing deadlines that federal habeas corpus petitioners must meet. Pursuant to 28 U.S.C. § 2244(d), prisoners must file federal petitions within one year after the latest of three events: (1) the date on which the state court judgment under attack becomes "final" by the "conclusion of direct review;" (2) the date on which an unconstitutional state impediment to filing is removed; or (3) the date on which the Supreme Court rec-

---

88. *Hoxsie v. Kerby*, 108 F.3d 1239, 1243 (10th Cir. 1997). The circuit court in *Hoxsie* borrowed this standard from *Granberry v. Greer*, 481 U.S. 129, 133 (1987), where the Supreme Court used it to describe the circumstances in which states' attorneys can waive the exhaustion requirement—on the theory that state courts have no serious interest in passing on claims in advance of the federal courts. In cases otherwise controlled by *Lundy*, district courts may be able to save petitions for immediate consideration, if it happens that the claims that prisoners have not yet presented to the state courts are so worthless that they can be dispatched on the merits pursuant to § 2254(b)(2). Where that is true, the prisoners concerned need not choose between the usual options. Premature claims can be eliminated on the spot for lack of merit.

89. 481 U.S. 129 (1987).

90. Notwithstanding § 2254(b)(3), it is questionable whether states' attorneys are free to withhold any argument about prisoners' satisfaction of the exhaustion requirement until the federal courts have invested resources in a consideration of the merits or, worse yet, until the federal courts have found prisoners' claims meritorious and are poised to award relief. See *Harding v. North Carolina*, 683 F.2d 850 (4th Cir. 1982) (refusing to allow states' attorneys to waive exhaustion on the condition that the federal court would rule against the prisoner on the merits). Of course, if a claim is so frivolous that it can be denied on the merits pursuant to § 2254(b)(2), it makes no difference whether the state waives exhaustion. The point here is that states' attorneys should not be able to manipulate the exhaustion doctrine with respect to potentially meritorious claims—allowing claims of that order to proceed in federal court in hopes that they will be rejected, but then insisting on exhaustion in the eleventh hour if it appears that prisoners are likely to win.

ognizes the "right" that a prisoner seeks to vindicate (provided that right has been "newly recognized" by the Court and "made retroactively applicable to cases on collateral review").[91] Filing deadlines necessarily encourage prisoners to seek federal habeas relief early, while the exhaustion doctrine demands that they postpone federal petitions until state court opportunities to litigate their federal claims have been tried. The *Lundy* doctrine contributes additional complications: Some claims may be made ready for federal habeas corpus without delay, but others may require time-consuming litigation.

In most instances, the first of the three starting points will control. Prisoners will have one year in which to prepare and lodge a federal habeas corpus petition, running from the date the state court judgment becomes "final." By conventional account, that is the date on which the Supreme Court of the United States disposes of a petition seeking *certiorari* review of the state appellate court's decision affirming the conviction (or, in cases in which prisoners do not file *certiorari* petitions, the date on which the time for filing such a petition expires).[92] If prisoners have satisfied the exhaustion doctrine at that point (by presenting their federal claims to the state appellate courts in connection with the direct review proceedings just completed), they can proceed to federal court, provided they get there within a year. If, however, they have claims that have not been fully aired in state court and can still be considered in state postconviction proceedings, they are obliged by the exhaustion doctrine to postpone their federal petitions until those opportunities for state court litigation are pursued. In that event, § 2244(d)(2) tolls the one-year filing period while a "properly filed" application for state postconviction relief "with respect to the pertinent judgment or claim is

---

91. Pursuant to § 2263, death row prisoners must meet a 180-day filing deadline, running from "State court affirmance of the conviction and sentence on direct review or the expiration of the time for seeking such review," but subject to tolling in certain circumstances. The filing periods in both § 2244(d) and § 2263 present interpretive difficulties. See Tushnet & Yackle, note 63, at 26-30 (offering a brief discussion); Yackle, note 63 (running on at some length). One of the most vexing is presented by § 2244(d)(1)(C), which makes the starting date contingent on the existence of a "newly recognized" right that is "retroactively" applicable and suggests that a decision by the Supreme Court itself may be necessary to identify a right as "new," to settle the "retroactivity" question, or both. Other provisions and amendments enacted as part of the 1996 Act depend on similar contingencies. See § 2244(b)(2)(A) (affecting prisoners' ability to file more than one federal petition); § 2254(e)(2)(A)(i) (affecting prisoners' ability to obtain a federal evidentiary hearing); § 2255 (affecting federal prisoners' ability to file a second or successive motion attacking a federal conviction or sentence). The text in each instance is ambiguous, and, to complicate matters, different (ambiguous) formulations appear in different provisions. Upon the whole, prisoners rarely advance claims that depend on novel, but retrospectively available, propositions of federal law. Yet there are cases in which the construction these provisions are given will make a practical difference. As a matter of policy, it would make sense to read § 2244(d)(1)(C) to require a Supreme Court decision to start the filing period running. That would comport with the apparent policy of that section and would make it comparatively easy to identify a date certain from which the period can be computed. It would not make much sense to read § 2244(b)(2)(A) and § 2254(e)(2)(A)(i) to require the Supreme Court itself to speak before prisoners can proceed. That would force delay (and inefficiency) for no legitimate pay-off. See Yackle, note 63 (explaining the benefits of reading the relevant provisions in the Act this way and the drawbacks of reading them any other way).

92. This is the definition the Supreme Court typically gives to "final" state judgments for other purposes. E.g., *Griffith v. Kentucky*, 479 U.S. 314, 321 n.6 (1987); note 170 and accompanying text. See *Alexander v. Keane*, 991 F. Supp. 329, 333 n.2 (S.D.N.Y. 1998) (using the same definition in this context).

pending."[93] Prisoners have time, then, to press claims in state postconviction proceedings—time that does not count against the filing period that generally urges them on to federal court.

This said, it must also be said that another statute, 28 U.S.C. § 2264, arguably dispenses with the exhaustion requirement once a petitioner under sentence of death files a federal petition. Under § 2264(a), a district court entertaining an application from a death row prisoner must determine at the threshold whether federal adjudication is foreclosed because a claim was not presented in state court. If the court determines that a claim is not precluded because of default, the next section, § 2264(b), instructs the district court to consider the claim "properly before it" in light of three specified paragraphs of § 2254, covering various aspects of litigation in cases in which state prisoners challenge their convictions or sentences collaterally. Importantly (or so it would seem), the paragraph that codifies the exhaustion doctrine, § 2254(b), is not listed. One available inference is that § 2264 jettisons the exhaustion requirement in the interests of speeding capital cases through the federal courts.[94] If this is what § 2264 means, however, the implication is startling: District courts in capital cases controlled by § 2264 are neither obliged nor *permitted* to enforce the exhaustion requirement, even if the state asks that the state courts be given the chance to consider a prisoner's claim.[95]

---

93. Since § 2244(d)(2) tolls the filing period while a state postconviction petition is filed with respect to a particular claim *or* the "pertinent judgment," it operates for all the claims a prisoner possesses regarding a conviction—both the claims the prisoner advances in state postconviction proceedings and other claims that are themselves ready for federal habeas adjudication but are held in abeyance while the claims the state courts have yet to consider catch up. Then, when all state postconviction proceedings are completed with respect to all claims, the prisoner can aggregate them all in a single petition in the manner prescribed by *Lundy*.

94. Since § 2264 appears in the optional Chapter 154, it is applicable only to capital cases and then only in cases arising from states that have triggered that chapter. See note 62. For a discussion of § 2264's implications for procedural default in state court, see notes 125-30 and accompanying text.

95. Startling though it may be, this is precisely what the Powell Commitee recommended. See Powell Committee Report, note 62, at 51-53. Recall that some features of the optional Chapter 154 established by the 1996 Act build on the Powell Committee's proposals—§ 2264 included. In one related respect, the Act attempts to expedite federal adjudication of capital cases in a way that the Powell Commitee did *not* recommend. Under § 2266, federal district and circuit courts must handle petitions filed by death-sentenced prisoners on fixed timetables. The initial provision of Chapter 154, 28 U.S.C. § 2261(a), limits the application of the new chapter to "cases arising under section 2254 brought by prisoners in State custody who are subject to a capital sentence." Nevertheless, § 2266(a) also extends timetables for federal court action to § 2255 motions from federal prisoners under sentence of death. Legislatively imposed timetables for Article III court action can be problematic. See William F. Ryan, *Rush to Judgment: A Constitutional Analysis of Time Limits on Judicial Decisions*, 77 B.U. L. Rev. 761 (1997). In this instance, however, federal courts have more flexibility than it at first appears. Under § 2266(b)(4)(B), (c)(4)(B), a state is authorized to "enforce" the timetables by petitioning for a writ of mandamus. An appellate court can mandate only that the court before which an issue is pending must decide that question, not that the court must reach a particular outcome. *Will v. United States*, 389 U.S. 90, 98 n.6 (1967). The contemplation of § 2266, then, is that the timetables established for federal court action on capital habeas petitions only encourage courts to act as quickly as they can to discharge their Article III duties. This also appears to be the contemplation of § 2266(b)(5), (c)(5), which calls on the Administrative Office of United States Courts to file periodic reports on compliance with the timetables.

C. Procedural Default in State Court

Petitioners satisfy the exhaustion doctrine if, at the time they file federal habeas corpus petitions, there is no available and effective state court opportunity to litigate their federal claims. It often happens that no state court opportunities are *currently* open, but only because petitioners failed to advance their claims in previous proceedings in the manner prescribed by state law, and, for that reason, the state courts are no longer willing to entertain them. For example, defense attorneys frequently fail to comply with contemporaneous objection rules during trial. The defendants concerned then forfeit any other state court opportunities to litigate the claims that counsel neglects. State courts are generally entitled to penalize defaulters in that way, and their ultimate judgments rest, accordingly, on adequate state procedural grounds—even if meritorious federal claims are ignored because of counsel's blunders. Adequate state grounds of decision usually prevent the Supreme Court from considering underlying federal claims on direct review.[96] They also (usually) bar federal district courts from considering those claims in habeas corpus proceedings. Commonly, then, petitioners satisfy the exhaustion doctrine (and thus avoid a postponement of their claims), but only for a reason that bars federal adjudication entirely. They escape the exhaustion doctrine's frying pan only to fall irretrievably into the procedure default doctrine's fire.

The idea is *not* that federal courts have their own ideas about the way prisoners should litigate federal claims in state court and that, if prisoners fail to proceed in that manner, they lose the opportunity they would otherwise have to seek federal habeas corpus relief. Instead, federal default doctrine reinforces *state* procedural rules and, to that end, gives effect to forfeitures that the state courts impose for default as a matter of state law.[97] If states' attorneys wish to contend that claims are barred because of default, they must advance that contention in federal court. Since federal jurisdiction is not at stake, a federal district court has no obligation is raise the matter *sua sponte*.[98] Then again, to the extent federal default doctrine gives effect to state law rules cutting off claims, it produces results that would be expected if federal district courts were simply to apply state preclusion rules—notwithstanding the exemption federal habeas corpus enjoys from the Full Faith and Credit Statute.[99]

---

96. See Chapter VII, notes 140-66 and accompanying text (describing state contemporaneous objection rules and the process model the Supreme Court employs to determine whether forfeitures imposed for violating rules of that kind are adequate to foreclose appellate review).

97. These *state* law matters establish the conditions that bring the *federal* doctrine governing access to federal court into play. If the state courts do not initially find a prisoner in default and refuse to consider a claim for that reason, but, instead, determine the claim on the merits, a federal district court will equally proceed to the merits. *Ulster County*, 442 U.S. at 148 (making it clear that a federal habeas court will decline to consider a claim only if the state courts have refused or would refuse to do so); *Rezin v. Wolff*, 439 U.S. 1103 (1979) (White, J., dissenting) (explaining that the Supreme Court's default doctrine does not "impose its own contemporaneous objection rule independent of state rules").

98. In *Trest v. Cain*, 118 S.Ct. 478 (1997), the Court held that federal courts are not *required* to take up the default issue *sua sponte*, but found it unnecessary to decide whether they *can*.

99. See note 4 and accompanying text.

There is no general statute governing the effect that federal courts entertaining habeas corpus petitions should give to procedural default in state court.[100] The Supreme Court has fashioned its own body of doctrinal rules for the occasion. By all accounts, those doctrinal rules have shifted with the ebb and flow of the Court's enthusiasm for habeas corpus over time. In the 1960s, the Court was suspicious of state procedural schemes that denied federal claims any judicial forum at all and thus threatened to frustrate implementation of "incorporated" constitutional safeguards. The Warren Court largely (though sometimes grudgingly) granted that state courts could visit forfeitures on criminal defendants for procedural default in state proceedings. And that Court largely (though sometimes grudgingly) respected the adequate state ground doctrine as a limit on its own appellate jurisdiction to review state court judgments directly.[101] But the Warren Court insisted that state procedural grounds of decision would not commonly foreclose adjudication of federal claims by federal district courts in habeas corpus proceedings.

Recall that, in theory, federal courts entertaining habeas petitions do not *review* state court *judgments* at all. In *Fay v. Noia*,[102] Justice Brennan gave that theoretical conception of the writ practical significance. He explained that district courts could act on habeas petitions without upsetting the state convictions that wardens offered to justify prisoners' detention. Even if those judgments were formally valid (in the sense that they rested on adequate state grounds), district courts could look behind them and examine federal claims that the state courts refused to consider. Brennan recognized that would-be habeas petitioners had an obligation to exhaust state court opportunities to litigate their federal claims and acknowledged that some device was necessary to discourage prisoners from ignoring the state courts, accepting forfeiture under state law, and then presenting their claims for the first time in federal court. Accordingly, he said that federal district courts should decline to entertain claims that prisoners intentionally withheld from the state courts "for strategic, tactical, or any other reasons that [could] fairly be described as the deliberate by-passing of state procedures." Yet the "deliberate bypass" standard contemplated that petitioners could be shut out of federal court only if they themselves decided to forego state court opportunities to advance federal claims. That standard thus permitted prisoners to seek federal relief on the basis of claims that state courts found to be barred because of procedural default ascribable to defense counsel's ignorance or neglect.[103]

---

100. But see notes 94-95, 125-30 and accompanying text (discussing § 2264 governing death penalty cases arising in states that trigger Chapter 154); notes 139-42 and accompanying text (discussing § 2254(e)(2) governing default with respect to fact-finding in state court); notes 234-39 and accompanying text (discussing § 2244(b)(2) governing second or successive federal petitions).

101. Recall the Warren Court's occasional decisions finding state procedural grounds inadequate in cases in which it appeared that litigants' race figured in the dispositions in state court, as well as the *Henry* and *Williams* cases in which the Court encouraged state courts to relax local forfeiture rules. See Chapter VII, notes 148-66 and accompanying text.

102. 372 U.S. 391 (1963).

103. Justice Brennan described the paradigm case as one in which a prisoner "after consultation with competent counsel or otherwise, understandingly and knowingly forewent the privilege of seeking to vindicate his federal claims in the state courts." A deliberate bypass could be found, he said, only on the basis of a "considered choice of the petitioner." A "choice made by counsel not participated in by the petitioner" would "not automatically bar relief." Id. at 439. Taken literally, then, Brennan had it that default could not foreclose

When the Supreme Court began to curtail habeas corpus in the 1970s, the deliberate bypass rule for default cases was one of the first features of the Warren Court's structure to go. In *Wainwright v. Sykes*,[104] then-Justice Rehnquist said that *Noia* failed to give sufficient respect to the state interests served by contemporaneous objection rules, invited petitioners and their lawyers to "sandbag" the state courts, and generally treated state criminal trials as a "tryout on the road" to federal habeas corpus rather than as the "main event" for the adjudication of all issues pertaining to criminal cases.[105] He therefore discarded the deliberate bypass rule and substituted a doctrinal formulation that revived (but added to) the adequate state ground doctrine.[106] Generally speaking, *Sykes* and subsequent decisions establish a new baseline. While the *Noia* approach to default cases prevailed, procedural default in state court did *not* foreclose federal habeas corpus, except in cases in which there was good reason for *penalizing* a failure to comply with state procedural rules. Under *Sykes* and its progeny, procedural default in state court *does* foreclose federal habeas corpus, except in cases in which there is good reason for *excusing* a failure to comply with state procedural rules.

Current doctrine can be complicated. At the outset, a federal district court must make the same assessments that the Supreme Court makes when it determines whether a state judgment rests on an adequate state ground. The initial questions are matters of state law: There must *be* a state procedural rule requiring a prisoner to raise a federal claim in a particular way or at a particular time. The prisoner must have failed to comply with that rule. And, for that reason, the state courts must be unwilling to consider the claim.[107] Next, the district court must determine whether the state courts' procedural disposition of the claim would constitute an adequate state ground of decision that would defeat jurisdiction in the Supreme Court, if the case were before the Court on direct review. In this respect, current law departs from the Warren Court, which found the adequate state ground doctrine inapplicable in habeas corpus. The adequate state

---

federal habeas even if counsel deliberately withheld claims for tactical purposes, unless prisoners themselves were consulted and approved. He probably meant that aspect of the deliberate bypass rule as a hedge against the tendency to presume that counsel's actions have a tactical basis and to impute that tactical purpose to their clients.

104. 433 U.S. 72 (1977).

105. See Chapter VII, note 141 and accompanying text (describing the sandbagging argument). The deliberate bypass rule itself addressed the very problem that concerned the Court in *Sykes* inasmuch as that rule cut off federal habeas if prisoners intentionally withheld claims from the state courts. Yet since the deliberate bypass rule demanded that petitioners themselves must have participated in a decision to forego state court litigation, it drastically limited the occasions on which federal courts could actually find federal habeas foreclosed. By most accounts, it was unrealistic to think that counsel could consult with their clients in the heat of a trial, and, if they did, it was difficult to prove it. See *Sykes*, 433 U.S. at 93 (Burger, C.J., concurring); *Henderson v. Kibbe*, 431 U.S. 145, 512 (1977) (Burger, C.J., concurring). Accordingly, while the deliberate bypass rule prevailed, tactical decisions to bypass the state courts may have escaped without detection. Then again, by some accounts, it is unlikely that defense lawyers actually engage in sandbagging.

106. Justice Rehnquist did not act abruptly in *Sykes*, but built upon other decisions handed down since *Noia*. For contemporaneous commentary, see Yale Rosenberg, *Jettisoning Fay v. Noia: Procedural Defaults by Reasonably Incompetent Counsel*, 62 Minn. L. Rev. 341 (1978); Ralph Spritzer, *Criminal Waiver, Procedural Default and the Burger Court*, 126 U. Pa. L. Rev. 473 (1978); Peter W. Tague, *Federal Habeas Corpus and Ineffective Representation of Counsel: The Supreme Court Has Work to Do*, 31 Stan. L. Rev. 1 (1978).

107. See note 97 and accompanying text.

ground doctrine is not jurisdictionally controlling in habeas corpus cases, as it is when the Court itself exercises appellate review. Nevertheless, that doctrine applies in habeas cases in the interests of "federalism and comity."[108] If, then, the state courts' refusal to consider a federal claim because of procedural default would establish an adequate state ground cutting off Supreme Court review, the district court will typically refuse to entertain the claim in a habeas corpus proceeding.

There are, however, two exceptions. A district court can consider a claim on the merits if: (1) the prisoner shows both "cause" for having failed to raise the claim properly in state court and "actual prejudice" resulting from the default;[109] or (2) the prisoner demonstrates that the federal error that went uncorrected in state court "probably resulted in the conviction of one who is actually innocent."[110]

Cause. Statutes and court rules commonly allow exceptions for "cause shown" and contemplate that courts will exercise *ad hoc* judgment about whether litigants offer a sufficient excuse for failing to meet procedural requirements. In this context, however, cause has a more definite meaning. Certainly, petitioners cannot demonstrate cause by showing that they or their attorneys inadvertently overlooked federal claims that should have been raised in state court. The very point of *Sykes* is that petitioners now routinely forfeit the opportunity to litigate claims in both state and federal court, even though neither they nor counsel knowingly meant to do so. Justice O'Connor explained in *Murray v. Carrier*[111] that petitioners can establish cause only by showing that "some objective factor *external to the defense* impeded counsel's efforts to comply with the state's procedural rule."[112] For example, cause can be shown: (1) if, at the time counsel might have advanced a claim in state court, the factual or legal basis for

---

108. *Lambrix v. Singletary*, 117 S.Ct. 1517, 1522 (1997). Notice that the revival of the adequate state ground doctrine for use in habeas cases can improve some prisoners' chances of obtaining a foothold in federal court. If a prisoner can persuade a district court that the procedural ground on which a state court purported to rest would *not* be adequate to bar Supreme Court direct review, the prisoner can avoid dismissal for default in a habeas corpus proceeding without going further. In this vein, Robson and Mello point out that *Sykes* actually (and perhaps surprisingly) resurrects *Henry v. Mississippi*. Ruthann Robson & Michael Mello, *Ariadne's Provisions: A "Clue of Thread" to the Intricacies of Procedural Default, Adequate and Independent State Grounds, and Florida's Death Penalty*, 76 Calif. L. Rev. 87, 118 (1988). See Chapter VII, notes 162-66 and accompanying text (discussing *Henry*).

109. *Sykes*, 433 U.S. at 85. The "cause" and "prejudice" ideas initially appeared in *Davis v. United States*, 411 U.S. 233 (1973), a case involving a federal prisoner's § 2255 motion attacking a federal conviction and thus implicating Rule 12 of the Federal Rules of Criminal Procedure. In that case, then-Justice Rehnquist drew upon Rule 12 for the cause standard and on precedents for the prejudice test, but reworked the latter into an additional hurdle for prisoners to clear. The precedents interpreting Rule 12 had it that federal prisoners who could not show cause for failing to comply with procedural rules could avoid a forfeiture by showing prejudice. In *Davis*, by contrast, Justice Rehnquist insisted that § 2255 movants must show *both* cause *and* prejudice. See Louis Michael Seidman, *Factual Guilt and the Burger Court: An Examination of Continuity and Change in Criminal Procedure*, 80 Colum. L. Rev. 436, 463 (1980). Next, in *Francis v. Henderson*, 425 U.S. 536 (1976), Justice Stewart imported the cause-and-prejudice doctrine into habeas corpus actions involving state prisoners. For a critique, see Alfred Hill, *The Forfeiture of Constitutional Rights in Criminal Cases*, 78 Colum. L. Rev. 1050, 1056 (1978).

110. *Murray v. Carrier*, 477 U.S. 478, 496 (1986).

111. *Id.*

112. Id. at 488 (emphasis added).

the claim was not "reasonably available;"[113] (2) if state authorities interfered with counsel's ability to comply with a rule, making compliance "impracticable;"[114] and (3) if counsel's failure to follow a procedural rule was so fundamentally incompetent and prejudicial as to constitute ineffective assistance of counsel in violation of the sixth amendment.[115]

Prejudice. Prisoners who hope to avoid dismissal on the basis of procedural default typically must establish both cause and actual prejudice. Justice O'Connor said in *United States v. Frady*[116] that in cases in which prisoners claim that jury instructions given in state court violated due process, prejudice is established

---

113. Id. In *Reed v. Ross*, 468 U.S. 1 (1984), the Court held that a prisoner established cause by showing that the claim he wished to advance in federal habeas corpus (an attack on a burden-shifting jury instruction) was novel and that his attorney could not reasonably have anticipated it in time to raise it at trial in state court (fifteen years earlier). While *Reed* has never been overruled, its value as precedent is questionable. Justice Brennan wrote the Court's opinion in that case, and that alone is reason enough for pause. Justice O'Connor has explained that while defense attorneys need not be "visionaries," they must use the "tools" they have to identify and appreciate creative claims and have no cause for withholding any claim simply because it *is* novel and thus unlikely to succeed. *Engle v. Isaac*, 456 U.S. 107, 131 (1982). Accord *Smith v. Murray*, 477 U.S. 527, 535 (1986). Since *Reed*, moreover, the Court has held that habeas petitioners usually cannot advance claims based on new rules of federal law, even if they *did* press those same claims in state court. See notes 165-98 and accompanying text (discussing the *Teague* doctrine); Marc M. Arkin, *The Prisoner's Dilemma: Life in the Lower Federal Courts after Teague v. Lane*, 69 N. Car. L. Rev. 371, 407-19 (1991) (describing *Teague's* effect on *Reed* in the lower courts); Yackle, *Primer*, note 61, at 419 n.124 (suggesting that conservative justices' dissatisfaction with *Reed* may have produced *Teague*). There are exceptions, however, in which "new rule" claims remain cognizable, and *Reed* may support an argument for cause in cases of that kind. Then again, the jury instruction claim in *Reed* itself would be unlikely to qualify. See notes 186-91 and accompanying text (discussing the exceptions recognized in *Teague*).

114. *Carrier*, 477 U.S. at 488. In *Amadeo v. Zant*, 486 U.S. 214 (1988), the Court found cause for counsel's failure to raise a jury discrimination claim at trial, because prosecutors had concealed crucial evidence supporting that claim and thus interfered with counsel's ability to identify and advance the claim in compliance with state procedural rules.

115. Justice O'Connor conceded this for the Court in *Carrier*, 477 U.S. at 488, and again in *Coleman v. Thompson*, 501 U.S. 722, 755 (1991). The point is not that defense lawyers can perform so poorly that they cease to be defendants' agents, but that the state bears overarching responsibility for ensuring that the defense function meets minimal constitutional standards. Accordingly, ineffective assistance in the constitutional sense qualifies as a factor "external to the defense" itself. Of course, habeas petitioners who prove that their sixth amendment rights were violated in state court can seek federal habeas relief on that independent basis—whether or not they can also advance the federal claims that counsel failed to raise. Justice O'Connor recognized as much in *Coleman* and then quickly added that prisoners who press ineffective assistance claims as the basis for establishing cause must satisfy the exhaustion doctrine with respect to those claims. 501 U.S. at 756. The constitutional standards for effective assistance are notoriously low. In *Strickland v. Washington*, 466 U.S. 668 (1984), the Court explained that counsel's performance need only be minimally competent and that even when it is not there is no constitutional violation unless the defendant is actually prejudiced. Moreover, the constitutional right to effective assistance attaches only at the trial and appellate stages of the process in state court and not to the crucial postconviction stage. Invoking a "greater power" argument in *Coleman*, Justice O'Connor said that since prisoners have no constitutional right to demand counsel in state postconviction proceedings, they equally have no right to demand that the lawyers they are given as a matter of grace perform effectively. Accordingly, the most egregious negligence of counsel at the postconviction stage cannot establish cause for procedural default.

116. 456 U.S. 152 (1982).

only if the instructions "so infected the entire trial that the resulting *conviction*" was unfair.[117] That formulation of prejudice insists that a prisoner must show not only that federal error affected the fairness of the proceedings in state court, but that it affected the outcome—the accuracy of the determination of guilt. Justice O'Connor did not explain precisely how great the effect on the outcome must be, nor even whether an effect on outcome is necessary with respect to other kinds of claims.[118]

Innocence. Justice O'Connor expressed confidence in *Carrier* that the cause-and-prejudice formulation will typically capture cases in which a genuine miscarriage of justice would ensue if default were not excused. Yet "in an extraordinary case, where a constitutional violation has probably resulted in the conviction of one who is actually innocent," she said that a federal court can address the mer-

---

117. Id. at 169 (emphasis added). Justice O'Connor explained in *Frady* that the cause-and-prejudice formulation elaborated in *Sykes* and other cases involving state prisoners also applies to cases (like *Frady*) involving federal prisoners pursuing § 2255 relief. That was unremarkable, given *Davis v. United States*. See note 109. Yet since the Court explains and defends the *Sykes* doctrine primarily on the basis of the comity federal courts owe to the states, it is not self-evident that collateral attacks on federal convictions should be reflexively handled in the same way.

118. Justice O'Connor was at pains in *Frady* to limit her discussion of prejudice to the circumstances in that case and to disclaim any more general elaboration of the prejudice idea for other cases and claims. 456 U.S. at 168. Professor Jeffries and Professor Stuntz suggest that the formulation O'Connor gave for prejudice in *Frady* approximates the formulation the Court gives for the prejudice element of ineffective assistance of counsel claims, where prisoners must show a "reasonable probability that, but for counsel's unprofessional errors, the result of the proceeding would have been different." In that context, a "reasonable probability" is a "probability sufficient to undermine confidence in the outcome." *Strickland*, 466 U.S. at 694. Jeffries and Stuntz think that is about right—an effect greater than what would create a "reasonable doubt," yet less than what would make an acquittal "more likely than not." John C. Jeffries, Jr. & William J. Stuntz, *Ineffective Assistance and Procedural Default in Federal Habeas Corpus*, 57 U. Chi. L. Rev. 679, 684-85 (1990). The intellectual difficulty is redundancy. If prisoners must typically establish an independent constitutional violation of their right to effective counsel in order to place claims that counsel did not raise before a federal court, they scarcely need to advance those underlying claims at all. Once they exhaust state remedies with respect to their sixth amendment claims, they should be entitled to habeas corpus relief on that basis alone. But see notes 199-229 and accompanying text (discussing the effect that federal districts courts must give to previous state court adjudication on the merits). Jeffries and Stuntz propose that the Court should abandon its focus on compliance with state procedural rules and attend to the nature of the claims prisoners advance in federal court—and should suspend rigid procedural bar rules when federal courts have the chance to correct an erroneous conviction or sentence of death. Professor Dooley proposes that the Court should jettison default rules altogether, allow federal courts to consider especially compelling claims, and simply foreclose other claims on the theory that they are by nature insufficient to warrant consideration in federal court. Laura Gaston Dooley, *Equal Protection and the Procedural Default Bar Doctrine in Federal Habeas Corpus*, 59 Fordham L. Rev. 737, 769-70 (1991). Professor Marcus offers a nuanced appraisal of both cause and prejudice and proposes that the two ideas should operate more closely together. For example, Marcus contends that defense counsel's neglect (short of a sixth amendment violation) should constitute cause, if the prisoner makes a showing of significant prejudice—namely, "factual innocence or a defect in the truth-seeking process." Maria L. Marcus, *Federal Habeas Corpus After State Court Default: A Definition of Cause and Prejudice*, 53 Fordham L. Rev. 663, 733 (1985). See note 109 (noting that older interpretations of Rule 12 allowed prejudice to make cause unnecessary). For a discussion of the various meanings the Court can assign to prejudice (and the confusion that can result), see Yackle, note 29, at 226-28 (Supp. 1997).

its of a claim and grant relief, "even in the absence of a showing of cause."[119] A safety valve for cases in which prisoners show "probable innocence" is hard to reconcile with the traditional understanding of habeas corpus or, for that matter, with federal jurisdiction generally. Virtually everyone agrees that it is for state courts (and juries) to determine whether defendants actually committed the criminal acts with which they are charged and that federal courts should limit their purview to the constitutionality of the legal procedures by which state courts set about reaching those judgments.[120] Nevertheless, there is some appeal in the idea that genuine concerns about prisoners' guilt should justify reaching legal claims that would otherwise be dismissed on procedural grounds.[121]

Even as the Court brooks some attention to actual innocence in habeas, however, the Court plainly hesitates to invite petitioners to advance innocence arguments routinely. In an apparent effort to keep this last escape route within narrow bounds, the Court has stated the controlling test in some of the most Byzantine language in all the law of federal courts. Writing for the Court in *Schlup v. Delo*,[122] Justice Stevens said that a prisoner who hopes to satisfy the "probable innocence" standard must "support his allegations of constitutional error with new reliable evidence—whether it be exculpatory scientific evidence, trustworthy eyewitness accounts, or critical physical evidence—that was not presented at trial." On the basis of that evidence, the prisoner must show that "it is *more likely than not* that *no reasonable juror* would have convicted him in light of the new evidence."[123] It is hard to think that district judges can comprehend that

---

119. *Carrier*, 477 U.S. at 496. Justice O'Connor did not mention the usual requirement that petitioners must also show prejudice. Prisoners who show probable innocence demonstrate prejudice *a fortiori*. See note 123 (discussing Justice Stevens' explanation of the relationship between prejudice and probable innocence in *Schlup*).

120. In the *Isaac* case, Justice O'Connor summarily rejected the argument that the *Sykes* approach to default should be relaxed when prisoners advance claims going more directly to factual innocence. *Isaac*, 456 U.S. at 129 (explaining that the habeas corpus statutes do not distinguish among federal claims).

121. See notes 147-48 and accompanying text (discussing the *Herrera* case).

122. 513 U.S. 298 (1995).

123. Id. at 327 (emphasis added). Dissenting in *Schlup*, Chief Justice Rehnquist said that Stevens' formulation mixed a "quintessential charge to a finder of fact" (the "more likely than not" standard) with "an equally quintessential conclusion of law" (the "no reasonable juror would have convicted" standard). Id. at 339. That was a fair point. Yet the Chief Justice himself proposed an alternative formulation even less intelligible—the formulation that Justice Kennedy had previously articulated for use in cases in which prisoners contend that they have been erroneously sentenced to death. In that context, a prisoner must show "by clear and convincing evidence that but for constitutional error, no reasonable juror would [have found] the petitioner eligible for the death penalty." *Sawyer v. Whitley*, 505 U.S. 333, 348 (1992). Justice Stevens, for his part, explained that prisoners like *Schlup* (whose claims go to the validity of a conviction) must make a showing that is stronger than what is needed to establish prejudice, but not so strong as what is required of prisoners in cases like *Sawyer* (whose claims go only to their eligibility to receive a death sentence). Both *Schlup* and *Sawyer* involved second or successive federal petitions from a single prisoner and thus formally elaborated the doctrine applicable to cases of that kind. Yet at the time those decisions were rendered, the Supreme Court used the same rules both to determine the effect of default in prior state court proceedings and to determine the effect of default in prior federal proceedings. See note 239. Baroque as the Court's standards may be, they are beacons of simplicity and clarity by comparison to related statutes. See, e.g., text accompanying notes 126, 139, 234.

standard, distinguish it from other standards with which they are familiar, and systematically use it to sort cases.[124]

Apart from the Supreme Court's decisions on the effect of procedural default in state court, there is one federal statute in point, albeit its application is limited: 28 U.S.C. § 2264.[125] Initially, § 2264(a) restricts a federal district court to claims that were previously "raised" and "decided on the merits" in state court, unless "the failure to raise the claim properly" was: (1) "the result of State action in violation of the Constitution or laws of the United States;" (2) "the result of the Supreme Court's recognition of a new Federal right that is made retroactively applicable;" or (3) "based on a factual predicate could not have been discovered through the exercise of due diligence in time to present the claim for State or Federal post-conviction review." Then, pursuant to § 2264(b), "[f]ollowing review subject to subsections (a), (d), and (e) of section 2254, the district court shall rule on the claims properly before it."[126]

This provision does not codify the Court's default doctrine in so many words. But it does largely incorporate the Court's illustrations of cause.[127] The first exception excuses default that can be ascribed to the state. It covers both cases in which state authorities interfered with counsel's ability to comply with

---

124. The doctrine is actually more complicated still. In *Bousley v. United States*, 118 S.Ct. 1604 (1998), the Court elaborated the "innocence" safety valve for cases in which prisoners attack pleas of guilty. The prisoner in *Bousley* (actually a federal convict proceeding under § 2255) initially pled guilty to a charge of using a firearm in connection with a drug offense—on the mistaken understanding that mere possession of a gun constituted "use." Thereafter, the Supreme Court held that "use" demanded more active employment of a weapon. The prisoner then contended that his failure to insist on that interpretation of the statute should be excused, because he was actually innocent. In the Supreme Court, Chief Justice Rehnquist acknowledged that the prisoner was entitled make a showing of "actual innocence," if he could. But the Chief Justice explained that the task would not be easy. The government would be able to rebut the prisoner's argument regarding his innocence with any additional (admissible) evidence of his guilt, even if that evidence had not been presented at the earlier proceeding in which the guilty plea was taken. Moreover, the Chief Justice anticipated that the government might have withheld additional charges at that time in connection with a plea agreement. If that was so, when the prisoner attempted to show that he was innocent of the "use" offense, the government would be entitled to introduce evidence of his guilt on those other charges. And in order to succeed, the prisoner would have to establish his probable innocence of those offenses, as well.

125. Since § 2264(a) forms part of the optional Chapter 154, it applies only in death penalty cases arising from states that have triggered that chapter. See note 62.

126. See notes 94-95 and accompanying text (discussing the implications of this section for the exhaustion doctrine).

127. Recall that the Court's own default doctrine only reinforces *state* default rules. See notes 97-98 and accompanying text. This statutory provision on default is not (expressly) conditioned in the same way and thus might be read to establish an entirely independent federal law of default that cuts off federal adjudication of federal claims, whether or not the state courts refused, or would refuse, to explore them. A construction of that kind would be extraordinary, however. It would vanquish an elaborate body of settled doctrine without explanation (and only by negative implication). And it would contemplate that federal courts must construct yet another body of *federal* default law to be applied to *state* criminal proceedings in order to determine whether federal habeas adjudication should be available. It is more plausible to read § 2264 to presuppose the familiar environment, in which the federal law of default is contingent on a threshold determination that a claim was, or would be, foreclosed in state court. In this vein, § 2264(a) refers (ambiguously) to claims that were not raised "properly" in state court. That suggests a state law definition of what counts as "proper."

state procedural rules and cases in which defense counsel's performance violated the sixth amendment.[128] The second exception covers cases in which counsel could not reasonably anticipate the emergence of a new claim. The third covers cases in which counsel could not discover facts to support a more conventional claim.[129] None of the three exceptions explicitly captures the Court's "probable innocence" safety valve.[130]

D. Evidentiary Hearings

Prisoners seeking federal habeas corpus relief typically advance fact-sensitive federal claims. Several statutes and a special set of court rules prescribe the means by which district courts can develop the factual record.[131] The Court held in *Townsend v. Sain*[132] that, as a general matter, a federal court is under an obligation to conduct an evidentiary hearing if a habeas corpus petition alleges facts that, if true, would entitle the applicant to relief, and the respondent, in turn, disputes those allegations.[133] Nevertheless, pursuant to 28 U.S.C. §2254(e), federal courts often decline to hold hearings, because: (1) the relevant facts were previously determined in state court; or (2) the prisoner committed procedural default with respect to fact-finding in state court and, for that reason, is not entitled to a hearing in federal court.

1. State Court Findings of Fact

Pursuant to §2254(e)(1), federal courts must typically presume that state findings of fact are correct.[134] Once that presumption is engaged, it can be re-

---

128. See notes 114-15 and accompanying text.

129. See note 113 and accompanying text.

130. The Court excuses default in "probable innocence" cases in an abundance of caution to ensure that no miscarriage of justice occurs. See text accompanying note 119. That suggests a constitutional footing. Professor Berger contends that, at the very least, death-sentenced prisoners have a constitutional right to seek relief (in some court) on the basis of new evidence undermining guilt and that ordinary procedural bar rules should not operate in cases of that kind. Vivian Berger, *Herrera v. Collins: The Gateway of Innocence for Death-Sentenced Prisoners Leads Nowhere*, 35 Wm. & Mary L. Rev. 943, 949-50 (1994). Accordingly, in order to avoid the delicate constitutional questions that would be presented if §2264 were read to foreclose prisoners who may actually be innocent, it may be sensible to read it to presuppose the "probable innocence" feature of the Court's doctrine. But see notes 41, 120 and accompanying text (recalling that habeas corpus is not traditionally concerned with guilt or innocence).

131. See Rules Governing Section 2254 Cases in the United States District Courts; Rules Governing Section 2255 Proceedings in the United States District Courts. For a discussion of pleading, discovery, and other preliminary matters, see Yackle, note 29, at 429-78.

132. 372 U.S. 293 (1963).

133. Id. at 317.

134. Under previous law, the presumption in favor of state findings was contingent on a written statement of the state court's conclusions, sound process in state court, and fair support in the evidentiary record. Taken literally, §2254(e)(1) preserves the presumption, but eliminates the contingencies. Still, it is hard to think that federal courts must accept state court findings at face value—no questions asked. Moreover, §2254(e)(1) must be reconciled with §2254(d)(2), which has it that a federal court may award relief on the merits if a previ-

butted only by "clear and convincing evidence" that the state courts reached erroneous determinations. In effect, § 2254(e)(1) recognizes a kind of issue preclusion with respect to state findings of fact, as distinct from conclusions of law. Ordinarily, courts with jurisdiction to determine claims have authority to decide all the material issues. In this instance, however, Congress has allocated responsibility for particular issues within an individual case: In the main, questions of fact are given to state courts, while questions of law and "mixed" questions of law and fact remain with federal courts. The resulting division of authority places heavy weight on the familiar fact/law distinction. It is one thing to accept state findings of historical facts and quite another to accept state court applications of law to those historical facts. Findings of fact rest in the main on credibility choices; applications of law are the crux of judicial judgment on the merits of claims.[135]

The Supreme Court is acutely aware that the characterization of an issue as factual or mixed determines the court that will have primary adjudicatory responsibility. When issues are plainly mixed, the Court acknowledges as much and finds the presumption in favor of factual findings inapplicable.[136] Neverthe-

---

ous state court adjudication "resulted in a decision" that was "based on an unreasonable determination of the facts in light of the evidence presented in the State court proceeding." See notes 224-25 and accompanying text. Under § 2254(d)(2), a federal court can scarcely be indifferent to the process by which a state court reached a factual finding or the evidentiary support that finding enjoyed. In order to determine whether findings of fact were reasonable in light of the evidence presented in state court, a federal court must have something in the way of a state record of that evidence. Recall, too, that in the context of preclusion, the Supreme Court has said that federal courts need not respect state judgments unless litigants had a full and fair opportunity to litigate their claims. See Chapter VI, notes 175-79 and accompanying text. Similarly in this context, federal courts presumably must hold the process by which state courts reach factual findings to some minimal procedural standards of fairness and regularity—standards demanded by due process at the very least. In a statement issued on the day he signed § 2254(e)(1) and related sections into law, the President said this: "If [§ 2254(e)] were read to deny litigants a meaningful opportunity prove the facts necessary to vindicate Federal rights, it would raise serious constitutional questions. I do not read it that way." Statement of the President, Office of the Press Secretary (April 24, 1996). See Larry W. Yackle, *Federal Evidentiary Hearings Under the New Habeas Corpus Statute*, 6 B.U. Pub. Int. L.J. 135, 140-41 (1996) (discussing these issues).

135. Then again, in most instances federal adjudication substitutes for state adjudication and does not follow state court litigation *seriatim*. In the special context of habeas corpus, federal litigation comes later. By the time a prisoner negotiates the state system and seeks habeas corpus relief from a federal court, the state courts have typically already heard what the witnesses have to say about the facts underlying federal claims and have chosen to believe one version of the story over another. In this context, moreover, it is not just that one set of courts has already found the facts and it appears wasteful and potentially antagonistic to propose that another set of courts should start over on a clean slate. Federal habeas typically comes some time after state court proceedings are complete. The passage of time since the critical events occurred may frustrate another round of fact-finding. Witnesses may be unavailable, memories may be faded, and physical evidence may be lost. Federal courts might restrict themselves to an appraisal of the state court record. Yet the judge who saw the witnesses first-hand was probably in the best position to sort truth from falsehood. Accordingly, it may make some sense to accord state findings of fact a presumption of accuracy.

136. See *Sumner v. Mata*, 455 U.S. 591, 597 (1982) (acknowledging that the presumption applies only to questions of historical fact and not to mixed issues). See, e.g., *Thompson v. Keohane*, 516 U.S. 99 (1995) (holding that the "custody" of a suspect at the time of an interrogation is a mixed question to which the presumption does not apply); *Miller v. Fenton*, 474 U.S. 104 (1985) (holding that the "voluntariness" of a confession is a mixed question);

less, the Court is frank to say that it sometimes approaches cases from the opposite direction—first deciding as a matter of policy whether it would be best if state or federal courts decided a question and then characterizing the question as either factual or mixed in order to channel it to the courts the justices prefer.[137] Certainly, the Court often characterizes issues as factual when, in all candor, they require more than a relatively objective determination of what happened in the course of some historical episode.[138]

2. Procedural Default Revisited

Pursuant to § 2254(e)(2), federal courts may sometimes deny prisoners federal evidentiary hearings on the basis of default with respect to fact-finding in state court: "*If the applicant has failed to develop the factual basis of a claim* in State court proceedings," a federal court "shall not hold an evidentiary hearing on the claim," unless the applicant shows that: (A) the claim relies on (i) "a new rule of constitutional law, made retroactive to cases on collateral review by the Supreme Court, that was previously unavailable" or (ii) "a factual predicate that could not have been previously discovered through the exercise of due diligence;" "and" (B) "the facts underlying the claim would be sufficient to establish by clear and convincing evidence that but for constitutional error, no reasonable factfinder would have found the applicant guilty of the underlying offense."[139]

In cases in which the standards in § 2254(e)(2) control, prisoners seeking federal evidentiary hearings have a heavy burden. They must demonstrate *both* that they could not have anticipated the need for litigating factual issues when they were in state court (either because they could not anticipate novel claims or because they were unaware that more conventional claims were available them), *and* that the facts they failed to develop would have revealed their innocence.[140]

Cuyler v. Sullivan, 446 U.S. 335 (1980) (holding that the "effectiveness" of defense counsel is also a mixed question).

137. *Miller*, 474 U.S. at 114.

138. E.g., *Wainwright v. Witt*, 469 U.S. 412 (1985) (concluding that the "bias" of a juror is a matter of historical fact to which the presumption attaches); *Maggio v. Fulford*, 462 U.S. 111 (1983) (holding that a defendant's "competency" to stand trial is equally factual). See Chapter VII, notes 167-77 and accompanying text.

139. Whew. This provision, like the provision in § 2264, fails to state explicitly that its application depends on a threshold determination that the state courts have imposed, or would impose, a forfeiture as a matter of state law. See note 127.

140. These standards are similar to the standards that appear in 28 U.S.C. § 2244(b)(2), which governs cases in which prisoners file multiple federal habeas petitions. See text accompanying note 234. In that context, the prisoners concerned have already had one opportunity to litigate in federal court. That is not necessarily true in the case of prisoners seeking evidentiary hearings. One would have thought that the standard here would be less rigid. Instead, it appears to be even more demanding. Under § 2244(b)(2)(A), prisoners who wish to file a second habeas application may do so if they have a claim that rests on a "new" and "retroactive" rule of constitutional law—whether or not the claim is related to actual innocence. Here, by contrast, if prisoners seek a federal hearing on the ground that a claim relies on a "new" and "retroactive" rule, the "facts underlying the claim" must go to innocence. Notice, too, that § 2254(e)(2)(A) refers only to "constitutional" claims and thus suggests that prisoners advancing non-constitutional claims are entirely foreclosed, even if they meet the demanding standards that § 2254(e)(2) otherwise imposes. State prisoners can seek federal habeas relief on the basis of non-constitutional claims. See note 149 and accompanying text. It is hard, then, to

In many instances, however, the standards in § 2254(e)(2) may *not* control, because "the applicant" did *not* fail to develop the facts in state court. Instead, facts were overlooked for some other reason not ascribable to the prisoner. By making the applicant's own responsibility for default crucial, § 2254(e)(2) essentially incorporates the Supreme Court's decisions on cause for default in state court. The working idea, both in the Court's decisions and in § 2254(e)(2), is that prisoners should forfeit claims (or, in the case of § 2254(e)(2), the opportunity to present evidence regarding the facts supporting claims) only if they themselves (or their competent lawyers) fail to comply with state procedural rules and, for that reason, forego state court opportunities for litigation that would normally be open. If, by contrast, default cannot be ascribed to prisoners or their attorneys, but is attributable to factors "external to the defense,"[141] there is no basis for visiting a forfeiture on blameless individuals, and a federal evidentiary hearing into the facts may be conducted.[142]

E. Cognizable Claims

Federal district courts entertaining habeas corpus petitions are authorized to determine whether the custody of which prisoners complain is "in violation of

---

read § 2254(e)(2)(A) to mean that prisoners who failed to develop the facts with respect to a non-constitutional claim in state court are out of luck in federal court no matter how "new" a claim may be, no matter how difficult it would have been to discover its "factual predicate" earlier, and no matter how closely the claim is linked to innocence. Other related statutes also refer explicitly only to "constitutional" claims, but still others are not so limited. Under § 2264, for example, death-sentenced prisoners may advance claims under the "laws of the United States." See text accompanying notes 125-26. Statutes like § 2254(e)(2)(A) may employ the "constitutional" label loosely (to mean "federal," "cognizable," or, perhaps, "fundamental"). In many contexts, it would be untenable to read references to constitutional claims and issues to exclude non-constitutional matters by negative implication. For example, § 2253 requires prisoners to obtain a certificate of appealability in order to seek review of an unfavorable district court judgment. To do that, prisoners must make a substantial showing of the denial of a "constitutional right." If § 2253 were read to restrict appellate review to purely constitutional issues, it would follow that prisoners could press non-constitutional claims at the district level, but not higher. District court judgments on non-constitutional claims would be final. For a discussion, see Yackle, note 134, at 146-47.

141. See text accompanying note 112. In *Keeney v. Tamayo-Reyes*, 504 U.S. 1 (1992), the Supreme Court held that the doctrine the Court had previously created in *Sykes* for cases in which prisoners failed to raise claims in state court equally applied to cases in which prisoners raised claims, but neglected fully to develop the supporting facts. The *Tamayo-Reyes* decision predated the enactment of § 2254(e), which formed part of the 1996 Act. See notes 61-62 and accompanying text.

142. *McDonald v. Johnson*, 139 F.3d 1056, 1059 (5th Cir. 1998) (explaining that a petitioner can be held responsible only if a state court's failure to develop the facts was the result of the prisoner's "own decision or omission"); *Burris v. Parke*, 116 F.3d 256, 258-59 (7th Cir.) (similarly declining to read § 2254(e)(2) to establish a "strict liability" rule), *cert. denied*, 118 S.Ct. 462 (1997). The President made this point in his signing statement when he said that "[§ 2254(e)] applies to situations in which 'the applicant has failed to develop the factual basis' of his or her claim. Therefore, [§ 2254(e)] is not triggered when some factor that is not fairly attributable to the applicant prevented evidence from being developed in State court." Signing Statement, note 134.

the Constitution or laws or treaties of the United States."[143] When, accordingly, prisoners successfully clear the procedural hurdles set before them, they are typically in a position to contend that the criminal convictions and sentences that custodians offer to justify their detention are insufficient. In the run of cases, prisoners argue that their convictions or sentences are invalid because they were obtained in violation of prisoners' federal rights before, during, or after trial.

1. Constitutional Claims

Prisoners almost always advance constitutional claims anchored in the procedural safeguards prescribed by the Bill of Rights, applicable to state cases via the fourteenth amendment. For example, habeas petitioners may allege that they were convicted on the basis of involuntary confessions, that their trials were corrupted by racial discrimination, or that their defense attorneys rendered ineffective assistance.[144] Recall that federal district courts do not review the judgments the state courts reached on prisoners' constitutional claims. Instead, district courts entertaining habeas petitions go directly to the merits of claims and decide for themselves whether prisoners' rights were violated. In the leading case, *Brown v. Allen*,[145] the Court explained that previous state court judgments on federal claims are entitled only to the "weight that federal practice gives to the conclusion of a court of last resort of another jurisdiction."[146]

Recall, too, that federal district courts do not typically concern themselves with prisoners' guilt or innocence. They consider evidence going to criminal acts or moral blame only when prisoners' substantive federal claims entail that kind of inquiry. In *Herrera v. Collins*,[147] for example, a prisoner advanced the claim that he was innocent of the offense of which he had been convicted and that it would therefore violate the fourteenth amendment to put him to death. In the Supreme Court, Chief Justice Rehnquist took pains to separate federal habeas corpus from any routine assessment of prisoners' guilt. Yet he assumed for purposes of analysis that "in a capital case, a truly persuasive demonstration of 'actual innocence' made after trial would render the execution of a defendant unconstitutional, and warrant federal habeas relief if there were no state avenue open to process such a claim."[148]

---

143. See text accompanying note 29.

144. For a survey of illustrative claims, see Ira P. Robbins, Habeas Corpus Checklists, Ch. 6 (1998). The federal courts' jurisdiction to consider prisoners' federal claims for habeas relief does not include supplemental jurisdiction to take up related state law claims.

145. See note 52 and accompanying text.

146. 344 U.S. at 458. The *Brown* case is conventionally taken to stand for the proposition that federal court adjudication in habeas corpus begins on a clean slate, *de novo*. That is the way Justice Jackson characterized the Court's analysis in his separate opinion concurring only in the dispositions of the consolidated cases at bar. Id. at 546. But see notes 165-229 and accompanying text (discussing the *Teague* doctrine and the effect that §2254(d) gives to previous state adjudication on the merits).

147. 506 U.S. 390 (1993).

148. The opening the Chief Justice allowed for free-standing claims of actual innocence is extremely narrow, if it exists at all. Even so, it has excited interest in academic and political circles. It may seem sensible to lawyers that federal courts should attend only to federal legal issues and should leave assessments of guilt to juries. Yet the point of procedural safe-

2. Non-Constitutional Claims

Prisoners who press non-constitutional federal claims for habeas corpus relief can encounter difficulty. Non-constitutional claims are cognizable only if they reveal "fundamental defects" that "inherently" result in "a complete miscarriage of justice."[149] Moreover, one extremely important non-constitutional claim is by nature unenforceable in habeas corpus, except in extraordinary circumstances. In *Stone v. Powell*,[150] the Supreme Court held that prisoners cannot ordinarily attack their detention on the ground that they were convicted on the basis of evidence obtained in violation of the fourth amendment. Justice Powell explained in *Stone* that the fourth amendment exclusionary rule is not a personal right, but is rather a judicially fashioned evidentiary standard meant to enforce the fourth amendment by deterring police misconduct. It is applicable only to proceedings in which that deterrent purpose is served sufficiently to make it worthwhile to forego the conviction of defendants who are demonstrably guilty. If unlawfully seized evidence is excluded at trial, or if a violation of the exclusionary rule forms the basis for reversal on direct review, the Court is satisfied that the officers whose conduct is faulted will get the point and mend their ways. If, by contrast, federal courts grant habeas corpus relief on the basis of the exclusionary rule, the Court is not convinced that the rule's deterrent purpose is achieved. Habeas corpus adjudication often comes too late to carry any genuine deterrent impact.[151]

Justice Powell explicitly disclaimed any intention of touching federal court jurisdiction, even when prisoners seek habeas relief on the basis of exclusionary rule claims.[152] The point of *Stone* is not the nature and scope of habeas corpus,

---

guards is chiefly (though not entirely) to avoid erroneous convictions. It is small wonder, then, that some limited attention to the accuracy of criminal judgments should be admitted in federal habeas. Recall that courts administering procedural default doctrine have occasion to address prisoners' arguments that they are probably innocent. See notes 119-24 and accompanying text. There, however, a showing of probable innocence only serves as a "gateway" to the consideration of conventional legal claims and does not itself count as a claim on which habeas relief may be issued. *Schlup*, 513 U.S. at 315. If it offends the Constitution to execute an innocent person, it must equally offend the Constitution to imprison such a person. Accordingly, the suggestion in *Herrera* that innocence claims may be cognizable in death penalty cases cannot be limited to that context. Professor Steiker has developed an argument that "bare-innocence" claims should be cognizable. Jordan Steiker, *Innocence and Federal Habeas*, 41 UCLA L. Rev. 303 (1993). By contrast, Professor Berger concludes (reluctantly) that federal courts should not ordinarily second-guess trial court determinations of guilt. Berger, note 130.

149. *Reed v. Farley*, 512 U.S. 339, 354 (1994) (involving a claim that state authorities had violated an interstate compact). Of course, state prisoners rarely have non-constitutional claims at all. Federal prisoners proceeding under § 2255 are much more likely to complain that their convictions or sentences rest on violations of federal statutes or court rules. There, too, however, only "fundamental defects" will suffice. *Hill v. United States*, 368 U.S. 424 (1962) (involving an alleged violation of Fed. R. Crim. P. 32); *United States v. Timmreck*, 441 U.S. 780 (1979) (involving an alleged violation of Fed. R. Crim. P. 11).

150. 428 U.S. 465 (1976).

151. Id. at 493.

152. Id. at 494 n.37.

but the nature and purpose of the exclusionary rule. Nevertheless, when Justice Powell described the exceptional circumstances in which federal courts can entertain exclusionary rule claims, he relied on a familiar device for allocating judicial authority: the process model.[153] Federal district courts can consider exclusionary rule claims if prisoners are initially denied an "opportunity" for "full and fair adjudication" in state court.[154] By making an "opportunity" for state court adjudication critical, Justice Powell declared that federal courts should rebuff not only claims previously treated and rejected in state court, but also claims that were not, but might have been, determined there. He thus interpreted the exclusionary rule to introduce both issue and claim preclusion into habeas corpus cases involving exclusionary rule claims: If state courts consider a prisoner's claim and find it wanting, the prisoner is typically barred from attempting to relitigate that claim in federal court. If state courts offer a prisoner a means of litigating an exclusionary rule claim and the prisoner does not seize that opportunity, federal habeas corpus is also foreclosed.[155]

3. Harmless Error

If federal courts determine that prisoners' claims are meritorious, they nonetheless withhold relief if the error was harmless. Some "structural defects" so undermine the integrity of the process that they can never be harmless.[156] In most instances, however, federal courts identify errors at trial that can be overlooked if they had no significant impact on the proceedings. When the Supreme Court considers cases on direct review of state court judgments, it employs a demanding test: The state must demonstrate that error was harmless "beyond a

---

153. See Chapter I, notes 61-65 and accompanying text.

154. *Stone*, 428 U.S. at 481-82.

155. The consequences of *Stone* were immediate and dramatic. Federal enforcement of the exclusionary rule in habeas corpus proceedings ground to a halt. See Philip Halpern, *Federal Habeas Corpus and the Mapp Exclusionary Rule After Stone v. Powell*, 82 Colum. L. Rev. 1 (1982). Thereafter, some members of the Court contended that other claims should be handled in the same way. E.g., *Duckworth v. Eagan*, 492 U.S. 195, 205 (1989) (O'Connor, J., concurring) (joined by Scalia, J.) (offering *Miranda* claims as candidates). Yet the full Court explained in a series of decisions that *Stone* is limited to the fourth amendment exclusionary rule. E.g., *Withrow v. Williams*, 507 U.S. 680 (1993) (holding that *Miranda* claims are cognizable in the ordinary course). See *Kimmelman v. Morrison*, 477 U.S. 365 (1986) (holding that prisoners can contend that their sixth amendment rights were violated when defense counsel failed to raise an exclusionary rule objection to unlawfully seized evidence). In 1982, the Reagan Administration proposed an amendment to 28 U.S.C. §2254, which would have barred federal district courts from awarding habeas relief on the basis of any claim that had previously been "fully and fairly" adjudicated in state court. The Reagan Administration's Proposed Reforms in Habeas Corpus Procedures (1982); see note 61. That initiative would have made issue preclusion the rule for all manner of claims advanced in federal habeas proceedings. Attorney General Smith conceded at the time that the point of the scheme was "simple abolition" of the writ for state prisoners. William F. Smith, *A Proposal for Habeas Corpus Reform*, in Criminal Justice Reform: A Blueprint (McGuigan & Rader eds. 1983). The Reagan Administration's plan was unsuccessful in Congress. See Yackle, note 49, at 2357-64.

156. See *Arizona v. Fulminante*, 499 U.S. 279, 290 (1991) (citing a violation of the right to counsel as an illustration).

reasonable doubt."[157] In *Brecht v. Abrahamson*,[158] the Court concluded that a "less onerous" standard is applicable to cases reaching federal court via petitions for federal habeas corpus relief. In habeas cases, trial errors are harmless if they had no "substantial and injurious effect or influence" on the outcome of a prisoner's trial.[159] In habeas, too, the burden of showing error to be harmless lies with the state. Writing for the Court in *O'Neal v. McAninch*,[160] Justice Breyer said that when the evidence is in "equipoise," and a district court is in "grave doubt," the court should treat an error as if it had the necessary substantial effect on the verdict.[161]

Chief Justice Rehnquist acknowledged in *Brecht* that the habeas corpus statutes prescribe no standard for harmless error. Accordingly, he fashioned an appropriate test as a matter of judicial policy. As Rehnquist explained it, the benefits of applying the "beyond a reasonable doubt" standard to habeas cases would be modest: State courts generally enforce constitutional rights and require no strong measures to "deter" them from committing constitutional error at trial.[162] The costs of employing that more demanding standard would be significant by comparison—namely, the demonstrable interference with state judgments, the bother and expense of curative state proceedings, and the possibility that guilty prisoners may escape punishment if the evidence supporting their guilt has become stale and they are acquitted after retrial.[163] Those costs attend any case in which a federal court awards relief. Chief Justice Rehnquist's explanation for *Brecht* is thus another illustration of the current Court's tendency to curb federal habeas corpus for state prisoners.[164]

F. New Rules of Law

Prisoners seeking federal habeas relief also encounter difficulty if they advance constitutional claims that depend on new rules of law. The Supreme Court draws a sharp line between cases the Court itself accepts on direct review from

---

157. *Chapman v. California*, 386 U.S. 18, 24 (1967). Since the Supreme Court itself uses the "beyond a reasonable doubt" standard on direct review, the state courts below are equally obliged to use that standard when they review trial errors directly. The *Chapman* approach to harmless error in cases on direct review has constitutional overtones. But see Daniel J. Meltzer, *Harmless Error and Constitutional Remedies*, 61 U. Chi. L. Rev. 1, 26 (1994) (arguing that *Chapman* states a proposition of federal common law—applicable both in the Court itself and in state court); see Chapter VIII, notes 32-78 and accompanying text (discussing federal common law).

158. 507 U.S. 619 (1993).

159. Id. at 637, quoting *Kotteakos v. United States*, 328 U.S. 750, 776 (1946). Under this standard, error is harmless in the absence of a determination of "actual prejudice." *Brecht*, 507 U.S. at 637.

160. 513 U.S. 432 (1995).

161. Id. at 444-45.

162. *Brecht*, 507 U.S. at 636.

163. Id. at 637.

164. For critiques of *Brecht*, see James S. Liebman & Randy Hertz, *Brecht v. Abrahamson: Harmful Error in Habeas Corpus Law*, 84 J. Crim. L. & Criminology 1109 (1994); Yackle, note 49, at 2408-15.

state court, on the one hand, and cases that arrive in federal court by means of petitions for the writ of habeas corpus, on the other. In direct review cases, the Court handles novel claims routinely and formulates the rule of law it thinks appropriate, however much it may depart from the past. That rule controls the instant case, future cases, and any cases pending at trial or on direct review—including cases in which the state courts have already rejected the same claim in light of prior precedents, but in which their judgments are still subject to Supreme Court review. It would violate "basic norms of constitutional adjudication" to refuse to apply a newly declared constitutional rule to a criminal case that is pending when the rule is announced.[165] When, by contrast, habeas corpus petitioners advance novel claims, virtually the opposite default position obtains: Claims based on new rules of law are *not* usually cognizable. It is typically enough if the state courts properly applied the law as it was previously.

The explanation for the apparent inconsistency lies in the different functions served by direct review and habeas corpus. When the Supreme Court itself reviews state court judgments directly, it performs its function as the system's final referee. In that posture, the Court properly engages any innovative claims the parties may have in order to articulate the supreme law in an accurate and uniform manner. Habeas corpus, by contrast, serves a different purpose. In *Teague v. Lane*,[166] Justice O'Connor explained that, theory to one side, the practical function of the federal writ is "deterrence"—namely, to give state courts an incentive "to conduct their proceedings in a manner consistent with established constitutional standards."[167] State courts, in turn, can only be expected to recognize rules of federal law that are well established at the time they act on defendants' claims. If federal district courts enforce new rules that are announced after a conviction becomes final on direct review, they achieve no deterrent effect. Accordingly, federal courts ordinarily do *not* entertain creative claims in habeas corpus proceedings. They do not announce and apply new rules of constitutional law, but hold state courts only to the law as it was reflected in the precedents in

---

165. *Griffith v. Kentucky*, 479 U.S. 314, 322 (1987). The Court takes the same view of changes in the law affecting ordinary civil litigation. See *Harper v. Virginia Dep't of Taxation*, 509 U.S. 86 (1993).

166. 489 U.S. 288 (1989).

167. Id. at 306, quoting *Desist v. United States*, 394 U.S. 244, 262-63 (1969) (Harlan, J., dissenting). Justice O'Connor generally relied for her analysis on Justice Harlan's opinions objecting to the Warren Court's enthusiasm for habeas corpus in the 1960s. See also *Mackey v. United States*, 401 U.S. 667, 692-93 (1971) (concurring opinion). Recall that in traditional theory habeas corpus does not focus on previous court judgments at all, but attaches to the prisoner's current detention. See notes 42-43 and accompanying text. Obviously, there is a certain rhetorical tension between Justice O'Connor's opinion in *Teague*, which has it that the point of federal habeas is to "deter" state courts from ignoring federal rights, and Chief Justice Rehnquist's insistence in *Brecht* that state courts need nothing to "deter" them from violating federal rights. But that tension is entirely verbal and bears no programmatic implications. At the end of the day in *Teague*, Justice O'Connor did not bring heavier weaponry to bear on state courts in order to achieve deterrence, but (once again) curtailed the authority of federal courts entertaining petitions from state prisoners. Professor Hoffmann explains that the deterrence theory of habeas corpus embraced in *Teague* has conceptual implications. Joseph L. Hoffmann, *The Supreme Court's New Vision of Federal Habeas Corpus for State Prisoners*, 1989 Sup. Ct. Rev. 165. Professor Lee has compared and contrasted the deterrence theory of the writ with the approaches suggested in prior decisions and in the academic literature. Evan Tsen Lee, *Theories of Federal Habeas Corpus*, 72 Wash. U. L.Q. 151 (1994).

place when prisoners were still seeking reversal of their convictions on direct review.[168]

The *Teague* doctrine is a choice of law rule: Federal courts entertaining habeas corpus petitions apply the rule of law that prevailed when a prisoner's conviction became final on direct review, not (necessarily) the rule that prevails when the prisoners appears in federal court later.[169] The first order of business, then, is to ascertain the date on which the prisoner's conviction became final. That is not the date on which the state appellate court affirmed the conviction. It is the date on which the Supreme Court denied *certiorari* or, if no petition for *certiorari* was filed, the date on which the time for filing a petition expired.[170] The next task is to determine whether the prisoner seeks relief on the basis of a

---

168. The Warren Court, too, sometimes denied retroactive effect to novel principles of constitutional law. In the 1960s, when that Court frequently gave constitutional safeguards an innovative interpretation, there was a very practical reason for giving at least some of those new ideas prospective effect only. If the establishment of a new rule of law inevitably meant that cases decided under previous understandings had to be revisited, the Court would have hesitated to be so creative in the first place. If, however, the Court could avoid upsetting old convictions, it could move the law along more readily. When, accordingly, the Warren Court reached a decision that made a "clear break" with precedent, the Court sometimes declared that the new rule would not apply retroactively. *Desist*, 394 U.S. at 248. If a "clear break" decision was not essential to protect the innocent, and if its application would upset reliance interests, the Court denied its benefits to prisoners whose claims rested on prior events or judgments. Because the fourth amendment exclusionary rule announced in *Mapp v. Ohio*, 367 U.S. 643 (1961), clearly broke with the past, and because it did not advance the accuracy of criminal judgments but potentially disrupted settled arrangements, the Court held that it was enforceable only in the particular case at bar and in future cases. *Linkletter v. Walker*, 381 U.S. 618, 636-37 (1965). By contrast, since the right to counsel was so vital to the fairness of criminal trials, the Court gave *Gideon v. Wainwright*, 372 U.S. 335 (1963), retrospective application. *Pickelsimer v. Wainwright*, 375 U.S. 2 (1963). In every case, the Warren Court wrestled with retroactivity by, first, deciding whether a rule was truly new (and thus presented a retroactivity question at all) and, second, weighing the values served by retrospective application against the disruption of state reliance interests. To the Warren Court, the retroactive applicability of a new rule was a property of the rule itself and had *nothing* to do with whether a case reached the Court on direct review from a state court judgment or via habeas corpus proceedings in the lower federal courts. In *Teague* and related decisions, however, the current Court has reconceptualized the very idea of retroactivity in criminal cases. Now the retrospective reach of a change in the law has *everything* to do with whether a claim arrives in federal court on direct review in the Supreme Court or in habeas corpus.

169. See *Wright v. West*, 505 U.S. 277, 310-13 (1992) (Souter, J., concurring). Professor Fallon and Professor Meltzer contend that *Teague* should, instead, be understood as an attempt to adjust the remedies available in circumstances in which the law is in flux. Richard H. Fallon, Jr. & Daniel J. Meltzer, *New Law, Non-Retroactivity, and Constitutional Remedies*, 104 Harv. L. Rev. 1731, 1766, 1813-20 (1991). See notes 199-205, 228-29 and accompanying text (discussing the way in which § 2254(d) appears to codify *Teague* as a doctrine governing the availability of federal habeas relief).

170. *O'Dell v. Netherland*, 117 S.Ct. 1969, 1973 (1997). Of course, the Supreme Court might hand down a decision concededly announcing a new rule between the date on which the state appellate court affirms a prisoner's conviction and the date on which *certiorari* is denied. In that event, the prisoner is entitled to the benefit of the new rule in federal habeas, even though the state courts have had no opportunity to address it on direct review. Professor Hoffmann argues, by contrast, that the "theoretical underpinnings" of *Teague* "virtually compel" making the crucial point the date on which the state courts act on a prisoner's claim. Joseph L. Hoffmann, *Retroactivity and the Great Writ: How Congress Should Respond to Teague v. Lane*, 1990 B.Y.U. L. Rev. 183, 216 n.135. See note 220 (discussing § 2254(d)).

rule of law that was not yet established on that benchmark date. That question is typically presented in two kinds of cases: (1) cases in which prisoners ask a federal district court to award habeas relief on the basis of some recent precedent that arguably changed the law from what it was at the time their convictions became final on direct review; and (2) cases in which prisoners do not rely on any particular recent precedent, but ask a federal court to award habeas relief on the basis of a legal theory that the district court can accept only by itself announcing and applying a change in the law.

Recent precedents. Cases in which prisoners rely on recent precedents lend themselves to a retroactivity analysis fairly readily. In the paradigm case, a prisoner files a habeas corpus petition citing a recent Supreme Court decision that has just resolved a division among the lower courts on a legal issue. It is fair to ask whether that decision changed the law from what it was previously. If it did *not*, but, instead, merely explained that some lower courts were mistaken about the issue in question, then the prisoner does not need the recent decision in order to prevail. The district court can rely on earlier precedents that the Court has reaffirmed. If, by contrast, the Court's recent decision *did* change the law, the situation is altered. Pursuant to *Teague*, the district court usually cannot give that change retrospective effect in a habeas corpus action.

If the *Teague* doctrine barred prisoners from invoking decisions that obviously establish new propositions of law, its practical effect would be modest and its intellectual foundations largely non-controversial. According to the Court, however, decisions do not have to be especially creative in order to establish new rules. In *Teague*, Justice O'Connor said that "a case announces a new rule when it breaks new ground or imposes a new obligation" on the government.[171] In other cases, the Court has explained that while "clear breaks" from precedent are sufficient, they are not necessary to the creation of new rules: "[G]radual developments in the law over which reasonable jurists may disagree" can also produce entirely new rules of law.[172]

Innovative claims. Cases in which prisoners cite no particular recent precedent do not immediately appear to present a retroactivity problem at all. But on examination, the same policy is at stake: Just as *Teague* bars a federal district court from giving retroactive effect to a recent Supreme Court decision announcing a new rule, *Teague* equally bars a district court from itself fashioning a new rule and then applying that rule to resolve a prisoner's pending habeas corpus action. To assess the novelty of the rule of law on which a prisoner relies, a district court must do essentially the same thing that it would do to determine the novelty of a recent Supreme Court decision. The task is to look back at the precedents that were in place at the time the prisoner's conviction became final and to determine whether those precedents stood even then for the legal rule that the prisoner wishes to enforce. If so, then the district court can apply that rule without doing anything new. If not, the district court must itself announce and apply a new rule of law in order to grant the prisoner relief. That, of course, is what *Teague* prohibits.

---

171. *Teague*, 489 U.S. at 301. Justice O'Connor explained in *Teague* itself that since the Court had previously held that racial groups need not be proportionately represented on juries, a rule requiring juries to reflect the racial make-up of the community would be new.

172. *Sawyer v. Smith*, 497 U.S. 227, 234 (1990).

Here, too, the Supreme Court's conception of new rules is expansive. Habeas corpus petitioners do not have to ask a federal district court to be very imaginative at all in order to be charged with asking the court to create a new rule of law. Unless previous precedents "dictated"[173] or "compelled"[174] the conclusion that a prisoner's claim was valid even then, a district court would have to create a new rule of law in order to find the prisoner's claim meritorious today. Moreover, the district court's "application" of a settled rule of law to the facts of an analogous case may also "involve a new rule of law."[175] That is so, because even a settled rule can be "extended" if it is applied in a "novel setting."[176] A district court thus establishes a new rule whenever it reaches a decision different from an "outcome" that was "susceptible to debate among reasonable minds" at the time a prisoner's conviction became final.[177]

The *Teague* doctrine has come under intense criticism in academic circles. By some accounts, *Teague* is a contrivance for circumnavigating the traditional understanding that federal courts exercise independent judgment on the merits of federal claims. Taken for all they are worth, the Court's various descriptions of new rules threaten to capture *all* claims advanced in federal habeas petitions—both claims seeking incremental developments in the content of legal standards and claims seeking the application of settled standards to different factual circumstances. Claims calling for any kind of serious judgment on questions of law, and equally claims calling for the resolution of mixed questions of law and fact, appear to demand the creation of entirely new rules of law that, given *Teague*, are typically unenforceable in habeas proceedings.[178] Moreover, the *Teague* doc-

---

173. *Teague*, 489 U.S. at 301.
174. *Saffle v. Parks*, 494 U.S. 484, 488 (1990).
175. *Sawyer*, 497 U.S. at 234.
176. *Stringer v. Black*, 503 U.S. 222, 228 (1992).
177. *Butler v. McKellar*, 494 U.S. 407, 415-17 (1990). Justice Harlan, for his part, recognized that a decision regarding the novelty of a rule would often be close. In his view, the "content" of constitutional principles rarely changes "dramatically from year to year." What may appear on first glance to be the announcement of a "new rule," may, instead, be "simply" the application of a "well-established constitutional principle" to a "closely analogous" case. *Desist*, 394 U.S. at 263 (dissenting opinion). Harlan insisted that a rule is not new for retroactivity purposes unless, at the time a case was in state court, the Supreme Court of the United States would have *rejected* the legal standard on which a prisoner relies. Under the current Court's formulations, a rule is new unless it can be said that, when the case was in state court, the Supreme Court would have *accepted* the prisoner's argument—and the state courts unaccountably failed to comprehend as much. While the Court may rely on Harlan for the general framework in *Teague* (i.e., the general prohibition on "new rule" claims in habeas corpus), the Court plainly draws no support from Harlan regarding the crucial question whether a rule is genuinely new. Professor Heald contends that the *Teague* doctrine would be more sensible if the Court were to revive Justice Harlan's understanding of what qualifies as new law. Paul J. Heald, *Retroactivity, Capital Sentencing, and the Jurisdictional Contours of Habeas Corpus*, 42 Ala. L. Rev. 1273, 1321 (1991). Professor Hoffmann, too, advocates a narrower definition of new rules that conforms more closely to Harlan's views. Hoffmann, note 170.
178. For criticisms of *Teague* in this vein, see Barry Friedman, *Habeas and Hubris*, 45 Vand. L. Rev. 797 (1992); James S. Liebman, *More Than "Slightly Retro": The Rehnquist Court's Rout of Habeas Corpus Jurisdiction in Teague v. Lane*, 18 N.Y.U. Rev. L. & Soc. Change 537 (1991); Kathleen Patchel, *The New Habeas*, 42 Hastings L. J. 939 (1991); Yackle, note 49, at 2386-93. On the wider jurisprudential implications of the Court's insistence that rules of law change so easily and rapidly, see Markus Dirk Dubber, *Prudence and Substance: How the Supreme Court's New Habeas Retroactivity Doctrine Mirrors and Af-*

trine undermines the conventional understanding that federal courts do not second-guess previous state judgments on federal claims: District courts must trace
the precedents back to the time when the state courts passed on a prisoner's
claim and determine whether, at that time, "reasonable minds" might have arrived at the "outcome" the state courts, in fact, reached. The Supreme Court itself has acknowledged the point, explaining that the very point of *Teague* is to
"validate reasonable, good-faith interpretations of existing precedents made by
the state courts."[179]

The justices explored *Teague's* implications in *Wright v. West*,[180] an otherwise obscure case from Virginia. In that case, the Court asked the parties to brief
not only the issues they had presented to the lower courts, but also a general
question that the justices identified on their own: Should a federal court entertaining a habeas petition from a prisoner in custody pursuant to the judgment of
a state court "give deference to the state court's application of law to the specific
facts of the petitioner's case" or "review the state court's determination *de
novo?*" That question posed a choice between two possibilities, neither of which
was consistent with conventional understanding. District courts had never (formally) purported to "give deference" to state court determinations of mixed
questions. Nor had they (formally) purported to "review" state court decisions.
Nevertheless, the question captured the gist of the controversy surrounding
Teague.

After wrestling with its own question, the Court disposed of *West* without
reaching and resolving it. In an opinion announcing the Court's judgment on the
prisoner's individual claims, Justice Thomas made it clear that he would have
district courts "defer" to state court determinations of all factual, legal, and
mixed issues and would rely on *Teague* and its progeny for support. In his view,
it is enough if federal courts retain authority to decide "independently" whether
the state courts reached a "reasonable" judgment.[181] Other justices explained
Teague differently. According to Justice O'Connor, *Teague* is genuinely concerned with changes in the law. District courts have the duty and responsibility
to determine whether state court judgments were "correct" in light of the law as
it was at the time. By O'Connor's account, the Court has never allowed "a state
court's *incorrect* legal determination" to stand "because it was reasonable."[182]
Justice Kennedy also denied that *Teague* is on a "collision course" with federal
court authority to decide mixed questions independently. By his account, *Teague*
spares the states from a regime in which their judgments are effectively upset by
"changing a rule [of law] once thought correct but now understood to be deficient on its own terms." Justice Kennedy added that some rules are by their nature general, meant to guide judgment in a variety of fact patterns. Rules of that
kind infrequently yield results that forge a new rule for *Teague* purposes.[183]

---

fects Substantive Constitutional Law, 30 Am. Crim. L. Rev. 1 (1992); Fallon & Meltzer,
note 169; Linda Meyer, *"Nothing We Say Matters": Teague and New Rules*, 61 U. Chi. L.
Rev. 423 (1994).

179. *Butler*, 494 U.S. at 414.
180. 505 U.S. 277 (1992).
181. Id. at 287-88. The Chief Justice and Justice Scalia joined Justice Thomas on this
point.
182. Id. at 305 (O'Connor, J., concurring in the judgment) (emphasis added).
183. Id. at 306-08 (Kennedy, J., concurring in the judgment).

In light of the opinions in *West*, it appears that *Teague* does not threaten habeas corpus fundamentally, after all. The very concept of a "new" rule of law contemplates that not every rule is new and that settled rules remain available to be applied in habeas corpus proceedings. The *Teague* doctrine contemplates a largely abstract appraisal of the content of legal rules as they were articulated and applied in the past. The idea is to make an objective determination of whether a rule was so well established that any court (including the state court that passed on the instant prisoner's claim) must have reached an erroneous judgment if it denied relief to a prisoner whose claim fairly rested on that rule. The crucial analytical question is the level of generality at which a rule of law is articulated. The higher the level of generality, the broader a rule's apparent reach, and the harder it is to say that a federal district court has changed the rule by reaching a result in a particular case. The lower the level of generality, the more fact-sensitive is a rule's character, and the easier it is to say that a court has changed the rule by reaching a result in a similar (but not identical) case.[184] The Supreme Court has provided numerous illustrations of the proper analysis. Usually, the Court has concluded that prisoners' claims are *Teague*-barred, but very often there have been vigorous dissents."[185]

Justice O'Connor identified two exceptions to the usual prohibition on "new rule" claims: (1) new rules that place "certain kinds of primary, private individual conduct beyond the power of the criminal law-making authority to proscribe;" and (2) rules "without which the likelihood of an accurate conviction is seriously diminished."[186] The first exception is narrow, meant primarily to cover cases in which federal *substantive* law develops to insulate citizens from criminal punishment at all.[187] The Court held in *Penry v. Lynaugh*,[188] however, that it captured a claim that a prisoner with the mental capacity of a child could not be executed. Justice O'Connor acknowledged that the claim in *Penry* did not fit the first exception precisely. But she candidly expanded that exception to reach new rules that bar certain punishments for a "class of defendants" identified by "status or offense."[189] The second exception is also narrow, here again importing an explicit attention to guilt or innocence into habeas corpus doctrine. Justice O'-

---

184. See Chapter X, notes 275-78 (discussing the same phenomenon in connection with qualified immunity).

185. In *Gray v. Netherland*, 518 U.S. 152 (1996), for example, Justice Ginsburg insisted that "*Teague* is not the straightjacket the Commonwealth misunderstands it to be" and does not bar federal habeas courts from "applying, in a 'myriad of factual contexts,' law that is settled." Id. at 183 (dissenting opinion) (joined by Stevens, Souter & Breyer, J.J.), quoting *West*, 505 U.S. at 309 (Kennedy, J., concurring in the judgment).

186. *Teague*, 489 U.S. at 311, 313. Justice O'Connor borrowed these two exceptions from Justice Harlan, but in a modified form. Harlan would have extended the second exception to any rule requiring "procedures" that are "implicit in the concept of ordered liberty." *Mackey*, 401 U.S. at 693 (concurring opinion), quoting *Palko v. Connecticut*, 302 U.S. 319, 325 (1937). Justice O'Connor rejected that possibility as too generous and substituted the requirement that rules covered by the second exception must go to the accuracy of the guilt-determination function.

187. One of Justice Harlan's examples was the rule announced in *Griswold v. Connecticut*, 381 U.S. 479 (1965), where the Court held that Connecticut violated substantive due process by making it a crime for married people to use contraceptives. *Mackey*, 401 U.S. at 692 n.7 (concurring opinion).

188. 492 U.S. 302 (1989).

189. Id. at 330. On the merits, the Court rejected the prisoner's claim.

Connor said in *Teague* that it is "unlikely" that there are many new rules so essential to accurate decision-making, but yet to emerge.[190] In the current climate, that was understatement worthy of the British aristocracy. The Court has found no rules that fit the second exception, and it may ultimately prove to be a null set.[191]

The limitation that *Teague* imposes on federal habeas corpus is not jurisdictional. The custodian must object that a prisoner's claim is barred because it necessarily depends on a new rule.[192] When the custodian raises a sufficient objection, the district court addresses the "new rule" question as a threshold matter— before considering the merits of the prisoner's claim.[193] The Supreme Court is plainly concerned that previous judgments by state courts should be accorded due respect. Yet a federal court's determination of whether a rule is new for *Teague* purposes does not depend on anything the state courts said or did in the instant case. Instead, the federal court examines the precedents that were in place at the time the prisoner's conviction became final and decides whether those precedents compelled a judgment in the prisoner's favor.

The *Teague* doctrine shares intellectual features with the qualified immunity doctrine.[194] In both instances, federal courts hold officials to account only for violating federal law as it was on a previous occasion. There are, however, important differences. In one respect, qualified immunity doctrine contemplates a more conventional adjudicatory role for inferior federal courts than does the *Teague* doctrine. Recall that in an immunity case, the court first decides whether the plaintiff has alleged a violation of a federal right and *then* turns to the different question whether that right was established earlier. In a *Teague* case, by contrast, the court has no occasion to elaborate the content of a legal rule at present, but, instead, only articulates and applies the law as it was when the prisoner's conviction became final. Once the custodian raises an objection that a claim rests on a new rule, the district court deals with that question before, and perhaps instead of, determining whether the prisoner has a meritorious claim in light of the law as it now stands. By the Court's own account, *Teague* eliminates habeas corpus as a mechanism for the development of federal law.[195]

In another respect, it is *Teague* that contemplates a more conventional role for inferior federal courts. Recall that in an immunity case, the court will hold an executive officer personally liable only for behavior that was so abusive that the officer must have known that it violated the plaintiff's federal rights. That standard is low, because the Court recognizes that executive officers (particularly the

---

190. *Teague*, 489 U.S. at 313.

191. Professor Hoffmann has suggested that the much broader exception that Justice Harlan proposed should be adopted. See note 186; Hoffmann, note 170, at 213.

192. *Collins v. Youngblood*, 497 U.S. 37, 40-41 (1990). See *Goeke v. Branch*, 514 U.S. 115 (1995) (concluding that the state had sufficiently preserved a *Teague* issue below); *Schiro v. Farley*, 510 U.S. 222 (1994) (indicating that a belated *Teague* argument might be heard as a means of defending a lower court judgment on alternative grounds).

193. *Caspari v. Bohlen*, 510 U.S. 383, 389 (1994) (summarizing the analysis in *Teague* cases). While any *Teague* issues in a case should be treated before a federal court reaches the merits of a claim, any procedural bar issues should be treated before *Teague. Lambrix*, 117 S.Ct. at 1523.

194. See Chapter X, notes 266-92.

195. *Teague*, 489 U.S. at 316. But see note 228 and accompanying text (discussing the effect that 28 U.S.C. § 2254(d) may have on *Teague* in this respect).

police) cannot sort through complex legal issues before taking action in the field. In a *Teague* case, by contrast, the state officers in question are judges, who have the resources, time, and professional credentials to make reasoned judgments. Moreover, the stakes are different: State judges are not personally exposed to liability, and it is hard to think that qualified men and women will be discouraged from accepting positions on state courts simply because prisoners are granted new trials when federal courts find their federal claims to be meritorious.[196] Under *Teague*, accordingly, federal courts conduct a more conventional appraisal of the contemporaneous precedents and determine whether they were distinguishable from the prisoner's case in a meaningful way.[197] The Court uses similar verbal formulations to describe the standards in the immunity and *Teague* contexts. But it seems clear that federal courts expect comparatively little of cops on the beat and comparatively more of state judges with lawyers and libraries at their disposal.[198]

G. Previous Adjudication in State Court

According to conventional theory, federal courts determine the merits of claims independently, giving due (but not binding) effect to previous state judgments on the same claims.[199] The *Teague* line of cases maintains that structure, albeit largely eliminating claims resting on new rules of law. Another statutory provision also leaves the essential architecture of habeas in place, but limits the circumstances in which federal courts can award relief on the basis of claims they find to be meritorious. Pursuant to 28 U.S.C. § 2254(d), "an application for a writ of habeas corpus on behalf of a person in custody pursuant to the judgment of a State court shall not be granted with respect to any claim that was adjudicated on the merits in State proceedings" unless the "adjudication" of the claim: (1) "resulted in a decision that was contrary to, or involved an unreasonable application of, clearly established Federal law, as determined by the Supreme Court of the United States;" or (2) "resulted in a decision that was based on an unreasonable determination of the facts in light of the evidence presented in the State court proceeding."

---

196. Dissenting in *Snead v. Stringer*, 454 U.S. 988 (1981), then-Justice Rehnquist actually proposed that "fewer and fewer capable lawyers [could] be found to serve on state benches when they [might] find their considered decisions overturned by the ruling of a single federal district judge." Id. at 993. That was a stretch.

197. See *West*, 505 U.S. at 303-05 (O'Connor, J., concurring in the judgment).

198. The Supreme Court does not cite qualified immunity and *Teague* cases interchangeably as though the two doctrines were essentially the same. Of course, the claims advanced in § 1983 actions for damages and habeas corpus petitions are often different. The former commonly involve fourth amendment or substantive due process claims against the police; the latter can implicate all manner of procedural safeguards attending criminal cases. Yet there is a not insignificant overlap, too. See notes 240-53 and accompanying notes (discussing the Court's efforts to deal with cases in which prisoners have claims that can be cognizable both in § 1983 actions and in habeas). For a discussion of the similarities and differences between immunity doctrine and *Teague*, see Kit Kinports, *Habeas Corpus, Qualified Immunity, and Crystal Balls: Predicting the Course of Constitutional Law*, 33 Ariz. L. Rev. 115 (1991).

199. See text accompanying note 146.

Under § 2254(d), federal courts *do* take explicit account of prior state court decisions. They do so, however, only after they have reached their own judgments regarding the merits of claims and are poised to award *relief* to prisoners whose claims they determine to be valid.[200] Accordingly, § 2254(d) preserves the conventional understanding that habeas corpus is an original civil action in which federal jurisdiction is based on detention alleged to be in violation of federal law—rather than on a previous state court judgment said to be erroneous.[201] Federal courts thus take up the merits of claims in the ordinary course, ascertain the material facts subject to the provisions of § 2254(e),[202] and come to a preliminary determination whether prisoners are confined in violation of federal law. At that point, federal courts turn to any previous state court adjudications on the merits, which may forestall the actual award of federal relief.

A limitation of the federal courts' authority to grant relief can diminish the consequences of habeas corpus in virtually the same way as a limitation on the substantive scope of the federal courts' purview. Certainly the prisoners who file

---

200. Judge Easterbrook explains that § 2254(d) "preserves rather than undermines federal courts' independent interpretive power" inasmuch as federal courts "are free to express an independent opinion on all legal issues in [a] case." This statute "does no more than regulate relief." *Lindh v. Murphy*, 96 F.3d 856, 868-69 (7th Cir. 1996), *rev'd on other gr'ds*, 521 U.S. 320 (1997). When the Senate debated the bill containing what became the 1996 Act (including a section that would become § 2254(d)), Senator Kyl offered a substitute that would have provided that "an application" for the writ "shall not be *entertained*" in federal habeas corpus, unless state court opportunities are "inadequate or ineffective to test the legality of the person's detention." 141 Cong. Rec. S7829 (June 7, 1995) (emphasis added); see Yackle, *Primer*, note 61, at 398-400. That amendment was soundly defeated. One key difference between the amendment that was defeated and the statute that was passed, that is, § 2254(d), is that the enacted statute retains the federal courts' authority to *entertain* claims and only limits their authority to award *relief* with respect to claims they find to be meritorious See notes 139-42.

201. Consider, for comparative purposes, 28 U.S.C. § 1257, which confers appellate jurisdiction on the Supreme Court to "review" state court judgments for error. See Chapter VII, text accompanying notes 57-58. There is no serious argument that § 2254(d) confers on federal district courts an appellate jurisdiction to superintend state courts as though they were inferior tribunals situated beneath district courts in a radical new hierarchical structure. Federal habeas corpus has always had an appellate quality, coming as it typically does after state courts have passed on prisoners' claims. And a number of academics promote an appellate model for the writ. See note 43. Yet the state courts' station within the federal judicial system is well established, and it would take more than the elliptical language in § 2254(d) to change it. See Chapter VI (explaining the many ways in which the co-equal status of state courts and lower federal courts plays out). By one account, § 2254(d) *does* adjust the traditional conception of habeas corpus by instructing federal courts to focus on any previous state court judgment on the merits and to determine whether that judgment was erroneous. By that account, § 2254(d) retains the federal courts' authority to make independent judgments, but targets federal court attention differently: Previously, federal courts had no occasion to focus on prior state judgments, but rather took up prisoners' claims and decided them afresh. Under § 2254(d), by contrast, federal courts examine previous state court decisions and determine whether they were correct at the time they were rendered. Yackle, *Primer*, note 61, at 411-13.

202. In many instances, there will be no occasion for a federal evidentiary hearing. Under § 2254(e)(1), federal courts ordinarily presume that state court findings are correct. And under § 2254(e)(2), federal courts deny evidentiary hearings to prisoners who failed to develop facts when they had an opportunity to do so in state court. When, however, § 2254(e) permits federal fact-finding proceedings, federal courts ascertain the facts as part of the adjudication of claims on the merits. See notes 134-42 and accompanying text.

federal habeas petitions do so in order to obtain a practical remedy. Realistically speaking, then, § 2254(d) covers much of the same ground that *Brown v. Allen*[203] and the *Teague* cases also occupy.[204] Nevertheless, Congress often adjusts the remedies that federal courts may award in cases within their jurisdiction, and § 2254(d) is not, on its face, anomalous merely because it contemplates that federal courts may adjudicate the merits of a federal claim, decide that the claim is meritorious, but still withhold a certain form of relief. It is not unimportant that by adjudicating the merits of claims in advance of applying § 2254(d), federal courts specify the current status of federal rights.[205]

Once a federal court decides that a prisoner's claim is valid, the court must turn to § 2254(d) to determine whether relief can be awarded. Initially, the court must ascertain whether a state court conducted an "adjudication" of the claim "on the merits." The burden of demonstrating a qualifying adjudication presumably falls on the custodian, who stands to benefit if a prior state adjudication is established. An adjudication is not a "decision." Under § 2254(d), a decision is the *result* of an adjudication. An adjudication, accordingly, is something more than a disposition that concludes judicial consideration of a claim. It is a decision-making process for *reaching* a dispositive judgment. The custodian must therefore demonstrate that the state court employed a process sufficient to count as an adjudication within the meaning of § 2254(d)—namely, an adjudication of sufficient quality that it can forestall federal habeas corpus relief that would otherwise be forthcoming.[206]

---

203. See text accompanying notes 145-46.

204. There is an argument that § 2254(d) displaces the *Teague* doctrine. In the *Teague* cases, the Supreme Court has fashioned a response to the practical problem that arises when federal law develops between the time that a state court rejects a prisoner's claim and the time that a federal court considers the claim in habeas corpus proceedings. In the main, according to *Teague*, a federal court should not give effect to a change in the law that, by hypothesis, the state court could not have anticipated. Arguably, however, Congress has approached the same problem in a different way. By establishing filing deadlines and other mechanisms for expediting habeas proceedings, the 1996 Act ensures that federal habeas proceedings come closely on the heels of state court adjudication, thus dislodging the premise on which the *Teague* doctrine rests. Given a faster and more efficient process, there may no longer be a need for a special judicially crafted doctrine for ameliorating the tensions that attend slower litigation and legal rules that perpetually develop underfoot. See Yackle, *Primer*, note 61, at 417-19. It is more likely, however, that § 2254(d) essentially codifies *Teague*, though with differences worthy of note. See notes 228-29 and accompanying text.

205. Recall that this is the pattern in official immunity cases. See Chapter X, notes 287-92 and accompanying text. Federal courts can determine the merits of federal claims in habeas proceedings even if, in the end, they have no authority to award relief. See Chapter X, note 289 (discussing standing in the qualified immunity cases). On the relationship between qualified immunity and § 2254(d), see notes 218-20, 228-29 and accompanying text.

206. Since § 2254(d) itself prescribes no standard for federal courts to apply, the occasion may call for the conventional process model. See Chapter I, notes 61-65 and accompanying text. District courts should find a qualifying state court adjudication if the state court process provided a prisoner with an opportunity for full and fair litigation of the claim in question. This is not to suggest that § 2254(d) incorporates the process-based approach to habeas corpus advanced by the Reagan Administration. See note 155. Under § 2254(d), a federal courts does not withhold relief simply because a state court employed adequate process, without pausing to examine the result the state court reached. Instead, the court initially determines the substantive merits of a claim in the ordinary course. Then, the court appraises the process the state court engaged to reach its decision only in order to determine whether that process constituted an adjudication on the merits within the meaning of

That adjudication must have been on the "merits" of the claim. An examination of adjacent procedural matters may have led the state court to dispose of a claim without determining its substantive persuasive power. That will not do. An adjudication for purposes of § 2254(d) focuses on whether a claim has sufficient factual and legal support to establish a violation of federal law.[207] The working idea in § 2254(d) is that federal courts should withhold relief because a state court has already considered the merits with care and has reached a reasoned decision that a prisoner is not imprisoned in violation of federal law. In any particular instance, then, § 2254(d) contemplates that a federal court will determine whether the state court has actually done that. If a qualifying state court adjudication on the merits is shown, § 2254(d) bars federal relief, unless that adjudication "resulted in a decision" resting on either: (1) mistakes of law; or (2) mistakes of fact.

1. State Court Mistakes of Law

Paragraph (1) of § 2254(d) contemplates four overlapping inquiries: (1) whether the state court decision was "contrary to" federal law; (2) whether the decision "involved an unreasonable application" of federal law; (3) whether the federal law in question was "clearly established;" and (4) whether, if it was, it

---

§ 2254(d). If the court concludes that the state court did adjudicate the claim on the merits, the court turns to the further question whether the outcome the state court produced meets the standards in paragraphs (1) and (2). The proponents of the Reagan Administration plan repeatedly failed to win sufficient votes in Congress. In the end, § 2254(d) was a compromise meant to pacify members who feared that the Reagan Administration plan would curb federal habeas too much. See Yackle, *Primer*, note 61, at 426-38

207. If the state court disposed of a claim on the basis of procedural default, federal habeas consideration of the claim may be foreclosed under the default doctrine. See notes 96-130 and accompanying text. By hypothesis, however, when a federal court turns to § 2254(d), it has already decided that the claim in question is not procedurally barred. At this later stage, the only kind of state court action that matters is an adjudication on the merits. See *Liegakos v. Cooke*, 106 F.3d 1381, 1385 (7th Cir. 1997) (opinion of Easterbrook, J.). The prerequisites for merits adjudication in state court may be informed by the decisions on the exhaustion of state remedies. Prisoners can satisfy the exhaustion doctrine only by alerting state courts to the nature of their claims, so that the state courts can comprehend their federal character and adjudicate accordingly. Likewise, a state court adjudication of the merits should indicate that the state courts appreciated the nature of the claim and ruled on its *bona fides* as a federal matter. In one way, the decisions on the default doctrine may also be helpful by analogy. Recall that if a state court passes on the merits of a federal claim despite a prisoner's default, the prisoner does not forfeit the opportunity to press the claim in federal court. When it is not clear whether the state court rested judgment on the merits or default, federal courts presume a judgment on the merits—if the state court judgment fairly appears to rest primarily on federal law. See Chapter VII, note 126 and accompanying text. Federal courts attempting to decide whether a previous state adjudication was on the merits for purposes of § 2254(d) may sensibly follow the same course, finding a qualifying adjudication only if the state court *explained* its decision *primarily* as a determination of the validity of the claim. Notice that § 2254(d) reverses the state's interests in the basis of a prior state court judgment. In the default context, custodians typically seek to establish that a state court judgment was *not* on the merits, in hopes of forestalling federal consideration of a claim. In this context, by contrast, custodians typically wish to prove that a prior state court adjudication *was* on the merits, in hopes of persuading a federal court to withhold habeas relief.

was clearly established "by the Supreme Court." On examination, those four inquiries boil down to the analysis courts employ in the *Teague* line of cases. Upon the whole, § 2254(d) essentially codifies the *Teague* doctrine—not as a choice of law rule for determining whether federal courts can entertain claims at all, but as a mechanism for determining whether federal courts may issue habeas corpus relief.

State decisions contrary to federal law. The phrase "contrary to" law is typically understood to describe judicial error—as when one court determines that another court has simply made a mistake.[208] The "contrary to" formulation in paragraph (1) of § 2254(d) thus may allow a federal court to grant habeas relief with respect to a claim, notwithstanding a prior state court adjudication on the merits—if that state court adjudication produced an erroneous decision.[209] Notice, however, that the state court decision must have been erroneous in light of "clearly established" law at the time it was rendered. In that, the "contrary to" formulation incorporates the basic thrust of the *Teague* doctrine—namely, that federal courts should not surprise state courts by invoking new rules of federal law.

State decisions unreasonably applying law. The "unreasonable application" phrase is ambiguous by comparison. By inserting that additional formulation after the "contrary to" phrase, paragraph (1) may signal that the two ideas are distinguishable. Accordingly, paragraph (1) may not state a single exception to the general rule against federal relief, but may itself be bifurcated—identifying two different ways in which a previous state court decision may be found wanting and prescribing different standards for a federal court to apply to each. By some accounts, the "contrary to" formulation applies only to a state court decision resting on an articulation of a purely legal rule, while the "unreasonable application" formulation applies to a state court decision resting on the application of a legal rule to the facts of a particular case. It may be, then, that a state court decision regarding a purely legal issue was "contrary to" federal law if it was erroneous. But a state court decision regarding a mixed question of law and fact was "unreasonable" only if it was not only wrong, but *unreasonably* wrong. Recall that Justice Thomas suggested such a standard in *Wright v. West.*[210] It is possible to construe the "unreasonable application" language in paragraph (1) of § 2254(d) to revisit *West* and to side with Thomas over Justice O'Connor and Justice Kennedy.[211]

---

208. Liebman and Ryan contend that the "contrary to" phrase is a "statutory term of art for one court's independent review of another court's legal or mixed rulings under governing law." James S. Liebman & William F. Ryan, *"Some Effectual Power": The Quantity and Quality of Decisionmaking Required of Article III Courts*, 98 Colum. L. Rev. 696, 866 (1998). They cite the Federal Magistrate's Act as an illustration. See Chapter V, note 30. In that context, a ruling that is "contrary to" law is simply a ruling that is erroneous as a matter of law. *Saltarelli v. Bob Baker Grp. Med. Trust*, 35 F.3d 382, 385 (9th Cir. 1994).

209. Judge Easterbrook reads the "contrary to" phrase this way. In his view, the only "novelty" in this part of § 2254(d) is the direction to consult only Supreme Court precedents. See *Lindh*, 96 F.3d at 869.

210. See note 181 and accompanying text.

211. Judge Kanne suggests this understanding in *Gomez v. Acevedo*, 106 F.3d 192, 198 (7th Cir. 1996). Judge Easterbrook has it that a state court's "fact-specific answer cannot be called 'unreasonable' even if it is wrong." *Lindh*, 96 F.3d at 876-77. See also Note, *Rewriting the Great Writ: Standards of Review for Habeas Corpus Under the New 28 U.S.C. § 2254*, 110 Harv. L. Rev. 1868, 1882 (1997) (reading § 2254(d) to establish a "reasonableness" standard for mixed questions but failing to mention Justice Thomas). Judge Jolly does not explicitly argue that § 2254(d) incorporates Justice Thomas' position in *West*. But he

Alternatively, the "unreasonable application" phrase can be read in conjunction with the "contrary to" phrase. The two formulations appear brigaded together in paragraph (1), not in separate and independent paragraphs of their own.[212] By this alternative account, they work in tandem to underscore a single point—namely, that federal courts can grant habeas corpus relief in the face of a prior state court decision if (and only if) the state court made a serious mistake, *either* in identifying the governing legal rule *or* in applying the proper rule in the instant case. There are at least two ways to understand how this might be so. One takes the "unreasonable application" formulation to refer to a state court decision resting on an "unreasonable" determination of a mixed question; the

---

does contend that the "unreasonable application" formulation bars federal courts from awarding relief unless "it can be said that reasonable jurists considering the question would be of one view that the state court ruling was incorrect." *Drinkard v. Johnson*, 97 F.3d 751, 769 (5th Cir. 1996), *cert. denied*, 117 S.Ct. 1114 (1997). Professor Lee argues that even if Judge Jolly's general approach to § 2254(d)(1) is valid, his account of an "unreasonable application" of federal law is flawed in two related ways. Initially, Jolly's account mistakes what it is that must be unreasonable if federal relief is to be awarded. The statute, § 2254(d)(1), contemplates that a state court "decision" must "involve" an unreasonable application of federal law. That focuses attention on the accuracy of a judicial judgment in the conventional way. Jolly, by contrast, has it that federal relief can be granted only if state judges themselves are unreasonable. That focuses attention on state judges' competence and sincerity. Relatedly, according to Professor Lee, Judge Jolly's account is far too grudging. If federal relief can be awarded only when federal courts are willing to say that state judges have lost their senses, it is hard to think that federal relief will ever be granted at all. That, presumably, is not what § 2254(d)(1) means to accomplish. See Evan Tsen Lee, *Section 2254(d) of the New Habeas Statute: An (Opinionated) User's Manual*, 51 Vand. L. Rev. 103 (1998). But see text accompanying note 177 (noting that the Supreme Court has used the kind of language that Judge Jolly employs in describing what counts as a new rule for *Teague* purposes).

212. Just before the Senate took up the bill that would become the 1996 Act, the House of Representatives debated a bill containing the Republican "Contract with America." In the course of the debate on that bill, Rep. Cox introduced an amendment on habeas corpus, which would have addressed federal habeas relief in a different way:

An application for a writ of habeas corpus on behalf of a person in custody pursuant to the judgment of a State court shall not be granted with respect to any claim that was decided on the merits in State proceedings unless the adjudication of the claim—

(1) resulted in a decision that was based on an arbitrary or unreasonable interpretation of clearly established Federal law as articulated in the decisions of the Supreme Court of the United States;

(2) resulted in a decision that was based on an arbitrary or unreasonable application to the facts of clearly established Federal law as articulated in the decisions of the Supreme Court of the United States; or

(3) resulted in a decision that was based on an arbitrary or unreasonable determination of the facts in light of the evidence presented in the State proceeding.

141 Cong. Rec. H1424 (Feb. 8, 1995).

The House adopted the Cox amendment, but the bill itself went no further. See Yackle, *Primer*, note 61, at 433-35. There are obvious differences between the Cox amendment in the House and § 2254(d), which ultimately passed in both bodies. One difference is that, in the Cox version, state court decisions based on incorrect interpretations of law and state court decisions based on unreasonable applications of law appear in different categories, indicating that they were conceived to advance different ideas. In § 2254(d), by contrast, the "contrary to" and "unreasonable application" formulations appear together. To treat them as separate, Judge Jolly and Judge Easterbrook must impose the structure of the failed Cox amendment on the different structure of the statute that Congress actually enacted. Judge Selya has pointed this out. *O'Brien v. DuBois*, 145 F.3d 16, 22-23 (1st Cir. 1998).

other takes that formulation to refer to a state decision resting on an extension of a legal principle to alien circumstances where it has no bearing. Both understandings lead to the conclusion that § 2254(d)(1) essentially codifies the *Teague* doctrine as Justices O'Connor and Kennedy described that doctrine in *West*.

Even if the "unreasonable application" formulation refers to a state court decision resting on an application of law to the facts, it does not follow (ineluctably) that paragraph (1) distinguishes neatly between a state court decision resting on the identification of an abstract legal standard, on the one hand, and one resting on the application of a purely legal standard to a particular case, on the other. By its terms, paragraph (1) instructs a federal court to withhold habeas relief in light of a prior state court "decision." A decision, in turn, necessarily embraces both the state court's identification of the pertinent legal rule and the court's application of that rule to the particular circumstances of a case.[213] By some accounts, accordingly, paragraph (1) merely employs two mutually reinforcing phrases to manifest the position that Justice O'Connor and Justice Kennedy adopted in *West*: A previous state court decision was not correct (enough) if it was reasonable; it was reasonable if it was correct.[214]

Then again, the "unreasonable application" formulation may not refer to a state court determination of a mixed question at all. By its terms, paragraph (1) states only that federal relief must be withheld in light of a prior state court decision that "involved" an unreasonable "application" of federal law. It does not specify that an "application" must necessarily be an application of law *to the facts of a case*. By some accounts, the "unreasonable application" formulation actually refers to a state court decision resting on an ill-advised attempt to apply a legal principle or rule outside its ordinary context in circumstances in which it cannot reasonably serve.[215] Recall that in the *Teague* cases, the Supreme Court has said that when courts extend a settled legal rule to a truly novel context, they do not merely misapply that rule to the facts of a particular case, but actually create an entirely new rule.[216] If that is what paragraph (1) captures in the "un-

---

213. Of course, a decision also encompasses a determination of the underlying historical facts. See Note, *The Path to Habeas Corpus Narrows: Interpreting § 2254(d)(1)*, 96 Mich. L. Rev. 434, 447 (1997). Yet since § 2254(e) independently addresses the effects of state court findings of fact, state court decisions for purposes of § 2254(d) can sensibly be limited to the judgments the state courts made regarding the legal significance of the facts.

214. Judge Wood has explained, accordingly, that § 2254(d)(1) preserves the federal courts' authority to consider *de novo* both questions of law and mixed questions of law and fact. *Hall v. Washington*, 106 F.3d 742, 748 (7th Cir.), *cert. denied*, 118 S.Ct. 264 (1997). See *Mata v. Johnson*, 99 F.3d 1261, 1268 (5th Cir. 1996) (reading § 2254(d) to "codif[y]" the Supreme Court's *Teague* doctrine insofar as that doctrine delineates "the scope of the Great Writ"); cf. *Fern v. Gramley*, 99 F.3d 255, 260 (7th Cir. 1996) (finding a *Teague* analysis to "suffice" for purposes of § 2254(d) insofar as that analysis focused entirely on Supreme Court precedent). For a discussion, see Lee, note 211. Writing prior to *West*, Professor Hoffmann proposed that Congress should codify the essentials of *Teague*, but should make it clear by statute that state courts are obliged to decide federal claims in "conceptual faithfulness" to extant precedents. See Hoffmann, note 170, at 217.

215. This is the way Professor Liebman reads the "unreasonable application" phrase. Liebman & Ryan, note 208, at 871-72. See *O'Brien*, 145 F.3d at 23-25 (largely embracing this interpretation). The unsuccessful Cox amendment in the House *did* refer to a state court's "unreasonable application" of clearly established law "to the facts." See note 212.

216. See note 176 and accompanying text.

reasonable application" formulation, then, here again, that paragraph codifies the essentials of the *Teague* doctrine.[217]

Clearly established law. Prior state court adjudications bar federal habeas relief if they produced decisions consistent with "clearly established" federal law. That same phrase appears in the cases on qualified immunity.[218] But just as the policy considerations that drive the meaning of "clearly established" law in qualified immunity cases do not travel well to habeas corpus cases governed by *Teague*, they do not travel well to cases implicating § 2254(d), either. All three related bodies of doctrine can best be reconciled if § 2254(d) is understood once again to borrow from the most closely analogous preexisting source—namely, *Teague*. The point is that state courts can be expected to apply only the rules of law that are well established at the time they address prisoners' claims.[219] If a state court adjudication resulted in a decision that comported with the precedents as they stood at time the state court acted, § 2254(d) instructs federal habeas courts to withhold federal relief.[220]

Supreme Court precedents. Prior state court decisions need only respect clearly established federal law "as determined by the Supreme Court." That contingency is problematic. Article III judges at every level operate as independent jurists, not as agents of the Supreme Court. They are duty-bound to make their best judgments about what federal law demands, and those judgments stand until they are overturned, either at the circuit level or in the Supreme Court itself.

---

217. This is where Judge Selya comes out. *O'Brien*, 145 F.3d at 24. Judge Luttig recognizes this different understanding of the "unreasonable application" formulation, but he grants it no analytical significance. *Green v. French*, 143 F.3d 865, 870 (4th Cir. 1998).

218. See Chapter X, notes 268-78 and accompanying text.

219. Both Judge Easterbrook and Judge Selya suggest that courts handling habeas cases pursuant to § 2254(d)(1) should rely on habeas corpus precedents applying the *Teague* doctrine rather than on § 1983 precedents applying qualified immunity doctrine. *Lindh*, 96 F.3d at 869-70; *O'Brien*, 145 F.3d at 24-25. In *United States v. Lanier*, 117 S.Ct. 1219 (1997), the Supreme Court construed 18 U.S.C. § 242, which makes it a criminal offense to "deprive a person of rights protected by the Constitution or laws of the United States." The circuit court had reversed a conviction under that statute, in part on the theory that the defendant could be criminally responsible for depriving his victim of a federal right only if that right was even more clearly established than it would have had to be to defeat qualified immunity in a civil action. In the Supreme Court, Justice Souter rejected that construction of § 242. He explained that defendants can be held either criminally liable under § 242 or civilly liable under the qualified immunity doctrine on the same showing of a violation of "clearly established" law. The decision in *Lanier* may have implications for the way in which the "clearly established" phrase in § 2254(d) should be understood. On the one hand, *Lanier* may suggest that the Court is inclined to treat the idea of clearly established law in the same way in all contexts. On the other, *Lanier* may underscore how generous that standard is to executive officers in qualified immunity cases—who elude civil liability for damages only if they take actions that would also support a criminal prosecution. That is not the standard that the *Teague* cases employ to determine whether state courts reached correct decisions on the basis of existing precedents. And it seems equally inapposite for purposes of § 2254(d). The Court cited no *Teague* cases in *Lanier*.

220. Judge Cox has explained that *Teague* and § 2254(d) call for a "similar analysis" of whether a rule of law was clearly established at the crucial time. *Neelley v. Nagle*, 138 F.3d 917, 922-23 (11th Cir. 1998). Recall, however, that under § 2254(d), by contrast to *Teague*, the benchmark is the date on which the state court adjudication produced a decision—not the date on which the Supreme Court denied *certiorari*. See note 170. Liebman and Ryan count that as one difference between § 2254(d) and *Teague*. Liebman & Ryan, note 208, at 867-68. Professor Lee agrees and considers the difference important in that it can turn actual cases. Lee, note 211, at 118-22.

There is an argument, then, that Congress intrudes upon Article III independence if it presumes to prescribe the sources that federal judges can consult—even if Congress specifies Supreme Court precedents *en masse*. Some courts and commentators have taken this feature of § 2254(d) to heart and run out the constitutional implications.[221]

There may be a far less threatening way to read § 2254(d): The idea is only to remind inferior federal courts that state courts are their co-equals in a single system, that state courts do not answer to federal district and circuit courts, and that both state and inferior federal courts *do* answer only to the Supreme Court.[222] If, then, a state court declined to follow precedents in the lower federal courts, that alone is insufficient to condemn its judgment as mistaken. A state court decision can be regarded as erroneous only if it neglected federal *law* as it then stood. That federal law was reflected in any existing Supreme Court decisions, as well as in the decisions of other courts (state and federal) that presumably hoped to interpret the law in the way the Supreme Court would. A previous state court decision was wrong, then, if it was inconsistent with any precedents (from whatever court) that accurately portrayed the law at the time—that is, the law that the Supreme Court itself would have brought to bear, if the case had reached the Court on direct review of the state court decision.[223]

---

221. The thought is that, under § 2254(d), a prior state court decision must be sufficient to foreclose habeas relief in any instance in which there was no plainly dispositive Supreme Court precedent at the time and thus no clearly established law "as determined by the Supreme Court" that the state court might have neglected. Judge Easterbrook responds that the federal judiciary is not unitary and that all Article III judges exercise independent judicial power. Easterbrook does not take § 2254(d) to deny that. *Lindh*, 96 F.3d at 869-70. Accordingly, he does not read § 2254(d) to enact the formalistic proposition that in the absence of a Supreme Court precedent squarely on point, there was no clearly established federal law from which a state court could depart. Judge Ripple *does* read § 2254(d) that way and insists that § 2254(d) is unconstitutional to the extent it restricts lower federal courts to an examination of existing Supreme Court precedents. Id. at 886-88.

222. See *Lockhart v. Fretwell*, 506 U.S. 364, 376 (1993) (Thomas, J., concurring) (explaining that state courts have no obligation to follow inferior federal court precedents).

223. By this account, § 2254(d) allows federal courts to compare prior state court decisions to contemporaneous precedents outside the Supreme Court—treating those decisions as evidence of what the Supreme Court itself would have declared the law to be, if the Court had taken the case for review. See *O'Brien*, 145 F.3d at 21 (expressing this view). Professor Jackson suggests that Article III guarantees inferior federal court decisions respect as precedents for *stare decisis* purposes, and that if § 2254(d) bars *any* consideration of lower court precedents at all, it may be inconsistent with that constitutional principle. Vicki C. Jackson, *Introduction: Congressional Control of Jurisdiction and the Future of the Federal Courts— Opposition, Agreement, and Hierarchy*, 86 Gtn. L.J. 2445, 2470 (1998). In *Lanier*, the circuit court below held that § 242 did not give fair warning of the behavior it condemned, unless the Supreme Court itself had issued a precedent or precedents clarifying a federal right and thus informing potential defendants of what would constitute a violation of that right. Justice Souter rejected that argument. Just as lower court decisions can clarify the law for purposes of determining whether defendants are immune from liability for damages, lower court decisions can equally clarify the law for purposes of determining whether defendants are criminally liable under § 242. 117 S.Ct. at 1226; see note 219. The *Lanier* decision rests on a construction of § 242. That case nevertheless indicates that the Court does not regard its own precedents as the sole authoritative source for federal law, and it may signal that the Court is unlikely to construe § 2254(d) to eliminate consideration of lower court decisions.

2. State Court Mistakes of Fact

Subsection (2) of § 2254(d) contemplates only one inquiry: whether a prior state court decision "was based on an unreasonable determination of the facts in light of the evidence presented in the State court proceeding." The idea at work in this second exception is plain enough: If the state court misapprehended the underlying facts, the court may have reached an unreliable decision regarding a claim, even if its handling of the legal issues was otherwise flawless. The reference in subsection (2) to an "unreasonable" determination of the facts repeats the ambiguity of the reference in subsection (1) to an "unreasonable" application of law. Here again, it is possible to understand § 2254(d) to contemplate state decisions that were not only wrong, but unreasonably wrong. Alternatively, this section may be read to allow federal habeas relief if a previous state court decision was premised on a seriously mistaken account of the material facts.

This portion of § 2254(d) must be reconciled with § 2254(e)(1), which instructs federal courts to presume that state court findings of fact are accurate.[224] There is no necessary conflict between the two. Even if some state findings of fact are taken to be correct, the decision the state court ultimately reached regarding a federal claim might still have been based on an unreasonable determination of other facts. Moreover, prisoners can rebut the presumption in § 2254(e)(1) by presenting clear and convincing evidence that the state courts were mistaken. In cases in which prisoners do that, federal courts may award relief on the theory that the prior state court decision was based on an unreasonable determination of the facts. Nevertheless, it would be hard to say that § 2254(d)(2) and § 2254(e)(1) complement each other in a neat and coherent framework. It is not clear, for example, that a federal court can decide that a prior state decision was based on an unreasonable determination of the facts *only* if the prisoner adduces clear and convincing evidence that the state court's factual findings were erroneous. Nor, for that matter, is it clear that if a prisoner makes that kind of showing, it follows ineluctably that the state court decision *was* based on an unreasonable determination of the facts.[225]

This portion of § 2254(d) must also be reconciled with § 2254(e)(2), which contemplates a federal evidentiary hearing if the facts were not developed in state court for reasons that cannot be ascribed to the petitioner.[226] The two provisions operate sequentially. A federal court must first ascertain the facts as provided in § 2254(e)(2) and *then* decide whether relief can be awarded under § 2254(d)(2). When § 2254(d)(2) comes into play, it limits a federal court's attention to the "the evidence presented in the State court proceeding." It would not do, then, for a district court to take up that section before expanding the state court record to

---

224. See notes 134-35 and accompanying text.

225. The two provisions derive from different prior legislative bills and were brought together in the bill that became the 1996 Act without any public discussion or explanation of how they would function together. See Yackle, *Primer*, note 61, at 427 (tracing the idea of an "unreasonable" determination of the facts to a Justice Department memorandum explaining the Reagan Administration's program).

226. See notes 139-42 and accompanying text.

the extent allowed by § 2254(e). To do that would be to render § 2254(e)(2) superfluous in precisely the cases in which that provision contemplates federal fact-finding—namely, cases in which previous state court proceedings were deficient. In a case in which § 2254(e)(2) authorizes federal fact-finding, previous proceedings in state court were by hypothesis incomplete. It follows, accordingly, that a federal habeas court has no occasion to decide whether, judged exclusively in light of that flawed record, the state court's determination of the facts was unreasonable. Even if the state court made perfectly sensible determinations on the basis of incomplete evidence, the federal court must take account of any further evidence generated in a federal hearing that § 2254(e)(2) permits.[227]

In the end, then, § 2254(d) fits fairly well into the landscape previously marked off by qualified immunity and *Teague*. In effect, § 2254(d) is a mix-and-match composite, borrowing from both the other doctrines in order to orchestrate an approach to habeas cases that attends to the interests at stake. The statute adopts one key feature of immunity doctrine for use in habeas cases: Under § 2254(d), a federal court first determines whether a prisoner has a meritorious federal claim and only then turns to the further question whether, if so, federal habeas relief can be awarded.[228] In that important respect, § 2254(d) displaces *Teague*, which would have a federal court begin by ascertaining the law as it was previously. The statute does not adopt, for use in habeas corpus, the standard that qualified immunity doctrine employs for determining whether executive officers can be held personally liable for damages. On that point, § 2254(d) embraces *Teague* as the more analogous body of precedent: Federal courts withhold habeas relief if a previous state court adjudication on the merits produced a decision that was correct in light of the law as it was at the time.[229]

---

227. See also Note, note 211, at 1875-76 (wrestling with the connection between § 2254(e)(2) and § 2254(d)(2)).

228. In a qualified immunity case, a federal court determines only whether a plaintiff has alleged facts that, if true, would make out a violation of a federal right. At the threshold, the court does not actually determine whether the plaintiff's allegations *are* true. In a habeas corpus case, by contrast, § 2254(d) contemplates that a federal court *will* ascertain the facts (within the limits prescribed by § 2254(e)) and thus will actually adjudicate the merits of a claim. See notes 200-02. Only if the federal court concludes that a claim is valid on the merits will the court have occasion to decide the further question whether § 2254(d) permits federal relief.

229. There are, however, some differences between § 2254(d) and *Teague* at this level. Again, the baseline date for purposes of § 2254(d) is different from the baseline date for purposes of *Teague*. See notes 170, 220. Moreover, § 2254(d) does not explicitly embrace the two exceptions that *Teague* recognizes to the general rule against the enforcement of new rules. See notes 186-91 and accompanying text. Liebman and Ryan are satisfied that if § 2254(d) is understood roughly to codify *Teague*, it does not intrude upon the authority of Article III courts to adjudicate. Liebman & Ryan, note 208, at 879. See also Scheidegger, note 58 (contending that § 2254(d) is constitutional inasmuch as it affects only the availability of habeas relief). If, however, § 2254(d) were read to require federal courts essentially to rubberstamp state court decisions on the merits of constitutional claims, its validity presumably would be questionable. See notes 30-31 (noting that the Supreme Court occasionally suggests that the Suspension Clause guarantees federal habeas jurisdiction to entertain petitions from state convicts); Chapter IV, notes 73-82 and accompanying text (discussing Article III limits on congressional authority to affect judicial outcomes).

H. Multiple Petitions

Just as habeas corpus is exempt from the Full Faith and Credit Statute, habeas is equally exempt (formally speaking) from the federal common law preclusion rules that ordinarily restrict litigants' ability to file multiple federal lawsuits against the same defendant, pressing claims arising from a single trans-action.[230] Nevertheless, second or successive federal petitions are restricted by statutes and judicial decisions that typically give preclusive effect to an initial federal habeas proceeding, in fact if not in name.

Under 28 U.S.C. § 2244(b)(1), a claim that was presented in a previous federal habeas petition "shall be dismissed." This does not mean, however, that *any* claim that was contained in a prior application is barred, irrespective of the disposition. The Supreme Court explained in *Stewart v. Martinez-Villareal*[231] that dismissals for "technical procedural reasons" do not trigger § 2244(b)(1)'s prohibition on petitions raising the same claim a second time.[232] If, for example, a claim was dismissed on a prior occasion because the prisoner failed to exhaust state opportunities for litigating the claim at that time, the disposition was without prejudice. When the prisoner satisfies the exhaustion doctrine with respect to the claim, § 2244(b)(1) permits another petition.[233]

Under § 2244(b)(2), a claim raised for the first time in a second or successive habeas petition may be considered, but only in certain circumstances. The prisoner must show either: (A) that the claim rests on a "new" rule of "constitutional" law, "made retroactive to cases on collateral review by the Supreme Court, that was previously unavailable;" or (B)(i) that its "factual predicate" could not have been discovered earlier by the exercise of due diligence "and" (ii) that "the facts underlying the claim, if proven and viewed in light of the evidence as a whole, would be sufficient to establish by clear and convincing evidence that

---

230. *Salinger v. Loisel*, 265 U.S. 224 (1924). For a discussion of the common law backdrop, see Yackle, note 29, at 551-52.

231. 118 S.Ct. 1618 (1998).

232. Id. at 1621-22.

233. Id. But see note 87 and accompanying text (discussing claims that prisoners deliberately abandon in order to avoid dismissal under the *Lundy* decision). The prisoner in *Martinez-Villareal* filed a federal petition advancing several claims, including a claim that he was incompetent and thus could not be executed. See *Ford v. Wainwright*, 477 U.S. 399 (1986) (holding that it is cruel and unusual punishment to execute an insane prisoner). Counsel for the custodian urged the district court to dismiss the *Ford* claim on the theory that it was premature: The prisoner was not scheduled for immediate execution, and his condition might change. The district court agreed to dismiss the *Ford* claim on that basis, but noted that the dismissal would not affect the prisoner's ability to advance the claim later. Then, when the prisoner revived the *Ford* claim at a later time, counsel for the custodian contended that it was barred by § 2244(b)(1). In the Supreme Court, Chief Justice Rehnquist explained that the prisoner's renewal of the *Ford* claim did not qualify as a successive application for habeas relief on the basis of the same claim. Dissenting in *Martinez-Villareal*, Justice Scalia and Justice Thomas insisted that the literal text of § 2244(b)(1) barred the prisoner's *Ford* claim and that the Court could not justifiably construe the statute another way merely because it found that result "perverse." 118 S.Ct. at 1625. For a discussion of cases in which claims are dismissed on procedural grounds and therefore can be presented in subsequent petitions, despite § 2244(b)(1), see *Benton v. Washington*, 106 F.3d 162 (7th Cir. 1996).

but for constitutional error, no reasonable factfinder would have found the applicant guilty of the underlying offense."[234]

A prisoner who wishes to file a second or successive federal application under § 2244(b)(2) must be authorized to do so by a panel of three circuit judges. Pursuant to § 2244(b)(3), the prisoner must move the circuit court for an order permitting the district court to entertain another application. A three-judge panel can authorize a prisoner to proceed in the district court only if the panel "determines that the petition makes a prima facie showing" that it meets the standards established by § 2244(b)(2). The panel must act within thirty days after the prisoner files a motion for authorization. A panel decision is neither "appealable" nor "subject to a petition for rehearing or for a writ of certiorari."[235] If a panel authorizes a prisoner to proceed in the district court, that court, in turn, to determines whether the application actually satisfies § 2244(b)(2)'s standards for second or successive applications.[236]

---

234. This last is roughly the same standard that § 2254(e) establishes with respect to prisoners seeking federal evidentiary hearings. See text accompanying note 139. In one way, this standard in § 2244(b)(2) is more demanding inasmuch as it refers to proof of the relevant facts and instructs the court to view those facts "in light of the evidence as a whole" — presumably the evidence at trial. Of course, this standard governs prisoners who have by hypothesis already had one opportunity to be in federal court. In other way, however, the standard in § 2254(e) is more demanding, even though the prisoners affected by that provision have *not* (necessarily) been before a federal court on a prior occasion. See note 140.

235. Timetables for federal court action can present constitutional difficulty. See note 95. This statute, § 2244(b)(3), does not specify what a panel is to do if, at the end of thirty days, it is not yet able either to grant or deny authorization. Only three possibilities are open. A panel might be compelled to authorize the prisoner to proceed in the district court. That course would have the virtue of ensuring that prisoners are not erroneously denied a judicial forum, but it would sacrifice obvious state interests. Moreover, a compelled disposition (even one favoring the individual) might run afoul of the separation principle and Article III. Congress cannot force an Article III court to reopen a judgment the court considers to be final. *Plaut v. Spendthrift Farm*, 514 U.S. 211 (1995); see Chapter IX, notes 30-32 and accompanying text. It may follow that Congress cannot force an Article III court to make a judgment final when the court has an issue under advisement. Alternatively, a panel might be compelled to *deny* the prisoner's request. That response to the timetable would raise even more constitutional problems. The Article III point would be the same, and the court's treatment of the prisoner might violate due process. *Logan v. Zimmerman Brush Co.*, 455 U.S. 422, 433 (1982) (holding that a state cannot terminate a party's claim simply because a hearing has not been held within a specified time and that the party is entitled to an "opportunity to present his case and have its merits fairly judged"). The only other option is to read the thirty-day timetable to be hortatory only and thus to allow a panel to render a proper decision when it can. Mechanically, a panel may enter a place-keeping order, but stay that order pending further study. Then, when the panel is able to dispose of the applicant's request, it can revisit the matter *sua sponte* and substitute a final order. The provision in § 2244(b)(3) declaring that a panel decision "shall not be the subject of a petition for rehearing" may only bar one of the parties from seeking reconsideration of an order the court considers to be final. The circumstances are different if the panel itself has stated that a previous order is *not* final and the panel acts without receiving a "petition" from one of the parties. E.g., *Triestman v. United States*, 124 F.3d 361 (2d Cir. 1997) (following this procedure).

236. Pursuant to § 2255, federal prisoners attacking federal convictions or sentences equally must obtain a circuit panel's permission to file more than one application. The precise language in § 2255 does not track perfectly with the language in § 2244(b)(3), however, and there may be cases in which federal prisoners receive different treatment. See Yackle, Part III, note 63 (identifying the discrepancies between § 2244(b)(3) and § 2255). The "gatekeeping" mechanism is presumably meant to promote efficiency by screening unjustified petitions out of the district courts at the door. Yet it also generates a welter of procedural ques-

The Supreme Court held in *Felker v. Turpin*[237] that § 2244(b)(3) eliminates the ordinary *certiorari* avenue to the Court itself, but preserves the Court's independent jurisdiction to entertain habeas applications as an "original" matter. If, then, a circuit panel denies a prisoner's request to file a second or successive petition, the prisoner can seek leave to file a petition for a writ of habeas corpus, issued originally from the Court.[238] In passing, Chief Justice Rehnquist said that § 2244(b)(2)'s standards for multiple federal petitions "constitute a modified res judicata rule." They may place a "restraint" on what federal courts conventionally call an "abuse of the writ." But the "added restrictions" they impose on multiple habeas petitions are "well within the compass" of the "evolutionary process" by which the availability of habeas relief has always been developed.[239]

I. The Ku Klux Klan Act Revisited

There are obvious parallels between habeas corpus proceedings authorized by § 2241 and civil rights actions authorized by § 1983. In both instances, individual litigants can initiate original lawsuits in federal court, contending that state officials have violated their federal rights—typically fourteenth amendment rights. Both § 2241 and § 1983 establish rights of action. The habeas corpus statute, § 2241, also confers jurisdiction on federal courts.[240] The Ku Klux Klan

---

tions and problems. Prisoners typically have no lawyers to explain to them that they must go first to the circuit level before they can proceed at the district level. They thus may file second or successive petitions in the district court and suffer dismissal for want of permission from a circuit panel. Pursuant to 28 U.S.C. § 1631, a district court can transfer a premature petition to the circuit court. The circuit court, in turn, can notify the prisoner that panel permission is necessary and fix a schedule. By the terms of § 1631, the one-year statute of limitations established by § 2244(d)(1) is met if the petition is timely when filed initially (though erroneously) in the district court. See notes 91-93 and accompanying text (discussing filing deadlines in connection with the exhaustion doctrine). The thirty-day timetable for circuit panel action on the motion for authorization begins to run when the prisoner files a proper motion in response to notification of the need to do so. See *Liriano v. United States*, 95 F.3d 119 (2d Cir. 1996) (outlining this process).

237. 518 U.S. 651 (1996); see Chapter IV, notes 67-70 and accompanying text.

238. Recall that the Court considers its authority to issue the writ originally as a species of appellate jurisdiction, thus defusing any Article III difficulty. See Chapter IV, note 70.

239. 518 U.S. at 664. Prior to the enactment of this provision in § 2244(b) in 1996, the Court used the doctrine formulated in the procedural default cases to determine the circumstances in which prisoners could file second or successive petitions containing claims that might have been, but were not, presented in prior applications. See *McCleskey v. Zant*, 499 U.S. 467 (1991); notes 96-124 and accompanying text. There are differences between those standards and the standards established by § 2244(b)(2). Recall that in the procedural default cases, prisoners who establish that they were probably convicted erroneously because of violations of their federal rights are excused from default in state court even if they cannot demonstrate cause. See text accompanying note 119. In § 2244(b)(2), however, there is a conjunctive "and" between the two elements of paragraph (B). It appears, then, that prisoners must show *both* something akin to cause *and* evidence undermining factual guilt—unless they proceed under paragraph (A), which requires a new rule of constitutional law, retroactively applicable.

240. Federal jurisdiction to entertain habeas corpus petitions is conferred by § 2241, which derives from the 1789 and 1867 Acts. Another provision in Chapter 153, § 2254(a),

Act, § 1983, does not do that independent work. But, of course, the general federal question jurisdictional statute, § 1331, invariably fills the void.[241] There are instances, then, in which litigants insist that they are entitled to advance federal claims touching previous state criminal prosecutions in a § 1983 lawsuit—in addition to (or as a substitute for) a § 2241 habeas corpus petition.

Ordinarily, § 1983 actions offer nothing that habeas corpus does not also deliver, and usually a good deal less. Recall that § 1983 suits are *not* exempt from the Full Faith and Credit Statute and therefore usually cannot be employed to revisit state criminal judgments.[242] In any event, the Supreme Court has construed § 1983 not to be available to most litigants who are in a position to seek habeas relief.[243] The ostensible idea is that habeas corpus is the traditional device for contesting unlawful deprivations of liberty. Various features of the habeas process, particularly the exhaustion doctrine, are meant to ensure that prisoners use the habeas corpus mechanism in a proper way at the proper time. It would be inconsistent, then, routinely to allow § 1983 lawsuits into the picture—lawsuits that do not entail the same bundle of defining rules and practices.[244]

In *Preiser v. Rodriquez*,[245] state prison inmates claimed that they had been deprived of "good time" credits[246] in prison disciplinary proceedings that failed to meet fourteenth amendment due process standards. They filed a § 1983 action in federal court, seeking an injunction ordering prison officials to restore the credits. In the Supreme Court, Justice Stewart regarded the prisoners' suit as a stratagem for eluding the exhaustion doctrine. If the prisoners had advanced their claim in a petition for habeas corpus relief, they would have been required to exhaust state opportunities for litigating that claim before going to federal court. Stewart insisted that they could not avoid that requirement "by the simple expedient of putting a different label on their pleadings." He did not simply hold that, in the circumstances in *Preiser*, the plaintiffs must exhaust state procedures before filing a § 1983 action for injunctive relief. Instead, he rested on a narrow construction of § 1983. Since the prisoners challenged the "fact or length of their confinement," their suit "fell squarely within [the] traditional scope" of habeas corpus. They were therefore limited to habeas, which occupied the field: The "general" statute (§ 1983) must give way to the more "specific" statute (§ 2241).[247]

---

contains language that appears to have jurisdictional significance. Yet Congress first enacted that provision in 1966, evidently to reinforce the understanding that habeas is available to prisoners held in state custody.

241. See Chapter VIII, note 94 and accompanying text.

242. See Chapter VI, notes 165-68 and accompanying text.

243. Prisoners can use § 1983 actions to attack the *conditions* under which they are held in confinement. *Wilwording v. Swenson*, 404 U.S. 249 (1971).

244. Recall that litigants need not exhaust state administrative remedies prior to filing federal § 1983 lawsuits. See Chapter XI, notes 48-52 and accompanying text. Recall, too, that the Court has also construed § 1983 narrowly in other contexts, ostensibly to avoid conflicts with other statutory and doctrinal arrangements. E.g., *Fair Assessment in Real Estate Ass'n v. McNary*, 454 U.S. 100 (1981) (refusing to allow litigants to circumvent the Tax Injunction Act by attacking state taxes in a § 1983 action); Chapter XI, notes 45-47 and accompanying text.

245. 411 U.S. 475 (1973).

246. See id. at 477-78 (explaining that "good time" credits are awarded for exemplary behavior in confinement and can substantially reduce the time prisoners must serve).

247. Id. at 487-90.

The prisoners in *Preiser* conceded that they would not have been able to substitute a § 1983 suit for a habeas corpus petition if they had sought injunctive relief from the convictions and sentences that sent them to prison in the first place. Justice Stewart insisted that the result must be the same where the prisoners hoped to reduce the duration of their terms by obtaining injunctive relief from the judgment of the prison disciplinary board. Writing for the Court in *Heck v. Humphrey*,[248] Justice Scalia went further. In that case, a state prison inmate filed a § 1983 action seeking damages from state police and prosecution officials on the theory that they had violated his federal rights in the course of their investigations and preparation for trial. The prisoner did not seek an injunctive order affecting the "fact or length" of his confinement and thus did not come within *Preiser*. Yet as Justice Scalia understood his complaint, the prisoner did challenge the "legality of his conviction." He premised his claim for monetary relief on allegations of misconduct that, if true, would obligate the state to release him, even if he did not explicitly seek a release order. Viewing the complaint in that way, Scalia said that § 1983 would not support it, unless and until the prisoner first established that his conviction was invalid by some other means—for example, by means of a successful habeas corpus action.[249]

Neither *Preiser* nor *Heck* absolutely bars § 1983 actions in all instances in which convicts wish to sue state officials for violating federal rights in connection with state criminal prosecutions. If plaintiffs advance claims that can be sustained without also drawing a prior conviction into question, § 1983 will answer, subject to any other limitations that may apply—for example, abstention[250] or preclusion pursuant to § 1738.[251] Suits are foreclosed only if litigants press claims that "*necessarily*" imply that a conviction is invalid.[252] Even then, according to *Heck*, § 1983 actions still can be maintained later—after convicts show that their convictions have been dislodged in some other way. Nevertheless, *Preiser*

---

248. 512 U.S. 477 (1994).

249. Justice Scalia mentioned other possibilities as well. A prisoner may show that the conviction has been reversed on direct appeal or expunged by executive order. Id. at 486-87. Recall that Scalia interpreted § 1983 by analogy to the common law tort of malicious prosecution, which required plaintiffs to prove that the relevant prosecution had been terminated in their favor. See Chapter X, note 227.

250. Justice Scalia mentioned this possibility in *Heck*. 512 U.S. at 487-88 n.8. He cited *Colorado River Water Conservation Dist. v. United States*, 424 U.S. 800 (1976); see Chapter XI, notes 118-29. Ordinarily, the only form of abstention that is warranted with respect to federal suits for damages is a postponement of federal adjudication, not the kind of complete relinquishment associated with *Younger v. Harris*, 401 U.S. 37 (1971); Chapter XI, notes 132-89 and accompanying text. For a discussion, see Chapter XI, note 62.

251. Justice Scalia noted, but declined to consider, the possibility that the action in *Heck* might have been foreclosed by state preclusion law. 512 U.S. at 480 n.2.

252. Id. at 487 n.7 (emphasis in original).

and *Heck* make § 1983 litigation more complex and time-consuming and thus discourage litigants from filing suit.[253]

---

253. Litigation will almost certainly be necessary to draw the distinction that *Heck* requires. Justice Scalia invited plaintiffs to show that their claims, even if successful, would not draw their convictions into question for any of a number of reasons—including that any violation of federal rights would be ruled harmless. See notes 156-64 and accompanying text. Convicts whose claims do go to the validity of a conviction and who must first unseat that conviction face a significant burden. There may be no remaining mechanism for asking state courts to revisit the matter, and federal habeas corpus is itself freighted with complexities of heroic proportions. The decision in *Heck* presupposes that litigants who wish ultimately to sue for damages have some near-term access to habeas corpus. If, then, *Heck* is to be reconciled with the *Teague* doctrine and § 2254(d), those features of habeas corpus law cannot desiccate the writ. Concurring in *Heck*, Justice Souter argued that prisoners who are barred from suing for damages by *Heck* must, at the very least, be in custody and thus in a position to apply for federal habeas relief. Justice Scalia explicitly rejected that friendly amendment in *Heck* itself. 512 U.S. at 490 n. 10. But in *Spencer v. Kemna*, 118 S.Ct. 978 (1998), Justice Ginsburg gave Souter another vote for his position. Id. at 990. After *Spencer*, it appears that § 1983 does authorize lawsuits by convicts who are no longer in custody and thus have no access to federal habeas corpus. Then again, those lawsuits may falter on any of a host of other bases that bedevil § 1983 actions at large. Between *Preiser* and *Heck*, the Court decided *Wolff v. McDonnell*, 418 U.S. 539 (1974). In that case, inmates sued prison officials under the authority of § 1983 both for damages and for an injunction ordering the defendants to restore "good time" credits. Justice White found § 1983 to authorize the suit for compensatory relief, but concluded that *Preiser* barred the injunction. In *Heck*, Justice Scalia set *Wolff* aside on the ground that the prisoners there sought damages on the theory that the defendants used "the wrong procedures" and not because they reached the "wrong result," i.e., an erroneous denial of good time credits. After *Heck*, the Court found a § 1983 action for damages not to be authorized where inmates sued prison officials on the kind of claim advanced in *Preiser*—a violation of procedural due process in prison disciplinary hearings. *Edwards v. Balisok*, 520 U.S. 641 (1997). With an eye on *Heck*, the prisoners in *Edwards* were careful not to attack the disciplinary committee's judgment, but only its procedures. Nevertheless, Justice Scalia insisted that if the prisoners were right that the procedures violated due process, they "necessarily" implied that the committee's judgment was also invalid. Analogizing the disciplinary committee judgment in *Edwards* to the criminal conviction in *Heck*, Scalia concluded that § 1983 did not authorize the *Edwards* suit.

Table of Cases

Abbott Laboratories v. Gardner, 305
Ableman v. Booth, 126-128
Adams v. Robertson, 152
Adamson v. California, 354
Adler v. Bd. of Ed., 304
Aetna Life Ins. v. Haworth, 230, 250
Air Courier Conf. v. Amer. Postal
  Workers Union, 290
Alabama Pub. Svc. Comm'n v. Southern
  Ry., 381, 383
Alabama v. Pugh, 327
Albright v. Oliver, 353-354
Alexander v. Keane, 435
Alfred L. Snapp & Son v. Puerto Rico,
  148, 272
Allegheny County v. Frank Mashuda Co.,
  385
Allen v. McCurry, 137-140, 403
Allen v. Wright, 259, 267-280, 292
Amadeo v. Zant, 441
Amalgamated Clothing Workers v.
  Richman Bros., 367
Amer. Ins. Co. v. Canter, 93
Amer. Fire & Cas. Co. v. Finn, 205
Amer. Nat'l Red Cross v. S.G., 184, 199
Amer. Well Works Co. v. Layne & Bowler
  Co., 213-214, 217-220, 234
Ames v. Kansas, 143, 146
Anderson v. Creighton, 358-359
Anderson v. Harless, 432
Ankenbrandt v. Richards, 381, 383, 401
Antoine v. Byers & Anderson, 357
Arizona v. California, 145
Arizona v. Evans, 169
Arizona v. Fulminante, 451
Arizona v. San Carlos Apache Tribe, 387
Arizona v. Washington, 432
Arizonans for Official English v. Arizona,
  308, 339, 378
ASARCO v. Kadish, 247
Ashcroft v. Mattis, 360

Ashwander v. TVA, 8
Ass'n of Data Processing Svc. Orgs. v.
  Camp, 264-272, 276, 289, 291-294,
  297-298, 301
Assoc. Indus. v. Ickes, 263
Atascadero State Hosp. v. Scanlon, 317,
  323-324, 326
Atchison, T. & S.F.R. Co. v. O'Connor,
  118
Atherton v. FDIC, 195
Atlantic Coast Line R.R. v. Brotherhood
  of Locomotive Engineers, 364, 366
Atlas Roofing Co. v. Occup. Safety and
  Health Review Comm'n, 105, 107
Avco v. Aero Lodge, 240-241
Ayers, In re, 313, 331-332, 338

Babbitt v. Farm Workers, 303-304
Bacon v. Rutland R.R, 371
Baggett v. Bullitt, 377
Bakelite Corp., Ex parte, 96-97
Baker v. Carr, 256-258
Baker v. McCollan, 348, 361
Banco Nat'l de Cuba v. Sabbatino, 256
Bank of America Nat'l Trust & Savings
  Ass'n v. Parnell, 195
Bank of United States v. Planters' Bank,
  185
Barlow v. Collins, 301
Barney v. City of New York, 333
Barr v. City of Columbia, 173
Barrows v. Jackson, 284
Bartlett v. Bowen, 74
Battaglia v. General Motors, 74
Bd. of County Comm'rs v. Brown,
  346-347, 349
Beal v. Missouri Pac. R.R, 373
Behrens v. Pelletier, 360
Bell v. Hood, 208-209, 212, 215-216,
  226, 244
Bellotti v. Baird, 378, 402

Bennett v. Spear, 290, 292, 294-295, 301-302
Benton v. Washington, 471
Berkovitz v. United States, 316
Bivens v. Six Unknown Named Agents, 204, 209-212, 316
Blackburn v. Portland Gold Mining Co., 218
Blessing v. Freestone, 206-207, 329
Blonder-Tongue Laboratories v. University of Illinois Foundation, 137
Bogan v. Scott-Harris, 356
Bollman, Ex parte, 37, 70, 420-421
Bors v. Preston, 143
Bose Corp. v. Consumers Union, 175-176
Boston Stock Exchange v. State Tax Comm'n, 292
Boerne, City of v. Flores, 327
Bousley v. United States, 444
Bowen v. Johnston, 430
Bowsher v. Synar, 5
Boyle v. Landry, 403
Boyle v. United Technologies Corp., 114, 189, 193, 196, 403
Braden v. 30th Judicial Circuit Court, 432
Bradley v. Fisher, 357
Brady v. Maryland, 154
Bragdon v. Abbott, 179
Brandon v. Holt, 335
Brecht v. Abrahamson, 452-453
Brinkderhoff-Faris Trust & Savings Co. v. Hill, 172
Briscoe v. LaHue, 356
Broadrick v. Oklahoma, 287
Brockett v. Spokane Arcades, 288, 378
Brooks v. Dewar, 128
Brown v. Allen, 16, 426, 433, 449, 462
Brown v. Bd. of Ed., 20, 179
Brown v. Gerdes, 122
Brown v. Western Ry. of Alabama, 125
Buck v. Colbath, 126
Buck v. Green, 433
Buckley v. Fitzsimmons, 357
Buckley v. Valeo, 51
Burford v. Sun Oil Co., 375, 380-387, 391, 410-411
Burns v. Reed, 357
Burris v. Parke, 448
Bush v. Lucas, 211
Bushell's Case, 420

Butler v. McKellar, 456-457
Butz v. Economou, 355, 358

Calderon v. Ashmus, 201, 250
Calderon v. Thompson, 363
Califano v. Sanders, 201
California v. Arizona, 144-145
California v. Deep Sea Research, 335
California v. Southern Pac. Co., 144
California v. Stewart, 154
California v. West Virginia, 147
Caminetti v. United States, 9
Campbell v. Louisiana, 285
Cannon v. University of Chicago, 203-205
Canton, City of v. Harris, 346
Capital Cities Media v. Toole, 169-170
Carafas v. LaVallee, 430
Cardinale v. Louisiana, 151
Cary v. Curtis, 198
Carey v. Piphus, 349
Carlson v. Green, 208, 210, 272
Carnegie-Mellon v. Cohill, 245
Carr v. United States, 314
Caspari v. Bohlen, 459
Caterpillar v. Williams, 241-242
Celotex Corp. v. Catrett, 360
Central Vermont Ry. Co. v. White, 125
Chandler v. Judicial Council, 55-56, 66
Chapman v. California, 452
Chappell v. Wallace, 211-212
Charles Dowd Box Co. v. Courtney, 112
Chauffeurs, Teamsters & Helpers Local No. 391 v. Terry, 108
Chevron v. Natural Resources Defense Council, 11, 89
Chicago, City of v. Internat'l College of Surgeons, 215, 227-228, 242-245, 383
Chicago & Southern Air Lines v. Waterman, 252-253
Chicago R.I. & P.R. Co. v. Stude, 243, 383
Chick Kam Choo v. Exxon Corp., 367-368
Chisholm v. Georgia, 318-323, 325
Church of Latter Day Saints v. Hodel, 93
Claflin v. Houseman, 110, 112, 115-116
Clarke v. Secur. Indus. Ass'n, 201, 204, 290-292
Clay v. Sun Ins. Office, 374

Clearfield Trust Co. v. United States, 193-195, 204-205, 209

Cleavinger v. Saxner, 357

Cleveland Bd. of Ed. v. Loudermill, 96

Clinton v. City of New York, 177, 274, 276

Clinton v. Jones, 357

Coates v. City of Cincinnati, 288

Cohens v. Virginia, 121, 143, 150, 312, 319-320

Colegrove v. Green, 256

Coleman v. Miller, 256, 262

Coleman v. Thompson, 424, 441

Collins v. City of Harker Heights, 350

Collins v. Youngblood, 459

Colorado River Water Conservation Dist. v. United States, 381-391, 411-412, 475

Commodity Futures Trading Comm'n v. Schor, 100-104, 107

Connecticut v. Massachusetts, 147

Conroy v. Aniskoff, 11

Corey v. White, 335-336, 339

Cort v. Ash, 203-205

Costarelli v. Massachusetts, 151-152

County Court of Ulster County v. Allen, 433, 437

Cox Broadcasting Corp. v. Cohn, 152-156, 176

Craig v. Boren, 283, 285-286, 294

Crawford-El v. Britton, 345, 351, 357

Creswill v. Grand Lodge Knights of Pythias, 165

Crowell v. Benson, 81, 86, 88-91, 94, 97, 100-101, 103

Cuyler v. Sullivan, 447

D'Oench, Duhme & Co. v. FDIC, 10, 190, 192, 195

Dalton v. Specter, 74

Daniels v. Williams, 348-349, 353

Darby v. Cisneros, 370

Davis v. Passman, 210, 292

Davis v. United States, 440, 442

Davis v. Wechsler, 171

Deakins v. Monaghan, 390

DeFunis v. Odegaard, 308

Delaware v. Prouse, 167

Dellmuth v. Muth, 326

Dennis v. Higgins, 207, 292

Desist v. United States, 453-454, 456

Diamond v. Charles, 283

Dice v. Akron, Canton & Youngstown R.R., 125

District of Columbia Court of Appeals v. Feldman, 135-136, 141-142, 364, 371, 379, 410-411, 424

Doe v. Commonwealth's Attorney, 180

Dombrowski v. Pfister, 25, 365, 389-390, 396, 400

Donovan v. City of Dallas, 127-128

Dooley v. Korean Air Lines, 191

Doran v. Salem Inn, 403-405

Dorchy v. Kansas, 159

Doremus v. Bd. of Ed., 269

Dorr, Ex parte, 420

Douglas v. City of Jeannette, 390, 401

Dove v. United States, 308

Dowling v. United States, 190

Drinkard v. Johnson, 465

Duckworth v. Eagan, 451

Dugan v. Rank, 312

Duke Power Co. v. Carolina Envt'l Study Group, 277-280, 291, 293, 303, 305-306

Duncan v. Henry, 432

Duquesne Light Co. v. Barasch, 154

Durley v. Mayo, 168

Durousseau v. United States, 66

Eastern Enterprises v. Apfel, 316

Eastlake, City of v. Forest City Enterprises, 277

Eastland v. United States Servicemen's Fund, 356

Edelman v. Jordan, 207, 329, 338-340

Edelmann v. Triple-A Specialty, 234-236, 238-239

Edgar v. MITE Corp., 405

Edwards v. Balisok, 476

Elder v. Holloway, 360

Ellis v. Dyson, 307, 392

Employees v. Dep't of Pub. Health, 122-123, 323, 330

England v. Louisiana State Bd. of Med. Examin'ers, 379-380, 392

Engle v. Isaac, 431, 441, 443

Enterprise Irrigation Dist. v. Farmers Mutual Canal Co., 166, 168

Epperson v. Arkansas, 305

Erie R.R. Co. v. Tompkins, 189-190, 193

Estep v. United States, 63, 422
Eustis v. Bolles, 159, 161
Examining Bd. of Engineers v. Flores de
Otero, 378

Fair Assessment in Real Estate Ass'n v.
McNary, 372, 390, 474
Fairfax's Devisee v. Hunter's Lessee,
149-150
Falbo v. United States, 63
Farmer v. Brennan, 349
Fay v. Noia, 159, 161, 420, 423, 426,
429, 438-439
FCC v. Sanders Bros. Radio Station,
263-265, 299, 302
FDIC v. Meyer, 208, 311, 316, 359
FEC v. Akins, 270-271, 282, 290, 300
Federated Dep't Stores v. Moitie, 137,
240
Felder v. Casey, 117, 125, 345
Felker v. Turpin, 69-70, 422, 473
Feltner v. Columbia Pictures, 105
Feres v. United States, 316
Fern v. Gramley, 466
Finley v. United States, 243
Firestone Tire & Rubber Co. v. Risjord,
176
First English Church v. County of Los
Angeles, 118
Fiske v. Kansas, 175
Fitzgerald v. Green, 52
Fitzpatrick v. Bitzer, 326-327
Flast v. Cohen, 266-267, 269-270,
292-294, 296
Ford Motor Co. v. Dep't of Treasury,
327, 329, 338
Ford v. Wainwright, 471
Fornaris v. Ridge Tool Co., 374-375
Forrester v. White, 357
Fox Film Corp. v. Muller, 162,
165-166
Franchise Tax Board v. Constr. Laborers
Vacation Trust, 202, 213, 227,
232-238, 241-242, 369
Francis v. Henderson, 440
Frank v. Mangum, 426
Franklin v. Massachusetts, 74
Franks v. Bowman Trans. Co., 310
French v. Hay, 367
Freytag v. Commissioner, 82, 84
Frothingham v. Mellon, 262, 269

Garcia v. San Antonio Metro. Transit
Auth., 179
Garlotte v. Fordice, 430
Garrett v. Moore-McCormack Co., 112
Gebser v. Lago Vista Ind. School Dist.,
203
General Motors v. Washington, 175
General Oil Co. v. Crain, 120-121
Georgia R.R. & Banking Co. v.
Musgrove, 121
Georgia v. Rachel, 132-134
Gerstein v. Pugh, 310
Gibson v. Berryhill, 396
Gideon v. Wainwright, 454
Gilligan v. Morgan, 256
Gladstone, Realtors v. Village of
Bellwood, 294
Glidden Co. v. Zdanok, 69, 81, 93
Goeke v. Branch, 459
Golden State Transit Corp. v. City of
Los Angeles, 201, 206-207
Goldwater v. Carter, 256
Gomez v. Acevedo, 464
Gomez v. Toledo, 357, 359
Gooding v. Wilson, 288
Goodyear Atomic Corp. v. Miller, 156
Gov't & Civic Employees Org. Comm. v.
Windsor, 379
Graham v. Connor, 354
Granberry v. Greer, 434
Granfinanciera, S.A. v. Nordberg, 97,
104-108
Gray v. Netherland, 458
Green v. French, 467
Green v. Mansour, 339
Greenwood, City of v. Peacock, 132-134
Gregory v. Ashcroft, 123
Griffith v. Kentucky, 435, 453
Griswold v. Connecticut, 458
Growe v. Emison, 379, 387
Gruber, Ex parte, 144
Guaranty Trust Co. v. York, 399
Gulf Offshore Co. v. Mobil Oil Corp.,
112-113
Gulfstream Aerospace Corp. v.
Mayacamas Corp., 388
Gully v. First Nat'l Bank, 221-222
Gutierrez de Martinez v. Lamagno, 187

Hafer v. Melo, 335, 339
Hagans v. Lavine, 244

Hale v. Bimco Trading, 365
Hall v. Washington, 466
Hans v. Louisiana, 317, 320-325, 327, 331, 341
Hardin v. Kentucky Utilities Co., 297-299
Harding v. North Carolina, 434
Haring v. Prosise, 140
Harlow v. Fitzgerald, 358-359
Harper v. Virginia Dep't of Taxation, 453
Harris County Comm'rs Court v. Moore, 378-379
Harris v. Reed, 168
Harrison v. NAACP, 375
Havens Realty Corp. v. Coleman, 272, 278, 293-294, 297, 300
Hawaii Housing Auth. v. Midkiff, 377, 405
Hawaii v. Gordon, 315-316
Hayburn's Case, 44, 252-253
Heck v. Humphrey, 349-350, 390, 475-476
Heckler v. Ringer, 313
Heflin v. United States, 424
Henderson v. Kibbe, 439
Henderson v. United States, 316
Henry v. Mississippi, 171, 174, 438, 440
Henry v. Williams, 174
Hensley v. Municipal Court, 429
Herb v. Pitcairn, 124, 161
Hernandez v. New York, 175
Herndon v. Georgia, 172
Herrera v. Collins, 449-450
Hess v. Port Auth., 329
Hicks v. Miranda, 391, 404-406
Hill v. United States, 424, 450
Hilton v. Guyot, 363
Hilton v. South Carolina Pub. Ry. Comm'n, 124, 206, 326
Hodgson v. Bowerbank, 64
Hohn v. United States, 177, 179
Holt v. Indiana Mfg. Co., 336
Home Telephone & Telegraph v. Los Angeles, 332-334, 343, 345, 352
Honig v. Doe, 309
House v. Mayo, 177
Houston, City of v. Hill, 377-378
Howlett v. Rose, 114, 116-117, 119-120, 123-124, 325
Hoxsie v. Kerby, 434
Hudson Dist. v. Eli Lilly, 152
Hudson v. Palmer, 351

Huffman v. Pursue, 391-392, 406-407, 411, 413-414
Hughes v. Rowe, 346
Hunt v. Washington State Apple Adv. Comm'n, 272
Hunter v. Bryant, 360
Hurley v. Irish-American Gay, Lesbian and Bisexual Group of Boston, 162, 176
Hurn v. Oursler, 244
Hutto v. Finney, 326, 335, 339, 346

Idaho v. Coeur d'Alene Tribe, 120-121, 333, 335-337, 401
Illinois v. Milwaukee, 189
Imbler v. Pachtman, 356
Imperial, County of v. Munoz, 365
Indiana ex rel. Anderson v. Brand, 167-168
INS v. Chadha, 5
Internat'l Brotherhood of Electrical Workers v. Public Svc. Comm'n, 376
Internat'l Primate Protection League v. Administrators of Tulane Ed. Fund, 247
Internat'l Science & Tech. Inst. v. Inacom, 124-125
Invest. Co. Inst. v. Camp, 293, 301
Iowa Mut. Ins. Co. v. LaPlante, 387

J.I. Case v. Borak, 203-204, 209
Jackson v. Georgia Dep't of Transp., 339-340
James v. Kentucky, 173
Janklow v. Planned Parenthood, 287
Japan Whaling Ass'n v. Amer. Cetacean Society, 256
Jefferson v. City of Tarrant, 156
Johnson v. Fankell, 360
Johnson v. Jones, 360
Johnson v. Mississippi, 132
Joint Anti-Fascist Refugee Comm. v. McGrath, 251, 262
Jones v. Cunningham, 422, 429
Juidice v. Vail, 396, 407-409, 411
Justices of Boston Municipal Court v. Lydon, 429

Kaiser Steel Corp. v. W.S. Ranch Co., 385
Kamen v. Kemper Financial Svc., 195
Kansas v. Colorado, 147, 328

Katchen v. Landy, 106
Keeney v. Tamayo-Reyes, 448
Kentucky v. Graham, 339
Kentucky v. Indiana, 147, 193
Kerotest Mfg. Co. v. C-O-Two Fire Equip. Co., 386
Kimmelman v. Morrison, 451
King v. St. Vincent's Hosp., 9
Kline v. Burke Constr. Co., 363-364, 367
Kolender v. Lawson, 282, 287
Kotteakos v. United States, 452
Kremens v. Bartley, 310
Kremer v. Chem. Constr. Corp., 138, 140-141, 370, 399, 417
Kugler v. Helfant, 396-397

Lake Carriers' Ass'n v. MacMullan, 238, 377
Lambrix v. Singletary, 440, 459
Lampf, Pleva v. Gilbertson, 253
Landgraf v. USI Film Products, 10, 72
Lane v. Pena, 316
Langenkamp v. Culp, 106
Larson v. Domestic & Foreign Commerce Corp., 312, 314-316, 331-332, 340
Lauf v. Shinner, 64
Lear v. Adkins, 130
Leatherman v. Tarrant County Narcotics Unit, 357
Lebron v. Nat'l R.R. Passenger Corp., 185
Lehman Bros. v. Schein, 378, 385
Leiter Minerals v. United States, 365
Lewis v. Casey, 267
Library of Congress v. Shaw, 316
Liegakos v. Cooke, 463
Lincoln County v. Luning, 328
Linda R.S. v. Richard D., 280, 296-299
Lindh v. Murphy, 179, 428, 461, 464, 467-468
Linkletter v. Walker, 454
Liriano v. United States, 473
Little v. Barreme, 312
Livadas v. Bradshaw, 206
Local 174 v. Lucas Flour Co., 195
Lochner v. New York, 334
Lockerty v. Phillips, 62-63
Lockhart v. Fretwell, 468
Logan v. Zimmerman Brush Co., 472
Los Angeles, City of v. Heller, 347

Los Angeles, City of v. Jews for Jesus, 287
Los Angeles, City of v. Lyons, 209, 281-283, 307-308
Louisiana Power & Light Co. v. City of Thibodaux, 381, 384-387, 391
Louisiana v. Cummins, 147
Louisiana v. Jumel, 320
Louisiana v. Mississippi, 148
Louisville & Nashville R.R. Co. v. Mottley, 188, 217, 222, 230, 239
Louisville & Nashville R.R. Co. v. Rice, 221
Lugar v. Edmondson, 343, 409
Lujan v. Defenders of Wildlife, 259, 272, 276, 281, 295-299, 301
Lujan v. Nat'l Wildlife Fed., 264, 279, 290
Luther v. Borden, 255-256
Lynch v. Household Finance Corp., 336

Mackey v. United States, 453, 458
Magana-Pizano v. INS, 423
Maggio v. Fulford, 447
Maher v. Gagne, 346
Maine v. Thiboutot, 206-207
Maleng v. Cook, 429-430
Malley v. Briggs, 358-359
Malone v. Bowdoin, 315-316
Mapp v. Ohio, 451, 454
Marbury v. Madison, 16-17, 21-22, 37, 66, 70, 145, 254, 256-257, 293, 313
Marrese v. Amer. Academy of Orth. Surgeons, 137-138
Martin v. Hunter's Lessee, 59, 149-150, 164, 175
Martinez v. California, 117, 352
Maryland v. Baltimore Radio Show, 180
Maryland v. Joseph H. Munson Co., 286-287
Maryland v. Louisiana, 148
Massachusetts v. Upton, 164
Mata v. Johnson, 466
Matsushita Elec. Indus. Co. v. Epstein, 138
McCardle, Ex parte, 67-73, 417
McCarthy v. Bronson, 88, 106
McCarthy v. Madigan, 370
McClellan v. Garland, 386
McCleskey v. Zant, 473
McDonald v. City of West Branch, 141

McDonald v. Johnson, 448

McKart v. United States, 370

McKesson Corp. v. Div. of Alcoholic Beverages & Tobacco, 118-121, 320, 323

McKnett v. St. Louis Ry., 117

McMillian v. Monroe County, 347

McNally v. Hill, 420

McNeese v. Bd. of Ed., 381

McNutt v. GMAC, 188

Memphis Community School Dist. v. Stachura, 349

Meredith v. Winter Haven, 384

Merrell Dow Pharmaceuticals v. Thompson, 223-228, 238-239, 242, 244

Merrill, Lynch v. Curran, 203

Merryman, Ex parte, 419

Mesa v. California, 131

Mesquite, City of v. Aladdin's Castle, 309

Metropolitan Life Ins. Co. v. Taylor, 241

Miami Herald Pub. Co. v. Tornillo, 155-156

Michel v. Louisiana, 172

Michigan v. Long, 163, 168-170

Middlesex County Ethics Comm. v. Garden State Bar Ass'n, 412-413

Middlesex County Sewerage Auth. v. Nat'l Sea Clammers Ass'n, 206-207, 337

Migra v. Warren City School Dist., 139-141

Miller v. Albright, 285

Miller v. Fenton, 446

Miller v. Johnson, 275

Milligan, Ex parte, 67

Milliken v. Bradley, 339

Mills v. Alabama, 153

Milwaukee v. Illinois, 189

Minneapolis & St. Louis R.R. v. Bombolis, 125

Minnesota v. Hitchcock, 313

Miranda v. Arizona, 451

Mireles v. Waco, 357

Mississippi v. Louisiana, 148

Missouri ex rel. Southern Ry. Co. v. Mayfield, 124

Mistretta v. United States, 66

Mitchell v. Forsyth, 357, 360

Mitchum v. Foster, 139, 366-368, 372-373, 388-389, 393-394, 398, 408

Mondou v. New York R.R., 115, 117

Monell v. Dep't of Social Svc., 346-348

Monroe v. Pape, 118, 200, 343-352, 374-375

Montana v. Hall, 180

Montana v. United States, 140, 314

Moore v. Charlotte-Mecklenburg Bd. of Ed., 251

Moore v. Chesapeake & Ohio Ry., 167, 219-220, 223

Moore v. Dempsey, 426

Moore v. Sims, 396-398, 406-407

Moragne v. States Marine Lines, 191, 193

Morales v. TWA, 402

Morrison v. Olson, 5

Morse v. Republican Party, 10, 204

Moses H. Cone Mem. Hosp. v. Mercury Constr. Corp., 388

Moses Taylor, The, 111

Mt. Healthy City Bd. of Ed. v. Doyle, 346

Murdock v. City of Memphis, 157-161, 170, 186

Murray v. Carrier, 440

Murray's Lessee v. Hoboken Land & Improv. Co., 94-97

Musick, Peeler & Garrett v. Employ. Ins., 11

Muskrat v. United States, 250-251

Myers v. United States, 53

NAACP v. Alabama ex rel. Flowers, 154

NAACP v. Alabama ex rel. Patterson, 172-173

NAACP v. Button, 379

Nashville, C. & St. L. Ry. v. Wallace, 250

Nat'l Credit Union Admin. v. First National Bank, 289-290, 302

Nat'l Farmers Ins. Co. v. Crow Tribe, 189

Nat'l League of Cities v. Usery, 179, 329, 338

Nat'l Mutual Ins. Co. v. Tidewater Transfer Co., 65

Nat'l Private Truck Council v. Oklahoma Tax Comm'n, 114, 372

Nat'l R.R. Passenger Corp. v. Nat'l Ass'n of R.R. Passengers, 212

Nat'l Soc'y of Prof. Engineers v. United States, 192

Nat'l Socialist Party v. Skokie, 155

Neelley v. Nagle, 220

Nevada v. Hall, 317, 328

New Jersey v. New York, 148

New York Central & H.R. Co. v. New York, 151
New York v. United States, 122-123, 296
Newport v. Fact Concerts, 347
Newsweek v. Florida Dep't of Revenue, 120
Ngiraingas v. Sanchez, 342
Nishimura Ekiu v. United States, 422
Nixon v. Fitzgerald, 357
Nixon v. United States, 54, 257-258
NLRB v. Jones & Laughlin Steel Corp., 105
NLRB v. Nash-Finch Co., 365
NOPSI v. Council of New Orleans, 381-382, 385, 387, 395, 410-414
Norris v. Alabama, 175
Northeastern Florida Chapter of Ass'n Gen. Contractors v. Jacksonville, 275-276
Northern Pipeline Constr. Co. v. Marathon Pipe Line Co., 90-92, 97-104
Northern Secur. Co. v. United States, 410
Northwest Airlines v. County of Kent, 212

O'Brien v. DuBois, 465-468
O'Callahan v. Parker, 94
O'Dell v. Netherland, 454
O'Donoghue v. United States, 65
O'Melveny & Myers v. FDIC, 195-196
O'Neal v. McAninch, 452
O'Shea v. Littleton, 294, 306-307, 414-415
Ohio Bureau of Employment Svc. v. Hodory, 391
Ohio Civil Rights Comm'n v. Dayton Christian Schools, 413-414
Ohio Forestry Ass'n v. Sierra Club, 305
Ohio v. Wyandotte Chemicals Co., 147
Oklahoma Packing Co. v. Oklahoma Gas & Elec. Co., 371
Oklahoma Tax Comm'n v. Graham, 228
Oneida Indian Nation v. County of Oneida, 221
Oregon v. Mitchell, 144
Org. for a Better Austin v. Keefe, 155
Osborn v. Bank of United States, 183-188, 199, 221, 244, 313, 320
Osborne v. Ohio, 288
Owen v. City of Independence, 347, 360

Pacemaker Diagnostic Clinic of Amer. v. Instromedix, 87
Pac. R.R. Removal Cases, 185
Pac. Tel. & Tel. Co. v. Kuykendall, 371
Palko v. Connecticut, 458
Palmore v. United States, 94, 98-99
Papasan v. Allain, 339
Parden v. Terminal Ry., 124, 330
Parratt v. Taylor, 348-349, 351-354, 372, 374
Parsons v. Bedford, 105
Parsons Steel v. First Alabama Bank, 368
Pasadena City Bd. of Ed. v. Spangler, 148
Patsy v. Bd. of Regents, 142, 352, 372-373, 383, 413
Paul v. Davis, 350-351
Peacock v. Thomas, 242
Peck v. Jenness, 365
Pembaur v. City of Cincinnati, 347
Pennhurst State School & Hosp. v. Halderman, 207, 244, 317, 340-342, 375, 377
Pennsylvania v. Quicksilver Co., 144
Pennsylvania v. Union Gas Co., 324
Pennzoil v. Texaco, 343, 376, 391, 407-411
Penry v. Lynaugh, 458
Peretz v. United States, 88
Perez v. Ledesma, 391, 401
Perkins v. Lukens Steel Co., 260, 264
Pernell v. Southall Realty, 106
Peyton v. Rowe, 430
Philadelphia Newspapers v. Jerome, 168
Phillips v. Washington Legal Foundation, 168
Picard v. Connor, 432
Pickelsimer v. Wainwright, 454
Pierce v. Society of Sisters, 304
Pierson v. Ray, 356
Pilot Life Ins. Co. v. Dedeaux, 240
Pitchess v. Davis, 432
Planned Parenthood Ass'n v. Ashcroft, 378
Planned Parenthood v. Casey, 287
Plaut v. Spendthrift Farm, 73, 253, 472
Poe v. Ullman, 304
Poindexter v. Greenhow, 119
Port Auth. v. Feeney, 329
Powell v. McCormack, 257
Powers v. Ohio, 285

Preiser v. Rodriguez, 474-476

Prentis v. Atlantic Coast Line Co. 136, 371, 381, 413-414

Principality of Monaco v. Mississippi, 319, 328

Printz v. United States, 122-123

Propper v. Clark, 377

Public Svc. Comm'n v. Wycoff, 201, 232-233, 238

Puerto Rico Aqueduct & Sewer Auth. v. Metcalf, 330

Puerto Rico v. Russell, 219

Pulliam v. Allen, 356

Quackenbush v. Allstate Ins. Co., 372, 374-375, 384-385

Quern v. Jordan, 326, 339

Radio Station WOW v. Johnson, 152, 154

Railroad Comm'n of Texas v. Pullman Co., 342, 373-377, 379-384, 387, 389, 391, 410

Raines v. Byrd, 268, 274

Reece v. Georgia, 172

Reed v. Farley, 450

Reed v. Ross, 441

Reetz v. Bozanich, 378

Regan v. Taxation With Representation of Washington, 279

Regents of the University of California v. Bakke, 274-276

Regents of the University of California v. Doe, 327, 340

Reich v. Collins, 118-121, 323

Republic of Peru, Ex parte, 151

Reynolds v. Sims , 256

Reynoldsville Casket Co. v. Hyde, 358

Rezin v. Wolff, 437

Rhode Island v. Massachusetts, 147

Richards v. Jefferson County, 137

Richardson v. McKnight, 355

Rivet v. Regions Bank, 240

Rizzo v. Goode, 306-307, 414-415

Robb v. Connolly, 115

Robertson v. Seattle Audubon Society, 73

Robertson v. Wegmann, 345

Rochin v. California, 354

Roe v. Wade, 309

Rogers v. United States, 179

Rooker v. Fidelity Trust Co., 135-136, 141-142, 353, 364, 371, 379, 410-411, 424

Rose v. Lundy, 433-436, 471

Royall, Ex parte, 430

Runyan v. McCrary, 274

Ry. Co. v. Whitton's Adm'r, 329

Ryder v. United States, 358

Sacramento, County of v. Lewis, 354, 361-362

Saffle v. Parks, 456

Salinger v. Loisel, 471

Saltarelli v. Bob Baker Grp. Med. Trust, 464

Samuels v. Mackell, 387, 390-415

Sanders v. United States, 426

Sawyer v. Smith, 455

Sawyer v. Whitley, 443

Schiro v. Farley, 459

Schlesinger v. Reservists Committee to Stop the War, 271, 273

Schlup v. Delo, 422, 443, 450

Schoenthal v. Irving Trust Co., 105

Schweiker v. Chilicky, 211-212, 337

Screws v. United States, 343

Scripps-Howard Radio v. FCC, 263, 302

Seminole Tribe v. Florida, 253, 313, 324-327, 334-337

Shamrock Oil & Gas Corp. v. Sheets, 129

Shaw v. Delta Airlines, 233, 238-239

Shaw v. Reno, 275

Sheldon v. Sill, 60-61

Shields v. Utah Idaho Central R.R., 313

Shoshone Mining Co. v. Rutter, 217-219, 221, 223

Shuttlesworth v. City of Birmingham, 173, 288

Sibron v. New York, 308

Siegert v. Gilley, 361

Sierra Club v. Morton, 271-272, 297, 302

Siler v. Louisville & Nashville R.R. Co., 244, 340, 342, 377

Simon v. Eastern Kentucky Welfare Rights Org., 277-279

Singleton v. Commissioners, 180

Singleton v. Wulff, 285-286, 294

Skelly Oil v. Phillips Petroleum, 229-238

Slaughterhouse Cases, 158

Slayton v. Smith, 431

Slocum v. Mayberry, 128
Smith v. Digmon, 433
Smith v. Kansas City Title & Trust Co.,
  220-221, 223-227, 231, 239, 455
Smith v. Murray, 441
Smith v. Robinson, 206-207
Snead v. Stringer, 460
Snowden v. Hughes, 333, 374
Solorio v. United States, 94
Sosna v. Iowa, 188
South Carolina v. Katzenbach, 251
South Carolina v. Regan, 145
South Dakota v. Neville, 168
Southern Pac. R.R. v. Jensen, 191
Southern Pac. Terminal Co. v. ICC, 309
Southland Corp. v. Keating, 156
Spencer v. Kemna, 267, 308, 476
State Tax Comm'n v. Van Cott, 167
Staub v. City of Baxley, 173
Steel Co. v. Citizens for a Better
  Environment, 126, 188, 202, 251,
  272, 282-283, 299, 302
Stefanelli v. Minard, 390
Steffel v. Thompson, 233, 307, 391,
  400-402, 405
Stewart v. Martinez-Villareal, 471
St. Louis, City of v. Praprotnik, 347
Stone v. Powell, 25, 139, 450-451
Strauder v. West Virginia, 133
Strawbridge v. Curtis, 60
Street v. New York, 170
Strickland v. Washington, 441
Stringer v. Black, 456
Stump v. Sparkman, 357
Sullivan v. Little Hunting Park, 173
Sumner v. Mata, 446
Supreme Court of Virginia v. Consumers'
  Union, 356
Suter v. Artist M., 207
Swain v. Pressley, 420, 425
Swift v. Tyson, 189, 321
Switchmen v. Nat'l Med. Bd., 100

T.B. Harms v. Eliscu, 112, 234
Tafflin v. Levitt, 113-114, 196
Tarble's Case, 126-128, 419
Teague v. Lane, 441, 449, 453-460, 462,
  464-467, 470, 476
Teal v. Felton, 126
Tennessee Coal, Iron & R. Co. v.
  Muscoda Local No. 123, 74

Tennessee Elec. Power Co. v. TVA, 263
Tennessee v. Davis, 130-131
Tenney v. Brandhove, 357
Terrace v. Thompson, 394
Testa v. Katt, 111, 115-117, 122-124,
  199
Texas Indus. v. Radcliff Materials, 193
Texas v. New Jersey, 147
Texas v. New Mexico, 147
Texas v. United States, 251, 304
Textile Workers Union v. American
  Thread Co., 187
Textile Workers Union v. Lincoln Mills,
  187, 190, 193-194, 199, 204-205,
  209, 241
Textron Lycoming Reciprocating Engine
  Div. v. UAW, 9, 232-236, 238
The Fair v. Kohler Die & Specialty Co.,
  216
Thomas v. Amer. Homes Products, 181
Thomas v. Union Carbide, 99-104, 107
Thompson v. Keohane, 446
Thompson v. Louisville, 152
Thompson v. Thompson, 10, 204
Thurston Motor Lines v. Jordan K. Rand,
  222
Toth v. Quarles, 94, 98
Toucey v. United States, 365-367
Tower v. Glover, 140, 355-356
Townsend v. Sain, 426, 445
Trafficante v. Metro. Life Ins. Co., 296,
  298-299
Trainor v. Hernandez, 396, 406
Trest v. Cain, 437
Triestman v. United States, 424, 472
Truax v. Corrigan, 64
Tutun v. United States, 253
TVA v. Hill, 302

UAW v. Brock, 272
United Bldg. & Constr. Trades Council v.
  Mayor of Camden, 175
United Food & Commercial Workers
  Union v. Brown Group, 283
United Mine Workers v. Gibbs,
  242-244
United Public Workers v. Mitchell, 303
United States Civil Service Comm'n v.
  Nat'l Ass'n of Letter Carriers, 304
United States Dep't of Labor v. Triplett,
  286

United States Parole Comm'n v. Geraghty, 310

United States Savings Ass'n v. Timbers of Inwood Forest Ass'n, 9

United States v. Claiborne, 54

United States v. Classic, 343

United States v. Coolidge, 189

United States v. Frady, 441-442

United States v. Hastings, 54

United States v. Hayman, 420-421, 424

United States v. Hays, 270

United States v. Hudson & Goodwin, 189

United States v. Johnson, 189, 251, 316

United States v. Jung Ah Lung, 422

United States v. Kimball Foods, 195

United States v. Klein, 69, 71-73

United States v. Lanier, 467

United States v. Lee, 313-314

United States v. Little Lake Misere Land Co., 190

United States v. MacCollom, 422

United States v. Mendoza-Lopez, 63

United States v. Mitchell, 316

United States v. Morgan, 424

United States v. Nixon, 253

United States v. Padleford, 71-72

United States v. Raddatz, 87, 91

United States v. Richardson, 271

United States v. Salerno, 287

United States v. SCRAP, 273, 276, 278-279

United States v. Sioux Nation of Indians, 73

United States v. Standard Oil Co., 192

United States v. Stanley, 211

United States v. Texas, 146, 328

United States v. Timmreck, 450

United States v. W.T. Grant Co., 309

United States v. Wyoming, 147

University of Tennessee v. Elliott, 141-142, 370, 373

Valley Forge Christian College v. Americans United for Separation of Church and State, 270, 292

Vander Jagt v. O'Neil, 267

Vendo Co. v. Lektro-Vend Corp., 366

Verlinden B.V. v. Central Bank of Nigeria, 187-188

Village of Arlington Heights v. Metro. Hous. Develop. Corp., 278

Village of Bolingbrook v. Citizens Utilities Co., 114

Virginia v. Rives, 133

Virginia Coupon Cases, 320

Wade v. Mayo, 433

Wainwright v. Sykes, 427, 439-440, 442-443, 448

Wainwright v. Witt, 447

Wallis v. Pan Amer. Petroleum Corp., 195

Ward v. Bd. of County Comm. of Love County, 118, 165

Warth v. Seldin, 268, 276-280, 291, 296

Washington v. Davis, 278

Webb's Fabulous Pharmacies v. Beckwith, 168

Webster v. Doe, 74

Weinstein v. Bradford, 309

Weiss v. United States, 94

Welch v. Texas Dep't of Highways, 324, 330

West Va. Univ. Hosp. v. Casey, 9

Whitley v. Albers, 354

Whitmore v. Arkansas, 286

Wilder v. Virginia Hosp. Ass'n, 207

Will v. Michigan Dep't of State Police, 339, 342-343

Will v. United States, 436

Willcox v. Consolidated Gas Co., 395

Williams v. Georgia, 173-174, 438

Williams v. INS, 423

Williamson County Regional Planning Comm'n v. Hamilton Bank, 354, 372

Willing v. Chicago Aud. Ass'n, 249, 262

Wilson v. Garcia, 345

Wilton v. Seven Falls Co., 201, 387, 400

Wilwording v. Swenson, 474

Wingo v. Wedding, 87

Wisconsin Dep't of Corrections v. Schacht, 329

Wisconsin v. Constantineau, 376

Wisconsin v. Pelican Ins. Co., 38, 115, 147

Wisniewski v. United States, 176

Withrow v. Williams, 451

Wolf v. Colorado, 359

Wolff v. McDonnell, 476

Wood v. Strickland, 358

Wooley v. Maynard, 402-403, 405

Worcester v. Georgia, 319

Wright v. City of Roanoke, 206-207
Wright v. West, 9, 454, 457-458, 460,
    464, 466
Wyatt v. Cole, 355

Yakus v. United States, 62-63
Yazoo & Mississippi Valley R.R. v.
    Jackson Vinegar Co., 284, 287
Yazoo County Indus. Develop. Corp. v.
    Suthoff, 216
Yellow Freight System v. Donnelly, 114

Yerger, Ex parte, 69-70
Ylst v. Nunnemaker, 168-169
Young, Ex parte, 119-121, 239, 331-338,
    340, 342, 345, 351, 368, 401,
    404-405, 417
Younger v. Harris, 152, 363, 382,
    389-415, 475

Zablocki v. Redhail, 402
Zinermon v. Burch, 352-354, 372
Zwickler v. Koota, 307, 377

Index

Abstention:
  and civil rights actions, 388-406, 414-415
  and parallel state proceedings, 386-388
  and state executive activities, 414-415
  and the eleventh amendment, 375, 377
  and the process model, 395-399
  in administrative cases, 380-384
  in state sovereign interest cases, 384-385
  regarding federal questions, 388-415
  regarding state questions, 373-380
  when state court proceedings are anticipated, 399-406
  when state proceedings are pending, 388-399
Adequate and independent state grounds:
  adequate state grounds for, 170-174
  and ambiguous state decisions, 168-170
  in habeas corpus cases, 438-440
  independent state grounds for, 161-168
  origins of, 159-160
Administrative agencies:
  as non-Article III adjudicators, 81-82, 88-90, 94-104
  judicial review of, 84, 89-90, 103-104, 260-268, 288-291, 294-300
Administrative Office of United States Courts, 42, 88, 436
Administrative Procedure Act, 42, 198, 200, 264-265, 289-291, 316, 370
Advisory opinions, 161, 169, 178, 230, 248-252, 254, 263, 283, 308-309, 402
All-Writs Act, 177-178, 313, 365, 367, 429
American Bar Association, 52
American Law Institute, 45, 130, 222, 236, 243, 366, 378-380

Ancillary jurisdiction, 164, 242; see Supplemental jurisdiction
Anti-Federalists, 6, 29, 32-33, 35, 47, 318
Anti-Injunction Act, 41, 139, 364-368, 372, 388-389, 393, 398, 408-409
Antiterrorism and Effective Death Penalty Act, 69, 369, 428
Appellate jurisdiction:
  of district courts, 135-136
  of Supreme Court, 148-181
Appointments Clause, 30, 48, 50-52, 82
Articles of Confederation, 28-29, 35, 59
Attorney fees, 283, 346, 350, 356

Bankruptcy courts, 20, 42, 90-92, 97-98, 103, 105-106, 112, 131

Capital punishment, 427-428
Caseload, 43-46
Cases and controversies:
  content of, see Advisory opinions; Standing
  original understanding of, 32
Cause of action:
  and jurisdiction, 214-216
  explanation of, 196-198
Certification:
  and Supreme Court jurisdiction, 176
  of state questions, 378
Certiorari, in Supreme Court, 70, 177-181
Chancery, 373, 418
Checks and balances, 48, 58, 61
Chief Justice, 30, 39
Circuit courts:
  modern, 42
  original, 37
  review of by Supreme Court, 176-177
Circuit-riding, 37, 253
Cities, as defendants in federal court, 346-347

Civil Justice Reform Act, 44
Civil War, 39-40, 67, 71, 127, 421
Class actions:
  and mootness, 309-310
  in civil rights cases, 20, 306-307,
    414-415
Clear statement, doctrine of, 12-13
Colonial period, 27, 418
Comity:
  definition of, 363
  in abstention cases, 390
  in habeas corpus cases, 430
Confirmation of judicial nominees,
  48-52
Congress, authority for:
  creating federal courts, 29-30, 58-59
  creating rights of action, 198-202
  granting standing, 293-300
  prescribing inferior federal court
    jurisdiction, 60-65, 71-75
  prescribing state court jurisdiction,
    122-124
  prescribing Supreme Court
    jurisdiction, 66-70, 71-75
Constitutional torts, 348-354
Convention, 29-32
Council of revision, 29, 31
Counties, as defendants in federal court,
  346-347

Declaratory Judgment Act:
  and abstention, 390-391, 400-406
  and advisory opinions, 249-250
  and federal question jurisdiction,
    228-240
  and right of action, 201-202
  and ripeness, 307
  history of, 249-250
Discipline, of federal judges, 53-56
District courts:
  modern, 42
  jurisdiction of, 60-65
  original, 37
District of Columbia, courts of, 64-65,
  93-94
Diversity jurisdiction, 57
Domestic relations cases, 383
Due Process Clause:
  as a claim in litigation, 348-354
  as a guarantee of access to court,
    118-122

Eleventh amendment:
  academic theories of, 320-323
  and civil rights actions, 334
  and officer suits, 331-341
  and state law claims, 340-342
  and the fourteenth amendment,
    332-334
  congressional power over, 323-327
  exceptions to, 327-329
  history of, 33, 317-320
Equitable remedies, 373-375, 389-390
Establishment Clause, 269-270, 292, 294
Evarts Act, 41, 178
Exceptions Clause, 66-70, 76
Exclusive jurisdiction, 111-112
Exhaustion doctrine:
  in general, 369-373
  in habeas corpus cases, 430-436

Fact-finding:
  appellate review of, 175-176
  in habeas corpus cases, 445-448
Fair Labor Standards Act, 74, 330
Federal Circuit, Court of Appeals for, 42
Federal common law:
  conditions for, 189-196
  in state court, 195
Federal Courts Study Committee, 43-46
Federal government:
  as defendant, 312-316
  as plaintiff, 252-253, 311
Federal Judicial Center, 42
Federal question jurisdiction:
  constitutional prerequisites for, 183-188
  of district courts, 212-240
  of state courts, 109-114
Federal Tort Claims Act, 192, 208, 243,
  316
Federalism, 6-7
Federalist papers, 34-36
Federalists, 6, 22, 29-30, 33, 37, 39
Final judgment rule, 152-156, 176-177,
  330, 360
Formalism, 83
Fourteenth amendment:
  and the eleventh amendment, 332-334
  as a claim in litigation, 41, 200, 223,
    449
Full Faith and Credit Statute:
  exceptions to, 417
  in general, 136-142

Greater power syllogism, 8

Habeas corpus:
  and civil rights actions, 473-476
  and the Suspension Clause, 37, 419-422
  custody doctrine in, 429-430
  effect of previous state court adjudication in, 423-424, 460-471
  evidentiary hearings in, 445-448
  exhaustion doctrine in, 430-436
  function and history of, 417-418
  harmless error in, 451-452
  in criminal cases, 423-428
  in death penalty cases, 427-428
  in executive detention cases, 422-423
  in immigration cases, 422-423
  issues cognizable in, 448-451
  multiple federal petitions for, 471-473
  new rules of law in, 452-460
  procedural default doctrine in, 437-445, 447-448
  Supreme Court original jurisdiction of, 69-70, 473
Hamilton, Alexander, 34-36
Hart and Wechsler, 13-15
Hohfeld, Wesley, 261

Impeachment:
  as a political question, 257-258
  of federal judges, 53-54
Independence of federal courts:
  safeguards for, 47-54
  values served by, 47
International Trade, Court of, 42

Jaffee, Louis, 261
Johnson Act, 369
Judicial Conference of the United States, 42, 428
Judicial Councils Reform Act, 55
Judiciary Act of 1789, 37-39
Judiciary Acts of 1790 and 1793, 39-40
Jury trial:
  history of, 27, 33
  in legislative courts, 104-108
Justiciability: See Advisory opinions; Standing

Ku Klux Klan Act:
  and abstention, 375, 388-415
  and standing, 294
  and the Anti-Injunction Act, 366-367
  and the eleventh amendment, 335-337
  and tort law, 345, 348-354
  as a device for enforcing federal statutes, 206-207
  as a device for enforcing the fourteenth amendment, 41, 200, 336-337, 342-354
  color of law requirement for, 343-345
  history of, 41
  in officer suits, 336-337, 342-354
  in state court, 114, 116-117
  in suits against cities and counties, 328, 346

Legal process, 10, 13-14
Legislative courts, 81-86, 92-104
Legislative history, 9-12
Long range plan, 44-46

Madison, James, 3, 16, 28, 251
Madisonian Compromise, 29-31, 58-61, 110, 127, 148
Magistrate judges, 20, 42, 44, 87-88
Magna Charta, 418
Military courts, 42, 94
Military Reconstruction Act, 67-69
Mootness, 248, 308-310

National Commission on Judicial Discipline and Removal, 54
New Deal, 39, 47

Officer suits:
  to affect the government, 313-315, 331-337
  to impose personal liability, 312-313, 347
  to obtain injunctive relief, 314, 331-337
  to obtain compensatory relief, 337-339, 347-354
Official immunity:
  absolute, 356-357
  qualified, 358-362
Original jurisdiction, of Supreme Court, 57, 143-148

Parity, between state and federal courts, 23-26

Pendent jurisdiction, 242; see
  Supplemental jurisdiction
Political questions, 248, 254-258, 271,
  274
Portal-to-Portal Act, 74
Powell Committee, 428, 432-433, 436
Preclusion:
  and full faith and credit, 136-142
  and the process model, 137, 140-141
  regarding administrative agency
    actions, 141-142
Preemption of state law, 130, 240-242
Preservation requirement, 151-152
President:
  executive authority of, 4, 72, 296
  immunity of, 357
Private attorneys general, 211, 262-266,
  294-296, 301-302
Private rights:
  and legislative courts, 89, 94
  model of, 15-17
Process model:
  and abstention, 395-399
  and the adequate state ground
    doctrine, 171-174
  in general, 18-19
  in habeas corpus cases, 426-427, 437,
    451, 462
  in preclusion cases, 137, 140-141
  in removal cases, 134-135
Protective jurisdiction, 131-132, 186-187
Public choice, 262
Public rights:
  and legislative courts, 94-104, 106-107
  model of, 19-23

Ratification, 32-34
Reconstruction, 40-41
Removal:
  by federal officers, 130-131
  in civil rights cases, 132-135
  relation to original jurisdiction, 130,
    213
Right of action:
  and federal question jurisdiction,
    214-217, 224-228
  and standing, 294-300
  congressional authority over, 198-202
  implied in constitutional provisions,
    207-210
  implied in statutes, 202-207

to enforce constitutional provisions,
    207-208
  to enforce statutes, 206-207
Ripeness, 303-307

Separation of Powers, 3-6
Sovereign immunity:
  of the federal government, 259-260,
    312
  of the states in federal court, 317-320
  of the states in state court, 116-117,
    119-124
  waiver of, 315-316, 329-330
Specialized federal courts, 44-45, 85
Standing:
  and abstention, 414-415
  and mootness, 308
  and overbreadth, 287-288
  and ripeness, 303
  and the merits, 300-302
  and the zone test, 288-293
  causation requirement for, 258,
    276-280
  congressional power over, 293-300
  constitutional prerequisites for,
    258-259
  in Administrative Procedure Act cases,
    264-268, 288-293
  in generalized grievance cases,
    270-274
  in taxpayer cases, 269-270
  injury requirement for, 258, 265-276
  of private attorneys general, 211,
    262-266, 294-296, 301-302
  on behalf of third parties, 284-288
  prudential prerequisites for, 283-293
  redressability requirement for, 280-283
State courts:
  authority in federal question cases,
    109-114
  authority regarding federal officials,
    125-128
  authority regarding state law, 159-160
  civil rights actions in, 116-117
  concurrent jurisdiction of, 109-114
  congressional authority over, 122-124
  obligation in federal question cases,
    114-125
States:
  as defendants in federal court,
    317-320

as plaintiffs in federal court, 311
Statutory construction, 8-13
Supplemental jurisdiction:
  and removal, 243
  of district courts, 242-245
  of Supreme court, 160
Supremacy Clause, 31, 110, 116-117,
  122-123, 125, 148, 150, 239
Supreme Court:
  appellate jurisdiction of, 57, 66-71,
  148-181
  discretionary jurisdiction of, 147-148,
  177-181
  original jurisdiction of, 57, 143-148

Suspension Clause, 37, 419-422

Tax Injunction Act, 120, 238-239, 369,
  372, 399
Territorial courts, 42, 85, 92-93
Three-judge court statutes, 368

Well-pleaded complaint rule, 217-224,
  228-240